This Book
Purchased
In
Memory
Of

Louis E. Neff

What Will Work

ENVIRONMENTAL ETHICS AND SCIENCE POLICY SERIES
General Editor: Kristin Shrader-Frechette

Experts In Uncertainty
Expert Opinion and Subjective Probability in Science
Roger Cooke

Acceptable Evidence
Science and Values in Risk Management
Edited by Deborah Mayo and Rachelle Hollander

Privatizing Public Lands
Scott Lehmann

Democracy, Risk, and Community
Technological Hazards and the Evolution of Liberalism
Richard P. Hiskes

Environmental Justice
Creating Equality, Reclaiming Democracy
Kristin Shrader-Frechette

In Nature's Interests?
Interests, Animal Rights, and Environmental Ethics
Gary E. Varner

Across the Boundaries
Extrapolation in Biology and Social Science
Daniel Steel

Taking Action, Saving Lives
Our Duties to Protect Environmental and Public Health
Kristin Shrader-Frechette

Is a Little Pollution Good for You?
Incorporating Societal Values in Environmental Research
Kevin C. Elliott

A Perfect Moral Storm
The Ethical Tragedy of Climate Change
Stephen Gardner

What Will Work
Fighting Climate Change with Renewable Energy, Not Nuclear Power
Kristin Shrader-Frechette

What Will Work

Fighting Climate Change with Renewable Energy, Not Nuclear Power

KRISTIN SHRADER-FRECHETTE

OXFORD
UNIVERSITY PRESS

OXFORD
UNIVERSITY PRESS

Oxford University Press, Inc., publishes works that further
Oxford University's objective of excellence
in research, scholarship, and education.

Oxford   New York
Auckland   Cape Town   Dar es Salaam   Hong Kong   Karachi
Kuala Lumpur   Madrid   Melbourne   Mexico City   Nairobi
New Delhi   Shanghai   Taipei   Toronto

With offices in
Argentina   Austria   Brazil   Chile   Czech Republic   France   Greece
Guatemala   Hungary   Italy   Japan   Poland   Portugal   Singapore
South Korea   Switzerland   Thailand   Turkey   Ukraine   Vietnam

Published by Oxford University Press, Inc.
198 Madison Avenue, New York, New York 10016

www.oup.com

Oxford is a registered trademark of Oxford University Press

Library of Congress Cataloging-in-Publication Data
Shrader-Frechette, K. S. (Kristin Sharon)
What will work : fighting climate change with renewable energy, not nuclear power / Kristin Shrader-Frechette.
    p.   cm.
Includes bibliographical references.
ISBN-13: 978-0-19-979463-8 (alk. paper)
1. Climatic changes.   2. Nuclear energy—Environmental aspects.   3. Radioactive pollution of the
atmosphere.   4. Renewable energy sources.   I. Title.
QC903.S57 2011
333.792'4—dc22   2010042383

1 3 5 7 9 8 6 4 2

Printed in the United States of America
on acid-free paper

For Emily Anne,
that we may leave you with an even better world
than the one into which we brought you

CONTENTS

ACKNOWLEDGMENTS

As this book goes to press, my heart is with my many Japanese friends who are heroically facing the nuclear crisis at Fukushima. May there be no more Fukushimas— and instead an even greater blossoming of wind, solar, and other renewable technologies.

Thanks to the US National Science Foundation for decades of research funding for my work in human health risk assessment. Special thanks for my 2007–2009 NSF grant, SES-0724781, "Three Methodological Rules in Risk Assessment," and my 2000–2003 NSF grant, SES-98-10611, "Nuclear Technology, Ethics, and Worker Radiation Risk," during which much of the work in this book was done. Any errors, however, are my responsibility and not that of the US NSF.

To the Autonomous University of Mexico; Boston University; the University of California, Berkeley; the University of Chicago; the University of Delaware; Hebrew University, Jerusalem; Hokkaido University, Japan; Kings College, London; Lehigh University; London School of Economics; Michigan State University; the State University of New York; the University of Pittsburgh; Santa Clara University; Virginia Polytechnic University; Purdue University; Villanova University; and Yale University—thank you for the invitations and the audiences that allowed me to present and refine many of the findings and arguments in this book. Thanks especially to the many philosophers of science and scientists at these universities who were kind enough to provide helpful comments on earlier drafts of various chapters of this book, especially Steve Gardner, Peter Machamer, Deborah Mayo, Sandy Mitchell, and my husband, Maurice.

May there be brilliant, compassionate, kind, strong, and dedicated physicians, magnificent healers like our son Eric and my research assistant Michelle Patzelt. This book is better than it would have been because of both of you. Thank you, too, to the world's most wonderful daughters, Danielle and Natalie, and to the love of my life—my bearded, mathematician husband who somehow has always managed to inspire me and to love me, even when I don't deserve it. Thanks, too, to my parents and brothers and sisters. Your idealism and courage continue to lead me. Thanks to the very best students I have ever taught, especially all the scientists, physicians, and pre-meds at the University of Notre Dame. Thanks especially to all the Notre Dame students who repeatedly have joined me for pro-bono environmental-justice work throughout the world. You all make everything worthwhile.

—University of Notre Dame, April 10, 2011

GLOSSARY

Terms in boldface type have a separate entry in the glossary.

Alpha particles

A form of **ionizing radiation** consisting of positively charged helium atoms; alpha particles contain 2 protons and 2 neutrons. The most densely ionizing of alpha, beta, and gamma rays, it is potentially the most dangerous of these 3 forms of radiation, although it is the least penetrating. If an alpha emitter like plutonium enters the body, e.g., through inhalation, it can cause significant cellular damage or death.

Beta particles

A form of **ionizing radiation** that has the same charge and mass as electrons. Streams of beta particles, such as those from strontium-90 and cesium-137, can cause skin burns.

Carbon-dioxide-equivalent emissions

A quantity (usually measured in metric tons) that describes, for a given mixture and amount of **greenhouse gas**, the amount of CO_2 that would have the same global warming potential, when measured over a specific time frame, usually 100 years. By using measures of carbon-dioxide-equivalent emissions, the global warming potential of different greenhouse gases can be combined and compared, in terms of a common metric.

Commercial nuclear fission

When nuclear reactors fission or split uranium or plutonium atoms, they create heat, which boils water, which in turn makes steam to run a turbine to generate electricity through nuclear fission.

Commercial radioactive waste

Waste created by **commercial nuclear fission**, including more than 80 different radioactive fission products (e.g., iodine-131, cesium-137), each of which is capable of releasing **ionizing radiation**, and each of which has a different **half-life**. According to the US National Academy of Sciences, spent reactor fuel and high-level radioactive waste must be secured for at least 1 million years; otherwise it can cause severe health harms, including death.

Curie

The most common measure of the intensity of radioactivity, abbreviated Ci and named after Marie Curie, who, with her husband, Pierre, discovered radium in 1898. A curie is the quantity of a radioactive isotope that decays at the rate of $3.7 \times 10E10$ disintegrations per second. One nuclear reactor may contain over 10,000 megacuries (a megacurie is a million curies) of radioactivity. In general, the greater the intensity of radioactivity, the more damage it can inflict.

Direct costs

Costs for activities or services that benefit specific projects (e.g., salaries for project staff and materials required for a particular project), whereas indirect costs are costs that are not directly accountable to a cost object (e.g., a particular function or product). Indirect costs may be either fixed or variable. Indirect costs include taxes, administration, and personnel and security costs, and are also known as overhead.

Gamma rays

A form of **ionizing radiation** consisting of high-energy, short-wave-length radiation that is a highly penetrating form of electromagnetic radiation. Either lead or several feet of concrete or rock are required for shielding against them; otherwise they cause health harms like cancer if they are inhaled, ingested, or somehow incorporated into the body. Iodine-131 is an example of a gamma emitter. Gamma rays are especially dangerous because they can damage or kill living tissue from a distance of several feet or more.

Germ-line mutation

Any detectable and heritable variation in the lineage of germ cells. Mutations in these cells are transmitted to offspring, while those in somatic cells are not.

Greenhouse-gas (GHG) emissions

Releases of carbon dioxide, methane, nitrous oxide, ozone, perfluorocarbons, or water vapor, all of which have different abilities to cause climate change or global warming because they trap heat near the Earth.

Half-life

The period of time it takes for a substance undergoing decay to decrease by half.

Ionizing radiation

Radiation (the energy transferred as particles or waves move through space, through bodies, or from one body to another) is ionizing when it is able to remove orbital electrons from other atoms or molecules and hence able to change their structure and molecular charge. The fact that any non-zero dose of ionizing radiation can change the structure of atoms or molecules is what accounts for its ability to cause carcinogenic, mutagenic, and teratogenic damage—to induce, respectively, cancer, genetic defects, and birth defects. Ionizing radiation may consist of **alpha particles, beta particles,** or **gamma rays**.

Ionizing radiation, health effects

Short-term effects of exposure to radiation are radiation sickness—nausea, vomiting, dizziness, headache, and so on. Long-term effects of chronic radiation exposure are cancer, reproductive failure, birth defects, genetic effects, and death. One reason why effects of radiation exposure are so serious is that there is no safe, non-zero dose of ionizing radiation. Instead, the scientific consensus (see the US National Academy of Sciences' BEIR Report, cited in chapter 1) is that health effects of ionizing radiation are both cumulative and LNT— linearly related to dose, with no threshold for increased risk-harm.

Logistic regression

Also called the logistic model or logit model, it is a generalized linear model that is used to predict the probability of an occurrence of an event by fitting data to a logit function logistic curve.

Negawatts

Amory Lovins's term for energy efficiencies that actually save electricity by reducing consumer use.

Odds ratio

The ratio of the odds of an event occurring in one group (e.g., those exposed to some pollutant) to the odds of its occurring in another group (e.g., those not exposed).

Rad

A measure of the absorbed dose (energy absorbed per gram of tissue) of ionizing-radiation exposure. A sievert is the amount of radiation required to produce the same biological effect as 1 rad of high-penetration X-rays, equivalent to a gray for X-rays. For most exposures (e.g., gamma rays, X-rays), absorbed and effective doses are the same. Thus 1 gray or sievert = 1 joule per kilogram (J/kg) = 100 rad or rem = 100,000 millirad or millirem. The typical background-radiation dose is about 360 mrad or millirem, or 3.6 mgray or msv per year.

Radioactive waste

See **commercial radioactive waste**.

Reference man

Health effects of **ionizing radiation** are assessed in terms of risks-harms to a person (reference man) defined as being male, Caucasian, between 20 and 30 years old; weighing 70 kg (154 pounds); being 170 cm (5 feet 7 inches) tall; living in a climate with average temperatures of 10–20 degrees C; and being Western European or North American in habitat and custom. Women, children, and others have higher risks from ionizing radiation.

Relative risk

In epidemiology, the risk of an event, relative to exposure, where the unexposed person has a relative risk of 0.

Rem

A measure of the effective dose (energy absorbed per gram of tissue, considering health effects) of ionizing-radiation exposure. A sievert is the amount of radiation required to produce the same biological effect as 1 rad of high-penetration X-rays, equivalent to a gray for X-rays. Thus 1 gray or sievert = 1 joule per kilogram (J/kg) = 100 rad or rem = 100,000 millirad or millirem. The typical background-radiation dose is about 360 mrad or millirem, or 3.6 mgray or msv per year.

Standard mortality ratio

The ratio of observed to expected deaths for a given population.

Statistical significance test

A statistical test of how likely an event is to have occurred, other than by chance.

Z test

Any statistical test for which the distribution of the test statistic under the null hypothesis can be approximated by a normal distribution.

What Will Work

CHAPTER 1

Why Climate-Change Skeptics Are Wrong

On January 14, 2010, the board members of the *Bulletin of the Atomic Scientists*, including 19 Nobel Prize winners, voted to move the minute hand of their famous "Doomsday Clock" to 6 minutes before midnight. They say the clock indicates how close society is to midnight, to the 2 catastrophes that could destroy civilization – climate change or nuclear war.[1] In 2007, Viktor Danilov-Danilyan, of the Russian Academy of Sciences, likewise warned that climate-change impacts could be equal to those of nuclear war.[2] Yet increasing the use of atomic energy for electricity, as a way to address climate change, means increasing the risks of weapons proliferation, therefore the threats of nuclear war. Can society avoid both climate change and nuclear war? Or does society face a dilemma, either to expand atomic fission technology, or to endure global climate change?

A Tale of Two Threats:
Commercial Nuclear Fission and Climate Change

This apparent dilemma has caused some people to re-think their opposition to atomic energy. During one week in 2009, 3 leading environmentalists claimed nuclear power is needed to help address climate change, in part because they claim reactors release few greenhouse gases. Stephen Tindale, a former Greenpeace director; Chris Smith, the chair of the UK Environment Agency; and Chris Goodall, a Green Party activist, all changed their positions to support fission.[3] Physician James Lovelock, Greenpeace co-founder Patrick Moore, former Friends of the Earth board-member Hugh Montefiore, Whole Earth Catalogue founder Stewart Brand, and others say expanded nuclear power is necessary to avoid climate change.[4]

Physicist Amory Lovins and most environmentalists disagree. He claims that no major "green" groups have accepted atomic energy, that only industry "front groups" and a few self-proclaimed, individual "environmentalists" accept nuclear fission.

Besides, he says the reactor industry has been "stricken by a fatal attack of market forces"; because private investors will not touch it, the nuclear industry needs massive taxpayer subsidies; as of 2009, these subsidies cover 60–90 percent of the costs of nuclear-generated electricity.[5] Yet because of economics, safety, and proliferation problems, Lovins warns that subsidizing fission is "like defibrillating a corpse: It'll jump, but it won't revive."[6] Instead, he says, "climate change can be prevented by taking markets seriously," by pursuing the cheapest responses to global warming, namely, renewable energy (like wind) and energy efficiencies ("negawatts").[7] Market proponents seem to agree. The Economist observed that "nuclear power, once claimed to be too cheap to meter, is now too costly to matter." And, like virtually all private investors, Warren Buffet claims fission energy "does not make economic sense." This book argues that nuclear power also does not make "safety sense," in part because scientists agree that health effects of any non-zero radiation dose are risky and cumulative, proportional to dose. (Effects are linear, with no threshold for increased risks). As a consequence, higher radiation doses near reactors cause higher nearby health harms. This book likewise argues that fission energy does not make "climate sense" because its full-fuel-cycle, greenhouse-gas emissions are high, roughly the same as natural gas. Nor does atomic power make "ethics sense," because its heaviest, disproportionate health burdens fall on children, developing nations, minorities, and poor people.[8]

The upshot? These chapters show that there is no "devil's choice" between expanding nuclear fission or enduring climate change. Both are Faustian bargains. They are what logicians and Bridge players call a "Morton's Fork," a forced choice between two equally undesirable, non-exhaustive alternatives. A false dilemma, Morton's Fork is named after John Morton, Chancellor of England under Henry VIII. In 1487, Morton used this fallacy as a way to collect more taxes. If subjects lived in luxury, Morton said they had sufficient income to pay large taxes. If they lived in poverty, Morton said they must have large savings, in which case they also could afford to give much of it to the King. Either way, Morton claimed the subjects could pay the King. Just as Morton used a false dilemma, this book shows there is a false dilemma between increasing nuclear fission, or enduring climate change (CC). There are better alternatives, including energy efficiencies and renewable energy, and people want them. After all, when university psychologists surveyed Britain in 2008, they found that 91 percent of people say CC is real, that 62 percent believe "every possible action should be taken against climate change," that 68 percent think renewable energy should be expanded to address CC, and that only 14 percent say nuclear power should be used. In the same survey, roughly the same percentage of people who support using renewable energy, to stop CC, also want increased energy efficiencies.[9]

Energy efficiencies are especially needed in the United States. Each US citizen, per capita, uses about twice as much energy as a citizen in France, Germany, Italy,

Japan, or the UK. Each US citizen thus is responsible for about four times as much per-capita energy use, therefore four times as many greenhouse-gas emissions as a citizen in countries like Sweden or Switzerland. As this book shows, such energy-use patterns contribute to CC. In fact, governments encourage fossil-fuel use by keeping energy prices artificially low, through enormous subsidies to highly-polluting technologies, like coal, oil, and nuclear energy. The US government, in particular, has subsidized its citizens' oil addictions by artificially lowering the price of gas. Taking into account government subsidies, tax credits, and externalities such as air-pollution costs, economists say the real cost of gas is roughly $12 per gallon, and $13 per gallon, considering inflation.[10] Yet as of December 2009, average US gas prices were $2.68 per gallon; average UK prices were $6.66 per gallon; and average German prices were $7.19 per gallon.[11] Just during 2002–2008, US fossil-fuel industries received taxpayer subsidies totaling $72 billion, while all renewable-energy subsidies, together, were $29 billion – the majority of which supported corn-based ethanol, not cleaner technologies like wind and solar.[12] According to the US Energy Information Administration, one result of such misguided fossil-fuel subsidies is that the US annually uses about 335 million Btu of energy per person, whereas nations like Japan use 178.7, and the UK, 161.7 million Btu.[13]

Chapter Overview

As this chapter reveals, flawed government energy policies are a result of flawed science, poor ethics, short-term thinking, and special-interest influence. This book shows how and why addressing all four problems is necessary to avoid climate-related catastrophe. Introducing the problem of CC, this chapter has 7 main sections. The first shows that the energy crisis includes at least four components – oil addiction, non-CC-related deaths from fossil-fuel pollution (even from alleged "clean coal"), nuclear-weapons proliferation, and catastrophic CC. The second and third sections argue that the evidence for global CC is overwhelming, and that Western nations, especially the US, are most responsible for it. The fourth section shows why CC skeptics – "deniers" who doubt that CC is real, and "delayers" who say that CC should not be addressed yet – have no valid objections. They all err scientifically and ethically. The fifth section reveals that all current scientific methods confirm the reality of global CC, and virtually all expert-scientific analyses, published in refereed, scientific-professional journals, accept the reality of CC. Yet, as the sixth section shows, the CC debate continues largely because fossil-fuel special interests have paid non-experts to deny CC. The seventh section of the chapter provides an overview of the entire book, chapter by chapter, as well as some caveats about what it does and does not contain, in addressing various solutions to CC.

Four Components of the Energy Crisis

To understand alternative responses to CC, one first must understand the global-energy crisis. At least since the 1970s, this crisis has presented four distinct problems, each of which will be surveyed in subsequent paragraphs:

(1) oil addiction – massive demand for costly, insecure oil supplies, especially from the Persian Gulf;
(2) pollution-related deaths – hundreds of thousands of annual fatalities caused by using fossil fuels, including alleged "clean coal";
(3) nuclear-weapons proliferation – resulting partly from using commercial-nuclear fission; and
(4) catastrophic CC – caused by greenhouse gases, mainly from fossil fuels.

All four energy problems are especially acute for the US. Regarding (1), because the US must import more than 60 percent of the oil it uses, it has spent billions of dollars, many lives, and military force (in places like Iraq) to try to secure its oil imports. Regarding (2), largely because the US provides half its electricity with coal – and supplies most of its vehicles with oil – it faces massive increases in cancer, heart disease, and respiratory disease, including a doubling of US childhood asthma rates in the last decade (see later paragraphs). Regarding (3), partly because the US has more atomic-energy plants than any other nation, it also faces greater risks of nuclear terrorism and proliferation. The more reactors a nation has, the more terrorist targets it has. Already the US has uncovered terrorist hideouts containing diagrams for attacks on US reactors. Regarding (4), the US has emitted the greatest volume of greenhouse gases to date, and it emits more gases, per capita, than other nations. Moreover, most Chinese greenhouse-gas (GHG) emissions are attributable to exports consumed in the West. For all 3 reasons, this book agrees with most scientists and ethicists, that the US ought to bear the greatest burden of GHG emissions reductions. Scientists say that to avert climate catastrophe, the West must move to a near-zero, carbon-dioxide-equivalent (CO_2) emissions. Already by the year 2000, many official government and UN reports, like the UK government's Stern Report, showed weather-related CC effects (droughts, floods, hurricanes) were killing 150,000 people annually. Stern and climate ethicists say the West is responsible for most of these deaths. Why? Receiving many fossil-fuel benefits, each person in the developed world nevertheless causes about 11 tons per year of CO_2, and each ton has a social cost (harm to others) of about $85. Although each person in the West enjoys many advantages because of fossil fuels, Stern says each such person causes about $935 in damages to global-CC victims, many of whom are both poor and innocent of causing CC. A 2009 report of the US National Academy of Sciences says something similar. Although the Academy was unable to count many fossil-fuel, pollution-related deaths and CC harms, although many costs could not be monetized, and although its figure is an underestimate, the Academy says US fossil-fuel use causes more than $120 billion annual damages. These damages amount to more than 3.2 cents per kWhr, just for non-CC-related health costs that US coal plants impose on US citizens.[14]

OIL ADDICTION

Regarding problem (1), oil addiction and oil security, later chapters suggest that moving to near-zero CO_2 emissions would help the economy over the long term, eliminate most foreign-oil imports, and reduce incentives for military actions. After all, the US admits that part of the reason for the Gulf War was to secure US oil supplies. Not counting the human lives that were lost or irrevocably damaged, the direct costs of the Iraq War are about $100 billion per year, equivalent to about $100 for each barrel of oil imported by the US from the Persian Gulf region. Yet as already mentioned, economists say the real price of gas is about $13 per gallon, although US consumers pay less than $3 per gallon. Because the US annually uses more than 100 billion gallons of gas, the disparity between real gas costs, and gas-station prices, takes a large toll on the US economy. This toll includes more than $1 trillion annually in gasoline subsidies and health and environmental costs, for which consumers do not pay at the pump. Economists say that in 2006, the last year for which data are available, the total unpaid costs of US gasoline, including subsidies, health effects, and so on, were up to $1.49 trillion annually.[15]

One of the worst things about the high costs of the US oil addiction is that they are unnecessary. Later chapters provide market data to show that economic expansion can occur despite (and indeed because of) a transition to renewable energy and to per-capita declines in energy use. Moreover, since the 1950s, the amount of US energy–required to produce a dollar of GDP growth–has declined. Energy use, per dollar of GDP, is now about half of what it was 50 years ago. California provides an excellent example. Although per-capital electricity use has increased nationally, it has remained constant in California. The reason is not the state's milder climate but its greater energy efficiencies (motion detectors, photoelectric switches, efficient electric motors, compact fluorescent bulbs, energy-conserving appliances). For instance, despite superior features, the typical refrigerator now is larger, costs less, but consumes only about one-fifth of the per-foot energy that it consumed 25 years ago.[16]

NO "CLEAN" COAL

Apart from the harmful effects of CC, the use of fossil fuels also threatens life and health, not just climate and pocketbooks. Energy problem (2) is that, apart from the more than 104,000 Americans who have died in coal-mining accidents, fossil-fuel pollution – from sources like coal-fired plants and gas-powered vehicles – has caused massive air pollution. Even if carbon were removed from coal, later arguments show that "clean coal" is oxymoronic because there are numerous, seriously harmful coal pollutants, in addition to carbon. A ground-breaking 2010 report by a major physicians' association warned that "coal contributes to four of the five top causes of mortality in the US" – and most of those deaths are not merely carbon-related; a 2009 US National Academy of Sciences report placed the annual health and climate costs, of US coal plants, at more than $120 billion annually, even before all costs were counted; a 2007 Cornell University study concluded that air, water, and soil pollution, together, prematurely cause at least 40 percent of all deaths worldwide, killing 3.7 billion people annually, many from fossil-fuel pollution.[17] In 1999, the World Health Organization estimated that about 3 million people annually die prematurely because of air pollution – more than 8,000 deaths each day.[18] One European-Union (EU) scientific study calculated that 25–40 percent of all UK deaths were "thought to be directly attributable to the effects of air pollution," mostly from fossil fuels.[19] Likewise, the American Public Health Association (APHA) notes that there is an "epidemic" of asthma among US "children and young adults under the age of 35," and that ambient air pollution is the major culprit.[20]

Fossil fuels are the major air-pollution problem because together, vehicles and coal-fired plants are responsible for most of the particulates, nitrogen oxides, reactive hydrocarbons, and ozone that foul the air, yet there are no safe doses of either ozone or particulates.[21] Scientists say that roughly half of US particulate pollution is from petroleum-fueled vehicles and half from fossil-fueled electricity; together this particulate pollution causes 30,000 to 100,000 premature US deaths each year, especially among children. In 2009, the US National Academy of Sciences said that burning fossil fuels costs the US at least $120 billion a year, just in health costs, not counting lost workdays, environmental harms, and other economic losses.[22] Even US consultants, hired by the pro-fossil-fuel Bush administration in 2000, admit this problem. Although the administration weakened air-pollution regulations and enforcement, its own consultants admitted airborne-particulate pollution, alone, most from fossils fuels, causes at least 30,000 annual, preventable US deaths. A 2003 US National Cancer Institute (NCI) study drew even more disturbing conclusions. Studying more than half a million people over 16 years in 156 cities, it showed there is no safe level of air pollution, that exposure to fine-particulate pollution (mostly from fossil fuels) is as risky as being overweight or exposed to cigarette smoke. Even if one excludes cancer and effects of water pollution, pesticides, and other air pollutants – like volatile organic compounds – the NCI study says each 10 micrograms of fine-particulate pollution, alone, causes an 18-percent increase in heart-related deaths, an 8-percent increase in lung-related deaths, and a 4-percent increase in US overall deaths. These NCI results mean that in Chicago, for instance, particulates are responsible for roughly 10 percent of the city's deaths.[23]

In fact, fossil-fuel pollution causes similar problems everywhere. Polluted air costs EU nations $161 billion annually in lost workdays, deaths, and economic damages because of heart attacks, cancer, asthma, and respiratory disease; EU scientists say the average European loses about one year of life because of air pollution.[24] While one year may seem trivial, this figure really means that members of sensitive groups, like children, lose many years of life, while the most robust members of the population lose none. As the preceding APHA statement illustrates, air pollution harms the youngest, most vulnerable people first.

Scientists have long known the hazards of fossil-fuel air pollution, yet subsequent chapters show that government has done little about them, partly because of special interests. In the early 1960s, US studies showed air pollution increases mortality, lung cancer, and respiratory problems.[25] More than 40 years ago, economists, writing in *Science*, showed that a 50-percent reduction in air pollution could cut annual US health costs by 5 percent – and cut costs of illness and death by at least $2 billion. Yet little was done. A 1980 study showed that about 50,000 people in the US died that year from air pollution alone, and the figures are even higher now.[26] Scientists say the health costs of ignoring a half-century of scientific data on air pollution are massive. Globally, air pollution kills 3 million people annually.[27] A World Health Organization assessment concluded that more than two-thirds of these premature, otherwise-avoidable, air-pollution-caused deaths – more than 2 million (of 3 million) premature deaths annually – are caused by fossil fuels, especially coal. Yet, as already explained, merely removing carbon from coal would not avoid most of these deaths, even if this removal could be done cost-effectively.[28]

NUCLEAR PROLIFERATION

An energy-related catastrophe whose magnitude is perhaps even greater than that of fossil-fuel-related pollution deaths is problem (3), nuclear-weapons proliferation. As chapter 2 explains in more detail, one theme of this book is that it makes little sense to address CC by building more reactors. Why? In attempting to use fission to reduce the probability of CC catastrophe, one increases the probability of a nuclear-proliferation catastrophe. Why would expanding atomic energy increase risks of nuclear proliferation? The main reason is that with increased fission technology, there will be more weapons-grade plutonium in circulation, able to be diverted to either terrorism or proliferation. Also, as chapters 2 and 7 discuss in more detail, the main motivation for most nations' beginning commercial fission programs is that they want nuclear-weapons' capabilities. Because the same, 14-stage, fuel cycle (see chapter 2) is used for both military and commercial nuclear production, commercial fission programs often are a convenient cover-up for military activities. Even if they are not, their very existence increases proliferation risks.

Of course, other non-fission nuclear technologies (such as proton-lithium reactions and fusion) might provide energy in the distant future and yet might have lower proliferation risks. Because these other technologies have not yet been shown to work safely and cost-effectively, on an industrial scale, fission is the only nuclear option discussed here, and it is known to have proliferation problems. Given these problems, as well as concerns about GHG emissions, costs, safety, health harms, radioactive wastes, and environmental injustice (higher pollution impacts on vulnerable populations, like children), this volume argues that nuclear risks and costs far exceed those associated with renewable-energy sources like wind and solar photovoltaic (PV).

CLIMATE CHANGE

Energy problem (4), CC, presents a possible global catastrophe because GHG emissions have increased by more than one-third in the last 150 years. Although 2010 data are not yet available, mean CO_2 emissions in 2009 were 387 ppm, and 386 ppm in 2008.[29] As a consequence, glaciers are disappearing across the globe, Arctic ice is diminishing, Siberian permafrost is melting, species like the polar bear are endangered, many ecosystems (such as coral reefs) are being extensively damaged, and sea levels are rising, threatening low-lying populations. Extreme climatic events, like Hurricane Katrina, also are increasing and becoming more intense; millions of acres of northern forests are dying from insect infestations during longer, warmer summers; more people are dying of vector-borne diseases whose range is expanding with warmer temperatures; and poor people throughout the world are those harmed most by CC-induced floods, hurricanes, and droughts. The most recent findings of the international Intergovernmental Panel on Climate Change (IPCC) are that cumulative GHG emissions must remain within the range of 445–490 ppm in order to limit mean (or average) global-temperature rise to 2–2.4 degrees Celsius or 3.6–4.3 degrees Fahrenheit. (The range is needed because of future, unknown climate variables, such as water-vapor and cloud feedbacks.)[30]

If global-average-temperature increases reach 2–2.4 degrees Celsius, the IPCC, the 2009 US National Academy of Sciences, and the classic, UK-government analysis, the Stern Report, argue that 1 in 6 people will be without water, and tens-to-hundreds of millions of people will be climate refugees, made homeless by droughts, storms, flooding, and sea rise. Part or all of the Amazonian rainforest – the lungs of the planet – will collapse. Billions of people will suffer water shortages by 2080. Crop yields will fall in many developing countries, causing 20–60 percent increases in hunger by 2080, especially in Africa and west Asia. Small-mountain glaciers will disappear, further jeopardizing water supplies. Sea-level rise will threaten London, Shanghai, New York City, Tokyo, Hong Kong, and other coastal cities. Coral-reef ecosystems will become irreversibly damaged. Many other ecosystems will become unable to maintain their current form, and 20–50 percent of species will face rapid extinction. Increases in hurricane intensity and frequency likewise will double current US-damage costs. The Atlantic thermohaline-circulation system will weaken; the Greenland ice sheet will irreversibly melt; and risks of abrupt, large-scale climate shifts, such as the collapse of the West Antarctic ice sheet, will occur. As already noted, despite the many benefits of fossil fuels, the Stern Report warns that in addition to hundreds of thousands of annual deaths from fossil-fuel pollution, already by the year 2000, weather-related CC effects were causing 150,000 annual deaths from drought, floods, and other CC-related threats. Who causes most of this climate-related global death and destruction? Stern says each person in the developed world contributes about $935 in annual, CC social costs, most of which are imposed on the poorest people – results that are consistent with the 2009 US National Academy of Sciences' report.[31]

To prevent further catastrophic climate effects, and to limit global-average-temperature increases to about 2 degrees Celsius, IPCC estimates that by 2040, global CO_2 emissions must be reduced by 50–85 percent, relative to year-2000 levels. This 50–85-percent reduction is the EU climate goal. However, IPCC says a 50-percent reduction would give only a 15-percent chance of limiting global-temperature rise to 2 degrees, and that an 85-percent reduction is necessary to obtain an 85-percent chance of limiting global-temperature rise to this amount.[32] As already noted (and as later paragraphs argue), because the West, especially the US, historically has caused most of the CC problem, any equitable solution requires the US to achieve almost-total elimination of fossil-fuel emissions.[33] In the US, roughly 85 percent of GHG emissions are caused by burning fossil fuels, including 44 percent from oil. Globally, 55 percent of GHG emissions arise from fossil-fuel use. Methane emissions from landfills, pipelines, and agriculture cause 16 percent; nitrous-oxide emissions from fertilizer use cause 9 percent; forest burning and other land-use changes cause 19 percent; and emissions of halocarbons cause 1 percent of global GHG emissions.[34]

Given the economic, ethical, political, and military desirability of moving to near-zero, US GHG emissions, what is the best way to achieve this goal? This book argues that because employing the nuclear-fuel cycle is more carbon intensive, costly, unsafe, and inequitable than pursuing energy efficiencies and renewable power, fission cannot solve CC. To understand why not, consider first the evidence for CC, and thus what is necessary to solve it.

IPCC Evidence for Climate Change

CC first came to public attention in 1988, when the United Nations (the World Meteorological Association and the UN Environment Programme) created the IPCC. Its purpose has been to bring together climate scientists from throughout the world to assess possible global-warming or CC risks. The main IPCC work has been to evaluate peer-reviewed-scientific literature on CC, to publish special reports assessing it, and to inform and implement the 1992 UN Framework Convention on Climate Change – which the US ratified in 1992. This UN convention is an international treaty designed to stabilize GHG emissions at levels that would prevent dangerous anthropogenic (human-caused) CC. Implementing this UN convention led to the 1997 Kyoto Protocol, which established legally-binding obligations for developed nations to reduce GHG emissions. Underlying and guiding these UN agreements are the four reports of the IPCC – issued in 1990, 1995, 2001, and 2007. Each report scientifically assesses CC risks to date.[35]

By 1995, the IPCC concluded there was strong scientific evidence that human activities were affecting global climate, a position affirmed more strongly in subsequent IPCC reports. In 2000, the American Association for the Advancement of Science (AAAS) warned that "the world is warming up. Average temperatures are a half a degree centigrade higher than a century ago.... Pollution from 'greenhouse gases' such as carbon dioxide (CO_2) and methane is at least partly to blame."[36] In 2001, the IPCC stated unequivocally that human activities are having detectable effects on Earth's climate, on the atmosphere and water of Earth. It said "most of the observed warming of the last 50 years is likely to have been due to the increase in greenhouse-gas concentrations."[37] By 2003, all major scientific organizations (whose research expertise bears on CC) had ratified this 2001 IPCC conclusion. In 2001, the US National Academy of Sciences confirmed:

> greenhouse gases are accumulating in Earth's atmosphere as a result of human activities, causing surface air temperatures and subsurface ocean temperatures to rise.... The IPCC's conclusion that most of the observed warming of the last 50 years is likely to have been due to this increase in greenhouse-gas concentrations accurately reflects the current thinking of the scientific community on this issue.[38]

The IPCC and other scientific groups also have emphasized the duty to take collective global action to address CC because of its potentially catastrophic consequences. They warn that 20th-century temperature increases were the largest of any century during the past 1,000 years.[39] As already noted, largely because anthropogenic GHG emissions have increased by one-third over the last century and a half, harmful agricultural, biological, hydrological, medical, economic, and weather-related consequences already have occurred. Even a 1–2 foot sea rise would severely harm tens of millions of people living on lowland islands and in coastal areas like Florida and Bangladesh. As already noted, to limit such destruction, climate scientists say mean-global-temperature increases must be no greater than about 2 degrees Celsius or 4 degrees Fahrenheit.[40] In February 2003, the American Meteorological Society again emphasized these warnings and echoed the duty of collective responsibility to address CC:

> There is now clear evidence that the mean annual temperature at the Earth's surface, averaged over the entire globe, has been increasing in the past 200 years. There is also clear evidence that the abundance of greenhouse gases has increased over the same period.... Because human activities are contributing to climate change, we have a collective responsibility to develop and undertake carefully considered response actions.[41]

Likewise, the UK's Stern Report says CC is the largest, most significant failure of the market system that has ever occurred. As already noted, apart from the many benefits of fossil fuels, the report (consistent with the US National Academy of Sciences' 2009 report) says that because each person in the developed world annually causes about $935 in CC damages to global citizens – most of whom are poor – developed nations bear primary responsibility for addressing CC.[42]

Responsibility for Climate Change

What ethical reasons show that developed nations, especially the US, are most responsible for CC? Given the requirements of the UN Framework Convention on Climate Change, given the small US population (5 percent of the globe's people), and given that US GHG emissions are the largest of any nation, most climate ethicists say equity requires a near-total (96-percent) US elimination of fossil-fuel emissions by 2050. Moreover, the sooner this zero-emissions economy is achieved, scientists say the smaller will be the costs. There are at least four different ethical frameworks that clearly demonstrate this responsibility of developed nations. The first, or historical, principles of ethics are based on the maxim of "you broke it, you fix it," or on fair access to a common resource. Following the views of John Locke on property rights, historical ethical principles require those – who appropriate or destroy common property (such as clean air) – to leave "as much and as good for others" to use. However, developed nations obviously have violated this principle because, if other nations emit the same per capita GHG emissions as the US, the planet will be destroyed. Thus, developed nations have caused the majority of harmful CC emissions and have not left "as much and as good" clean air for other countries to use. Such historical ethical principles are the Lockean basis of the US Constitution and Bill of Rights. Provided one accepts these principles, because the US has created roughly 30 percent of GHG emissions, the US is responsible for correcting about one-third of the problem.[43]

A second set of ethical principles, so-called time-slice or a-historical principles, likewise show that developed nations, especially the US, are mainly responsible for CC. These ethical principles ignore past causes of CC, mostly emissions from the West. Instead they presuppose GHG emissions should be stabilized at current levels, and that every currently-existing person should have an equal-emissions allotment. They presuppose each person should be permitted to cause the same amount of GHG emissions, up to the point that total emissions risk global catastrophe. However, using this second set of ethical principles, the US would have to reduce 80 percent of its current emissions, because it releases far more GHG emissions than allowed, given its relatively small population.[44]

A third set of ethical principles for assessing CC responsibility are those of the late Harvard philosopher John Rawls. For Rawls, the rich can have more goods or produce more pollution emissions, provided their goods and emissions benefit the worst-off people of the world, rather than disproportionately benefit themselves. However, Rawlsian principles show that developed nations are mainly responsible for correcting CC because they use the lion's share of natural resources, like clean air, and their use does not benefit mainly the poor. For instance, 89 percent of the goods and services produced in the US are consumed there. More generally, most of the global poor cannot afford goods produced by developed nations. Besides, US GHG emissions are inefficient, producing less per-capita GDP than the average GHG emissions of the rest of the world. All these facts mean that US emissions are more likely, than other nations' emissions, to harm others because each US pollution-unit produces less development. Hence, the US and developed nations must drastically reduce GHG emissions, because they are dangerous, disproportionate to their small populations, and do not significantly benefit the rest of world, especially poor people.[45]

A fourth, or utilitarian, set of principles also shows that developed nations, especially the US, are primarily responsible for CC and ought to remedy it. Utilitarian principles dictate that people should act so as to produce the greatest amount of good for the greatest number of people. Because developed nations are a minority of the world's people, yet have caused most GHG emissions, and because their fossil-fuel use primarily benefits them, not the majority (the poor), developed nations' CC behavior fails to satisfy utilitarian principles. Also, because of the diminishing marginal utility of the benefits of fossil-fuel use by developed nations, these benefits do not outweigh CC harms to the majority of the world. Thus, on utilitarian grounds, developed nations are mainly responsible for correcting CC.[46]

If one ignores past harms from developed nations' massive GHG emissions, even the most modest egalitarian ethical principles show that developed nations bear primary responsibility for CC. Such modest principles affirm that, because people finally know the harms of CC, the initial GHG emissions allocation rule should affirm equal, per-capita GHG emissions for each global inhabitant (given GHG emissions limits necessary to avoid global catastrophe). A subsequent rule might permit trading as a way to reduce emissions in developed nations. Even on this scheme, however, which is the most generous to developed nations and which ignores past responsibility, the US would be required to cut 75 percent of current emissions. Thus, all major ethical schemes – including historical, a-historical, Rawlsian, utilitarian, and egalitarian – show that developed nations, especially the US, are mainly responsible for correcting CC.[47]

What does this CC responsibility entail? In the US, it requires massively reducing fossil-fuel burning by automobiles, electric utilities, and manufacturers – because 84 percent of US GHG emissions come from fossil fuels.[48]

Climate-Change Skeptics

In response to overwhelming scientific evidence for anthropogenic CC, some claim CC is uncertain. These CC skeptics are either "deniers" or "delayers." Either they deny CC, or they admit it, but claim that action to avert CC can be delayed without causing catastrophe. A 2006 poll, reported in *Time* magazine, found that many Americans are deniers. Only about 56 percent believes average global temperatures have risen. The same article reported, "64 percent of Americans thinks scientists disagree with one another about global warming."[49] Many of these public doubts about CC have been orchestrated by fossil-fuel industries, as later paragraphs show. Oil, coal, and automobile industries,in turn, invoke these "public doubts" to justify US failure to join the rest of the world in addressing CC. CC skeptics also point to the fact that, just as scientists have been wrong in the past, they could be wrong about CC. Max Planck's advisors were wrong when they told him not to go into physics, because all the important questions had been answered. Copernican astronomers were wrong when they said the Sun revolved around the Earth. Medical doctors were wrong when they gave people arsenic for stomach ailments. Geophysicists were wrong when they said that continents could not drift. Gynecologists were wrong when they gave women hormones for menopause. Are those who assert anthropogenic CC also wrong?[50]

One way to answer this question is to examine all technical analyses of CC, published in refereed, expert-scientific journals, so as to compare the views of scientists who do technical CC research. University of California, San Diego, scientist Naomi Oreskes did just that. She examined one of the most important databases, the Web of Science of the Institute for Scientific Information (ISI). ISI indexes scientific articles published globally, in more than 8,500 different refereed-scientific journals. During 1993–2003, ISI indexed 928 articles that presented CC research. Oreskes evaluated these 928 articles and found surprising results. None of the articles advanced findings that explicitly refuted or challenged CC. Instead, 20 percent explicitly endorsed CC, and 50 percent implicitly endorsed CC by assessing various CC impacts. Another 15 percent evaluated various methods for analyzing climate; 10 percent discussed the historical record of climate, or paleo-climate change, and the remaining 5 percent of articles likewise implicitly endorsed CC by discussing scientific strategies for mitigating CC. Thus, of all papers published by climate researchers during this decade, and indexed in the classic ISI database, none – not one – challenged the existence of anthropogenic CC. The main reason more articles did not *explicitly* endorse anthropogenic CC is that scientists typically analyze only disputed or unanswered questions. They do not focus on areas on which everyone already agrees. In fact, scientific journals refuse to publish material that is not new. Moreover, because scientists typically do not take votes on their views, their technical papers (in refereed-scientific journals) reveal their beliefs. Thus, the Oreskes journal-survey shows there is virtually no expert-scientific disagreement about the existence of anthropogenic CC, at least among the scientists who do the basic research in the field, because none of the papers challenges the existence of anthropogenic CC. (However, as later paragraphs show, scientists do disagree about minor details regarding precisely how this admitted CC is taking place.) The Oreskes result means that the record of scientific publications appears consistent with the consensus statements of all major scientific groups: CC is real and is mainly human-caused. Scholars say that, by 1995, the reality of anthropogenic CC was a matter of expert-scientific consensus among technical researchers in the field.[51] "The basic reality of anthropogenic climate change is no longer a subject of scientific debate."[52]

Common Objections to Taking Action on Anthropogenic Climate Change

But if the reality of anthropogenic CC is no longer a subject of expert-scientific debate, why do many Americans think CC is disputed? To answer this question, consider 8 fossil-fuel-industry objections to the existence of CC and why these objections mislead people.

Some spokespersons claim, *first*, that CC may be a result of natural climate variability.[53] However, this objection errs because scientists have been able to separate CC "signals" from the "noise" of natural-climate variability. Indeed, scientists' success in doing so, coupled with the magnitude of human-caused change, are the main reasons that virtually all climatologists agree about anthropogenic CC. Scientists know that, from roughly 10,000 BC until about 1750 AD, CO_2 levels in the atmosphere were stable at about 280 parts per million (ppm). In the middle of the 18th century, however, people began to burn fossil fuels to power industry. As a result, average CO_2 concentrations began increasing. Concentrations went from 316 parts per million (ppm) in 1959, to 387 ppm in 2009. By the end of this century, expert-scientific consensus (following the IPCC) says that anthropogenic CC will cause global-temperature increases of 1.1–6.4 degrees Celsius, depending on other climate variations that have not yet taken place. Of course, both CC and greater natural climate variability could be occurring, but anyone who rejects anthropogenic CC errs on at least three grounds. For one thing, she erroneously assumes that massive increases in atmospheric CO_2 have had negligible effects, although laboratory experiments clearly show increased warming from increased GHG emissions. That is, laboratory measurements show how much infra-red radiation, at which wavelengths, CO_2 molecules absorb. These measurements then enable one to calculate warming levels for each CO_2 increment. A second problem with natural-variability objections is their erroneous assumption that repeatedly confirmed correlations, between increased CO_2 and increased temperature, are either strange coincidences or inexplicable – contrary to what physicists have long accepted about the behavior of gas, pressure, and temperature. A third problem is that natural-variability objections reject all scientific theory behind long-ago predictions that burning fossil fuels would increase CC. A century ago, Swedish chemist Svante Arrhenius made this prediction. By 1950, many other scientists agreed – on purely theoretical grounds – that fossil-fuel burning would cause global warming. Part of their rationale is thermodynamics. It dictates that, if the planet is to remain at a constant temperature, amounts of energy (absorbed as sunlight) and amounts of energy (emitted back to space, in the longer wave lengths of the infra-red spectrum) must be the same. Thermodynamics also dictates that if this energy is trapped and cannot be emitted back to space, Earth temperatures will increase. Given thermodynamics, one does not need massive temperature measurements to recognize CC is predictable. When someone uses standard scientific theory (e.g., thermodynamics) to make predictions that later come true, one cannot reject the predictions without rejecting basic science. Thus, if CC objectors appeal to natural variability, they are fundamentally unscientific in rejecting thermodynamics, what scientists have confirmed for centuries. These objectors are like people who see someone shoot another person with a gun, but who nevertheless claim the victim could have died of natural causes. If objectors make such anti-scientific claims, contrary to the evidence, at a minimum they must explain why they believe much Western science is wrong.[54]

A *second* objection, according to some oil-industry claims, is that even if CC exists, it is not harmful because people prefer warmer climates, and the climate changes at the low end of the IPCC predictions may not be severe.[55] However, this warming-is-good part of the objection errs because the problem is not merely global warming, but CC and the fact that increased CO_2 concentrations make it more difficult for planetary energy, absorbed as sunlight, to be emitted back to space. As a consequence, this greenhouse effect increases average temperatures of the lower atmosphere – which disrupts normal energy flows from the planet's surface to the atmosphere, and from equator to poles. This energy-flow disruption, in turn, changes ocean, wind, rainfall, and weather patterns – causing increased frequency and intensity of hurricanes, tornadoes, droughts, floods, crop failures. These weather changes, in turn, annually cause millions of climate refugees and thousands of climate-related deaths. As noted earlier, already by the year 2000, the UK government's Stern Report showed that weather-related, climate-change effects (droughts, floods, hurricanes) were killing 150,000 people annually. Stern showed that despite many fossil-fuel benefits, each person in the developed world was causing about \$935 in annual climate-related damages to others. Moreover, the Stern results are consistent with the 2009 US National Academy of Sciences' conclusions. Such massive disruptions obviously are not beneficial. As later paragraphs reveal, the main groups who say CC is beneficial are either fossil-fuel industries that profit from CC – or those they pay to do PR. Of course, the second part of this objection is partly correct. Warming at the low end of the IPCC range would not be as catastrophic as high-end warming. However, the problem with this low-end objection is that no one can guarantee where, in the range of future climate effects, actual effects will occur, given various future climate events of unknown magnitude, such as water-vapor and cloud feedbacks. This low-end objection thus amounts to saying that given future variables, uncertainties about the precise nature of future CC argue for doing nothing to avert CC. This is the same as objection 7, which will be analyzed shortly.[56]

A *third* objection is that scientists apparently disagree about CC.[57] However, this objection misunderstands the precise nature of scientific disagreement. As anyone (who understands science) knows, scientists often agree about the *existence* of some reality, like CC, before they agree on the precise *mechanisms* and *timing* to explain it. For instance, people usually agree about the reality of someone's death, but without an autopsy, they may disagree on what caused the death. Similarly, people often recognize auto problems before they understand precisely what caused them. The same is true of CC. Virtually all scientists – who do expert research on climate – agree that anthropogenic CC is real. Nevertheless, some disagree about the *precise* timing (or tempo) and mechanisms (or mode) causing CC, such as the precise degrees to which clouds amplify water-vapor feedbacks at specific temperatures, and therefore CO_2 warming. Yet CC skeptics claim that, because of such minor disagreements and uncertainties, CC is doubtful. They confuse disagreement on minor CC details with disagreement on CC itself.[58] However, as noted, disagreement on precisely *why* someone died – does not entail disagreement *that* she is dead. Likewise, disagreement on precisely *when* a cancer patient will die – does not entail disagreement *that* she has cancer. The same is true in debates over evolution. By the middle of the 20th century, virtually all biologists accepted evolution. Nevertheless, disagreement continues on very *precise* details about it – on what paleontologist George Gaylord Simpson calls the "tempo and mode" of evolution. One reason for similar CC disagreements is that CO_2 is not the only influence on global warming. Some aerosols and particles of air pollution cool the atmosphere, while others warm it. The precise effects of all these agents are difficult to precisely predict, partly because one cannot conduct experiments on entire climate systems, and partly because some future phenomena are unknown. Nevertheless scientists agree on the range of CC effects, even if they cannot always narrow that range precisely. Thus, although climate skeptics are correct that there are uncertainties in climate science, they err in thinking these uncertainties challenge the existence of anthropogenic CC. Belief in anthropogenic CC is therefore no less reliable than belief in evolution, DNA, HIV, or fractional-electrical charges. As scientists recognize, confirmed science is reliable, but it is neither certain nor perfect. Climate critics err in assuming climate science must be perfect. Yet no area of science is without minor disagreement.[59]

A *fourth* CC objection is that some people claim Earth has natural-feedback mechanisms, self-regulating processes, that protect it from catastrophic, anthropogenic CC.[60] However, this objection errs on at least three grounds. First, it begs the question to say that humans cannot have damaging CC effects. Second, because no known scientific mechanism protects Earth from catastrophic CC, this objection has no empirical support. Third, the objection is inconsistent with thousands of scientific findings, confirming average-global-temperature rises, hurricane increases, and so on. Obviously this purely-hypothetical protective mechanism either does not exist, or has failed. Besides, no self-regulating mechanism protected Earth, centuries ago, from meteors that caused massive deaths and extinctions. No self-regulating mechanism protects people from their massive pollution. Instead, scientists say roughly 90 percent of the 600,000 annual US cancer deaths are anthropogenic, "environmentally induced and theoretically preventable."[61] Likewise, no mechanism protects people from eating too much and getting fat. Few reasons thus suggest that a CC mechanism protects Earth. Of course, there are some negative-feedback mechanisms that help mitigate CC, as already mentioned, mechanisms like those associated with some aerosols and particular pollution. However, the magnitude of none of these mechanisms comes remotely close to being large enough to stop or prevent climate change.

A *fifth* possible objection is that some climate scientists "omit much contrary evidence," are guilty of bias and "alarmism," and are not reliable sources of CC information.[62] For instance, in November 2009, emails among scientists, at the Climatic Research Unit (CRU) of the UK's University of East Anglia, revealed these scientists apparently did not want to share information with climate critics, contrary to the UK's Freedom of Information Act. Critics said CRU researchers were overstating CC evidence, so as to support corrective action.[63] Also, the latest IPCC report inadvertently made a false claim that Himalayan glaciers were going to disappear by 2035, instead of 2350.[64] Do such problems give climate skeptics grounds for rejecting CC? Fossil-fuel-industry representatives say they do. Although they cite the work of climate scientists who affirm anthropogenic CC, many industry representatives misrepresent that research; they claim that minor uncertainties show the research "is inconsistent with or directly contradicts" anthropogenic CC.[65] However, at least three reasons suggest climate skeptics err when they use scientific error, uncertainty, or disagreement as grounds for rejecting CC. First, rejecting CC, because of the Himalayan mistake, confuses the general scientific consensus about the *existence* of anthropogenic CC, with particular scientific misrepresentations about specific CC *timing, mechanisms, or data points.* Misrepresentations or uncertainties about specific data points do not negate the reality of CC itself, in part because CC is confirmed by much independent data. At least three different, independent records of land-surface-temperature readings exist, only one of which is compiled at East Anglia CRU. All accounts generally agree with each other and are accepted as reliable.[66] Thus, even if CRU data were flawed, this would not jeopardize claims about the existence of CC. This objection also errs in presupposing no misbehavior or uncertainty in science. Yet every area of science (and life) includes some misbehavior and uncertainty. The possible errors of a few researchers are insufficient to jeopardize the results of a majority of CC scientists – provided the majority has independent data to show it is right. As already noted, scientific validity does not require perfect worlds or perfect people. To think otherwise confuses the reliability of people with the reliability of scientific claims. This confusion is like saying there is no God because some religious leaders are pedophiles, or that there is no good rock music because some musicians are drug addicts. All beliefs must be evaluated in their own right, not merely in terms of who professes them. Otherwise, one commits the genetic fallacy – confusing the quality of a belief with the quality of those who accept it. Thus, the CRU errors have not changed climate *science*, or the reality of anthropogenic CC, but only people's *perceptions* of CC. Besides, if people do not want to rely on any climate scientists, because a few climate scientists apparently have behaved badly, they ought to practice what they preach. When they are sick, they ought to reject all medical opinions, simply because some physicians behave badly or give wrong diagnoses. Yet no reasonable people would reject all medical scientists. Instead they would seek the best medical scientists and listen to them. Listening to the best climate scientists amounts to following the best, refereed, scientific journals, as Oreskes did.

A *sixth* possible objection to the existence of anthropogenic global-warming is focused on recent, extremely cold, weather. Objectors might deny CC because the winter of 2010 was so cold.[67] This objection, however, fails because it confuses average, with individual, temperatures. It also generalizes on the basis of only one case that occurred only in the Northern Hemisphere. As every logic student learns, it always is fallacious to generalize from one instance. Thus, one ought not infer that all whites are less intelligent than all blacks, merely because of one unintelligent white person. Likewise, one ought not deny CC because of some cold weather.

A *seventh* objection is that uncertainty about CC tempo and mode might argue for inaction, for not acting immediately to curb CC.[68] However, when people face the possibility of catastrophic events, they do not wait to act, until they are certain about precisely when, where, and how catastrophe will occur. If they did, they could not avert catastrophe. People get medical check-ups, even when they feel fine. They do not wait until they are sick to see doctors. People buy home insurance. They do not wait until they have a fire, or smell smoke. Another, already-mentioned, problem with this objection is its presupposing that uncertainty about minor CC details is grounds for political inaction and doing only research. Yet uncertainty is precisely the reason, especially in cases of potential catastrophe, that people ought to take protective action. If people have repeated car trouble, they should not drive alone, in a dangerous neighborhood, late at night, because they are uncertain about how the car will perform. Instead they should take precautions. If doctors disagree on whether some patients have fatal cancers, the patients ought not "do nothing." Possibly facing death, reasonable patients instead take precautions. They avoid the worst outcomes. Indeed, facing even trivial harms, people take precautions. They carry umbrellas if the sky is cloudy. They don't wait for rain to do so. As scientists have recognized, at least since the 1980s, a better, more precautionary, CC approach is following no-regrets strategies – taking actions that would be beneficial, or at least minimally damaging, regardless of the precise nature of CC.[69]

Ethical tradition also argues against the seventh objection, that uncertainty demands inaction. According to this tradition, articulated by the late Harvard ethicist John Rawls and many moral theorists, when one faces both uncertainty and potentially catastrophic losses, one ought to take the "maximin" action that averts the worst harm. Why? In potentially-catastrophic cases, magnitude of possible harm trumps concerns about minor uncertainties. Besides, when known groups (e.g., fossil-fuel users and sellers) cause potentially catastrophic harm, ethics doubly requires action. First, in order to take precaution, one must act to avert catastrophe. Second, those who put others at risk have duties to compensate their victims and avert further risks, not deny their risks. It is a common tactic of polluters, attempting to avoid responsibility for their harms, to deny them, to claim the relevant science is uncertain.[70] Thus, even when CC science is uncertain in minor details, fossil-fuel industries and users who put innocent people at risk have duties to take action to avert that risk. Risk imposers never have rights to impose involuntary risks on innocent others, merely because of some uncertainties about those risks. If not, uncertainty about minor CC details does not justify inaction, especially when those who appeal to uncertainty are precisely those who profit most from inaction (see later paragraphs).[71]

An *eighth* objection arises from people who accept the existence of anthropogenic CC. Sometimes they say it would be too expensive to address CC.[72] However, this objection errs ethically and scientifically. It begs the question, "too expensive for whom?" Addressing CC may be too expensive for profit-oriented, fossil-fuel industries and users, but not for CC victims. The objection also erroneously presupposes that, when one group harms others, offenders can simply claim restitution is too expensive. Yet, if offenders could simply claim it was too expensive to pay fines, or to go to jail, there would be no justice, especially no compensatory or retributive justice. Instead, companies could sell tainted food and then, instead of correcting the problem with a recall, claim it was too expensive to fix the problem. Virtually no one accepts such food-company objections, and the same is true for CC objections. People have no rights to harm others, simply to enhance profits.

On the scientific side, the "too-expensive" objection errs because addressing CC is not extraordinarily expensive. Even CC skeptics, like Bjorn Lomborg, admit that the total costs of addressing CC are equal merely to deferring global economic growth for one year.[73] However, the total cost of doing nothing about CC is far greater, comparable to the hardships and expenses of World War II.[74] Moreover, addressing CC is not extraordinarily economically detrimental for anyone except fossil-fuel-related industries. The objection thus errs in confusing costs to fossil-fuel interests with overall costs to everyone. Indeed, addressing CC immediately could give a nation a green-technology-development edge, not harm it. As chapter 6 argues in detail, using mainly energy efficiencies and sustainable technology to address CC would help the economy far more than either doing nothing or increasing nuclear fission. Chapter 6 shows that pro-nuclear, US government agencies have demonstrated that energy efficiencies, alone, could have enabled the US to cut GHG emissions to 1990 levels by 2010, at no net economic cost. After all, during 1973–2004, US industrial-energy use was flat, while production doubled. This doubling showed that economic growth requires no energy growth, in part because of increased efficiencies. Chapter 6 also explains market assessments that show global-energy demand can be cut by 50 percent over the next 15 years, at zero net economic cost. Likewise chapter 6 shows that renewable technologies, like wind and solar-PV, are more cost-effective than current energy sources, and that fossil-fuel "special interests" (neither high costs nor underdeveloped renewable-energy technologies) are mainly blocking the transition to clean, sustainable energy.[75]

The "expense" objection to CC-abatement also errs in ignoring the monumental health toll taken by fossil-fuel emissions, as well as the lives that could be saved by energy-efficient, renewable technologies. As already noted, particulate pollution alone, nearly all from fossil fuels, causes 30,000 to 100,000 premature US deaths each year, especially among children. Otherwise, these deaths would not have occurred. *Lancet* authors say that particulate-air pollution, alone, annually causes 6.4 percent of children's deaths, ages 0–4, in developed nations; particulates, alone, annually kill 14,000 EU toddlers, and double that number in the US; US Environmental Protection Agency data show that fossil-fuel pollutants annually kill about 400,000 people globally who otherwise would not have died.[76] Government data likewise show that 1 in 5 women of child-bearing age has blood levels of mercury, mainly from coal-fired plants, that can cause neuro-developmental problems (like autism and ADHD) in her unborn children; mainly because of mercury from coal plants, waters in 48 US states have fish-consumption advisories.[77] As noted earlier, fossil-fuel use causes ozone, the major cause of asthma, and asthma is now the leading cause of childhood school-absenteeism and the most common chronic-childhood disease. In the last decade, US asthma has increased by 40 percent – costing the nation about $6.2 billion in annual damage. This asthma epidemic is mostly from fossil fuels, from nitrogen oxides and reactive hydrocarbons that combine, in sunlight, to produce ozone, which has no safe dose. In 2005, Harvard, Yale, and NYU scientists showed that for every 10 parts-per-billion (10ppb) daily-ozone increase, deaths increase 10 percent over the subsequent three days, deaths that otherwise would not have occurred.[78]

As also noted earlier, children, poor people, and minorities bear the heaviest burdens of air pollution, mostly from gasoline vehicles and coal plants. The US Centers for Disease Control say that children are the largest and most vulnerable population subgroup that is harmed by such air pollution and that it causes up to half of all childhood cancers. Considering this health and environmental-injustice toll of fossil fuels, addressing CC would save both thousands of lives and billions of dollars annually, just in US health costs. The expense objection thus has CC costs exactly backwards.[79]

Scientific Methods Show Anthropogenic Climate Change

Apart from answering those who reject action on anthropogenic CC, one also can show that all scientific methods confirm anthropogenic CC. The most common scientific method is induction, as explained by logicians such as John Stuart Mill. It generalizes from many particular cases to all cases, from claims that all observed swans are white to claims that all swans are white. Although inductive methods yield no absolute certainty, they are widely used in science, and they support the thesis of anthropogenic CC. Why? For over 150 years, global-temperature records have inductively shown warming of 0.6–0.7 degrees Celsius since the Industrial Revolution. Widespread inductive data from independent sources – tree rings, ice cores, coral reefs, instrumental water measurements, instrumental land measurements – agree on the fact of anthropogenic CC.[80]

Hypothesis-deduction (HD), a method discussed by Carl Hempel and others, likewise shows the reality of anthropogenic CC. In HD, scientists develop hypotheses, then set up situations in which they can test these hypotheses. They do so by determining whether or not predicted consequences, that follow logically from the hypotheses, are realized. The more these predicted consequences are confirmed, the more reliable is the hypothesis from which they follow. If predicted consequences do not occur, the hypothesis is rejected. As already noted, a century ago Swedish chemist Svante Arrhenius used HD and thermodynamics to predict CC. By 1950, many other scientists (e.g., G. S. Callendar, Roger Revelle, Han Suess) also assessed fossil-fuel use, then predicted both warming and ocean-level rises. Inductive measurements of global warming and ocean rises clearly have already confirmed their predictions. Likewise scientists, such as Suki Manabe, predicted CC-warming effects would be strongest, first, in polar regions because of polar amplification – a deduction from theoretical principles of ice-albedo (reflectivity). Because ice has a high albedo, it reflects much sunlight back into space. As ice disappears, increased open water and bare ground decrease reflectivity. As a result, more heat energy is absorbed on Earth, not reflected into space. In 2004, the Arctic Climate Impact Assessment confirmed Manabe's prediction. Many other HD predictions likewise confirm CC. Yet many people misunderstand the role of theory and prediction in science. They forget that the theory underlying why something happens is as important as practical measurements that it happened. Affirmation of anthropogenic CC thus is dependent not only on precise temperature measurements, but also on basic scientific theory, including thermodynamics, as already argued. Thermodynamics predicts increased, CO_2-caused warming, which has occurred. Because HD has confirmed many different CC predictions, someone who rejects CC thereby rejects one of the most widely used scientific methods, HD.[81]

Besides induction and HD, Karl Popper's falsificationism is a third scientific method that likewise confirms the reality of CC. For a theory to be genuinely scientific, falsificationists recognize that it must be capable of being falsified. That is, the *theory* must produce testable hypotheses whose consequences could be falsified and thus cause rejection of the original hypothesis. The hypothesis of anthropogenic CC passes this test of falsificationism because, as seen in the HD case, CC theory has produced hypotheses whose predicted consequences (e.g., increased Arctic effects of CC will appear first) are capable of being falsified, but were not falsified. Perhaps the best illustration that CC meets criteria for falsificationism is that many critics have tried to falsify it, but have failed to do so.[82]

A fourth scientific method, consilience of evidence, has been promoted by Harvard biologist E. O. Wilson, and it too confirms the reality of CC. To confirm a theory, proponents of consilience say one needs a variety of independent sources of evidence. Because different sources of independent CC data (sea temperature, land temperature, ice cores, tree rings, boreholes, coral reef-data) agree with each other, despite differences in measurement methodology, and because these data agree with thermodynamic theory and CC models, consilience also supports the thesis of anthropogenic CC.[83]

Inference to the best explanation is a fifth scientific method that might be used to assess CC. It consists of discovering a number of possible explanation for phenomena, such as Arctic ice melt, determining whether those explanations are consistent with all data, then supporting the scientific explanation which best explains the phenomena. The "best explanation" is determined by whether it is consistent with all known evidence, scientific laws, multiple independent lines of data, and whether some mechanism underlies operation of the phenomena. This method thus employs all the criteria of the previous four scientific methods. It assesses theories according to how well they meet these criteria. Because anthropogenic CC is consistent with all available evidence and scientific laws, is based on known mechanisms (e.g., thermodynamics), and is supported by many independent measurements, inference to the best explanation confirms it.[84]

Why People Sometimes Misunderstand Climate Change

But if 5 different scientific methods and expert-scientific consensus confirm anthropogenic CC, and if CC skeptics err, why do some laypeople think not all experts accept CC? Laypeople may be misled by the previous 8 *objections,* all of which are flawed. They also may be misled because experts often have *poor scientific-communication skills.* After all, advanced-scientific researchers are trained to do demanding technical work and make new discoveries, not to popularize science. They are trained to produce knowledge, not disseminate it. Indeed, if scientists become popularizers, they typically become suspect among other experts – who may think they cannot do technically-demanding work. Poor expert communication thus can leave science open to misrepresentation – a point to be discussed later. A *third* reason laypersons may be misled about CC is that they may be uncomfortable with *uncertainty.* Yet, there is no absolute certainty in science, only confirmation of claims. Laypeople may misunderstand this fact. Or they may prefer simple falsehoods to complicated truths.[85]

A *fourth* reason some people misunderstand CC is their *misunderstanding science.* As already noted, uncertainty about CC tempo and mode will continue for some time, partly because large-scale CC experimentation is impossible. Consequently, as already explained, laypeople may erroneously believe good science should be certain. Yet science is reliable, not infallible. As *The Economist* put it, minor CC uncertainties and disagreements lead some scientifically-uninformed people to focus on the holes in theories, while others focus on the wholes. Some focus on missing CC evidence they think destroys (what they see as) a house of cards. Others focus on finding missing pieces of a partly-completed jigsaw puzzle. Yet scientific understanding is required to know whether CC is a house of cards (false claims of anthropogenic CC) or a jigsaw puzzle (correct claims of anthropogenic CC, with minor details missing), and many people do not have this understanding.[86]

A *fifth* reason laypeople may be misled about anthropogenic CC is that *mass media* have paid attention to a handful of CC dissenters, perhaps because controversy sells newspapers and gains TV watchers. Yet virtually no CC dissenters do peer-reviewed-expert climate research. Most of them are scientifically uninformed, and most are paid by special interests, like the oil lobby. For instance, on March 30, 2010, the *New York Times* ran a front-page story, "Scientists and Weathercasters at Odds over Climate Change."[87] The title and article were misleading because they suggested climate-change controversy. Yet climate scientists are Ph.D.s, mostly at universities, who do technical research, which they publish in peer-reviewed-scientific journals. Weathercasters, however, are TV personalities, not scientists. They do not publish in refereed-expert-scientific journals. Indeed, the article admitted that half of weathercasters have no undergraduate degree in meteorology, much less a Ph.D. Hence, non-expert TV personalities should not be viewed as "disagreeing" with expert climate scientists, but as being scientifically uninformed. Obviously, biology Ph.D.s typically have no authority from which to criticize advanced-physics research. However, media personalities may not realize that scientists like Frederick Seitz – who have never done climate research – have no authority from which to disagree with climate scientists who spend their lives doing advanced climate research. Other media-trumped CC critics, like Michael Crichton, are merely novelists who have inadequate CC expertise. Yet because media and the public may be unaware of what scientific expertise requires, they fail to understand that virtually all CC critics produce no new, peer-reviewed research and thus invalidly attack CC. While a few scientists (like Richard Lindzen of MIT) are in the minority, in thinking that CC effects are likely to be in the "low-end" range predicted by IPCC, those who deny all CC cannot publish their work in scientific journals because it fails basic tests of scientific method. These tests include being based on evidence, avoiding the genetic fallacy, not equivocating, and not confusing the existence of CC with its tempo and mode. Those who deny all CC are thus a bit like proponents of astrology. They criticize mainline scientific views, but they typically have no valid scientific evidence, argument, or theory to legitimately document their claims. As a result, mass media may give them an undeserved forum, partly because media people often fail to realize (as later paragraphs document) that most CC deniers are paid by front groups funded by fossil-fuel interests.[88]

A *sixth* reason laypeople may be misled about CC is *misrepresentation*. Many CC critics are disingenuous, and they deliberately misrepresent CC science because they are paid to do so. As noted regarding CC objections, the American Enterprise Institute (AEI), funded by chemical and fossil-fuel interests, repeatedly misrepresents CC research. AEI claims CC work is "inconsistent with or directly contradicts" the thesis of anthropogenic CC. Yet none of the scientific authors, cited by AEI, rejects anthropogenic CC. Instead they merely discuss alternative accounts of CC tempo and mode.[89] When Harvard physicist Willie Soon published a paper outlining some predictive limitations of some CC models, CC critics erroneously and widely cited his work and claimed it discredited CC; yet, Soon himself explicitly said his work "does not disprove a significant anthropogenic influence on climate change."[90] In other words, as already noted, no CC experts – who actually do advanced climate research – challenge it. Instead they debate minor claims regarding CC tempo and mode. Often misrepresenting CC research, CC critics thus commit logical, scientific, and ethical errors, already criticized earlier.[91]

A *seventh* reason laypeople may be misled about CC is that special interests – like the oil, coal, and automobile industries – have paid lobbyists, PR firms, and non-specialist scientists to promote confusion about CC, to make CC appear unsettled. Because special interests' profit motives make the public suspicious of their CC stance, these special interests create and fund artificial "front groups" to do their PR. The groups have scientific-sounding names, like "The Advancement of Sound Science Coalition," and they produce CC-skeptic op-ed pieces, articles, advertisements, and PR. For decades, industry-funded think tanks, like AEI and the George Marshall Institute, have been actively communicating CC messages that contradict expert-scientific consensus.[92] One well-known example of a special-interest campaign, designed to create uncertainty about CC, is that of ExxonMobil. It has run highly-visible advertisements in magazines and newspapers like the *New York Times*, so these ads look like news reports. The thrust of these ads has been that because CC is uncertain, scientists ought to do more CC research, but take no action against it.[93]

People Who Are Paid to Deny Climate Change

At least 5 groups of special interests profit from CC and thus challenge its existence. These are (1) carbon polluters, (2) politicians paid by carbon polluters, (3) lobbyists paid by carbon polluters, (4) media personalities paid by carbon polluters, and (5) scientists who do no climate research but are paid by carbon polluters.

Among group (1), carbon polluters, are Don Blankenship, CEO of Massey Energy, the fourth-largest US coal-mining operation, often using mountain-top removal. Massey Energy was responsible for the April 2010 West-Virginia coal-mine accident that caused the deaths of 29 miners, because of repeated safety violations. Blankenship, the nation's highest-paid coal executive and a union-buster, says CC is "a hoax and a Ponzi scheme," yet he admits climate legislation "would probably cut our business in half." Other carbon polluters and CC denouncers include Warren Buffett, CEO of Berkshire Hathaway (BH). BH has massive fossil-fuel holdings, and in 2009, for instance,spent $26 billion to buy the top US coal hauler, Burlington Northern Santa Fe RR. The same year, BH also bought 1.3 million shares of the biggest US climate polluter, ExxonMobil. A BH subsidiary, MidAmerican Energy, also has the worst CO_2-intensity of any US utility, 65 million tons in 2008. Yet, BH is the largest US firm not to disclose its CC pollution. Another carbon polluter and CC denouncer is Jack Gerard, President of American Petroleum (AP). AP represents ExxonMobil, Shell, BP, Halliburton, and 400 other member oil companies. Gerard created a fake industry "front group," the "Global Climate Science Communications Action Plan" – to fund non-experts to dispute climate change. Tea Partiers Charles and David Koch do something similar. They run Koch, the nation's largest private-energy company, and they pay non-experts to dispute CC. Charles Koch also founded the Cato Institute, which is largely funded by CC polluters. Interestingly, of any corporate groups anywhere, the Koch brothers and ExxonMobil give the most dollars to anti-climate front groups, like the Cato Institute, AEI, and Heritage Foundation. In 2009 alone, Koch Industries spent $8.5 million on anti-CC lobbying before the US Congress. David Ratcliffe, CEO of the Southern Company (SC), is another major CC polluter and funder of CC critics. Because SC is the second-dirtiest of all US utilities, Ratcliffe has financial reasons to avoid CC-controls. SC's largest coal plant is so dirty that it produces more CC pollution than all Brazilian power plants combined. Ratcliffe, however, claims Earth will "adapt" to CC, and he employs 63 anti-CC lobbyists in Washington, DC. Another typical carbon polluter is Rex Tillerson, CEO of ExxonMobil, the world's largest oil company. ExxonMobil is also the largest CC polluter in the US. It annually causes 397 million tons of CO_2, more than double the GHG emissions of the dirtiest US coal utility. Alone, ExxonMobil causes 7 percent of all US CC pollution. To continue its business as usual, ExxonMobil spent $29 million in 2008 alone, lobbying against CC legislation in the US Congress. Although ExxonMobil funds the Heritage Foundation (an industry front group) to challenge CC, it presents itself as "green." In 2007, ExxonMobil spent $100 million on ads, to boast about its renewable-energy investments. However, the total renewable-energy investments of ExxonMobil have been only $10 million (only one-tenth of its renewable-energy-advertising, or "greenwash" costs for one year).[94]

A second group of CC-deniers are hundreds of US politicians who accept donations from fossil-fuel companies. Joe Barton, Republican Representative from Texas, has accepted $1.4 million from oil-and-gas companies. In return, he has opposed CC, severely harassed climate scientists, and argued in Congress for letting private oil-and-gas companies drill on US public lands. US Senator James Inhofe, from Oklahoma, claims CC is "the greatest hoax ever perpetrated on the American people," perhaps because he has received $1.1 million in gifts from the oil-and-gas industry. Claiming CO_2 is "not a real pollutant," Inhofe forced all US Senate Republican committee members to boycott Congressional debate on CC legislation. He promised that Republicans would block all curbs on carbon pollution. US Democratic Senator Mary Landrieu, from Louisiana, likewise has blocked curbs on GHG emissions, perhaps because she too receives oil-industry money. In 2008, alone, she received $272,000 from the oil industry and voted to give big oil $12 billion in tax breaks. Although her coastal state likely will be ravaged by CC, she has worked in the US Senate to kill climate legislation. The League of Conservation Voters calls her one of the "Dirty Dozen" of pro-pollution US politicians. Other politicians, like Republican Senator John McCain, change their stances after receiving oily money. After he lost the year-2008 race for the US Presidency, and no longer had to appeal to all voters, McCain rejected his earlier, anti-pollution stance. Campaigning for president, McCain supported carbon-cap legislation. After receiving large donations from polluters, however, his views changed. In June 2008 alone, from the state of Texas alone, McCain received $1.214 million in donations from the oil-and-gas industry. McCain now says he opposes CC legislation because it imposes a "corporate tax" on US fossil-fuel companies. He also erroneously claimed the US House 2010 CC bill would impose a $630 billion tax on CC-polluting corporations. However, the bipartisan Congressional Budget Office and other "fact-checkers" show the legislation actually provides $690 billion in CC-pollution subsidies.[95]

A third group of CC deniers are lobbyists paid by fossil-fuel polluters. Lobbyist Tom Donohue is President of the US Chamber of Commerce (COC), the largest US-Congressional-lobby group. It represents many carbon polluters. In the first 9 months of 2009 alone, COC (dominated by 3 major coal companies) spent $65 million to lobby Congress against limits on GHG emissions. Donohue's CC claims are so extreme that COC members, such as Apple, Exelon, Nike, and the California utility PG and E, accuse him of "disingenuous attempts to distort" CC dangers. Dick Gephardt, former US House of Representatives Democratic Majority Leader, also apparently does some distorting, at the behest of his polluter clients. Gephardt heads the Gephardt Group – lobbyists representing many large coal utilities that deny CC, such as Peabody Coal, the world's largest, private-sector coal company. Gephardt also lobbies for the COC, the second-largest-US-lobby group that opposes CC legislation, and for Ameren, the fourth-dirtiest US utility. From Peabody alone, Gephardt received $1.7 million in the last several years. He is paid to deny CC and to oppose CC legislation. Another typical fossil-fuel lobbyist is Marc Morano. Paid by oil-industry heir Richard Mellon Scaife, Morano runs a CC-denying website ("Climate Depot"). His former paid positions include promoting "Swiftboat" lies about Senator John Kerry's military service, being producer of Rush

Limbaugh's radio show, and working for climate-change denier (and oil-industry "gifts" recipient) Senator James Inhofe.[96]

Media owners are a fourth group that is paid to deny CC, through advertising by CC polluters. Rupert Murdoch, recipient of massive, CC-polluter-advertising money, is CEO of World News Corporation. It owns Fox News, the *Wall Street Journal*, the *New York Post*, and other media. Given Murdoch's polluter-advertising dollars, his *Wall Street Journal* has condemned CC legislation. His *New York Post* condemned the Copenhagen CC meetings as only a meet-up for "shamsters, scam artists, and assorted global-warming opportunists" who wanted to "transfer a trillion bucks from the economies of the world's developed nations to Third World Kleptocrats ... with cash sticking to the fingers of well-connected UN bureaucrats." Murdoch media personalities, like Sean Hannity of Fox News, also deny CC and misreport it. For instance, Hannity said 2009 was "one of the coldest years on record," yet it was the fifth-hottest year in the last 130 years. Similarly, in 2009 Fox News featured an extended "news" show called "The Carbon Myth." In it, Fox used carbon-polluter-paid spokesmen, who do no CC research, to claim more CO_2 is "good for the environment." Similarly, ABC-TV receives millions of advertising dollars annually from CC polluters, and ABC's George Will (of "This Week") denies CC. Will criticizes "environmental Cassandras" who "indoctrinate" the public about "hypothetical" CC. Will also was funded by oil-industry representative George Bush, to try to help prepare Bush for the US-presidential-election-campaign TV debates. Despite his public prominence, Will has repeatedly misled the public about CC. In the *Washington Post*, he claimed, "there has been no recorded global warming for more than a decade." However, IPCC says 11 of the warmest years on record have occurred in the last 13 years. Will also claimed in the *Post* that "global-sea-ice levels now equal those of 1979." However, IPCC says researchers have documented massive decreases in global-sea-ice since 1979, a decrease bigger than the states of Texas and California combined. Although both the *Washington Post* ombudsman and the World Meteorological Association rebuked Will for repeated CC factual errors, he has neither run corrections nor admitted these errors. Nevertheless, Will accuses climate scientists (but not corporate polluters) of "perpetuating [CC] lies out of self-interest."[97]

A fifth group of CC deniers are non-expert scientists like Fred Singer, who publish no advanced climate research. An 85-year-old retired physicist, Singer denies CC but says global warming would be good, promoting plant growth. Most of Singer's CC criticisms are paid for by the Heartland Institute – which is funded by ExxonMobil, oil-baron Richard Scaife, and Koch (the nation's largest private-energy company). Earlier, the tobacco industry paid Singer to deny cigarette hazards, and CFC manufacturers paid him to deny ozone-hole hazards. Another CC-denier is Patrick Michaels, a biologist paid by the Cato Institute (an industry front group). Cato is largely funded by coal companies, and Michaels is typical of climate critics; he has never published climate research.[98]

The upshot? Scientific consensus, among experts who do CC research, is that anthropogenic CC is real. Because of special-interest funding, however, many members of the public have been misled about CC.

Overview of the Book

The public also has been misled about CC solutions. Would atomic energy provide an economical, effective, ethical – albeit partial – response to CC? This book uses market data, scientific studies, and ethical analyses to argue that it would not. It likewise shows that nuclear proponents employ flawed science in trying to make their case, and that increasing fission would worsen already-existing, nuclear-related environmental injustices and proliferation risks.

To provide a context for the later discussions in the book, chapter 2 outlines the origins and history of nuclear technology. Next it shows that, once one counts GHG emissions from all nuclear-fuel-cycle stages, fission has roughly the same GHG emissions as natural gas – far more than electricity produced by wind or solar-PV. Chapter 2 also shows that atomic energy is routinely misrepresented as "green" and "carbon free" because its proponents make fundamental scientific errors. They rely on many counterfactual assumptions in calculating greenhouse emissions. By misleadingly ignoring energy-input needs, and by counting GHG emissions only at point of electricity use, nuclear proponents ignore the fact that reactors produce only 25 percent more electricity that that needed, as input, to their 14-stage-fuel cycle. In fact, the chapter shows that most nuclear-emissions studies ignore the GHG emissions from the full, nuclear, 14-stage-fuel cycle. They count only a small fraction of these emissions, then erroneously claim atomic energy is a CC solution.

Chapter 3 reveals that atomic energy is also extremely costly. Even if one ignores taxpayer subsidies, fission is at least 3 times costlier than wind, and nearly twice the cost of solar-PV. Atomic energy likewise imposes many harms on the public, including government-mandated liability limits that make nuclear-accident victims, not industry, responsible for more than 98 percent of worst-case, nuclear-accident damages, even those caused by industry's intentional safety violations. The chapter also shows that fission proponents erroneously trim data on fission costs by making many counterfactual assumptions about nuclear-construction-interest rates, load factors, construction times, and so on. Indeed, the chapter shows that market proponents agree: atomic energy is uneconomical. Consequently, all credit-rating firms downgrade the credit of utilities with a nuclear plant. This costliness is one reason the nuclear industry cannot build any reactors without massive taxpayer subsidies, including covering half the costs of each $12–20-billion plant. Thus the chapter shows that atomic energy only appears economical – because most nuclear-cost studies (nearly all done by the reactor industry) ignore costs from the full, nuclear,

14-stage-fuel cycle. Instead they count only a small fraction of these costs, then erroneously claim atomic energy is an inexpensive CC solution.

Chapter 4 argues that nuclear power likewise is costly in terms of human health and scientific reliability. Because of industry cover-ups, scientific misrepresentation, and violating conflict-of-interest guidelines, the chapter shows that industry's atomic-energy-accident data are seriously flawed. Consequently, these data grossly undercount harmful nuclear consequences. As a result, the chapter shows the public has been seriously misled about atomic energy, as medical journals confirm. In particular, the Three Mile Island (Pennsylvania) nuclear accident and core melt caused a documented, 64-percent-cancer increase, especially childhood cancers. Yet because of industry PR, many people erroneously believe this was a minor accident that killed no one.

Chapter 5 shows that, even without any accidents, fission nevertheless causes many serious, pollution-induced health effects that are disproportionately imposed on children, radiation workers, and future generations. These environmental injustices, inequitable pollution impacts, include the facts that children living near normally-operating nuclear plants show statistically-significant increases in cancer, especially radiation-related cancers like leukemia. Moreover, these cancers decrease in proportion to distance away from the reactor. Likewise, because US regulations allow nuclear workers to receive 50 times the annual-radiation dose of the public, they are at especially high risk. Using US National Academy of Sciences (NAS) and International Agency for Research on Cancer (IARC) data, the chapter shows that allowable, annual, occupational-radiation doses can *annually* cause one fatal, otherwise-avoidable, premature cancer in every 80 workers who receives this dose. If nuclear workers receive the maximum-annual dose for 40 years, workplace-radiation exposures will cause nearly half of them to have premature, otherwise-avoidable, fatal cancers. Moreover, the chapter shows that, because contemporary US radiation-protection regulations do not satisfy risk-disclosure and voluntariness requirements, nuclear workers cannot give informed consent to these much-higher occupational risks. Finally, the chapter reveals that, because US radiation standards, for permanent, future, nuclear-waste management, are more than 4 times less protective than for current people, they subject future people to massive environmental injustices.

Chapter 6 discusses many CC solutions that avoid nuclear fission and alleged "clean" coal. These solutions include conservation, energy efficiencies, wind, and solar-PV. The chapter also explains at least 4 reasons that "clean coal" is an oxymoron – and thus not a viable solution to problems of CC. Using classic scientific studies from Harvard, Princeton, and the US Department of Energy, the chapter shows that renewables and energy efficiencies can supply all energy needs – and do so more cheaply than either fossil fuels or fission. Market proponents agree. Renewable-energy installations are doubling annually, while nuclear fission is declining.

Chapter 7 responds to numerous objections. These include the apparent success of the French nuclear-energy program, the intermittency of some renewable-energy technologies, and the alleged costs of renewable energy. The chapter shows that all these objections err, that the public has been grossly misled by nuclear-industry PR, and that efficiencies and renewable energy are cheaper, safer, more ethical, and less GHG emissions intensive than atomic power. Chapter 8 concludes with suggestions about how to promote cheaper, safer, more ethical, less carbon-intensive renewables, conservation, and energy efficiencies.

Several Caveats

Because no book can appeal to everyone, at least 5 caveats help explain the scope of this volume. *First,* because this book includes both scientific analyses (in every chapter) and ethical analyses (especially in chapters 3–5), ethicists may want more ethics, and scientists may want more science. However, the book does only the science and the ethics that are necessary to make its arguments about CC, atomic power, and renewable energy. To do anything else would require more than one book. A *second* caveat is that because the issues of CC, nuclear fission, and renewable energy are so broad, not all topics related to them can be treated here. Instead, the book focuses on nuclear, and other proposed, solutions to CC. *Third,* because the book seeks both a lay and scholarly readership, for the sake of clarity it includes some repetition, such as quick outlines at each chapter beginning, quick summaries at each chapter end, and listings of main points and arguments.

A *fourth* caveat is that, because the book aims to illuminate other cases of flawed science leading to flawed policy, it has several short methodological analyses that lay readers can skip. These analyses provide the technical underpinnings for 3 key themes. These themes include *how* conservation, efficiency, and renewable energy – not nuclear fission – can solve climate problems, *why* nuclear proponents' arguments about climate err, and *how* scientific-methodological understanding can advance energy policy. Because these scientific and ethical methods for analyzing faulty arguments can be applied elsewhere, in many different scientific-ethical cases, one goal of the book is thus pedagogical, to illustrate and document these methods carefully, so that others can use them elsewhere. Without missing the main points of the book, those less interested in scientific methodology can skip the short, chapter 1 section that shows how alternative scientific methods confirm the existence of anthropogenic climate change, the short, chapter 4 sections on how different causal accounts (mechanist, unificationist) all show that ionizing radiation from the Three Mile Island nuclear accident caused serious cancer increases nearby, and perhaps the short section in chapter 4 on "inference to the best explanation."

A *fifth* caveat is that readers may be misled unless they examine the sources for the scientific and technical claims being made or criticized throughout this volume. In general, the sources for the claims that are criticized in this book, e.g., scientists employed by the fossil-fuel or nuclear industries, appear to have financial conflicts of interest. However, the sources for claims that are praised in this book, e.g., university scientists, appear to have no financial conflicts of interest. That is, the analysis shows that those who are criticized in this book – who deny CC, who want to delay CC action, who support increased nuclear energy – are typically either funded by special interests and often guilty of doing flawed science, or misled by this flawed science. This flawed science includes collecting nonrepresentative data and samples, making implausible assumptions, using biased models, drawing invalid inferences, or performing incomplete analyses. Later chapters explain such scientific errors and show how they generate false conclusions. They also reveal four typical hallmarks of these questionable studies, especially their biased sources. Obviously, not all industry-funded research is questionable. However, the flawed research, criticized in this book, typically (i) is not peer-reviewed, (ii) does not appear in refereed scientific journals or peer-reviewed government documents, (iii) is funded and controlled by the nuclear or fossil-fuel industries, and (iv) has conclusions that are tainted by conflicts of interest because they serve the financial goals of their funders or authors. However, the scientific research, used by this book to criticize flawed studies, typically (1) is peer-reviewed, (2) appears in refereed scientific journals or peer-reviewed government documents, (3) is not funded or controlled by any special interests (instead typically is done by university or government researchers), and (4) has conclusions devoid of conflicts of interest because they serve no apparent financial goals of the funders or authors. As a result, readers need to heed both the sources of all information discussed here (see the notes), as well as their different methodological characteristics. As subsequent chapters show, the invalidity or validity of scientific studies is revealed in their biased or unbiased methods– which in turn often are revealed by their funders.

Time for Change

Although this book argues for greater conservation, efficiencies, and renewable-energy solutions to CC – and against nuclear fission – not all the problems it addresses are new. Energy-based pollution has plagued the human race for centuries. Since Roman times, for instance, inhabitants of the British Isles have faced fossil-fuel pollution from using coal for heating. For thousands of years, they scavenged soft, bituminous "sea coal" from veins exposed when the ocean eroded land near northeastern-coastal England. Even now, veins of coal are visible near beaches at places like Blackhall. By 1200, because available firewood was depleted and too expensive for most people, English sea-coal use skyrocketed, mostly for heat. Although Queen Eleanor tried to ban its burning, virtually everyone disobeyed, and air quality rapidly worsened. In 1247, coal fumes became so severe that they drove Queen Eleanor from Nottingham Castle.[99]

By 1271, coal smoke was killing so many people that Edward I banned selling or burning sea-coal, under penalty of torture or death.[100] Yet even executions did little to stop use of this cheap resource. Because people had no alternative fuel, they disregarded the ban. Because officials could not enforce a ban—that nearly everyone disobeyed – coal use increased, and London air quality worsened.[101] In Shakespeare's time, coal-induced air pollution forced people to sleep sitting up, in short beds. (Shakespeare's home has such short beds.) Otherwise, people found it difficult to breathe. Yet King Richard III (in the 1300s), King Henry V (in the 1400s), and Queen Elizabeth (in the 1500s) complained about filthy, coal-polluted air, even in Westminster Palace. All tried to ban coal. None was successful, given widespread coal use and near-universal violations of their bans.[102]

By the time of the Industrial Revolution, the coal ban was stopped in the name of economic progress. In 1800, more than a million Londoners were burning coal, and the city became even more notorious for its thick smog. Its 19th and early-20th-century air was so heavily laden with coal toxins that pollution-induced deaths increased massively during the winter, coal-burning months.[103] In 1873, a coal-smoke fog hovered over the city for days and killed nearly 300 people from ailments like bronchitis. In 1879, a coal-smoke fog lasted from November to March, blotted out the sun, and killed hundreds of people. Still things did not change. Indeed, the smog became permanent. In 1900, from the summit of St Paul's Cathedral, winter visibility was typically a half-mile. On the streets, visibility was often as little as 30 feet. Deaths mounted every winter. People tried to justify these pollution-induced fatalities, in the name of economic benefits. Progress came only in response to a dramatic number of short-term deaths. In only one week, a December 1952 London-coal-smoke fog killed more than 3,000 people. Largely as a result, in 1956 the British Parliament enacted the Clean Air Act.[104]

Similar coal-smoke problems faced other cities. In the 19th-and-early-20th centuries, in cold weather, most US cities were coated with thick, black, coal soot. Windows could not be opened because home furnishings would be covered with coal dust. Millions of people suffered from heart failure, cancer, asthma, bronchitis, emphysema, and other lung ailments. One of the most dramatic events occurred in 1948, when 18 people died within several weeks in the small town of Donora, Pennsylvania. An air inversion had trapped coal-polluted air in their town. Today, nearly 800 years after King Edward's warning, society is still killing people with coal pollution. It is time to stop the deaths. This book tells how to do so – and how to stop climate change at the same time.

CHAPTER 2

Trimming the Data on Nuclear Greenhouse Emissions

In the 13th century, a global climate change of only 1 degree caused massive famine and death from disruptions in agricultural, meteorological, and vector-borne-disease patterns. The infamous Black Plague or Black Death was one such effect.[1] Yet today, climate scientists warn that even if nations take action soon, the very best society can do will be to limit climate change (CC) to about 2 degrees Celsius. As the previous chapter showed, even a 2-degree CC will bring increasingly severe hurricanes, droughts, floods, and vector-borne dis-eases, plus millions of climate refugees and hundreds of thousands of additional annual deaths.

To avoid as much climate-related death and destruction as possible, and to reduce greenhouse-gas (GHG) emissions by curtailing use of fossil fuels, many people propose increasing atomic energy. In his 2010 State of the Union address, US President Barack Obama proposed increasing nuclear power and providing nearly $50 billion in new, taxpayer subsidies for atomic energy. Yet as this and sub-sequent chapters show, Obama and other nuclear proponents are making a big mistake. For one thing, chapter 1 revealed that scientists agree—there is no safe, non-zero dose of ionizing radiation. Chapter 1 also noted that the largest fission increase that industry says is possible would require tripling nuclear plants by the year 2050. This means the number of global commercial reactors could rise from about 450 to 1,000–1,500, supplying about 20 percent of year-2050 global elec-tricity,[2] compared to 14.8 percent now. Even with this unlikely nuclear tripling, fission would supply roughly 8–9 percent of total global energy, as compared to the current 2.1.[3]

Underlying the ethical question—whether it would be desirable to triple nuclear plants in order to reduce GHG emissions—are many scientific questions. One of the most prominent issues is whether this tripling is an effective way to avoid GHG emissions.

Chapter Overview: The Climate-Necessity Argument

Many nuclear-industry proponents say atomic energy is a needed solution to CC. Accepting the "climate-necessity" argument for increased atomic power, the US Department of Energy (DOE), the UK Environment Secretary, the classic MIT study, and others claim that nuclear energy is needed because fission-generated electricity is "carbon free" and thus necessary to help avoid CC—that "we don't really have any other choice" but to increase nuclear fission because it "has no carbon footprint."[4] Official US government, Nuclear Energy Institute, and World Energy Council documents, respectively, say nuclear power is needed because it is "clean" and "emissions free," "does not emit greenhouse gases," and is "not a source of carbon-dioxide."[5] Other versions of the climate-necessity argument, like those given by the UK Department of Trade and Industry (DTI)—which relies only on nuclear-industry data—are that atomic energy is needed to address CC, despite its risks, because it is the "only" large-scale available source to combat CC and thus the only "practical way" to address CC.[6] Still other nuclear proponents claim that fission is "the only existing power technology which could replace coal in base load" and "the only technology ready to fill the gap and stop the carbon-dioxide loading of the atmosphere."[7]

Is it? After providing a brief overview of nuclear technology and history, the chapter shows that the climate-necessity argument has many flaws that invalidate its conclusions. Among these flaws is the argument's counting GHG emissions only from reactors, rather than from the entire 14-stage nuclear-fuel cycle. By thus "trimming the data" on nuclear-related GHG emissions, proponents try to make fission look like a low-carbon technology, when it is not. A second flaw of the climate-necessity argument is failing to take account of the much higher nuclear emissions that arise because of using low-grade uranium ore to create reactor fuel. A third flaw is inconsistency. The climate-necessity argument fails to apply its own logic (to implement energy technologies with low GHG emissions) to electricity sources (like wind and solar photovoltaic) that are much better GHG-emissions-avoiders than is nuclear power. A fourth flaw in the climate-necessity argument is its self-defeating consequences. These include the fact that reactors generate only about 25 percent more energy, in their lifetime, than is required, as input, to the 14 stages of their fuel cycle. A fifth flaw in the argument is failure to take account of the fact that reactors massively increase risks of nuclear proliferation and terrorism. Thus using atomic power to help combat CC worsens another, and equally catastrophic, energy problem: nuclear proliferation and nuclear terrorism. A sixth flaw of using fission to address CC is failure to take account of the practical difficulties of tripling the number of global reactors. For all these reasons, the chapter shows that concerns about CC do not support using commercial atomic power. Instead, later chapters show that GHG-emissions reduction is better achieved by conservation, energy efficiency, and a variety of sustainable, low-GHG-emitting technologies like wind and solar photovoltaic (PV).

Origins and History of the Nuclear Industry

To understand why some people propose commercial nuclear fission as a partial solution to CC, and why those proposals err, it is important to understand the origins of this technology, its post–World War II history, and its current status. At present, reactors are being proposed as a partial way to address CC. Fission-industry representatives have called for more atomic energy, and in the US both the Bush and Obama administrations have provided enormous nuclear subsidies (tens of billions of dollars in 2005, 2007, and 2011). The governor of Maryland recently said that CC presented a "moral imperative" to build nuclear plants.[8] Currently reactors supply about 6 percent of global energy, down from 7 percent in the 1990s,[9] or about 14 percent of global electricity.[10] This is 2.2 percent of world net-energy overall, once full-fuel-cycle energy inputs are subtracted (see chapter 2).[11] To replace old nuclear and some coal plants, the nuclear industry proposes tripling global reactors from 435 to roughly 1,500 (1,000 Mwe), although it admits this "high" projection is unrealistic.[12] For the US, this "optimistic" nuclear-tripling would require building five fission plants a year for the next 50 years.[13] Given the postulated increases in global-energy demand—up to four-fold by 2050[14]—and the replacement of soon-to-retire reactors, this proposed nuclear-tripling would mean fission might supply 20 percent of year-2050 global electricity, slightly more than the 14 percent supplied now. Even this "high" estimate—that of the nuclear-industry lobby group, the World Nuclear Association (WNA)—is rejected by WNA as unrealistic; instead it proposes 740 new plants,[15] less than double the number of reactors currently operating, many of which will soon retire. The nuclear-industry "low" projection, for 390 new reactors globally by 2050, would not even replace current plants.[16] Yet, roughly 40 percent of US reactors—41—will end their lifetimes by 2015.[17] Nuclear advocates say these retirements will occur at least 5 years before new reactors could begin operation (2020), even if construction had begun in 2008.[18]

On one hand, the governments of Finland, France, India, Japan, Russia, South Korea, the UK, United States, and China support nuclear-plant expansion.[19] The US nuclear industry says it may seek permission to build 34 new reactors but admits many will not be built because of high costs, poor nuclear-credit markets, and cheaper sources of electricity.[20] These problems help explain why no new US nuclear plants have been ordered since 1974.[21] Even if all 34 proposed US plants were built, however, US nuclear electricity would massively decrease in the future, as new reactors would not replace the 41 plants that are retiring by 2015.

On the other hand, the governments of Austria, Belgium, Denmark, Germany, Italy, Netherlands, New Zealand, and Sweden either prohibit, or are phasing out, nuclear power.[22] The Saudis have joined these nuclear critics.[23] One of their key anti-nuclear arguments is that, if fission is safe and desirable, why does the nuclear industry demand a liability limit that makes it responsible for only 1–2 percent of worst-case-accident costs? If fission is safe, neither the public nor industry needs liability protection. If it is unsafe, both need protection. Yet, in most nations, the nuclear industry has liability protection, while the public does not—a good reason to question nuclear safety. Other critics of fission note that uranium is already running out and that, at most, fission could supply only 20 percent of year-2050 electricity, as already mentioned. Moreover, if the 2005 survey by the pro-nuclear UN International Atomic Energy Agency (IAEA) is correct, a majority of people and nations oppose new nuclear plants; the survey showed that only in South Korea do a majority of people support new reactors.[24] Warning that atomic energy is saddled with problems of high costs, long construction times, waste management, need for massive taxpayer subsidies, and nuclear proliferation, Shell Oil is pursuing renewable energy.[25] Shell argues that by 2050, 50 percent of electricity can come from renewables.[26] Shell and the EU also say that by 2010, renewables could supply 22 percent of global energy and an even higher percentage of electricity.[27]

Although most new nuclear plants are being built in developing nations and rely on older, less-safe technology, any new reactors in the West would be generation-III or -III+ plants designed in the last 15 years.[28] Incorporating more passive-safety (as opposed to engineered) features, these generation-III and -III+ plants rely more on processes, such as convection, for emergency cooling and safety features.[29] Although new designs "incorporate only incremental changes to designs previously built,"[30] engineers hope they will be safer and have longer lifetimes.[31] However, because all such designs are new, it will take decades to determine whether they perform as hoped. After all, previous generation-III plants, like the 1999 AP-600, went through a decade of full US-regulatory design and approval but were abandoned because utilities said they could never be economical.[32] Something similar could happen with other new designs. The only generation-III+ designs now under construction in the West are the Olkiluoto, Finland, plant,[33] and the Flamanville, France, plant, both being built by the French and subsidized by the French people.[34] Even if more reactors could be built, as already noted, the nuclear industry admits that, at best, fission could supply only about 20 percent of year-2050 electricity.

Nuclear technology also faces some unique problems because of its military history. The technology began in 1895 with Roentgen's discovery of the X-ray. Only three years later, during the Spanish-American War, the US was using 17 battleships outfitted with X-ray equipment. By the 1920s, X-rays were common in the US and other developed nations. However, vast nuclear technology and radioactive wastes were not created until the early 1940s, as the US raced to develop an atomic bomb before either its German or its Japanese World War II enemies were able to do so. During the war, for military purposes, both the US and the Soviet Union began developing nuclear technology, including uranium-enrichment plants to provide fuel for reactors—used to generate plutonium for nuclear weapons. This initial military use of fission technology was part of the famous US Manhattan Project, which by 1942 had produced the world's first nuclear-chain reaction. By 1943 the first atomic bombs were built in Oak Ridge, Tennessee, and Hanford, Washington. In July 1945 the US exploded the first atomic bomb in New Mexico, and one month later it dropped this weapon on Hiroshima and Nagasaki—an attempt to quickly end the war in the Pacific Theater. From 1940 to 1945, the US spent $2 billion to develop the first atomic bombs. From 1945 to 1965, the US spent more than $100 billion in subsidies to develop the first commercial reactors to generate electricity. In fact, immediately following the war, the US, Soviet, English, and other governments all began extensive subsidies of commercial nuclear-fission reactors, for three main reasons. (1) They wanted weapons-grade plutonium for military efforts. (2) The identical 14-stage nuclear-fuel cycle (see later paragraphs) is needed both to produce weapons and to generate electricity. (3) The government wanted a nonmilitary rationale (called "Atoms for Peace" in the US) for continuing nuclear-weapons development and obtaining weapons-grade plutonium. Given these three military motives for developing commercial nuclear fission, all revealed in US congressional documents of 1945–1955, atomic-energy technology developed quickly, partly because government has continued to subsidize at least half the costs of commercial reactors. In the 1940s–1950s government also put the same agency, the US Atomic Energy Commission (AEC), in charge of both military and commercial fission energy—and both nuclear promotion and nuclear regulation. Partly as a result of this dual charge, later paragraphs show that multiple US congressional and government-oversight reports say military and commercial atomic energy have shared a culture of secrecy, centralization, violations of safety laws, falsification of worker-radiation-exposure logs, cover-up, whistleblower harassment, and technocracy—which (some congressional investigators say) continues to the present day. As chapter 3 points out, one result of this culture of secrecy is that because of commercial-nuclear-industry appeals to "trade secrets" and "competitive advantage," only reactor owners know the actual costs of fission-generated electricity. Consequently, virtually all third-party nuclear-cost studies (see chapter 3) are forced to rely mainly on often-biased industry data about nuclear economics.[35]

The same nuclear-secrecy culture also typically enshrouds reactor-safety problems, as chapter 4 reveals. One reason is that when safety violations occur, congressional and government-oversight reports show they often are not corrected. Instead, the nuclear industry frequently harasses whistleblowers. For instance, whistleblower Karen Silkwood, working at the US Kerr-McGee nuclear facility in Oklahoma, was mysteriously murdered—after management failed to correct serious safety violations, and she threatened to reveal these violations. *Paris Match* called her the world's first anti-nuclear martyr. After her death, the US Nuclear Regulatory Commission verified 20 of her 39 health-and-safety allegations, and an Oklahoma jury ordered Kerr-McGee to pay $10.5 million in punitive damages to Silkwood's children because of her murder and radioactive contamination. Kerr-McGee appealed, but in 1986 finally paid a settlement of $1.4 million to Silkwood's four children. As later paragraphs and multiple government-oversight reports show, cover-up of safety problems, data falsification, and whistleblower harassment are common in the nuclear industry. Because of court-mandated gag orders, however, the US public has little access to such information. Secrecy problems are even more troublesome for military-nuclear technology because many documents are classified. For instance, in 1986, in response to US congressional demands for information about US-government nuclear experiments on civilians, the US energy department released tens of pages of formerly classified documents. They revealed that, for years, US military and military-funded researchers had conducted harmful radiological experiments on US civilians without their knowledge or consent. For years, the government also illegally released hundreds of thousands of curies (annually) of cancer-causing radioactive materials that harmed US citizens without their ever knowing the sources of their health problems. Perhaps the most worrisome aspect of these Silkwood, radiation-experiment, and other nuclear cover-ups is that nuclear secrecy and safety violations may be continuing. For instance, in 1982, Congress told the US National Cancer Institute (NCI) to assess fallout-related health effects from the 200+ above-ground nuclear-weapons tests the US conducted during the 1950s and 1960s. (At the time of the tests, government repeatedly told citizens that the fallout was harmless, even though it knew this was not the case.) In response, NCI did one small part of the fallout study but suppressed all results for more than a decade. After repeated pressure from Congress and the US Department of Health and Human Services, in 1997 NCI finally released part of the report, on effects of only one radioactive isotope released by the fallout, iodine-131. It said bomb-related iodine-131 fallout would cause up to 214,000 premature US thyroid cancers—apart from additional cancers caused by scores of other fallout-radionuclides. Although the US National Academy of Sciences and independent scientific associations criticized NCI estimates as possibly too low, again the crucial question was ethical. Why did government delay releasing the report? Because of the NCI delay, the statute of limitations has kept thousands of US nuclear-fallout victims from claiming government-guaranteed compensation for 13 different types of radiation-related cancers, especially leukemias. Although Congress called for fallout-dose assessment in 1982, and the full report on effects of all radionuclides was due in 2000, government still—as of 2011—has not released it. One government-committee hypothesis for this delay is that the health results could damage commercial and government nuclear interests. In fact, a recent US presidential commission warned that additional radiation experimentation on civilians—and citizen harm from radioactive pollution—was possible. Why? The commission cited "serious deficiencies" in government radiation protection and oversight.[36]

Such deficiencies, including government cover-up of nuclear-safety problems, appear to have characterized US implementation of commercial fission technology from the very beginning. For instance, to convince citizens that atomic energy was safe, the US government commissioned the 1956 taxpayer-funded Brookhaven Report. Concluding the opposite, the Brookhaven Report showed that a nuclear accident could cause 150,000 fatalities, catastrophic economic damages, and destruction of an area the size of Pennsylvania. Government studies also showed that the probability of a nuclear core melt, in one of approximately 100 US reactors during their lifetimes, was about 1 in 5. As a result, in 1956 the US energy department suppressed the taxpayer-funded analyses of the Brookhaven Report, instead claimed atomic energy was safe, and (during 1957–1974) licensed approximately 100 US nuclear plants. Although government no longer needs the plants' weapons-grade plutonium, it does have a military interest in keeping nuclear technology available and up-to-date. Consequently, in 1973 the US government predicted there would be 1,000 fission plants generating electricity in the US by the year 2000. Yet, as of 2011, there are roughly 100. In fact, one year after this 1973 prediction, the last US nuclear plant was ordered (although current, massive government subsidies have encouraged utilities to plan future orders). What happened? As chapter 3 shows, *Forbes*, the *Economist*, and credit-rating firms all say nuclear energy was killed by market forces— high costs, coupled with the fact that no nuclear plant has ever been built, anywhere in the world, without massive government subsidies. Yet despite subsidies that cut nuclear-electricity costs by 50–90 percent (see chapter 1), chapter 3 shows that Wall Street says the technology is not cost-effective. In the 1980s alone, US fission costs quadrupled, the massive government subsidies continued, and US commercial-fission minor accidents exceeded 34,000 in number. As chapter 4 explains, the 1979 Three Mile Island (TMI), Pennsylvania, nuclear accident raised additional safety concerns and caused a slew of cancers, infant mortalities, and childhood diseases. Even worse, the US Nuclear Regulatory Commission admitted that the US has a 50-percent chance of having another TMI (or larger) reactor accident. The 1986 Chernobyl nuclear accident in Ukraine made nuclear economics still worse. It contaminated much of Europe, already has cost more than $500 billion, and (according to UC Berkeley physicians and scientists) will cause 475,000 deaths, most from long-term cancers, and most occurring outside the former Soviet Union. (For comparison, note that Hurricane Katrina killed about 1,000 people and cost about $200 billion.) The obvious question is how such devastating nuclear accidents could occur—especially in technically advanced nations. As already mentioned, one reason is that the US government covered up the damning conclusions of the 1955 Brookhaven Report. Because it was not released until 1974 (after the 1966 Freedom of Information Act went into effect and government was forced to do so), the government was able to claim, at least until 1974, that atomic energy was safe. In fact, in the early 1950s, government told GE, Westinghouse, and other corporations that it was their "patriotic duty" to implement commercial nuclear fission because of its military applications, and that the technology was economical. Industry, however, knew better. In 1955, all US corporations refused to begin commercial US reactors unless government both assumed responsibility for permanent radioactive-waste storage and provided industry with full liability protection against nuclear accidents. Despite massive controversy, government did both, for the three military reasons listed earlier in this section. It passed the Price-Anderson Act, providing industry with liability protection against 98 percent of total possible damage claims from the public. It also agreed to accept responsibility for, and cover the bulk of the costs of, permanent radioactive-waste storage. As a result of these two government subsidies—for nuclear-liability coverage and permanent radioactive-waste storage—the first US commercial reactor opened in 1957, in Shippingport, Pennsylvania.[37]

Both government subsidies have generated substantial controversy. Critics say nuclear-liability limits (which most developed nations have) violate citizens' due-process rights, prohibit their suing negligent nuclear industries for full damages, and, in the US, allow coverage for less than 2 percent of possible nuclear-accident claims. Noting the $500-billion-plus costs of Ukraine's 1986 Chernobyl nuclear catastrophe, mentioned above, critics argue that it was not a worst-case accident. Yet because the Price-Anderson Act currently limits US nuclear liability to about $11 billion, they say innocent victims could bear more than 98 percent of nuclear-accident costs, even if a company were negligent. Critics also point to nuclear-exclusion clauses on all homeowners-insurance policies. They ask: Why should government admit that a US nuclear accident could kill 150,000 people—150 times more people than Hurricane Katrina—yet prohibit the public from recovering more than $11 billion total in nuclear damages? A negligent utility could bear only 1.5 percent of an accident's cost, while innocent citizens could lose everything. As chapter 3 explains in more detail, critics claim government has given industry a free ride at citizens' expense. They say this unfair situation arose because, after a constitutional challenge to the Price-Anderson Act, the US Supreme Court responded in part that the legislation does not violate citizens' due-process rights because a catastrophic nuclear accident is unlikely. However, neither the insurance industry nor credit-rating firms agree that a catastrophic nuclear accident is unlikely. Besides, if an accident were truly unlikely, the nuclear industry would not demand the protection of the Price-Anderson Act as a condition for fission-generation of electricity. In addition, private insurers say nuclear risks are far higher than the 1-in-5 probability of a core-melt alleged by the US government (see earlier paragraphs). As a result, obtaining private insurance would make commercial nuclear power prohibitively expensive. For instance, as chapter 3 reveals, EU reports show that, apart from massive other government subsidies, merely including the costs of full nuclear-liability insurance, alone, would triple current nuclear-electricity costs.[38]

The bottom line? As later chapters reveal, the US government (and perhaps other governments, such as those of France and the UK) appears to have given the nuclear industry freedom from liability, at citizens' expense; withheld fission-cost data and nuclear-safety information; falsified radiation-exposure records; suppressed scientific information; and violated the civil liberties of nuclear critics.

Because of such problems, by 1974 the US Atomic Energy Commission (AEC) was so embroiled in scores of nuclear-safety lawsuits that government had to abolish it and create a new agency, the Department of Energy (DOE). The 35-year-old DOE, however, has many of the same problems as the earlier AEC, in part because the leaders and employees merely switched agencies. As a result, the US National Academy of Sciences (NAS), the US Inspector General, the US Office of Technology Assessment (OTA), and another US government oversight agency, the Government Accountability Office (GAO), have all repeatedly criticized DOE for lax safety, information-suppression, failure to report full costs, and harassment of whistle-blowers. Beginning in 1991 and continuing to the present day, both of these government oversight agencies (OTA, GAO) and the Congress have repeatedly called for DOE abolition or external regulation—because it has the same problems of corruption, data falsification, poor safety practices, and whistleblower harassment as the AEC. The DOE uses a system of "self-regulation" that has been criticized repeatedly by Congress and these federal oversight agencies. As a result, Congress, the NAS, the GAO, and the OTA have condemned DOE-controlled facilities for repeated contamination, fires, explosions involving radioactive materials, and "significant and potentially widespread problems with ... not adhering to nuclear safety procedures." Congressional investigators likewise have said nuclear-worker dose-monitoring programs are "inaccurate, and in many cases nonexistent." In fact, the GAO discovered that 90 percent of DOE nuclear facilities had contaminated groundwater that exceeded regulatory standards by a factor of up to 1,000. In response, government did virtually nothing. In 1998, the GAO said: "We have long criticized DOE for weaknesses in its self-regulation of the environmental safety and health at its own facilities.... Widespread environmental contamination at DOE facilities ... provides clear evidence that [DOE] self-regulation has failed." Yet, to date, almost none of these problems has been corrected. In 2008, the GAO warned that despite repeated safety violations, nuclear facilities have not reduced the occurrence of over one-third of the most common reported safety violations in the last three years and that current reactors cannot meet fire safety rules, largely because of electrical and maintenance violations that have not been corrected, despite warnings for as long as 5 years. In 2008 the GAO also warned that many radioactive-waste-storage containers, without secondary containment, have had a long history of uncorrected leaks; that the DOE has not performed required safety analyses, even though accidents could be "catastrophic"; and that "persistent safety problems" and "violations of safety rules" occur at many US nuclear facilities, which in the last decade have had roughly 3 "serious accidents or near misses" per year. For all these historical and continuing nuclear-safety violations, the GAO cites 4 causes: (1) lack of independent or outside DOE review, (2) weak oversight, (3) "lax attitudes toward safety procedures," and (4) failure to correct known safety problems. Today, these same harsh criticisms of the DOE remain true, despite their having been repeated for 20 years, year after year, in new government-oversight reports. Yet nothing is done, perhaps because of the nuclear industry's ties to the military. DOE facilities remain totally self-regulated, although GAO officials say "DOE's credibility... [is] almost zero." Criticism of the DOE has been especially harsh in the last 15 years. Congress, the GAO, the OTA, and the NAS point to nuclear-industry falsification of worker-exposure records and cover-up of contamination and safety problems. They claim that DOE facilities even illegally exposed the public—including 13,000 children—to high doses of radiation. Congress also says the DOE has neither credible radiation-exposure records for 600,000 US nuclear workers nor adequate medical monitoring in 26 of its 33 types of facilities. In fact, because of flawed record-keeping and safety violations, in 2000 US President Clinton was forced to provide taxpayer-financed health care for all DOE nuclear workers, despite their employment as industry contractors.[39]

Where does this problematic nuclear history leave us? Recall that, beginning in 1991 and continuing to the present, the US OTA, the GAO, and Congress have repeatedly called for DOE's abolition or its external regulation. Neither recommendation has been followed. Instead, despite 6 decades of repeated violations and criticism by government oversight agencies, nuclear-safety problems continue. Commercial fission continues to receive the vast majority (more than 60 percent cumulative) of US government energy subsidies, yet it supplies only 19 percent of US electricity—6 percent less than renewables supply. As chapter 7 shows, the only nations with substantial atomic-energy programs are centrally planned and must heavily subsidize reactors—as France and all other nuclear nations do. Thus, although nuclear power has not been able to survive in the free market, nevertheless secrecy, cover-up, and subsidies protect it when economics cannot. As a July 2005 analysis in the *Economist* warned, nuclear costs, safety, and permanent waste storage make atomic energy "extremely risky." The publication noted that for decades bankers in London and New York have refused loans to nuclear industries. The *Economist* blames nuclear lobbyists and campaign contributors for the continuation of the economically indefensible multi-billion-dollar nuclear subsidies by the US government. It says a more economically efficient US energy choice would have been squeezing "polluting activities" and "taxing the use of carbon... to encourage energy consumers to switch to other sources." Similar conclusions recently came from MIT and EU scientists who say problems with cost, safety, proliferation, terrorism, security, and permanent waste storage are major obstacles to using atomic power. Given this "straight talk" of the *Economist* and EU scientists; nuclear bans by Sweden, Italy, Belgium, Germany, and other nations; the absence of new US commercial reactor construction since 1974; and the absence of an approved US facility for permanent nuclear-waste storage, the continuing billion-dollar US nuclear subsidies suggest a serious information problem. So does the 2005 revelation of falsified safety data at DOE's proposed waste-storage site, at Yucca Mountain, Nevada. Knowing the US government's problematic nuclear history, cities and states also are challenging proposals for hundreds of thousands of unguarded commercial-nuclear-waste shipments across US interstates to the proposed Nevada dump. They call the proposed transport "Mobile Chernobyl." Since the nuclear-core melts at Three Mile Island, Fukushima, and Chernobyl, critics say citizens will not accept atomic energy. Whether or not they will, the main point of this book is to get the science (including economics), the ethics, and the energy policy right. Congress, GAO, and OTA have criticized US nuclear-regulatory secrecy, deception, safety violations, and failure to do accurate cost accounting. A recent NAS committee likewise concluded that "lack of trust in the DOE and its [nuclear-industry] site operators is a major impediment to radiation protection." The US government oversight agency also faulted the nuclear industry, as late as 2008–2011, for long-uncorrected safety violations and its failure to do accurate nuclear-cost accounting. Given these continuing US nuclear problems, it is easy to see why later chapters need to criticize so many nuclear-cost and nuclear-safety studies done by industry and government. It also is easy to see that the nuclear record—on safety, emissions, and costs—needs to be set straight in order to evaluate CC-related proposals to expand atomic energy. [40]

Trimming Greenhouse-Gas Emissions from the Nuclear-Fuel Cycle

As already mentioned, at the heart of the CC case for expanding atomic energy is the climate-necessity argument: the claim that, because nuclear generation of electricity is carbon free, it is needed to help address CC. To understand this climate-necessity argument for increased nuclear fission, note first that the nuclear-fuel cycle has at least 14 stages. These include

(1) mining uranium ore—or leaching it out, by using hundreds of metric tons of chemicals such as sulfuric acid, nitric acid, and ammonia;

(2) milling the ore to extract the roughly 0.2 percent uranium oxide (U_3O_8) from it;

(3) converting the U_3O_8 to gaseous uranium hexafluoride (UF_6) by means of fluorine;

(4) enriching the UF_6 so that it becomes 3.5 percent U-235 (rather than 0.7 percent, as in natural uranium), and removing the 85 percent of the UF_6 which are enrichment tails;

(5) fabricating the fuel into ceramic pellets of uranium dioxide (UO_2), packing the pellets into zirconium alloy tubes, then bundling the tubes together to form fuel rods for reactors;

(6) constructing the reactor, which (as the next chapter shows) takes 12 years or more;

(7) operating the reactor;

(8) reprocessing waste fuel or spent fuel;

(9) conditioning the spent fuel;

(10) storing radioactive waste (in pools of water on the reactor site) until it is cool enough for transport and permanent storage;

(11) transporting the waste to a secure, permanent, storage facility;

(12) storing the waste permanently in a secure facility;

(13) decommissioning the reactor; and

(14) reclaiming the uranium mines, milling facilities, enrichment facilities, and so on.[41]

When proponents of the climate-necessity argument claim atomic energy is "carbon free," they err by ignoring GHG emissions from most of the 14-stage, nuclear-fuel cycle. Yet even under optimum conditions, only stage (7), reactor operation, is carbon free. Each of the remaining 13 stages creates high GHG emissions in using mainly fossil fuels for raw-materials, product-output, and radioactive-waste-storage transport. Each stage likewise releases many GHG emissions because most of its processes rely mainly on coal-generated electricity.[42]

Consider carbon emissions from nuclear-fuel-cycle stages (2) through (4)—uranium milling, conversion, and enrichment. One reason GHG emissions from nuclear stages (2) through (4) are so massive is that, because of the low concentration of usable uranium in ores (far less than 1 percent), the amount of uranium ore (by weight) that must be intensively mined and processed, per year, to feed one nuclear plant is greater than the coal tonnage that is needed annually to feed a coal plant that generates the same amount of electricity.[43] For instance, more than 1,000 tons of (high-grade) 0.1 percent (uranium-235) uranium ore must be processed, in highly energy-intensive ways, to produce 1 ton of uranium usable in a nuclear reactor.[44] Virtually all of this ore-processing is done by means of fossil fuels that release massive amounts of GHG emissions. Moreover, later paragraphs show that, if low-grade ore is used—and most uranium ore *is* low-grade—10,000 tons of uranium ore must be processed (using fossil fuels) to produce 1 ton of uranium for a reactor.

Stage-(2) milling alone requires roughly 1,000 metric tons of uranium ore to produce 1 ton of yellowcake (about 80-percent uranium oxide or U_3O_8); milling uses mainly coal-generated electricity to grind ore into small particles, chemically leach it, and process it.[45] Fuel-cycle stage (3), conversion and purification of yellowcake into uranium hexafluoride (UF_6), likewise releases substantial GHG emissions because it employs mostly fossil-based electricity for extraction, fluorination, and fractionation processes and because yellowcake often has 20-percent impurities and is only about 60-percent uranium ore.[46]

Stage (4) of the nuclear-fuel cycle, which includes UF_6 enrichment and concentration into (roughly 5-percent) U-235, releases substantial GHG emissions, both because its processes use mainly coal-generated electricity and because UF_6 is only about 0.7-percent usable, fissionable U-235.[47] Consequently, stage-(4) enrichment and concentration create many radioactive wastes that must be reclaimed, secured, shipped, and managed. Processing each 1,000 metric tons of UF_6 in a modern gaseous-diffusion (enrichment) plant produces only 124 tons of enriched UF_6—but 876 tons of radioactive-waste tailings that must be secured and managed, so as to minimize their damaging environmental impact. For instance, just the uranium-238 in the tailings has a half-life of 4.5 billion years. Processing 124 metric tons of UF_6 also requires 951,542,500 kWhr of electricity. Thus, obtaining only 1 kg of enriched UF6, just at nuclear-fuel-cycle stage (4), requires 7,674 kWhr of electricity, virtually all from fossil fuels.[48]

Because each reactor annually uses about 15 metric tons of enriched UF_6, each reactor therefore requires roughly 19,230 megawatt-hours (MWhr) per year of largely fossil-fueled electricity, just for fuel-cycle-stage-(4) processes, namely uranium enrichment.[49] For all 104 US commercial reactors, stage-(4) electricity needs, alone, are (104) times (19,230), or 1,999,920 MWhr/year; nuclear-fuel cycle, stage-(4) electricity needs are thus alone about 2,000,000,000 kWhr/year, largely from fossil fuels.[50] Yet each kWhr of US coal-generated electricity produces (on average) more than 2 pounds (0.91 kg) of CO_2.[51] Consequently, because US nuclear-fuel-cycle-stage (4) relies mainly on coal-generated electricity, US CO_2 emissions from nuclear enrichment, alone, are 4 billion pounds (1,814,369,000 kg) per year.

Similar to what occurs in stages (2) through (4) of the nuclear-fuel cycle, 13 of the 14 stages have large GHG emissions, waste products, and fossil-fuel transport needs. One reason for these high GHG emissions and wastes is that light-water reactors have a lifetime uranium utilization of less than 0.6 percent; this means that for every kilogram of uranium that comes from a mine, "994 grams leave the nuclear reactor as depleted uranium in highly radioactive spent fuel."[52] Yet, as already noted, this waste must be stored and managed in perpetuity. Nuclear-fuel-cycle stage (12), permanent waste storage, requires massive energy, in part because each spent-fuel waste canister (weighing more than 10 times as much as the waste it contains) must be carefully fabricated and lined with lead, steel, and pure electrolytic copper. Moreover, the energy needed—to produce the canisters to contain the lifetime wastes of only one reactor—is roughly the same as the energy needed to build the reactor itself. Just the storage, cleaning, and cooling—required in nuclear-fuel-cycle stage (13), reactor decommissioning—produces about 1,000 cubic meters of high-level radioactive waste. Total decommissioning (including dismantling the reactor and cutting it into small pieces for permanent storage) requires about 50 percent more electricity—mostly from fossil fuels—than that required for reactor construction itself.[53]

These massive energy requirements of the 14-stage nuclear-fuel cycle help explain why each reactor takes at least 11 years to "pay back" energy used prior to start-up; by contrast, payback for natural-gas plants is only 6 months.[54] As the next chapter shows in more detail, the average lifetime of all already-closed nuclear plants is 22 years.[55] This means half of average-lifetime reactor output is needed to repay the pre-start-up nuclear-energy "debt." University of London economist David Fleming calculates that roughly one-quarter of reactor-electricity production is required to pay back the front-end nuclear-energy debts from mining, fuel fabrication, and reactor construction; that another one-quarter is required to pay the back-end energy debts of reactor decommissioning, waste storage, and so on; and that another one-quarter is required to process and store the backlog of existing wastes. This means that three-fourths (75 percent) of current nuclear-energy electricity production is currently needed for energy payback. But Fleming shows that if processing the backlog of radioactive wastes is delayed until 2025, the energy and emissions costs of this cleanup will mean that 100 percent of nuclear-energy output will be required to cover its full fuel-cycle energy inputs. In other words, if the radioactive-waste backlog is not addressed until 2025, at that date the nuclear-fuel cycle will face energy bankruptcy. Its nuclear-energy output will not exceed its energy inputs.[56]

Even if the nuclear-waste backlog is processed immediately, Fleming explains, nuclear-energy bankruptcy nevertheless could occur by midcentury. Why? Because a "severe shortage" of uranium will occur by 2013, and because reprocessing (to create mixed-oxide [MOX] fuel) cannot be increased, more reactors will be forced to use low-grade, uranium-ore supplies (below 0.02 percent), rather than higher-grade ore. As a result, energy requirements of the "front end" of the nuclear cycle will increase massively (see discussion later in the chapter). Consequently, reactors soon will produce less energy than their nuclear-fuel cycle requires. Energy bankruptcy will result. In technical, economic terms, the massive energy needs of the nuclear-fuel cycle create a very low "energy return on energy invested" (EREI) for atomic energy. Either delay in treating the backlog of nuclear wastes, or use of low-grade uranium supplies, is alone sufficient to cause nuclear-energy bankruptcy. In short, Fleming shows that because the entire nuclear-industry electricity output is insufficient both to meet all nuclear-fuel-stage requirements (including processing and permanently managing the backlog of radioactive waste) the nuclear industry will become a net *user* of energy, mostly from fossil fuels, just to manage its own radioactive waste.[57]

This "energy debt" of the nuclear-fuel cycle is significant for at least four reasons. One reason is that the debt shows atomic energy is self-defeating. It needs as much energy as it creates. A second reason is that (as later chapters explain in more detail) massive nuclear expenditures of energy and money could delay a global transition to clean, sustainable, inexpensive forms of energy. A third reason this nuclear-energy bankruptcy is significant is that it shows reactors face a uranium-depletion problem, similar to that of the oil industry.[58] Because of this fuel depletion, energy debt, and permanent radioactive-waste management, fission obviously is not a sustainable technology. A fourth reason the nuclear-fuel-cycle energy debt is significant is that this debt is created mostly by use of fossil fuels in various stages of the nuclear-fuel cycle, as already illustrated. This means that when proponents of the climate-necessity argument (such as the Nuclear Energy Institute, the US DOE, the UK DTI, the World Energy Council, and so on) say nuclear power is carbon free and thus needed to address CC, they err. Moreover, given the massive energy debt of fission, they err in egregious ways because they consider only some of the GHG emissions of the nuclear-fuel cycle—usually only those of stage (7), reactor operation.

When one counts all 14 nuclear-fuel stages, what are total fission GHG emissions? If one excludes all analyses (of fuel-life-cycle GHG emissions) that rely on secondary sources, are unpublished, or fail to explain GHG-emissions estimation and calculation methods, only 103, post-2000 analyses remain. These calculate nuclear-fuel-cycle GHG emissions ranging from 1.4 g to 288 g carbon-dioxide-equivalent emissions per kWh of electricity (gCO_2/kWh), depending on how many stages of the nuclear-fuel cycle are considered in their calculations. For instance, both the classic, otherwise-excellent German study of GHG emissions[59] and the International Energy Agency (IEA) studies[60] calculate GHG emissions from various energy sources, but they ignore GHG emissions associated with nuclear stages (10), (11), (12), and (14)—respectively, interim waste storage, waste transport, permanent waste storage, and uranium-mine reclamation. They omit these GHG emissions on the grounds that there are no empirical data for them, because full and permanent waste storage and so on have not yet taken place. Scientists who ignore these GHG emissions thus effectively count them as zero. Yet earlier paragraphs showed that this "back end" of the nuclear-fuel cycle is associated with fossil-fuel emissions whose energy needs are massive—roughly one-fourth those of total nuclear-plant output (see earlier details). Such fossil-fuel needs obviously cause massive GHG emissions. As a result of ignoring many nuclear-fuel-cycle emissions, IEA scientists erroneously conclude that nuclear GHG emissions are roughly the same as total emissions from solar PV. However, it is obviously fallacious to compare partial nuclear-fission GHG emissions with total solar GHG emissions.

Many nuclear-industry studies tend to give total fission-fuel-cycle GHG emissions as 1.4 g, but they consider only one or two nuclear-fuel-cycle stages, typically (7), and sometimes stages (4) or (5). Some environmental groups tend to give total atomic-energy GHG emissions as 288 g, but they sometimes appear to double-count some emissions. However, the average, total-nuclear-fuel-cycle GHG emissions calculated by the most reliable 103, post-2000 studies (see caveat 5, in the previous chapter) is 66 gCO_2/kWh (although University of London economists calculate 88–135 gCO_2/kWh).[61] This 66 g also is roughly the figure obtained by independent university scientists (at schools such as Columbia, Oxford, and Singapore) who are without financial conflicts of interest and who are funded neither by industry nor by environmentalists. Unlike the nuclear-industry studies mentioned earlier (see caveat 5, about sources, in the previous chapter), they use current, refereed, published, empirical data on nuclear facilities' lifetimes, efficiency, enrichment methods, plant type, fuel grade, and so on. Their calculations (fairly consistent across universities) show mean, total-fuel-lifecycle, per-kWhr GHG-emissions ratios, for COAL : COMBINED-CYCLE NATURAL GAS : NUCLEAR : SOLAR PV : WIND, as 1,010 : 443 : 66 : 32 : 9. This is a GHG-emissions ratio of roughly

112 coal : 49 gas : 7 nuclear : 4 solar : 1 wind.

If correct, these university GHG-emissions calculations show that although fission, using high-grade ore, emits 16 times less GHG than coal, it releases about 2 times more GHG emissions than solar, and about 7 times more than wind.[62]

Because proponents of the climate-necessity argument fail to count most of the emissions from the nuclear-fuel cycle, they commit a fallacy of composition: an invalid inference from GHG emissions in 1 or 2, to all 14, nuclear-fuel-cycle stages. They assume that because 1 stage (reactor operation) of the nuclear-fuel cycle can be carbon free, therefore all 14 stages are always carbon free.

Why do nuclear proponents engage in such invalid data trimming? One reason may be their desire to promote atomic power, despite its massive energy debt and GHG emissions. Another reason may be that trimming nuclear GHG-emissions data may arise partly from Kyoto Protocol conventions. These conventions assess carbon content in nuclear fuels at their consumption-point (electricity generation); consequently, they unrealistically ignore full, 14-stage-fuel-cycle carbon content.[63] The result? This major climate convention (Kyoto), while designed to help avert CC, actually provides an unrealistic and counterfactual means of assessing contributions to CC.

Unrealistic Uranium-Ore Assumptions in the Climate-Necessity Argument

Even when fission proponents consider GHG emissions from many of the 14 nuclear-fuel-cycle stages, they typically trim atomic-energy GHG emissions through unrealistic assumptions. For instance, often they erroneously assume that reactors use only higher-grade uranium ores (those with at least 0.1 percent uranium oxide—yellowcake U_3O_8), not lower-grade ores (those below 0.02-percent U_3O_8). The German, IEA, Japanese, and US DOE studies, for example, and virtually all nuclear industry studies make this high-grade-uranium-ore assumption.[64] Yet because high-grade ores create much less radioactive waste (to be transported and managed), and require much less energy for mining and milling, they cause much fewer GHG emissions. As a consequence, this high-grade-ore assumption is used by the industry, German, IEA, Japanese, US, and other studies—to justify their failing to calculate full GHG emissions from at least 3 stages of the nuclear-fuel cycle (mining, milling, and waste management). Because of this and other faulty nuclear-data-trimming assumptions, the German, IEA, DOE, and industry studies conclude that GHG emissions from nuclear fission and solar PV are roughly the same.

How reliable is this crucial assumption that only high-grade-uranium ore is used in reactors and therefore that only minimal GHG emissions result from the front end of the nuclear-fuel-cycle processing? This assumption is questionable because the vast majority of uranium ores are lower-grade, whereas cleaner, higher-grade ores are nearly gone.[65] In fact, as already noted, economists say shortages already are occurring and a "severe shortage" of high-grade uranium will occur by 2013. Consequently, when reactors use lower-grade uranium ores, they cause much higher nuclear-fuel-cycle GHG emissions. One reason for these higher GHG emissions is that converting 1 metric ton of uranium into an enriched form requires about half a metric ton of fluorine (to produce UF_6, as already mentioned). The lower the ore grade, the more fluorine must be used, and the more GHG emissions are released. Because only the enriched fraction of UF_6 can be used by reactors, depleted hexafluoride gas (hex) is left as waste, much of which escapes into the atmosphere. In fact, scientists say most of this hex is likely to escape, precisely because it is not being stored in secure containers deep underground. Yet hex is a halogenated compound (one of several that is used in the nuclear-fuel cycle), and halogenated compounds are potent greenhouse gases. As greenhouse gases, they are up to 10,000 more potent than carbon dioxide. Thus whenever a nuclear-fuel-cycle process uses lower-grade uranium ore, it requires more hex, which causes more GHG emissions.[66]

A second reason that lower-grade uranium ores cause more nuclear-fuel-cycle GHG emissions is that much more (lower-grade) radioactive rock must be mined, milled, and stored as waste, in order to extract small amounts of ore that can be processed into reactor fuel. As already noted, Australian, British, Dutch, US, and other university scientists, especially economists, point out that high-grade uranium ores require roughly 1 metric ton of high-grade ore to be mined, milled, enriched, fabricated, and so on, in order to extract 1 kg of uranium fuel, whereas the roughly 10-times-less-concentrated, low-grade uranium ores require about 10 metric tons of low-grade ore to be mined, milled, enriched, fabricated, and so on, in order to extract 1 kg of uranium fuel. These scientists show that, when one uses low-grade ore, fossil energy for mining and milling, as well as greenhouse emissions, increases by roughly a factor of 10. They point out that because "the vast majority of the world's known uranium resources are low-grade" and because new reactors are being built, usable (high-grade) uranium could be gone within several years.[67]

Part of the reason for the shortage of usable uranium is not only that most of the known uranium ore is low-grade, but also that this uranium is unable to provide a practical return on energy investment (PREI) in nuclear power. Factors limiting PREI include the great depth of some uranium deposits, their being located in underground water or where there is insufficient water for processing, their trivial contribution to supplies, the lack of available investment capital for uranium mines (see chapter 3), and so on. Thus, although some uranium is now being mined that is as poor as 0.03, economists warn that uranium of at least 0.1 percent is required for a positive PREI. More uranium may be discovered, but economists also warn that, after 70 years of uranium exploration and mining, remaining deposits are likely too poor to yield a positive PREI.[68]

What is the significance of the increase in GHG emissions whenever low-grade uranium ore is used in the nuclear-fuel cycle? Whenever reactors are forced to use low-grade uranium ore, average-nuclear-fuel-cycle GHG emissions are *higher* than average-fuel-cycle GHG emissions from natural-gas-fired plants.[69] Economists say that remaining uranium ores are of "such poor quality that the gas and other fossil fuels used in the nuclear-life-cycle would produce less carbon dioxide per kilowatt-hour if they were used directly as fuels [instead of used to fabricate uranium for reactors] to generate electricity."[70] Moreover, as already mentioned regarding the "energy bankruptcy" of nuclear fission , below 0.02 percent uranium ore, scientists say nuclear GHG emissions increase massively because more power is needed to produce atomic energy than is gained from it.[71] As one British scientist put it, "Lifetime costs in energy and greenhouse emissions go up exponentially as ore grade goes down."[72] Nuclear-fuel cycles using 10-times-less-concentrated ore (<0.01 percent yellowcake) thus have total GHG emissions that are equal roughly to those for natural-gas-fuel cycles; all other things being equal, low-grade-uranium-ore nuclear cycles release 12 times more GHG emissions than solar cycles, and 49 times more than wind cycles.[73] That is, when reactors use low-grade-uranium ores, the full-fuel-cycle-GHG emissions ratio =

112 coal : 49 natural gas : 49 nuclear : 4 solar : 1 wind.

Note that the GHG emissions ratio given earlier, of 112 coal : 49 natural gas : 7 nuclear : 4 solar : 1 wind, applies only when reactors use high-grade uranium ore. As already noted, many scientists say nuclear-fuel cycles that rely on low-grade-uranium ore could require more energy than they produce.[74] For all these reasons, proponents of the climate-necessity argument err when they trim nuclear-fuel-cycle GHG emissions by assuming they can ignore GHG emissions from low-grade uranium ore.

Inconsistency in the Climate-Necessity Argument

Apart from trimming nuclear GHG emissions and accepting counterfactual assumptions about uranium-ore grade, proponents of the climate-necessity argument also fall into several inconsistencies. These inconsistencies arise from the fact that the climate-necessity argument is built on the reasonable assumption that one should promote energy technologies that are effective in avoiding GHG emissions. Yet if the preceding data and ratios (about fuel-cycle-carbon emissions) are correct, wind and solar PV are more effective in avoiding GHG emissions than is atomic energy. But if so, proponents of the climate-necessity argument ought to promote wind and solar PV before nuclear power. Yet they do not, as already noted earlier. Instead they say "we don't really have any other choice" but to increase nuclear fission.[75] They say atomic power is the only energy source that is "readily available,"[76] "the only existing power technology which could replace coal in base load,"[77] "the only technology ready to fill the gap" to address CC,[78] "the most viable [energy] alternative."[79]

How could proponents of the climate-necessity argument know that atomic energy is the best CC solution, when most industry (and many government) reports analyze GHG emissions only from coal, natural gas, atomic energy, and petroleum?[80] Climate-necessity proponents thus are inconsistent. They claim to want to address CC, yet they fail even to consider and assess more effective GHG-emissions-avoiding technologies, like wind and solar PV. They also are inconsistent in a second way. They promote nuclear fission on the grounds that it helps avoid GHG emissions, yet from a purely economic point of view, building reactors interferes with the most effective ways of avoiding GHG emissions. As chapter 6 argues in more detail, UK business-school studies show that because capital-intensive, heavily subsidized nuclear plants undermine funding for energy-efficiency programs, conservation, and renewable energy—all of which are more effective than nuclear fission in reducing GHG emissions—they delay more-effective technologies for GHG-emissions-avoidance.[81] UK government reports also repeatedly warn of the opportunity costs of nuclear development; they say fission investments "depress the market" for renewables and divert government subsidies to less effective and more costly strategies for CO_2 abatement.[82] Besides, if energy efficiencies and using (geographically) distributed renewable-energy technologies will save from 2 to 10 times more carbon, per dollar of investment, than will nuclear power, and do so more quickly,[83] the major opportunity cost of fission investment is that it makes it harder to address CC. Obviously, if finite dollars are available to spend on energy development, and if those dollars are spent in ways (atomic energy) that are less effective at reducing GHG emissions, fission expenditures actually promote CC.

Why does atomic-energy investment promote CC? As chapter 6 explains in more detail, the famous Harvard Energy, US OTA, and Presidential Commission studies all concluded that energy efficiency was the cheapest, most reasonable way to address energy needs; in fact, the commission showed that every federal dollar spent on energy-efficiency programs would generate a 40-to-1 return on the initial investment.[84] Just one current, inexpensive, US DOE energy-efficiency program annually saves electricity equivalent to what nearly 7 nuclear plants would generate.[85] In 2007, McKinsey and Company, one of the world's leading management-consulting firms, likewise showed that global energy demand could be cut by 50 percent over the next 15 years without compromising any economic growth, that is, at a net cost of zero, because cutting demand would be cost-effective. The same study showed that 28 percent of current energy demand could be reduced immediately, with existing technology; in 2008, McKinsey showed that a $520 billion investment in US energy efficiency would produce $1.2 trillion in energy savings by 2020.[86] As chapter 6 also explains, Germany's Oko Institute shows that efficiency programs, wind, and gas-cogeneration all have negative costs of GHG-emissions-avoidance because they are inexpensive and cut energy demand.[87] US government reports agree. The pro-nuclear US DOE, NAS, and OTA say that, using energy efficiencies alone, "the US could [have] cut carbon emissions to 1990 levels by 2010 with no net cost to the nation's economy."[88] The classic Princeton University study shows that of more than 7 options—including technological efficiencies, conservation, natural gas, wind, solar-photovoltaic (PV), biomass, and hydrogen—each option could alone, cost-competitively, with fewer emissions, and "at an industrial scale," supply as much energy as nuclear tripling.[89] This fact may be one reason that wind generates 20 percent of electricity in midwestern US states, such as Iowa, and in many nations, like Denmark.[90] If the preceding university data on GHG emissions are correct, if nuclear proponents are consistent, and if their primary goal is avoiding GHG emissions, then those who support the climate-necessity argument should assess and promote conservation, efficiency, wind, and solar PV—before nuclear fission—because they are cheaper and less carbon-intensive. Otherwise, if proponents of the climate-necessity argument promote costly (see chapter 3), carbon-intensive technologies like nuclear fission, they threaten CC abatement.

Self-Defeating Consequences of the Climate-Necessity Argument

The Germans recognize this fact and say they can avoid fission and instead use wind to become carbon neutral; the Swedes say they can become carbon neutral by avoiding fission and instead using biomass.[91] They recognize that even if atomic energy were safe and cheap, had places to store radioactive waste, and so on, it would remain a self-defeating technology. Why? One reason, already discussed here, is the "energy bankruptcy" of fission, given its energy-intensive, carbon-intensive fuel cycle; its low-grade uranium ore; its failure to deal with the backlog of radioactive waste; and its low EREI. As already mentioned, the fossil-fuel-based energy needed to recover uranium from rocks in the earth's crust increases with decreasing ore grade. Thus, even if the radioactive-waste backlog is addressed immediately, if nuclear plants are tripled, degraded uranium-ore quality means that nuclear-generated electricity will become self-defeating by 2050, during the lifetime of any plants whose construction was begun in 2010 or later.[92]

Atomic energy also is self-defeating because, even under the most optimistic and unrealistic conditions, fission would supply too little electricity too late. As already mentioned, even with an unrealistic nuclear tripling, atomic energy could reduce only about 20 percent of year-2050 GHG emissions, could provide only 20 percent of needed electricity,[93] and could supply only 8–9 percent of total energy. As the MIT authors put it, without fission or any other means of addressing CC, greenhouse emissions will be 200 percent greater in 2050 than they are now. With nuclear tripling, these emissions will be 175 percent greater.[94] Moreover, new reactors begun in 2010 could not come online until at least the middle 2020s.[95] Average US nuclear construction time is 11–12 years,[96] and as the next chapter shows, the last US reactor took 23 years to build. Yet as chapter 1 showed, CC needs to be addressed immediately, not in 11, 12, or 23 years. Given its small energy contribution and its long lead times, nuclear fission is obviously a "too little, too late" contribution to addressing CC. It would make only an "insignificant contribution" to lowering greenhouse emissions, in part because of its energy debt.[97]

A third reason that fission is a self-defeating way to address CC is that it is not sustainable. It has problems both with permanent radioactive-waste management (see chapter 5) and with uranium shortages, as already discussed.[98] If all the world's electricity could somehow be generated by nuclear power, the world's known high-grade uranium reserves would last only 3.5 years.[99] This is why even scientists conducting analyses for the pro nuclear US DOE argue that the world's uranium supply would fall short of meeting future nuclear-tripling demands; moreover, the US itself produces less than 5 percent of the total uranium needs of its current reactors.[100] This means that if nuclear reactors were tripled, uranium imports could cause many of the same problems as oil imports. Pro-nuclear MIT and Harvard analyses admit that massive government support for uranium exploration would be needed if the US nuclear program were to expand.[101]

What do the preceding data show? Increasing the number of reactors, in the name of averting CC, is self-defeating in at least three ways. It would worsen the energy debt, produce little or no "net energy," and lead to nuclear "energy bankruptcy." It would produce too little energy, too late, and it would not be sustainable.

Although increased nuclear fission is thus self-defeating in these three ways, there are several alternative-energy technologies that could supply more energy, cheaper, faster, without onerous fuel requirements.[102] As chapter 6 argues in more detail, these alternative technologies include solar PV and wind. Neither of these technologies is likely to be self-defeating, because there will never be a solar or wind production-decline curve. They have no fuel that can become scarce or difficult to extract from ore. Thus if one is convinced of CC, the question is why one would use a self-defeating fission technology to address it. It took only 25 years (from 1975 to 2000) to phase out use of chlorofluorocarbons; with a similar commitment, it should also be possible to phase out fossil fuels and nuclear power.[103] Besides, as chapter 6 reveals, already scientists have spelled out detailed strategies for achieving massive reductions in GHG emissions, strategies that require no fossil fuels, no coal without sequestration, and no increase in the percent of the GDP used in energy services.[104]

Implementation Problems with the Climate-Necessity Argument

Despite the three ways in which tripling global atomic energy would be self-defeating, some proponents claim that reactors can be implemented quickly and easily. As noted earlier in this chapter, they say atomic power is the only energy source that is "readily available" to address CC,[105] "the only technology ready to fill the gap" and help avert CC.[106] Nuclear proponents also claim that wind and solar energy are incapable of being implemented immediately,[107] a claim that chapters 6 and 7 will show is false. Thus nuclear proponents say atomic energy is "the most viable [energy] alternative" to address CC.[108]

How legitimate are these claims of quick nuclear-fission implementation? When proponents of the climate-necessity argument make these implementation claims, they face a dilemma. On one hand, if they argue that nuclear energy can be implemented more quickly now than in the past, they beg the question because they ignore actual empirical data on reactor-construction times. As noted earlier, the US National Academy of Sciences says the average reactor-construction time is 11 years, and the last US plant took 23 years to build. On the other hand, if they follow actual empirical data and thus argue that nuclear energy cannot be implemented more quickly than in the past, they lose the supposed nuclear advantage, the speed of implementation mentioned by nuclear proponents in the previous paragraph. As a result, these proponents are forced to follow the path of most current energy investors—toward solar and wind, and away from atomic power. Virtually all fission proponents admit that the main CC debate is over the short term. Over the intermediate and long term, virtually everyone agrees that renewables are the only answer. Thus claims about rapid nuclear implementation either beg the question or lose the short-term nuclear argument.

Why do climate-necessity proponents beg the question if they claim fission can be implemented more quickly now than in the past? *First*, the most obvious reason is that they ignore actual empirical data, like those of the National Academy of Sciences, cited earlier. As already noted, the last reactor built in the US took 23 years to build.[109] Of the last 6 power plants brought online in Japan, the 5 five brought online in the 1980s averaged 17 years to plan and build, whereas the one brought online in the 1990s took 26 years.[110] Eastern European nuclear plants using Soviet technology have taken an average of 15 years to build, and the average time taken in France is 8 years,[111] perhaps because members of the public have little voice in the decision and in overseeing safety checks. In 2007, one of the top business-management consulting firms, McKinsey, estimated that it would take 9–11 years to bring a new nuclear plant online.[112] Thus no empirical data show that decreased reactor-construction time is likely. Any claims of shortened construction times are purely speculative.

A *second* reason nuclear proponents err if they claim future reactor-construction times will decrease is that newer reactor designs are untested. As the eminent investment and credit-rating firm Standard and Poor's put it in its 2006 assessment of nuclear energy, "Given that construction would entail using new designs and technology, cost [and time] overruns are highly probable."[113] Yet according to top management-consulting firm McKinsey, if future nuclear plants have cost (and time) overruns, this would limit any nuclear expansion.[114] A *third* problem is that the US, at least, has lost most of its nuclear expertise, given that no US nuclear plants have been ordered for nearly 40 years.[115] *Fourth,* even the nuclear industry predicts future nuclear-fission decline, and consequently no rapid implementation of atomic energy.[116] After all, in the early 1990s, atomic energy supplied 17 percent of global electricity, but as of 2006, this percentage was 14.8 and declining.[117]

A *fifth* reason that rapid future fission implementation is unlikely is that a majority of members of the public (60 percent according to the 2003 MIT study)[118] rejects nuclear power and, instead, has long supported efficiency and renewables.[119] Thus any possible future nuclear installations may be slowed by public protest, particularly because many members of the public view themselves as victims of a US DOE "DAD" strategy—"decide, announce, defend"—rather than a strategy that involves them.[120] The pro-nuclear MIT study showed that, for decades, 77 percent of Americans has favored the expansion of solar and wind, while less than 30 percent has supported nuclear power.[121] After all, more than a thousand people repeatedly have been arrested at a single US nuclear plant, in a single year, in protests.[122] More than 300 national, state, and local citizens' organizations have issued a statement outlining their reasons for opposing use of nuclear power to address CC, and not a single environmental group supports nuclear power.[123] As the pro-nuclear International Atomic Energy Agency notes, environmental opposition to nuclear power puts even uranium mining at risk, especially in the US and Australia; this is partly because all uranium mines would need to be secured, in order to protect against clandestine uranium enrichment for weapons.[124] Thus public opposition could delay or prohibit not only reactor construction but also uranium mining.[125]

A *sixth* reason that rapid, future implementation of nuclear fission is unlikely is that the logistics required for implementing atomic energy are daunting. If all coal-fired plants in the world were to be replaced by nuclear plants, this would require building a gigawatt-sized nuclear reactor every two and one-half days for 38 years.[126] Yet this is something that seems unlikely in the face of uranium shortages (already noted), lack of full nuclear-liability insurance (discussed in later chapters), high atomic-energy costs (discussed in chapter 3), and public opposition that is likely to lead to delays. Even if nuclear power tripled globally, the pro-nuclear MIT authors note that, for 4 decades, one reactor would have to come online every 15 days—something that seems quite unlikely,[127] especially given that no nation has ever brought online more than one or two commercial reactors in any given year. Moreover, as the next chapter shows, more reactors have been cancelled after they were begun than have actually been built—imposing financial losses on investors that make them even more wary of atomic energy.

A *seventh* problem facing any rapid nuclear increase is that there is no approved, accepted way to permanently store nuclear waste. With no assurance of what to do with radioactive waste, utilities will be even more reluctant to build reactors, a fact that argues against rapid construction. The US long ago exceeded the 63,000-metric-ton statutory limit on the proposed Yucca Mountain waste repository,[128] and because of predicted leaks, seismic hazards, and volcanic activity, funding was cut on the Yucca Mountain facility in 2010. As the MIT authors note, if nuclear power were tripled globally, this would require building a waste facility the size of Yucca Mountain every three or four years; yet no commercial-waste repository anywhere, including Yucca Mountain, has ever been approved.[129]

For all the preceding reasons, rapid nuclear implementation seems unlikely. But if so, atomic energy would lose any apparent temporal advantage over renewable energy sources, like wind and solar. As chapter 6 discusses in more detail, the classic 2004 Princeton University study, published in *Science*, shows that any 6 of 9 renewable technologies already deployed at an industrial scale could completely solve the climate problem by 2050; a later US DOE study is even more optimistic, showing that technology already is available for renewable energy resources to provide 99 percent of US electricity generation by the year 2020.[130] Yet 2020 is earlier than the date by which any nuclear plant would be finished, if it were begun in 2010. The British say that they can supply well over 30 GW (the equivalent of more than 30 nuclear plants), using only solar and wind, by the year 2020; already the Germans have more wind-power capacity than the entire UK nuclear component, although they have fewer wind resources than the UK.[131] Scientists have shown that virtually all global energy needs could be supplied through renewable energy.[132] As already mentioned, Princeton University and other studies agree with the Intergovernmental Panel on Climate Change (IPCC). They show that renewable energy alone could address CC and that "a portfolio of technologies now exists to meet the world's energy needs over the next 50 years and limit atmospheric CO_2."[133] "None of the options is a pipe dream or an unproven idea," say the authors, since "today one can buy electricity from a wind turbine, PV array, gas turbine," and "every one of these options is already implemented at an industrial scale and could be scaled up further over 50 years."[134] As chapter 6 explains in more detail, other scientists say three-fourths of all US electricity could be saved through energy efficiency that would cost, on average, about 1 cent per kWh; already firms like DuPont, Dow, and IBM are saving billions of dollars annually by cutting energy intensity by as much as 6–8 percent per year.[135]

Moreover, implementation of these renewables, according to US DOE government studies, assumes no storage for solar PV energy and accepts current grid reliability, grid stability, and wind variability concerns. Nevertheless, under these assumptions, US government studies show that solar photovoltaic (PV) could supply 12 percent of total US electricity in 2020, while wind could supply 20 percent. Beyond the year 2020, government says new battery-storage options would allow solar and wind to supply far more of US electricity.[136] The National Renewable Energy Laboratory also has estimated that the entire electricity demand of the US could be supplied with solar from less than one-third of the land currently used for military purposes.[137] Market investors agree with the preceding facts. As chapter 6 explains in more detail, global manufacture of solar PV cells has been growing as much as 50 to 60 percent per year over the last few years.[138] Solar potential on only 1 percent of US landmass (e.g., mostly on rooftops and parking lots),[139] converted at 20 percent efficiency, is 3 times larger than wind potential—or 8 times current US electricity needs.[140] Because of a variety of new manufacturing techniques, including non-silicon thin film cells and increased manufacturing scale, the pro-nuclear US DOE says the cost of solar PV electricity will go from year-2007 costs of $0.18–0.23 per kWh to $0.05–0.10 by the year 2015 and that US PV manufacturing capacity will increase 12 times in the next five years—making solar PV competitive in all markets nationwide by 2015.[141]

Given these government data on the ease of rapid transition to renewable energy, the flaws in claims about rapid nuclear implementation are especially obvious. As already emphasized, unless nuclear power can be implemented quickly, it loses any supposed advantages to renewable energy. But if rapid nuclear implementation is not likely, this is yet another reason that the climate-necessity argument fails.

Proliferation Problems with the Climate-Necessity Argument

In supporting the climate-necessity argument, proponents also err because they promote nuclear fission as a way to help avert the catastrophe of CC, yet their nuclear promotion increases the likelihood of another catastrophe, nuclear-weapons proliferation, and nuclear terrorism. In fact, many people view the nuclear-proliferation and terrorism problem as the most severe difficulty confronting atomic energy.[142] In at least three ways, the commercial use of fission technology encourages terrorism and weapons proliferation. The first reason is that, in nuclear-fuel-cycle stage (4), uranium-235 is enriched to about 90 percent, rather than the 3.5 percent that is absolutely required for a reactor; this enrichment creates the higher-grade uranium needed for nuclear weapons. The second reason that a rise in the number of commercial reactors provides a technological platform that increases the risk of nuclear terrorism and weapons proliferation is that nuclear-fuel-cycle stage (8), waste-fuel reprocessing, also generates weapons-grade materials. This reprocessing isolates and purifies plutonium, a fuel for nuclear weapons. The third reason is that, the more reactors one has, the greater the supply of radioactive materials that can be stolen and used to create a dirty bomb—a weapon that disperses radioactive materials using a conventional explosive.[143]

Atomic-energy proponents often attempt to get around problems of terrorism and proliferation by saying that not all such problems can be avoided. Or they say that, even if there were no nuclear plants, there would still be problems of terrorism. While these responses are true, they ignore the fact that increasing the number of nuclear plants increases the likelihood of terrorism and weapons proliferation. The bottom line is that if nuclear proponents want to satisfy the climate-necessity argument, they must encourage nuclear expansion, so as to avoid more CC. However, if they want to satisfy concerns about proliferation and terrorism, they must avoid any nuclear expansion. They cannot have it both ways. They cannot argue both that nuclear energy adequately addresses the catastrophe of CC and that it avoids the catastrophe of nuclear proliferation and terrorism.

At least 10 reasons suggest that increasing the number of nuclear facilities would increase terrorism and proliferation risks. *One* reason is that terrorists need succeed only once to shut down nuclear energy or cause a catastrophe, but security services have to succeed every time.[144] Yet it is very difficult for security services to succeed every time. Humans cannot avoid all human error. One need only recall the 2009 African terrorist who attempted to blow up a plane headed for Detroit. Although the US was warned long ahead of time about this man, the warning fell through the cracks, and only passengers' rapid responses prevented a tragedy. Moreover, government defense groups say that terrorism is likely to become more widespread, extreme, autonomous (with non-state actors), and international.[145] Given such autonomy, it is arguably more difficult for security experts to succeed every time.

A *second* reason that nuclear expansion would increase the likelihood of nuclear terrorism and proliferation is that, if reactors become more numerous, proliferation and terrorism risk will increase, in part because there will be more terrorist targets. Terrorist groups like Al Qaeda have already targeted nuclear installations and tried to obtain nuclear materials.[146] Already people have been arrested for trying to sell poorly guarded Russian nuclear materials, such as weapons-grade uranium.[147]

Besides, most research reactors, as on university campuses, have only minimal security.[148] One indicator of the success of terrorist groups is not only their past catastrophic actions, as in Tokyo in 1995 and New York in 1993 and 2001, but also the fact that (as late as 2011) terrorists continue to keep oil production, safe drinking water, and electricity in Baghdad far below the levels enjoyed when Saddam Hussein was in power.[149] Even heavily guarded oil plants in Saudi Arabia have been successfully attacked, and terrorist groups have had particular success with attacking transport routes, as in Madrid, that are essential to nuclear-waste transport.[150]

A *third* reason that nuclear expansion would increase the likelihood of nuclear terrorism and proliferation is that expanded atomic-energy production would make every step in the nuclear-fuel cycle more vulnerable. Yet many of these fuel-cycle stages are located in nations with little or no security. For instance, to protect against clandestine nuclear enrichment, experts say every single uranium mine in the world—and most of these are in developing nations—must be secured.[151] More generally, increased nuclear power would cause massive increases in nuclear materials available for bomb materials. Globally, already more than 1,500 metric tons of plutonium have been generated, all of which can be used for nuclear weapons; by 2010, the world had enough plutonium for 110,000 nuclear weapons.[152] Japan alone, for instance, has enough separated and stored plutonium for 4,750 bombs. Yet only 0.0025 percent of the MOX nuclear fuel that would be manufactured annually, under a nuclear-tripling scenario, would be enough for a bomb; this is an amount of material that can be kept in a container measuring 9 inches on each side.[153] Similarly, only 1 percent of the plutonium that would be processed annually, under the nuclear-tripling scenario, is enough to produce 149 weapons each year.[154] This is one reason that many experts, including those at Los Alamos National Laboratories and the International Atomic Energy Agency, say that nothing can completely prevent the risks of proliferation and nuclear terrorism once there is fission-generated electricity.[155] Nuclear proliferation and terrorism risks, they say, are "simply uncontrollable."[156] The IPCC also says that the increased security threat would be "colossal" if nuclear power was used extensively to tackle CC.[157] More available bomb materials mean more potential misuse of those materials, especially if only a few kilograms (e.g., 10 kg) of plutonium are enough to make a nuclear bomb that is powerful enough to destroy a city.[158]

A *fourth* reason that fission expansion would increase the likelihood of nuclear terrorism and proliferation is that, if experts are right (as discussed earlier) that there is not enough high-grade uranium ore to fuel an increase in nuclear power,[159] reactors would have to rely on recovered fuel (MOX) and plutonium from reprocessing to fuel reactors,[160] as nations like Japan are already doing. Yet this reliance on MOX fuel creates massively more available fissile materials and increases the cost of already-expensive nuclear electricity by 4 percent to 12 percent.[161] This reliance, in turn, creates an even more unstable situation.[162] After reprocessing, these materials are much more available, because no more than 99 percent of MOX materials ever can be accounted for, even under the best of reprocessing circumstances; even a single, state-of-the-art reprocessing plant typically has enough material-unaccounted-for (MUF) to create one nuclear weapon each month.[163] Before reprocessing, the spent nuclear fuel is so radioactive that it must be handled with remote equipment, although its volume is easy to ensure; during and after reprocessing, however, the complicated calculations and processes themselves make it difficult to know whether any plutonium or other materials are missing; at least 50 kg/year, or 1 percent of total nuclear materials, are unaccounted for, even in the best reprocessing facilities.[164]

This amount of MUF, of course, is small, compared to the actual levels of weapons-grade plutonium that is lost in reprocessing, simply because of carelessness and human error. The Japanese, in a state-of-the-art plutonium facility, admitted in 2003 that they were missing 276 kg of plutonium just from the years 2003–2004, and the British admitted that they were missing 40 kg of plutonium. The US Department of Energy has already admitted that, in its 50 years of producing plutonium in the US, hundreds of kilograms have gone missing, and the DOE is not even sure why. For one thing, normal-operating losses of plutonium at only a single lab, like Los Alamos National Labs (LANL), are as high as 92 kg/year. Apart from missing nuclear materials, another problem is that the plutonium inventories listed at US DOE headquarters do not match the inventories listed at the thousands of government sites, such as LANL; the LANL discrepancy, alone, is 765 pounds, enough to make 150 nuclear bombs. One problem is that the US plutonium-waste-inventory numbers, given from within a security perimeter, and those numbers given at the outside site to which the plutonium is sent do not match. Yet another MUF discrepancy is that different US labs produce different amounts of plutonium waste, even when they do essentially the same reprocessing. The Rocky Flats facility, for instance, processed about 250,000 kg of plutonium and created about 5,600 kg of plutonium waste, whereas LANL has processed about 3,000 kg of plutonium and created about 610 kg of waste. This means that 20 percent of the LANL plutonium has ended up as waste, whereas only about 2 percent of the Rocky Flats plutonium ended up as waste. Such discrepancies reveal the difficulty of using actual empirical data, across facilities, to try to establish how much nuclear material is MUF. This difficulty, in turn, shows massive security problems with increased reprocessing and therefore with a nuclear-energy buildup. Overall, US DOE nuclear-waste records indicate that the US is missing about 310 kg—one-third of a ton—of plutonium, which is enough for about 60 nuclear bombs.[165]

These US plutonium-discrepancy numbers also pose a *fifth* reason that increased atomic energy will increase nuclear proliferation and terrorism risks. This reason is that US policies for preventing proliferation and terrorism are politically flawed and unlikely to work, because they are unfair and inconsistent. Because the US is pursuing nuclear weapons but not allowing most other nations to do so, it is sitting on a barstool preaching temperance to others. This inconsistent US position also involves its demanding that Iran renounce its nuclear program, while it rewards India's armaments program with a supply of uranium.[166] The US likewise wants other nuclear nations—like Russia, France, the UK, Israel, India, Pakistan, North Korea, and Japan—to secure their plutonium, but the US appears unable to do so itself, as the preceding paragraph shows. All these facts clearly show that atomic-energy facilities cannot secure nuclear materials to prevent their being used for weapons or terrorism. Moreover, the International Atomic Energy Agency has held Japan's single reprocessing plant to a strict plutonium-discrepancy standard of about 200 kg—less than a third of the plutonium that is missing at only one of many US facilities.[167] This means that under the current atomic-energy regime, other nations are being held to standards that even the wealthiest nation in the world (the US) cannot meet. All these inconsistencies are part of the reason that non-nuclear-weapons states are unlikely to go along with restricting enrichment and reprocessing to those states that already have it.[168] But if so, nuclear proliferation and terrorism are likely to increase. As the US OTA warned, restricting enrichment and reprocessing to nuclear-weapons states aggravates the discriminatory nature of the nonproliferation regime and makes it "politically untenable."[169] Even the pro-nuclear International Atomic Energy Agency warned: "We must abandon the unworkable notion" that some countries can pursue nuclear weapons of mass destruction, to count on them for security, while others cannot; this means that, without a workable, verifiable program to eliminate nuclear weapons, no nonproliferation policy will work.[170] If not, increased nuclear power will obviously lead to more proliferation problems.

A *sixth* reason that increased atomic energy will increase nuclear-proliferation and terrorism risks is that there is no reliable way to separate peaceful and commercial uses of atomic energy. Consequently, with commercial nuclear tripling, proliferation and terrorism problems are likely to get worse, in part because less reliable nations will be using fission-generated electricity and facing unrealistic nuclear-materials-safeguard requirements. In fact, additional nuclear-electricity states already have increased existing nuclear-security and terrorism problems, like those with Iraq, Iran, Pakistan, and North Korea.[171] India's nuclear-weapons program, for instance, was begun as a result of fuel and technology supplied through a Canadian commercial reactor.[172] In fact, former US Vice President Al Gore noted recently that every single weapons-proliferation problem that the US had during his 8 years in the White House was "connected to a civilian-reactor program."[173] The reason? As the case of Iran shows, it is virtually impossible to distinguish a civilian nuclear program from a military one.[174] Even inspections cannot stop nuclear-weapons proliferation, and the case of Iran shows that they often don't work. Iran purchased a research reactor from the US in 1959, and for many years it has pursued a secret, very extensive enrichment program. Yet because of flawed inspections, it took at least 20 years for this enrichment program to be detected in 2005.[175] As Hannes Alven, a Nobel Prize–winning Swedish physicist, put it: "The military atom and the civil atom are Siamese twins."[176] We have to close the stable door (stop commercial atomic energy) if we don't want the nuclear-weapons horse to bolt.[177] We must phase out nuclear power, or at least stop reprocessing and limit enrichment—none of which has been done.

A *seventh* reason that fission expansion would increase the likelihood of nuclear terrorism and proliferation is that, once poor nations have commercial nuclear technology, some of them are likely to see nuclear weapons as cost-effective. Poor nations cannot afford to train and equip a conventional military force or to develop space-based weapons. However, building nuclear weapons would be much cheaper and easier if more commercial atomic energy were available.[178]

An *eighth* reason that nuclear proliferation and terrorism would increase if atomic energy increases is that an industry-dominated UN agency, the International Atomic Energy Agency (IAEA), is charged with protecting against nuclear-weapons proliferation and terrorism. The IAEA is unlikely to be effective in providing adequate protection (against terrorism and proliferation) because it is dominated by nuclear-industry representatives and because it has financial conflicts of interest. It is responsible both for promoting and for regulating nuclear technology. In fact, the IAEA has repeatedly exhibited its financial conflicts of interest in its biased reports, for instance, on the massive human-health harms done by the 1986 nuclear accident at Chernobyl. The IAEA claimed, for instance, that the Chernobyl accident caused at most 50 to 56 fatalities.[179] Contrary to this Chernobyl claim, however, a UN public-health investigation of Chernobyl health effects called the accident "the greatest technological catastrophe in human history."[180] Because of the long half-lives of many of the radionuclides, the investigators warned that the radioactivity released by Chernobyl would never disappear completely from the biosphere.[181] They said that "during 1986–1990 in the zone of strict control [of radiation pollution in the former USSR, 30 km from the reactor], only four years after the accident, there was a 50 percent increase in the average frequency of thyroid disorders, malignancies, and neoplasms (leukemia increased by 50 percent), and a serious increase in the number of miscarriages, still births, and children born with genetic malformations."[182] Less than 6 years after the accident, already there was a 100-fold increase in thyroid cancers in Belarus, Russia, and Ukraine.[183] Scientists documented a doubling of germline mutations in children born only 8 years after, and 400 km away from, the Chernobyl accident.[184] Twenty years after the accident, the journal *Nature* documented a doubling in breast cancer in the most heavily Chernobyl-exposed areas of Belarus and Ukraine, and an excess of several thousand Chernobyl-induced cancers in the three nations most affected by Chernobyl; yet because of the long cancer latency, full Chernobyl cancers will not appear for at least another 20 years.[185] Even more disturbing, scientists have confirmed Chernobyl-induced genomic instability (GI). GI is the phenomenon in which ionizing radiation not only increases mutation rates in the exposed somatic cells, but also causes elevated mutation rates many cell divisions—and generations—after the initial radiation damage.[186] These delayed transgenerational effects of ionizing radiation also cause increased cancers and many other damaging health effects in later generations—in people not even exposed to the offending radiation.[187]

For all the preceding reasons, it is especially troubling that the industry-dominated IAEA could claim no more than 50 Chernobyl fatalities. The agency knows that the radionuclides deposited by the Chernobyl accident have half-lives from tens, to hundreds of thousands, to millions of years. These airborne, soilborne, foodborne, waterborne, and ingested radionuclides will cause serious long-term effects and will continue to re-expose citizens for centuries,[188] especially given that millions of people are still living in areas of "wide-scale contamination" by Chernobyl, such as in Belarus. This ongoing contamination will add to human and environmental radiation doses for many years to come.[189] These effects will be substantial, as many nations still require Chernobyl-caused quarantines on local crops and farm animals, often because of cesium-137 contamination: for example, sheep in the UK;[190] reindeer in Finland, Norway, Russia, and Sweden;[191] and berries, mushrooms, and fish in many European countries, all likely to be quarantined at least until 2050.[192] At the current time, biologists continue to show reduced numbers of animals near Chernobyl, as a function of radiation dose, a fact indicating that the accident's effects on animals has been massive.[193]

Once one takes account of the preceding latent, internal-dose or food-chain, statistical, future, genomic-instability, global, and disease-related casualties, some scientists say that total Chernobyl-induced fatal cancers may rise to about 475,000.[194] If one ignores cancers caused by ongoing mutations throughout future generations, one might obtain a reduced Chernobyl-fatality count like that published in *Nature*: 125,000 deaths.[195] Just from cesium-137, a single radioactive isotope of the hundreds of types of radioisotopes released at Chernobyl, the nuclear-industry research group (the Electric Power Research Institute) and the US Lawrence Livermore Laboratories calculate between 17,400 and 51,000 additional, fatal, Chernobyl-induced cancers in this generation.[196] Obviously, therefore, the IAEA claim of 50 Chernobyl fatalities is false. Its falsity shows that, because of conflicts of interest, this industry-dominated IAEA may be equally unlikely to protect citizens against nuclear proliferation and terrorism. After all, such protection would threaten the commercial atomic-energy industry and make fission even more expensive (see the next chapter).

A *ninth* reason that fission expansion would increase the likelihood of nuclear terrorism and proliferation is that commercial nuclear technology encourages an arms race, a domino effect. Particularly in the Middle East, the Gulf Cooperation Council (Bahrain, Kuwait, Oman, Qatar, Saudi Arabia, and the United Arab Emirates) has already pointed to Iran and Israel and stated that it will acquire civilian nuclear technology; in making the announcement, the Saudi foreign minister pointed to Israel's nuclear reactor, used for weapons, as the "original sin."[197] If more nations build nuclear plants, then still more nations, including Egypt, Syria, and others, also will want nuclear reactors.[198] Yet such behavior arguably increases the arms race and thus the risk of nuclear terrorism and proliferation. Already about 3 dozen nations (including Iran, Japan, Brazil, Argentina, Egypt, Taiwan, South Korea, and Turkey) have the technological capability to make weapons.[199] Increasing this capability arguably increases terrorism and proliferation risks. For instance, Japan's reprocessing capability, stocks of commercial plutonium, and technological infrastructure mean that it could become a nuclear-weapons state in only 6 months.[200] As one scientist put it, building more nuclear plants makes the proliferation problem move from "difficult" to "intractable."[201] A top business-management consulting firm, McKinsey, said something similar. It warned that nuclear proliferation has the potential to present "unforeseen challenges" to anyone who proposes new commercial nuclear plants.[202]

A *tenth* reason that nuclear expansion would increase the likelihood of nuclear terrorism and proliferation is that even US nuclear reactors are not designed to withstand the impact of a large commercial aircraft.[203] The US Nuclear Regulatory Commission itself admits that onsite spent-fuel pools at reactors are vulnerable to attacks; if they caught fire, they could cause casualties as far as 500 miles away.[204] Also, nuclear explosives are very devastating and very easy to make, using either plutonium or enriched uranium. With weapons-grade uranium, for instance, there is a good chance of an explosion if one simply drops half the material onto the other half.[205] A crude nuclear weapon made of enriched uranium could explode with a power equivalent to a few hundred tons of TNT; this impact is roughly 10 times larger than that of the largest bomb used in World War II.[206] A terrorist attack on the Sellafield reprocessing facility in the UK, an attack that released either about 17 percent of the high-level waste or 1–3 percent of the plutonium, would be roughly 10 times as devastating as Chernobyl.[207]

The preceding 10 reasons show that, if more atomic-energy facilities are built, more nuclear proliferation and terrorism will result. Yet if the world stopped building commercial reactors, bomb ingredients would be harder to get. People and nations also would more conspicuous if they tried to get them. Thus people and nations would face much greater political costs if they were caught trying to get nuclear materials, because the motive for wanting them would be unmasked as military, not civilian.[208] The upshot? Proponents of the climate-necessity argument cannot consistently argue both that increased nuclear plants are needed to address CC and that this increase poses no security threat. If proponents claim that nuclear can make a substantial contribution to CC, more than the current roughly 2 percent of total net-energy needs, they must admit that as the contribution to CC increases, the contribution to proliferation and terrorism also increases. In short, nuclear proponents cannot have it both ways. They cannot use the climate-necessity argument to defend commercial nuclear expansion without falling into a greater security threat, from nuclear proliferation and terrorism. Yet they cannot reliably reduce security threats without reducing commercial nuclear fission. If not, the climate-necessity argument fails—both because it cannot adequately reduce GHG emissions, given its energy debts, and because it cannot easily be implemented and brings security risks. But as later chapters show, solar PV, wind, conservation, and efficiency have none of these problems.

Objections

In response to the preceding arguments, what if proponents claim that atomic energy ought to be considered for its potential to fight CC, even if its net energy contribution of global nuclear tripling is less than about 2 percent of global needs? What if someone says that, despite its problems, commercial fission ought to be embraced because of the great severity of CC?

In part, these questions have already been answered. That is, atomic energy is less effective at addressing CC than technologies like solar PV and wind—and programs achieving conservation and energy efficiencies. Because fission is much more expensive than renewable technologies like solar PV and wind (as chapter 3 shows), increasing atomic energy actually would harm these more effective CC-fighters, such as solar and wind. Also, even if nuclear fission were theoretically desirable, this chapter showed that it is self-defeating and provides too little net energy, too late. Worst of all, atomic energy increases problems of weapons proliferation and terrorism. For additional responses to various nuclear and CC arguments, especially the argument that an "energy mix" of various technologies, including nuclear, is needed, see chapter 7.

Conclusion

This chapter reveals flaws in perhaps the major argument—of those who wish to use nuclear fission in order to address CC. They are wrong to say that nuclear-related GHG emissions are minimal. Instead, nuclear-fuel-cycle GHG emissions are massive, roughly the same as those of natural gas, a fossil fuel. Nuclear proponents avoid this fact because they focus on emissions only from the reactor stage of the 14-stage nuclear-fuel cycle. In ignoring most nuclear GHG emissions, they invalidly trim the data on nuclear GHG emissions, commit fallacies of composition, rely on inconsistent claims, make arguments with self-defeating consequences, and ignore problems of increasing nuclear proliferation and terrorism. For all these reasons their climate-necessity argument errs—the argument that implementing more nuclear fission is necessary to help avoid climate change. . This chapter shows that atomic energy is not one of the more feasible, effective, and desirable ways to avoid GHG emissions. In fact, this and later chapters show that conservation, efficiency, wind, and solar PV are all more effective ways to help avert CC. The next chapter shows that fission also is neither a cost-effective nor a safe way to avert CC. Yet obviously society ought to take the most effective, safest, and cheapest ways to stop CC.

US astronauts returning from outer space warned that our efforts to address CC already are long overdue. From their distant spacecrafts, they saw not only a beautiful blue planet but also large swaths of coal-generated brown smoke, covering entire regions and entire nations.[209] Our lives and health, and the life and health of the planet, rely on our changing what they saw.

CHAPTER 3

Trimming the Data on Nuclear Costs

Merck Pharmaceuticals suppressed data on harmful effects of its drug Vioxx. As a result, many people died. Guidant Corporation suppressed data on electrical flaws in one of its heart-defibrillator models, and it too caused many patient deaths. Many similar examples reveal how financial conflicts of interest (COI) can skew biomedical research—especially when companies suppress data that could jeopardize their pharmaceutical profits. As a result, scientists and ethicists have long recognized the harm done by such COI. An *Annals of Internal Medicine* study recently showed that 98 percent of papers based on industry-sponsored studies reflected favorably on the industry's products; a *Journal of the American Medical Association* article likewise concluded that industry-funded studies were 8 times less likely to reach conclusions unfavorable to their drugs than were nonprofit-funded studies.[1] Does something similar happen in energy studies done by electric utilities?

Both coal and nuclear utilities appear to massively underestimate the costs of their activities. For instance, an association of coal utilities and producers, the World Coal Institute, said in 2009 that coal is "cheaper per energy unit than other fuels," but as chapter 1 documented, the US National Academy of Sciences says that annual costs of coal-generated electricity often exceed their benefits, especially for older, dirtier coal plants. The academy noted that annual US health-related and CC damages from US coal plants are more than $120 billion annually, including tens of thousands of coal-induced deaths per year. Even in market terms, coal benefits often do not pay for its costs. A recent report of the Mountain Association of Community Economic Development showed that, for a typical coal-producing state, like Kentucky, annual state revenues from coal are $528 million, but they cost $643 in state expenditures—and these figures do not include any health damages.[2]

Nuclear-industry cost estimates are just as misleading. Jonathan Porritt, chair of the UK Sustainable Development Commission and adviser to Gordon Brown, says, "Cost estimates from the [nuclear] industry have been subject to massive underestimates—inaccuracy of an astonishing kind consistently over a 40-, 50-year period."[3] A UK government commission agrees, claiming that these "massive underestimates" have arisen because virtually all nuclear-cost data can be "traced back to industry sources"; the main US oversight agency, the Government Accountability Office, says something similar, repeatedly faulting the nuclear industry for greatly underestimating the full costs of its activities.[4] Why do these flawed nuclear-fission cost estimates occur? The preceding chapter gave some of the historical reasons, namely the military legacy of secrecy and data falsification. It also noted that typically only the industry is privy to full nuclear-cost data. University of Greenwich business professor Stephen Thomas says the same thing: because the nuclear industry controls virtually all the economic data, it is difficult for others to check it or even obtain it; fission companies "are notoriously secretive about the costs they are incurring."[5] If these government and university charges are correct, they suggest the need to scrutinize nuclear-industry claims that, to address climate change (CC), fission is "the most cost-effective power source."[6] Is it?

Overview of the Chapter

This chapter argues that nearly all nuclear-fission-cost estimates (most of which are produced by the industry) are examples of grossly flawed science. The studies not only violate standard COI guidelines, widely accepted in scientific research, but also "trim the data" on nuclear costs. Just as chapter 2 showed that industry calculations of greenhouse-gas (GHG) emissions err in usually including only emissions from 1 (reactor operation) of the 14 stages of the nuclear-fuel cycle, this chapter likewise shows that industry calculations of nuclear costs err in usually including only costs from 1 (reactor construction and maintenance) of the 14 stages of the nuclear-fuel cycle.

Attempting to show that increased atomic energy can help address CC, many industry advocates claim reactors are an inexpensive way to generate low-carbon electricity. However, surveying all 30 nuclear-electricity analyses, post-2000, this chapter shows that all of the industry-funded (but not the university-funded) studies appear to fall into COI and to illegitimately trim relevant cost data in several vital ways. Most exclude costs of full-liability insurance, underestimate interest rates and construction times by using "overnight" costs, and overestimate reactor load factors and lifetimes. Yet if these studies correct only these 5 false cost assumptions, market costs (excluding subsidies) of fission-generated electricity can be shown to be roughly 6 times more expensive than most nuclear-economics studies claim. Although there are legitimate situations in which scientists ought to trim scientific data, the chapter shows that trimming nuclear-cost data fails to satisfy standard scientific guidelines. After answering several objections, the chapter shows that nuclear fission is actually far more expensive than conservation, efficiency programs, and renewable-energy sources, like wind and solar photovoltaic (PV).

The Economics Argument of the Nuclear-Fission Industry

As chapter 1 revealed, scientists agree that there is no safe, non-zero dose of ionizing radiation, and as chapter 4 shows, there are higher cancer rates around nuclear plants, given their normal radioactive emissions. Safety concerns, however, are not what caused no new US nuclear reactors to be ordered since 1974. Instead, naming "financial hurdles" as the biggest contemporary obstacle to new atomic-energy plants, economists say the "rebirth of the US nuclear power market will be greatly influenced by its associated costs."[7] Hence it is not surprising that when nuclear proponents promote using fission to help address CC, they make the economics argument. That is, they say atomic energy is inexpensive, "the most economical way to generate baseload electricity,"[8] "some of the cheapest power available,"[9] "very high yield,"[10] and "cost effective."[11] A top business-management-consulting firm, McKinsey, praises nuclear energy for "low operational and maintenance costs."[12]

Current CC concerns are one reason many hope the economics argument is correct. However, past nuclear performance is one of many reasons to doubt it. Nuclear proponents, economic consensus, and credit-rating firms agree that the "excessive costs" of "uneconomic" nuclear plants are what caused the industry to cancel hundreds of reactors and to order no new US plants since 1974.[13] Over 2 decades, the 2 top US reactor vendors, GE and Westinghouse, each lost money on every reactor that they delivered for a fixed price,[14] yet those prices have risen substantially, and no reactor vendor still offers fixed-price contracts—a telling fact. Industry proponents say the latest Western nuclear plants each will cost at least $12 billion,[15] while future reactors will cost even more because of new, untested designs. Nuclear advocates also admit that consumers are still paying for the reactor problems of decades ago. Many plants were canceled after billions of dollars had been spent on them, and some were completed but never opened because of safety problems. For instance, decades ago, the $5.5 billion Shoreham (New York) plant was closed the same year it opened, and the $9 billion Watts Bar (Tennessee) plant—the last constructed in the US, and completed in 1996—took 23 years to build. Because of numerous financial problems, nuclear proponents admit that US nuclear "ratepayers were left responsible" for "some of the highest electric rates in the country." However, the same proponents say that things have changed, that nuclear power is now one of the cheapest electricity sources available.[16] Are they right? This chapter shows that they are not.[17]

Nuclear-Cost Studies

To assess the economics argument for nuclear fission, consider all 30, post-2000 prominent, international, nuclear-cost studies that are original economic analyses.

None is merely a summary or derived from earlier reports.[18] These 30 analyses include all original nuclear-cost studies that are publicly available in scientific journals, books, nongovernmental-organization (NGO) analyses, industry reports, and government documents since the year 2000. The list of 30 appears both balanced and comprehensive, as it includes all 7 studies that are reviewed by the global-nuclear-industry lobby group,[19] the World Nuclear Association (WNA).[20] The list also includes all 9 nuclear-cost studies reviewed[21] in a prominent 2006 UK government report,[22] and all 12 nuclear-cost studies reviewed[23] in a 2007 Greenpeace International report.[24]

One interesting fact about these 30 prominent nuclear-economics studies is that a majority appear to trim nuclear-fission costs in at least 3 ways. Subsequent paragraphs argue that they ignore taxpayer subsidies, ignore long reactor-construction times and interest costs, and inflate reactor capacity (or load factor) and lifetime data. As a consequence, they grossly underestimate the real costs of fission-generated electricity.

Ignoring Taxpayer Subsidies for Nuclear Fission

Consider first the way that most nuclear-cost studies ignore taxpayer subsidies. The largest ignored subsidies are those for nuclear-liability insurance. The European Commission (consistent with WNA and Cato Institute figures) recently showed that, if commercial reactors had to purchase full-insurance-liability coverage on the market, this would triple fission-generated-electricity prices.[25] As already mentioned in chapter 2, this means a majority of nuclear-economics studies underestimate costs by a factor of 3, merely because they exclude full-insurance costs, presumably because these insurance costs are not market-related, but mainly paid by governments and taxpayers. Yet without these subsidies (and resulting liability protection), utilities vehemently agree they would never use risky atomic energy.[26] Why not? Fission-insurance rates, available on the market, accurately reflect high nuclear-accident risks. The US-government-calculated, lifetime-core-melt probability for all US commercial reactors is 1 in 5,[27] and government says a worst-case accident could cause roughly $660 billion in damages, excluding medical costs.[28] Given these high risks and costs, utilities, governments, and credit-rating firms universally confirm that no nuclear plants, anywhere, operate on the market, and none could exist without massive government subsidies, including an accident-liability limit.[29] In effect, utilities have said, "Give us subsidies, or give us death." As chapter 1 revealed, US government subsidies for nuclear fission—alone—cut nuclear electricity prices by 50–90 percent. Yet, almost no government, industry, or university analyses of nuclear-electricity costs take account of subsidies, and almost no studies include the costs of industry's transferring (through nuclear-liability limits) its serious atomic-energy risks to the people.

The world's 443 commercial reactors fall into 3 camps regarding nuclear-accident-liability coverage. The vast majority of reactors are in the first camp (e.g., in China, India, Iran, and Pakistan), where operator nuclear liability is 0, and accident victims could bear 100 percent of nuclear-accident costs. One-third of reactors (many in Western Europe and the US) are in the second camp, where operator liability is minimal. US reactors are protected by the Price-Anderson Act, and they have the highest (minimal) liability, $10.8 billion—roughly 1.5 percent of government-calculated, worst-case-accident damages of $660 billion.[30] In this second case, accident victims could bear roughly 98 percent of nuclear-accident costs. The third camp includes 13 percent of reactors (in Germany, Japan, and Switzerland), all having government-guaranteed, unlimited liability.[31] There taxpayers and utilities, not only victims, would bear all nuclear-accident costs. The upshot? All global reactors have either direct (87 percent of global reactors, those in camps 1 and 2 above) or indirect (13 percent of global reactors, those in camp 3 above), government-mandated nuclear-accident-liability protection. In the direct-liability case, government transfers either 100 percent or 98 percent of nuclear-industry-accident risks, costs, and negligence mainly to potential accident victims. In the indirect-liability case, government transfers industry risks, costs, and negligence to taxpayers through guaranteed government subsidies.[32]

Although nuclear-liability limits mean that 87 percent of global nuclear ratepayers bear financial and health risks from nearby reactors, surprisingly none of the major government, industry, or university nuclear-cost studies include these liability-related costs. Not even the classic 2004 MIT and University of Chicago studies include them.[33] Neither do assessments by the main international nuclear-lobby group, the WNA,[34] or the UN's Nuclear Energy Agency.[35] In fact, energy-cost studies done by Rice University,[36] Lappeenranta University,[37] the UK,[38] the UK Royal Academy,[39] the US Department of Energy (DOE)–funded Scully Capital,[40] OXERA Consultants,[41] and most nuclear economists trim nuclear-liability-related cost data.[42] What is their rationale?

They have 3 main arguments for trimming nuclear-insurance costs. The first, their market argument, is that neoclassical economic analyses should include only market costs;[43] because government allows industry to buy no full nuclear-accident insurance on the market, they claim the nuclear-accident-liability limit is an externality, not counted in market calculations. The second, their responsibility argument, is that industry bears no financial or legal responsibility for full nuclear-accident-liability coverage because government requires "no payment" for full coverage.[44] The third, their subsidy argument, is that, because nuclear-liability limits require no full-nuclear-insurance coverage, no taxpayer costs are involved: the limits are a subsidy from potential radiological victims.[45]

How reasonable are these industry arguments for nuclear-liability cost-trimming? The market argument fails because, even if cost-trimming is consistent with neoclassical economic procedures, energy-policy decisions require total-cost accounting, not merely market prices. For instance, the real cost of gasoline is not merely its market price, but its market price plus all taxpayer subsidies, which equals more than $15 per gallon; in the US, these subsidies include percentage-depletion allowances, fuel-production credits, enhanced oil-recovery credits, foreign-income deferrals, export-financing subsidies, and so on.[46] If policymakers fail to consider the full costs of goods (like gasoline), externalities can cause market exchanges to generate false economic signals, cause misuse of resources, and jeopardize efficiency, societal welfare, sustainability, distributive equity, fairness, reasonableness, and other values.[47] Because of nuclear-liability-limit subsidies or externalities, accident victims could face death, injury, financial harm, injustice, and other uncompensated costs. Besides, if atomic-energy investments were economically efficient, it would be unnecessary to subsidize and therefore socialize nuclear-industry risks and costs—transferring them to taxpayers—while allowing privatized nuclear-industry profits.[48]

As chapter 2 already suggested, the main problem with the responsibility argument (for trimming nuclear-insurance-subsidy costs) is that it begs the question against nuclear-industry financial responsibility for its accidents, contrary to virtually all liability law. This argument also assumes that legal actions (like government-allowed, nuclear-liability-cost limits) are always ethical. Yet obviously this assumption errs. Much ethics is not covered by law, and the law can be ethically wrong (as in government-mandated segregation or sexism). Consequently, people are ethically responsible for harms and costs they impose on others, regardless of what the law says. But if so, nuclear industries are ethically responsible for accident costs, and therefore these costs ought not be trimmed, even if the law limits liability. Because victims' nuclear-accident costs are not limited to roughly 1.5 percent of worst-case-accident coverage, up to the $10.8 billion for which industry is liable,[49] cost calculations ought not be limited to this amount.

The subsidy argument likewise errs, in begging the question that taxpayer subsidies should be excluded from nuclear-electricity-cost calculations simply because they are subsidies. For all the reasons already stated, nuclear-accident-insurance subsidies should be included in nuclear-economics calculations because they are real costs. In fact, if they were not real costs, the nuclear industry would not demand protection from 98.5 percent of worst-case-accident liability as a condition of operation, as already mentioned. Without protection from accident costs, industry and government admit, nuclear-electricity generation would stop.[50] Yet if these costs are so substantial that industry requires protection from them, it is inconsistent to trim them from cost calculations merely because citizens, not industry, is forced to bear them. Because someone must bear nuclear-accident costs, because even pro-nuclear governments say nuclear-liability limits impose "potential" liability on taxpayers,[51] and because (as mentioned earlier) both government-calculated, nuclear-accident probabilities and nuclear insurance are very high, full-liability costs arguably ought not be trimmed from nuclear-economics assessments. After all, prospective investors would not want nuclear-liability-cost data trimmed, because trimming could obscure the difference between desirable and undesirable investment risks.

At least 4 other considerations likewise suggest that nuclear-liability-data trimming is not reasonable. I call these, respectively, the rationality, misleading-science, sensitivity, and economic-risk arguments. According to the rationality argument, rational energy choices presuppose full cost-benefit accounting because decision-makers should minimize economically inefficient choices, potential risk victims need full information to protect themselves, and investors need it to make economically efficient decisions. For instance, if people were offered job A or job B, but only job A provided health-insurance coverage, obviously the prospective employees would not want job offers to trim insurance information, because such information is needed for making reasonable job choices. The same is true for energy choices.

According to the misleading-science argument, full insurance-liability costs ought not be trimmed from nuclear-cost calculations, because this could mislead the public. The public probably is unaware of the nuclear-liability limit and how the US Price-Anderson Act sanctions a financial and medical risk-transfer from nuclear utilities to taxpayers. Marvin Fertel, senior vice president of the Nuclear Energy Institute, has admitted that because this law removes "the cost for insurance against the liability" from utilities, this cost is "passed on in part to consumers."[52] Yet, since at least 1987, the American Public Health Association,[53] scientists, and bioethicists all have reaffirmed the public's right to know about science-related health risks imposed on it. This right requires that nuclear-liability costs not be trimmed from energy assessments.

According to the sensitivity argument, costs of nuclear-liability insurance arguably ought not be trimmed, both because they are substantial and because nuclear-cost calculations are extremely sensitive to them. On the substantial point, as already mentioned, the European Commission showed that requiring full-nuclear-liability coverage would triple fission-generated-electricity costs.[54] The global nuclear-industry-lobby group, the WNA, admits these EU calculations are correct. WNA says average annual-liability-insurance premiums for typical Western commercial reactors are each about $400,000 per $300 million in coverage,[55] and the US government says a worst-case nuclear accident could cost $660 billion. If additional nuclear-liability-insurance coverage were purchased at the same ($300 million) rate, full $660 billion coverage could cost about $880 million ($400,000 × 2,200) per reactor per year. This figure is consistent with Canadian economists' claims that full nuclear-liability insurance equals "half the capital costs of nuclear reactors,"[56] consistent with inflation-adjusted Cato Institute estimates of $200 million per reactor, per year[57] (but higher than the $33 million per reactor, per year, estimates of US economists Jeffrey Dubin and Geoffrey Rothwell).[58] Regardless of the exact figure, because nuclear-insurance data-trimming is substantial, because law has transferred this industry risk to taxpayers, because insurance rates provide reasonable societal-risk estimates, and because nuclear-electricity prices are extraordinarily sensitive to these high-liability-insurance costs, the public arguably ought to know them. Besides, US Securities and Exchange Commission rules require the absence of a nuclear-liability limit (and resulting financial costs) to be disclosed to nuclear investors.[59] Potential victims deserve the same protection. Consequently, nuclear-liability costs arguably ought not be trimmed from fission-cost calculations.

According to the economic-risk argument, because all pro-nuclear cost assessments trim full nuclear-liability-insurance costs, they ignore various economic risks associated with serious accidents: planned reactors might be scrapped, others might be shut down, and people might be vulnerable to baseload-electricity shortages. A single event (an earthquake, terrorist attack, or accident) could financially derail the entire nuclear industry.[60] Trimming nuclear-insurance-cost data thus errs because it encourages assessors to ignore accident-related economic risks.

In summary, because a majority of the 30 nuclear-cost studies mentioned above trim taxpayer-subsidized, nuclear-liability-insurance costs from their energy-cost calculations, they encourage flawed economic signals, inefficient markets, questionable research ethics, and unequal treatment. Moreover, it seems inconsistent and unethical for assessors to trim (and not disclose) full-nuclear-liability costs that increase taxpayer risks,[61] while because of the associated financial risks, the US Securities and Exchange Commission requires disclosing lack of nuclear-liability limits to investors.[62]

Trimming Nuclear Costs by Ignoring Nuclear-Interest Rates

Another strategy of most nuclear-economics studies is to assume "overnight" plant-construction capital costs, currently at least $12 billion in the US.[63] Overnight costs assume 0-percent interest rates and 0 construction times. For instance, although the WNA says "the case for nuclear energy is now solid on economics alone," its economics calculations include only "overnight costs"—costs that exclude construction time, finance, and interest charges on construction capital— as if the reactor were built overnight, without any construction inflation or interest charges on capital. The WNA says overnight-cost estimates of at least "$2000 per kW of capacity" "have been produced by [nuclear-reactor] vendors and their partners." Attempting to justify this cost-trimming (i.e., using only overnight costs), the WNA says "most studies of the competitiveness of nuclear power base their estimates of capital costs on...recent reactors in Asian countries [whose safety standards are weaker than in the West, as later paragraphs show] and use overnight costs."[64]

Likewise, perhaps because official US national policy and relevant federal-agency policies are pro-nuclear, even US government agencies trim cost data on nuclear plants, as the Tennessee Valley Authority did recently. It used "overnight costs only" to quote prices for its reactors.[65] Following most nuclear-cost analysts, the authors of the 2009 MIT study also quote total nuclear-plant costs as "overnight costs"— then say "this total [nuclear-power-plant] cost, which is exclusive of financing cost, is $4,706/kW."[66] Noting that earlier MIT analyses employed overnight costs, "as described in the MIT (2003) *Future of Nuclear Power* study," the 2009 MIT authors attempt to justify cost-trimming by saying that using overnight costs "represents the standard basis for quoting comparable costs across different plants."[67]

This "standard" procedure of the nuclear industry, however, is deeply flawed economic science. There are problems with assuming both that nuclear-interest rates are 0 and that construction times are 0. First consider interest rates. As already noted, the latest Western nuclear plants each cost at least $12 billion.[68] Because construction costs account for three-fourths of ratepayer prices for nuclear electricity,[69] these prices are extremely sensitive to data-trimming assumptions about construction-interest costs. By how much do economics-argument proponents trim the cost of capital, the interest rates on nuclear-construction loans? To answer this question one needs to know (1) typical interest rates for risky projects such as nuclear plants; (2) interest rates that nuclear proponents presuppose in their calculations; and (3) full economic effects of ignoring differences between actual and assumed interest rates.

Regarding (1), typical risky-project interest rates, most private investors and banks are unwilling to invest in fission except at rates of at least 15 percent.[70] Citing poor credit ratings, high construction costs, numerous plant cancellations, a competitive energy market, and a long history of cost overruns, delayed plants, and equipment malfunctions, the World Bank, European Bank for Reconstruction and Development 2006, Asian Development Bank 2000, African Development Bank, European Investment Bank, Inter-American Development Bank, and others say nuclear power is "uneconomic"; as a matter of policy, they refuse nuclear loans or investments.[71] Citigroup, Credit Suisse, Goldman Sachs, Merrill-Lynch, Morgan Stanley, and virtually all other investors also refuse long-term credit to the financially risky nuclear industry.[72] Consequently, if nuclear utilities can obtain private-market loans, they typically pay rates of 15 percent, a telling admission that nuclear economics is very fragile. Credit-rating companies, such as Moody's and Standard and Poor's, also downgrade credit ratings of utilities with reactors, claiming that even massive taxpayer subsidies often cannot make reactors economical.[73] Moody's recently calculated that, even if one ignores costs associated with reactor decommissioning, reprocessing, and permanent waste storage, nuclear-generated electricity still costs 3 times more than that from new natural-gas plants and double that from scrubbed, coal-fired plants.[74] Nuclear proponents admit that decommissioning one reactor costs $2–6 billion,[75] that reprocessing raises nuclear costs 33–58 percent,[76] and that permanent US radioactive-waste storage will cost $1 trillion—that is, $50 billion for each of 104 US nuclear plants.[77] Although none of the preceding, additional, trimmed costs (mentioned in this paragraph) will be included in this chapter's analysis, nevertheless one can easily see that including these additional costs would make atomic energy even more uneconomical than this chapter argues—and yet even without including them this chapter is able to show that nuclear costs are underestimated by 600 percent.

Regarding (2), interest rates that economics-argument proponents typically assume, they never assume 15 percent, the "going rate" for nuclear utilities.[78] Even (normally more reliable) university nuclear-cost studies, like those from MIT[79] and Chicago,[80] assume nuclear-interest rates of 11.5–12.5 percent, and these too are underestimates. Instead, the main international-nuclear-lobby group admits "most studies" of nuclear costs assume 0 interest costs (0 interest rate)—and only the lower capital costs for cheaper, more dangerous, poorly designed Asian reactors, not Western ones.[81] They trim nuclear costs by including only a cheaper plant's "overnight costs," those occurring if the reactor were built overnight, without interest charges and construction-cost increases. Yet the latest US commercial reactors have taken 23 years to build, during which interest charges accrue.[82] When nuclear proponent Steve Berry,[83] a former US Argonne National Laboratory adviser, calculated fission costs in 2007, he presupposed year-2002 dollars and included only overnight costs. Nuclear proponents say studies by the World Nuclear Association,[84] Rice University,[85] US DOE–funded Scully Capital,[86] OXERA Consultants,[87] and the US Energy Information Agency routinely use only overnight costs.[88] Yet because atomic power has the highest construction costs and longest construction times of any energy technology, using overnight costs substantially trims cost data. Even the pro-nuclear lobby admits that "overnight costs" underestimate real fission expenses, which "mainly depend" on interest costs and construction time—neither of which is included in overnight costs.[89] Nevertheless, the WNA uses overnight costs.

Regarding (3), differences in nuclear economics, when one omits typical 15-percent nuclear-interest rates, standard amortization formulas show this data-trimming cuts nuclear-construction costs by 250 percent. If a utility had 15-percent interest rates, made quarterly payments, and had typical, 15-year loans, its construction costs (principal and interest) would be about $30 billion, not $12 billion in overnight costs. This conclusion is consistent with the WNA admission that even very low interest costs double nuclear-construction costs.[90] If all other operating costs remain the same—and if capital costs (principal plus interest) are 75 percent of operating costs, as most nuclear advocates indicate—then moving from 0- to 15-percent interest rates would increase operating costs, thus consumers' nuclear-electricity prices, by at least 188 percent.[91] This conclusion is consistent with the pro-nuclear International Energy Agency's admission that each 5-percent interest increase raises generation costs 50 percent,[92] as other pro-nuclear studies confirm.[93]

Interest costs are not the only data trimmed when industry uses "overnight costs" to assess nuclear-electricity economics. The main international-nuclear-industry lobby group admits the US had a 50-percent increase in construction material, equipment, and labor from 2004 to 2008; that it had a 100-percent increase from 2000 to 2008; and that nuclear-construction costs increase through time.[94]

Proponents likewise say that using new reactor designs, with un-worked-out "bugs," will drive up costs.[95] World Energy Council studies also show trends of increased nuclear-construction time, cost overruns, and interest charges.[96] Despite multi-billion-dollar government subsidies, every nuclear plant ever built thus has run over budget—often by 400 percent—and had longer-than-predicted-construction times.[97] This is why no reactor vendors offer fixed-price, or "turnkey," plants.[98] Given all these factors, nuclear-plant costs are likely more than $30 billion for principal and interest. Yet the pro-nuclear US DOE–Scully Capital study showed that fission plants provided typical electric-utility rates of return on their investment[99] only if nuclear-construction costs (principal and interest) did not exceed $1 billion.[100] If the pro-nuclear DOE–Scully Capital study is correct, it explains nuclear-proponents' incentives to include only overnight costs in fission assessments.

The reluctance of private banks and investors to lend to the nuclear industry, and the DOE–Scully Capital study's warning about low returns on nuclear investments, are both consistent with findings of the US government oversight office, the DOE Inspector General. It said taxpayer-financed nuclear-loan subsidies impose significant risks on American taxpayers.[101] Nevertheless, government gave nuclear-loan subsidies of $18.5 billion in the 2005 US Energy Act,[102] and President Obama promised another $54 billion in his 2011 budget, mainly because Wall Street would not do so. Similarly, the UK government repeatedly has bailed out nuclear utilities when they went bankrupt.[103] Likewise, the French government, which holds majority interest in the French nuclear industry (e.g., Areva), has had to finance French nuclear-construction programs.[104] As a result, Finland's Areva (generation-III+) nuclear plant has a 2.5-percent, French-taxpayer-subsidized interest rate on its construction loan,[105] when the "going rate" is 15 percent. As already noted, no nuclear plant has ever operated without massive taxpayer subsidies. Thus the industry itself admits that high nuclear-capital costs (principal and interest) will rule nuclear fission "out of consideration" in the future; it admits that because of escalating costs, by 2030 the amount of electricity supplied by atomic energy will decrease from its current 16 percent to 9 percent globally,[106] and from 25 to 20 percent in the UK.[107] The preceding data mean nuclear proponents are trying to trim (or cover up) the very capital costs that are killing the industry, presumably to encourage nuclear investment.

Trimming Nuclear Costs by Ignoring Nuclear-Construction Time

As just noted, because nuclear-generated-electricity costs are so sensitive to interest rates, they also are sensitive to construction times. Yet long nuclear-plant-construction times are a global phenomenon. The most experienced nuclear operators, such as Florida Power and Light, say current US new-nuclear-plant construction time is

12 years.[108] A pro-nuclear US National Academy of Sciences report estimates at least 11 years.[109] A pro-nuclear business-management-consulting firm, McKinsey, estimates 9–11 years.[110] Nuclear advocates admit the last US nuclear plant, Watts Bar (Tennessee), took 23 years to construct and went billions of dollars over budget.[111] Comanche Peak (Texas) went billions of dollars over budget and took 16 years; Nine Mile Point (New York) went billions of dollars over budget and took 14 years; Seabrook (New Hampshire) went $6 billion over budget and its delays caused utility bankruptcy;[112] and so on.[113]

In the UK, average nuclear-plant-construction time is 11 years.[114] The 4 French plants completed between 2000 and 2002 averaged more than 10 years to build and 14 years to produce commercial electricity.[115] The 5 Japanese nuclear plants completed in the 1980s averaged 17 years to build, whereas the one built in the 1990s took 26 years.[116] Eastern European nuclear plants, completed after 2002 and using US technology, have taken 15 years to build,[117] as have Eastern European plants using Soviet technology.[118] Moreover, several factors, already noted in discussing nuclear-interest rates, suggest new reactors will have longer construction times. Because no US plants have been ordered since 1974 and nuclear technology has been declining globally,[119] new fission technologies are untested.[120] Infrastructure, manufacturing facilities, and trained workforces are lacking. Costs for basic materials, like steel and concrete, also are spiraling upward.[121]

Despite the preceding data, industry lobbyists say most nuclear-economics studies assume overnight costs and therefore trim interest rates and construction times to 0,[122] as already mentioned. For instance, Rice University,[123] University of Lappeenranta,[124] UK,[125] and OXERA studies assume 0 nuclear-construction time.[126] The pro-nuclear MIT authors assumed 5-year nuclear-construction times,[127] as did Scully Capital,[128] the Royal Academy,[129] and the International Energy Agency.[130] The pro-nuclear University of Chicago assumed 7 years,[131] while other studies used 3 years.[132]

The economic effects of such nuclear-construction-time trimming are to erroneously lower calculated fission costs. Yet nuclear proponents admit that each 5-year nuclear-construction-time increase raises capital (principal plus interest) costs 100 percent.[133] This suggests that assuming 10, not 0, years of nuclear-construction times increases capital costs 200 percent. But if capital costs are 75 percent of operating costs,[134] then assuming 10-year reactor-construction times increases nuclear-electricity-operating costs 150 percent (0.75 times 200).

Given nuclear-cost sensitivity to construction times, it is disconcerting that official WNA nuclear-construction-time tabular data err. Instead of averaging construction times of all plants being built, WNA data do "not include plants on which construction has stalled."[135] Yet 22 plants are being built, and construction is "stalled" on 12; this suggests that construction has about a 50-percent probability of stoppage. Given how the WNA trims nuclear-construction-time data by including only 10 of 22 plants,[136] its construction-time study is comparable to a pharmaceutical-industry drug study that throws out all cases showing harmful drug effects, yet claims the drug is beneficial.

Accurate, untrimmed nuclear-construction-time data are crucial to energy choices because even proponents admit fission is an interim technology, useful only until efficiencies and renewable energy supply all needs.[137] Thus, as chapter 6 shows, if reactors cannot be built quickly, they are of little use, especially because the classic Princeton study, published in *Science*, shows that only 6 of 9 renewable or efficiency technologies, "already deployed at an industrial scale," could easily solve the climate problem by 2050; a 2006 study by the pro-nuclear US DOE claims that already-available renewable technology can provide 99 percent of US electricity generation even earlier, by the year 2020.[138] As chapter 6 reveals, already by 2005 the annual global-growth rate of non-hydro renewable energy was 7 times greater than nuclear,[139] partly because renewables like wind are inexpensive and their investments can be paid off in 10 years.[140] In the last year, 60 percent of new added US electricity capacity was wind , as measured by peak summer demand ,[141] Trimming nuclear-construction-cost data thus could mislead energy decision-makers, especially given that nuclear market costs are 3–4 times higher than those for wind, as chapter 6 shows.

Trimming Nuclear Costs by Inflating Reactor-Load Factors

A fourth fission-cost-trimming strategy, used in a majority of the 30 studies, is over-estimating reactor-load or capacity factors (plant-output percentages, compared to 100-percent output). For instance, WNA claims that "capacity factors of nuclear plants around the world have increased....Levels of 90% and above have been achieved by many plants in Europe and Asia for many years."[142] Likewise, the 2009 MIT study presupposes a "capacity factor of 85%."[143] Yet what do actual empirical data say about nuclear-load factors?

The first atomic-energy plants began generating electricity in 1955. After 30 years of commercial experience, nuclear proponents say they ran about half the time and had average load factors of 50 percent.[144] Low-load-factor reactors—like Fort St. Vrain (Colorado), at 14 percent—closed early because they were uneconomical.[145] With more nuclear reactors (104) than any other nation, all US plants have an average-lifetime nuclear-load factor of 71 percent.[146]

Atomic-energy load factors are poor, proponents say, because even flawless performance and perfect components allow, at best, 90-percent load factors over a very short time, given needed debugging, refueling, and maintenance.[147] Yet no nation's average-lifetime nuclear-load factor has ever been close to 90 percent because of leaks, equipment failures, and human error. In 2000, generator-tube ruptures at Indian Point reactor shut it down for 10 months, and replacement power averaged

$600,000 per day; boric-acid leaks and a football-sized corrosion hole in Ohio's Davis-Besse steel cap shut down the reactor for 2 years; replacement-power costs were $450,000 per day.[148] Japanese, Canadian, UK, and other authorities likewise have ordered fleetwide reactor shutdowns in the face of systemic safety lapses.[149] For instance, in 2005, when cracks in the graphite cores of AGR reactors caused safety compromises, 14 (of 23 total) UK reactors were shut down prematurely.[150] Steam generators and reactor-pressure vessels, each costing $100 million, are just 2 of the "most-often-replaced parts" of a nuclear plant. Pro-nuclear, US DOE economics estimates are that 10 percent of all reactor components must be replaced every 10 years.[151] On average, this means 1 percent of reactor components must be replaced each year, costing $120 million annually (assuming principal = $12 billion). Because the US GAO, the government oversight office, warns that nuclear-plant managers often defer such maintenance in order to keep reactors running and to save money , despite the resulting safety risks,[152] only lifetime, national, fleet-average nuclear-load factors provide reliable data.

Will new, improved reactor designs increase nuclear-load factors and reduce shutdown times? Three facts suggest the opposite. *First*, standard, pro-nuclear IAEA databases reveal that new-reactor designs always have lower initial load factors (like 50-percent load factors for the first 30 years of US plants, already mentioned), although these often improve with reactor-operator experience and "debugging."[153] *Second*, because even vendors admit new-reactor designs typically have 50-percent load factors, at least for 4–5 years, they never guarantee specific load factors for clients.[154] *Third*, industrial history reveals that after 50 years of commercial implementation, most technologies have achieved all likely design improvements, efficiencies, and cost savings; because commercial reactors have operated for more than 50 years, it is unlikely their load factors will improve significantly.[155]

Despite the preceding 3 facts, most fission-cost assessments assume much higher nuclear-load factors (thus lower costs) than the current 71-percent US average and 79-percent global average.[156] Yet as already mentioned, the pro-nuclear IAEA excludes load-factor data for stalled or already-closed plants.[157] It misleadingly calculates load-factor averages (US and global) by basing them only on the most economical nuclear facilities. Also, the 79-percent global nuclear-load-factor average is misleadingly high because of data from less-safe reactors (not allowed in the US), which are operated under lax regulations in the developing world.[158] Consequently, US, UK, and French load-factor data are more accurate.

Past experience of Western nations also confirms that new-reactor designs (generation-III and -III+) do not have improved load factors. No generation-III+ plants in the West have been completed, as of 2010. The load factor for Finland's generation-III+ plant (being built by the French) will not be known until after many years of operation. Besides, previous generation-III nuclear plants (e.g., the US AP600) already have been abandoned as uneconomical[159] or have suffered numerous breakdowns, months-long technical shutdowns, and operation at 15 percent below their standard load factor (e.g., the Japanese ABWR-III's).[160]

Although load factors associated with some technological designs improve over time, the latest reactors, now fully implemented commercially (generation-II designs), have worse load factors than their predecessors. In France, which supplies more electricity (75 percent) from atomic energy than any other country,[161] generation-II reactors have worse load factors than the French nuclear-fleet average. Given generation-II design and corrosion difficulties, most UK reactors (and all newer AGR-II reactors) operate at 71-percent load factors; half of UK reactors have load factors averaging 54 percent. Globally, three-fourths of the 414 operating reactors (having at least 1 year's service, and therefore higher load factors) have lifetime load factors below 80 percent. Only 7 of all 414 global reactors (1.7 percent)—mostly those with lax design, standards, and enforcement—and delayed maintenance in the Third World — have individual load factors of at least 90 percent.[162]

How close are pro-nuclear load-factor assumptions to the 71-percent US average or the 79-percent global average? As already noted, nuclear-load factors assumed in most of the 30 current nuclear-cost calculations, 90–95 percent, are physically impossible for any sustained period that includes maintenance. Yet 2 recent studies, from Finland's Lappeenranta University[163] and OXERA,[164] respectively, assume load factors of 91 and 95 percent. Five other recent, prominent, pro-nuclear studies—from the nuclear-lobby group WNA,[165] US DOE–Scully Capital,[166] the Royal Academy,[167] and the Canadian Nuclear Association[168]—assume load factors of 90 percent—something never achieved by the average performance of any nation's reactors. Five other prominent studies also assume average load factors never achieved by any nation. The later WNA,[169] UK,[170] MIT,[171] University of Chicago,[172] International Energy Agency,[173] and UK studies all assume average load factors between 80 and 85 percent.[174]

The most-commonly-assumed load factors, 90–95 percent, have been attained, only temporarily, by only 1.7 percent of all reactors, after deferred maintenance and many years of operation. They do not represent all-reactor, lifetime, national averages. Based on the current average load factor in the US (71 percent), these studies overestimate nuclear reliability by 19–25 percent. Even the 5 "more realistic" nuclear-load-factor assumptions (80–85 percent) overestimate fission reliability by 9–14 percent. Obviously, though, nuclear-economics studies should use average, lifetime, national load factors, not single-year load factors for the top 1.7 percent of non-US reactors. Using this fallacious 1.7-percent strategy, one could just as well trim all but the lowest load factors, then claim a 14-percent US nuclear-load factor, based on the closed Fort St. Vrain plant.[175]

What are the erroneous cost-savings of massively overestimating nuclear-load factors? The pro-nuclear MIT study calculated that, if nuclear-load factors decreased 10 percent, this alone would increase overall ratepayer costs 10–15 percent.[176] MIT thus estimates roughly 1–1.5 percent ratepayer-price savings per 1-percent load-factor improvement. All other things being equal, this suggests that using the most common load-factor assumption (90–95 percent), not the average US nuclear-load factor (71 percent), erroneously cuts nuclear-ratepayer prices 19–36 percent.

This load-factor data-trimming not only assumes that temporary performance of top-performing 1.7 percent of third-world reactors are typical of all reactors, but also obscures the fact that fission faces the same power-intermittencies as renewables like wind or solar. Correcting for load-factor data-trimming alone could raise nuclear-ratepayer prices 19–36 percent; yet the pro-nuclear UK government says wind-intermittency increases wind-generated-electricity costs only 6 percent, and wind is several times cheaper than nuclear energy.[177] According to credit-rating firms, nuclear-energy prices are more than 15 cents per kWhr,[178] while the pro-nuclear US DOE says actual US wind prices, on average over the last 7 years, are about 4.8 cents per kWhr.[179] Because decision-makers need reliable cost data on energy-intermittencies, overestimating nuclear-load factors appears unjustified— and thus likely to lead to poor energy choices.

Trimming Nuclear Costs by Inflating Reactor Lifetimes

Estimated nuclear-fission costs also artificially drop when assessors overestimate reactor lifetimes. Given high-temperature, heavy-radioactive bombardment of reactor materials, current plants were designed to last 30 years. To save utilities money, some licenses have been extended longer,[180] because it can be cheaper (assuming no major repairs) to spread nuclear-electricity costs over longer lifetimes.[181] However, the global-average lifetime of all 119 already-closed reactors is 22 years.[182] Safety and economic problems caused 19 US fission plants (20 percent) to retire early, and more than $20 billion was spent on 121 plants that were later canceled.[183] Thus more US reactors (140) were closed prematurely or canceled (during construction) than are now operating (104).

Rather than actual, global-average reactor lifetimes of 22 years, however, virtually all nuclear-cost studies counterfactually assume much longer lifetimes. The WNA claims, for instance, that nuclear plants "can offer electricity at predictable low and stable costs for up to 60 years of operating life."[184] Such industry data-trimming obscures the 22-year global-average nuclear lifetime for at least 3 reasons. One reason is that published industry tables of reactor lifetimes omit canceled and early-retirement plants, then calculate average lifetimes only for remaining plants.[185] Another reason is that all nuclear-industry and government cost assessments assume hypothetical, counterfactual longer lifetimes. The Lappeenranta University study assumed a 60-year lifetime;[186] the WNA,[187] US DOE–Scully Capital,[188] Royal Academy,[189] University of Chicago,[190] International Energy Agency,[191] OXERA,[192] and UK studies assumed 40-year lifetimes.[193] MIT studies assumed 25–40 years.[194] The vast majority of nuclear-cost studies assume reactor operating-lifetimes of 40 years or more. A third reason nuclear-industry data-trimming obscures accurate data is that, even if reactors lasted 30 to 50 years rather than 22, University of London economist David Fleming shows that, at best, reactors can "produce electricity at full power for no more than 24 years." This 24-year limit occurs because of 4–8 years of start-up debugging and because corrosion and intense radioactivity soon make reactors "impossible to repair." Consequently, Fleming says new-reactor designs will not have longer lifetimes.[195]

What are the economic effects of artificially overestimating reactor operating-lifetimes? The pro-nuclear MIT study calculated that increasing plant lifetimes from 25 to 40 years would reduce overall nuclear-electricity costs 5 percent.[196] Erroneously trimming reactor lifetimes, however, not only underestimates costs but also ignores rate-payer economic burdens from early closures. New York's Shoreham plant, for instance, was shut down the year it opened, and taxpayers paid the bill. Washington Nuclear defaulted on $2.25 billion in bonds for a reactor,[197] and ratepayers again paid. As already mentioned, typical nuclear-cost studies—which illegitimately trim expenses through counterfactual assumptions, such as longer plant lifetimes—are like pharmaceutical-company studies that claim drug safety, yet rely on trimmed drug-trial data that exclude subjects who were forced to quit the trials early because of adverse drug effects.

Effects of Trimming Nuclear-Cost Data with Five Counterfactual Assumptions

How does economic-data-trimming affect fission-electricity prices? The preceding data show that including full nuclear-liability-insurance expenses could—alone — increase atomic-energy costs 300 percent above most published nuclear-cost estimates, which were above $0.15/kWhr in 2008, according to credit-rating firms,[198] and roughly $0.21/kWhr in late 2009.[199] Including full 15-percent nuclear-interest charges rather than assuming 0-percent interest could alone raise costs 188 percent. Including 10-year rather than 0-year reactor-construction times could alone increase costs 150 percent. Using historical-average (71-percent) rather than hypothetical (90- to 95-percent) nuclear-load factors could raise costs 19–36 percent. Finally, using actual historical (22-year) rather than hypothetical (40-year) nuclear-plant lifetimes could increase costs 5 percent. Provided effects of these 5 types of data-trimming are independent, correcting them could increase atomic-energy costs nearly 700 percent—more precisely, 662–679 percent (300 + 188 + 150 + (19 – 36) + 5)—to about $1.47/kWhr (or 7 × $0.21/kWhr). Although this cost is far above all published estimates, it may be too low because it excludes expenses such as full nuclear-waste storage, reactor decommissioning, and the 15-percent annual increase in nuclear-construction costs caused by labor and materials increases.[200]

Guidelines for Scientific Data-Trimming

Given these massive economic effects of atomic-energy data-trimming, is data-trimming ever defensible? What do scientists say? Methodological controversies over data-trimming have a long scientific history. Mathematician Robert Babbage long ago warned of scientists who "cook" and "trim" data, yet many researchers, even famous scientists, appear to have done so. Robert Millikan conducted experiments with oil drops to measure the smallest electrical charge on an electron. He dripped oil through electrically charged plates and measured the effect of plate charges on the oil drops. Later, in a published paper on the charge of an electron, he reported only 140 of the 189 oil-drop observations recorded in his lab notebooks. Consequently, some scientists say Millikan unethically trimmed his data. Others disagree. The historical record likewise suggests that Mendel's peas had some assistance in sorting themselves in ways that agreed with Mendel's theory. Today, in areas like neuroscience, researchers debate whether some data plots have been omitted, smoothed, or shaped.[201]

On one hand, data-trimming proponents say not deleting outliers could lead to misleading conclusions,[202] or to indefensible variability in the data.[203] They note many largely accepted techniques for case-specific, scientific-data trimming.[204] In statistical studies, proponents say data-trimming often can give higher-power, more-precise results;[205] reduce error in the mean; or make sample means less variable in heavy-tailed distributions.[206] Besides, they say that "with a normal distribution ... the power loss" is quite small, that data "trimming shows great promise and should have wide usefulness," and that sometimes it "can make a silk purse from a sow's ear."[207]

On the other hand, although most scientists say data-trimming to fit some predetermined theory is unacceptable, some say data-trimming is always wrong.[208] They claim it makes many statistical inferences inoperable,[209] often lowers statistical power, may delete important data, and is an "extreme" measure that ignores the theoretical importance of outliers. They say one should never trim data but should instead attempt to minimize outliers' misleading effects.[210]

If one assumes there are at least some circumstances in which data-trimming might be legitimate, the key questions are whether, when, and how to trim data. The scientific literature provides 5 prominent guidelines.[211] The first 2 guidelines suggest *when and whether* to trim, and the next 3 suggest *how* to do so.

(1) Typically data should be trimmed only when they are rare, extreme data points; all other things being equal, "the more nonnormal, the greater should be the trimming,"[212] because extreme data points may reflect measurement error.

(2) Typically data should be trimmed only when doing so is necessary to prevent error: for example, when outliers overly influence the mean or come from a different population.[213]

(3) Data-trimming typically should be accomplished by means of cuts that are symmetrical: for example, removing the upper and lower x percent of the data

set, then finding the arithmetic mean of what is left. One ought not "trim just the high values or just the low values," because this would bias results.[214]

(4) Data-trimming typically should be accomplished by means of techniques that allow documenting and evaluating associated error and uncertainty. Techniques include using standard formulae to calculate standard deviations or error bars for trimmed means, comparing confidence intervals for trimmed and untrimmed data, assessing different types of trimming by giving error bars for alternative degrees of trimming, and reporting "auxiliary information" on how well trimming worked.[215]

(5) Data-trimming typically should be accomplished by means of techniques that include communicating trimming results to ensure they do not mislead: for example, noting the presence of outliers and the effects of trimming on results.[216]

Obviously there are many questions about how to use and interpret the preceding guidelines. How can one satisfy both guideline (3), regarding symmetrical cuts, and guideline (2), if measurement error apparently affects only upper-tail data? When should one employ guideline (1), if outlier data can reveal evidence of low-probability, high-consequence risks? While such questions deserve answers, they are beyond the scope of this chapter. The point here is to give a preliminary answer regarding whether nuclear-related data-trimming appears consistent with noncontroversial aspects of the guidelines.

Economics-Argument Data-Trimming and the Five Guidelines

Is nuclear-liability-related data-trimming defensible? Although guideline (1) suggests trimming only extreme data points, the earlier analysis shows that full nuclear-liability-insurance-cost data are not rare outliers, but consistent data possibly warning of needed liability protection. Thus, this trimming appears not to follow guideline (1). Nor does it follow guideline (2); eliminating liability-related costs is not necessary to avoid nuclear-cost errors. Rather, the trimmed costs are real, transferred from industry to the public. With the exception of parts of MIT analyses, most pro-atomic-energy studies likewise fail to follow guideline (3), regarding liability-insurance costs, because their trimming is not symmetrical: they trim only high-end nuclear-insurance costs. They also fail to follow guideline (4), which requires documentation of trimming-related error and uncertainty, because the majority of studies provides no documentation. Nor does this trimming follow guideline (5), which requires public communication of trimming effects so that taxpayers are not misled. The majority of studies includes discussion of neither nuclear-liability limits nor cost-trimming effects on citizens when nuclear-liability risks are transferred from industry to the public. One of the only pro-nuclear studies that attempts to follow guidelines (4) and (5) is the 2003 (but not the 2009) MIT analysis,[217] although it errs in other ways. The 2003 MIT authors justify trimming liability-related-cost data by erroneously claiming that (i) the nuclear-insurance subsidy "is very small" and (ii) US law does not require firms to carry full insurance.[218] However, if (i) were correct, the nuclear industry would not require liability-insurance subsidies as a prerequisite for operation, yet obviously these subsidies are massive, half of reactor capital costs, as discussed earlier. Similarly, (ii) fails to justify insurance-cost data-trimming, because the law's not requiring something (full-liability coverage) does not mean analyses ought not include it. Legal and economic requirements are 2 different things; otherwise, legal and economic analyses would be identical, and they are not. Besides, as previous paragraphs showed, the US Securities and Exchange Commission follows guideline (5); it requires that investors be told whether there is a nuclear-liability limit (which reduces their investment risk). This requirement suggests the public deserves the same risk-information cost-trimming effects. Thus, almost all nuclear-liability data-trimming fails to follow guidelines (1)–(3), while most fails to follow guidelines (4)–(5).

Regarding the second and third types of nuclear-cost data-trimming—assuming interest-rate and construction-time data are 0—all pro-nuclear economic analyses likewise run afoul of data-trimming guidelines. They fail to follow guideline (1) because trimmed interest-rate and construction-time data are not rare outliers, but typical; all plants have non-0 values for both. Likewise, interest- and construction-time trimming fails to follow guideline (2) because it does not prevent, but actually causes, error—a 250-percent underestimate of nuclear costs when interest is trimmed to 0, as is typical. The trimming also fails to follow guideline (3) because these data cuts are not symmetrical. As previous paragraphs showed, the trimming is biased in cutting only lower-end interest-rate and construction-time data. Nearly all pro-nuclear studies likewise fail to follow guideline (4)—which requires the documentation of trimming-related error and uncertainty—and guideline (5)— which clarifies the effects of data-trimming. As already mentioned, however, 2 studies followed guidelines (4) and (5) and showed precise, erroneous cost decreases because of failure to use actual, 15-percent interest rates.[219] Thus, virtually all interest- and construction-time data-trimming fails to follow guidelines (1)–(3), while most studies likewise fail to follow guidelines (4)–(5).

With respect to the fourth type of nuclear-cost data-trimming—assuming higher, counterfactual load factors—almost all atomic-energy-cost studies likewise fail to follow guideline (1) because they trim actual load-factor data, rather than rare outliers. They also fail to follow guideline (2) because using hypothetical load-factor data is not necessary to prevent errors, but likely generates them. Likewise, this trimming fails to follow guideline (3). The data cuts are not symmetrical: they trim only low-end load factors, biasing nuclear-cost calculations. Almost all nuclear-economics studies likewise fail to follow guideline (4), which requires the documentation of trimming-related error and uncertainty, and guideline (5), which warns against misleading the public about trimming effects. Ignoring guideline (5), most of these studies fail to analyze the cost effects of using counterfactual nuclear-load factors. One exception is the MIT study, as already noted; it showed that each 1-percent load-factor decrease caused a 1.5-percent nuclear-ratepayer-cost increase.[220] Thus virtually all pro-nuclear load-factor data-trimming fails to follow guidelines (1)–(3), while most fails to follow guidelines (4)–(5).

Finally, regarding the fifth type of nuclear-cost-data trimming, as earlier paragraphs revealed, almost all fission-economics studies trim costs by assuming longer, contrary-to-fact nuclear lifetimes of 40–60 years, not the 22 years shown by historical data. This trimming fails to follow guideline (1), because instead of deleting rare outliers, it omits factual, in favor of counterfactual, data on lifetimes. This data-trimming also violates guideline (2) because it is not necessary to prevent error, but rather generates it by using contrary-to-fact lifetime data. Lifetime-related data-trimming likewise fails to follow guideline (3) because instead of deleting symmetrically, assessors cut only low-end lifetimes. One exception is the UK (2002) Performance Unit study, which employs 15- to 30-year lifetimes. However, almost all nuclear-economics studies fail to follow guideline (4), which requires the documentation of trimming-related error and uncertainty, and guideline (5), which warns against misleading the public regarding trimming effects, because (with the exception of MIT scientists, as noted) nearly all failed to analyze load-factor-trimming effects on nuclear cost. MIT authors calculated that, if average-nuclear-operating lifetimes increased from 25 to 40 years, this would reduce overall-nuclear-electricity costs 5 percent,[221] an admission that follows guidelines (4)–(5). Thus virtually all pro-nuclear, load-factor data-trimming fails to follow guidelines (1)–(2), while most fails to follow guidelines (3)–(5).

If preceding paragraphs are correct, the least-followed guidelines are (1)–(2), and assessors trim typical, not rare, data points. In trimming 4 of 5 types of nuclear-cost data (liability, interest-rate, load, and lifetime-related) nearly all these analyses also trim asymmetrically and thus fail to follow guideline (3). This suggests biased data-trimming, perhaps done to lower apparent costs. Although most pro-nuclear studies appear flawed in all 25 ways (failing to follow 5 guidelines regarding 5 types of data-trimming), the 2003 MIT study does follow 6 guidelines, namely guidelines (4)–(5) for 3 of the 5 types of data—liability, load-factor, and reactor-lifetime.[222] Thus despite its serious shortcomings (failure to follow 19 apparent guidelines for scientific data-trimming), this MIT study is less flawed than the other 29 studies that trim nuclear-cost data in 25 questionable ways.

Studies That Do Not Trim Nuclear Costs

Because so many nuclear-economics analyses trim cost data, and do so in illegitimate ways, at least 2 questions arise: "Do any studies get nuclear costs right?" and "What can explain why so many nuclear-cost studies have erred so badly?"

Regarding the first question, many analyses do include more complete nuclear costs. For instance, although most studies ignore massive nuclear subsidies (e.g., for accident-liability insurance), analyses done by university professors and by NGOs often include them.[223] Authors from the University of New South Wales and the University of Melbourne, for example, claim that nuclear subsidies are "market distortions" and that taxpayer subsidies cover 60–90 percent of new nuclear-construction costs.[224] In Britain, they say, nuclear subsidies are about $2.6 billion annually. As a result, these university authors note that "ignoring the huge subsidies from government to nuclear energy also makes the technology look less expensive," although "the current economics of nuclear power make it an unattractive option for new generating capacity."[225]

Similarly, many studies done by NGOs or university professors neither trim interest costs and construction times nor use overnight costs.[226] Instead they note that "choosing an unrealistically low interest rate can make nuclear energy look much less expensive."[227] Thus, these authors use full market interest rates for nuclear construction, in part because many of them obtain data from banks and from Standard and Poor's, Moody's, and other credit-rating agencies. As one University of California, Berkeley, engineering PhD claims, nuclear plants "pay more on the margin for credit. Federal support of construction costs will do little to change that reality."[228]

Likewise, many university and NGO studies use empirical, historical-average load factors and nuclear-plant lifetimes. For instance, one Technical University of Eindhoven scholar criticizes the assumption of a "very long operational lifetime [for a nuclear plant], as MIT proposes" in its nuclear-cost analyses. He says instead that today "only a few reactors in the world reached an operational lifetime of 24.6 FPY [full power years] today. Extensive refurbishments are required to reach even this lifetime.... The reliability of the reactor vessel determines the operational lifetime of a NPP. The quality of the vessel deteriorates over time by corrosion and neutron capture." Thus "the lifetime of one reactor," even with extensive refurbishment, is "30–40 years" at best; "the average operational lifetime of the reactors to be decommissioned on the list of the UK Nuclear Decommissioning Authority...is 18.7 FPY."[229]

As the previous examples show, university-based nuclear-cost studies often provide more reliable cost figures, based on historical-average data, bank estimates, and credit-rating figures. Reliable nuclear-cost data are difficult to obtain, however, for reasons that become clear once we address the second question.

What May Explain Nuclear-Cost-Data Trimming

Regarding the second question, what can explain why so many studies err so badly in underestimating nuclear-electricity costs? At least 7 reasons come to mind. One reason, obvious from chapter 2, is that those who calculate nuclear costs ignore both full-fuel-cycle GHG emissions and costs. Examining only part of the fuel cycle, they grossly underestimate atomic-energy costs. Yet, as chapter 2 showed, the massive energy requirements of all 14 nuclear-fuel-cycle stages mean reactors produce only 25 percent more energy than that needed throughout their fuel cycles. These large energy inputs cause energy bankruptcy, which in turn translates into financial bankruptcy. Thus, failure to calculate full-fuel-cycle energy debts is one reason that atomic-energy economic analyses err so badly.[230]

A second reason for nuclear-cost errors is that current turnkey or fixed-price data for nuclear-plant construction are not available because no utilities have been willing to build turnkey nuclear plants, as they did with early reactors. Nuclear proponents say this unwillingness has arisen because every utility has had cost- and construction-time overruns on all reactors; every utility has lost money on turnkey plants.[231] Instead, "cost-plus" contracts have become the norm.[232] Yet, given various types of fission-cost overruns, it can be difficult to account for all construction costs. Thus, the Congressional Budget Office recently revealed that average US nuclear-plant-cost overruns have been 207 percent and that reactors cost triple their original estimates.[233] Although the Finnish reactor (now being built by French-government-owned Areva) is a turnkey plant, it is mostly taxpayer-subsidized; only 3.5 years after its construction began, it already was 50 percent over budget and 3 years late.[234] In February 2010, project manager Jouni Silvennoinen said the reactor's estimated start date will be delayed to June 2012. By 2010, market construction costs were $7.2 billion and rising—already 200 percent over budget.[235] Because this and another Areva plant are the only latest-design nuclear plants under construction in Western Europe or North America,[236] good nuclear-cost data are difficult to find.

A third reason most nuclear-economics studies underestimate costs is that utilities are allowed to quote different nuclear prices to different groups, at different stages of the nuclear-fuel cycle, and they know that low-price quotes help sell reactors. These different price quotes cause confusion and cost misstatement. For instance, when a utility applies to build a nuclear plant and tries to show its cost-competitiveness, it quotes highly trimmed economic data that omit many charges— for example, interest and transmission-system upgrades—that are not paid to the reactor vendor. These trimmed data are "how the cost is typically quoted by the [nuclear- plant] vendor"; however, once the plant is built, the utility quotes much higher costs to the Public Service Commission, including inflation, interest, upgrades, cost overruns, and so on, because "the regulated utility will be allowed [by the commission] to recover this total cost through customer charges." Yet as revealed earlier, interest charges alone more than double "the [nuclear-plant] vendor's EPC [engineering, procurement, and construction] overnight cost" that was quoted before the plant began. Moreover, the trimmed nuclear-cost figures, submitted to the commission to gain building approval, typically have "all detailed information about this cost figure" redacted from filings. Thus nuclear-price data often are underestimated because government allows them to be quoted in different ways, depending on their audience and use (either to convince utilities to purchase allegedly low-cost reactors, or to convince public-service commissions to allow full nuclear-cost recovery from ratepayers). Given no universally accepted, canonical studies for what nuclear-cost assessments ought to include and how they ought to be represented, obviously it is in the reactor vendor's financial interest to underestimate nuclear costs in order to sell reactors. As already mentioned, the 2009 MIT authors say that using overnight costs "represents the standard basis for quoting comparable costs across different plants"; they are "how the cost is typically quoted by the [nuclear plant] vendor."[237] Given this norm and earlier comments on different nuclear audiences and data uses, there are no universally accepted, canonical studies for how and what nuclear-cost assessments ought to include.

Moreover, a fourth reason for underestimated nuclear costs is that many industry analyses do not clarify precisely what is included in their cost tabulations. Given this fact, and nuclear-industry control of most nuclear-cost data, misrepresentation seems likely. For instance, one prominent UK government study, done at the University of Sussex, noted that although industry-funded studies exclude financing and other costs, [238] often "it is not known" (e.g., in the pro-nuclear Finnish analysis)[239] what costs are included or excluded.[240] Consequently, Sussex University researchers claimed that even government nuclear-cost reports, such as the UK Department of Trade and Industry's 2006 study,[241] "leave no clear audit trail."[242] Scientists from the University of Melbourne and the University of New South Wales agreed. They said "published [nuclear] capital-cost estimates...derive from studies...from vendors of reactor systems....The data are supplied...by the nuclear industry itself and are not open to objective verification."[243] More generally, the Sussex University authors (of a UK government report) criticize the "[cost] appraisal optimism" of most nuclear studies. Under the heading of "capital costs," they note that "all of the [nuclear capital-cost] data is traced back to industry sources, usually reactor vendors, and the number of these sources is very few....Reactor vendors inevitably and legitimately have an interest in presenting costs in a way that maximizes their chances of commercial success."[244]

A fifth reason for underestimated nuclear costs is that nearly all studies are either performed or funded by the nuclear industry, which has financial incentives to minimize costs. Of the 30 post-2000 nuclear-cost studies analyzed here, at least 18—or 60 percent—come directly from nuclear interests.[245] Virtually all have been either *performed* by,[246] or at least partly *funded* by, the nuclear industry[247] or pronuclear government agencies, like the US DOE.[248] For instance, the 2009 MIT study notes it has been funded by the pro-nuclear or lobby groups EPRI and INEEL, but admits, "None of the figures reported [by the nuclear industry] for these [nuclear] plants represent actual costs."[249] Instead all of the cost figures are too low and have trimmed data.

A sixth reason for underestimated fission-electricity costs—another result of studies' being funded or performed by the nuclear industry—is that industry typically claims fission-cost assumptions are either "privileged information" (and thus kept secret by the industry) or purely counterfactual. Regarding secrecy, the 2009 MIT authors reported that, in Public Service Commission filings before nuclear-plant approval, nuclear-industry-cost figures (e.g., those provided by Georgia Power in 2009, when it considered building 2 nuclear plants) typically have "all detailed information about this cost figure" redacted,[250] even though taxpayers subsidize nuclear-electricity costs and ratepayers cover the remainder. Likewise, a recent University of Greenwich nuclear-cost assessment noted that, for industry-performed or industry-funded studies,[251] "many of the [cost] assumptions are not fully specified, being classified as commercially sensitive."[252] The same university researchers charge that one pro-nuclear UK government-commission study errs;[253] it merely "reports the forecasts provided by [the 2 nuclear companies] British Energy and BNFL" and "uses BNFL's assumptions…[although] many of the assumptions, such as for construction cost, are categorized as commercially sensitive and not published.…On load-factor, the figures are also confidential, although the PIU states the assumed performance is significantly higher than 80 percent."[254]

Yet, as already noted, actual nuclear-load factors are about 70 percent—not "significantly higher than 80 percent," as cited by the preceding pro-nuclear government study. Another UK government report, done by University of Sussex researchers but not funded by the nuclear industry, says many industry-dominated studies—including the earlier, pro-nuclear UK commission report[255]—use nuclear-industry data but keep them confidential, to protect the industry.[256] For instance, the UK Royal Academy of Engineering report,[257] done by nuclear-industry contractor PB Power,[258] states that "an allowance for [reactor] decommissioning cost is included in the capital cost, but it does not specify cost assumptions."[259] Both this study and the PB Power study are based on Finnish nuclear-industry data,[260] but even MIT-based, nuclear-industry contractors admit "there is no detail on what is included in this [Finnish-cost] figure, and so it must be handled carefully."[261] Such figures could be used to underestimate nuclear costs, particularly because they "leave no audit trail." As the same UK government report also emphasized, many studies "provide estimates of the overall generating cost of electricity using their own input assumptions," but "because [many industry-funded] published studies do not show the precise method by which different input costs are translated into generating costs, and because the assumptions made will vary and be of differing methodological quality, it is not possible" to evaluate their "robustness."[262]

Moreover, when secret nuclear-cost assumptions are revealed, typically they are counterfactual in a way that is favorable to the reactor industry. For instance, in the industry-funded Finnish nuclear-cost study,[263] done at Lappeenranta University of Technology, the authors assume a counterfactual 5-percent (rather than the actual 15-percent) interest rate, as already mentioned. They likewise assume a counterfactual 91-percent (rather than historical-average 71-percent) load factor, and a counterfactual 60-year (rather than historical-average 22-year) lifetime, as already mentioned. Consequently, the study arrives at low nuclear-power costs. Nevertheless, as already mentioned, the Royal Academy and PB Power studies accept these implausible Finnish assumptions and their confidential, contrary-to-fact data.[264]

What do the preceding 6 reasons for fission-cost underestimates suggest? Recall that these reasons include (1) the *absence of fixed-price or turnkey reactor contracts*, (2) the *price discrepancy* between vendor-quoted versus utility-quoted (to the Public Service Commission) nuclear costs, (3) the vendor and industry *standard practice* of quoting trimmed prices, (4) the lack of independent confirmation of most *nuclear-cost data*, mostly from industry, (5) the dearth of alternative analyses, because most *fission-nuclear-cost studies* are funded or performed by nuclear interests, and (6) the use of *counterfactual assumptions* and confidential assumptions by most studies. The preceding reasons, especially (4)–(6), suggest that nuclear-industry financial conflicts of interest (COI) also may help explain fission-cost underestimates.

Possible COI in Nuclear-Cost Studies

To investigate whether financial COI appear to be at least partly responsible for some fission-cost underestimates, one needs to understand what constitutes a COI. As defined in a classic 2009 US National Academy of Sciences (NAS) report, "conflicts of interest are defined as *circumstances that create a risk that professional judgments or actions regarding a primary interest will be unduly influenced by a secondary interest*. Primary interests include promoting and protecting the integrity of research," the quality of scientific education, and the welfare of the public, whereas "secondary interests include not only financial interests...but also other interests, such as the pursuit of professional advancement."[265] What happens when one applies this COI definition to nuclear-cost studies that are performed or funded by fission interests? If the nuclear industry performs or funds economic studies whose results could affect its profits, this may "create a [COI, a] risk that professional judgments or actions regarding a primary interest," scientific integrity, may be "unduly influenced by a secondary interest," fission-industry profits.

To assess whether nuclear-related COIs may be involved in these 30 studies, consider 2 questions: (1) whether nuclear-cost studies funded by fission interests appear to trim fission-cost data, and (2) whether studies *not* funded by nuclear interests appear *not* to trim fission-cost data. If the answers to (1) and (2) are negative, then no COI may be involved. However, if the answers to (1) and (2) are positive, then COI may be occurring.

Although complete conclusions require a more extensive analysis than can be given here, at least this chapter can provide some preliminary answers regarding (1) and (2). That is, regarding question (1), this chapter showed earlier that, of the 30 recent nuclear-cost studies, at least 18 (60 percent) were performed or funded by pro-nuclear interests (also see later analyses),[266] such as the US DOE. Moreover, most of these studies trimmed the cost data in the 5 ways discussed in this chapter. Regarding question (2), this chapter also showed earlier that most nuclear-economics studies—that were neither funded nor performed by the nuclear industry—include most fission costs and do not trim them. Building on this already-presented information, one can divide the 30 post-2000 nuclear-economics studies into 4 groups, A–D below, based on who funds them and what cost data they include or exclude. (Some studies do not list their funders, and they are categorized as such.)

- Group A (nuclear funders, pro-nuclear stance) consists of 18 analyses that (to varying degrees) are pro-nuclear and have been at least partly performed or funded by pro-nuclear interests (either industry or government).[267]
- Group B (unknown funders, pro-nuclear stance) consists of 1 nuclear-cost analysis that is pro-nuclear and whose funders are unknown because the study does not mention them.[268]
- Group C (nonprofit-NGO funders, anti-nuclear stance) consists of 4 nuclear-cost studies that are critical of high nuclear costs and whose funders are nonprofit NGOs.[269]
- Group D (university funders, anti-nuclear stance) consists of 7 nuclear-cost studies that are critical of high nuclear costs and whose (at least partial) funders are universities,[270] given that the lead authors of these studies are or were employed by universities.

To answer questions (1) and (2) above, consider characteristics of the nuclear-cost studies in each of these 4 groups.

Group A: 18 Studies with Nuclear Funders and a Pro-Nuclear Stance

The Group A studies—which are funded or performed by nuclear interests—represent most (18 of 30, or 60 percent) of the nuclear-economics studies.[271] What is especially interesting, however, is that typical industry, government, and NGO groups—even anti-nuclear groups—appear to take these 18 pro-nuclear, largely industry-funded studies as the nuclear-economics paradigm. For instance, a classic UK government report lists only 9 fission-cost studies,[272] all performed or funded by nuclear interests.[273] The WNA , a global nuclear-industry-lobby group, lists only 7 fission-cost studies, all performed or funded by nuclear interests.[274] Even environmental-group studies, like those of Greenpeace,[275] list only 12 fission-cost studies—and all of them were performed or funded by nuclear interests.[276] Thus, not only are most fission-cost studies done by pro-nuclear interests, but government, industry, and even environmentalists take these studies as dominant. Other interesting facts about these 18 nuclear-funded studies are that none of them includes nuclear-cost data (a) from credit-rating agencies, (b) that cover taxpayer nuclear subsidies, or (c) that correct counterfactual, industry-supplied nuclear-economics data. To see how flaws (a)–(c) affect typical Group A conclusions, consider the 2009 MIT atomic-energy-cost analysis.[277]

On the positive side, as already mentioned, these MIT authors admit their work is funded by the nuclear industry;[278] they note that, because of cost-data trimming, "none of the figures reported [by industry] for these [nuclear] plants represent actual costs." The authors thus deserve credit for blowing the whistle on fission-industry failure to report actual costs, to reveal assumptions used to calculate costs, to explain counterfactual nuclear-cost calculations, and to explain the doubling of overnight nuclear-construction costs during 2003–2008.[279]

Despite these strengths, however, the industry-funded 2009 MIT authors ignore problem (a), high fission costs calculated by credit-rating companies. Instead they follow overly optimistic nuclear-industry assumptions that lead to erroneously low fission-energy-cost conclusions, as will be shown below. Regarding problem (b), the MIT authors fail to take account of massive taxpayer subsidies that artificially reduce nuclear costs. They say their analysis "does not include any of the benefits from the production-tax credits or loan guarantees…of 2005," that is, a specific class of 2005 US taxpayer subsidies.[280] Yet they inconsistently incorporate economic effects of other cost subsidies that artificially lower their calculated nuclear-electricity costs. If the late MIT physicist Henry Kendall is correct, pre-2004 US nuclear-power subsidies amount to about $20 billion annually—all of whose effects were ignored by the MIT authors.[281] For instance, they ignore the billions of dollars in taxpayer subsidies needed annually for nuclear-waste storage, perhaps because these are not market costs. Instead the MIT authors assume that total costs of spent-fuel and waste disposal will be only "the statutory fee of 1 mil/kWhr currently charged" by government to the utility.[282] Over the last 10 years, this amounts to only $5 billion total.[283] Given the average 22-year lifetime of nuclear plants (see above), this statutory fee means the total collected from current US nuclear plants amounts to roughly $11 billion. Yet this amount, assumed by the 2009 MIT authors, is only a tiny portion of permanent waste-storage costs, most of which will be borne by taxpayers, per government agreement.[284] In 1996, the US National Academy of Sciences studies said the total was not $11 billion, but at least $350 billion,[285] and these costs now are $1 trillion.[286] Thus the MIT authors include only between 1 percent (assuming $1 trillion is needed) and 3 percent (assuming $350 billion is needed) of the total monies needed for US nuclear-waste management—because they ignore taxpayer subsidies. More generally, the MIT authors assume fission electricity includes no taxpayer-subsidized costs,[287] although "federal subsidies cover 60–90 percent of the generation cost for new nuclear plants[288] and, as already documented, US federal nuclear subsidies have already amounted to about $150 billion. The MIT failure to take account of nuclear subsidies in nuclear costs is troublesome both because utility executives say that "without [low-interest, taxpayer-subsidized] loan guarantees, we will not build nuclear plants,"[289] and because the study failure suggests its industry funding may have influenced its fission-cost underestimates.

Regarding problem (c), because the 2009 MIT authors use mainly uncorrected nuclear-industry data, they make many counterfactual and inconsistent assumptions that lower nuclear-cost estimates. They assume, for instance, that the "total cost" of a nuclear plant includes neither financing nor interest charges. Yet they inconsistently admit these charges can double construction costs, and they counterfactually assume that nuclear-plant construction takes only 5 years, although earlier paragraphs showed that historical-average nuclear-plant-construction time is 10–23 years. Likewise, these MIT authors assume a nuclear-load or "capacity factor of 85%," although earlier paragraphs showed that historical-average capacity factors are 71 percent. Likewise, the MIT authors assume annual inflation rates for future nuclear construction are 3 percent, although they admit that over the last 5 years, costs have increased 23 percent per year. They also assume that for fission, "the costs of capital [are] equal to those for coal." Yet this assumption appears wholly unrealistic; market-interest rates for nuclear loans, as already mentioned, are 15 percent, whereas coal loans are only about 25 percent of that figure. Moreover, as already noted, interest can add 250 percent to overnight reactor costs, whereas the MIT authors admit that coal-plant interest charges add only 17–21 percent to overnight coal-plant costs.[290]

The MIT authors likewise claim to "update the cost of nuclear power," although their nuclear costs are only half of those calculated by credit-rating firms like Standard and Poor's and Moody's.[291] Moody's says that, since 2008, it has taken "a more negative view for those issuers seeking to build new nuclear power plants" because of "the substantial execution risks involved."[292] The discrepancy between MIT and credit-rating-company figures should have caused the 2009 MIT authors to question their industry-friendly assumptions, which led to artificially low nuclear-cost conclusions.

Perhaps because the 2003 MIT nuclear-cost analysis likewise was partly funded by the nuclear industry, it too fell into counterfactual and inconsistent assumptions about nuclear costs.[293] It claimed to be funded by the "Alfred P. Sloan Foundation,…MIT's Office of the Provost, and [the MIT] Laboratory for Energy and the Environment."[294] However, "funding for this [laboratory that sponsored the] work comes from a variety of sources, including DOE, EPRI…[and] INEEL,"[295] all pro-nuclear interests. Like the 2009 MIT studies, this 2003 research includes no nuclear-cost data (a) from credit-rating agencies, (b) that takes account of taxpayer-provided subsidies, or (c) that justifies using uncorrected, nuclear-industry-supplied cost data. Regarding (b), this 2003 MIT report criticizes nuclear subsidies, yet proposes additional "modest" taxpayer subsidies for nuclear power, but excludes these subsidies from its cost accounting of nuclear power. Likewise, regarding (c), the 2003 MIT analysis assumes that nuclear-plant construction takes only 5 years, although earlier paragraphs showed historical-average nuclear-plant-construction time is 10–23 years. It also counterfactually assumes a nuclear-load factor of 85 percent, although earlier paragraphs showed that the historical-average load factors is 71 percent. Similarly, the 2003 MIT study assumes an 11.5-percent interest rate, although earlier paragraphs showed that 15 percent is the market rate. Finally, it assumes a 40-year lifetime for reactors, although earlier paragraphs revealed the historical-average lifetime is 22 years. Such implausible, inconsistent, and counterfactual nuclear-industry assumptions appear to have compromised the quality of MIT analyses.[296]

Group B: 1 Nuclear-Cost Study with Unknown Funders That Uses Uncorrected Industry Data

What about the other 12 nuclear-cost studies, those neither performed nor funded by nuclear interests? Group B studies consist of 1 nuclear-cost analysis,[297] done by Oxera Consultants in the UK, whose funders are not revealed by the authors. Like the Group A analyses, those in Group B appear to include no nuclear-cost data (a) from credit-rating agencies, (b) that take account of taxpayer-nuclear subsidies, or (c) that correct inconsistent, counterfactual, fission-industry-supplied cost data.

Regarding (a), the Oxera study says nothing about how credit-rating-company claims contradict Oxera's conclusions about low nuclear costs. Regarding (b), Oxera's authors say only that "economic investment [in fission] is likely to require government support"; regarding (c), they admit their data and assumptions are "according to industry sources," like Westinghouse, that supplied "related assumptions."[298] Unsurprisingly, the Oxera authors employ uncorrected nuclear-industry assumptions: for example, they use a nuclear-load factor of 95 percent,[299] although the historical-average figure is 71 percent, as shown earlier. They also assume reactor-construction "cost inflation per year" is 2 percent,[300] not 23 percent annually, documented for the last 5 years.[301] Likewise, they assume reactor construction takes 4 years, not the historical-average 10–23 years, shown earlier. Finally, they assume nuclear-interest rates are 5 percent, not 15 percent, as shown earlier. Because their assumptions are inconsistent with historical data, are biased, and minimize costs, Oxera authors conclude that "the potential investment in nuclear new build is likely to bring positive returns."[302]

Group C: 4 Studies with NGO Funders and Completely Corrected Industry-Cost Data

What about Group C fission-cost analyses? They are consistent with market data, like that from credit-rating firms, perhaps because their funders have no apparent

COI and are nonprofit NGOs.[303] Group C includes a study from a nonprofit think tank, the Rocky Mountain Institute (RMI).[304] RMI says, "Half our support comes from individual donors and foundation grants.... The other half comes from earned revenue—from consulting for corporations and governments."[305] A second study,[306] from the nonprofit NGO Nuclear Information and Research Service (NIRS), says it relies on "contributions from citizens across the world to support our efforts."[307] A third study comes from another nonprofit think tank, the Institute for Energy and Environmental Research (IEER).[308] The IEER website says its work is "supported by grants from foundations, concerned individuals and public-interest consulting contracts. Foundation funders include Colombe Foundation, Ford Foundation, Livingry Foundation, New-Land Foundation, Ploughshares Foundation, Stewart R. Mott Charitable Trust, Town Creek Foundation, and the Wallace Global Fund."[309] The fourth study in this group is funded by the Maryland Public Interest Research Group (PIRG).[310] To see how nonprofit NGOs approach nuclear-power costs, note that all Group C studies (a) include nuclear-cost data from credit-rating agencies (b) take account of taxpayer-nuclear subsidies, and (c) correct nuclear-industry-supplied cost data. For instance, consider the 2008 study done by RMI.[311]

Regarding (a), credit-rating data, RMI acknowledged poor fission-credit ratings and argued that "the private capital market isn't investing in new nuclear plants, and without financing, capitalist utilities aren't buying." Instead, poor nuclear-credit ratings mean "the few [reactor] purchases, nearly all in Asia, are all made by central planners with a draw on the public purse." RMI also shows that, when one relies on "evidence-based studies," like those done by Moody's and Standard and Poor's, the capital costs of fission-generated electricity are more than 3 times higher than the MIT-estimated nuclear costs, based on industry data.[312]

Regarding (b), taxpayer-subsidy data, RMI notes that even massive government subsidies have failed to make fission cost effective and that, once such subsidies are counted, authors "approach full costs." RMI thus shows that the nuclear industry relies mainly on taxpayer subsidies, not private investors:

> Taxpayers, who already bear most nuclear-accident risks[,] ... for decades have subsidized existing nuclear plants by ~1–5¢/kWh. In 2005, desperate for orders, the politically-potent nuclear industry got those US subsidies raised to ~5–9¢/kWh for new plants, or ~60–90 percent of their entire projected power cost, including new taxpayer-funded insurance against legal or regulatory delays. Wall Street still demurred. In 2007, the industry won relaxed government rules that made its 100-percent-loan guarantees (for 80%-debtfinancing) even more valuable—worth, one utility's data revealed, about $13 billion for a single new plant, about equal to its entire capital cost. But rising costs had meanwhile made the $4 billion of new 2005 loan guarantees scarcely sufficient for a single reactor, so Congress raised taxpayers' guarantees to $18.5 billion. Congress will soon be asked

for another \$30+ billion in loan guarantees, or even for a blank check. Meanwhile, the nonpartisan Congressional Budget Office has concluded that defaults are likely.[313]

Regarding (c), correcting industry-based data and assumptions, RMI challenges nuclear-industry-funded conclusions—like those of the MIT and University of Chicago studies—that assume as much as 85–95 percent nuclear-load factors.[314] The RMI authors say actual load factors are much lower because "even reliably operating nuclear plants must shut down" for roughly 8% of the time, "for refueling and maintenance, and unexpected failures" cause additional shutdowns for another "8% of the time." Thus the most reliable single reactors have average-load factors of 84 percent, but not all reactors are reliable. Why not? Only "132 . . . 52 percent of the 253 [reactors] originally ordered" were completed. Not-completed reactors (numbering 121) are excluded by industry from alleged load-factor averages. Also excluded are another 28 US reactors (21 percent of those built), because they were "permanently and prematurely closed due to reliability or cost problems." Industry likewise excludes yet another 27 percent of US reactors that "have completely failed for a year or more. Although surviving US nuclear plants," 68 in number and one-fourth of total US reactor orders, have short-term load factors of about 90 percent, RMI says this 90-percent figure is misleadingly quoted in industry studies. Industry studies fail to reveal that the load-factor figure of 90 percent represents only a short-term load factor, not lifetime-average load factor, and only for 25 percent of US reactors, not all 253 US reactors that were ordered. As already explained, the lifetime-average US nuclear-load factor is 71 percent, not 90 percent. RMI thus explains that erroneously high load-factor figures arise from excluding low-load-factor reactors, which comprise 73 percent of US reactors.[315]

Likewise, RMI shows that when industry-funded, nuclear-cost studies exclude reactor-construction time and interest charges, this data-trimming illegitimately represents nuclear-capital costs as more than 50 percent less than they are. Yet in reality, as RMI notes, quoting the *Economist*, nuclear power "is now too costly to matter."[316]

Group D: Seven 7 Studies That Are Partly University Funded and Use Fully Corrected Industry Data

Other studies likewise challenge the counterfactual assumptions in many industry nuclear-cost studies. Group D consists of 7 such analyses whose (at least partial) funders are universities, as lead authors are or were employed by universities.[317] A chemist at University of Greenwich, in London, did one study.[318] Another was done by "a Press Fellow at Wolfson College, Cambridge, during 2007/08."[319] MIT physics PhD Brice Smith, chair of the physics department at the State University of

New York (SUNY) at Cortland, did another analysis.[320] Unlike industry studies, these 7 university-funded analyses include nuclear-cost data (a) from credit-rating agencies (b) that account for taxpayer-nuclear subsidies and (c) that use corrected, nuclear-industry-supplied data. Consider the study by physicist Smith from SUNY.

Regarding (a), Smith repeatedly cites credit-rating-firm data in his cost analyses. He quotes Moody's or Standard and Poor's to show that if utilities build nuclear plants, their credit is downgraded, which prevents further construction; that reactors always have cost overruns; that even subsidies will not make fission economical; and that credit-rating firms reject atomic energy.[321] Given poor credit rating, Cambridge University professor Paul Brown likewise confirms that the high "cost of borrowing capital [for nuclear construction] in the open market" means that, "without government guarantees to hold down interest rates for new nuclear build," no new reactors will be built.[322]

Regarding (b), uncounted nuclear subsidies, SUNY physicist Smith notes that, throughout its history, nuclear power has had to be "pushed along by large government subsidies." Yet he warns: "Despite the magnitude of these [additional] proposed subsidies, they would still not be large enough to fully overcome the higher costs of nuclear power."[323] Brown concurs, noting that "without subsidy no new nuclear power station has ever been constructed";[324] he also warns that a "major public subsidy [of fission] is insurance against accident and the increasing bill for security."[325] In France, he says, "the public pays for the nuclear industry twice, through its electricity bills and again through its taxes. The true cost of nuclear energy in France is a state secret and has never been disclosed."[326] As already mentioned, taxpayer subsidies account for 60–90 percent of the cost of proposed new US reactors.[327]

Regarding (c), correcting nuclear-industry data and assumptions, SUNY physicist Smith criticizes the "highly optimistic assumptions" of industry. He criticizes the MIT 5-year reactor-construction assumption, because the US National Academy of Sciences says the figure is 12.2 years. Smith also shows that, given flawed interest and construction-time assumptions, industry has underestimated reactor-construction costs by 75 percent. In the overly optimistic MIT study (which assumed a nuclear-interest rate of 11.5 percent), Smith says MIT claimed interest charges represented only 20 percent of nuclear-capital costs; however, Smith argues that, if one raises this nuclear-interest rate to 12.5 percent (not even the "going rate" of 15 percent, as shown earlier), interest charges become 40 percent of nuclear-capital costs and make fission even less economical. After correcting many erroneous assumptions, Smith concludes: "It is unlikely that any significant improvements to the economics of nuclear power could be sustained."[328]

What follows from the 4 classes of nuclear-cost studies (Groups A–D), given that analyses in each group share comparable funding and make similar assumptions? One conclusion is that of the 30 studies whose funders are known, a majority (18 in Group A) appear to be performed or funded by pro-nuclear interests. A second conclusion is that, perhaps as a consequence, studies performed or funded by pro-nuclear interests (Group A) are most of those that trim fission-cost data. A third conclusion is that studies performed or funded by pro-nuclear interests are most of those that exclude evidence-based credit-rating data and taxpayer-subsidy data on high nuclear costs. A fourth conclusion is that most of the 11 analyses (Groups C and D) that include credit-rating and taxpayer-subsidy data and use actual empirical data for cost assumptions are studies that are at least partly university-funded (the 7 in Group D). A fifth conclusion is that 4 of these 11 analyses— the Group C studies, which are funded by nonprofit NGOs—also include credit-rating and taxpayer-subsidy data and empirically based cost assumptions. Thus, a sixth conclusion is that most nuclear-cost studies (the 18 in Group A) appear to underestimate nuclear costs, perhaps because they are either performed or funded by nuclear interests. A seventh conclusion is that a minority of nuclear-cost studies (4 in Group C plus 7 in Group D) more accurately assess fission costs because they use empirical data, not industry assumptions, and because their authors have no obvious financial COI.

Moreover, although most studies that "get things right" are university-funded analyses (the 7 studies in Group D), not all university work is unbiased. Rather, 6 of the 18 nuclear-funded studies were done at universities (Chicago,[329] Lappeenranta,[330] MIT,[331] Rice[332]), yet all exclude credit-rating and massive taxpayer-subsidy data; all use industry-projected and not historical-data-based assumptions; and all draw unrealistic conclusions about positive nuclear economics. Therefore, an eighth conclusion is that university-performed studies cannot protect against bias if industries with financial COI fund university research. However, a tenth conclusion is that, if funders of university-based studies have no obvious financial COI, these studies appear most reliable.

Why Nuclear-Cost Studies Fall into COI

Why do a majority of nuclear-cost studies apparently succumb to data-trimming and biased policy conclusions in favor of atomic energy? The answer may not be merely that they are performed or funded by those with apparent financial COI. Rather, part of the answer may be that COI are difficult to handle, so as to protect all legitimate interests.[333] Another answer may be that although traditional professional codes of ethics typically require professionals to protect the public, these codes do not require full public disclosure of financial COI. For instance, the US General Services Administration, in its Federal Acquisition Regulations (FAR), does not require that consultants publicly disclose COI when they perform government-sponsored research. Because federal officials are not required to publicly disclose COIs, they are handled privately, within government confines. Provisions like FAR thus may help explain problematic assumptions in many nuclear-cost studies, For instance, rather than requiring public disclosure of COI, instead FAR section 9.504(a)(2) says government officials should "avoid, neutralize, or mitigate significant potential conflicts [of interest]" or obtain waivers for COI when acquiring work from consultants or scientists. Rather than requiring full public disclosure of COI, FAR section 9.506(b) requires only that if a "government contracting officer" decides a particular action involves "a significant potential organizational conflict of interest, the contracting officer shall…submit for approval to the chief of the contracting office" a written analysis of the COI and how to mitigate or avoid it, so that the approving official can "approve, modify, or reject the recommendations in writing."[334]

Likewise, US National Science Foundation (NSF) policies do not require public COI disclosure in government-sponsored research. Instead NSF requires only that an institution such as a university have a written COI policy, "manage" all COI prior to expending NSF funds, and ensure that grantees disclose to a "responsible representative of the institution [e.g., university] all significant financial interests of the investigator," so the representative can certify to NSF that all COIs have been mitigated or avoided. Scientists need make no COI disclosure in their resulting research, to the public, or to NSF. NSF requires only that it be informed about any "unresolved conflict" of interest and that, otherwise, the institutional "representative" handle COIs.[335]

Similarly, the ethics code of the National Society of Professional Engineers (NSPE) does not require public disclosure of COIs. Instead section II.4 of the NSPE code requires merely that engineers "disclose all known or potential conflicts of interest to their employers or clients by promptly informing them of any business association, interest, or other circumstances which could influence or appear to influence their judgment or the quality of their services."[336] The Accreditation Board for Engineering and Technology (ABET) likewise requires (Guideline 1) no public disclosure of COI—only that analysts do work "consistent with…the safety, health, and welfare of the public and…disclose promptly factors that might endanger the public." Yet this disclosure does not include the public. Instead ABET says (Procedures) only that "copies of the conflict of interest records will be provided" to officers selecting the analysts and their evaluators. ABET also requires (Guideline 4) that analysts "keep confidential all…evaluations unless by doing so they endanger the public."[337]

How Energy-Cost Studies Should Be Done

However, if analysts knew that their possible COI could be disclosed publicly, they might avoid counterfactual or biased assumptions in their work. Given that scientists and engineers deserve privacy and yet that clients and affected parties (including the public) deserve protection from COI, how could the 30 nuclear-cost analyses examined in this chapter have avoided both COI and their questionable assumptions? As previous paragraphs explained, there is no canonical study of nuclear costs. Nevertheless, one can specify at least 5 necessary conditions that might make energy-economics analyses more reliable. Although specifying necessary and sufficient conditions is impossible, it clearly is wrong to exclude relevant data, as many nuclear studies have done.

Following the earlier brief discussion of COI, one necessary condition for reliable nuclear-cost analyses is attempting to avoid financial COI. In sections 9.505-2(b)(1)-9.508(a)-(e), US FAR for instance, clearly say that analyses ought not be done by those who have personal or organizational COI. These regulations specify that "contracts for the evaluation of offers for products or services shall not be awarded to a contractor that will evaluate its own offers for products or services"; that the same scientists who prepare "a work statement" for some system "may not supply the system"; that scientists who might "provide systems engineering and technical direction" to a government agency for a reactor "should not be allowed to supply any power-plant components"; or that the same consultants who "prepare data-system specifications and...criteria...should be excluded from" supplying any "information technology" for that system.[338] In other words, US government COI guidelines require avoiding situations in which those who assess some technology are the same scientists with financial interests in it.

Yet in the majority of analyses examined here (18 of the 30 nuclear-cost studies done since 2000)—including the majority of nuclear-cost studies cited by the WNA,[339] by the UK government commission,[340] and by the Greenpeace study—the same pro-nuclear groups who have financial interests in atomic energy assessed fission technology by radically trimming nuclear costs.[341] Moreover, virtually all of these COI-tainted studies were used to help justify partial government "acquisition" or subsidy of nuclear power. Thus it is not surprising, as one UK government study warned, that fission-industry "cost estimates need to be treated with some caution as the vendors' commercial incentive is clearly to estimate optimistically."[342]

A second necessary condition, for cost studies that cannot avoid COI, is to mitigate their effects by publicizing them. As the earlier discussion suggested, this requires at least reporting, in the study itself, the full personal and institutional financial ties of those who perform or fund the analyses. Obviously, this disclosure is not sufficient to help protect against COI, but it is necessary.[343] The public has a right to know about the quality of studies used to evaluate possible government subsidies, which are taxpayer dollars. Yet few studies funded by nuclear interests reveal full funding sources in their pages. For instance, in one MIT case,[344] the study said funding partly came from an MIT lab, yet failed to disclose who funded the lab—the nuclear industry. If relevant financial ties (as with the lab) are reported by scientists and their institutions, they more likely will perform studies that withstand COI scrutiny. As a recent US National Academy of Sciences committee put it: "The disclosure of individual and institutional financial relationships is a critical but limited first step in the process of identifying and responding to conflicts of interest."[345]

A third necessary condition, especially for energy-cost studies, is employing lifecycle-cost analysis. With fission, such analyses should at least include costs associated with uranium mining, milling, conversion to uranium hexafluoride (UF_6), enriching UF_6, fuel fabrication, reactor construction, reactor operation, waste-fuel processing, fuel conditioning, interim waste storage, waste transport, permanent storage, reactor decommissioning, and uranium-mine reclamation. Although this chapter showed that typical economic analyses include only several stages of the nuclear-fuel cycle (e.g., reactor construction and operation),[346] traditional codes of professional ethics, such as ABET Guidelines 5(c)-6(a), prohibit professionals from "omitting a material fact," from "distorting or altering the facts," and from "any conduct that deceives the public."[347] Yet this chapter shows that data-trimming nuclear costs omits material facts, distorts the facts, and may deceive the public. Lifecycle-cost analysis may help reduce these problems.

Doing lifecycle-cost analyses of energy systems also is important to ensure using limited resources efficiently, to avoid flawed and misleading accounting, to obtain the highest energy and environmental values for the lowest cost, to make rational energy-policy decisions, and to make energy-decision-making transparent and cost-effective.[348] In the US, the federal government says lifecycle-cost analysis is both necessary and the best way to implement Executive Order 13101 ("Greening the Government") and Executive Order 13423 ("Strengthening Federal Environmental, Energy, and Transportation Management).[349] In part to satisfy executive orders, the US National Institute of Standards and Technology (NIST) has long had a software program, BEES (Building for Environmental and Economic Sustainability), that enables government purchasers and policymakers to use lifecycle-cost analyses to make economic, environmentally sustainable decisions about acquiring products and services—as mandated by the International Organization for Standardization (ISO) 14040 requirements for measuring environmental and economic performance.[350] For all these reasons, the US National Academy of Sciences says "many federal acquisition policies...require life-cycle costing," and it too has recommended life-cycle-costing in order to achieve "performance standards," "preferable products," and "sustainable development and value engineering."[351] Without lifecycle-cost analysis, public decisions about energy choices may ignore externalities that dominate costs. For instance, the International Energy Agency (IEA) points out that, because nuclear subsidies and *negative* externalities (e.g., taxpayer funding of most reactor-construction costs and permanent waste storage) are typically not included in *nuclear-cost* calculations, this causes nuclear-cost *underestimates*. Likewise, IEA says that because the *positive* externalities that lower costs (e.g., no fuel waste, no electricity-generation emissions, no catastrophic insurance needed) are typically not included in *renewable-energy cost* calculations, renewable-energy costs are *overestimates*. Yet, "unrewarded [beneficial] environmental characteristics" of renewable-energy technologies, such as wind, are "the principal barrier to increasing the market share for renewable energy."[352]

A fourth necessary condition for reliable energy-cost assessment is ensuring that energy-cost estimates are consistent with credit-rating and market data. When one uses nuclear-cost estimates based on credit-rating data, as many apparently reliable studies do,[353] they are up to 350 percent higher than industry estimates (e.g., from the WNA),[354] and nearly 200 percent higher than those from groups (like MIT), funded by the nuclear industry.[355] Regarding the importance of credit-rating data, section 9.506(a) of US FAR note that if information is "necessary to identify and evaluate potential organizational conflicts of interest or to develop recommended actions [to mitigate COI]," government officials should seek information from both government groups, such as "audit activities and offices," and from nongovernmental sources, such as "publications...credit-rating services, trade and financial journals."[356]

A fifth necessary condition also comes from section 9.506(a) of the US FAR. It mandates that cost analyses should undergo reliable peer review by technical specialists and that federal officers who contract for studies, services, or products "should obtain the advice of counsel and the assistance of appropriate technical specialists in evaluating potential conflicts [of interest] and in developing any necessary...contract clauses."[357] Yet, there is no evidence that any nuclear-cost-study contracting groups, such as the US DOE—which funded the University of Chicago,[358] Scully,[359] and other nuclear-cost studies—had "technical specialists" evaluate them. Part of the reason for this failure may be that, at least since 1990, as chapter 2 showed, the US DOE has been repeatedly criticized by the US Congress, by government oversight agencies, and by the agency's own inspector general for its pro-nuclear biases and poor science; the COI criticisms of DOE have been so severe that the US Office of Technology Assessment and the Congress repeatedly have recommended either abolition of the US DOE or its regulation by an outside agency. Neither has occurred.[360]

The Climate Importance of Nuclear-Cost Assessments

Given CC problems, getting nuclear costs "right" is especially important because society needs economically efficient, low-carbon solutions, not inefficient guesses based on trimmed economic-cost data. However, if faulty fission analyses (like those just investigated) dominate CC discussions, they could jeopardize the groundswell of support for further increases in cheaper, cleaner technologies like wind.[361] As a recent UK government commission notes, "Plans for new nuclear generation can therefore be expected to depress the market's appetite" for renewable-technology "investment, relative to what it otherwise would be," because there would be "a trade off between funding of nuclear power and funding of renewable."[362] Given this trade-off, it is especially important to get nuclear costs right.

Even without considering the data-trimming assessed in this chapter, nuclear costs roughly triple those of wind. As already noted, credit-rating firms say nuclear-fission electricity cost more than $0.15/kWhr in early 2008,[363] and $0.21/kWhr in late 2009.[364] Yet the US DOE says US full-fuel-cycle wind prices, on average over the last 7 years, are $0.048/kWh,[365] and global wind potential is 35 times greater than current global electricity use.[366] As chapter 6 points out in more detail, IRA says wind costs have been dropping 18 percent (and solar-photovoltaic costs, 35 percent) for every installed-capacity doubling, while atomic-energy costs have been increasing.[367] By 2015 (a decade sooner than reactors, ordered today, could be operational), even the pro-nuclear US DOE says full-fuel-cycle centralized-solar-photovoltaic prices will be $0.05–0.10/kWh (depending on location), "competitive in markets nationwide," and much cheaper than nuclear.[368] Solar photovoltaics on only 7 percent of US land currently used for parking lots and buildings could provide all US electricity.[369] Given such data, it is not surprising that atomic energy has been losing private markets. As already noted, by 2005, non-hydro renewable energy was annually growing 7 times faster than nuclear.[370] In 2006, global added new wind capacity was 10 times greater than global added new nuclear capacity; in 2006, carbon-free renewable energy added 40 times more capacity globally than did nuclear; in 2007, carbon-free renewable energy gained more than $90 billion in global investment, and in 12 nations, renewable energy now provides between 17 and 50 percent of total electricity needs.[371] As already mentioned, US government data, for the latest year available, show that wind has been responsible for 60 percent of annual new-electricity capacity, as measured by peak summer demand.[372] Also as noted earlier, the classic 2004 Princeton University study shows that 6 of only 9 renewable technologies, already deployed at an industrial scale, could completely solve the climate problem by 2050; the US DOE is even more optimistic, arguing that available renewable technology can provide 99 percent of US electricity by 2020.[373] Given these other, cheaper, lower-carbon (see chapter 2) energy options, nuclear fission is especially questionable.

Objections

Objecting to the preceding conclusions, one might ask whether nuclear analyses should use actual, historical-average data (as done here), or projected data (as industry does). However, as already noted, governments of many nations, including the UK and the US, have repeatedly said nuclear-industry cost estimates have consistently (since the beginning of the technology) been underestimates by several hundred percent. This suggests that, while it might be reasonable to use some projected-cost data, the nuclear industry's own cost projections are not reliable. Besides, using projected cost data would require using hypothetical, untested data that have been provided by those who would profit from optimistic or low price estimates—a clear COI. For instance, the nuclear industry admits that reactors always have a minimum of 4–6 years of lower (50-percent) load factors, until "bugs" are removed.[374] If so, more optimistic, projected nuclear-fission price estimates make little sense, at least for the first 5 years. Moreover, if industry's projected-cost numbers were correct, most banks would make nuclear loans, and reactor vendors would guarantee specific lifetimes and nuclear-load factors for clients. Yet neither will do so.[375] Thus vendors, utilities, and the market itself all challenge projected counterfactual nuclear-fission-cost estimates. Also, as already mentioned, after 50-plus years of commercial implementation (as with fission), most technologies already have achieved all likely improvements.[376] The nuclear industry itself, at least in part, also appears to admit that future fission costs will increase, not decrease, because, despite taxpayers' massive atomic-energy subsidies,[377] the nuclear-industry lobby says high costs will rule nuclear "out of consideration" in the future; by 2030, the WNA says fission will decrease from its current 16 percent of global electricity to 9 percent.[378] For all these reasons, nuclear-industry proponents' low-cost projections seem practically unrealistic, economically unsound, and unethical, given the COI associated with these projections.

Second, one might ask why so many countries use fission-generated electricity if reactors are uneconomical. Likewise, third, one might ask whether this analysis ignores the intermittency of renewable technologies, like wind and solar. Finally, fourth, one might ask whether it seems plausible for nuclear-cost research to have erred as badly as this chapter argues. These additional objections, and several others, will be discussed in detail in chapter 7.

Conclusions

What follows from the preceding analysis? It showed that, although many industry advocates claim nuclear reactors are an inexpensive way to generate low-carbon electricity and thus address CC, nearly all nuclear-fission-cost estimates (most of which are produced by the industry) are examples of grossly flawed science. Surveying all 30 recent nuclear-electricity analyses, this chapter shows that all industry-funded studies fall into conflicts of interest and illegitimately trim relevant cost data. Most studies exclude costs of full-liability insurance, underestimate reactor-construction-loan interest rates and construction times by using "overnight" costs, and overestimate reactor load factors and lifetimes. Yet if these 5 false assumptions are corrected, market costs (excluding subsidies, which are billions of dollars per year) of fission-generated electricity can be shown to be roughly 6 times more expensive than most studies claim—and far more expensive than available renewable energy. If this chapter is correct, the proposed nuclear solution to CC is as trouble-some as CC itself.

This chapter shows that nuclear power is a market failure; yet governments should be subsidizing technologies that are, or will be, market winners. As the chapter reveals, it also makes no sense to use atomic energy when its fuel cycle produces only 25 percent more energy than what must be input to it. Nuclear power thus requires subsidizing an old, expensive, dirty, nonsustainable technology of the past. Wind, solar PV, and other renewable-energy sources allow us to embrace newer, cheaper, cleaner, sustainable technologies of the future. The market and common sense are on the side of the future.

CHAPTER 4

Fukushima, Chernobyl, Three Mile Island: Flawed Science and Accident Cover-Up

Multiple earthquakes. A tsunami.[1] Fires. At least 3 different nuclear core melts. At least 4 different explosions spewing highly radioactive debris for miles. Roofs and walls blown off reactors. Gaping holes ripped in nuclear containment. Hot, highly radioactive fuel demolishing layers of concrete and steel. Continuing releases of lethal radiation. Uncontrolled, runaway reactors and radioactive-spent-fuel storage pools. "Extremely intense radioactivity."[2] Doses of 500 millisieverts(mSv) per hour—enough to cause cancer fatalities in everyone exposed for only2 hours.[3] High radiation levels, making it impossible to control the situation for many months. Continuing radioactive contamination, and 700,000 refugees. People left for weeks without electricity, heat, or running water. Some victims receiving only one and a half rice balls daily for food. Empty stores. "Chronic shortages of everything from rice to gasoline." Sick people without medicines. Hospital patients irradiated by a miles-away nuclear disaster. Two million households without water. Many nations telling their citizens to leave Japan and warning others not to travel there.[4] Foreign airlines suspending flights to Japan. "Radioactive particles on the seafloor at over 1,000 times normal level—20 km from Fukushima." Harmful radiation releases "in Japan kept secret to avoid 'panic in the whole of society'." Months after the disaster began, performers continue canceling concerts scheduled in Japan. "Crew members on Justin Bieber's tour refuse go to Japan for upcoming shows in Tokyo, Osaka because of radiation."[5]

The drumbeat of bad news has continued, many months after Japan's Fukushima Daiichi (FD) accident began, largely because the offending nuclear plant still had not been brought under control by summer 2011. Unfolding on March 11, 2011, the disaster began partly as a result of the 9.0 earthquake and tsunami that hit Japan the same day. Roughly 12,000 people have been confirmed dead, and 16,000 people missing. Perhaps even worse, these seismic and flooding catastrophes knocked out the electricity required for the nuclear-core-cooling systems at FD's 6 reactors and 6 nuclear-storage pools. Without continuous operation of the cooling systems, radioactive fires, explosions, nuclear meltdowns, and massive radioactive contamination continue. The result? After several months of stopgap measures, by summer 2011 FD still had at least 5 uncontrolled nuclear installations, all still in crisis mode since March 11, 2011. Complete loss of containment in any 1 of the 12 FD facilities could alone kill 138,000 people; contaminate 2,170 square miles; and cause $550–700 billion in damages.[6] So far, the continuing disaster has irradiated people and the outside environment at lethal doses, up to 800 times the regulatory limit, "lofting the radiation in clouds that... spread the radioactivity."[7]

The most vulnerable continue to be hurt most. After several weeks, thousands of victims, too old or too sick to flee from the FD disaster, still faced "starvation... trapped in their homes or refugee shelters" because "delivery trucks refused" to come within tens of miles of FD.[8] They also were trapped, as the Japanese Prime Minister put it, because "The first priority is the accident response. Then it [government] needs to help those who have been affected."[9] "Bodies of hundreds of people... lay unburied near the plant because they were contaminated by radiation.... The police and morgue workers were unable to handle them safely."[10] Warned of radioactive contamination, many families also remained unable "to recover the remains of loved ones," even after months.[11] Rescue workers themselves, retrieving some of the dead, have been overcome with post-traumatic stress disorder.[12] US Navy helicopter crews, flying relief missions for the first 3 weeks of the disaster, have been contaminated.[13] Yet many Japanese who are still alive, but victimized by the nuclear disaster, have been "marooned" for weeks without roads, electricity, or water; they must "forage for firewood," "lug water from the marsh," and wait for relief workers giving them "their one meal a day"—a piece of bread, a can of tuna, and a pack of instant noodles. Some people have only several days of medicine and no way to get to the hospital to receive either medicine or medical care.[14]

Distant people also continue to be affected. Within 2 weeks after the accident began, FD radiation was "found everywhere" throughout the globe. Princeton University scientist Robert Socolow confirmed that the FD contamination will remain "measurable throughout the lifetimes of everyone alive today." Months after the accident began, experts at Stanford University and the University of Michigan continued to warn: "The situation remains serious, and radioactivity continues to be released."[15]

Tokyo, the world's most populous metropolitan area, has been particularly hard hit, although it is 140 miles from FD. Only a week after the accident and radiation releases began, Tokyo's 40 million people faced radiation levels 20 times above normal. Months after the Fukushima disaster began, Rotterdam officials warned that radioactive contamination—found on containers from Japan at levels 50 times greater than the maximum limit—"could be dangerous," In the San Francisco Bay and many other areas, scientists reported that levels of the dangerous and long-lived cesium -137 from FD were continuing to rise in their topsoil. In fact, scores of US and European radiation detectors continue to signal that the FD accident is contaminating their air, their water, and their food.[16]

Given continuing radiation releases and continuing inability to control the FD reactors and spent-fuel pools, it is not surprising that only weeks after the accident began, the Japanese utility, the Japanese nuclear commission, and international scientists all were forced to warn that FD radioactive leaks would "exceed Chernobyl" in their levels of contamination. Yet assessments published by the New York Academy of Sciences in 2009 showed that Chernobyl will cause roughly 1 million additional premature fatalities throughout the world. One reason FD contamination will exceed that of Chernobyl is that, months after the accident and releases began, the United Nations' International Atomic Energy Agency (IAEA) warned that nuclear explosions could still be continuing; that heavy radioactive "smoke continues to be emitted" from FD; and that health hazards to the US would have to be reassessed. International scientists agree that the Japanese government has "covered up" the high levels of FD radioactive contamination, especially contamination far outside the 12-mile, government-evacuation zone, Yet, less than 2 months after the FD contamination began, the US government "abandoned efforts to monitor elevated levels of radiation that infiltrated the nation's water and milk in the wake of" the FD disaster. Responding to this lack of monitoring, University of California scientist Dan Hirsch said he was "horrified." He warned that abandoning US monitoring "is quite staggering, and it seems to be part of the pattern of... trying to make sure that there are no measurements that could cause people to be concerned".[17]

Overview of the Chapter

What does the continuing Japanese nuclear disaster tell us about reactor safety and whether atomic energy can contribute to addressing climate change? Answering this question, the chapter explains what went wrong in Japan, why these same weaknesses plague reactors throughout the world, and why—decades earlier—similar, unheeded weaknesses caused the Three Mile Island (TMI) accident and the Chernobyl accident, from both of which regulators and industry have failed to learn all their lessons. After investigating the radiation doses, health effects, and economic consequences of the FD accident, the chapter argues for 6 main claims. (1) The FD nuclear disaster in Japan, like the TMI accident in Pennsylvania, was not a rare or black-swan event, but predictable because of weak regulation, industry's cost-cutting, deferred maintenance, ignoring earlier "near misses," and "spinning the science." (2) Likewise, neither FD nor TMI nor Chernobyl radiation releases were as trivial as government and industry tried to claim in their blame-the-victim arguments. Rather, all 3 accidents caused measurable cancers and injuries that government and industry have tried to minimize by "spinning the science." (3) In particular, flawed inductive methods help explain why the accepted causal hypothesis S (that TMI-related stress and not radiation caused most observed TMI health problems) is less plausible than alternative hypothesis R (that TMI-accident radiation and not stress more likely caused these injuries and deaths). (4) Many scientists erroneously reject R and accept S because of conflicts of interest (COI) and their misuse of classical statistical tests. (5) However, because TMI data are non-experimental, inference to the best explanation, especially contrastive explanation, illuminates competing causal hypotheses S and R better than do standard statistical tests. (6) Once scientists use correct scientific methods, it is clear that hypothesis R and not S is more likely, that nuclear fission is an extremely risky technology, and that it ought not be used to try to address climate change.

Fukushima's Economic, Environmental, and Health Effects

Perhaps most surprising about the FD disaster is that it is occurring in the world's third-largest economy, worth $5 trillion: in a nation with virtually unlimited resources, with advanced education, and with technology as sophisticated as any in the world. It also seems surprising that the best scientists from France, Japan, the US, and elsewhere still cannot control the Japanese and American nuclear technology that is continuing the FD disaster. After the 1986 Chernobyl accident, some people claimed that a commercial-reactor catastrophe could never happen in a highly developed country. Yet FD proves than it can.

FD also proves that the economic effects of nuclear disasters can be massive. Perhaps it is not surprising that the stock of the FD owner, Tokyo Electric, fell 80 percent within 2 weeks after the accident began, and that only government bailout can prevent the destruction of the company; it is more surprising, however, that a wealthy nation like Japan needs an emergency tax increase "to help finance relief and recovery work," that a nuclear meltdown is leading to a financial meltdown.[18] Likewise, perhaps it is not surprising that, within weeks, radioactive contamination has forced the government to ban the crops of more than 70,000 Japanese farmers who annually produce more than $2.4 billion worth of milk and vegetables. Yet it does seem surprising that if "all the agriculture is gone," the Japanese utility and government are unlikely to compensate these farmers.[19] As later paragraphs show, perhaps the reason is that, not counting farm losses, FD accident damages alone will be in the hundreds of billions of dollars.

In Tokyo, 140 miles from the accident, the water supply is radioactively contaminated, forcing officials to distribute bottled water.[20] The Tokyo area also faces months of rolling blackouts, factory closures, fuel shortages, and an economy of nearly 40 million people trying to live with Japan's bullet trains running only at 20 percent of their normal schedules.[21] The world's largest fish market, in Tokyo, also is "finished.... Gone. Hopeless."[22] Rejecting all Japanese fish and produce, many nations, restaurants, and food importers throughout the world have purchased radiation detectors to test all imported produce, especially any grown anywhere with fish-emulsion fertilizers.[23] Countless global supply chains have been impacted. Only weeks after the accident, digital chips jumped 40 percent in price because the disaster destroyed factories of a major supplier, Toshiba. From Subaru in Indiana, to GM in Louisiana, automakers face stopped or slowed production because of inability to get Japanese parts. Canon, Fujitsu, Honda, Mazda, Mitsubishi, Nissan, Sony, Subaru, Suzuki, Toshiba, Toyota, and many other companies have closed factories for weeks because of parts problems.[24]

The economic effects of the FD disaster are not surprising, however, once one realizes the enormity of Japanese radioactive contamination. At the plant, long-lived cesium-134 and other radioactive isotopes have poisoned soils at levels up to 7.5 million times the regulatory limit; radiation outside plant boundaries has been found at doses up to 12 mSv per hour, the equivalent of getting about 4 years' worth of radiation each hour—or getting about 7 chest X-rays per hour.[25] Cumulative in their effects, many of these doses are ongoing and will be lethal. Later paragraphs show they could get even worse. Also, outside the plant perimeter, other doses have been measured at 8.22 mSv per hour.[26] After several months of exposure at this hourly dose, all the fatal cancers of those exposed would be attributable to FD radiation.[27]

About 19 miles northwest of the FD plant, air-radiation readings have been 0.8 mSv per hour; after 2.5 days of this exposure, roughly 1 in 20 of the fatal cancers of those exposed would be attributable to FD radiation; after 5 days of this exposure, 1 in 10 of the fatal cancers of those exposed would be attributable to it; after 2 months of this exposure, 19 miles from the plant, most of the fatal cancers of those exposed would be attributable to FD radiation. Yet residents in this 19-mile area are not within the mandatory evacuation zone of the Japanese government.[28] Even farther outside the 12-mile evacuation zone—and less than 2 weeks after the accident began—soil 25 miles northwest of the plant had cesium-137 levels "twice as high as the threshold for declaring areas uninhabitable around Chernobyl"; this level of contamination suggests "the land might need to be abandoned."[29] Still, months after the FD disaster began, the Japanese government insisted that it had plans neither "to expand the [12-mile] zone" of evacuation, nor to begin soil cleanup of cesium. Yet, to avoid poisoning the entire food chain for thousands of years, soil "decontamination has to be done very quickly," or it cannot be done at all. Instead, Japanese authorities have ordered the evacuation only of areas that were receiving more than 20 mSv per year from the damaged FD reactors and storage pools. Yet this evacuation policy and dose limit are problematic for at least 10 reasons. For one thing, (1) this allowed dose is 20 times higher than allowable public exposures to radiation, and as the chapter later explains, (2) there is no safe dose of ionizing radiation. (3) *Each year* of this allowed 20 mSv dose of FD radiation would cause an additional 2 percent of adults' lifetime fatal cancers to be attributable to FD exposures—and an additional 20 percent to

76 percent of children's fatal cancers to be attributable to FD exposures. This means that (4) children will be hurt most by such lax Japanese radiation standards because the FD dose limit covers "schools for younger children, including elementary and junior high." After less than 2 years of such exposure, 100 percent of the children's fatal cancers will be attributed to FD exposures. Moreover, (5) these FD standards are set to avoid only immediate, "observable health risks," not to avoid later cancers, genetic defects, and deaths. (6) The weak standards also ignore the fact that FD doses are cumulative in effect and continuing. Instead, (7) the FD dose limit is driven by "a cramped nation with little space to spare," rather than by "public safety." As a consequence, standard radiation-dose-response calculations reveal that (8) Japanese officials err when say the 20 mSv allowed-dose limit would "raise the rate of cancer deaths by far less than one percent," At a minimum, (9) the IAEA and US have urged Japan to evacuate people up to 50 miles, not 12 miles, from the continuing leaking, out-of-control reactors. Besides, (10) the Fukushima reactors and spent-fuel-storage pools have "been dispersing radioactive material...far longer than the 10 days during which the Chernobyl plant" released radiation in 1986.[30]

Apart from air and soil contamination, tons of irradiated water have leaked from FD into the Pacific, at doses of 1,000 mSv per hour; because there is no room to store tons of other contaminated water, Japanese officials deliberately have dumped it directly into the Pacific.[31] Yet a 1,000 mSv radiation dose is massive, enough to cause nausea and vomiting. Because triple this dose is lethal, people could die after only 3 hours of exposure. In the open seas, FD radiation levels have been measured at 5 million times the legal limit. Seaweed and fish concentrate radiation further, up to 10,000-fold above the water's radiation level. This biomagnification is why, within weeks after the accident began, Japanese fisherman discovered fish contaminated with at least double the regulated limit of radiation. Even 19 miles from the crippled plant, the IAEA said waterborne-radiation doses were thousands of times above normal.[32]

The health effects of such massive FD radioactive contamination have been worsened, as already noted, because of Japanese coverup and failure to implement adequately protective health standards. For instance, 5 weeks after the disaster began, Japan said contaminated schools would not be cleaned up, but could be used, if their radiation levels were below 3.8 microsieverts per hour. This allowed dose is equivalent to exposures of about 20 mSv per year, or about 20 times higher than allowable public exposures. Yet, as chapter 5 explains in more detail, children are roughly 10 to 38 times more sensitive to ionizing radiation than adults are. This means, as already noted, that *each year* of allowed FD radiation doses of 20 mSv would cause an additional 2 percent of adults' lifetime fatal cancers to be attributable to FD exposures—and an additional 20 percent to 76 percent of children's fatal cancers to be attributable to FD. Given such data, on April 30, 2011, nearly 2 months after the Fukushima disaster began, Toshiso Kosako, a University of Tokyo radiation-safety expert and government advisor resigned. "During a tearful news conference...he charged that the government was not adequately protecting the population from radiation" and that children should not be allowed to receive 20 mSv annual FD doses. Besides condemning Japanese-government radiation standards for children, Kosako also criticized "an overly high limit on radiation exposure for workers who have spent weeks struggling to keep the plant under control" and government "lack of transparency in releasing radiation levels around the Fukushima Daiichi plant." He said "many Japanese suspect [the government] of understating the true danger at the plant," in order to save cleanup money, avoid panic, and prevent people from shunning Japanese fish and agriculture.[33]

Fukushima Is Forever: "Worse Than the Chernobyl Accident ... Could Persist Indefinitely"

Two of the most disturbing aspects of the FD disaster are that its cleanup will take roughly a century, and that effects of its continuing contamination will continue nearly forever, given the massive amounts of long-lived radioactive isotopes that are still being released, as of summer 2011. "Fukushima is forever" because long-lived FD radiation not only will cause additional cancers for up to 60 years for those exposed, but also is causing germline mutations that will increase cancer, other diseases, and death for centuries. At least 4 FD nuclear-fuel-pool explosions already have occurred, and physicians say that even one such explosion causes "millions of new cases of cancer in the Northern Hemisphere." Particularly fortunate FD cancer victims may go into remission from the disease, but as this chapter explains, the human gene pool will almost never be rid of the FD mutations that will cause future cancer rates to increase. As radiation expert and physician Helen Caldicott puts it: "The mutations caused in cells by this radiation are generally deleterious.... There are now more than 2,600 genetic diseases on record, any one of which may be caused by a radiation-induced mutation, and many of which we're bound to see more of, because we are artifially increasing background levels of radiation."[34]

"Fukushima is forever" also because it will require roughly a 100-year cleanup, a "Chernobyl-like effort" during which additional radiation releases will occur, causing increased cancers, other diseases, germline mutations, and deaths. After all, the Chernobyl (Belarus) nuclear accident occurred in 1986, and its clean-up is scheduled through 2065, with delays likely. Similarly, the earliest the final cleanup of the 1957 Windscale, UK nuclear accident will occur is 2032, yet no commercial accidents have caused contamination as massive as that at FD. The Japanese cleanup will be enormous and lengthy (a) because FD explosions have spewed highly radioactive debris for many miles; (b) because lethal contamination means it will take years before anyone can even look inside the cores; (c) because robots will be needed for the work; (d) because multi-billion-dollar buildings must be built around each of the 6 damaged FD reactors and 6 storage pools; (e) because only the government, not the utility, can afford the massive, multi-billion-dollar cleanup; and (f) because the absence of working core-cooling systems has required continually flooding the reactors and continually creating thousands of tons of new, highly radioactive waste water that has either escaped or been deliberately dumped into the environment. Only weeks after the FD disaster began, the Japanese deliberately dumped "more than 10,000 tonnes" (11,023 tons) of radioactive water "into the Pacific Ocean to make way for more-radioactive cooling water".

Robert Alvarez, the US secretary of energy during the Clinton administration, says the FD catastrophe is likely to be the worst-ever nuclear disaster to date, worse than the Chernobyl accident because it has not been brought under control; because it involves 12 facilities, not 1 reactor, as at Chernobyl; and because it includes nuclear-fuel-pool accidents. Fuel-poor accidents are worse than reactor meltdowns because they involve explosions that shoot intense radioactivity for extraordinarily great distances. Yet, fires, explosions, and nuclear melts could occur at FD for a long time. It will take "years to stabilize the 6 reactors and spent-fuel pools" that have been in runaway mode since the March 11, 2011, earthquake, tsunami, and nuclear disaster.[35] Even "after the fission process has stopped," the reactors and fuel pools will be unstable for years if they have no continuous cooling.[36] In fact, the Japanese government has repeatedly admitted that "it could not predict when the nuclear complex would be brought under control"; that levels of nearby radiation in air and seawater were continuing to rise to thousands of times above the legal limit; and that measures taken so far were "stopgaps not solutions" to the crisis.[37]

The Reactor Safety Team of the US Nuclear Regulatory Commission (NRC) also has warned that the runaway FD reactors and fuel-storage pools face "threats that could persist indefinitely"[38] and that there could be additional "catastrophic explosions."[39] Former US energy secretary Alvarez said the FD disaster could cause "a catastrophic release of radiation that will not necessarily happen all at once, worse than the Chernobyl accident," and could make contaminated areas of land "uninhabitable for decades."[40] Consequently, as Japanese Chief Cabinet Secretary Yukio Edano warned, it is "unlikely that evacuations will be resolved soon."[41] Why not? As the Japanese Nuclear Safety Commission warned, "radiation levels are unlikely to decline for some time."[42] Of course, there are international plans for a century-long FD cleanup, "but no one knows when it can begin" because lethal radiation at the site prevents corrective action.[43] Even this cleanup, however, cannot address the widespread, long-lived global contamination, far from the plant.

Black-Swan Lies about Fukushima and Other Nuclear Accidents

Given the obviously hazardous radiation releases from FD, nuclear proponents would have a difficult time trying to argue that fission is a completely safe, reliable technology. What can they argue? As this chapter shows, they often attempt 2 types of justifications. One is the black-swan argument that, although nuclear accidents occur, they are very rare. The other attempted justification is the blame-the-victim argument—that although injuries or casualties occurred because of various nuclear disasters, most of these casualties were psychologically induced by the victims, not by radiation. Both of these flawed arguments were used after the Chernobyl accident and the TMI accident, and now they are being used after the FD accident. The remainder of this chapter shows how special interests often manipulate science in order to promote these flawed arguments and to claim nuclear safety. Consider first the black-swan argument.

Reporting on the 2011 FD disaster, both scientists and newspapers repeatedly quoted industry experts who claimed that the FD accident and any core melt were black-swan events, flukes, completely unpredictable.[44] Government representatives themselves, relying almost completely on industry-supplied data, also have repeatedly claimed that major nuclear accidents, core melts, are very rare events. In 2011, for instance, the Japanese Atomic Energy Commission has claimed that "the situation at the Fukushima Daiichi nuclear power plant continues to be unpredictable,"[45] suggesting that the FD accident could never have been foreseen.

Yet the opposite is the case. FD was not a black-swan event. Two weeks before the beginning of the March 11, 2011, FD disaster, Tokyo Electric, the plant owner, admitted that "it had failed to inspect 33 pieces of equipment" for the cooling system at the 6 FD reactors, that regulators said "maintenance management was inadequate" and that the "quality of inspection was insufficient"; regulators pointed to Tokyo Electric's attempts to "manipulate data," to its "uneven safety records, and [to] a history of cover-ups."[46] In 2004, regulators forced Tokyo Electric to temporarily shut down 17 plants after they discovered that the company had "falsified inspection records and hid flaws over 16 years—to save on repair costs."[47] Eisaku Sato, who for 18 years (until 2006) served as governor of Fukushima, where the 2011 FD accident occurred, calls Tokyo Electric "an organization that is inherently untrustworthy."[48] Moreover, as David Brenner, director of the Columbia University Center for Radiological Research, put it, it is obvious that Japan has "a fleet of aging nuclear reactors," with outdated safety protections and inadequate technology—despite the Japanese technology's being roughly the same as in 31 US reactors, some also in seismic zones.[49] Moreover, 2 months before the Fukushima earthquake, Japanese seismologists warned that the plates were "poised to slip catastrophically," and 1 month before the March 11 earthquake and tsunami crippled safety systems at 6 FD reactors and storage pools, government regulators "approved a 10-year extension" of the oldest of these Japanese reactors (40 years old), "despite warnings about safety."[50] The Japanese safety-review committee also warned of "stress cracks" in the same FD diesel backup-engines that were knocked out by the tsunami and that are used to run the emergency core-cooling system; for years, engineers who designed the 40-year-old GE reactors said that because the FD reactors were "outdated," they were more susceptible to explosions, accidents, and radiation releases than newer reactor designs.[51] Because nuclear proponents did not heed such warnings, they continued to use black-swan arguments.

Promoting the black-swan claim, many US government and industry officials also say nuclear-core melts are rare. In 2003, the US NRC used only nuclear-accident-probability estimates that were supplied by industry, then claimed that, for all 104 US reactors, a core-melt accident could be expected only once every 1,000 years; instead of basing this figure on government inspections and independent analyses, it relied merely "on data submitted by plant owners."[52] The US NRC predecessor agency, the US Atomic Energy Commission also has a long history of making black-swan claims, including that the probability of a US nuclear core melt is only 1 in 17,000 per reactor-year.[53] Where do such low probabilities come from? As just mentioned, often these probabilities are based merely on industry guesses or opinions, not actual accident-frequency data that industry and government possess.

At least 3 major reasons show that these black-swan, nuclear-core-melt probability guesses are wrong—are gross underestimates of reactor risks. *First,* the guesses are not based on actual empirical data, actual frequency data about accidents, but taken from industry opinions. As just shown, when the NRC assessed nuclear accidents in 2003, it used industry-supplied guesses, not its own frequency data, from actual operating experience. Likewise, although the classic, MIT-authored, US-government-funded study of nuclear-reactor safety had access to actual frequency data about various types of nuclear accidents that already had occurred after 20 years of operating-experience in US reactors, it did not use these frequency data, collected at Oak Ridge National Laboratories; instead the MIT authors used industry assumptions, calculations, and conjectures about the probability of these 7 types of reactor accidents.[54] Yet when independent, university mathematicians compared US nuclear-accident-frequency data reported from actual operating experience, with industry-government probability guesses, they discovered that all the "guesses" were far too low, by several orders of magnitude. Moreover, all of the higher-risk data, based on actual reactor-operating experience, showed no accident frequencies that were within the theoretical, 90-percent confidence interval proposed by MIT-Rasmussen guesses. Yet, there is only a subjective probability of 10 percent that the true (frequency-based) probability values should fall outside this 90-percent interval. The conclusion? The mathematicians said MIT assessors were guilty of a massive "overconfidence" bias in assessing nuclear safety, a typical flaw in most industry-government nuclear risk analyses.[55]

Besides using "guesses" rather than actual, reported accident-frequency data, a *second* reason that black-swan, nuclear-safety assessments err is that atomic-energy proponents—including the US government, as this chapter shows later—cover up many nuclear fatalities, reactor core melts, and serious accidents, just as Japanese authorities continue to do at FD. Instead they mention only the widely known accidents, and the lay public typically is none the wiser. For instance, well-known nuclear proponents say that, because there have been only 2–3 reactor core melts globally (at Three Mile Island, Chernobyl, and Fukushima), therefore nuclear disasters are rare—unlikely.[56] Or they cite the US government's (NRC's) assertion that a core-melt accident in the 104 US reactors will occur only once every 1,000 years.[57] If such black-swan claims are correct, however, there should be only (i) 1 accident every 1,000 years for 104 US reactors, and thus (ii) roughly 1 accident every 250 years for 442 global reactors.

Yet, as explained below, (i) is doubtful because US research and commercial reactors have had at least 5 core melts in roughly 50 years—not the claimed 1 core melt in 1,000 years; (ii) is likewise doubtful because global research, commercial, and military reactors have had at least 26 core melts in roughly 50 years—not the claimed 4 core melts in 1,000 years. Recall that the classic MIT report, funded by a pro-nuclear US government agency, concluded that a core melt would be expected in a reactor only once every 17,000 reactor years and that the US NRC says a nuclear core melt for the 104 commercial reactors should occur only once every 1,000 years. Yet both in the US and globally, there have been many more core melts than government, industry, and industry-funded studies suggest. How many core-melt accidents have occurred?

This is a difficult question, given the financial and political incentives for cover-up of nuclear accidents. To provide a best-estimate answer, note that the lists below of nuclear core melts exclude (a) nonmelt accidents, even if serious; (b) intentional or deliberate core melts; and (c) supposed core melts not documented in reliable scientific literature. Regarding (a), the lists below of nuclear core melts do not include fuel-loss or criticality accidents, however serious, if they do not partially melt the nuclear-reactor core. Thus, many serious US accidents—such as the 1964 criticality accident at the Charlestown, Rhode Island, reactor; the fire at the Cook reactor in Michigan in 2003; the loss of cooling at the Ginna reactor in New York in 1982; or the reactor explosions at the Brownsville reactor in Nebraska in 1975, and at the Waterford reactor in Connecticut in 1997, for instance—are not included in the list of US core melts below because there appears to have been no melting in these and many other serious US reactor accidents.[58] Likewise, many non-US accidents—such as that in 1958 at the Vinca reactor in Yugoslavia, for example—are not included below because there appears to have been no partial melting in these and many other damaging reactor accidents. Regarding (b), the lists below of nuclear-core melts also exclude those that have been intentional, such as those at the Borax-1, SPERT, and TREAT reactors in Idaho in the 1950s–1960s. Such core melts are not included in the lists below because they were not results of apparent accidents or negligence. Regarding (c), the lists below of nuclear core melts likewise excludes incidents for which detailed accounts of alleged core-melt accidents were not available in the refereed scientific literature. As a consequence, many supposed core melts—such as at the WTR reactor in Pennsylvania in 1960—have not been included in the lists below. Given the previous 3 caveats, (a)–(c), *at least 5 unintentional, partial-nuclear-core melts—all resulting in radiation releases, death, and injury—appear to have occurred in the US:*

EBR-1 in Idaho in 1955
Santa Susana in Los Angeles in 1959
SL-1 in Idaho in 1960–1961
Fermi 1 in Michigan in 1966
Three Mile Island in Pennsylvania in 1979

Given the same 3 caveats already noted, at least 21 unintentional partial-nuclear-core melts appear to have occurred outside the US—all resulting in radiation releases, death, and injury:

Chalk River in Canada in 1952
Windscale in the UK in 1957
Chalk River in Canada in 1958
Lenin (ship) in Russia in 1966–1967
Chapelcross in Scotland in 1967
Saint-Laurent in France in 1969
Lucens in Switzerland in 1969
Greifswald in Germany in 1975
Saint-Laurent in France in 1980
8 in Soviet navy nuclear submarines: K-19 (1961), K-11 (1965), K-27 (1968),
    K-140 (1968), K-429 (1970), K-222 (1980), K-314 (1985), and K-431
    (1985)
Chernobyl in Ukraine in 1986
3, so far, in Fukushima, Japan, beginning in 2011[59]

Besides actual nuclear-core-melt frequency, a *third* reason that black-swan, reactor-safety claims likely err is that industry requirements for nuclear-accident-liability limits reveal that the industry knows core-melt accidents are likely. As chapter 3 explained, virtually all nuclear manufacturers and utilities have demanded and received a government-guaranteed liability limit, or else they refuse to generate nuclear electricity. In the US, this limit is only about 1–2 percent of total possible government-estimated losses. The effect of this government-guaranteed liability limit is to ensure that the public, not the nuclear industry, bears the cost of reactor accidents, even those that result from negligence or illegal activities. Thus, as chapter 3 already warned, while the nuclear industry tells the public that reactors are safe, it itself demands the 98-percent accident-liability limit as a conduction of doing business. Moreover, these demands continue in the US, the UK, France, and elsewhere—such as India. Currently India and China are the only 2 nations in major nuclear expansion,[60] largely because high costs have brought the commercial nuclear industry almost to a global standstill, as chapter 3 explained. Yet even Indian reactors may not be built because India has a nuclear-liability provision "that makes nuclear-power-plant suppliers, not just operators, liable if accidents occur"; GE, Westinghouse, and other reactor manufacturers, however, say they will "stay out of the Indian nuclear market unless the country changes its liability law" to confirm to those in the US, Japan, and other nations—where taxpayers, not nuclear suppliers, are liable for accidents.[61] But the GE-Westinghouse liability requirement suggests at least 3 points, all relevant to the black-swan argument. One point is that nuclear suppliers recognize atomic energy as very risky; otherwise, they would not demand the liability limit as a condition of doing business. A second point is that, given their liability-limit requirements, nuclear suppliers obviously recognize that commercial-fission accidents are not really black-swan, "fat tail," or rare events. A third point is that if reactor catastrophes are not rare, and if nuclear suppliers recognize this fact, something must be keeping the lay public from recognizing nuclear dangers. What is this something? As both chapter 3 and Harvard economist Robert Stavins argue, because governments have massively subsidized atomic energy and "capped the liability of nuclear power producers…markets have never really had a chance to price nuclear power." Consequently, the massively subsidized markets propping up the reactor industry may be one reason that laypeople are misled about the severity of nuclear-accident threats.[62]

Bankers, however, are not misled. Chapter 3 showed that virtually no bank in the world will give nuclear loans, that all credit-rating agencies downgrade utilities with nuclear plants, and that utilities admit they would never build reactors unless they received massive taxpayer subsidies to cover half their costs. Thus, other factors also must be misleading people about nuclear safety, making them erroneously think that reactors are very safe and that accidents are black-swan events. After all, there have been at least 26 documented core melts globally—and yet the US and other governments and the nuclear industry erroneously claim that none of these accidents was probable.

Blame-the-Victim Lies at Fukushima and Elsewhere

Of course, whenever reactor accidents cause apparent casualties, it is more difficult for nuclear proponents to use the black-swan argument. As a consequence, they often resort to another ploy: blaming the victim. This flawed argument is that because radiation risks are very low, any confirmed medical problems associated with nuclear accidents are a result of stress, anxiety, or nuclear phobia, not radiation. In other words, the erroneous blame-the-victim argument is that medical problems near reactor accidents are the nuclear victims' own fault. For instance, after the FD disaster, many newspapers quoted university scientists who had worked for the nuclear industry and who used the blame-the-victim arguments:

Although radiation escaping from a nuclear power plant catastrophe can increase the risk for many cancers and other health problems, stress, anxiety and fear ended up in many ways being a much greater long-term threat to health and well-being in Chernobyl, Three Mile Island, and other nuclear accidents, experts said Monday. "The psychological effects were the biggest health effects of all—by far," said Fred Mettler, a University of New Mexico professor emeritus.... "In the end, that's really what affected the most people."[63]

Contrary to the preceding claims and as already noted, New York Academy of Sciences researchers and many other scientists confirm that the Chernobyl nuclear accident caused roughly a million premature fatalities. Among the scientific community, these massive numbers of deaths are uncontroversial. Yet as late at 2011, a key industry lobby group, the World Nuclear Association (WNA), as well as many industry-funded scientists likewise used the flawed blame-the-victim argument. They claimed that at Chernobyl, "biological and health effects...cannot be attributed to radiation exposure...and are much more likely to be due to psychological factors and stress."[64] One scientific commentator writes: "Nearly 20 years after Chernobyl, nearly 20 percent of the women had post-traumatic stress disorder stemming from the disaster, compared to 7.5 percent of the control group. Nearly a third had faced major depression in the past year."[65]

Similar "blame games" occurred after the TMI and FD accidents. As this chapter later explains, for a full 11 years after the 1979 disaster, no TMI-area health studies were done except those focused on mental health, virtually all of them funded by the nuclear industry. Yet in 1980 the official presidential group studying the TMI accident, the Kemeny Commission, concluded: "The major health effect of the accident appears to have been on the mental health of the people living in the region of Three Mile Island and of the workers at TMI."[66] How can one know that the major health effects of TMI are psychological if nothing but psychological studies have been done? The chapter argues later that one cannot. Likewise, after the FD reactor crisis began, commentators used blame-the-victim arguments. They claimed that "many...[Japanese] women remained fixated on Chernobyl." They accused the women of "anxiety," predicting that "the [FD radiation] warning's psychological effects on Tokyo could cause lasting stress to a group particularly at risk during nuclear crisis: young mothers." They said that the women felt "health-related anxiety about their exposure, even if nonexistent, to radiation."[67]

What helped make it easy for blame-the-victim proponents to claim that many nuclear-accident victims were not really physically hurt, but instead had mental problems? Proponents were able to "get away" with such arguments mainly because industry and government officials routinely claim that nuclear-accident consequences are minor, and much of the lay public has too little scientific or medical expertise to challenge such claims. Thus, when Tokyo Electric officials claimed that "we do not feel that a critical [nuclear] event is imminent," and when US officials said that Japanese radiation drifting over the US was harmless,[68] many people believed them. Likewise, despite several different FD reactor explosions, many people probably believed the Japanese utility spokespeople when they said: "There has not been a particular problem."[69]

One of the most basic errors in all these blame-the-victim arguments is that they are merely examples of a classical logical fallacy, ad hominem—meaning literally "to the man." One commits this fallacy when one illegitimately attacks the person who makes some argument, rather than attacking her argument. Obviously an argument could be valid even if its proponent is questionable, and obviously a completely reliable person could present an invalid argument. The issue thus is not the type of person propounding an argument, but the quality of the argument itself. As this chapter shows later, government, industry, and many of the scientists they hire all attack the victims of the TMI accident and downplay nonpsychological harms attributed to it.

A second reason that blame-the-victim arguments err is that they often rest on false scientific claims. As the chapter later shows, government, industry, and many of the scientists they have hired have often "gotten away with" with their erroneous, ad hominem arguments about TMI, Chernobyl, Fukushima, and other nuclear accidents because of their scientific errors—because the lay public typically has not been able to recognize the scientific flaws in experts' arguments. Frequently such arguments err because they illegitimately "trim the data" on nuclear-accident casualties. As the chapter explains later, after the US TMI nuclear accident, industry scientists used flawed statistical methods to underestimate TMI-accident fatalities, then blamed the victims for their medical problems. Likewise, speaking of the continuing FD disaster, the US NRC erred in saying it expected that no "harmful levels of radioactivity" would reach the US from the Japanese catastrophe.[70] As the chapter later shows, however, this NRC claim errs and underestimates FD accident fatalities because it ignores the classic radiation dose-response curve. Virtually all scientists everywhere, including members of the US National Academy of Sciences, accept this curve, according to which there is no safe dose of ionizing radiation except zero, and resulting harms are linearly related to dose. Indeed, as the chapter later explains, virtually all radiobiologists agree that even the lowest non-zero doses of radiation increase one's risk of cancer. Yet if there is no safe dose of radiation except zero, then any non-zero levels of radiation increase health risks, contrary to what governments and industry often claim.

Another way that blame-the-victim proponents manipulate and misrepresent science so as to minimize nuclear-accident harms is by counting only immediate or acute radiation casualties. They ignore the more numerous, long-term fatalities— often from cancer—that appear years after radiation exposure. For instance, after the Chernobyl nuclear explosion and core melt in the Ukraine, the main international nuclear-industry lobby group, the Soviet government, and industry scientists all erred when they underestimated the accident fatalities. What did they do? They counted only "acute" fatalities following Chernobyl. Yet as the chapter reveals later, in hundreds of technical articles, scientists from dozens of countries in the world have documented thousands of Chernobyl nuclear-accident fatalities—most occurring years after the accident, most because of cancer. Instead of admitting all these cancer deaths, completely predictable on the basis of the classic radiation-dose-response curve, industry and government officials ignore later fatalities and claim that Chernobyl killed only "31 people." This is the number of Chernobyl acute fatalities among firefighters who died soon after trying to control the Chernobyl explosion and blaze.[71]

Obviously it makes no sense to blame the victims of nuclear accidents, especially if there is no safe dose of ionizing radiation except zero, and if radiation cannot *not* put those exposed at higher risk. Besides, 1 reactor itself contains enough radiation, if properly distributed, to kill everyone for thousands of miles around. As a former US EPA attorney, Sheldon Novick, points out, "A million-kilowatt nuclear power plant, after a year of operation, contains ten billion curies of radioactive material, enough (if properly distributed) to kill everyone in the US."[72] Thus it is hardly irrational or unduly phobic to be wary of nuclear power. Moreover, even paranoid or phobic people sometimes have real enemies. Similarly, even nuclear-phobic people sometimes face real nuclear dangers. The issue is not whether they are phobic, but whether they are legitimately phobic. By attempting to provide a robust scientific and mathematical analysis of nuclear safety, this chapter shows not only why blame-the-victim nuclear proponents err scientifically, but also why many radiation victims might be legitimately afraid of atomic energy.

Blame-the-victim arguments are especially worrisome in less-developed nations, partly because such countries are likely to have more technology-related accidents and fewer safety protections. Also, leaders in repressive nations seem more likely to get away with black-swan and blame-the-victim arguments, because their citizens may have fewer educational opportunities, thus less ability to challenge official pronouncements, and also fewer civil liberties to safeguard their challenges. For instance, consider what happened recently in China. In spring 2009, China's Jilin Connell Chemical Plant opened. It produces aniline, a highly toxic chemical used to make polyurethane, rubber, and herbicides. While making aniline, the plant also releases many chemicals, including carbon monoxide and hydrogen sulfide. As a result of exposures to these chemicals, many plant employees already have died from the fumes, and 1,200 other people, working near the Jilin Connell plant but for other employers, have been hospitalized with convulsions, vomiting, and temporary paralysis. Some of these nearby workers also have died from brain hemorrhaging. Following the "blame-the-victim" argument, however, Chinese officials say the thousands of fallen workers are merely victims merely of "hysteria," not chemical exposures.[73]

Are Chinese officials right? Their causal inferences, about the supposed psychogenic origins of Jilin Connell's worker illnesses, seem clearly wrong. After all, many different people experienced the identical medical symptoms, and all these symptoms are well known as being associated with precisely the chemicals released by the plant. Besides, the local government regulators—who accused workers of being victims of their own "hysteria" and not victims of toxic-chemical exposures—are the major private investors in the chemical plant.

Something similar to the Jilin Connell case may happen when nuclear profiteers speak about the ailments of nuclear-accident victims. Much of the remainder of this chapter investigates how US government and industry scientists have used illegitimate black-swan and blame-the-victim arguments to minimize the substantial risks from Pennsylvania's TMI nuclear accident. For several reasons, it is especially important to delve into the particulars of the TMI accident, rather than just those associated with the FD or the Chernobyl catastrophes. For one thing, it is easier to get reliable, scientific, accident-consequence information about TMI than about FD or Chernobyl. After all, the Soviet government suppressed much Chernobyl-accident information, as this chapter shows. Likewise the quotations, given so far, suggest that the Japanese government also has been guilty of FD-information suppression. Both for this reason and because the FD accident is still continuing, there are no reliable, long-term scientific studies of health effects of the FD nuclear disaster. To learn why nuclear proponents' reactor-safety arguments often fail, one of the best current options is to consider a clearer case, that of TMI.

The TMI Problem: Two Causal Hypotheses

Consider the Three Mile Island (TMI) nuclear accident, which began on March 28, 1979. The deadliest US commercial-reactor accident, to date, TMI occurred in rural Pennsylvania. Later paragraphs show that many scientists and physicians say TMI has caused health problems, including increased infant mortality, infant retardation, genetic defects, hypothyroidism, and cancer, partly because—as earlier chapters showed—scientists agree that there is no safe dose of ionizing radiation except zero.

If the TMI accident was really this serious, however, concerns about nuclear safety and cover-up could argue against using fission to address CC. After all, NRC reactor-technology instructor David Lochsbaum said in 2011 that, because of industry influence over the US NRC, "absent dead bodies, nothing seems to deter the NRC" from ignoring serious reactor problems. At Entergy's Vermont Yankee plant, similar in design to the FD plants in Japan, industy officials assured lawmakers and regulators that there were no underground pipes that could leak. Officials accepted the industry's claim, and months later, in 2010, they accidentally discovered that leaks from underground pipes had radioactively contaminated local soil and groundwater. "The only difference between [dangerous US nuclear plants such as] Byron and Fukushima is luck," says Lochsbaum. Similarly, it took 30 years for the NRC to get fireproofing installed at reactors after a massive fire and accident at an Alabama reactor. Why does such laxness continue? While US nuclear-industry safety violations have not declined, why have actual penalties paid by industry for these violations declined 80 percent since the 1990s"? Why does the NRC try "to avoid ruffling the feathers of the nuclear industry and its Washington lobbyists"? Why is it that "no [US reactor-]license renewal application has [ever] been turned down" by the NRC, despite many safety violations and despite the fact that the plants were designed to operate for 40 years, not 60, as the renewals request? One reason is that most NRC regulators are from the nuclear industry. They are like William Magwood, a former employee of Westinghouse Electric, nominated by President Obama to serve on the NRC. Another reason for NRC laxness, according to former investigators at the US Inspector General's office, is that US NRC regulators hope to eventually land much more lucrative nuclear-industry jobs. Consequently, during their NRC work, "they're not going to do anything to jeopardize that." Both these facts help explain why the US Nuclear Regulatory Commission says "potentially dangerous" carcinogenic radioactive-tritium leaks—many ongoing—already have occurred at 65 (of 104 total) US nuclear plant sites. Moreover, as later paragraphs reveal, even normally operating reactors emit radiation known to cause cancer. If so, does it make sense to say that the TMI accident caused no health harms?[74]

Although TMI scientists disagree on details about the accident's effects, most appear to reject the 2 initial positions on TMI health effects, as articulated by the Kemeny Commission and the nuclear industry. The industry position is that "no member of the public died" because of TMI; this industry position is at odds with the official government position put forth in the Kemeny Commission report, which is that excess TMI-cancer fatalities would be less than 10.[75] Instead, strong epidemiological evidence now suggests that both industry and Kemeny estimates of TMI-cancer fatalities are serious underestimates. Instead, even scientists (such as Maureen Hatch) who were most skeptical of any TMI-radiation effects have documented a variety of increased, agreed-upon health problems after TMI, including a 64-percent cancer-incidence increase within 10 miles of the plant, only 4 years after the accident. Thus, virtually all epidemiologists (such as those at Columbia, the University of Pittsburgh, and the University of North Carolina) who have studied TMI health effects—have been forced to agree that there have been increased local health problems since the TMI accident.[76]

The major causal difference between the various TMI epidemiologists is over what hypothesis better explains these increased health problems. Has stress (hypothesis S, the dominant/majority scientific position, adopted by epidemiologists at Pitt and Columbia) or radiation (hypothesis R, the minority position, adopted by epidemiologists at UNC) the more likely cause? The dominant position, which is also that of the US government and the nuclear industry, is that there was "no consistent evidence that radioactivity released during the nuclear accident has had a significant impact on the overall mortality experience of these [TMI] residents."[77] Instead, reminiscent of the official, blame-the-victim, Chinese response to the Jilin chemical-plant effects, the official US (and dominant or majority scientific) position is that TMI-related *stress* likely caused the post-accident increases in nearby cancer and mortality.[78] In fact, without doing any studies in response to documented post-TMI increases in infant mortality and low birth-weights, groups like the industry lobby, the American Nuclear Association (ANA), claimed that increased TMI-area infant health problems probably were caused by mothers who took excessive medication to counter stress during the accident.[79] The minority position is that TMI radiation is the more likely cause.[80] Which causal inference is more plausible, S or R? If S, then safety concerns about using atomic energy might be lessened. If R, then nuclear plants may not be a safe way to address CC.

Some scientists have gone wrong in studying TMI because they forget C. S. Peirce's warning: "bank balances and credit ledgers" are "exact," but real-world events are not; thus scientists should "stop trying to model the world, as we have done since the time of Descartes, on the transactions of shopkeepers."[81] Instead, we must "respect...the origins of the data."[82] Because many scientists studying health effects of the 1979 TMI, Pennsylvania, nuclear accident have both fallen into conflicts of interest and failed to respect the origins of their inductive accident-data, this chapter shows their dominant/accepted position about what has caused increased numbers of post-accident, TMI-related health problems is wrong. The most likely explanation is hypothesis R: TMI radiation has caused increased post-accident health harms. But if so, society has been grossly misled about reactor safety, just as it has been misled about nuclear greenhouse emissions (chapter 2) and nuclear costs (chapter 3).

The TMI Accident

To understand alternative causal hypotheses, S and R, that have been proposed to explain post-TMI increases in health harms, one must understand what happened during the accident and the effects of TMI-radiation releases. As early as the 1920s, scientists (publishing in the *Journal of the American Medical Association*) revealed that even small amounts of radiation caused genetic harm and damage to blood-forming tissues. In the 1950s–1970s, partly because scientists at US Livermore Laboratories and at the US National Academy of Sciences concluded that US nuclear-weapons fallout caused as many as 8,000 fetal and 4,000 infant mortalities and that US nuclear power "could cause the deaths of thousands of Americans from cancer every year," above-ground US nuclear-weapons testing ended. Yet, by 1970, President Nixon said that atomic energy could help the US meet all of its own energy needs, without depending on "foreign energy sources." In response, in 1974, the US EPA said that normal radiation releases, between 1970 and 2020, could cause as many as 24,000 additional US deaths. Today, scientific consensus, as noted in earlier chapters and as articulated by the US National Academy of Sciences, is that damaging effects of ionizing radiation are cumulative and LNT—additive, linear, proportional to dose, with no threshold for increased risk. This means that, all other things being equal, higher ionizing-radiation doses cause greater molecular damage (thus more cancer, genetic defects, immune deficiencies, etc.). Thus, all other things being equal, the higher the radiation doses at TMI, the more likely that R, not S, better explains increased post-TMI health harms.[83]

How is dose measured? Effects of ionizing-radiation exposures are measured either as rads or grays of "absorbed dose" (energy absorbed per gram of tissue), or as rems or sieverts of "effective dose" (energy per gram of tissue, considering biological damage). For gamma rays—which can penetrate far into the body from external sources—absorbed (rad) and effective (rem) doses are roughly the same. A sievert is the amount of radiation required to produce the same biological effect as 1 rad of high-penetration X-rays, equivalent to a gray for X-rays. Thus 1 gray or sv = 1 joule per kilogram (J/kg) = 100 rad or rem = 100,000 millirad or millirem. Doses of 600 to 1,000 rads would be lethal to nearly everyone receiving them. The typical background-radiation dose, about 360 mrad or mrem (3.6 mgray or mSv) per year,[84] causes roughly 6 percent of fatal cancers—36,000 annual US deaths that otherwise would not have occurred. Ionizing radiation, from TMI or elsewhere, adds to these background-radiation risks.[85]

What caused the TMI radiation doses? The accident caused more than half the core to melt, according to US Nuclear Regulatory (NRC) estimates, and reactor-core temperatures reached 2,800 degrees Celsius (more than 5,100 degrees Fahrenheit), the melting point of uranium dioxide.[86] In part because the TMI utility had no inexpensive way to store accident-caused, radioactive-pollutant releases that filled several onsite buildings, official government reports say the utility made deliberate, uncontrolled, illegal, offsite releases of radioactive iodine and noble gases (e.g., krypton and xenon).[87] Because of its illegal radiation releases, accident cover-up, data falsification, "148 violations of NRC operating, procedural, and reporting requirements," the utility was convicted of accident-related "criminal misconduct" and destroying TMI-safety data–for which it received the maximum fine allowed under US law.[88]

How much TMI radiation was released? The utility's radiation dosimeters provided incomplete coverage because most utility radiation-monitors went "off-scale" only hours after the weeks-long TMI accident began; the utility also says it lost dosimetry data for the days of highest radiation releases.[89] Nevertheless, for 2 reasons, government claims TMI-radiation releases were low, only about one-third of annual-background radiation doses.[90] *First*, government currently uses "official [utility] exposure estimates as 'best estimates' of the [maximum] level of [TMI] radiation" released; *second*, industry bases estimates on data from the few distant, widely separated monitors "that remained on scale for most of the accident."[91] (Yet if most monitors went off-scale, those that remained on scale do not reveal maximum doses.) Because they follow TMI-industry claims about maximum TMI-radiation releases, both the official presidential 1979 Kemeny Report (which later paragraphs show to be both internally inconsistent—and externally inconsistent with later epidemiological data confirming TMI-area cancer increases) and official 1990 government reports err. They say TMI-radiation releases were 13 million curies, causing no more than 100-mrem-maximum doses to any person.[92]

However, some scientists and physicians say TMI releases were 56–106 million curies, in part because the official US Nuclear Regulatory Commission (NRC) report recorded off-site doses of 20–25 mrem *per hour,* during the weeks-long accident, and because, as chemist Chauncey Kepford warned, a "stagnant" air mass prevented TMI exposures from decreasing rapidly, with increasing distance from the plant; thus "the largest and most serious population exposures occurred beyond the fifteen-mile perimeter" where dosimeters were located; yet President Carter and his wife, after only a minutes-long site visit, had recorded-dosimeter doses of 100 mrem.[93] Likewise, as later paragraphs show, TMI-area physicians say that, based on clinical data from their patients, thyroid-radiation doses to the public had to be at least 100 times greater than industry and government (which uses industry's dose estimates) allege, and total-radiation doses had to be at least 1,000 times greater.[94] Of course, such clinical-medical evidence relies on no information about the source term. Such direct evidence is not available. However, based on the state of TMI's air-filtration system, the damaged reactor core, and the radionuclides remaining in the core, experienced, non-TMI, nuclear-industry executives and engineers claim TMI released 1 billion curies.[95] That is, they say TMI released 1/16 of total-core-radiation inventory, because once the core melted, many other radionuclides were released, in part because (as the official government report, by the US Nuclear Regulatory Commission, admitted) "the major source of increasing radiation in the atmosphere of the auxiliary building and of release to the environment was the flow of [contaminated] coolant between the core and the auxiliary building.... Leakage...produced high levels of radiation in the auxiliary building, some of which was released outside the plant through a ventilation stack." Within an hour or 2 after the accident began, TMI's onsite-filtration systems were quickly overloaded and nonfunctioning for nearly the entire accident (i.e., for several weeks). Likewise, only hours into the accident, "radioactive gas had begun to leak into the control room.... This forced the twenty to thirty Met Ed employees in the control room to wear respirators and greatly complicated" the situation. Moreover, as the official US NRC report explains, given "the growing presence of radioactive gas in the plant's auxiliary building, produced by damage to the reactor core," plant operators reduced the pressure in the system by "opening a vent to 'burp' the [radioactive] gas." They "agreed to keep the vent open for an extended period...[to] release more radiation to the environment." After about an hour of radioactive venting on March 30, 1979, "the [company] helicopter recorded a maximum reading of 1200 millirem per hour 130 feet" away from "the stack through which radiation was leaving the auxiliary building." The venting readings the day before "were at least as high," and a week after the accident began, the official NRC report notes that "radiation readings in the containment dome were still at the exceedingly dangerous level of about 30,000 rad an hour." The NRC report likewise notes that the US NRC said "aerial off-site readings were in the range of 20–25 millirem per hour." The report likewise notes that because "the containment structure was too heavily contaminated for entry," "the NRC staff concluded that the best method [of decontamination] was to vent the gas into the atmosphere."[96]

Other official US government reports also confirm that TMI's outside-air vents released enough radiation to kill someone within seconds—that is, utility-recorded doses of 30,000 rad per hour. The Kemeny Commission itself notes:

> Filters in the auxiliary and fuel-handling buildings did not perform as designed because the charcoal-filtering capacity was apparently partially expended due to improper use before the accident. Required testing of filter effectiveness for the fuel-handling building had been waived by the NRC. There were no testing requirements to verify auxiliary-building-filter effectiveness.[97]

Thus both official US government studies (the 2004 Walker report of the US Nuclear Regulatory Commission and the 1979 Kemeny Commission report commissioned by President Carter) say TMI's air filters were not functioning during most of the accident. Although the TMI reactor had a containment dome, it failed to be adequately protective because faulty air filters allowed nonfiltered radionuclides to pass out into the open air. Considering TMI air-filtration problems, who is right about TMI radiation releases, the industry (claiming low releases) or independent scientists and physicians (claiming high releases)? To answer this question, consider the release-data disagreements between these 2 groups.

Data-Based Disagreements over S and R

Scientists who accept S (that stress, not radiation, caused most TMI cancer increases) accept the industry-government claim (see above) that TMI released about 13 million curies of radiation. However, scientists accepting R (that radiation, not stress, caused most TMI cancer increases) say releases were much higher. Their disagreement is compounded by the fact that the Kemeny Commission report is both externally inconsistent with later, epidemiologically confirmed, cancer increases—and internally inconsistent about TMI-radiation releases. Kemeny claimed that noble-gas releases (the supposed bulk of TMI-radiation releases) were 13 million curies, that I-131 releases were 13–17 curies, and that I-131 releases were 8–12 percent of total releases. Yet (deducing by the logical inference of transitivity, that if a = b, and if b = c, then a = c), *if* the Kemeny Commission was correct that TMI I-131 releases = 8–12 percent of total releases of 13 million curies, and *if* 8–12 percent of total releases of 13 million curies = 1.04–1.56 million curies, *then* Kemeny-estimated TMI I-131 releases = 1.04–1.56 million curies of I-131, not 13–17 curies. Thus government's Kemeny Commission itself admits that I-131 releases could have been 6 orders of magnitude higher than industry and government claim.[98]

As this chapter demonstrates, at least 10 considerations suggest TMI-radiation releases could be much higher—perhaps 3–6 orders of magnitude higher—than industry and government claim. (1) As just argued, the Kemeny Commission's own statements reveal TMI's I-131 releases could be 6 orders of magnitude higher than industry and government claim, and (2) official government reports admit TMI air-filtration systems stopped working within an hour or 2 after the accident began.[99] (3) Industry radiation-monitoring data are missing for most of the TMI accident, and even when monitors existed, they were too close to the plant to record the highest doses. (4) The utility has a massive financial conflict of interest (COI), encouraging it to underestimate releases. (5) The utility suspiciously claimed it lost the first 2 (heaviest) days of radiation-monitoring data, when most monitors went off-scale. Later paragraphs also reveal that (6) the utility used false assumptions (e.g., regarding beta dose, plume rise, and the inside-outside air temperature differential, causing underestimates of calculated dose), and that (7) utility dose estimates are inconsistent (by a factor of at least 1,000) with independent, confirmed, offsite-dose measurements made both by US Nuclear Regulatory Commission officials and by industry employees themselves, and inferred by physicians as a result of radiation-related ailments in the local population. Later paragraphs likewise show that (8) while the Kemeny Commission had many excellent and competent members, its inconsistencies (see earlier paragraphs) might be explained by its being the product of group negotiation among scientists with different opinions; its being done in 1979, before any TMI-health-effects studies and before the NRC affirmed, in 1988, that more than half the TMI core melted; its being done "under stringent time constraints [6 months]," and its not being released in its entirety (government feared that doing so would end the nuclear industry). As subsequent paragraphs reveal, (9) the Kemeny Commission Advisory Committee charged both the TMI utility and the US government with TMI-accident cover-up; and (10) TMI-radiation-release claims by industry/government (that the accident released only about 13 million curies of radiation, killed only 1 person, and certainly killed fewer than 10 people) are inconsistent with those of the United Nations (UN).[100]

Regarding reason (10) for doubting the TMI-utility and US government radiation-release estimate of 13 million curies, independent radiation data from an industry group, the World Nuclear Association (WNA), and a UN group, the World Health Organization (WHO), can help clarify the situation. That is, if one assumes

(1) that TMI utility/US government TMI-radiation-release estimates of 13 million curies ($48 \times 10E16$ Bq) are correct;
(2) that WNA is correct that $14 \times 10E18$ Bq of radiation were released at the 1986 Chernobyl nuclear accident,[101] largely because of the reactor and building explosion and fire lasting 10 days; and
(3) that the WHO is correct that the Chernobyl accident released about 200 times more radiation than did the Hiroshima and Nagasaki bombs,[102]

then it logically follows

(4) that the Chernobyl accident released about 300 times more radiation than TMI, and
(5) that TMI may have released two-thirds as much radiation as did the Hiroshima and Nagasaki weapons.

That is, the TMI-utility/government, WNA, and WHO statements above mean that the rough ratios of these radiation releases is as follows:

Chernobyl 600: Hiroshima – Nagasaki 3: TMI 2.

Yet excluding bomb-blast effects, radiation from Hiroshima and Nagasaki is well known to have caused thousands of fatalities, not including the continuing increase in the Japanese cancer rate, in part because of increased germ-line mutations induced by bomb radiation.[103] Yet if TMI released two-thirds as much radiation as the 2 Japanese bombs, then despite several caveats,[104] it is unlikely that TMI caused no more than 10 radiation-induced fatalities, as the TMI utility and US government both claim. Thus, if independent industry (WNA) and UN experts (WHO) are correct, Hiroshima and Nagasaki radiation releases may be roughly the same as those from TMI, despite the earlier caveats and the fact that the Japanese health effects likely occurred over a wider geographic area than those from TMI. Japanese university scientists have calculated the cumulative-maximum-radiation dose from the bombs as 1.2 Gy (120,000 mrem) at Hiroshima, and 0.6 Gy (60,000 mrem) at Nagasaki—or 180,000 mrem total,[105] as compared to the 100 mrem TMI-maximum-radiation dose alleged by the TMI utility and the US government. Yet if the preceding data are correct (if, as WNA and WHO suggest, TMI released two-thirds as much radiation as the bombs), and if maximum doses are proportional to overall releases, then WNA and WHO claims suggest that maximum TMI-radiation doses could have been 118,800 mrem ($0.66 \times 180,000$ mrem). This dose is 3 orders of magnitude higher than the 100-mrem-maximum TMI dose alleged by the TMI utility and the government, and—as later paragraphs show—this higher dose is consistent with both epidemiological and clinical-medical data from TMI physicians.

Regarding reason (7) above for errors in TMI-utility/government-dose claims, these claims are inconsistent with the few, independent, confirmed, offsite-dose measurements, some of which already were mentioned. The chair of the pro-nuclear US NRC said he measured a TMI-radiation-dose plume whose "husky" hourly dose was 120 mrem/hour.[106] Even after the worst releases ended, NRC said TMI's offsite-radiation-dose readings were 365 mrem/hour, and the authors of the official, "most elaborate of the NRC's studies of Three Mile Island," done by "more than 50 professionals from the NRC and twenty-five outside attorneys," confirmed this dose.[107] In court the TMI utility admitted, under oath, that TMI-radiation doses to the public exceeded 500 mrem/hour.[108] Yet all the preceding *hourly* doses exceeded the alleged, *weeks-long* 100-mrem-maximum-radiation doses alleged by the TMI utility and the US government (see above). Moreover, the official NRC report notes that the dosimeters may not have captured the highest TMI doses because all of the dosimeters were located too close to the plant, whereas maximum doses may have occurred at least 15 miles beyond the plant. If TMI residents received 500 mrem/hour for 2 days, their doses would be 24,000 mrem; officials admit this dose would have caused premature cancer in 10 percent of those exposed. This conclusion is roughly consistent with scientists' claims that "thousands" of people likely died "as a direct result" of the TMI accident.[109]

Regarding reason (6) for TMI-utility and government radiation-dose errors, correcting only 2 flawed (industry and government) assumptions (about beta doses and radioactive-plume rise) would increase those radiation doses by 2 orders of magnitude. Because both the utility and government ignored TMI beta-ray doses, no TMI-radiation dosimeters were programmed to measure them; nevertheless, government admits beta doses comprised 90 percent of total-TMI-radiation releases.[110] If one uses government radiation models, but includes government-admitted TMI-beta-radiation levels, this would raise maximum-TMI-radiation doses by a factor of 10. Likewise, only the utility/government's erroneous assumption that the temperature differential between the outside air and the escaping radioactive plumes was 10 degrees enabled it to assert that radioactive-plume rise and dispersion were minimal; consequently, utility/government officials claimed maximum-TMI-radiation doses were 100 mrem, although (a) average TMI outside-air temperatures, during the accident, were 50s–60s Fahrenheit; although (b) reactor-core fuel melts at 5,100 degrees;[111] and although (c) the last confirmed temperature printout from the reactor building (before going off-scale) was 750 degrees, as confirmed in the best official NRC reports.[112] If one uses the same utility/government radiation-meteorology models,[113] but assumes that outside-air temperature was 50 degrees (confirmed by March temperature records), that reactor-building plumes were at least 750 degrees, and that the temperature differential was 700 degrees, this correction alone increases alleged maximum-TMI-radiation doses by a factor of 10. Correcting plume-rise and beta-dose assumptions alone, therefore, increases total-TMI-maximum-radiation doses by a factor of 100.

What explains the apparent utility/government underestimate of 100-mrem-maximum TMI-radiation doses? One possible answer is reason (4), utility financial conflicts of interest (COI). Facing billion-dollar TMI-damage claims, the utility quietly (with required gag orders on TMI-radiation-accident victims) paid $80 million to many victims of TMI cancer, retardation, and infant mortality—then used its 100-mrem-maximum-dose claims to deny damages to all other victims.[114] Another explanation is that most TMI-health-effects studies "were funded by the nuclear industry and conducted under court-ordered constraints" whose required "apriori assumptions precluded interpretation of [TMI-related dose] observations as support for the hypothesis" of TMI-radiation-induced harms; TMI utility insurers also had to "concur" on TMI-study designs, and the insurers required scientists to accept the industry/government 100-mrem-maximum-radiation dose.[115] Because TMI scientists (who accept S) were forced to use this court-ordered, question-begging radiation-dose assumption to assess TMI-health effects, they arguably had no testable hypothesis. The scientists appear to have been forced into circular reasoning and an anchoring bias (that no radiation doses were greater than 100 mrem) that caused them to accept S over R.

An Objection

In response to the preceding 7 arguments that the utility and the government grossly underestimated TMI-radiation doses, someone might claim that only reliable estimates of source-term releases provide sufficient evidence for reliable TMI-dose information. However, because there are no available data on source-term releases (industry controls the data and has financial COI regarding them), scientists must examine other sources of reliable information—like the 7 reasons just given for believing that utility/government estimates of TMI-radiation releases are too low. Given these 7 reasons, the obvious question is whether utility/government estimates are correct, or whether actual releases were at least 2 orders of magnitude higher, as reasons (1)–(7) argue. Later sections of the chapter show that, when one makes an inference to the better explanation, increased TMI-related health effects are better explained by higher-radiation-dose estimates. In other words, the chapter reveals epidemiological grounds for challenging the inconsistent industry/government/Kemeny low-dose claims. Moreover, in the absence of actual source-term data, one begs the question to assume that the TMI utility and the government correctly estimated TMI-radiation doses.[116]

Who are the main epidemiologists who support or accept the majority, dominant, industry/government claim about low-TMI-radiation exposures, and thus accept causal hypothesis S? TMI researchers from Columbia University and University of Pittsburgh generally accept the industry/government low-TMI-radiation-dose claim, and therefore majority hypothesis S, about causes of increased TMI-related health effects. TMI researchers from the University of North Carolina generally question the low-dose claim, therefore accept minority hypothesis R.

Although various smaller or single-cancer studies also have found excess cancer, mortality, thyroid problems, and so on, after TMI,[117] 3 main groups of epidemiological scientists have done comprehensive TMI-area health studies. All 3 groups, from Columbia,[118] the University of North Carolina,[119] and the University of Pittsburgh,[120] agree with the Hatch findings that TMI-cancer-incidence rates within 10 miles of the plant rose 64 percent in the 4 years after the accident, as compared to 4 years before; that these increases were especially observed in the radiation-sensitive cancers of leukemia, lung cancer, and non-Hodgkin's lymphoma; and that within a 10-mile radius, all types of cancers increased for all persons under age 25. Even the data of scientific skeptics, like those at Columbia (who deny both R and TMI-radiation-induced health problems) showed that 4 years after the accident, as compared to 4 years before it, the rates of leukemia, lymphoma, lung cancer, and all childhood cancers doubled.[121]

As preceding paragraphs show, the industry/government/consensus scientific position (S) contradicts claims of no TMI-area health effects after the accident. The only major TMI-related causal disagreement among the main groups of epidemiologists is over hypotheses S versus R. To see how these hypotheses differ, consider the 3 main sets of TMI studies, respectively (and chronologically) from Columbia, UNC, and the University of Pittsburgh.

The Columbia University TMI Studies

The Columbia University researchers, who are proponents of hypothesis S, accepted the industry/government/majority assumption of low, 100-mrem-maximum TMI-radiation doses. Based on this assumption, they assigned hypothetical, relative-radiation exposures to TMI-area residents who lived within 10 miles of the facility, and used a 6-year cancer follow-up. Based on initial wind patterns for the first few hours of the accident, they assigned highest total TMI-radiation doses to areas north–northwest of the plant, and lowest doses to the downwind areas north–northeast of the plant. Next they employed local hospital and TMI-registry data to study cancer incidence. Using odds ratios derived from logistic-regression estimates, as well as average cancer-incidence rates for the entire nation, they determined expected rates of cancer, before and after the accident, and compared them to actual rates.[122]

Although the Columbia researchers found post-TMI increased cancers, they concluded that "the pattern of results does not provide convincing evidence that [TMI] radiation releases" influenced these increases. Part of their reason for rejecting R appears to be that, using the industry/government low-radiation-dose assumption, they hypothesized that cancer rates after TMI increased notably "in 1982, persisted for another year, and then declined" somewhat for the next 2 years. After some increased-cancer results failed tests of statistical significance,[123] the researchers said assumed "radiation emissions, as modeled mathematically, did not account for the observed increase" in cancer. The Columbia researchers thus supported S with a post-accident cancer odds-ratio of 1.4 and a 95 percent confidence interval, and claimed a "modest association...between post-accident cancer [incidence] rates and [stress, as indicated by the assumed stress measure of] proximity of residence to TMI."[124]

Despite 5 important strengths of the Columbia studies (see previous note), their validity is compromised by at least 14 weaknesses, all of which caused them to underestimate TMI-radiation health effects.

(1) They explored TMI effects only within a 10-mile radius, although airborne radionuclides travel hundreds or thousands of miles (see later discussion), and official NRC reports of TMI warned that maximum TMI doses could occur at least 15 miles from the plant;

(2) They assumed the *lowest* radiation doses were northeast (the prevailing wind direction) of TMI, although *most* post-TMI cancers, hypothyroidism, and infant/neonatal mortality increases were found there;[125]

(3) They used a short follow-up, 6 years, although "most radiosensitive cancers have long latencies,"[126] up to 6 to 10 times longer; and

(4) They both ignored radiation-exposed people who left the TMI area after the accident, and assumed all current residents were exposed to TMI, although many were newcomers.[127]

(5) They failed to do detailed analyses of possible TMI effects on neonates, children, thyroid disease, thyroid cancer, and other well-known consequences of radiation exposure, although state public-health officials confirmed large post-TMI increases in infant mortality, infant-neonatal hypothyroidism, and thyroid cancer, and children are far more sensitive to radiation.[128]

(6) They used low-power statistical studies, unlikely to detect cancer increases.[129]

(7) They used national cancer data for comparisons and failed to correct for the lower pre-TMI-area cancer rates typical of rural areas.[130]

(8) They begged the question by assuming low TMI-radiation exposures that could not have caused the increased cancers.[131]

(9) They used observational rather than experimental studies.

(10) Their studies assumed that stress, not radiation, caused post-TMI cancer increases, but they had had no measure of stress except proximity to the reactor (a measure typically used, instead, to assess radiation dose).[132] They also ignored pre-TMI increased cancer near the reactor; ignored disproportionate, post-TMI increases in radiosensitive cancers; ignored the distant down-

wind TMI-radiation plumes; ignored disproportionate post-TMI increases in lung cancers (although TMI releases were gaseous); and ignored confirmed findings that contradicted their stress hypothesis.[133]

Later paragraphs show that, contrary to the Columbia researchers, R and not S better explains the increased incidence of post-TMI-area cancers.

The University of North Carolina TMI Studies

The University of North Carolina (UNC) epidemiologists, proponents of hypothesis R, used the same TMI-radiation-dose estimates, 10-mile radius, wind assumptions, hospital and TMI-registry data, 6 years of follow-up, and 69 study tracts as the Columbia University scientists. Why? The UNC researchers wanted to show both the flaws in the Columbia studies and the likelihood of TMI-radiation-induced cancers. However, instead of dividing radiation-exposure groups into 4 cardinal dose-levels, as Columbia scientists had done, they divided them into 9 ordinal, radiation-exposure groups. This 9-level grouping allowed for better sensitivity of cancer-incidence to relative dose than did the Columbia University groupings. Besides correcting several Columbia data-reporting errors, the UNC scientists also corrected 5 methodological problems in the Columbia work, such as using low-power studies that were unlikely to detect any cancer increase. As a result, the UNC scientists were able to show that, using the low TMI-radiation doses assumed by Columbia researchers, TMI areas receiving at least median ordinal radiation doses had ratios of observed to expected cancer cases, for the 4-year period after the TMI accident, of 1.49. Using corrections, such as grouping all similar cancers together (e.g., all leukemias), UNC scientists also discovered that cancer-incidence and radiation-dose associations were strongest for leukemia, perhaps the most radiosensitive of all cancers. In study tracts estimated to have received the highest radiation doses, they showed that the observed to expected-leukemia ratio was 4.0; 4 years later, it was 7.[134]

Besides correcting 5 methodological problems (see above) of the Columbia studies, the UNC research appears strong because, although it was undertaken in response to post-TMI citizen harm, UNC scientists refused financial support from the court-mandated TMI Public Health Fund. Why does this refusal likely make their research better? The TMI utility and insurer control this TMI fund, and they require all researchers who receive money from it to accept the industry/government assumption that TMI-radiation doses were low—only 100 mrem maximum.[135] In part because the UNC researchers (unlike those at Columbia and Pitt, who accepted the TMI-fund money, and therefore the question-begging assumption) did not beg the question, their studies are stronger in this respect.[136]

Although the UNC studies arguably are some of the best TMI research done so far, they share many Columbia-research flaws, precisely because they used the same

TMI data that Columbia used (but alternative methods of assessment), so they could show flaws in Columbia conclusions. However, the unavoidable UNC-study weaknesses (arising from their goal of correcting Columbia errors, such as the small study radius) cause ND studies also to underestimate increased TMI-radiation health effects.[137] For instance, they used a short, 6-year follow-up, although "most radiosensitive cancers have long latencies,"[138] up to 6–10 times longer. Also, because they based cancer-incidence rates on place-of-residence residence at diagnosis, they counted "unexposed" people as TMI-radiation exposed, even though they did not live at TMI at the time of the accident—and they ignored radiation-exposed people who left the area. (Yet, all other things being equal, emigrants may have left because they received higher radiation doses/injuries than others.) Likewise, despite state health officials' confirming large post-TMI increases in infant death/disease, especially thyroid disease,[139] the UNC studies (intentionally using Columbia data) also failed to analyze possible TMI effects on neonates, children, thyroid disease, thyroid cancer, and other well-known radiation effects. However, the UNC scientists recognized that, if they had not accepted key Columbia assumptions, they could have shown TMI radiation caused even worse health effects than claimed by Columbia researchers.[140]

The University of Pittsburgh TMI Studies

Like Columbia epidemiologists, University of Pittsburgh researchers also are S proponents. They used death-certificate and TMI-registry data to study post-TMI mortality within 5 miles of TMI and employed an 18-year follow-up. Like Columbia scientists, they accepted the industry/government low-TMI-radiation-dose claims (100 mrem max) and assumed that the lowest TMI-radiation doses were downwind, north–northeast of the reactor. Partly because of such assumptions, they concluded there was "no consistent evidence that radioactivity released during the [TMI] nuclear accident has had a significant impact on the overall mortality experience of these residents."[141]

Despite at least 6 important strengths (see note) of the Pittsburgh studies,[142] they have at least 12 weaknesses, all of which apparently cause underestimates of negative TMI-radiation health effects.

(1) They examined mortality, not disease incidence, although researchers recognize that "mortality is not a valid surrogate for [cancer] incidence," partly because mortality underestimates cancer-incidence risk.[143]

(2) They included only those potential victims who lived within 5 miles of TMI, although airborne radionuclides travel hundreds to thousands of miles and, as noted earlier, even the NRC says maximum TMI doses may have occurred at least 15 miles from the plant.

(3) They oversimplified wind direction, assuming that atypical winds, toward north–northwest, occurred throughout the accident, although north–north-east is both the prevailing wind direction and where most post-TMI excess cancers, hypothyroidism, and infant/neonatal mortality appeared.[144]

(4) Although they used a longer follow-up (18 years) than many scientists did, as already noted, latency periods for radiation-induced cancers often are 2 or more times longer.

(5) They both ignored TMI-exposed people who left the area, and counted unex-posed people (who had moved into the area after the accident) as exposed, because they used residency-at-time-of-diagnosis as the criterion for TMI harm.

(6) They failed to analyze TMI effects on neonates and children, especially thy-roid disease, thyroid cancer, and other well-known radiation-exposure conse-quences, although state public-health officials confirmed increased post-TMI harms in these areas.[145]

(7) On grounds of inadequate data, they excluded all nonwhites from their stud-ies, although TMI-area nonwhites have higher post-TMI cancer-incidence and mortality rates than whites.

(8) On grounds of inadequate confounder information, they excluded children under age 18, although children are roughly 3–38 times more sensitive to ion-izing radiation than are adults.[146]

(9) Because they accepted the industry/government assumption of 100 mrem TMI-maximum dose, and assumed TMI health harms were proportional to this assumed dose, they begged the question of increased TMI-radiation health harms, likely had no testable hypothesis, and had an anchoring bias.[147]

(10) They used cardinal values for various groups' radiation-dose estimates (given 100 mrem maximum dose), despite uncertainty about actual TMI-radiation-release data.

(11) They say they were forced to ignore analyses of central-nervous-system (CNS) cancers because of their small numbers,[148] yet arguably they could have grouped them with other radiosensitive cancers.[149]

(12) Although they admitted that TMI radiation exposures predicted some can-cers—that TMI males had statistically significant increases in respiratory-system cancer, bronchus cancer, trachea cancer, lung cancer, respiratory-system nonmalignant disease, heart disease, and all-cause mor-tality; that white females had statistically significant increases in all-cause mortality, heart disease, and nonmalignant respiratory disease; and that white females aged 50–69 (and all females during 1985–1989) had statisti-cally significant increases in lymphatic and hematopoietic-cancer rates[150]—the Pittsburgh epidemiologists denied that radiation exposures predicted all excess TMI cancers, because they aggregated all cancer-mortality data, then rejected R.

Columbia and Pitt epidemiologists studying TMI also failed to investigate hypotheses S and R relative to each other. For instance, as later paragraphs argue, researchers should have questioned their support of S, given largely gaseous TMI-radiation releases (xenon and krypton), and given the disproportionate appearance of post-TMI respiratory cancers. If S were the better hypothesis, why would post-TMI cancers be disproportionately respiratory? They also should have questioned their support of S, given the predominance of post-TMI radio-sensitive cancers. If S were the better hypothesis, why would post-TMI cancers be predominantly radiosensitive? The Columbia and Pittsburgh researchers also should have examined their statistical inferences more carefully before support-ing S over R.

Flawed Statistical Inferences

In particular, the dominant-camp Columbia and Pittsburgh epidemiologists should have questioned their conclusion that—despite increased-post-TMI odds ratios for cancers, especially leukemia—their non-experimental results were not statistically "significant," or were statistically significant but not "consistent," or had wide confi-dence intervals.[151] Similar questionable inferences (using classical statistical-signifi-cance tests to deny pollution-disease associations in non-experimental data) occur frequently. For instance, Chevron-Texaco funded UCLA epidemiologists to fight a $27 million court verdict in favor of 30,000 Amazon-cancer-risk victims; they were harmed by substandard oil-drilling practices that contaminated Rhode Island–sized areas of the Amazon.[152] The epidemiologists used statistical-significance tests of non-experimental data, then denied any associations between "oil-extraction activi-ties and adverse [Amazon-region] health outcomes."[153] As subsequent paragraphs argue, Chevron-Texaco did what the TMI utility and US government did. It funded questionable observational studies, then used them to deny legal responsibility for pollution victims.

This questionable practice (relying on classical statistical tests in non-experi-mental studies), the one used by proponents of TMI hypothesis S, is standard among dominant-school, "black-box" epidemiologists. These epidemiologists argue for methodological rigor; emphasize specific population behaviors and disease-related exposures (risk factors); argue for increased emphasis on robust statistical analysis; and pay little attention to pathogenic mechanisms or social-cultural influ-ences on disease, such as poverty, greed, or COI.[154] Inputs to their black box include the counts of diseased and nondiseased people, classified by exposure status; out-puts include relative-risk estimates, based on the formula for the odds ratio. Responding to regulators' demands for alleged causal "proof" of harm, black-box epidemiologists, such as Savitz,[155] thus argue for increased use of statistical analysis, even in non-experimental studies, such as those of TMI. They also note that many famous epidemiological results have come from non-experimental studies that employ classical statistical tests, like the Framingham (Massachusetts) research used to show that smoking predicts heart-disease risk.[156]

Because the dominant school of black-box epidemiologists rejects observational results as biased and unscientific—unless they are subjected to statistical-significance tests—most TMI epidemiologists (those at Columbia and Pittsburgh, not UNC) subject observational TMI data to statistical-significance tests. Courts too have followed this trend. Most US courts—hearing toxic-torts cases based on observational (non-experimental) pollution studies—require that population-level evidence satisfy statistical-significance tests; otherwise they throw it out.[157] Is it reasonable for black-box-epidemiologists, for TMI epidemiologists, and for most toxic-torts courts to accept this requirement of statistical-significance testing for non-experimental data?

Randomization Arguments

On one hand, black-box epidemiologists say conventional-statistical tests often are best-case interpretations of non-experimental results. Besides, because experimental studies must be large and expensive and cannot be done after accident-exposure, non-experimental studies (such as Framingham) are often the only studies that can be done; they dominate epidemiology.[158]

On the other hand, when epidemiologists derived Framingham tobacco-risk functions from statistical-significance tests of observational data, then used those function in Belfast and France, they could not predict heart disease there.[159] Likewise, when epidemiologists use statistical-significance tests (on non-experimental data) to show "the cardio-protective effects of [moderate] alcohol [consumption],"[160] their causal inferences also are flawed. Why? Because non-experimental studies are purely observational, they cannot avoid confounders (e.g., sick people do not drink; moderate drinkers are socially advantaged, thus healthier). Consequently, although authors of observational studies (such as those at TMI) have no experimental results to justify causal inferences, they sometimes employ statistical-significance tests of purely observational data, then use these tests to draw erroneous causal inferences (e.g., imbibing a carcinogen, alcohol, improves health; TMI radiation did not cause increased cancer).[161] They arguably confuse *correlations* (e.g., drinking is something that healthy people do; stress was elevated prior to TMI health harms) with *causes* (e.g., drinking is something that makes people healthy; stress caused TMI health harms).

Apart from problems with confounders, using classical statistical tests on non-experimental data also provides no unbiased way to select representative samples, exposure levels, or experimental conditions because the data are not randomized.

Yet randomization in experimental design provides the "link between inferential statistics and causal parameters."[162] Without randomization, no reliable interpretations, statistical-significance tests, power, confidence intervals, or inferences from samples to larger populations are possible; as Fisher recognized, randomness helps scientists avoid bias, apply probability laws, and make rationally based statistical inferences.[163] Why? Randomization helps destroy previously existing causal relationships—like those associated with confounders. It helps "break the mechanism" between earlier causes (e.g., healthy immune systems) and effects (e.g., recovered health), so that new cause-effect relationships (e.g., cures from pharmaceuticals) can be assessed.[164]

Another epistemic argument against using classical statistics tests to assess causal inferences in non-experimental (observational) studies, like those at TMI, is that this allows no precise *definition* for the parent population, because *so many* factors affect subjects' responses to study conditions. That is, because scientists *do not know* (in observational studies) what the most relevant factors are, they *do not know* everything in the parent population of which the sample is supposed to be a sample. For Framingham studies, is it Massachusetts residents? Only Massachusetts males? Only nondiabetic Massachusetts males? Only non-overweight, nondiabetic Massachusetts males? And so on. All such descriptors could signal confounders, yet non-experimental studies have no way to control for them. Consequently, the most relevant homogeneity relationships between sample and parent populations (e.g., being diabetic or not) may not hold. Yet these homogeneity relationships are what make statistical inferences "work." Without ways to ensure representative samples by randomizing subject and exposure selections (as experimental studies do), doing unbiased, non-experimental studies requires knowing all major homogeneity details ahead of time. Not knowing them, scientists ought not use classical statistical tests in non-experimental studies. The upshot? Trying to define non-experimental, parent populations more precisely, via descriptors like "diabetic," the Framingham studies illustrate that conclusions will be inapplicable to other groups.[165] Trying to ensure study applicability by avoiding narrow-parent-population definitions fails to ensure representative samples. Thus, non-experimental studies can have applicability, or parent-population definability, but not both. This is another way of saying that models (statistical-significance tests) are only as good as their underlying assumptions (e.g., homogeneity assumptions for exposed and control groups). Because non-experimental researchers cannot control all strong risk factors, they cannot know these homogeneity assumptions are satisfied. Therefore they cannot know that classical statistical tests provide valid results—at TMI or anywhere else.

Scientists also err in their inductive or statistical inferences when they fail to find statistically significant associations in non-experimental studies and therefore deny evidence for health-related effects and attribute these effects to "chance." For instance, a US National Academy of Sciences Committee evaluating non-experimental studies claimed that excess cancers near commercial-nuclear and nuclear-weapons-testing facilities were "all caused by chance," because they were not statistically significant.[166] However, knowing something occurred by chance (not because of exposures, study bias, etc.) requires knowing a priori probability distributions for relevant events. But knowing these distributions requires experimental control over study materials and circumstances, therefore ordering them (e.g., through randomization) to avoid systemic bias. But non-experimental studies provide no such experimental control, therefore no information about a priori probability distributions, therefore no knowledge that something occurred by chance. In the absence of randomization, in a fair experiment, it is impossible to distinguish whether test statistics reflect bias, or the exposure under investigation.[167] For this reason, the Columbia and University of Pittsburgh researchers ought not have used statistical-significance tests of their observational TMI data as grounds for rejecting hypothesis R.

Inference to the Best Explanation (IBE), Especially Contrastive Explanation (CE)

How should one use observational (non-experimental) data to assess TMI-causal hypotheses S and R? If one is not an inductive skeptic, is willing to set aside the absence of uncontroversial accounts of causality, and admits there are noncausal explanations, as in mathematics, how might one justify particular inductive (causal) hypotheses over others? By appeal to other inductive principles. After all, both Noam Chomsky and Thomas Kuhn argued for unacknowledged principles of induction. They realized that, insofar as induction is methodical, it must use additional rules or principles.[168] What other inductive principles can be used to assess hypotheses S and R?

At least 4 prominent scientific traditions provide such principles for weighing evidence for competing inductive or causal hypotheses, such as S and R. These include (a) inference to the best or better explanation (IBE), (b) the mechanism tradition, (c) the unificationist tradition, and (d) the interventionist-counterfactual tradition. Subsequent sections investigate (a) and apply it to TMI—but suggest why full analysis of (b)–(d) also would likely provide results consistent with (a) analyses.

According to (a) IBE, one infers what would, if true, better explain scientific evidence. For causal hypotheses, the better explanation links cause and effect by providing information about an effect's causal history—for example, increased TMI-area cancers after the TMI accident. However, most information about an effect's causal history (e.g., a plane crash) is explanatorily irrelevant (e.g., the plane's color). How can one account for the causal selectivity (relevance) of explanatory practices? As Carl Hempel recognized, examining *aspects* of effects (e.g., post-TMI cancer increases) can pare causal factors to explain these effects. One way to examine aspects of effects is via contrastive explanation (CE), using a fact and a foil (control) to explain why x, not y, causes some phenomenon.[169]

Like Mill's Method of Difference, the choice of IBE-CE foils (controls) helps select explanatory causes. For Mill, a cause lies among antecedent differences between cases where effects do, and do not, occur. Thus to explain why R, and not S, one must cite an event (contrast) in R's history, and the absence of a corresponding event in S's history. This explanation involves 2 main steps. *First*, one must filter potential explanations so that they satisfy all conditions of actual explanations (e.g., logical compatibility with observations), except possibly truth. *Second*, one must select the best (the likeliest and most explanatory) of potential explanations. Provided one is willing to accept reasonable defenses of why interest-relativity in choosing foils is not subjective in a damaging sense, one can use IBE-CE to assess TMI hypotheses S and R. By inferring whether S or R better explains various contrasts, one can infer a likely cause of increased post-TMI health problems. Peter Lipton illustrates guidelines for IBE assessment by looking at how Ignaz Semmelweis discovered the cause of childbed fever. Recall that in showing "cadaveric matter" was the cause of childbed fever, Semmelweis investigated many other causal hypotheses, such as rough patient handling, epidemic influences, fear of death, and so on. As IBE-CE guidelines for assessing competing hypotheses, consider the 5 below, as illustrated via Semmelweis and his 1847 discovery in Vienna General Hospital.[170]

(1) The "best" causal explanation (e.g., cadaveric-matter exposure causes childbed fever) cites *common antecedent* events (e.g., patients' being in hospital) that it shares with other explanations (e.g., rough handling of patients).

(2) The "best" causal explanation (e.g., cadaveric-matter exposure) cites some *difference or contrast* (e.g., higher childbed-fever rates in the first, not the second, hospital-maternity divisions) between it (cadaveric matter exposure causes childbed fever) and competitor explanations (e.g., epidemic influences cause childbed fever), such that the better explanation better accounts for this contrast.

(3) After *removal* of the supposed cause (e.g., removing cadaveric matter by physician hand-washing), the supposed effect (e.g., childbed fever) disappears.

(4) *Reject hypotheses* (e.g., epidemic influences) that fail to explain differences or contrasts (e.g., the higher childbed-fever rates in first-maternity division, despite divisions' similar crowding and therefore epidemic influences).

(5) To prevent false inferences and reduce potential hypotheses, use further observations and conjectures to produce *new differences or contrasts* to test causal hypotheses.

How might one use the 5 preceding IBE-CE principles to assess TMI hypotheses S and R?

Evaluating TMI Hypotheses via IBE-CE Principles (1) and (2)

Consider first IBE-CE principle (1), finding common antecedents among TMI hypotheses. TMI hypotheses S and R share much TMI causal history. For instance, both have been potentially affected by the same nuclear accident, the same human population, and the same geographic area.

What about IBE-CE principle (2), finding causal-history contrasts to account for why S or R better explains post-TMI-cancer increases? One contrast (already mentioned) is that post-TMI-cancer increases are mostly and disproportionately radiosensitive ones (e.g., leukemia, lymphoma, lung cancer).[171] This contrast supports R over S. But if R, not S alone (whose proxy = reactor proximity), better explains post-TMI-cancer increases (odds ratio 1.4), then several consequences follow: (a) resulting cancers should be mainly and disproportionately radiosensitive, and (b) non-radiosensitive cancers (e.g., chronic lymphocytic leukemia)[172] should not disproportionately increase. Moreover, (c) odds ratios for (radiosensitive) lymphoma should increase, for example, to 1.9.[173] If S alone, not R, better explains TMI effects, then effects (a)–(c) should not occur. Because (a)–(c) did occur, R explains post-TMI health effects better than S does.

Following principle (2), a second contrast (already mentioned) is that post-TMI-cancer increases are mostly and disproportionately respiratory. This contrast also supports R, not S. Because TMI-radiation releases were mostly noble gases, affecting respiratory systems,[174] R explains at least 2 aspects of this contrast, while S cannot. *First*, R explains why post-TMI-area males had statistically significant respiratory-system-, bronchus-, trachea-, and lung-cancer increases; why post-TMI male lung cancers had 1.7 odds ratios; while all post-accident cancers in the TMI area had 1.4 odds ratios.[175] *Second*, R explains why males (more likely working outdoors, thus receiving heavier respiratory exposures) showed more respiratory cancers than females. Therefore R, not S, better explains 2 contrasts—disproportionately radiosensitive and disproportionately respiratory cancers.

Can S proponents cite any TMI contrasts to support their hypothesis? Columbia scientists claim that the association (odds ratio 1.4)—between reactor proximity (the stress proxy) and increased cancers—supports S, not R.[176] However, this contrast faces at least 5 problems. These include (a) disproportionately radiosensitive and respiratory post-TMI cancers,[177] (b) the absence of any reliable or accepted stress-cancer measures, and (c) no uncontroversial associations between psychosocial stress and particular cancers. Radiation, however, is uncontroversially known to cause at least 20 different types of cancer.[178] Regarding (c), oxidative stress or pro-inflammatory cytokines reveal associations between *molecular or biochemical* stress and disease.[179] However, most randomized, case-control studies deny any associations between *psychosocial* stress and cancer-onset, although psychosocial stress likely worsens already-existing conditions.[180] Also, only questionable scientifically studies allegedly show associations between psychosocial stress and cancer onset. They employ no representative samples, no case controls, no consideration of confounders, no distinctions between *stressful events* versus *feeling stress* from events, no analysis of cancer-onset data, and no objective measures of stress.[181]

Other problems with S proponents' using the reactor-proximity contrast to support S over R are that (d) cancer rates for post-TMI hilltop residents (living within 3–8 miles of TMI) were 7 times higher than the 1.4 post-TMI area cancer-odds ratio.[182] Although hilltop-cancer numbers were small (2 rising to 19), making scientific interpretation difficult, R, not S, better explains these high numbers of hilltop cancers because TMI-radioactive plumes more likely hit hilltops, while stress effects were allegedly proportional to reactor proximity. Moreover, R, not S (measured via reactor proximity), better explains distant-downwind-cancer increases hundreds of miles away, in other states.[183] Besides, (e) most radiation researchers use reactor proximity to measure effects of radiation, not stress, because even normally operating reactors release radiation. Thus, pre-TMI-accident, presumably a low-stress time, Columbia data show an association (odds ratio 1.2) between increased TMI-area cancer and reactor proximity.[184] Likewise, many studies show an association between increased cancers and nuclear-facility proximity. Normally operating reactors presumably do not induce stress, yet they are allowed to release 25 mrem/year of ionizing radiation.[185] This amount is only one-fourth the amount that was alleged (by industry and government) to have been released at TMI, yet numerous researchers show 25 mrem causes massive health hazards. Although normal-reactor emissions are highest downwind, well-confirmed normal-reactor-operation studies in England, France, Germany, Scotland, and the US show increased near-reactor infant- and fetal-mortality and increased childhood cancers, especially leukemia, lymphoma, and brain cancers. The official history of the US NRC, for instance, reveals 4-times-higher leukemia rates around the Pilgrim, Massachusetts, nuclear plant; there are 14-times-higher leukemia rates in children who live 3 miles from the Seascale, UK, nuclear facility; and 3 percent of the Hanford, Washington, nuclear workers had died from occupational radiation exposure that was within normal limits. Once normally operating nuclear facilities close, however, all health effects return to normal.[186] Such studies suggest that pro-S contrasts, such as TMI-reactor-proximity, actually support R better than S because cancer increases also occur during normal, presumably low-stress, reactor operation.[187]

S proponents also claim a second contrast: low-TMI-accident radiation doses (industry's 100 mrem maximum), which they say cannot explain the post-TMI cancer increases.[188] However, as earlier sections of this chapter argued, this proposed low-dose contrast has many problems. These problems include incomplete dosimetry coverage; most dosimeters' quickly going off-scale; no onsite air-filtering; the utility's financial COI and "losing" data for the heaviest days of radiation releases; inconsistent dose claims by utility and government officials; flawed radiation-dose assumptions (e.g., regarding beta doses and plume-rise); and the government's claiming the utility was unreliable, falsified data, withheld evidence, and was guilty of "criminal misconduct" at TMI. As already noted in the chapter, the UN WHO says TMI released two-thirds as much radiation as Hiroshima and Nagasaki, and nuclear-industry executives and engineers say TMI releases were 100 times what the US government and industry claimed. Besides, if TMI-accident-radiation doses were low, it is unclear why the utility spent $80 million, quietly settling out of court (requiring gag orders on victims who were financially compensated) with many TMI victims of cancer, birth defects, retardation, and infant mortality.[189] All of these factors suggest that TMI doses could have been quite high, not low, as S proponents claim.

Additional problems with S proponents' low-dose contrast is its inconsistency with other reliable data. Dr. Joseph Leaser and other TMI-area physicians reported that hundreds of citizens (including those unaware of any nuclear accident, and especially the 450 hilltop residents who lived 3–8 miles from TMI) had health symptoms consistent with acute high-dose gaseous-radiation exposure, including metallic taste, hair loss, nausea, vomiting, diarrhea, and erythema.[190] TMI residents would have had to receive 400 rad for hair loss, 200–300 rad for erythema, and 100+ rad for vomiting.[191] Yet 100–400 rad are 1,000–4,000 times greater than the 100-mrem-maximum TMI-radiation doses alleged by industry and the US government. Moreover, these 100- to 400-rad doses are consistent with the fact that the TMI utility settled (out of court, with required gag orders) with parents whose children were born retarded, shortly after TMI.[192] Why? Each sv (100 rad/rem) of in-utero ionizing-radiation exposure, during brain-formation stages, causes permanent 25-point IQ drops.[193] If TMI induced retardation, accident doses must have been at least 100 rad or rem (consistent with the doses required for metallic-taste and hair-loss effects, as reported by Dr. Leaser). But doses of 100 rad or rem are at least 1,000 times greater than doses that industry and the US government claim were released at TMI.

Dr. Leaser also reported many patients with higher eosinophils, white-blood-cell counts characterizing high-radiation exposure; Russian scientist V. A. Shevchenko, who diagnosed and treated many Chernobyl and Soviet high-radiation-exposure victims, likewise confirmed that many TMI residents had chromosome aberrations that indicated they had received TMI radiation doses 2,000 times higher than industry and the US government claim.[194] Although some of this evidence is anecdotal and clinical, it is consistent with much other data (see above), especially data revealing courtroom-documented high-radiation-dose claims.

TMI-area childhood-mortality increases also contradict S proponents' low-dose contrast. The former Pennsylvania state health director, physician Gordon MacLeod, showed that in Harrisburg (10 miles from TMI), the neonatal (1 month since birth) death rate *quadrupled* within 3 months post-TMI, then increased *sevenfold* within 7 months post-TMI; within 6 months after the accident, MacLeod showed that infant mortality increased *sevenfold* within 5 miles of TMI, and *twofold* within

10 miles.[195] Because official TMI-cancer studies excluded children, given "lack of confounder information" on them,[196] S proponents cannot easily answer this child-mortality challenge to their contrast (their alleging that TMI released only low-dose radiation of 100 mrem maximum).

Evaluating TMI Hypotheses via IBE-CE Principles (3) and (4)

Because the TMI accident already occurred under uncontrolled conditions, one cannot assess cancer increases via controlled experiments that follow principle (3). That is, one is unable to follow principle (3) and thus remove TMI-related psycho-social stress, or TMI-radiation doses, and then assess the effects of these removals. However, one can employ sensitivity analysis, or "influence analysis," by using other studies about R or S, to investigate how hypothesized causal relationships change under perturbations of R or S.[197] This perturbation is the central strategy in the interventionist-counterfactual causal account of James Woodward (see below). How might one use this principle (3) perturbation to assess R and S?

The classic, well-confirmed, ionizing-radiation dose-response curve illustrates this principle (3) assessment of perturbation—evaluating the effects of removing or varying radiation, a putative TMI-cancer cause. As already mentioned, virtu-ally all scientists accept the LNT-radiation dose-response curve, based on Japanese-atomic-bomb data[198] and on decades-long, actual IARC-radiation-dosimetry data from 600,000 nuclear workers facing normal conditions[199] Whether radiation subjects are under high-psychosocial-stress conditions, as after Japanese bombing (NAS/ICRP studies), or under normal/low-psychoso-cial-stress conditions, as in normal (non-accident) workplaces (IARC studies), the levels of negative health effects from ionizing radiation remain virtually iden-tical, LNT. Moreover, health harms resulting from ionizing radiation are not reduced in the lower-stress situations, those of the IARC studies, as compared to the higher-stress Japanese situations of the NAS/ICRP studies. IARC workplace data show that about 6 additional fatal cancers occur annually for each 500 people exposed to the maximum-allowable-occupational-radiation dose of 50 mSv/year. Thus, if radiation-dose-response studies (such as those of IAEC) are "quasi-exper-iments," in which radiation dose is varied (as IBE-CE principle (3) directs), then R, not S, better explains post-TMI health harms because negative health effects are proportional to radiation dose, and stress appears to play little or no role. Likewise, scientists have shown other effects of R removal and perturbation. For children under age 5, leukemia risk decreases with increased distance from nuclear plants and thus with reduced radiation exposure.[200] As already mentioned, the fact that cancers drop when radiation is removed or varied—for example, when normally operating reactors close—also suggests that R, not S, better explains increased post-accident TMI-area health harms.

How might one follow the second part of principle (3), removing or varying stress and then examining resulting cancer effects? The effects of removing stress were illustrated (see the previous section) by the 20-percent-higher cancer rates (odds ratio 1.2) near normally operating global reactors that caused no stress, because no accidents took place. This stress "removal" also shows that R, not S, better explains resulting TMI-related health harms because cancers increased as a function of radiation emission, even though no apparent stress was involved. Likewise, earlier sections of this chapter showed another principle-(3) stress removal. It revealed elevated cancer and mortality effects from TMI, hundreds of miles downwind from TMI.[201] Yet presumably only R, not S, had such distant effects, given that TMI scientists measured stress via reactor proximity. These distant, increased TMI cancers were a function not of proximity to the reactor (as S requires), but of being far downwind of TMI, as even Columbia (S proponents) authors admit.[202] In Albany, New York (230 miles downwind), radioactive gas xenon-133 was 3 times greater than normal for the first 5 days of the TMI accident; elevated post-TMI radioactivity also was detected in Portland, Maine, 430 miles downwind from TMI.[203] After the TMI accident, infant-mortality increases likewise occurred in downwind cities such as Syracuse, Rochester, and Albany.[204] However, if one "removes" radiation, by looking upwind (but within 10 miles) of TMI, where stress levels were presumably high, one discovers proportionate (to radiation dose) cancer reductions.[205] Both the distant, downwind S removals (and higher cancers) and the nearby, upwind R removals (and lower cancers) thus suggest that R, not S, better explains increased TMI-cancer rates. The upshot?

If the earlier treatment of IBE principle (2) is correct, S is a poorer explainer than R of at least 2 contrasts. The first contrast is (a) disproportionate TMI-area cancer increases in radiosensitive cancers (consistent with R, not S). The second contrast is (b) disproportionate TMI-area cancer increases in respiratory cancers (consistent with R, not S, given radioactive-gaseous releases). Likewise, if preceding IBE principle-(3) analyses are correct, S is a poorer explainer than R of at least 5 contrasts. These are (c) why TMI-cancer incidence is proportional to radiation dose (given the classic radiation-dose-response curve), rather than to some unknown stress level (given no stress-dose-response curve); (d) why nearby cancer rates return to normal once reactors close and radiation releases stop; (e) why (as already noted) children's leukemia rates decrease (under age 5) as distance from normally operating reactors increases; (f) why TMI-cancer incidence is proportional to downwind location rather than to distance from the reactor; and (g) why cancer incidence is increased and proportional to radiation releases near normally operating nuclear facilities rather than to nearby residents' presumed low stress levels. Therefore, following principle (4), one ought to reject S because it is less able than R to explain contrasts (a)–(g).

Evaluating TMI Hypotheses via IBE-CE Principle (5)

How might one apply IBE-CE principle (5), producing new contrasts to "test" putative causes (S and R) of TMI health harms? One might follow at least 3 strategies. These include finding S-versus-R contrasts that involve *heterogeneous evidence*, finding contrasts that provide *mechanisms* to explain contrasts, and finding contrasts that support explanatory-scheme *unification*.[206] Consider these 3 strategies in order.

Heterogeneous evidence (for increased TMI-area cancers and negative health effects) might provide contrasts that address heterogeneous *victims*, heterogeneous investigative *methods*, or heterogeneous health *effects*. Regarding *heterogeneous victims*, R and not S better accounts for the contrast of why TMI-area botanicals (TMI victims without psychosocial-stress effects) exhibited post-TMI harm. Botanist Dr. James Gunckel found numerous instances of oversized, deformed post-TMI plants. He argued that 100 mrem radiation doses (alleged by industry and the US government) could not have caused such phenomena. Russian radiation-science expert V. A. Shevchenko likewise argued that at least 60–90 rem (TMI-radiation doses 600–900 times what industry and the US government claim) were required to cause observed TMI-area tree damage.[207]

Regarding *heterogeneous health effects*, again R and not S better explains a number of TMI health effects. Recall that, besides cancer and mortality, such post-TMI health effects include increased hypothyroidism, birth defects, genetic defects, immune-system defects, and infant retardation.[208] Yet R, not S, arguably better explains increased genetic, immune, and IQ contrasts. Why? No literature links psychosocial stress to effects such as genetic effects, whereas radiation is a common cause of genetic defects.

Regarding *heterogeneous methods* for investigating TMI-causal hypotheses S and R, again R appears the better explainer because diverse and unflawed methods support R rather than S. Recall that the latest, longest-term government- and industry-approved (University of Pittsburgh) TMI studies relied on data from the 1979–1997 TMI registry.[209] These studies are flawed because they (1) were short term (18 years, given cancer latency of 50 years or more); (2) addressed mortality (not cancer or disease incidence); (3) covered 93 percent of people living within a 5-mile TMI radius, 18 years after TMI (which ignores exposed people who moved from TMI, victims who have not died yet, and those harmed by distant (250 miles away) TMI effects); (4) ignored beta-radiation exposures, as already noted; (5) used small-sample, low-power studies because they considered different cancers separately; (6) ignored effects on blacks, Harrisburg, and children under age 18; and (7) used industry-estimated radiation doses to deny TMI-radiation harms, and therefore to support S over R.

However, if one uses more reliable methods than (1)–(7), methods such as cohort analysis, then R and not S better explains post-accident TMI-related health harms. Rather than requiring statistical-significance tests for observational populations, cohort analysis examines precise information about exposed subgroups (e.g., children's relative disease and death risks, before and after some event); it seeks differences in cohort members' health, compared to that of others.[210] For instance, for the cohort of infants under 1 year old on March 28, 1979 (when the TMI accident began), in the 2 counties (Dauphin and Lebanon) immediately downwind (northeast) of TMI, all-cause mortality (excluding accidents, suicides, and homicides) has been 26–54 percent higher than that of statewide age-group peers, throughout this cohort's childhood, adolescence, and young adulthood. This cohort's cancer rate is 46 percent higher than that of statewide peers, although the local pre-TMI-accident cancer rates were below statewide rates, given TMI's rural location.[211] Yet R rather than S better explains the higher cancers in this TMI child-cohort because children are known to be many times more sensitive to radiation than are adults, whereas they are not known to be many times more sensitive to psychosocial stress.

The higher cancer and death rates in this TMI child cohort are important because the industry- and government-approved Pittsburgh studies ignored TMI effects on children, the subpopulation that is most sensitive to radiation. Instead the Pittsburgh researchers (doing the latest and longest official TMI studies) excluded children who were 18 and younger at the time of the accident; rather, the Pittsburgh scientists examined only those people living within a 5-mile or 10-mile radius of TMI, 10 years after the TMI accident, and they also ignored downwind (north/northeast)effects.[212] Because of all these biases, their methods arguably failed to detect many post-TMI negative health effects. These child-cohort results, however, provide at least 2 possible reasons that R, and not S, better explains post-TMI health harms. *First*, children—who are up to 38 times more vulnerable than adults to identical ionizing-radiation doses—experienced worse TMI harm than did adults.[213] *Second*, distant-downwind radionuclides affected children, whereas (by definition) stress-related TMI effects (measured via reactor proximity) did not.[214] Thus, by using alternative methodologies, like cohort analysis, one is able to provide contrasts, heterogeneous evidence, showing that R better explains TMI health harms than does S.

IBE-CE Principle (5):
Mechanisms, Explanatory Unification, and TMI

Contrasts that specify underlying mechanisms likewise suggest that R, not S, better explains post-TMI-accident cancer increases. Why is this the case? As earlier sections of this chapter showed, a stress-dose-response curve has not been confirmed, and "the mechanisms of the possible oncogenic effects of psychosocial stress have not been established."[215] However, the radiation-dose-response curve, and mechanisms for radiation-induced cancer, are well known. That is, ionizing radiation has sufficient energy to change molecular structure, including DNA within the bodily cells. Because some of these changes cannot be repaired, they initiate cancer processes (e.g., gene deletion), explaining why radiation causes at least 20 different cancers.[216]

Several contrasts also show that R, not S, better unifies explanatory schemes for post-TMI cancer increases. As already noted, scientists have tied increased cancer risks to increased radiation doses—for atomic-bomb victims, for civilian nuclear workers, for radiation-therapy patients, for US military "atomic veterans," and for nuclear-weapons workers.[217] If one hypothesizes that TMI-accident radiation doses also increase cancer, by similar mechanisms, this hypothesis would help unify radiation-exposure situations (medical, workplace, wartime, etc.), radiation-exposure types (different radionuclides/rays), and radiation-exposure effects (carcinogenic, neurological, cardiac, immunological, etc.). Moreover, as was already shown, at least 7 other pieces of scientific evidence show that R, not S, better unifies explanatory schemes for post-TMI cancer increases. This evidence includes (1) the molecular effects of high-energy radionuclides; (2) the LNT thesis; (3) the radiation-induction of 20 different cancers; (4) the heightened radiation effects on children; (5) the 700 percent, post-TMI cancer increase in TMI-area hilltop residents; (6) the absence of nearby, upwind cancer increases; and (7) the hundreds of TMI residents' having metallic taste and hair loss. All 7 pieces of evidence are thus unified and illustrated by R. However, S accomplishes no comparable unification, given no known S mechanism, no S measure, no legitimate S proxy, and no known stress-dose-response curve. Therefore, application of IBE-CE principle (5) suggests that R, and not S, better explains post-TMI health harms.

TMI Hypotheses and Other Causal Accounts

Many of the conditions imposed on IBE and CE—such as IBE principle (5), which postulates that causal inferences have greater plausibility when they rely on an underlying explanatory mechanism—are similar to conditions imposed on causal claims by other philosophers and scientists. Consequently, these other causal accounts may provide additional (or very similar) reasons to support R or S. Three main strands of contemporary work on causal explanation are the interventionist-counterfactual tradition,[218] the mechanist tradition,[219] and the unificationist tradition.[220] All 3 traditions are guided by the idea that a cause is something that makes a difference to its effects. On the interventionist-counterfactual account, counterfactual interventions or manipulations are the difference-maker, and 2 events are causally related if and only if actual or counterfactual interventions on causes make a difference to effects. On the mechanistic account, the difference-maker is mechanisms, and 2 events are causally related if and only if there is a mechanism that connects them. On the unificationist account, the difference-maker is greater explanatory unification, and 2 events are causally related if and only if they promote the superior unification of relevant scientific theory.

Brief considerations suggest that these other causal accounts also might support R over S, just as preceding IBE-CE analyses have done. First, consider James Woodward's account. His interventionist-counterfactual account provides grounds for evaluating alternative causal hypotheses, such as S and R, because his account is able to explain a difference or contrast between S and R.[221] Woodward's account of explanation seems particularly important because it recognizes that "causal relationships are often established in the absence of information about intervening mechanisms," as when we know that some drug cures illness but we don't know the mechanism by which it does so,[222] and because it improves on David Lewis's causal account.[223] Various reasons suggest that a full analysis of Woodward's interventionist-counterfactual account also would support R over S as the better causal hypothesis.[224]

Likewise, full mechanist analyses also might support R over S.[225] This is because R, but not S, has underlying mechanisms (e.g., the radiation-dose-response curve) that can explain contrasts among alternative causal hypotheses (see earlier sections).[226] Similarly, full unificationist analyses likewise might support R over S. This is because R better unifies empirical cancer research.[227] Also, because R does a better job than S of unifying "consistent results of [other] epidemiological studies" on nuclear workers, children, atomic-bomb victims, and so on,[228] using a full unificationist analysis likewise might support R over S as a better causal hypothesis.

Answering Objections

In response to the preceding TMI arguments, several possible objections arise. A *first* objection is that, because some R evidence is anecdotal-clinical (e.g., post-TMI hair loss), R actually may not explain TMI health harms better than S does. However, this objection errs in forgetting that relevant case-controlled experiments cannot be done after pollution-related accidents have occurred; anecdotal, clinical, and observational data are the only data that can be obtained. Moreover, both the former Pennsylvania health director (physician Gordon MacLeod) and the Kemeny Advisory Commission charged the TMI utility and the US government with TMI-accident-effects cover-up; with failure to do scientist-requested post-TMI studies (e.g., on TMI respirable-dust exposures to confirm radiation dose);[229] and with not releasing relevant TMI-accident data.[230] Given this apparently deliberate industry/government failure to obtain better data, and given industry/government cover-up of TMI health harms, anecdotal and clinical evidence for TMI harms arguably ought not be ignored.[231] In such a situation, there are at least 5 additional reasons that help justify the use of anecdotal data in assessing causes of TMI health harms.

(1) These anecdotal data are neither the only data, nor the bulk of the data. Indeed, they are dwarfed by the abundance of data from the National Academy, IARC, and so on, on effects of ionizing radiation.

(2) In some few cases, like the TMI-area physicians' claims about their patients' hair loss and metallic taste, often the only available and relevant data have been anecdotal-clinical; consequently it seems important to use them but to mention their epistemic status.

(3) Not to use anecdotal information, especially whenever it sometimes is the only evidence available on a specific point, is to encourage people to beg the question against TMI-radiation-related health effects. This is because people often erroneously assume that the absence of evidence for some effect is the same as evidence for the absence of an effect.

(4) Using anecdotal information, when it might help illuminate some specific health problem, is also important as an incentive, because it increases the probability that government will do official, fully funded, comprehensive studies assessing this problem, to see if anecdotal reports are borne out.

(5) Because this discussion addresses *relative* IBE evaluation of alternative causal hypotheses, not inference to *a nearly certain* explanation, using anecdotal information seems defensible, particularly information from otherwise-reliable sources, such as local physicians.

A *second* possible objection to supporting causal hypothesis R over S is that using classical statistical tests to assess non-experimental inferences seems more likely to reveal TMI-radiation harms than to cover them up, given that the TMI samples were disproportionately composed of exposed people. This objection seems partly correct. Obviously if sampling is not random, but biased by including mainly exposed populations, results should reflect this bias. However, at least 7 reasons suggest that other TMI-study flaws overwhelm this exposed-population bias toward finding radiation effects. Consequently, these TMI-study flaws prejudice researchers against R.

(1) Sections 4–5 in the chapter revealed flawed TMI-radiation data and assumptions that obviously lead to TMI radiation-dose underestimation (e.g., about beta dose and plume rise).

(2) Section 5 showed that restricted, industry-controlled TMI scientific funding, through the TMI Public Health Fund, required scientists to accept low (industry's 100-mrem-maximum) TMI-radiation doses.

(3) Section 9 revealed that bias against R, in TMI-radiation-effects studies, came partly from black-box epidemiologists who erroneously use classical statistical tests in non-experimental studies, and from toxic-tort courts' requiring classical statistical tests of non-experimental data to establish harm.[232]

(4) Section 10 argued that, without randomization, non-experimental TMI studies have no reliable interpretation. Instead they merely reflect the biases of the models: for example, assuming that TMI evidence at the time of cancer diagnosis, 15 years after TMI, accurately reflects TMI-induced cancers.

(5) Section 12 revealed that most TMI studies ignore post-TMI occurrence of disproportionately radiosensitive and respiratory cancers.

(6) Section 13 showed that most TMI studies ignore distant, downwind (250 miles away), TMI-induced cancers.

(7) Section 14 revealed that most TMI studies ignore plant, animal, and acute radiation-exposure effects that occurred after the TMI accident.

(8) Section 15 showed that the official, supposedly best, TMI-radiation studies exhibit biases against R (e.g., excluding blacks and children; considering mortality and not disease incidence; ignoring long-latency cancers).

(9) Section 15 revealed that, because most TMI-radiation-effects studies considered rare cancers separately and ignored the fact that the rural TMI area would typically have had lower cancer rates, they had inadequate power and sample size to detect possible R effects of TMI.[233]

(10) TMI-study bias against R also likely arises because, as the American Association for the Advancement of Science warns,[234] two-thirds of all US science is funded by special interests in order to promote their financial goals.

Because of (10), finding (and funding) non-experimental studies that corroborate R over S is more difficult because corporations control, and may manipulate, at least some scientific research.[235] Thus studies—that show pollution harms—are far more difficult to find than those denying such harms. If so, contrary to objection (2), externally controlled science may bias post-accident TMI-health-effects studies against inferring R as the more important cause of TMI-related health harms.

A *third* possible objection to the preceding arguments is that a non-experimental US National Cancer Institute (NCI) study allegedly showed no higher cancer rates near US nuclear plants, contrary to earlier claims. The NCI study admitted it could support no definitive conclusions, yet claimed its evidence showed no higher cancer rates in US counties having nuclear plants.[236] Comparing cancer rates in counties with and without reactors, the NCI authors assumed that all reactor-radiation-exposed residents resided in counties with reactors, while all non-reactor-radiation-exposed residents resided in counties without reactors. Calculating all-county standard mortality ratios (SMRs) for these 2 populations (populations in exposed and in non-exposed counties) before and after nuclear-facility startup, the authors found no overall SMR difference.

Unfortunately this study has at least 5 biases against finding harmful effects from power-plant radiation releases. *First*, because the study used only *countywide data* to examine nuclear-plant-health effects, it biased samples in many ways. For one thing, it counted residents of counties without reactors as non-reactor-radiation-exposed, while it counted residents of counties with reactors as reactor-radiation-exposed. Yet many reactors are at counties' eastern or northern borders, a fact that causes downwind radiation mainly in other counties (whose residents were counted as non-exposed). These same reactors cause nearly 0 radiation in their reactor-home counties (whose residents were counted as exposed). Also, because the typical countywide-study area was 1,200 square miles, the distant low-dose, or 0-dose radiation-dose "victims" diluted the radiation health effects on closer, higher-dose victims. Similarly, because half of the population examined lived more than 20 miles from reactors, the more-harmful radiation effects on closer residents were diluted by lesser radiation effects on faraway residents. *Second*, because the NCI study ignored wind direction, its nearly 0 upwind health effects dilute mostly downwind health harms from radiation. *Third*, the study used cancer-mortality, not cancer-incidence, data, even though many scientists have demonstrated statistically significant associations between radiation and cancer incidence—despite the lack of associations (in short-term studies) between radiation and cancer mortality.[237] After all, premature-cancer-mortality effects take up to 50 or more years to appear and are biased by quality of medical care. Consequently, such mortality studies are confounded by different quality of health care, and they do not measure only the effects of radioactive pollution. A *fourth* problem with the NCI study is that it admits there are increased, statistically significant, radiation-related-mortality risks near some nuclear facilities, yet it denies these effects by averaging overall mortality for all facilities. *Fifth*, as already argued, the NCI study's conclusions (no increased cancers in counties with nuclear facilities) are inconsistent (see above) with well-confirmed LNT radiation-dose-response curves that show there is no safe dose of radiation; thus if reactors emit any levels of radiation, the health harms from this radiation should be detectable, given proper studies.

A fourth possible objection to this chapter's conclusions is that supposed TMI-related cancers appeared too early, within 4 years after the accident, although most cancers have a latency period of at least 5 years. This objection errs, however, for at least 6 reasons. (1) Radiosensitive cancers, like leukemia and thyroid cancer, do not always have a long latency period, and radiosensitive cancers represented the bulk of the TMI-cancer increase. (2) Post-TMI cancers did not merely appear within 4 years. Instead, the earlier discussion showed that for more than 3 decades, the TMI-child (at time of accident) cohort has had significantly higher death and cancer rates, throughout their lifetimes. Moreover, (3) because the earlier discussion showed most TMI epidemiological studies have methodological flaws, their failure to confirm R is questionable. For instance, they excluded children (the most radio-sensitive group), had low-power problems, studied only mortality, and so on, as argued earlier. (4) Because the 4-year rapid-cancer increases also are consistent with findings, cited earlier, of rapid, early, TMI-area increases in infant mortality, infant hypothyroidism, and child retardation, radiation, not stress, better explains all these effects (5) The early (4 years post-accident) cancer increases likewise appear consistent, as noted earlier, with physician reports of post-TMI massive hair loss, vomiting, and nausea—for which at least a 400 rad exposure would be neces-sary—clearly an exposure high enough to cause early-onset cancer, as already argued. Finally, (6) the early-cancer onset is consistent with radiation causation, rather than stress causation, because TMI cancers were disproportionately respira-tory (and TMI-radiation releases were mainly gaseous), because radiation can explain many distant, downwind post-TMI health effects—as far away as Maine—and because the TMI utility quietly settled with numerous TMI victims for $80 million and required gag orders of them.

What about more theoretical objections to the IBE-CE and interventionist-counterfactual accounts of causal explanation?[238] For instance, one might object to the deterministic nature of the interventionist-counterfactual account of causal explanation, given that much of the world is indeterministic.[239] However, as Woodward notes, "most functional relationships in most areas of science" are deter-ministic, and "the great majority of our best theories in the biomedical and the social sciences are deterministic," especially regarding "causal modeling techniques" where statistical information is used. Even in statistical areas, the underlying models often are deterministic, and this deterministic account can be extended to indeter-ministic situations: "In many, many cases deterministic theories describe how nature works, up to a reasonable (sometimes very great) degree of approximation, and that should be good enough for all of us."[240]

Another possible objection is that the interventionist-counterfactual accounts of scientific explanation work best when there is only one cause that is sufficient for some effect, although this is often not true in the world. There are many causes of some types of cancer, for instance.[241] However, one can employ a combination of different interventions or contrasts to assess causal relationships that are character-ized by many different contributing causes. Because one can hold other variables (or potential causes) fixed, and thus check the effects of different interventions, one can address this objection.[242] How might one use multiple interventions to assess multiple possible causes? This already has been done in applying IBE-CE principle (2). That is, assuming that both ionizing-radiation exposure and stress can possibly cause cancer, one sees the effects of natural manipulations of these 2 alleged causes in the Hiroshima-Nagasaki atomic-bomb-radiation data.[243] There, both stress and radiation exposures increased, and so did the cancers. But if one looks at the effects of natural manipulations of these 2 alleged causes in the TMI case, where both stress and radiation exposures increased, one can observe (as already noted) the increased cancers. However, because these were predominantly radiosensitive and respiratory cancers, the differences in the effects suggest that R, not S, is the more likely cause of increased TMI cancers. This conclusion also is supported by another manipulation. Assuming that both ionizing-radiation exposure and stress are possible causes of TMI-cancer increases, as already discussed, one sees the effects of natural manipulations of these 2 alleged causes by observing the increase in radiation exposure (to downwind but hundreds-of-miles-distant populations), under conditions of low stress (because downwind populations are very distant from the TMI accident, presumably they have no TMI stress effects). Here one observes that the very-distant-from-TMI downwind cancer rate increases, despite the absence of increased stress. This contrast, in turn, suggests that R, not S, is a better explainer of TMI-cancer increases. Likewise, as already discussed, one sees the effects of quasi-manipulating these 2 alleged causes, S and R, by observing the decrease in radiation exposure (to near-TMI, upwind populations), under conditions of high stress (because nearby upwind populations live very close to TMI). Here one observes that nearby, upwind cancer rates do not increase, despite proximity to TMI. This fact also suggests that R, not S, is a better explainer of TMI-cancer increases.

Conclusion

What has this chapter taught us? According to the dominant scientific position on health effects of the TMI nuclear accident, stress, not TMI radiation, was more likely responsible for increased deaths and health problems after the accident. However, this chapter has shown that the dominant/majority/industry/government position is wrong. Instead, the minority position is the better causal hypothesis: TMI radiation, not accident-related stress, is more likely responsible for the negative health effects of the accident, and for 4 main reasons. (1) Flawed inductive methods help explain why the dominant causal hypothesis S (that nuclear-accident-related *stress*, not radiation, more likely caused the increase in post-TMI-accident cancers), is less plausible than alternative hypothesis R (that TMI-accident *radiation*, not stress, more likely caused these harms). (2) Many scientists erroneously reject R, and accept S, partly because they fall into COI or misunderstand randomization requirements (not met in TMI studies) for use of statistical-significance and other tests. (3) However, given non-experimental TMI data, inference to the best explanation (IBE), not statistical-significance tests, may better illuminate the statistical underpinnings of competing causal hypotheses S and R. (4) Avoiding erroneous, statistics-related causal inferences, like those at TMI, thus requires fundamental shifts in epidemiological method. Scientists need less black-box epidemiology and more IBE-CE. When scientists use correct methods to assess nuclear accidents, it is clear that atomic energy is a very risky technology, thus a very poor way to help address climate change.

People cannot see, hear, taste, touch, or smell ionizing radiation, but they need to learn that it can hurt them. They need to learn that so long as radiation-induced diseases, like cancer, cannot be cured, they must prevent them. Just as engineers used their technical training to begin commercial nuclear fission, citizens and especially physicians must use their understanding and wisdom to help end it.

CHAPTER 5

Nuclear Energy and
Environmental Justice

Commercial atomic energy has many problems as a proposed solution to climate change (CC). Chapter 2 showed that its fuel-cycle greenhouse-gas (GHG) emissions are roughly equal to those of natural gas, and many times higher than those of wind, solar photovoltaic (PV), and other renewable-energy sources. GHG emissions ratios, per kWhr of electricity, are roughly coal 60 : gas 9 : nuclear 9 : solar 2 : wind 1. Chapter 3 revealed that, provided one uses actual market and credit-rating data for cost assumptions and includes all fuel-cycle costs, nuclear fission is by far the most expensive source of current electricity, many times more expensive than wind, solar photovoltaic (PV), and other renewable energy sources. Chapter 4 likewise showed that atomic energy is unsafe. Accidents like those at Fukushima Daiichi, Japan; Chernobyl, Belarus; and Three Mile Island, Pennsylvania, have caused up to a million deaths and additional health problems, and they help explain the government-guaranteed accident-liability limit, which forces nuclear-accident victims, not the industry, to cover 98 percent of worst-case-accident costs. Without this liability limit, industry says it would not use nuclear power.

Given the emissions, cost, and safety problems of fission, as documented in earlier chapters, it is easy to see why atomic energy is declining, why most banks refuse nuclear loans, why credit companies downgrade the credit rating of utilities with reactors, why fission can survive only if taxpayers pay most of its costs, and why accidents like Three Mile Island have caused so many fatalities. As the previous chapter explained, these fatalities occur partly because radiation has no safe dose and induces many cancers and genetic effects—such as increased rates of long-term, germ-line mutations, which in turn induce health problems, such as cancer, for hundreds of future generations.[1]

Even in cells not directly hit by ionizing radiation, exposure causes bystander effects and genomic instabilities. This means radiation increases mutation rates, raises propensity for disease in later generations, and weakens the human genome—not only in exposed cells, but also in unexposed cells, even many cell divisions and many generations after radiation exposure.[2] Radiation's delayed, transgenerational effects thus explain why cancer *rates*, not merely cancer *incidences*, continue to increase in Japan, even among those born several generations after the Hiroshima and Nagasaki exposures. Such transgenerational effects also explain harms to children who were born many years after parental radiation exposure, as in the large cluster of leukemia cases in children living near the Sellafield, UK, nuclear facility.[3]

Chapter Overview

This chapter argues that such ionizing-radiation effects are not equally distributed. Instead, atomic energy is responsible for significant environmental injustice, that is, for disproportionately higher pollution effects on the weakest, most vulnerable people—children, blue-collar workers, minorities, and members of future generations.[4]

Outlining these environmental injustices, the chapter argues for 4 main claims. *First*, the nuclear-fuel cycle, including uranium mining, milling, enrichment, and so on, imposes unjust and uncompensated radiation burdens on indigenous people and minorities. *Second*, US commercial reactors are disproportionately sited in the poorest part of the US: in the Southeast and in communities having statistically significantly more people living below the poverty line. *Third*, even without accidents, normally operating reactors cause radiation-induced diseases and fatalities. *Fourth*, the chapter shows that radiation standards themselves are environmentally unjust because they protect many US children almost 200 times less well than adults—and blue-collar workers 50 times less well than other members of the public. They also protect future generations at least 4 times less well than current people.

Environmental Injustice in the Nuclear-Fuel Cycle

Recall the 14 stages of the nuclear-fuel cycle, presented in chapter 2, and consider first the environmental injustices (EIJ) associated with stage (1), mining uranium. In most major uranium-producing nations (e.g., Canada, Australia, Kazakhstan, Niger, Russia, Namibia, Uzbekistan, and the US), indigenous peoples have been harmed by working in unregulated uranium mines, by exposure to uncontrolled uranium wastes on native lands, or by risky uranium mining and processing on their lands, although they have not consentedto these operations.[5] In Canada, for instance, all uranium mining is on lands claimed by, or directly affecting, indigenous groups.[6] In the US, Native American uranium miners (e.g., Navajos) face 14 times the normal lung-cancer risk, "most" of which, the government says, has been caused by their uranium mining, not by smoking.[7]

The US government also admits that it failed to require uranium-mine ventilation, failed to disclose radiation risks to Navajo miners, and had "no plausible justification" for allowing massive exploitation of Native American uranium miners.[8] In 2005, the Navajo Nation demanded a moratorium on uranium mining and processing on its lands until ongoing uranium-mining and -processing damages have been assessed and remedied. These damages include inadequate compensation for radiation-induced disease among native miners, neither permanent closure nor decontamination of hundreds of uranium-mining or processing sites that continue to expose native peoples, and no ongoing medical studies of the health status of Native Americans affected by uranium mining.[9]

EIJ also occurs in stages (2)–(5) of the nuclear fuel cycle, respectively, (2) milling uranium, (3) converting it to uranium hexafluoride (UF_6), (4) enriching the UF_6, and (5) fabricating nuclear fuel. Employees in these stages of the fuel cycle— tens of millions of radiation workers, including nearly 2 million in the US[10]—also face EIJ. As this chapter reveals, US nuclear-facility owners legally may expose workers to annual radiation doses up to 50 times higher than those allowed for members of the public,[11] although there is no safe dose of ionizing radiation.[12] Yet these employees often receive no hazard pay or compensating wage differential,[13] and they typically fail to give informed consent to their higher workplace risks; instead they perform dangerous nuclear jobs out of economic necessity,[14] or because they do not realize the risks, given government-contractor falsification of worker radiation doses.[15] The chapter shows that flawed radiation standards, flawed risk disclosure, and flawed workplace-radiation monitoring all have caused employees to underestimate radiation risks.[16] Yet the risks are substantial. The International Agency for Research on Cancer (IARC) shows that every time 100 workers are exposed to the maximum-allowable annual occupational-radiation dose of 50 mSv, 2.5–5 percent—up to 1 in 20—of their lifetime fatal cancers will be attributable to their workplace-radiation exposure,[17] or that the radiation exposure gives them a 1 in 80 chance of dying from premature cancer. After 40 years of exposure to maximum-annual-radiation doses each year, workers would have a 50-percent chance of lifetime fatal cancer, induced by their occupational-radiation exposure.[18]

US nuclear-waste policies in fission-fuel-cycle stages (8)–(9)—radioactive waste transport and storage—likewise have already caused EIJ at US nuclear-waste facilities such as Hanford (Washington), Maxey Flats (Kentucky), and Savannah River (South Carolina); this chapter shows that further EIJ is likely when future radioactive-waste canisters fail—long before the million years that the US National Academy of Sciences says they must be completely secured.[19] Future EIJ is even more likely because the US government has admitted falsifying and manipulating data on radioactive-waste risks.[20] In fact, UN and nuclear-industry studies warn that the US government has underestimated future waste-repository-radiation doses by 9–12 orders of magnitude.[21] Much of this risk will be borne by Appalachian, Latino, and Native American populations—who live in higher proportions near existing and proposed nuclear-waste-storage sites. Besides, even if these sites meet US nuclear-waste standards, their leniency likely will impose EIJ on future generations. They would allow future radioactive-waste-facility exposures that are 10 times higher than those now allowed at US Department of Energy facilities. They also require only the mean or average radiation dose to meet regulatory requirements. As the chapter shows, this means the regulations allow higher, even fatal, radiation doses to some people.[22]

Nuclear-Related Environmental Injustice in Reactor Siting

Nuclear-waste-related EIJ occurs not only because members of future generations are likely to be harmed by leaking radionuclides but also, as just mentioned, because government both mandates less-protective radiation standards for future people and typically places radioactive-waste facilities in poor or minority communities. The now-stalled Yucca Mountain waste repository is surrounded by disproportionate numbers of Native American, Latino, and poor residents; the Savannah River site, by disproportionate numbers of blacks and poor people; the Maxey Flats waste dump, by Appalachian and poor residents.[23] What about reactors themselves? Are they often sited in poor or minority communities?[24] Many citizens' groups say they are.[25] Are these groups correct?

Consider the proposed Vogtle reactors in Waynesboro, Georgia. These reactors are important because, if they are actually finished, they will be the first new, highly subsidized US reactors ordered since 1974, when massive financial problems stalled the nuclear industry. In 2006 Southern Nuclear Operating Company (SNOC) proposed 2 additional reactors for Waynesboro.[26] Currently SNOC's Early Site Permit Application,[27] as well as its Combined Construction Operating License, are under Nuclear Regulatory Commission review.[28] However, because SNOC uses at least 3 flawed criteria for assessing EIJ, it likely errs when it denies that the Vogtle facility will cause any EIJ.[29] According to these criteria, SNOC claims EIJ exists only if

(1) census blocks within the full, 50-mile radius of the Vogtle facility include high minority or poverty-level populations;

(2) these census blocks have either (a) a population that is more than 50 percent minority or poor, or (b) a minority or poor population that exceeds the averages for Georgia or South Carolina by at least 20 percentage points;[30] and

(3) the Vogtle facility is located amid dense population.[31]

Yet all 3 criteria are seriously flawed. Criterion (1) dilutes potential EIJ effects by using a 50-mile radius,[32] instead of assessing closer minority and poor populations.

Obviously the greater the distance from a risky facility, the less likely are facility-related health risks, therefore the less likely is EIJ. Besides, the National Cancer Institute (NCI) study (of cancer rates near nuclear plants, discussed in the previous chapter) says areas 30 miles (not 50 miles, as the Vogtle study claims) from a nuclear plant are those most likely affected by radioactive emissions.[33] Criterion (1) also ignores wind patterns relative to minority and low-income census tracts. Yet areas downwind of the Vogtle reactors likely would experience greater risks.

Criteria (2a) and (2b) likewise are unrealistic and unfair. According to criterion (2a), EIJ exists only if there is a 50-percent minority or low-income population within a 50-mile radius of Vogtle. Yet in the US, average state low-income populations range from 4.3 to 16 percent.[34] This means that showing income-related EIJ, under Vogtle criterion (2a), would require showing local low-income populations that were 3–12 times greater than the Georgia average. Even a doubling of low-income groups near Vogtle would not count as EIJ, under criterion (2a). Similarly, according to alternative criterion (2b), EIJ exists only if percentages of minority or low-income populations are 20 percentage points above the respective averages for Georgia or South Carolina. Yet Georgia and South Carolina already have minority populations of about 30 percent.[35] To show EIJ, criterion (2b) thus requires nearly doubling (over the state average) the percent-minority population residing near Vogtle. Yet obviously EIJ could exist without a near-doubling of the percentage of nearby minority or poor people.

Using unrealistic and unfair EIJ criteria (2a)–(2b), SNOC says that 183 census-block groups (37.3 percent of those within a 50-mile radius) meet criterion (2a) for minority populations; that 14 census-block groups (2.8 percent) meet criterion (2a) for poverty-level populations; that 168 census-block groups (34.2 percent) meet criterion (2b) for minority populations; and that 72 census-block groups (14.7 percent) meet criterion (2b) for poverty-level populations.[36] Relying on these data and anecdotal evidence collected from 2 phone interviews, SNOC admits: "Some existing communities within the [50-mile-radius] area exhibit disproportionately high percentages of minority (primarily Black races) and low-income populations."[37] However, because SNOC says these high-density minority and low-income areas are "scattered," it concludes that "there were no environmental justice effects to consider with respect to densely populated minority or low-income peoples."[38] However, as this quotation reveals, EIJ criterion (3) of SNOC is flawed because it recognizes only residents in "densely populated" groups as EIJ victims. Yet whether EIJ victims live in sparsely populated (rural) or densely populated (urban) areas is irrelevant to whether they are EIJ victims. Criterion (3) thus is unfair and misleading in excluding all rural cases of EIJ.

SNOC is just as biased when it uses criterion (3). It defines a "population center" as having greater than 25,000 residents; lists Augusta, Georgia (population 195,182), as the nearest (26 miles away) population center to Vogtle;[39] then claims the Vogtle facility is located in a sparsely populated area.[40] Yet Vogtle is directly located in largely minority, largely low-income Waynesboro, Georgia, whose population is 5,813.[41] By thus assuming a town (Waynesboro) of 5,813 residents is sparsely populated, SNOC can ignore its EIJ violations—which it defines as applying only to "densely populated" areas. The result? SNOC says the Vogtle nuclear siting satisfies none of its 3 EIJ criteria. Yet because all 3 criteria are scientifically and ethically suspect, siting the Vogtle reactors could well involve EIJ.

Apart from questionable EIJ criteria used in the Vogtle case, does EIJ typify other US nuclear-reactor-siting cases? Consider the Grand Gulf Nuclear station, in Port Gibson, Mississippi. Some citizens' groups claim this reactor was sited under EIJ conditions because its home-county population is 85-percent African American, and 33-percent poverty-level.[42] However, if one examines census data from zip codes in which the 104 US nuclear facilities are located, roughly half are located in zip codes having higher percentages of African American/Hispanic/minority/poverty-level residents than is average for their home states, and roughly half are not.[43] This suggests that, although these data tell nothing about how far above (or below) average are the percentages of vulnerable populations near nuclear plants, they provide no obvious EIJ evidence. However, if one considers EIJ victims separately—respectively grouping African Americans, Hispanics, minorities, and poverty-level residents—and if one considers US regions separately, Z-tests show apparent EIJ. They show that the 38 commercial nuclear reactors in the Southeast (Arkansas, Alabama, North Carolina, South Carolina, Georgia, Florida, Mississippi, Virginia, Louisiana, and Tennessee) are sited disproportionately in zip codes having higher percentages of poverty-level residents. Moreover, Z-tests show that this poverty-area reactor siting has a greater-than-99-percent likelihood of not being due merely to chance ($p < 0.001$).[44]

Besides apparent EIJ against poor people, reactor siting also may involve regional inequity. Over 36 percent of US nuclear reactors are located in the Southeast, 25 percent in the Northeast, 23 percent in the Midwest, and 15 percent in the West. However, census data show that the Southeast contains only about 26 percent of the US population, while the Northeast has 23 percent; the Midwest, 19 percent; and the West, 31 percent. If the percentage of commercial reactors in each region were proportional to its population, only 26 (not 36) percent of reactors should be in the Southeast. This means the number of southeastern reactors is 38 percent greater than expected—a disproportionately high percentage of fission plants, given the regional population. In comparison, reactor numbers are only 7 percent greater than expected in the Northeast, and 19 percent greater in the Midwest. Reactor numbers are 52 percent less than expected in the West. Such data suggest the Southeast may bear more nuclear-fission burdens than the rest of the nation.[45] This may be an important EIJ, given that the Southeast has a disproportionately higher percentage (than other US regions) of both African Americans and poverty-level populations.[46]

Nuclear-Related Environmental Injustice in Normal Reactor Operation

Even if nuclear plants were never sited in poor or minority communities, they would still be responsible for much EIJ, mainly because of the disproportionately harmful effects of their emissions on children. What are these emissions? Normal reactor-operation involves airborne and waterborne releases of many radioactive isotopes, including hydrogen-3 (tritium), carbon-14, and plutonium-239; only recently have people recognized that these allowable-radiation releases already have contaminated local air and water supplies.[47] Because US (and most other Western) nuclear facilities are allowed to emit 25 mrem of radiation annually,[48] scientists have detected statistically significant increases in infant and fetal mortality near US reactors;[49] in childhood cancers and leukemias near US reactors;[50] in childhood leukemias near German reactors;[51] in childhood leukemias near French nuclear-reprocessing plants;[52] and in childhood leukemia, child lymphoma, child brain cancer, and cancer generally, near English and Scottish nuclear facilities.[53] Studies also show that, once nuclear reactors shut down, nearby rates of infant health ailments, cancers, and deaths decrease.[54] In particular, as already noted, scientists have shown a decreasing leukemia risk, for children under 5 years of age, with increased distance from nuclear plants.[55] The upshot? Virtually all scientists (except several paid by the nuclear industry) have reached a consensus on confirmed, peer-reviewed journal studies showing increases in child-leukemia and non-Hodgkins-lymphoma clusters, with up to fivefold and tenfold increases, at least near nuclear facilities in Seascale, England; Dounreay, Scotland; and Elbmarsch, Germany.[56] As these data indicate, radiation effects on young people are especially severe,[57] even with supposedly safe conditions of normal reactor-operation. Later paragraphs show that these disproportionate effects occur partly because children are up to 38 times more radiosensitive than adults.

Some people (mostly those paid by the nuclear industry) have objected to the preceding findings of increased negative health effects near normally operating reactors, claiming that a US National Cancer Institute (NCI) study suggested no higher cancer rates near nuclear plants. However, the preceding chapter explained why this NCI study is scientifically flawed and draws invalid conclusions. At least 2 additional reasons show that even normally operating reactors likely impose higher risks on children. One reason is that heightened risks have been confirmed by many different peer-reviewed, scientific-journal studies in many different countries, as already noted. The other reason is that increased health harms are required by the standard, well-confirmed radiation-dose-response curves, already discussed in the previous chapter. Virtually all radiation scientists and professional associations (including the influential US National Academy of Sciences committee that assesses biological effects of ionizing radiation) accept the linear, no-threshold (LNT) dose-response curve for radiation. They say that health effects of any non-zero radiation dose are risky and cumulative, hence that health consequences of radiation are LNT, proportional to dose. Thus, higher radiation doses near reactors cause higher nearby health harms.[58] As noted in the previous chapter, the NAS committee estimates that, on average, each 10 mSv (100 mrem) per year of radiation exposure, over a 70-year lifetime, causes roughly a 5-percent (lifetime) increase in fatal cancers. This is roughly 1 additional annual fatal cancer in every 300 people exposed to 10 mSv. Using a different data set, the International Commission on Radiological Protection (ICRP) likewise supports LNT and draws a similar conclusion. It says every exposure to the maximum-allowable US occupational-radiation dose, 50 mSv/year, induces about 1 extra fatal cancer per year in every 500 people exposed— or 1 fatal cancer in every 49 people over their lifetimes.[59] The NAS and ICRP radiation-dose-response curves thus reveal what happens when radiation levels are varied—reduced or increased. Negative health effects are proportional to dose. This proportionality argues strongly, as scientific consensus affirms, that effects of ionizing radiation are LNT with respect to dose.

Yet because both NAS and ICRP dose-response curves are based on dose estimates and extrapolations derived from atomic-bomb survivor data, the previous chapter argued that these data may not be as reliable as actual empirical data from the largest study of nuclear workers to date.[60] Conducted by IARC, the nuclear-worker assessment provides the basis for the best-confirmed, most empirical radiation-dose-response curve. It evaluates numbers of cancers, diseases, and deaths associated with actual, individual, radiation-dosimeter readings, over several decades, for 600,000 nuclear workers. Moreover, the workers had no idea what their radiation-dosimeter readings were, at least during employment, and they engaged in normal occupational activities. In this IARC study, scientists again confirmed that negative health effects of radiation exposure are LNT, proportional to dose, but they discovered that radiation is even riskier than NAS and ICRP studies suggested. As already mentioned, empirical IARC data show that every time 100 workers are exposed to the maximum-allowable annual occupational-radiation dose of 50 mSv, up to 1 in 20 of their lifetime fatal cancers will be attributable to their workplace-radiation exposure,[61] or that the radiation exposure gives them a 1 in 80 chance of dying from premature cancer; after 40 years of exposure to maximum-annual-radiation doses each year, workers would have a 50-percent chance of lifetime fatal cancer, induced by their occupational-radiation exposure.[62] Thus the IARC cancer-fatality rates are several times higher than those estimated by NAS and ICRP, although all 3 dose-response curves confirm that radiation effects are LNT, with no safe dose except zero. Given this well-confirmed LNT radiation-dose-response curve, it is impossible that even small radioactive emissions from normally operating reactors would not cause increased negative health effects. Moreover, well-confirmed studies have shown that every 10 mrem increase in gamma radiation can cause a 50-percent increase in cancer risk for children under age 15.[63] This means radiation doses of less than half the amount that nuclear facilities are allowed to release annually are able to cause significant health problems for children—even when there are no radiation accidents.

Nuclear-Related Environmental Injustice from Flawed Radiation Standards for Children

Children are at risk from commercial fission, however, not merely because of accidents and normal emissions from the nuclear-fuel cycle. Current national and international radiation-protection standards also fail to protect them adequately. In fact, for most pollutants, children are at roughly a 10-times-higher risk than adults, because their organ, metabolic, and detoxification systems are not fully developed; 80 percent of their alveoli, for instance, are formed after birth. Children also have much higher rates of cell multiplication and division than adults, and their unformed gastrointestinal tracts can absorb far more radionuclides than can those of adults.[64] Because children take in more air, water, food, and pollutants, per body-mass unit, than do adults, their pollution doses are proportionately higher. Children likewise have higher heart and respiration rates, in part because of their smaller airways. For all these reasons, children are more sensitive to pollutants. The World Health Organization says that, while children under age 5 represent only 10 percent of the global population, they represent 40 percent of the world's victims of disease.[65] Children likewise represent roughly 70 percent of global human deaths. Even in developed nations, pollution is causing adult cancer rates to increase roughly 1 percent per year, while children's cancer rates are increasing 40 percent faster, at 1.4 percent annually.[66]

Children likewise are far more radiosensitive than adults,[67] and infants are especially sensitive. As already mentioned, if an infant receives the same thyroid exposure to plutonium-139 as an adult, she will receive a dose that is 39 times higher than that of the adult; if both receive the same dose, her thyroid-cancer risk will be 33 times higher than that of the adult.[68] If a female infant, and a female adult of age 30, both receive the same dose of ionizing radiation, the infant is 21 times more likely to contract breast cancer than the adult.[69] Likewise, if an infant and an adult each drink milk with the same radioactive-iodine dose, the infant would receive a 13-times-higher thyroid dose than would the adult.[70]

Given children's much higher radiosensitivity, it is surprising that international and national radiation standards fail to protect them adequately. One of the central reasons they fail is that hazards of ionizing radiation are assessed in terms of the reference-man model. As ICRP put it: "Reference man is defined as being between 20–30 years of age, weighing 70 kg [154 pounds], is 170 cm [5 feet 7 inches] in height, and lives in a climate with an average temperature of from 10° to 20° C. He is a Caucasian and is a Western European or North American in habitat and custom."[71] In fact, the reference-man model is built into the main US computer program, RESRAD, used to assess radioactive risks after remediation of radioactively contaminated sites.[72] Yet RESRAD and reference-man models for radiation risks focus only on male cancer risks, although women's cancer risk is roughly 50-percent higher when both receive the same radiation dose.[73] Moreover, because the reference-man model focuses only on cancer, it also ignores noncancer harms. These radiation harms include genetic defects, immune-system damage, blood diseases, spontaneous abortion in the early weeks after conception, birth defects up to 14 weeks after conception, and higher risks of neonatal mortality—after radiation exposure.[74] The reference-man model likewise ignores the permanent 25-point drop in IQ for every sievert (100 rem) of in-utero ionizing-radiation exposure during the critical weeks (8–26) of brain formation.[75]

US radiation regulations governing children are especially suspect because they protect many children less well than adults—and US children less well than European children. According to US regulations, female nuclear workers need not declare their pregnancy unless they choose to do so. If they do, they and their fetus are allowed to receive annual radiation doses of 500 mrem (rather than 5,000 rem that radiation workers may receive annually); however, this dose to the fetus is 5 times higher than the 100 mrem annually that members of the public are allowed to receive, and 5 times higher than the 100 mrem annually that the fetus is allowed to receive in most of Europe (e.g., Germany).[76] The obvious question is why US fetuses are less well protected than European fetuses, and why US children are less well protected than adults, when infants are up to 38 times more radiosensitive than adults (see preceding paragraphs), and fetuses are even more sensitive than infants. If US fetuses and infants were to be protected at the same level as US members of the public, their annual radiation dose would have to be no more than $(1/38) \times$ (100 mrem), or 2.6 rem. Because the actual US fetal standard is 500 rem, the US fetus is $500 \div 2.6$ or 192 times less protected from radiation than US adults. If children are the most vulnerable members of our society, if current US radiation regulations protect children several hundred times less well than adults, and if they protect female adults half as well as they protect adult males, this suggests that radiation regulations may follow the preferences of the powerful, not the needs of the vulnerable.

How might US regulators respond to these criticisms of radiation-protection standards for children? They might claim different pollution standards for children are not able to be implemented, or would hinder economic production that benefits children, or that the regulations take account only of cancer risks mainly because adequate data are lacking for many other health effects of ionizing radiation. These objections might be called the implementability, economics, and data claims.

The implementability claim, that more protective childhood-radiation standards cannot be implemented for practical reasons, seems questionable on at least

4 grounds. *First,* in the last half-century, radiation standards for the public have become 500 percent more protective, moving from maximum-acceptable doses of 500 to 100 mrem annually.[77] If these standards have been progressively tightened, partly through improved radiation-protection technology, why cannot they be tightened further? *Second,* radiation standards are now 5 rem (50 mSv) annually for workers, but 500 mrem (5 mSv) annually for women who declare their pregnancy; federal regulations mandate that pregnant women be moved to lower-radiation areas during their pregnancies.[78] If contemporary employers implement a 10-times-stricter differential standard to protect fetuses, why cannot government extend such protection to all children? *Third,* current radiation-protection standards are based not on what can be easily implemented, but on what is ALARA—as low as reasonably achievable, taking into account economic considerations.[79] Thus, there is no in-principle limit to greater radiation protection, but only a federal-regulatory limit based on the costs of reducing radiation exposures. If it costs more than $1,000 to avoid an additional person-rem (0.01 person-Sv) of radiation, typically a polluter need not make the improvement.[80] This means radiation protection is largely a matter of economic trade-off. If so, the question of stricter radiation protections for children is largely a matter of economics and ethics, not implementability. This means those who claim more-protective radiation standards for children cannot be implemented must show that it is ethically defensible for a polluter to save money by not controlling radiation that disproportionately harms children. Because polluters gain by imposing risks on innocent people, it is difficult to see how this justification could work. After all, polluters ought to pay the costs of doing business, and those who use polluting products also ought to pay full price for them, not impose costs on innocent pollution victims, children. Note that, by federal regulation, radiation-pollution standards do not apply to medical therapy, only to industrial releases. Hence, by definition, it would be difficult to show that a child put at risk by radiation gained therapeutically.

A fourth reason to doubt the implementability claim is that the US government provides additional protections to children who are research subjects because it recognizes their medical vulnerability and political powerlessness.[81] Arguably, the same reasons justify expanded radiation-pollution protection for children. Moreover, the case for children's radiation-pollution protection is even stronger than that for their medical protection as experimental subjects. Why? At least in some medical research, children are sometimes allowed to be experimental subjects if there is a chance of direct medical benefits for them.[82] Yet no obvious direct benefits come to children when they are exposed to pollution merely because it is cheaper for polluters not to control it. Hence if government gives children special experimental-subject protections even when they benefit, and yet if children receive less protection against industrial-radioactive pollution even without any pollution-related benefits, then consistency and fairness require that children receive greater protection from ionizing radiation.

What about the economics claim—that weakened radiation-pollution standards may promote economic production that benefits everyone, including children? This claim begs the question that unequal radiation protection for children is worth increased economic benefits for society. That is, it begs the question that utilitarian benefits for many people can outweigh inequities suffered by children. The correctness of this ethical question-begging is doubtful, partly because children are the most vulnerable members of society and less able to speak for themselves. It also is doubtful because great inequities to the most vulnerable among us arguably harm everyone and damage the common good. Besides, from a purely factual point of view, it is questionable whether weakened radiation-pollution standards for children actually benefit society—that is, whether weaker pollution laws clearly cause increased welfare. As noted earlier, radiation protections for fetuses are 5 times more stringent in the EU than in the US. Does that mean the EU is 5 times worse off, in every way, than the US? Besides, if weak pollution control brings economic benefits, profits could find their way into CEO pockets and shareholder earnings, not the paychecks of everyone else. Thus tax structure and regulation, not just pollution, help determine pollution-related economic welfare. US census data for the last 40 years support this point. They cast doubt on the thesis that economic growth, even if it is promoted by weaker pollution laws, actually makes people better off. Why not? Given problematic taxation rules and questionable access to goods like health care, schooling, legal assistance, and so on, census data show that, since 1975, US economic welfare has improved, while more than 80 percent of Americans have become less well off.[83]

In response to the data claim, that adequate scientific evidence may be lacking for radiation-induced diseases other than cancer, it is important to note that the classic 1990 report, of a committee of the US National Academy of Sciences, noted much evidence for noncancer radiation-induced diseases. The report even provided radiation doses associated with various health effects. For instance, radiation-induced chromosome changes were tied to immunodeficiencies, in the scientific literature, as early as 1984–1988, as was radiation-induced cancer.[84] Likewise the report gave extensive lists of various radiation doses associated with different germ-line mutations, birth defects, and genetic defects—data based on Japanese atomic-bomb survivors that were clear in 1972.[85] In addition, the report noted that radiation's causing cataracts was evident by 1982; causing life-shortening was evident by the 1940s; and causing sterility was evident by the 1970s.[86] By the early 1960s, the report said scientists knew that radiation caused motor defects and hyperactivity; by the early 1970s, that it caused learning deficits and mental retardation; by 1977, that radiation could kill the embryo, cause central nervous system abnormalities, retard growth and development, and cause sterility; and by 1987, that radiation could cause many central-nervous-system disorders, such as hydrocephaly and anencephaly, as well as diseases such as spina bifida.[87] Hence, for all these reasons, it seems difficult to justify US regulatory neglect of virtually all radiation-induced diseases, except cancer, particularly given that scientific evidence for radiation-induced, noncancer harms has been accepted for more than 2 decades. If the preceding arguments are correct, the implementability, economics, and data objections provide no valid reason for regulations to provide children with less radiation protection than adults receive. Therefore radiation-protection standards for children may illustrate EIJ because they are roughly 200 times less protective than those for adults.

Nuclear-Related Environmental Injustice from Flawed Occupational-Protection Standards

Subsequent paragraphs show that US radiation standards for workers likewise illustrate EIJ because they are 50 times less protected than the public, and workers are likely unable to consent to these higher risks. US regulations allow members of the public to be exposed to 100 mrem (or 1 mSv) of radiation annually, while radiation workers may receive 5 rem (or 50 mSv) annually.[88] These differences are important because most scientists, including members of the influential US National Academy of Sciences BEIR Committee, already mentioned, say any radiation dose is risky and cumulative, no matter how small—and hence that radiation health effects are linear, with no threshold (LNT).[89]

According to the academy's estimates, every exposure to the maximum-allowable occupational-radiation dose—50 mSv per year—induces about 1 additional lifetime cancer in every 175 people exposed. Two years' exposure to this maximum-allowable occupational-radiation dose induces roughly 2 cancers in 175, or 1 cancer in every 88 people exposed; 3 years' exposure, 3 cancers in every 175, or 1 cancer in every 58 people exposed; and so on. According to the academy, if nuclear workers had 40 years of exposure, at the maximum-allowable annual dose, this would cause 1 in every 4–5 of them to have workplace-induced cancer, and roughly 1 in every 9 to die from that workplace-radiation exposure.[90]

As already mentioned, the largest study of nuclear workers to date (2005), conducted by IARC and based on actual dosimetry data, implies an even higher risk. IARC says up to 5 percent of lifetime fatal cancers, among workers exposed to the maximum-allowable annual occupational-radiation dose of 50 mSv, will be attributable to their workplace-radiation exposure,[91] or that each 50 mSv of radiation exposure gives them a 1 in 80 chance of premature, fatal cancer; after 40 years of maximum-annual-radiation exposures annually, workers would have a 50-percent chance of lifetime fatal cancer, induced by their occupational-radiation exposure.[92] According to the National Academy's estimated models, if nuclear workers had 40 years of exposure, each year at the maximum-allowable annual dose, this would give them a 1 in 10, or 10-percent, chance of dying from premature, workplace-induced cancer. In the IARC study, although the average worker's exposure is relatively low (about 20 mSV cumulative radiation dose), the authors say 1 percent to 2 percent of the cohort's lifetime fatal cancers (roughly 4,100 to 8,100 cancers in 407,391 people) are attributable to these occupational doses. For comparison, the average US public exposure is about 3 mSv per year, roughly 80 percent from natural background radiation and 20 from human-made-radiation sources.) This group of workers thus has a 17-year-lifetime-total dose of background radiation of $(3 \text{ mSv} \times 70) = 210$ mSv. When added to the 20 mSv occupational exposure, their total background and workplace-radiation exposure = 230 mSv. Thus, their total occupational dose (20 mSv) gives them a radiation dose 10 percent higher $(230 \div 210)$ than people without workplace-radiation exposure. Radiation workers who receive the maximum-annual occupational-radiation dose for 40 years thus could receive lifetime doses, from occupational and background exposure, that are about 11 times higher than doses to the public.[93]

How many people receive occupational-radiation exposures? In Canada, whose population is one-tenth that of the United States, there are more than 550,000 radiation workers in more than 80 occupations. Switzerland's radiation workers number 60,000; South Korea's, 65,000. In the United States, 1.5 million workers are annually occupationally exposed to ionizing radiation, and 300,000 of these workers are employed in the commercial nuclear industry.[94]

If millions of global workers are exposed to ionizing radiation at higher doses than members of the public, this raises at least 2 important ethical issues—whether worker regulations should be less protective, and whether workers actually consent to these higher doses. The first question asks whether nations like the US are justified in having a double standard that allows workers to receive higher radiation doses than the public. Most other nations maintain that justice requires equal protection for both, mainly because those who take risky jobs are unskilled, poorly educated, and unable to protect themselves. Who is right? On one hand, many economists defend the US double standard, saying that higher pay for riskier work compensates workers for taking higher risks, promotes worker welfare, allows more efficient job-risk trade-offs, and allows greater worker autonomy. On the other hand, ethicists note that, empirically, most workers receive no extra compensation (compensating wage differential or CWD) for riskier jobs, unless they are male, white, and unionized or college-educated. They say that when workers accept higher radiation-pollution risks, their decision harms innocent people, such as later victims of genomic instability and cancer who were harmed by ancestors' radiation-induced mutations, and that, in principle, blue-collar workers are likely unable to consent to higher workplace risks because of their poorer education, lower job skills, lower socioeconomic status, and need for employment. If correct, such arguments suggest it is ethically questionable for the US to allow blue-collar workers to bear higher radiation risks than the public.[95]

Apart from the defensibility of the double standard for radiation exposure, obviously radiation exposures are unethical if workers do not consent to them. Two factors that can block occupational consent are a lack of *individualized* radiation-dose data and of *cumulative* radiation-dose data. Unlike other developed nations, which require radiation workers to have personal air monitors, the US has little individualized radiation-dose data because it allows employers to use general air monitors (single, fixed, air samplers for assessing internal-radiation dose and regulatory compliance) and to report only mean-radiation exposures in work areas.[96] Consequently, US reports of occupational-radiation doses frequently underestimate exposures and mask uncertainties and variations in radionuclide concentrations and doses. In some workplaces, radiation concentrations change 4 orders of magnitude over 2 months and 3 orders of magnitude within a day.[97] The National Council on Radiation Protection and Measurement warns that general air samplers can underestimate radionuclide concentrations and *individual* doses by 3 orders of magnitude, especially if they are located far from employees who receive higher exposures.[98] Consequently, unless there are other means of assessing doses, radiation workers may be unable to know or consent to their individual radiation doses.

Lack of data on *cumulative* radiation doses likewise threatens occupational consent. Suppose 2 workers, one a cancer survivor who had received radiotherapy, and another who had not received it, were deciding whether to continue radiation work. If the risks (from a given radiation exposure) increase on a scale of the excess relative risk, as is often assumed, suppose both workers receive the same occupational dose. However, according to the accepted LNT model, expressed on a relative-risk scale,[99] risk differences associated with this same dose are larger at higher cumulative doses. This is why, all other things being equal, Hall confirms that prior radiotherapy could give the first worker a 10-year-average cancer risk 6 times higher than that of the second worker.[100] Yet as the NAS notes, depending on the type of cancer and therapy, a therapeutic radiation dose could be 200–1,200 times greater than the maximum-annual-occupational dose of radiation.[101] If so, this would give the first worker a cancer risk much higher than that of the second worker. Likewise, because about 60 percent of human-made-radiation exposures are from medical X-rays, suppose the first worker had 1 whole-body computed tomography (CT) scan, with exposures of about 10 mSv.[102] This CT scan would give him about half the cumulative radiation dose (10mSv) of the workers included in the IARC study,[103] or one-fifth of the US maximum-allowable annual occupational-radiation dose.[104] A diagnostic abdominal-helical-CT scan, performed in childhood, would increase the first worker's cancer risk about as much as receiving half the US maximum-allowable annual dose of occupational radiation; even X-rays taken as part of required worker-health exams would contribute to radiation risk.[105]

Despite these 2 workers' radically different radiation-exposure histories, they probably would not receive quantitative information about their different relative risks. Because all nations require employers to disclose only occupational-radiation doses (those relevant to employer regulatory compliance), employees typically have incomplete information about their individual, cumulative, and relative radiation doses and risks.[106] Protecting US radiation workers thus relies on one type of information—*average occupational dose*—to achieve *employer compliance* with regulations. Achieving *employee consent,* however, also requires another type of information—*individual cumulative dose.* All bioethics codes, such as the famous Helsinki Declaration, require potential risk recipients to be adequately informed of, and consent to, the risk.[107] Implementing this requirement, the classic doctrine of informed consent mandates 4 necessary conditions. The risk imposer must fully disclose the risk; risk recipients must fully understand the risk, be competent to assess it, and voluntarily accept it.[108] If cumulative and individual radiation doses partly determine occupational-exposure risks, but workers know only their average occupational dose, obviously risk disclosure is incomplete. Workers may misunderstand the different relative risks associated with the same average occupational dose of radiation.

Consider the 2 radiation workers in the earlier example. Receiving the same occupational-radiation exposures, they are like 2 nighttime drivers on a foggy mountain road without a guardrail. The distance to the edge represents the odds ratio (which is linear) of getting radiation-related cancer, although cell sterilization and death may be more likely at high doses.[109] The edge represents malignancy, and the fog represents difficulties with radiation-risk assessment and workers' understanding of their relative risks. The driver closer to the edge is like the higher-exposure worker who has accumulated all radiation hits except the last 1 required for malignant transformation. The driver farther from the edge is like the lower-exposure worker who has not accumulated these hits. If both drivers move 2 feet toward the edge (both workers get another radiation hit), they may be unaware that the effects will not be the same for each of them. Worker information and consent also are limited because ICRP and national laws mandate no overall radiation-dose and risk limits, only limits within single exposure classes (e.g., medical, occupational, public doses) and from single sources, like a nuclear power plant.[110] Consequently, no nation routinely measures cumulative-radiation dose and risk from all sources and exposure classes, even for high-exposure workers.

Most nations also have not followed Canada and instituted a reliable, centralized radiation-dose registry (RDR) for radiation workers. The US has a variety of registries,[111] some run by groups alleged to have conflicts of interest, such as the Department of Energy (DOE), the Nuclear Regulatory Commission, the Department of Veterans Affairs, and individual facilities. No one has systematically studied radiation-induced disease by combining and improving all US registries, partly because different groups control them. One result has been flawed occupational-dose data, difficulties in reconstructing doses under the Energy Workers' Compensation Act, inadequate occupational-dose disclosure and consent, repeated human and environmental contamination by radiation, and avoidable deaths, as in the case of hundreds of Navajo uranium-miner fatalities.[112] In 1991, confirming contamination and radiation-dose falsification among 600,000 nuclear workers at 3,500 US DOE facilities, the Office of Technology Assessment recommended DOE abolition or outside regulation.[113] Neither occurred. Again in 1994, 1999, 2001, 2002, 2007, and 2008, Congress criticized DOE and its contractors for radiation-safety violations, falsification of worker-dose records, contamination, and cover-up.[114] In 1998, the Government Accountability Office (GAO) warned: "Widespread environmental contamination at DOE facilities...provides clear evidence that [DOE] self-regulation has failed"; in 2007 GAO again warned that "persistent safety problems" at US nuclear facilities have continued to occur because of "lax attitudes toward safety procedures," failure to correct known safety problems, and very weak oversight; again GAO recommended abolition of DOE and creation of a new agency because of DOE's long history of safety violations, cover-up, falsification of worker doses, and so on—all already documented in chapter 2.[115]

One remedy for flawed US radiation-worker policies would be a reliable, centralized RDR, independent of agency conflicts of interest, perhaps within the US Centers for Disease Control and Prevention. At a minimum, this RDR would include activities of centralized radiation-dose collection, epidemiological analysis, risk assessment, risk communication, and verification of dose measurement. Creating an RDR would not by itself resolve most problems of radiation-dose accuracy. Excellent research traditions are also required, as at Japan's Radiation Research Effects Foundation. A first step might be congressional hearings to evaluate an in-principle commitment to RDR. A second step might be building on National Academy work, commissioning a US National Research Council study of radiation epidemiology and charging it with developing scientific and practical recommendations for implementing a reliable RDR, perhaps modeled on the Canadian registry.[116] A third step might be implementing National Academy recommendations. A fourth step might be encouraging other nations to develop similar registries, as the academy suggested. This fourth step would enlarge the radiation-data set and help resolve international controversies over radiation-dose fluctuations and uncertainties.

The needed academy *scientific* recommendations (second step) would include those for achieving accurate, complete data; learning from Canadian experience; improving on excellent research like the 2005 IARC study; deciding which covariates—like smoking and dietary history—to include; evaluating confounders and effect modifiers; using meta-analysis and pooling to resolve controversies; and centralizing and improving data from existing general registries. The needed *practical* recommendations would include those for privacy, cost, liability, potential litigation, access to data, and similar registries in other nations.

The National Academy of Sciences is a logical place to develop RDR-implementation strategies, given that RDR is relevant to the goals of the academy committee that does the classic reports on radiation-exposure effects.

Recommending prospective collection of exposure data and citing the particular importance of nuclear-worker doses, the committee called for extensive radiation-epidemiological studies—including follow-ups of CT-scan cohorts—to resolve theoretical and practical problems of low-dose radiation. It also recommended global-radiation consortia using similar methods of data collection and follow-up; individualized, real-time estimates of radiation doses; national radiation-worker registries; and linking these registries with sets of other exposure data, including those in tumor and disease registries.[117] A reliable RDR would facilitate all of these academy recommendations. Because reconstructing diagnostic and therapeutic radiation exposures is difficult, if not impossible, RDR data collection could be implemented in stages, beginning with occupational-radiation-exposure data. Following NAS recommendations, a second stage might add workers' medical-exposure data. At a third stage, the RDR might include medical and occupational radiation exposures for the entire US population. At a fourth stage, all fallout, accident, consumer-product, and other exposures for the US population might be added. The Centers for Disease Control and Prevention and National Cancer Institute websites already reveal precedents for small parts of the RDR, like the National Cancer Institute's online radiation-dose calculator, which lets citizens estimate their fallout-related iodine-131 thyroid doses.[118]

Benefits of a reliable RDR include promoting worker consent, because workers would have better information about their radiation risks. Other benefits include giving authorities the ability to implement required annual, 5-year, and lifetime radiation-dose limits within exposure classes.[119] Without an RDR, one could never know whether these allowable limits were exceeded, especially because workers can move among nuclear plants and accrue maximum-allowable annual radiation doses at several different plants. Some high-risk workers, "jumpers," work at several facilities each year. Without a registry, they bear sole responsibility for reporting past radiation exposures. The RDR also could clarify radiation-dose distribution among members of the public, providing sounder bases for regulation and resolving scientific controversies. In addition, a reliable RDR could help improve direct, empirical information about low-dose-radiation effects. This improvement is especially needed for 3 reasons. *First,* many current low-dose-radiation standards rely on imperfect cancer estimates obtained by extrapolating from epidemiological studies of higher doses and higher dose-rates, like those that characterize the classic cohort of atomic-bomb survivors. *Second,* historically scientists have repeatedly shown the need to raise radiation-risk estimates. *Third,* empirically derived radiation-dose data often conflict with extrapolated radiation-dose data. For instance, the 2005 empirical-dose study by the IARC has central-risk estimates of cancer mortality that are several times higher than linear extrapolations from dose-estimates for atomic-bomb survivors, although the IARC estimates are statistically compatible with the bomb estimates, given wide confidence intervals.[120] Empirical data from the 2005 Techa worker-cohort likewise has produced much higher estimates of excess relative risk than atomic-bomb extrapolations, but Techa data have problems with confidence intervals and dose estimates.[121] The fact that IARC and Techa studies found higher radiation-risk coefficients than are currently accepted is a good reason to promote the RDR and further radiation-risk assessment. At a minimum, such assessment needs to include accounting for diagnostic X-ray exposures; improving information and follow-up on vital status in the Techa cohort;[122] and extending IARC results—especially because 98 percent of the collective radiation dose was to males, to 90 percent of the cohort.

A RDR also might help illuminate other controversies, like that over doses and confidence limits in Canadian worker research showing excess relative cancer risks per 100 mSv that are 13 times higher than radiation risks revealed by atomic-bomb studies, and 33 times higher than radiation risks revealed by the British worker study.[123] By controlling for factors like confounders, healthy-worker effects, and dose misclassifications; providing direct, individualized, exposure data; offering larger samples and longer exposure periods; and building on worker studies,[124] the RDR could facilitate exploratory-data analysis, clarify low-dose controversies, make radiation studies cheaper and easier, and provide a model for other nations to follow.

If a US RDR is, in principle, scientifically and ethically defensible, why has it not been adopted? Some objectors say employers should not have to ensure that radiation employees are informed about, and consent to, occupational, cumulative, and relative radiation doses and risks, because employers have no control over nonoccupational risks. Yet neoclassical economics recognizes that workplace-risk imposition requires employees' consent and their full receipt of information, and that economic efficiency obliges employers to help meet these requirements.[125] Ethics likewise requires employers to promote employee-risk disclosure, consent, and protection—because employers profit from employee radiation exposures; rights to profit entail corresponding responsibilities.[126] ICRP and many nations also recognize this employer responsibility, as illustrated by laws requiring employers to monitor pregnant radiation workers and to take workers' medical histories.[127]

A second objection to the RDR is that because it could open highly exposed radiation workers to occupational discrimination, like that used against chemical-industry employees with genetic predispositions to chemically induced disease,[128] radiation workers might avoid radiotherapy or diagnostic X-rays. However, worse consequences (than occupational discrimination) could follow from allowing some individuals' fears of discrimination to trump everyone's rights to know and consent to radiation risks. If this trump were allowed, fear of resulting mistreatment could be used to justify nonrecognition of human rights. If this trump were allowed, society could be guided by expediency and emotion, not by ethics and law. A better solution is working to protect victims of discrimination, as in cases of workplace mistreatment based on race, religion, or gender. Besides, just as radiation workers decide whether to report their pregnancies, and British nuclear employees can exclude their radiation doses from the registry,[129] employees might avoid potential discrimination by sometimes retaining rights not to disclose their non-occupational-radiation exposures.

A third objection to the RDR is that it might not be needed because most occupational-radiation exposures are low. However, if earlier IARC data are correct, many doses are not low. IARC says about 400 IARC-cohort members received cumulative occupational-radiation doses greater than 500 mSv, which NAS models say will cause at least 24 cancers, or, in other words, cause about 5 percent of them to get cancer; IARC models say this 500 mSv will cause at least 104 additional cancers.[130] Likewise, IARC says about 41,000 cohort members received cumulative occupational-radiation doses greater than 50 mSv, which the NAS ties to 234 additional cancers, roughly 117 fatal—and which IARC ties to 1,026 additional cancers, roughly 513 fatal. Thus, just these few supposedly "low" doses are responsible for at least 1,300 radiation-induced cancers that otherwise would not have occurred. Even the cumulative occupational-radiation dose for members of the IARC cohort, averaging about 20 mSv, is responsible for 1–2 percent of all fatal cancers in the IARC cohort.[131] Thus, allegedly "low" radiation doses will cause at least 1,300 workers to have cancer. Earlier accounts of DOE's lax safeguards and occupational-dose falsification also suggest that some US worker doses might be high. Otherwise, why has the United States (with its 50 mSv allowable-annual-radiation dose) not adopted the stricter 20 mSv occupational standard of other nations, or the 12.5 mSv limit recommended by British authorities?[132] Even if most US occupational-radiation doses were low, this third objection errs in assuming that not everyone has rights to equal protection, that only utilitarian or majority protection is necessary—the greatest good for the greatest number of workers.[133] The objection also erroneously assumes that the size of radiation doses alone is always sufficient to make doses ethically acceptable. This second error, described by British ethicist G. E. Moore,[134] is known as the naturalistic fallacy. Those who commit this fallacy attempt to reduce *ethical* questions (e.g., is the imposition of workplace risk just?) to *scientific* questions (e.g., how high is workplace risk?). The 2 questions are irreducible because even small risks may be ethically unacceptable if they are easily preventable, or imposed unfairly, without adequate compensation, through rights violations, and so on. Besides, risk bearers ultimately must judge whether risks are low—by giving or withholding their consent.

A fourth objection to the RDR is that there is less reason for disclosing workers' full radiation doses and risks than for disclosing sometimes-larger risks—like smoking. Epidemiologically, this is often correct. As already mentioned, risks like smoking are important covariates whose inclusion in the RDR is probably essential to accurate dose information. Ethically, however, disclosing alcohol or tobacco risks is less important than disclosing individual, cumulative, and relative risks associated with occupational radiation. Why? Despite pressures like cigarette advertising, largely personal risks like smoking are more ethically legitimated than workplace-radiation exposures, because they typically involve more individual choice, consent, and control. However, occupational-radiation risks often involve less individual choice, consent, and control, partly because of inadequate disclosure and the frequent absence of alternative employment options.[135] Whenever risk imposition involves less choice, consent, and personal control, as in workplaces, even small risks can require more ethical and societal attention than larger risks that involve more choice, consent, and control.[136] Government also has greater duties to regulate risks that one party imposes on another than to regulate self-chosen risks affecting mainly the chooser.

If science defines effects of any level of radiation exposure as both risky and cumulative, and if workers have rights to know and consent to their additional workplace-radiation exposures, society should ensure that workplace regulations are consistent with its science and ethics—and neither jeopardize worker consent nor impose EIJ. In principle, improving disclosure requirements for workplace-radiation regulations, assessing the double standard for worker and public exposure, and implementing an RDR could help promote workplace consent to radiation. Without these improvements, radiation workers appear to be victims of EIJ—victims of a situation in which US workers bear 50 times more radiation risk than the public, and nearly 3 times the radiation risk of workers in the EU.

Nuclear-Related Environmental Injustice from Flawed Radiation Standards for Future Generations

Another group threatened with EIJ because of less-protective radiation standards is members of future generations who will be exposed to releases from nuclear-waste facilities. The US government has planned to store commercial-reactor waste underground at Yucca Mountain, Nevada, although President Obama challenged this plan in 2010, suggesting instead that it might be stored onsite at reactors around the country or in other centralized facilities. Although not all US nuclear-reactor waste will fit at Yucca Mountain, no other US site has been studied. However, in 2008 government published radwaste regulations for permanent US (underground) nuclear-waste storage. Because this spent fuel and high-level radioactive waste must be safely stored for at least a million years, according to the US National Academy of Sciences,[137] government officials admit it is certain to leak from its containers and from its underground geological medium, even in relatively dry areas, like Yucca Mountain. The most likely route is groundwater migration.[138]

Would a site like Yucca Mountain protect nearby residents from radiation exposure? Arguably it would not—because US waste-related regulations for future people are far less protective than those for other nuclear facilities. Regulations for current US nuclear-related facilities require that no member of the public receive more than 25 mrem annually from any US facility, and no more than 100 mrem (1 mSv) annually from all radiation-releasing facilities.[139] (Using the current, *empirical,* IARC dose-response curve for ionizing radiation, explained earlier, if members of the public were annually exposed to 25 mrem, for a lifetime of 70 years, this facility alone would cause roughly 1 in every 125 people exposed to have cancer. If people were exposed for only 35 years, this would cause 1 in every 250 people exposed to have cancer.)[140] However, for 10,000 years after a permanent-underground-waste facility is closed, the US standard allows annual public exposures of 15 mrem (150 uSv); for 10,000–1,000,000 years after closure, the standard allows annual public exposures of 100 mrem (1 mSv)—4 times more annual exposure than now allowed from a US nuclear facility.[141] According to the IARC dose-response curve, future people who received the lifetime-allowable-radiation dose (from the waste facility) would have a 3.2-percent chance, or 1 in 31 chance, of getting cancer, just from that facility.[142]

There are at least 9 ethical problems with this fourfold US weakening of radiation-waste protections for future generations.

(1) Future generations arguably receive no benefit from bearing this generation's nuclear-waste risks, so the weaker radwaste standards arguably violate intergenerational equity and the government's own neutrality criterion. According to this EPA criterion, adopted in 1980, no generation should be forced to bear higher government-imposed risks than another, and no nuclear-waste risks should ever be higher than those arising from natural uranium.[143]

(2) Future generations arguably would not consent to this higher radwaste-risk imposition; psychometric studies confirm that present generations do not want radioactive waste in their regions, although it is less risky now than it will be in the future, when it escapes.[144]

(3) Because lifetime-allowable standards (see above) could cause 3.2 percent of exposed people to contract radwaste-induced cancer, and nearly 2 percent to die from it, they amount to Russian roulette against the weakest people, those most sensitive to radiation. As already shown, because women are 50 percent, and children about 1,000 percent, more radiosensitive than adult men,[145] such regulations could allow nearly 5 percent of exposed women, and 32 percent of exposed children, to contract cancer from the waste facility.

(4) Virtually all US environmental and public-health protections typically ensure protection against threats whose annual probability of fatality exceeds 1 in 100,000–1,000,000.[146] Annual allowable radwaste doses (1mSv) for future people are inconsistent with these protections because they provide protection that is 100 times weaker, allowing nearly a 1 in 4,000 chance of dying from premature cancer.[147]

(5) Virtually all US environmental and public-health regulations guarantee individual protection against specific levels of pollutants. However, the new radwaste standard requires only that average or mean doses meet the 25 mrem standard, and those receiving higher-than-average exposures would get no protection. That is,

EPA adopted "the arithmetic mean as the statistical measure to be applied at all times" to the radwaste-pollution standard of 25 mrem annually.[148] Thus, if 6,000 nearby residents annually received waste-related-radiation doses of 1 mrem, but 1 person received a fatal dose of 600 rem (6 Sv), this death would be allowable, despite its environmental injustice. Using average doses as the criterion for acceptable pollution levels is thus like accepting the claim of a city police chief who says he will prosecute no murderers unless the city's number of murders exceeds the per-capita national average.

(6) A related ethical flaw in the new radwaste standards is that the US Nuclear Regulatory Commission will use "projected doses presented by DOE" to determine regulatory compliance.[149] Such projections have 3 flaws. First, by expanding dose distributions, DOE could lower calculated means and thus claim high doses were acceptable. Second, dose projection could be manipulated more easily than dose measurement, especially by those who might profit by not controlling nuclear pollution. Third, as chapter 2 showed, multiple US congressional investigations have revealed massive DOE safety violations, dose falsifications, and persecution of whistleblowers; repeatedly since 1990, US government oversight agencies and professional associations have called for either abolition or external regulation of DOE.[150] Neither has occurred, but DOE arguably has no business monitoring radiation-dose compliance.

(7) The new US nuclear-waste standard also is ethically and scientifically flawed because it excludes high-dose persons from the calculations showing average doses. That is, it excludes all radwaste doses higher than those to the "Reasonably Maximally Exposed Individual" (RMEI).[151] Yet because the RMEI is defined as neither drinking water, nor eating food grown, near the site, this RMEI would not have the highest radwaste exposures, as pointed out in a US National Academy of Sciences report.[152]

(8) The new radwaste standards likewise allow EIJ because they include no groundwater-protection regulations after 10,000 years, allegedly because the courts have not required it.[153] However, this omission violates the Clean Water Act and suggests that an underground repository could not meet the act's standards. Because groundwater migration is the most likely route for radiation-waste exposure, the standards arguably ought to include groundwater protection, or they would fail to protect people.

(9) The new radwaste standards also are flawed because they exclude consideration of waste-intrusion risks, through accident, terrorism, or other activities.[154] Yet given the million years that nuclear waste must be secured, intrusions seem likely. By ignoring intrusions, it follows that government cannot guarantee it can meet the radwaste standard it dictates. If not, future people will face waste-related EIJ.

In response to the preceding 9 problems with US nuclear-waste regulations, how has government responded? If one groups these 9 waste-regulation problems into 3 major categories—arbitrariness (being subjective, incomplete, and based only on projected doses), unfairness (not protecting equal rights of future persons), and inconsistency (contradicting current regulations), consider how EPA has responded to each of these 3 major areas of concern. Regarding the arbitrariness of radiation-waste regulations, EPA admits this problem but defends itself by saying its calculations of specific radiation doses in the distant future are purely "qualitative" because they are "overwhelmed by fundamental uncertainties" about actual future doses.[155] As the National Academy of Sciences admits, even the best future-dose calculations contain "a residual, unquantifiable uncertainty."[156] Similarly, because of "uncertainties" in the disposal-system performance, EPA says people "cannot easily make distinctions at such incremental levels" of radiation exposure as 15 or 100 mrem.[157] Why not? Government admits that dose uncertainties will increase over time.[158] Given that nuclear-waste standards will have to be met a million years into the future, EPA justifies its qualitative approach to waste-related radiation standards by saying, "It is better to be roughly accurate . . . than it is to be precisely wrong in spurious aspirations" to protect future people. How successful is this government defense of arbitrariness in its nuclear-waste regulations? Given EPA's admission that knowledge of future radiation doses is purely "qualitative" and unable to guarantee precise regulatory adherence to waste standards, including the 100 mrem standard, it logically follows that setting any future quantitative standard is meaningless. EPA thus has admitted that its nuclear-waste regulations are incoherent and unable to guarantee future protection. But if so, these arbitrary standards are both scientifically flawed and likely to lead to EIJ against future people.

In response to concerns that government's nuclear-waste regulations are unfair and fail to guarantee equal rights because members of future generations are less well protected than present persons, government has made several responses. One is that intergenerational equity does not require "the same compliance standard" for present and future generations.[159] This response is partly correct. Fairness need not require sameness of treatment. However, moral philosophers recognize that, for any deviations from the default position, same treatment, to be morally justified, at least 1 of 4 sorts of justification is needed; merit, special compensation for earlier injury or risk, incentives, or individuals' special needs can justify treating them differently.[160] Yet because government provides no justification for not treating present and future people the same, it begs the question. Moreover, at least 2 of these 4 justifications suggest that future people deserve more (not less) radwaste protection. One reason is that future people should be compensated for bearing this generation's radwaste burdens, because they will receive no benefits from it. Another reason is their need; they may have to spend substantial sums to protect themselves from this waste, given that leaks will increase over time. Thus, on grounds of compensation and need, future generations arguably deserve more, not less, protection from current radioactive waste.

Another government response to charges, that its radwaste regulations are unfair to future people, is that "no consensus" exists regarding obligations to future generations.[161] However, this response errs on at least 2 counts. First, consensus is not necessary to establish the morality of actions. Racism would be wrong even without consensus that it is wrong. Similarly, duties to future generations arguably exist even without consensus that they exist. Consensus reveals only what people believe, not what they ought to believe, and not what can be rationally justified. A second problem is that the "consensus" response ignores the government's neutrality criterion, mentioned earlier.[162] It is illogical and unfair to say that an existing government policy (the neutrality criterion) can be ignored whenever no consensus supports it. This stance is just as inconsistent and unfair as claiming that, although the 1964 Civil Rights Act forbids racism, whenever no consensus against racism exists, government can promulgate racist policies.

A third way government responds to charges of unfairness in its radwaste standards is by claiming that, when waste-related doses are added to background-radiation doses, total doses will be within the "variation in the existing levels" of natural-background radiation.[163] EPA also says annual waste-related-radiation doses will give about the same risk as annual cancer risk from all natural sources.[164] These responses, however, have at least 3 problems. One problem is their assumption that natural-background radiation is an acceptable norm for acceptable radiation risk, although all non-zero doses of radiation are risky and lead to higher cancer rates, as noted earlier. Making this assumption is like saying murders are permissible, provided their number does not exceed the natural-background murder rate. In assuming the ethical acceptability of natural-background radiation, the government commits the naturalistic fallacy, mentioned earlier. Those who commit this fallacy attempt to reduce *ethical* questions (e.g., is the imposition of higher future-radwaste risk just?) to *scientific* questions (e.g., how high is future-radwaste risk, compared to natural-background-radiation risk?). The 2 questions are irreducible because even small risks may be ethically unacceptable if they violate rights to equal protection, are easily preventable, are imposed unfairly and without compensation, and so on. Besides, risk bearers ultimately must judge whether risks are acceptable—by giving or withholding their consent. Because members of future generations cannot consent, arguably they ought to be given more protection than present people who can consent. Another problem with EPA's natural-background-radiation response is that it is inconsistent with earlier EPA claims that future radwaste doses are uncertain and can be known only qualitatively. If so, EPA cannot know they are within the range of natural-background radiation. A final problem with EPA's natural-background-variation response to alleged unfairness to future people is that regulators would not allow contemporary polluters to use this justification for violating regulations. Nuclear-plant owners are not allowed to avoid regulatory compliance by claiming that, when their plant's higher radioactive pollution is added to natural-background-radiation doses, total doses will be within the "variation in the existing levels" of natural-background radiation—analogous to what EPA claimed.[165] Yet if regulated entities cannot avoid responsibility for radiation exposure by appealing to natural-background-radiation variations, EPA cannot make this appeal without being unfair to future persons and violating its own regulations.

A fourth way that government responds to charges of unfairness in its radwaste standards is by claiming permanent nuclear-waste disposal is safer than all other waste-handling options.[166] Yet this response ignores the fact that even the safest option could be ethically wrong or too risky. It also begs the question at hand, just as would someone who tried to justify murder by saying, "Strangling is the safest way to murder Joe." This EPA "safest" response begs at least 3 questions: that permanent disposal is safest, when EPA gives no evidence for this claim; that additional nuclear waste should be generated; and that future generations should bear this generation's nuclear-waste burdens. Moreover, this question-begging response is irrelevant to fairness, because even the safest technologies may not be safe enough or fair enough. If they are not, nuclear-waste generation may impose EIJ on future people.

In response to charges that US nuclear-waste regulations are inconsistent with (i.e., less protective than) other pollution standards, government claims that because the US National Academy of Sciences recommended no specific future radiation-dose standard, this is one of the "regulatory-policy issues left to EPA's discretion."[167] However, this EPA response fails for at least 3 reasons. First, it is not the duty of a scientific group, the academy, to make ethical or policy decisions about acceptable pollution levels. Such decisions belong to the people themselves, or to their elected representatives, who have delegated this decision to EPA. Second, even if the academy had the right to make policy decisions, it could be wrong. Therefore, instead of committing the logical fallacy of appealing to the authority of the national academy, EPA should have defended its regulatory standard for future people. Third, this "discretion" response fails because an inconsistent policy-decision does not miraculously become consistent merely because those (who made it) claim discretionary power to be inconsistent. Not all discretionary power is exercised wisely. If it is not, EPA must show that its inconsistent radwaste regulations, which place heavier risks on future persons, represent an ethically and scientifically defensible use of discretionary power. Instead it has begged the question of legitimate discretionary power, erroneously assuming that such power can override concerns about consistency, equal treatment, and environmental justice.

Other government responses to charges that its nuclear-waste regulations are inconsistent with established pollution standards fare no better. Trying to defend itself, EPA claims "the potential for [future] doses higher" than the regulatory standard "has always been implicit in the concept of geologic disposal" because radionuclides will escape, and "barrier failures" will occur.[168] EPA also says higher future doses are possible because the system "will evolve over 1 million years."[169] However, this EPA higher-dose defense of its less-protective, radioactive-waste regulations is questionable for several reasons. One reason is that, in appealing to waste-system evolution, and geological-barrier failure, government defends its inconsistent and weakened nuclear-waste regulations on the grounds that it cannot meet any specific, future, radiation-protection standards. This higher-dose defense not only shows that waste-related regulations are a sham, but also is inconsistent with the government's own repeated claims that its radiation regulations will protect public health.[170] Thus, EPA admits in this response that it cannot protect public health from radioactive waste, contrary to its own claims. If it cannot, government should stop generating nuclear waste immediately—because its own responses show that it knows its own radiation-waste standards cannot be met, and therefore that future radiation-waste-related EIJ is likely.

Conclusion

Where do this chapter's arguments leave us? *First,* they show that the nuclear fuel cycle, including uranium mining, milling, enrichment, and so on, imposes unjust and uncompensated radiation burdens on indigenous people and minorities. *Second,* US commercial reactors are disproportionately sited in the poorest part of the US, the Southeast, and in communities having statistically significantly more people living below the poverty line. *Third,* even without accidents, normally operating reactors cause radiation-induced diseases and fatalities. *Fourth,* radiation standards themselves are environmentally unjust because they protect some US children almost 200 times less well than US adults, and several times less well than European children. Radiation standards also protect blue-collar workers 50 times less well than members of the public, and they protect future generations at least 4 times less well than current people. As a consequence, using nuclear fission to address CC increases not only scientific problems, but also fundamental ethical problems. This chapter shows that radiation standards themselves appear severely flawed regarding environmental justice, equal treatment for vulnerable groups.

Of course, these higher radiation-exposure risks to children, blue-collar workers, and future people might be defensible if victims could consent to them. Yet children and future generations obviously cannot consent, and this chapter has showed that, because of inadequate individual and cumulative radiation-dose disclosure, blue-collar workers cannot legitimately consent. Thus, no apparent reasons justify US government regulations that allow the weakest, most vulnerable people—children, blue-collar workers, and future generations—to bear the worst EIJ. Solving problems of climate change should not require the greatest sacrifices to be borne by the weakest and most vulnerable among us. Otherwise nuclear fission could cause more ethical problems than the CC it addresses.

CHAPTER 6

The Solution

USING RENEWABLE ENERGY, EFFICIENCY, AND
CONSERVATION TO ADDRESS CLIMATE CHANGE

The classic, pro-nuclear MIT energy study showed that, for decades, 77 percent of Americans have favored the expansion of solar and wind, while less than 30 percent have supported atomic energy.[1] Partly as a result, more than a thousand people repeatedly have been arrested at a single US nuclear plant, in a single year, in protests.[2] More than 300 national, state, and local citizens' organizations have issued statements outlining their reasons for opposing use of nuclear power to address CC, while not a single major environmental group (only various individuals who claim to be environmentalists) officially supports it.[3] In fact, in the 48 hours following President Obama's 2010 State of the Union address, over 3,000 clean-energy advocates wrote him letters protesting his assertions that atomic energy is safe and that the US should provide $54 billion in subsidies for new federal-loan guarantees for new reactors.[4] As the pro-nuclear International Atomic Energy Agency (IAEA) notes, massive environmental opposition to nuclear fission puts any reactor expansion at risk; it also jeopardizes uranium mining, which, in turn, could delay or prohibit use of uranium for nuclear plants.[5]

Chapter Overview

Are members of the public correct to reject nuclear power and instead to support greater efficiency and clean, renewable energy sources like wind and solar? This chapter argues that the public is right. It shows (1) that energy efficiency and conservation are the cheapest ways to address CC; (2) that wind is cheaper than nuclear power; (3) that solar photovoltaic (PV) also is cheaper than fission; (4) that market proponents confirm that renewable energy is cheaper than atomic power; (5) that renewable energy is becoming progressively cheaper, while fission is becoming progressively more expensive; (6) that renewable-energy sources could supply all global energy, while fission could not; (7) that renewable-energy sources can be implemented more quickly than atomic power; (8) that renewable-energy sources are sustainable and low-carbon technologies, while fission is not; (9) that renewable energy would make the nation and the planet more militarily secure than could nuclear power; (10) that alleged "clean coal" is neither clean, nor inexpensive, nor currently technically feasible, and that it causes severe health threats—even with the carbon removed; and (11) that the transition to 100-percent-renewable energy can be made easily and smoothly. Because wind and solar-PV power are fully developed, relatively inexpensive, and can provide electricity (which offers the greatest flexibility in energy use, including supplying electricity for plug-in hybrids), this chapter considers mostly wind and solar PV. Other renewables, however, like microalgae and switchgrass biomass, can provide baseload electricity and thus help in the transition to 100-percent-renewable energy.[6] Consider, in order, each of 10 arguments for using renewable energy and efficiency programs, rather than nuclear fission, to address CC.

Energy Efficiency and Conservation Are the Cheapest Ways to Address Climate Change

Greater energy efficiencies are needed to address climate change (CC) quickly and inexpensively and to avoid merely replacing high-carbon with lower-carbon technologies. Instead of merely "building our way" out of CC with renewable energy, efficiency requires developing technologies and programs that reduce demand. As chapter 2 documented, a 2008 report by McKinsey market consultants showed that a $520 billion investment in US energy efficiency would produce $1.2 trillion in energy savings by 2020.[7] Reducing energy demand and increasing efficiency involve actions like insulating drafty buildings; using more energy-efficient cars and appliances; taxing, regulating, or capping greenhouse-gas (GHG) emissions; and using compact-fluorescent lightbulbs and time-of-use electricity pricing. For instance, all-electric cars and trucks are now made with new lithium-ion batteries that can be charged in 10–15 minutes at a gas-station-like service stop. Even this first generation of all-electric vehicles can go 3–55 miles on a single kilowatt-hour of electricity, and plug-in hybrids can drive 70–100 miles on only 0.1 kWhr of electricity. Partly as a result, scientists have shown that, instead of requiring 1 percent of energy growth to support each 3 percent of economic growth, the same economic growth can be achieved by reducing delivered energy by 1 percent annually.[8]

Renewable-energy programs include government strategies, like California's "Million Solar Roofs," rebates for solar-PV installations and zero-emission cars,[9] or Germany's feed-in tariff that guarantees a price for each kilowatt-hour of electrical energy that is generated renewably and fed into the grid.[10] US national-electricity usage could be reduced by one-third if the 40 least-energy-efficient states were to match the efficiency of the top 10 most-efficient ones.[11] As such data reveal, nuclear power is not needed to address CC because there are cheaper, lower-carbon alternatives to building more fission plants,[12] alternatives such as implementing time-of-use pricing for electricity.[13] Montgomery County, Maryland, for instance, has reduced both electricity rates and carbon emissions by combining demand of multiple electricity consumers to create aggregate contracts for green power. This combined green-power purchase has saved the county and its aggregation partners over $25 million.[14] However, conservation and efficiency programs are even less expensive than supplying renewable energy to build our way out of CC, and they cause less natural-resource destruction, less pollution, and more investment-capital available for other uses—as the pro-nuclear US DOE, the US National Academy of Sciences (NAS), and the US Office of Technology Assessment (OTA) have shown. Merely by using energy efficiencies, they confirmed that the US could have "cut carbon emissions to 1990 levels by 2010 with no net cost to the nation's economy."[15] Fifteen percent of year-2008 global GHG emissions could be cut by 2020 simply by using more energy-efficient information technologies.[16] The market agrees. In 2007, McKinsey and Company, one of the world's leading management-consulting firms, showed that global energy demand could be cut by 50 percent over the next 15 years without compromising any economic growth—at a net cost of zero, because cutting energy demand would be cost-effective. The same study showed that 28 percent of current-energy use could be reduced immediately, with existing technology.[17] Industry and local governments already have learned this lesson. In 1999, Dupont announced its goal to reduce its GHG emissions by 65 percent; only 4 years later, it had used efficiency to reduce its emissions by 72 percent.[18] As one of its 2010 sustainability goals, Dupont plans to reduce its energy and waste intensity by 15 percent over 2010.[19] Firms like Dow and IBM are saving billions of dollars by cutting their energy intensity by as much as 6–8 percent annually.[20] Similarly, the city of Bellingham, Washington, decided in 2006 that it would use only green power to meet its electricity needs, and it succeeded less than a year later. By 2012, it is on track to reduce its GHG emissions to 64 percent below 2000.[21]

The famous 2009 Harvard, 2004 Princeton, US OTA, and 1997 Presidential Commission energy studies all concluded that efficiency programs were the cheapest, most reasonable way to address energy needs; in fact, the commission showed that every federal dollar spent on energy-efficiency programs would generate a 40-to-1 return on the initial investment.[22] In 2009 Obama's administration announced a $346 million investment in energy-efficiency programs for both commercial and residential settings; the administration showed the programs were easy and cost-effective and avoided GHG emissions.[23] In fact, just 1 current US DOE energy-efficiency program annually saves electricity equivalent to what nearly 7 nuclear plants would generate.[24] Overall, energy efficiencies and using distributed renewable energy technologies could save from 2 to 10 times more carbon (per investment dollar) than fission could do, and they could do so more quickly and more cheaply. Scientists say three-fourths of all US electricity could be saved through energy-efficiency programs that would cost, on average, about 1 cent per kWhr.[25]

Energy-efficiency and conservation programs better address CC because they are more complete and more profitable. On the completeness side, efficiency programs can reduce emissions from cars and factories, not just electric utilities[26]— which cause only 9 percent of GHG emissions.[27] Efficiency programs thus tackle the total-emissions problem, not merely the 8 percent of global energy that nuclear power supplies—and not merely the 2.2-percent net energy from fission, if one counts the energy used in the 14-stage nuclear fuel cycle (see chapter 2).[28]

On the profitability side, energy efficiency is so lucrative that it has been growing faster than the US economy—something that cannot be said about nuclear power.[29] Since the mid-1990s, the rate of US energy growth has been about 2 percent less than the rate of growth of the GDP.[30] Consequently, the energy required in 2007 to produce the same unit of GDP was only 55 percent of what it was in the 1950s.[31]

However, as the next chapter shows in more detail, efficiency programs can be jeopardized by using government subsidies for commercial fission. Recent studies at UK business schools showed that because new reactors are capital intensive and heavily subsidized (as earlier chapters revealed), they undermine funding for efficiency and renewables, delay energy decentralization, and thus retard the most cost-effective means of addressing CC.[32] More specifically, every dollar invested in energy efficiency displaces 6.8 times more carbon-equivalent emissions than investments in nuclear power; this means that, because the same dollar can be used only once, any dollars invested in capital-intensive atomic energy divert expenditures away from efficiency; because of these facts, nuclear investments actually could contribute to CC, as compared to investments in efficiency.[33] Money thus could be used much more cost-effectively to increase appliance, automobile, and fuel-efficiency, for instance, to avoid the CC and political instability created by reliance on oil imports.[34] As Germany's Oko Institute and many other studies show, using money for energy-efficiency programs, wind power, and gas-cogeneration is both more cost-effective than using it for atomic power, and it has negative costs of greenhouse-gas abatement, because these technologies cut both energy demand and cost.[35] For instance, because decentralized solar-thermal energy and solar electric do not presuppose centralized generating facilities, they avoid up to one-third loss of electricity through long-distance-transport lines—and essentially get this saved electricity "free."[36] This is one reason Germany has a target of 46-percent renewable energy by 2050.[37] It also is one reason the US OTA says the US could immediately reduce electricity use 20–45 percent, by adopting currently available efficiency technologies such as efficient appliances, heat pumps, increased building insulation, and so on.[38]

Besides, the case of California shows that if energy-program subsidies are used, they ought not be for market losers but for market gainers, like greater efficiency. In the 1980s, when California let all energy technologies compete on an equal footing, without subsidies to fossil and nuclear energy, the 10 million people served by Southern California Edison cut the electricity-peak-load forecast by 8.5 percent annually, and they did so at about 1 percent of the long-run marginal-supply cost.[39] This is one reason California's per-capita use of electricity has been flat for 30 years,[40] while its per-capita real income has risen 79 percent.[41] Moreover, for 2 reasons, California's milder climate cannot explain this trend. One reason is that states with the lowest energy use, per unit GSP, do not always have the mildest climate, showing that energy use is linked mainly to the structure of the state economy.[42] The other reason is that, in 1976, the rest of the US used 15 percent less electricity, per capita, than Californians; yet by 2000, on average the US used 70 percent more per-capita electricity than Californians.[43] Californians thus show that saving electricity requires about 1,000 times less capital and repays it 10 times faster than supplying more electricity.[44] The rest of the US needs to learn from California—especially because 48 of the 50 US states erroneously reward utilities for selling more electricity and penalize them for cutting customers' bills through energy efficiencies. Even so, in 2006, the US cut electric intensity (energy consumption divided by economic output) by 3 percent, and primary-energy intensity by 4 percent.[45] Market "winners," like energy efficiency, thus give society more climate solution, at a cheaper cost, faster, than does nuclear power. Later sections of this chapter show that investors know this, and the market is investing massively in renewable energy, not nuclear power.

In 2010, more than $211 billion was invested in new renewable-energy capacity, plants, research, and development—up 30 percent from the previous year; in 2010, renewables supplied 20 percent of global electricity. In 2010, global solar-PV more than doubled over 2009, and Germany installed more PV in 2010 than the world added in 2009. Japanese and US PV markets doubled in 2010, over 2009. Globally, wind added the most new capacity in 2010. Developing countries have more than half of global renewable power, which now generates more electricity, both globally and in the US, than nuclear fission.[46] By 2011, at least 95 countries had policies (like feed-in tariffs) to promote renewable-energy generation. Annual renewable-energy investment represented about half of new capacity in 2010, and in 2010, power from renewable sources totaled 1320 GW.[47]

Wind Is Inexpensive

The public is especially investing in wind energy, one of the cheapest current sources of electricity. The International Energy Agency says global wind costs dropped to 2 or 3 cents/kWhr by 2010,[48] whereas credit-rating data from chapter 3 shows that just the market costs of atomic energy (excluding massive costs of taxpayer subsidies) are at least 21 cents/kWhr—roughly 8 times higher than wind-energy costs. The average price paid for wind power in the US in 2008 was 4.7 cents/kWhr and dropping; in many places, US wind prices are below 1 cent/kWhr.[49] In 2010, installed wind capacity grew globally faster than any power source, supplying 22 percent of electricity in Spain, and 21 percent in Portugal. In the US, despite a crippling recession, wind energy grew 39 percent in 2009, and by roughly the same percentages in 2007 and again in 2008. During 2002–2009, US wind capacity increased by 700 percent. Why the rapid growth?[50]

Since at least 1998, wind has been more economical than nuclear plants.[51] For many years, wind also has been more economical than natural gas.[52] Even fission proponents admit wind now costs 5 cents/kWhr or less.[53] The head of the UK company Ecotricity said that, with only £410 million (of the £850 million that UK taxpayers provided for the nuclear-bankruptcy bailout in 2002), his company could have provided 10 percent of UK electricity needs from wind power, at a tiny fraction of the nuclear cost.[54]

In 2007, when wind costs were even higher than they are now, Lawrence Berkeley National Laboratory assessed actual costs of wind-generated electricity and found that the median price of power provided by new US wind farms was 3.4 cents per kWhr in 2004 dollars; the cheapest wind farms provided power at less than 2 cents per kWhr.[55] As a result, the state of Minnesota found that it could cost-effectively produce 15 percent of its electricity by using wind, and the integration costs of wind energy (new transmission lines and taking account of intermittency) would be only $4.60 per MWh, or 0.46 cents per kWhr.[56] Even the median-cost US wind plants (3.2 cents/kWhr) produce power at far less than half the alleged market cost of current new nuclear plants.[57] Indeed, sophisticated utility analyses show that, when wind energy is added to the electricity supply, consumer (and utility) costs decrease massively.[58] Such facts and figures are disturbing, because fission has received 20 times more US government subsidies than has renewable energy, although nuclear energy is a "mature" technology, commercialized for more than 50 years.[59]

Investors understand the preceding wind-cost numbers. Positive wind economics are one reason that, for the last year for which data are available, 2008, wind energy has been responsible for 60 percent of annual added new US electricity capacity, measured as percentage of peak summer demand.[60] In 2009, the US wind industry installed 10,000 MW of new generating capacity—equivalent to 10 nuclear plants. Wind energy and natural gas together accounted for 80 percent of all new US electricity capacity added that year.[61] In January 2008 alone, $700 million in new wind farms went into operation in Texas.[62] In 2007, US installed-wind capacity grew 45 percent,[63] and wind enjoyed $9 billion in private US investments, while nuclear had no private investments.[64] In 2006, distributed renewables got $56 billion of private investment, while nuclear got zero. In 2009, despite economic recession, US wind-energy installations grew 31 percent.[65] In 2007 and 2008 US wind grew 45 and 50 percent, respectively.[66] From 2007 to 2011, largely emissions-free wind grew to supply 22 percent of all electricity in some midwestern states, like Iowa.[67] In 2006 alone, US installed wind capacity grew by 2,700 MW—equivalent to nearly 3 nuclear plants.[68]

> Worldwide in 2006, micropower generated more electricity than nuclear power; nuclear power brought online 1.49 GW, less than photovoltaics did (1.74 GW) and a tenth what wind power did (15 GW). Nuclear lost 0.5 net GW (retirements exceeded additions), while micropower added roughly 34 GW. Distributed renewables got $56 billion of private investment while nuclear got zero.... What part of this picture does anyone who takes markets seriously not understand? The small, fast options are triumphing in the global marketplace, because investors prefer their lower costs and risks. Their potential is enormous – for wind power alone, 35 times that of world electricity use – and they need less back-up than intermittent big thermal stations need now.[69]

Between now and the year 2015, wind is expected to generate $65 billion in private US investments.[70] Yet no US nuclear reactors have been ordered since 1974. The upshot? Nuclear lobbyists may be convincing politicians (to whom they gave campaign donations) that wind is expensive, but they are not convincing investors.

Globally, low wind costs explain why wind capacity grew 25 percent in 2006, and that much again in 2007.[71] In 2009 in the EU, wind capacity grew more than any other energy source, comprising 39 percent of all new electricity capacity, whereas EU nuclear capacity grew only 1.7 percent. EU solar power provided 16 percent of total EU capacity.[72] Global wind-capacity additions were 40 percent higher in 2007 than in 2006.[73] Globally, wind-energy installations grew 27, 29, and 31 percent, respectively, in 2007, 2008, and 2009.[74] In 2006, wind (15GW) brought 10 times more electricity online globally, than did nuclear.[75] In fact, each of just 3 nations (Germany, Spain, and India) annually adds more wind power (about 2 GW), in 1 country, than the entire world adds in nuclear power.[76] The Danes already use wind to generate 20 percent of their electricity, and it will generate half their electricity by 2030.[77] The British (with the best wind in Europe) say that by 2020, they can use wind to supply 6 times the planned nuclear increase of 6 plants.[78] Already the Germans have more wind-power electricity than the UK does from its entire nuclear component, even though German wind resources are less than those of the UK.[79] Germany is only 5 percent the size of the US, yet it has 2.3 times more installed wind—the equivalent of about 20 large coal-fired or nuclear plants.[80] Overall, the EU says it will generate 20 percent of its energy from renewables by the year 2020; Sweden says it will generate 49 percent; Finland, 38 percent; and Austria, 34 percent by 2020.[81] Offshore wind is even more reliable, and many European nations have already this capacity.[82]

Market investors confirm the preceding wind facts. McKenzie, a top business-management-consulting company, says that by 2030, global wind capacity will have grown by 700 percent above its 2005 level, while, at best, nuclear energy will have grown by only 13 percent above its 2005 level.[83] The US Energy Information Agency (EIA) estimates that US primary-renewable-energy production will experience a threefold increase from 2008 levels, while primary-nuclear production, at best, will be roughly the same as its 2008 levels.[84] Although more transmission capacity is needed to deliver wind energy in some nations,[85] the wind is cheap. Moreover, land with wind turbines can still be used for farming, grazing, recreation, commercial fishing, and so on.[86]

Wind energy is not merely inexpensive; it is also plentiful. A classic 2009 Harvard University study showed that, globally, wind could supply more than 40 times current worldwide energy uses.[87] In the US, only 3 US states (Kansas, North Dakota, and Texas) could supply all US electricity using wind power.[88] "The wind energy potential in each one of the top six [US wind] states—North Dakota, Texas, Kansas, South Dakota, Montana, Nebraska—is greater than the total nuclear-electricity generation from all 103 operating US nuclear power plants."[89] Overall USA wind potential, in only 20 states, is over 2.5 times the total of year-2005, US electricity generation.[90] In only 12 states, US wind potential is over 2.5 times the total of year-2000 electricity generation.[91] Even if one excludes Alaska, plus all US areas within 5 nautical miles of shoreline, plus two-thirds of US areas between 5 and 20 nautical miles, US offshore wind (at 35 percent capacity) could have supplied 70 percent of year-2005 electricity.[92] Moreover, much US wind is located in the midwestern farm belt, so that, as just mentioned, crops and grazing can be done on the same land.[93] The case of Texas rancher Louis Brooks is fairly typical. He is paid $500 per month to allow 78 wind turbines on his ranch, yet he can use virtually all of this land for grazing and farming.[94] Iowa, Minnesota, Colorado, and Oregon all get up to 20 percent of their power from wind farms.[95] By 2015, Texas wind generation is expected to be 5 times greater than it is today; one rancher, Boone Pickens, plans to invest $10 billion and install his own wind farm of 4,000 MW—equivalent to the electricity generated by 4 nuclear plants.[96]

Plentiful US wind resources are one reason that utility-industry studies, including those by GE Energy, say wind energy currently can supply 10 percent of US electricity inexpensively, and perhaps as much as 15 percent, with "no increase" in reserve capacity or backup.[97] In New York, GE concludes that if wind supplied 10 percent of electricity (3,300 MW), total utility costs would drop by $430 million annually; in fact, GE says additional gas storage (required to accommodate wind variability), when wind supplies 15 percent of electricity, would provide a winter-summer seasonal hedging benefit (better than the current system) that would save $1/MWh annually.[98] Likewise, the state of Minnesota showed that, if it dispersed wind farms geographically, it could supply 25 percent of its electricity inexpensively; its reserve power would have to increase from 5 percent (with no wind generation) to only 7 percent (with 25-percent wind).[99] Stanford University studies came to even better conclusions. Studying the states of New Mexico, Colorado, Kansas, Oklahoma, and Texas, the Stanford scientists found that up to 47 percent of baseload electricity could be supplied by wind, provided the generators were distributed geographically, to off-set wind variations.[100] Wind also could be backed up by pumped hydropower, batteries, hydrogen, and compressed-air-storage of energy, all already being used and providing greater efficiency, fewer emissions, and lower costs than conventional energy. Besides, as already mentioned, when wind provides less than 20 percent of utility electricity, no backup except the normal grid is needed.[101]

Despite the preceding government statistics on low wind costs, massive wind capacity, and rapid wind-market growth, nuclear proponents mislead people about the cost-effectiveness of renewable energy. They make claims such as that nuclear "generating costs are cheaper than wind turbines," allegedly because wind is "highly subsidized."[102] This claim errs in at least 3 respects. *First*, as chapter 3 showed, fission has received about 25 times more US-taxpayer energy subsidies than have wind and solar together. *Second*, nuclear-generating costs are trivial, compared to overall (14-stage) nuclear-fuel-cycle costs that include uranium mining, fuel enrichment, reactor construction, reactor decommissioning, waste storage, and so on. As chapter 3 showed, only full-fuel-cycle costs provide reliable economic information. Focusing on partial energy costs, as nuclear proponents do, commits a fallacy of division, a fallacy of assuming that the properties (e.g., cost-effectiveness) of part of a whole (nuclear-generation costs) are the same as the properties of the whole (full-fuel-cycle costs).

Because wind energy is so much more economical, plentiful, and easier to implement than atomic power, it is difficult to see how anyone could argue for using fission to address CC. But this point raises an obvious objection. If there is so much cheap wind capacity, why has wind not been implemented even more rapidly? As the next chapter reveals, one reason that even more wind energy is not now available has been disclosed by business publications like *Forbes* and the *Economist*. They point out that political-campaign donors in the fossil-fuel or nuclear business have manipulated US politicians, so that they have skewed US energy priorities away from what is most economical, sustainable, safe, and low carbon. A recent article in the *Economist* warned that nuclear costs, safety, and permanent waste storage made it "extremely risky"; that for decades bankers in London and New York have refused loans to nuclear utilities; that utilities should use "other sources" of electricity; but that atomic-energy lobbyists and political-campaign donors are responsible for mis-placed energy priorities and for the billions of dollars misspent on nuclear-energy subsidies, as in the US.[103]

A second reason that cheap, plentiful wind energy has not been implemented more quickly is that, as already mentioned in chapter 3, 96 percent of US energy subsidies (for solar, wind, and nuclear) have gone to nuclear energy. A year-2000 report by MRG Associates showed that, from 1947 through 1999, the US spent approximately $150 billion of (direct and indirect) energy subsidies for nuclear, wind, and solar power—96.3 percent of which went to nuclear.[104] Yet this figure does not include later subsidies like the $13 billion in the 2006 Energy Policy Act,[105] or the $54 billion in President's Obama's 2011 budget for nuclear-loan guarantees. In spite of US nuclear subsidies, which are 25 times greater than those given to wind and solar energy, the US led the world in exploiting wind energy. In 1985, the US had 95 percent of the world's installed wind capacity, with 18 times that of Europe. Yet because of poor US policies of subsidizing nuclear and fossil fuels (rather than renewable energy), by 2003 the US share of installed wind was only 16 percent. In 2003 alone, the EU added 15 percent more installed wind capacity to its grid than the cumulative amount installed in the US up to that time.[106]

A third reason even more wind energy has not been used is that instead of focusing on cheap, plentiful, sustainable wind energy, most nations have focused instead (as the next chapter shows) on the military uses of nuclear technology, which exclude wind. That is, the US went into nuclear generation of electricity for the same reason that China, France, India, Iraq, Israel, Pakistan, South Africa, the Soviet Union, the UK, and other nations did: "to open a nuclear weapons option."[107] The US and other nations have had a "not too hidden agenda" of claiming to use the commercial nuclear technology to develop nuclear weapons.[108] They wanted a "peaceful" excuse (and cover) for continued development of nuclear weapons, and government officials (such as the chair of the Joint Committee on Atomic Energy) and nuclear scientists (such as J. Robert Oppenheimer) explicitly admitted this fact.[109]

A fourth reason that wind energy has not developed more rapidly is that, as chapter 3 explains in detail, the nuclear and fossil-fuel industries have misleadingly emphasized the need for baseload power. They also have misrepresented the actual costs (including health and environmental costs) of nuclear and fossil fuels. Finally, they have erroneously claimed that because some individual, renewable-energy stations provide intermittent power, renewable energy is not reliable. (See the next chapter for responses to the intermittency objection.) Thus nuclear- and fossil-fuel special interests wrongly emphasize the minor costs associated with wind intermittency, yet they ignore much-higher costs associated with nuclear plants, such as 15-percent interest, for 11–23 years, on reactor-construction loans. According to the pro-nuclear UK government, only about 6 percent of wind costs derive from wind intermittency.[110] As chapter 3 showed, because wind already is about 5 times cheaper than fission, intermittency adds no significant costs to wind-energy prices.

Solar Is Inexpensive

Not only is wind energy a cheap and plentiful alternative to fission, but so is solar PV. Currently, intermediate-scale and large solar-PV costs are about the same as costs for peak-time, single-stage, natural-gas turbines.[111] The pro-nuclear US DOE estimates that, because of economies of scale, rapid solar-PV growth, and a variety of new manufacturing techniques (including nonsilicon thin-film cells and increased manufacturing scale), solar PVs will cost as little as 5 cents per kWhr by 2014,[112] and US solar-PV-manufacturing capacity will increase 12-fold in the next 5 years—making solar PV competitive in markets nationwide by 2015.[113] By 2015, even large-scale solar PV is expected to cost only 6–7.5 cents/kWhr,[114] and solar-PV-system reliability will increase to 20 years.[115] Already solar PV is competitive in many markets, and grid-connected solar PV is the fastest-growing energy technology in the world, with 50-percent annual increases in cumulative-installed capacity in both 2006 and 2007.[116] For instance, the US PowerLight Corporation installation of 750kW solar PV installation on parking-lot rooftops saves the company a quarter of a million dollars annually in peak-electricity costs.[117] In 2009, SolFocus began construction on a 10 MW solar field in Samaras, Greece; Opel completed 330 kW of solar PVs in Tarronga, Spain; and Everphoton made plans for a 1 MW installation in China.[118] Yet nuclear prices are increasing (see chapter 3). Fission already costs more than 21 cents/kWhr, as chapter 3 showed. Even the mass conversion of the entire US to largely solar power will cost only 8–9 cents/kWhr.[119]

As a consequence of low solar-PV and wind costs, especially where countries need to save money in order to develop, they prefer renewable energy. Economist Mark Cooper calculated that adding 100 new nuclear reactors to the US power grid would cost taxpayers anywhere from $1.9 to $4.1 trillion more than would renewable-power sources.[120] Even if one excludes massive taxpayer nuclear subsidies, reactors cost up to 29 cents/kWhr in the first year of operation, while wind costs 4–6 cents/kWhr.[121] That is why, as of 2007, developing nations as a group had more than 40 percent of existing renewable-energy capacity, more than 70 percent of existing solar-hot-water capacity, and 45 percent of biofuels production.[122] As of 2006, China had 7 times more energy from renewables (49 GW) than from nuclear power. China's renewables provided the equivalent of electricity from 49 large nuclear plants, except that the electricity was cheaper than that from fission.[123] Cheap renewable energy also is why the UK says it will use solar to supply 3 times the planned nuclear increase.[124] In Germany in 2009, 3 GW of new solar capacity was installed, double the amount added there in 2008.[125] Globally, during 2009 solar capacity increased from 6 GW to 10 GW.[126] In 2006, the pro-nuclear IAEA said global nuclear capacity shrank 0.43 GW, while even the costliest renewable, solar PV, had 1.74 new installed GW.[127] Between January 2008 and July 2009, 11.4 GW of new solar capacity was brought online globally, but from January to September 2008, not even 1 new nuclear plant was built.[128] Globally over the last few years, the manufacture of solar-PV cells has been growing as much as 50 to 60 percent annually.[129]

As already noted, such solar-PV-growth figures disprove the claim of nuclear proponents, that solar requires too much land. Solar potential, on only 1 percent of US land (e.g., rooftops and parking lots),[130] converted at 20 percent efficiency, is 3 times larger than wind potential—or 8 times current US electricity needs.[131] Moreover, installing solar PV on parking lots would require no new land use for solar and would provide vehicle-to-grid exchanges of electricity to facilitate both electric cars and a vehicle-backup for the grid; at 15-percent conversion efficiency, parking-lot solar-PV installations could supply more electricity than what is generated in the US today.[132] The US DOE National Renewable Energy Laboratory estimates that the entire US electricity demand could be supplied with solar from less than one-third of the land currently used for military purposes.[133] At least 640,000 square km of land in the southwestern US, alone, is suitable for solar-PV use, and a large fraction of this land (i.e., 85 percent in Arizona) is not privately owned. If all US land area—that is now used to produce coal power—was used instead to support solar-PV cells, energy production would increase, even at 2009 rather than later-solar-PV-efficiency rates.[134]

Market Proponents Say Renewable Energy Is More Economically Desirable Than Fission

As already mentioned, this chapter considers mainly wind and solar energy, because each is fully developed, is relatively inexpensive, and can provide electricity (which offers the greatest flexibility in energy supply, including use of solar and wind to supply electricity for plug-in hybrids). Many other energy sources also can help in the transition to renewable energy, such as microalgae and switchgrass biomass to provide baseload electricity,[135] but unfortunately there is no time to consider them all here. The important thing is that, as chapter 3 and the preceding sections have argued, commercial-nuclear fission is far more expensive than wind and solar energy. As a UK government committee showed, once all the hidden nuclear costs and taxpayer subsidies were actually counted, nuclear plants could be seen to be "wholly uneconomic."[136]

Poor nuclear economics, and excellent renewable-energy economics, are 2 reasons that market investors favor renewable energy. Year-2010 renewable sources generated 4,000 trillion kWhr, while nuclear sources generated only 2,800 trillion kWhr.[137] For the last few years, small-scale renewables, such as solar PV and wind, have been adding 10 times more capacity each year than has nuclear, and at far lower costs. As already mentioned, in 2009, global wind-power capacity grew 31 percent, adding 37.5 new GW to bring total global wind installations to 158 GW.[138] Yet no new nuclear capacity was added in 2008 or 2009.[139] In 2006, distributed-renewable power sources, like solar and wind, surpassed nuclear power's total global output, and wind alone added 15 GW.[140] In 2005, distributed-renewable power sources, such as solar and wind, added 4 times as much electrical output and 11 times as much capacity as nuclear power, and they now provide more energy globally than nuclear power.[141] Even the pro-nuclear US DOE admits that, by 2030, renewables are projected to supply 6,724 trillion kWhr, while, at best, nuclear will supply only 3,844 trillion kWhr.[142] Solar PV and wind have been surpassing nuclear growth largely because they are cheaper, and Wall Street understands this arithmetic.[143]

Given high atomic-energy costs and low renewable-energy costs, it is not surprising (as chapter 3 revealed) that credit-rating companies, like Standard and Poor's, downgrade nuclear-utility credit ratings,[144] whereas renewable-energy companies have extraordinarily high credit ratings and stock valuations.[145] Market-credit raters say even massive taxpayer nuclear subsidies might not provide enough incentive to build fission plants or to sustain their credit quality.[146] Consequently, even the pro-nuclear business community has flatly said that atomic energy is economically unviable without massive government subsidies.[147] The US Secretary of Energy likewise says that without financial incentives and massive subsidies, nuclear power is not an option.[148] As the US Assistant Secretary for Nuclear Energy admitted in 2008, new nuclear "plants are not capable of obtaining non-recourse project financing without federal guarantees."[149] Consequently, as pro-nuclear economists also admit, "to construct a new generation of nuclear reactors will require direct involvement from the federal government."[150] They claim these taxpayer subsidies "could amount to half the cost of financing and constructing the unit," subsidies that nuclear opponents call "corporate welfare."[151] Because everyone admits that commercial-nuclear power requires massive taxpayer subsidies, while renewable energy does not, nuclear proponents face a dilemma. Either they must claim fission is cheap and does not require massive taxpayer subsidies, or they must ask for subsidies on the grounds that fission is not cheap. They cannot have it both ways, as they apparently want. They cannot logically claim both that the nuclear industry needs massive subsidies and yet that the technology is inexpensive. Moreover, those who say future nuclear plants will be cheaper must explain why Wall Street is demanding 100-percent loan guarantees and full insurance,[152] and why no US reactors have been built for more than 3 decades.

As preceding paragraphs show, market proponents essentially agree with this book's cost analyses of nuclear power and renewable energy. They recognize that economics-related nuclear insecurities (created by high costs, long construction times, low load factors, and risks of accidents) are arguably greater than any energy insecurities created by renewable energy.[153] If an accident or terrorist attack occurs at a renewable-energy facility, the main cost/risk/insecurity is how to supply the missing electricity generated by the injured facility. However, if such an accident or attack occurs at a reactor, widespread contamination, radiological injury, and public fear also would occur. Planned nuclear plants might be scrapped, other reactors might be shut down, and the nation would be left vulnerable to a baseload electricity shortage—any of which could lead to higher costs and to energy insecurity. As a former US Nuclear Regulatory Commissioner put it: The "Three Mile Island [nuclear accident] taught Wall Street ... [that an accident] could turn a $2 billion asset into a $1 billion cleanup job in about 90 minutes."[154] That is, another accident could "up-end" nuclear investments, as a recent article in *Nature* put it.[155] A single event (an earthquake, terrorist attack, or accident, for instance) could financially derail the entire nuclear industry.[156] As the 2011 Fukushima accident (see chapter 4) showed, reactors are more economically risky than renewable energy.

Renewables Are Getting Cheaper, Nuclear Is Getting More Expensive

Another reason to address CC, by means of solar PV and wind, not fission, is that the pro-nuclear US DOE says costs of these renewable-energy technologies are decreasing, while atomic-energy and other conventional-energy costs are increasing—and have been more expensive than renewables since at least 2002.[157] The most recent nuclear costs are even higher than those cited in chapter 3. Generation costs alone for new nuclear power, excluding subsidies, are 25–30 cents/kWhr, while generation costs of wind are now as low as 1 cent/kWhr.[158] Market proponents say that, in the last 10 years, the cost-per-kWhr of wind electricity has fallen by 50 percent, and that of solar PV by 30 percent, while nuclear costs have increased, despite massive subsidies given to nuclear power but not to solar or wind.[159] For instance, during only 4 years, 2003–2007, nuclear costs increased 20 percent. The classic MIT study estimated total nuclear-capital costs in 2003 at roughly $3,200 per kW,[160] but by 2007, these had climbed $4,000 per kW.[161] A 2009 update to the MIT study showed that construction costs of nuclear plants have been increasing at a rate of 15 percent annually since 2003.[162]

Several reasons explain why the cost advantage of wind and solar PV will continue to increase, relative to atomic energy. One reason is that these renewables have no fuel costs. As a result, they will be unlikely ever to experience a production-decline curve or resource exhaustion. However, as chapter 3 showed, uranium is in short supply, and lower-grade uranium is more difficult, and more energy-intensive, to extract from ore. A second reason that nuclear costs are unlikely ever to decrease significantly is that 75 percent of nuclear costs (as compared to 25 percent of gas costs) are for construction costs, and prices of labor and materials continually increase.[163]

Renewable Energy Could Supply All Energy, but Fission Could Not

Yet another reason to prefer renewable energy is that it is capable of supplying a much larger portion of—indeed all—global-energy needs, while at best, nuclear fission could supply no more than 20 percent of electricity needs, and far less of total energy needs, as chapter 2 clearly showed. As already mentioned, the classic 2004 Princeton University study shows that 6 of only 9 renewable technologies, already deployed at an industrial scale, could completely solve the climate problem by 2050; the US DOE is even more optimistic, arguing that available renewable technology can provide 99 percent of US electricity by 2020—the earliest date by which a nuclear plant would be finished, if it had begun in 2008.[164] A 2009 study on global wind power found that China has the potential to increase its electricity supply 18-fold, relative to its 2005 consumption levels, by using onshore wind; in the US, wind power could be harnessed to increase electricity generation to levels 23 times larger than current consumption.[165] European studies likewise show that virtually all global-energy needs could be supplied through renewables.[166] Even wind alone, if developed to maximal capacity, could supply enough energy to power the world's current and estimated future energy needs.[167] By 2040, the European Renewable Energy Council says, renewables could supply 50 percent of the world's primary energy.[168] By 2050, this number is expected to increase to 56 percent, with a 50-percent reduction in carbon emissions from 1990 levels.[169] Even Shell Oil has said that by 2050, up to one-half of the world's energy can come from renewables.[170] Agreeing with the Intergovernmental Panel on Climate Change (IPCC), and showing that "a portfolio of technologies now exists to meet the world's energy needs over the next 50 years and limit atmospheric CO_2," the classic Princeton University study says renewables alone can solve CC.[171] As already mentioned, the Princeton authors show that more than 7 options (including technological efficiencies, conservation, natural gas, wind, solar PV, biomass, and hydrogen) could alone, cost-competitively, supply at least as much energy as nuclear tripling. "None of the options is a pipe dream or an unproven idea," say the authors, because "today one can buy electricity from a wind turbine, PV array, gas turbine," and "every one of these options is already implemented at an industrial scale and could be scaled up further over 50 years."[172] As already mentioned earlier, solar PV could easily supply all US energy needs, at competitive costs, by 2015–2020.[173] Onshore wind power is already even cheaper and, as noted earlier, could supply all global energy needs.[174] If only cost-competitive renewables were used, scientists say that by 2030 they could supply 40 percent of US electricity.[175] Moreover, studies by the pro-nuclear US DOE show that rapid implementation of renewable-energy sources, like wind and solar PV, assumes no storage for solar energy. US DOE data also accept current-grid reliability, and wind variability. Nevertheless, DOE data show that solar PV could supply 12 percent of total US electricity in 2020, while wind could supply 20 percent. Beyond 2020, government says battery-storage options would allow solar and wind to supply all US electricity.[176]

However, nuclear fission could never supply all energy needs, as already noted, because the largest-possible increase that atomic-energy proponents say is possible would lead to 1,000 plants globally.[177] If global-energy demand increases fourfold by 2050, and if old reactors are replaced, even 1,000 reactors would supply only about

20 percent of global electricity in 2050, only slightly more than it provides now.[178] As chapter 3 showed, because of long nuclear construction times, and no current US-reactor beginnings, even if some reactors began construction in 2011, they could not generate electricity before 2022.[179] This is in part because the National Academy of Sciences says nuclear construction time is 11 years or longer.[180] Yet wind and solar PV are already cheaper than nuclear fission, and by 2021, atomic energy will be even more costly, relative to wind and solar PV. Because of the small amounts of electricity that fission could supply (see chapters 2–3), the MIT authors warn that, without addressing CC, year-2050 GHG emissions will be 200-percent greater than they are now, yet if 1,000 global reactors are built, year-2050 GHG emissions will be 175-percent greater than they are now.[181] If electricity accounts for only 9 percent of total GHG emissions,[182] even tripling the number of reactors would not provide enough energy, in time, to address CC.

The upshot? At best, fission could supply only a small portion of future energy needs because of worsening nuclear economics, long and difficult reactor-construction times, and the increasing scarcity of uranium for fuel. The fuel problem could be alleviated through reprocessing spent-nuclear fuel, but reprocessing is very costly and dangerous. The one US reprocessing facility (in West Valley, New York), which operated from 1966 to 1972, was shut down because of safety, environmental, and economic concerns. It left taxpayers with a billion-dollar cleanup charge, a charge also not included in nuclear costs. Moreover, this reprocessing would create even more waste than current reactors, and would massively increase nuclear-weapons-proliferation risks—all of which would make atomic energy even more uneconomical than it is now.[183] Thus, even if commercial fission were economical, relative to wind and solar PV (and chapter 3 shows that it is not), it would make little sense to deploy it; it could address only a tiny fraction of CC problems, whereas renewable energy could address all CC problems.[184]

Renewable Energy Can Be Implemented More Quickly Than Nuclear Fission

Still another reason to prefer renewable energy to fission, as a way to address CC, is that renewable-energy sources like wind and solar PV can be implemented much more quickly than fission. Preceding paragraphs showed that, at best, atomic energy would provide "too little, too late" to address CC. Nuclear proponents, however, say fission is the only low-carbon energy source "readily available" until renewables are widely available,[185] "the only technology ready to fill the gap," to address CC,[186] "the only existing power technology which could replace coal in base load."[187] They claim that because wind and solar-PV sources are "intermittent and unpredictable," thus incapable of being implemented immediately,[188] atomic energy is "the most viable alternative" for addressing CC.[189] Thus nuclear proponents admit the lower full-fuel-cycle costs, lower fuel-cycle GHG emissions, greater speeds of implementation, and lower security risks of solar PV, wind, and other renewables, as compared to fission. Consequently even atomic-energy proponents admit that, at best, atomic energy is only a "transitional strategy" until there is full adoption of renewable energy.[190]

Should fission be a transitional energy supply? Given the preceding data (and that in chapter 3) on long nuclear-construction times; given that nuclear energy is getting more expensive, while solar PV and wind are becoming less expensive; and given that solar PV and wind are already cheaper than fission, it is difficult to see how atomic energy could be even a "transitional strategy." As already mentioned, this may be why the Germans say they can become carbon-neutral without nuclear energy, and instead are using wind; the Swedes also have rejected nuclear energy and say they can become carbon neutral by using mainly biomass, and so on, throughout the world.[191] Perhaps these nations recognize that fission proponents (who claim atomic energy can be a "transitional" electricity source) provide deeply flawed arguments. For one thing, nuclear proponents face a dilemma. *On one hand,* if they say nuclear energy can be implemented more quickly than in the past, they beg the question because (as chapter 3 showed) they ignore actual empirical data showing average reactor-construction times of 11–23 years. *On the other hand,* if they follow actual empirical data, and thus say atomic power cannot be implemented more quickly than in the past, they lose the supposed nuclear advantage—speed of implementation in addressing CC—and are forced instead to accept wind and solar PV, as the market and private investors already are doing. As already noted, all experts admit that the main debate about CC solutions is over the short term. Over the intermediate and long term, virtually everyone agrees that renewables are the answer because renewable fuel supplies are unlimited.

The second problem with nuclear proponents' claims about easy, rapid fission implementation is that they fall into inconsistency. They ignore massive intermittencies and energy insecurities associated with fission, yet emphasize minimal or nonexistent problems with wind and solar-PV intermittencies. After all, as already mentioned, when wind represents up to 20 percent of the electricity supply, no backup except the normal electrical grid is needed; thus, despite the thousands of MWe of installed US wind capacity (equivalent to many 1,000 MWe reactors), no wind installations have required any conventional baseload-power backup.[192] Yet as chapter 3 showed, during the first 2 decades of atomic power, its average load factor was only 50 percent. The current nuclear-load factor is 71 percent, revealing that fission has 30-percent downtime or intermittent-electricity generation. Moreover, as earlier chapters have warned, other nuclear intermittencies arise because of accident, terrorist, and financial risks. (See this chapter's "Objection" section for further discussion of the intermittency objection.)

Given the necessity to address CC quickly and effectively, not in a self-defeating way, why should one use reactors? Fission plants take decades to build, address only

2.2 percent of net global-energy needs, make only an "insignificant contribution" to lowering greenhouse emissions,[193] are not sustainable, and face uranium shortages.[194] Yet unless nuclear power can be implemented quickly, it loses virtually all its advantages to renewables. Even the market and investors recognize this fact. As chapters 2–3 argued, atomic energy is thus a self-defeating way of addressing CC. Its energy is too little, too late, too expensive.

Renewable Energy Provides More Security Than Fission

Besides the lower costs, lower carbon, and speedier implementation of wind, solar, and other renewable-energy technologies, another reason to prefer them over atomic power is that they offer more security, both with respect to nuclear weapons and with respect to energy supply. The pro-nuclear British government has data showing that a terrorist attack, such as a large plane crashing into a nuclear plant (or into nuclear-waste facilities), could release as much radioactivity as the 1986 Chernobyl accident and cause, at worst, several million fatalities.[195] The fact that the US government already has issued temporary no-fly zones, for 10 nautical miles (11.5 miles), around 86 nuclear sites, is testimony to the harm that planes could cause if they hit a nuclear installation.[196] Yet even 10-mile no-fly zones are useless, given that a plane could crash into a facility within 10 minutes, long before a military plane could be scrambled to stop it.[197] Thus, it is not surprising that the US Congress admits that fission plants are not designed to withstand attacks using large aircraft.[198] Such an attack on the Indian Point Reactor, near Manhattan, could cause 44,000 near-term deaths and 500,000 long-term deaths from cancer among those living within 50 miles.[199] Although the US Nuclear Regulatory Commission (NRC) did add a requirement in 2009 stating that *new reactors* be tested for their ability to withstand large-aircraft crashes, there is no specific test these reactors must pass. Instead, those responsible for building the reactors must describe how plant features might mitigate effects of a plane crash. This lack of a uniform nuclear-testing procedure, and dependence on the industry to police itself, obviously result in greater reactor vulnerability to terrorist attacks.[200]

Moreover, in force-on-force tests conducted by the US Nuclear Regulatory Commission to see if US nuclear reactors could meet terrorist threats, half of the plants failed.[201] In 2 cases, the simulated damage incurred by the nuclear reactor would have been enough to release unacceptable levels of radioactivity.[202] After most US atomic plants failed these force-on-force tests, the government did 2 things that further weakened nuclear security. *First*, it gave the contracts to conduct the force-on-force tests to the company, Wackenhut, that currently holds contracts to guard half of the commercial US nuclear sites—so there is an obvious conflict of interest regarding reliable force-on-force tests.[203] The same company that failed the terrorist tests thus was charged with conducting tests of US nuclear-facility ability to withstand terrorist attacks. After acting as the "adversary" in these force-on-force tests in 2004–2007, Wackenhut's contract was canceled after it cheated in these tests. Guards at some plants (e.g., the Peach Bottom reactor in York County, Pennsylvania) were even caught sleeping on the job.[204] *Second,* using the excuse of combating terrorism, the government in August 2004 said that it would no longer release any public information about nuclear-plant security.[205] As a result, the US National Academy of Sciences said, in a 2005 report on spent reactor fuel, that US government security restrictions on sharing information about reactor security were hindering progress in addressing vulnerabilities of onsite spent-fuel storage at nuclear plants.[206] This report found that successful terrorist attacks on spent fuel pools were possible and could result in the propagation of a zirconium cladding fire, which would result in the release of large amounts of radioactive material.[207] Yet renewable-energy sources face none of these terrorist threats of radioactive contamination and death.

If not, fission proponents thus face a security dilemma that proponents of renewable energy do not face. As chapter 2 argued, one can either increase nuclear energy to address CC, or one can decrease nuclear energy to reduce terrorism-proliferation risks. One cannot do both. The reason? More atomic plants would increase the very threats that nuclear weapons are intended to defeat.[208] The risks of terrorism and proliferation are directly proportional to nuclear capacity precisely because every single stage of the nuclear-fuel cycle must be secured, and because the more nuclear materials in circulation, the larger the terrorist and proliferation threat. Yet terrorism, proliferation, and nuclear war are perhaps the only risks that might be greater than those of CC. As the IPCC said, the security threat would be "colossal" if nuclear power were used extensively to tackle CC.[209] Again, as chapter 2 explained, many people view the proliferation-terrorism problem as the most severe difficulty confronting atomic energy.[210]

Nuclear proponents might object and claim that increasing commercial nuclear fission will not increase proliferation and terrorism risks. However, as chapter 2 showed, at least 10 reasons confirm that increasing nuclear plants increases terrorism and proliferation risks. Former IAEA Director General Mohamed ElBaradei warns, "The gravest threat the world faces today, in my opinion, is that extremists could get hold of nuclear or radioactive materials."[211] As chapter 2 showed, nuclear-fuel-cycle technology can be directly applied to produce nuclear weapons, granting potential weapons capabilities to all those involved with fission power.[212] As just mentioned, the IPCC says the security threat would be "colossal" if nuclear power were used extensively to tackle CC.[213] More-available bomb materials mean more-available misuse of them, especially if only 10 kilograms (about 22 pounds) of plutonium are enough to make a nuclear bomb—powerful enough to destroy a city.[214] The most recent US NRC estimate of total unaccounted-for contaminated waste and radioactive materials is 20 million pounds. In addition, NRC records show 18,740 documented cases of radioactive materials in consumer products due to improper use of recycled, radioactively contaminated metal in producing such items.[215] In 2009, the US government revealed that the amount of plutonium from Soviet-era Russia alone that has not been accounted for could produce 25 nuclear weapons as powerful as the one dropped on Nagasaki. Because the Soviets produced 140–162 tons of plutonium during the Cold War, to leave even one-tenth of 1 percent unaccounted for is to misplace 310–360 pounds.[216] Not surprisingly, the IAEA has documented at least 18 cases of plutonium loss or theft, none of which were detected until it was discovered that the materials were missing.[217] Already, reprocessing spent-nuclear fuel has resulted in the production of 270 tons of plutonium that is readily usable for weapons.[218] For all the reasons given here and in chapter 2, military-related nuclear insecurities (nuclear proliferation, sabotage, and terrorism) are arguably greater than any energy insecurities created by renewable energy, especially if one increases terrorist targets by building more nuclear plants.[219]

No "Clean Coal"

Earlier arguments on economics, GHG emissions, safety, ethics, ease-of-implementation, and security show that, to address CC, one should prefer renewable energy to nuclear fission. They also revealed that even pro-nuclear governments (like that of the US), university scientists, and market investors admit that renewable energy could easily and cost-effectively supply all needed global energy. If so, the pressing question is how to make the full transition to renewable energy. Although the specifics of such a transition to renewable energy are too extensive to be addressed here, it is possible to show briefly why alleged "clean coal" will not work, and what sorts of renewable-energy technologies will work.

For at least 4 reasons, this several-decades-long transition to renewable energy does not presuppose alleged "clean coal" with carbon-capture and sequestration. One reason is that, as noted in chapter 1, sequestering CO_2-equivalent emissions from coal burning would not resolve all the other (noncarbon) human-health problems associated with burning fossil fuels—such as increased asthma, heart disease, and cancer rates. Hence, more than carbon needs to be eliminated from the fuel supply, suggesting the need for stopping the burning of coal. Because much more than carbon needs to be removed from coal to make it clean, claims about "clean coal" are oxymoronic. A *second* reason that carbon-capture and sequestration appears implausible is that there is no assurance of long-term success—any more than there is assurance of long-term success in permanently securing high-level radioactive wastes. Untested carbon reservoirs could fail and suddenly emit CO_2-equivalent gases, possibly asphyxiating a nearby population, as occurred with natural venting of CO_2 from a lake in western Africa in 1986. A *third* problem with carbon sequestration is that there is no clear way to deal with both the health and the financial liability associated with venting from CO_2 sequestration. International guidelines for both problems are both unknown and arguably difficult to ensure, especially given the long time frames required—essentially forever. A *fourth* problem is that the costs of permanent sequestration—so as to achieve very low-carbon-leak rates—are uncertain. Many scientists say carbon sequestration would add between 1 and 4.2 cents per kWhr to the costs of coal-generated electricity, even if sequestration worked. The 2007 MIT study put the costs of carbon-capture alone (excluding sequestration) at 3 cents per kWhr,[220] yet this cost makes coal (with carbon capture and storage) far more expensive than renewable energy, as earlier chapters have argued.[221]

The Transition to Renewable Energy

As already noted in chapter 1, what is needed—instead of coal and nuclear fission— is an adequate response to a fourfold energy crisis: climate disruption because of human-caused GHG emissions, price volatility and insecurity of oil supply, fossil fuel pollution harms, and nuclear-weapons proliferation, encouraged by nuclear power. Scientists already have demonstrated the technical and economic feasibility of achieving 0 CO_2-equivalent emissions in the next 30–50 years, without nuclear power and without acquiring carbon credits from other nations. Scientists likewise have shown that net US oil imports could be eliminated in roughly 25 years.[222]

Many benefits of such a transition to renewable energy already have been out lined in this book. These include not only more energy security and reduction of proliferation threats, but also the elimination of much regional and local fossil-fuel pollution—like that from ozone and particulate pollution. As chapter 1 showed, ozone and particulate pollution are annually responsible for hundreds of thousands of avoidable deaths throughout the globe, and even US consultants hired in 2000 by the pro-fossil-fuel Bush administration admitted the severity of the problem; they said that, apart from sulfur oxides, nitrogen oxides, benzene, and other fossil-fuel pollutants, US particulate pollution alone causes at least 30,000 annual, preventable US deaths. Moving toward renewable energy would lessen both GHG emissions and many fossil-fuel-caused deaths.

Already, private companies, cities, and nations have illustrated how to begin the transition to renewable energy. As shown earlier in this chapter, the examples of Bellingham, Washington, and Montgomery County, Maryland, demonstrate that new, sustainable-energy policies can have environmental and economic benefits that are realized soon after implementation.[223] Countries like Denmark and Germany likewise have shown how federal initiatives such as tax exemptions for wind power and feed-in tariffs for solar PV can stimulate sustainable-energy growth.[224] More generally, many scientists and international-energy agencies have proposed detailed guidelines for the transition to a healthier, sustainable, non-coal, non-nuclear, almost 0 GHG emissions, renewable-energy framework.[225] Here are highlights of these guidelines:

(1) All nations should institute hard caps (measurement-based, fixed, enforced, physical-emissions limits) of CO_2-equivalent emissions, for some year prior to 2007, that decline each year until they reach zero, sometime before 2060. Emissions-allowances could be sold by the US government, for use only in the US, and resulting revenues could be used for energy-demonstration plants, research and development, and worker-community transitions to sustainable energy. However, allowing international emissions-allowances trading would undermine CO_2-equivalent reductions because rich nations could buy permits and continue heavy releases of GHG emissions.

(2) All subsidies, loans, and tax breaks for fossil fuels, nuclear power, and biofuels from food crops should be eliminated.

(3) All new coal-fired power plants that do not have carbon-capture and -storage should be banned.

(4) By mandating stringent, incentive-based, energy-efficiency standards for lighting, vehicles, appliances, and building design, already available today, nations easily could achieve a 2-percent annual increase in efficiency per unit of GDP—which would result in a 1-percent energy-use decline per year. Most of the additional efficiency reductions in GHG emissions can be achieved without incurring any cost penalties, as already argued earlier in this chapter.

(5) Federal, state, and local governments should mandate federal-contracting procedures that reward early GHG-emissions reductions by corporations and that make plug-in hybrids the standard US government vehicle by 2015.

(6) Federal governments should adopt vigorous research, development, and pilot-plant projects for newer technologies that could help eliminate GHG emissions (e.g., solar-hydrogen production, hot-rock geothermal power).

(7) Demonstration plants for key supply technologies, such as large-scale solar PV, should be built. Because the US renewable-energy base is vast and largely untapped, as already mentioned, wind energy in any one of the states of North Dakota, Texas, Kansas, South Dakota, Montana, and Nebraska could supply more electricity than all 103 US nuclear plants, and solar-energy resources on only 1 percent of US land (parking lots and rooftops) are roughly 3 times larger than all wind resources. Moreover, as already mentioned, installing solar PV on parking lots would require no new land use for solar, and it would allow vehicle-to-grid exchanges of electricity that would facilitate both electric cars and a vehicle backup for the grid. Thus, although wind alone, or solar alone, or both, could supply all US energy needs, because of the intermittency of these renewable-energy sources, they should be integrated into the grid together, and widely distributed so that adequate electricity from at least one of these sources is always available. For instance, the wind blows more at night, when solar is not available.

(8) Pumped hydropower and combined-cycle natural gas could provide stabilization standby capacity for the wind-and-solar system (which could supply at
least half of electricity without affecting reliability). Natural gas has less than
half the GHG emissions of coal, and yet it is at least 2.5 cents cheaper, per
kWhr, than nuclear power.[226] Moreover, natural gas is readily available because
electric utility and independent natural-gas-generator capacity utilization
was under 19 percent in 2006 in the US.[227]

(9) Geothermal and biomass could provide baseload electrical power.

(10) Federal, state, and local purchasing power should be leveraged to create markets for necessary advanced technologies, e.g., plug-in-hybrid automobiles.

(11) New batteries can enable plug-in hybrid cars and electric vehicles (parked in
large parking lots or owned by fleets) to provide inexpensive electricity storage, in a vehicle-to-grid system. Parked cars could be connected to the grid
and charged and discharged. New nanotechnology-based, lithium-ion batteries for vehicles allow about 15,000 deep discharges—far more than needed
for lifetime vehicle operation. Already in July 2007, Google's plug-in hybrids
were getting 73.5 MPG and using only 0.113 kWhr per mile of electricity.[228]
Besides, the collective installed power of automobiles is much greater than
that of the US electric power system.[229]

(12) Food-crop-based biodiesel and ethanol should be avoided because of social,
economic, environmental, and GHG emissions harms. Instead biofuels
should employ feedstock such as microalgae, water hyacinths, and prairie
grasses.

(13) Use of hydrogen, derived from wind power and possibly from solar power,
would reduce the land impacts from large-scale biofuels production.[225]

Conclusion

Following classic government analyses, like those from US DOE, and classic university analyses, like those from Princeton, this chapter has shown how to solve the
climate problem. It revealed (1) that energy efficiency and conservation are the
cheapest ways to address CC; (2) that wind is cheaper than nuclear power; (3) that
solar photovoltaic (PV) also is cheaper than fission; (4) that market proponents
confirm that renewable energy is cheaper than atomic power; (5) that renewable
energy is becoming progressively cheaper, while fission is becoming progressively
more expensive; (6) that currently available, industrial-scale renewable-energy
sources could supply all global energy, while fission could not; (7) that currently
available, industrial-scale renewable-energy sources can be implemented more
quickly than atomic power; (8) that currently available, industrial-scale renewable-
energy sources are sustainable and low-carbon technologies, while fission is not;

(9) that renewable energy would make the nation and the planet more militarily secure than could nuclear power; and (10) that the transition to a 100-percent-renewable energy can be made easily and smoothly, particularly by following guidelines like those given in the last section of this chapter.

Can such guidelines be achieved soon enough to address CC? It took only 25 years (from 1975 to 2000) to phase out use of chlorofluorocarbons. It took only 4 decades to transform the US energy economy, in the first 4 decades since 1900, from horses and coal-fired trains to electricity and oil-fueled vehicles.[230] It took only 20 years, 1970–1990, to reduce US coal plants' sulfur-dioxide emissions.[231] With a similar commitment, fossil fuels and nuclear energy could be phased out and replaced with renewable technologies, conservation, and efficiency programs.

CHAPTER 7

Answering Objections

Several years ago, when my husband and I were teaching a weekly Saturday-morning class for abused, poverty-level women at a local shelter, we learned that all of them had rock-bottom credit scores. None of them could engage in any financial transaction—like renting an apartment or opening a charge card—that required a good credit rating. We knew that all of them had been born into extreme poverty. None of them knew anyone, in their extended families, who had ever been married. Most had experienced 3 generations of living on welfare, in single-parent households. But why did none of them have good credit?

We learned that none of the women themselves had done anything to harm their credit. Instead, when they were only babies, each of their poverty-ridden mothers—whose credit had long ago been destroyed—applied for social-security cards in their babies' names. Next their mothers used these social-security cards to apply for credit cards in their babies' names. Only months later, by the time each of these women was only a toddler, her credit was ruined. Facing hardships of their own, the destitute mothers of these abused women had taken away their children's hopes for a secure financial future. From their earliest ages, these abused women knew that, no matter how hard they worked, no matter how long they studied, no matter how honest they were, their undeserved credit scores would haunt them. Even a sophisticated lawyer would need years to demolish the mountain of debts that the mothers of these women had dumped on them. The tragedy is not only that their own mothers betrayed these abused women when they were only babies, but also that these mothers destroyed the financial futures of their own children.

If the preceding chapters of this book are correct, unchecked climate change and nuclear expansion will destroy the future of our children. Like the abused women who now bear their mothers' debts, our children and their children's children will bear the irrevocable effects of this generation's climate-change debts. Because those debts will foreclose their futures, we must avert that foreclosure.

One way to do so is to discover and correct false beliefs and erring public policies about both climate change (CC) and nuclear power. This book has argued that many widely held beliefs about nuclear power are false. One of the most common is that atomic energy is emissions free and thus can provide major help to address CC.

As already noted, official US government and Nuclear Energy Institute documents, respectively, claim more nuclear power is necessary because it is "clean" and "emissions free" and "does not emit greenhouse gases."[1] Thus, in 2009 an MIT report noted that atomic energy is "a practical and timely option" for "climate-change risk mitigation."[2] The Intergovernmental Panel on Climate Change (IPCC) claimed that nuclear power could make "an increasing contribution to carbon-free electricity and heat in the future."[3] However, chapter 2 showed that once carbon emissions from all stages of the fuel cycle are counted, fission has roughly the same emissions (per kilowatt-hour) as natural gas, and many times more emissions than wind, solar photovoltaic (PV), and other renewables.

Likewise, many people erroneously believe that nuclear power is cost-effective. As already noted, industry proponents say it is "the most economical way to generate baseload electricity,"[4] and "some of the cheapest power available."[5] The World Nuclear Association bluntly says that atomic energy is "cost-effective."[6] However, chapter 3 showed that once full, fission-fuel-cycle costs are included, atomic energy is roughly 7 times more expensive, just in market costs that exclude subsidies, than its proponents claim. It is many times more expensive than conservation and renewable-energy sources, such as wind.

Chapter Overview

As earlier chapters revealed, CC and nuclear fission are complex issues, partly because much of the climate and nuclear debate has been dominated by financial conflicts of interest—by those who profit from fossil fuels and atomic energy. Consequently, many people have been misled about facts, like nuclear costs and emissions, and they may have questions about the preceding arguments. The purpose of this chapter is to answer all such major objections. Already chapter 2 (on nuclear greenhouse-gas emissions) answered the objection that, given the severity of CC, perhaps atomic energy is needed to help address emissions problems. Chapter 3 (on nuclear economics) likewise answered the objection that perhaps nuclear-cost analyses should rely on projected future costs, rather than actual, current costs, as chapter 3 has done. Similarly, chapter 4 (on reactor safety) answered 3 objections, explaining negative responses to each of the following flawed questions. Isn't much of the evidence about nuclear-accident harms anecdotal? Don't classical statistical tests overestimate radiation damage from accidents and normal reactor operation? Didn't a National Cancer Institute study fail to show any increased cancer risks near US reactors? Chapter 5 (on inequitable radiation protection and nuclear environmental injustice) likewise addressed 3 objections, explaining negative responses to each of the following misguided questions. Aren't more protective radiation standards unable to be operationalized by industry? Won't they be uneconomical? Aren't they based on hypotheses, rather than empirical data about radiation harms? Chapter 6 (on using renewable energy to address climate change) also gave detailed answers to 2 erroneous objections. If wind and other renewable-energy sources are so cost-effective and desirable, why have they not been implemented more widely? With proper safeguards, why would increasing the number of reactors increase terrorism and nuclear-proliferation risks?

This chapter answers 8 of the most common but flawed objections that nuclear advocates might make to the arguments of the preceding chapters. Why did the US even begin using atomic energy, if fission is as expensive and risky as the preceding chapters have argued? Why does France have an apparently successful atomic-energy program, if fission is as expensive and risky as the preceding chapters have argued? How is it plausible that official government and nuclear-industry cost estimates could err by 700 percent, as previous chapters have argued? Why is there now an apparent renaissance of nuclear-power construction, if this technology is expensive, carbon-intensive, and risky, as this book has argued? Why is renewable energy apparently growing so slowly, if it is both cheaper and safer than nuclear fission? How can renewable energy possibly take the place of coal or nuclear power—both of which supposedly supply baseload electricity—whereas renewables like wind and solar energy supposedly supply intermittent electricity? Given the severity of CC, why isn't a mixture of various technologies, including nuclear fission (rather than merely conservation, efficiency, and renewable energy alone), a more reliable way to address CC? Why can't other technologies, such as breeder reactors, address the uranium shortage? I call the preceding 8 questions, respectively, (1) the US Objection, (2) the France Objection, (3) the Implausibility Objection, (4) the Nuclear-Renaissance Objection, (5) the Growth-in-Renewables Objection, (6) the Intermittency Objection, (7) the Energy-Mixture Objection, and (8) the Uranium-Depletion Objection. This chapter answers each of these claims.

The First, or US, Objection

People may question why the US ever went into nuclear generation of electricity, if it is uneconomical and risky, as previous chapters argued. Yet both the US Atomic Energy Commission and virtually all electric utilities in the 1940s–1950s, prior to nuclear startup, repeatedly asserted that fission-generated electricity was "exceptionally costly and inconvenient."[7] Not surprisingly, US utilities emphasized that they did not want to go into nuclear-fission-generated electricity because of its costs, risks, and problems with radioactive waste. US utilities said that all 3 factors would bankrupt them. Nevertheless, US utilities began using atomic energy in 1955, mainly because of the prodding, financial incentives, and liability protections provided by the government. As chapter 2 explained, the US government said the utilities had a "patriotic duty" to help develop this technology, useful for nuclear weapons. Consequently, utilities agreed, but only on the condition that the US government guaranteed them 3 things. The first was free liability protection (through the 1955 Price-Anderson Act) against 98 percent of worst-case-accident losses, because market-based nuclear insurance was, and remains, prohibitively expensive— a fact that confirms the risks of atomic energy, as already argued. The second government guarantee was for taxpayer-funded responsibility for nuclear waste. The third guarantee was for massive and continuing taxpayer subsidies.[8]

Pressured into the nuclear-electricity business for military reasons, the utilities were proved right about wanting to reject atomic-energy costs and risks. Between 1972 and 1984, the US industry canceled 115 nuclear plants, despite the fact that they had already invested more than $20 billion in them; more US nuclear plants have been abandoned or canceled than have actually been built.[9] In fact, as chapter 3 noted, all US nuclear suppliers, such as GE and Westinghouse, lost money on their fixed-price reactors and had to move to cost-plus contracts.[10]

History thus reveals that the US government promoted nuclear-generated electricity not because it was supposedly cheap, cost-effective, and sustainable. Rather, chapter 2 revealed that government forced industry into fission-generated electricity for the same reason that most nations seek it today. US Atomic Energy Commissioner Thomas Murray pointed out in 1953 that the US government could derive "propaganda capital" from showing it had peaceful uses of a fission technology that was essentially military.[11] That is, the US went into commercial atomic energy for the same reason that China, France, India, Iraq, Israel, Pakistan, South Africa, the Soviet Union, the UK, and other nations did: "to open a nuclear-weapons option."[12] The US had a "not too hidden agenda" of claiming to use a supposedly commercial technology to develop nuclear weapons.[13] It wanted a "peaceful" excuse (and cover-up) for continued development of nuclear weapons, and government officials (such as the chair of the Joint Committee on Atomic Energy) and nuclear scientists (such as J. Robert Oppenheimer) explicitly admitted this fact.[14] After all, if a country has commercial atomic-energy programs, the technology is more likely to remain up-to-date and ready for joint military use. Also, the same nuclear-fission-fuel-cycle stages needed for electricity are also required for weapons production. Yet this joint technological capability would not be charged as a line-item in a military budget. Instead, electricity consumers would bear the costs. The upshot? The US nuclear program does not show that the atomic energy is safe, economical, or workable. Instead, US history shows that a military agenda has driven the commercial use of fission technology.

The Second, or France, Objection

In response to the preceding data on the US commercial nuclear program, proponents of atomic energy may point to France. It supplies 75 percent of French electricity and is the world's largest per-capita atomic-power generator; it also is the world's largest net exporter of energy.[15] Nuclear proponents say France, with 59 reactors, is "the poster child" for the commercial success of nuclear power.[16]

Unfortunately, for several reasons, France's nuclear data and claims of reactor success are not reliable. One reason is that France's atomic-energy program is state subsidized and does not operate on the market. In fact, French reactors are never expected to make a profit, even after subsidies, and this fact is true in all nations; French nuclear systems are run to attempt to attain energy independence—and to ensure the availability of technology needed for a nuclear arsenal.[17] That is why both of France's nuclear-electricity suppliers, Cogema and Électricité de France, are "state-controlled companies," "majority owned by the French government."[18] Thus, the generation-III nuclear plants currently being built in the West, those being constructed in France and Finland by the French company Areva, are 96-percent owned by the French government.[19] The French government also owns 82 percent of Cogema, which owns majority interest in the rest of the nuclear-fuel cycle (e.g., conversion, enrichment, fuel-fabrication, and uranium mining), much of which is done in former French colonies; for instance, Cogema owns 57 percent of the Somair uranium mine in Niger and 68 percent of the Comuf mine in Gabon.[20]

The preceding economic data illustrate how, in part to maintain nuclear-weapons capabilities, the French government repeatedly "bails out" its atomic-energy program whenever it goes bankrupt. Even in its heyday of building, when France completed more than 30 nuclear units, plant cost-overruns averaged 54 percent, although the facilities were almost completely state subsidized.[21] Now building its latest (Areva) plant in Finland, the French admit that, even in the beginning stages of construction, the plant is already several billion dollars over cost and 2 years behind in schedule, despite massive French-government subsidies.[22] Yet because its nuclear program is government-directed and not market-based, France was able to go from 8- to 77-percent nuclear electricity from 1973 to 1996, despite the fact that atomic energy is not cost-effective,[23] as chapter 3 showed. Even fission proponents admit that the government has financed the vast majority of the French nuclear program and owns a majority of the French nuclear utilities.[24] Moreover, because France uses plutonium rather than uranium fuel in its light-water reactors, its electricity costs an additional 2 cents per kWh more than nuclear electricity produced in countries like the US and the UK.[25] The result? The French nuclear industry is even less able to compete on the open market.

The French nuclear industry not only is taxpayer-subsidized, rather than profit-making, but also follows questionable safety standards. For instance, France (like England) cuts its nuclear costs by piping hundreds of millions of liters of liquid radioactive waste into the English Channel each year, instead of properly managing them. As a consequence, the French (and the British) have radioactively polluted the seas all the way to the Arctic Ocean. If these 2 nations dumped (rather than piped) barrels of the identical waste into the sea, they would violate the 1970

London Dumping Convention. Although 12 of the 15 nations who are parties to this London convention repeatedly have demanded that France and Britain stop their radioactive pollution, they have not done so.[26]

Apart from financial and safety concerns, the French nuclear-fission situation also is problematic from the point of view of energy independence, one goal of the French. Although the nation owns a percentage of many uranium mines, it is forced to import all its uranium.[27] Given the preceding facts, it is not surprising that the French people do not view the nation's nuclear-energy program as a success. Currently, the French can find no area of the country that is willing to accept French radioactive waste for permanent storage, and only 31 percent of the French now support nuclear energy; 54 percent oppose building any new reactors, while 84 percent instead support developing renewable energy.[28] As this French case illustrates, nations may use atomic energy to avoid dependence on foreign coal, or to support nuclear-weapons capability; as chapter 3 suggests, they also are victims of centralized planners who are swayed by the "propaganda campaign" of nuclear lobbyists.[29] However, no free markets anywhere in the world have ever built nuclear plants. Hence neither France nor the US shows that commercial atomic energy is desirable, economical, or safe. Instead, fission appears to be mainly government-prodded assistance to its nuclear-weapons agenda.

The Third, or Implausibility, Objection

As both the French and the US cases illustrate, nuclear utilities and governments (often because of a nuclear-weapons agenda) historically have promoted atomic energy and massively underestimated its costs.[30] Despite massive nuclear-cost underestimates, documented in chapter 3, many people might question the plausibility of the claim that government and industry routinely underestimate nuclear costs by 400 or more percent, as chapter 3 showed. Are such large errors plausible?

Massive nuclear-cost underestimates have been possible, in part, because electric utilities are rarely responsible for their financial mistakes, such as cost underestimates. As regulated monopolies, utilities often are bailed out by ratepayers, despite questionable investments and accounting. Moreover, chapter 3 showed that utilities routinely quote vendor prices when they want to build nuclear plants, but much higher actual costs when they want to get a full return on their investment from the local Public Service Commission. As corporations, utilities also can often claim trade secrecy (as chapter 3 showed) regarding their costs. Their corporate and regulated-monopoly status mean that nuclear utilities have rarely had to suffer the market consequences of their financial underestimates. As chapter 3 showed, at least 8 additional factors are evidence that nuclear-industry cost estimates err by a wide margin.

(i) The nuclear industry agrees to no fixed-price or "turnkey" reactor contracts, only "cost plus" contracts.

(ii) There are great price discrepancies between vendor-quoted, low prices (used to sell a reactor), versus utility-quoted, higher prices (used to pass on excess costs to ratepayers).

(iii) Vendor and nuclear-industry standard practice is to quote trimmed (e.g., "overnight") prices—that ignore all subsidies and life-cycle costs, including interest payments,. and that underestimate real prices by roughly 700 percent.

(iv) Most nuclear-cost data are from the industry, without independent confirmation.

(v) Most atomic-energy-cost studies are either funded or performed by nuclear interests.

(vi) Most nuclear-industry cost studies use counterfactual, confidential, cost-lowering assumptions.

(vii) Most nuclear-industry cost studies do not rely on market, credit-rating, and other, less biased data—that contradict industry's nuclear-cost underestimates.

(viii) Most nuclear-industry cost studies are not subjected to independent peer review.

As chapter 3 argued, the preceding reasons, especially (iv)–(viii), suggest that nuclear-industry financial conflicts of interest (COI) may help explain chronic, large, fission-cost underestimates and resulting industry failure to be responsible for its financial errors. The same nuclear industry—that stands to profit from atomic energy—has financial reasons to underestimate costs, often without bearing the financial consequences of doing so. This occurs because Public Service Commissions often force ratepayers to cover overruns. The commissions also have allowed nuclear utilities to charge interest costs on reactor-construction loans to ratepayers, even before the reactors are completed, as is now occurring in states such as Florida. Hence, because the nuclear industry often can avoid the market consequences of its PR-driven, profit-driven, cost claims, it often errs by an enormous margin, just as chapter 3 showed.

To illustrate these nuclear-cost underestimates, consider the case of Duke Power. Industry proponents erroneously say Duke Power produces nuclear-generated electricity, at its 7 reactors, at market costs lower than those of coal, at roughly 4 cents/kWhr, if one ignores costs of coal's health and environmental damage.[31] These claims have been made, in part, because the CEO of Duke Energy said capital costs of new nuclear plants were $2,500 to $2,600/kW.[32] Yet just as chapter 3 argued, such industry claims trim cost data by ignoring full fuel-cycle costs. What happens when one adds interest on the reactor-construction loan, plus fuel, operating, and maintenance costs,[33] as well as spent-fuel storage and reactor decommissioning—as calculated conservatively in year-2000 dollars by nuclear utilities and the pro-nuclear government agency, the Nuclear Regulatory Commission? Duke Power admits that the actual, market-based cost of nuclear electricity is 7–8 cents/kWh (even before one includes taxpayer subsidies; before one costs of all stages of the nuclear-fuel cycle, such as waste management; and before one corrects the 5 counterfactual cost assumptions criticized in chapter 3).[34] Thus, Duke's admitted partial nuclear costs are double what nuclear proponents claim. Credit-rating-firm data on Duke nuclear-energy costs, for the same year, 2007, are even more damning. Moody's, a premier Wall Street investment-ratings firm, says nuclear capital costs were $5,000 to $6,000/kW, bringing nuclear market costs (excluding enrichment, waste, and other taxpayer subsidies) to about 14 cents/kWhr,[35] as compared to the industry esti-mates of 4 cents/kWhr. Yet even the Moody's estimate does not include all nuclear costs. Thus, even before one counts all nuclear-electricity costs, the Duke Energy figures themselves are roughly double what nuclear proponents claim about Duke costs, and market-cost data are nearly quadruple what industry proponents claim about Duke costs. Hence, contrary to objection (3), massive nuclear-industry cost estimates appear not only plausible, but also supported by actual cases.

Other situations likewise support the massive nuclear-cost underestimates, documented in the Duke Energy case and in chapter 3. Consider the costs of one of only 2 Western reactors whose construction is well along: the Areva plant in Finland. Its costs are much higher than industry-PR estimates claim. The Areva plant is not being built on the market and is largely subsidized by French taxpayers and government, who are majority owners. Nevertheless, future Areva electricity costs were calculated in 2007 to be at least 11 cents/kWh, based on already-incurred costs; yet this plant is close neither to completion nor to full cost expen-ditures, so this 11 cents/kWhr estimate obviously will increase.[36] However, this subsidized Areva-electricity-cost figure is already 300-percent higher than industry-PR claims for the same plant. Likewise, when PacificCorp says its costs of nuclear-generated electricity are 5.1 cents/kWhr, its claims are not based on actual empirical data, and they exclude most of the nuclear-fuel-cycle costs, including costs outlined in chapter 3; they are about 300 percent lower than Wall Street and Areva cost data.[37] Repeated nuclear-industry cost underestimates thus confirm that the massive nuclear costs—outlined in chapter 3—are quite plausible, provided one is willing to believe market estimates, rather than the estimates of industry groups that profit from atomic energy.

Who should one believe about nuclear-cost estimates? Wall Street has no appar-ent conflicts of interest in giving nuclear-electricity costs that are roughly 350–700 percent higher than many industry claims. Besides, if the industry cost claims were correct, and not gross underestimates, industry ought to be willing to use its price claims as the amount it would be willing to take for building a fixed-price reactor.[38] Yet as already noted, industry refuses to build fixed-price nuclear plants. The only conceivable reason for this refusal is that industry knows that it has underestimated costs. It must know that there will be cost overruns, as there always have been in the past. Thus, when fission proponents say atomic energy is inexpensive, cheaper than most other sources of electricity,[39] at best they beg the question. At worst, they fall victim to financial conflicts of interest and to contradicting the actual historical record of atomic-energy costs.

Besides nuclear-industry conflicts of interest, and nuclear-industry cost estimates that are contradicted by market estimates and by empirical expenditures, a third important response to objection (3)—that massive, nuclear-industry cost underestimates seem implausible—is that both governments and the industry have repeatedly engaged in nuclear cover-up and misrepresentation—as chapter 2 already showed. Consequently, cover-up and misrepresentation also seem possible in nuclear-cost claims. In the US, citizens themselves were not told the truth about nuclear costs and risks when government began promoting atomic energy in the late 1940s, for military reasons. For 2 decades, the US government suppressed the results of its 1955 Brookhaven Report. Because of a request under the US Freedom of Information Act, the report was finally released. As chapter 2 explained, the report showed that a nuclear accident could destroy an area the size of Pennsylvania and kill 150,000 people. While the US government and the nuclear industry suppressed these results for 20 years, they claimed that atomic energy was cheap and safe. Yet at the same time, the US nuclear industry demanded (and received) government-guaranteed freedom from 98 percent of nuclear-liability claims. If atomic energy were safe, neither industry nor citizens would need the financial protection of a liability limit. Because industry says it needs the liability limit, it must believe that catastrophic nuclear accidents are both costly and probable, contrary to its own claims. Moreover, over the last 70 years (i.e., since atomic energy began), US government and industry cover-up of nuclear health, safety, and environmental violations (including falsification of radiation-worker radiation doses by the US government and its contractors) have been both continuous and severe. These violations have been documented in repeated congressional hearings, congressional studies, and reports by the US Government Accountability Office (GAO), as noted in chapter 2. These industry cover-ups and falsifications have been orchestrated even by government agencies, like the US Department of Energy (DOE), in part because these government regulators appear to have been co-opted by industry, and in part because government has sought to protect its military nuclear interests by protecting commercial nuclear interests. The ongoing cover-up of nuclear-industry costs, illegal acts, and safety violations has been so serious that ever since 1991, the US Congress, the US GAO, and the US Office of Technology Assessment repeatedly have called for either abolition of DOE (charged with regulating the nuclear industry) or outside regulation of DOE. Neither has occurred.

The extreme underestimates of nuclear-energy costs, outlined earlier in chapter 3, as well as chronic and very serious nuclear-industry violations of health and safety laws, also are consistent with 6 economic facts, all of which suggest how and why these nuclear-cost underestimates have occurred.

First, as chapter 3 noted, credit-rating companies downgrade the ratings of utilities with nuclear plants,[40] a fact suggesting that reactors are financially risky, not economical, as nuclear proponents allege in objection (3).

Second, as also noted in chapter 3, the preeminent credit-rating firm, Moody's, says nuclear-generated-electricity costs are triple those of natural gas, and double those of scrubbed coal—despite the fact that its nuclear calculations omitted full-fuel-cycle costs like decommissioning, waste storage, and those discussed earlier in chapter 3.[41] Consequently, Moody's shows that the nuclear-industry cost claims are underestimates.

Third, again as chapter 3 showed, the pro-nuclear, US DOE–Scully Capital study argued that fission plants could provide typical, profitable, electric-utility investment-return rates only if nuclear-construction costs did not exceed $1 billion.[42] Yet nuclear-construction costs are now $12–30 billion, as noted in chapter 3. Because industry economists themselves admit that nuclear technology is not cost-effective, staying in business requires the nuclear industry to use cost underestimates, contrary to objection (3).

Fourth, as also noted in chapter 3, despite taxpayers' massive atomic-energy subsidies,[43] the nuclear industry itself admits that high costs will rule fission "out of consideration" in the future; the industry lobby group, the World Nuclear Association, says that by 2030 the proportion of global fission-generated electricity will decrease from its current 16 percent to 9 percent.[44] Nuclear costs thus must be much higher than industry admits, or future nuclear declines would not occur.

Fifth, as already noted, no atomic-energy plant anywhere in the world operates on the free market, and all are massively subsidized by taxpayers and pulled out of bankruptcy. For instance, the UK government annually pays £184 million, just for spent nuclear-fuel liabilities, to prop up British Energy (BE); in 2003, the UK government was forced to bail BE out of bankruptcy.[45] In all nations with commercial reactors, taxpayer subsidies dominate atomic-energy costs. Fission is the most heavily subsidized of all energy technologies.[46]

Sixth, if nuclear plants were really cost-effective, they could operate on the market and would not need such heavy subsidies. Yet as chapter 3 showed, from 1947 through 1999, the US spent approximately $150 billion on energy subsidies for nuclear, wind, and solar power; 96.3 percent of those subsidies went to nuclear, but only 3.7 percent went (together) to wind and solar.[47] Since 2000, this US imbalance has continued, with $13 billion in US nuclear subsidies in the US Energy Policy Act of 2005,[48] another $18.5 billion in 2007,[49] and another $85 billion promised by President Obama.

Consistent with the preceding 6 facts is that, in 1976, only 20 years after nuclear-generated electricity began, the *Wall Street Journal* proclaimed nuclear power an "economic disaster" because it was unable to operate on the market. Yet 25 years later, this "economic disaster" worsened, so that nuclear-generated-electricity costs increased by 800 percent above its 1976 rates.[50]

Not only do the previous considerations show that objection (3) errs in suggesting that massive nuclear-cost underestimates seem implausible. The preceding considerations also force one to ask why politicians have provided the bulk of taxpayer energy subsidies to a market loser, nuclear power. The military rationale again may provide a reason. Yet as chapter 3 revealed, even this rationale may fail because Standard and Poor's (a top credit- and investment-ratings firm) says that, given enormous costs, massive nuclear subsidies might not provide enough incentive either to build future nuclear plants or to sustain credit quality in the nuclear industry.[51] If not, then contrary to objection (3), nuclear costs appear both high and underestimated, as chapter 3 has argued.

Would new nuclear plants with more advanced technology be more cost-effective than current ones? Lower nuclear costs seem unlikely for several reasons. One reason is that even the pro-nuclear business community admits that atomic-energy costs are increasing, while solar and wind costs are decreasing—which means that new nuclear plants are becoming even more expensive.[52] For instance, in 2003 the classic MIT study estimated market-based nuclear capital costs at roughly $3,200/kW.[53] Yet in 2007, the McKinsey business-management report estimated these same market-based nuclear capital costs at $4,000/kW.[54] Market-based capital costs of nuclear-generated electricity thus increased roughly 20 percent in only 4 years. The industry lobby group, the World Nuclear Association, also noted that between 2004 and 2008, finance or interest charges *alone* doubled the cost of nuclear plants.[55] In addition, in the US, there was a 50-percent increase in construction material, equipment, and labor from 2004 to 2008, and a 100-percent increase from 2000 to 2008,[56] all of which are symptomatic of continuing increases in nuclear-construction costs. As already mentioned, World Energy Council studies show that the trend over time has been increased construction-time and prices for fission plants, and therefore increased nuclear costs, because of the increased interest on the capital borrowed.[57]

A second and related reason that nuclear costs are unlikely ever to decrease significantly, even with new technology, is that 75 percent of nuclear costs (as compared to 25 percent of gas costs) are for building and construction.[58] Given that labor and materials prices are continually increasing, as just noted, this 75 percent of nuclear costs is almost certain to increase. Economically savvy nuclear proponents also dismiss any idea of a decrease in future atomic-energy costs because these new plants are "first-of-a-kind reactors,"[59] plants that must rely on "untested engineering,"[60] with costly, unworked-out "bugs."[61] Likewise, chapter 3 and Standard and Poor's shows that, during the first decade of operation, because reactor lifetimes and load factors are typically decreased, as bugs are being worked out, future reactors are sure to have higher costs and many cost overruns.[62] Moreover, those who say future nuclear plants will be cheaper must explain why Wall Street is demanding 100-percent loan guarantees and full taxpayer-covered financial insurance for all new reactors.[63] As already noted, even the pro-nuclear business community has flatly said that nuclear power is economically unviable without government subsidies.[64] All of the preceding points help explain why no new US reactors have been ordered since 1974 and why objection (3) is misplaced.

Even carbon-tax subsidies would not help nuclear energy, relative to wind and solar, in part because (as chapter 3 showed) wind is already currently much cheaper than nuclear power.[65] Of course, industry groups, such as the World Nuclear Association, claim that atomic energy could compete with coal and natural-gas technologies if there were a carbon tax of \$45/ton CO_2-equivalent emissions.[66] However, the pro-nuclear MIT study says that even a carbon tax of \$100/ton CO_2-equivalent emissions would bring atomic energy only to the breakeven point, financially, as compared to other dirty technologies like coal.[67] Given such economic data, it is not surprising that special interests have massively underestimated nuclear costs, contrary to what objection (3) claims.

The Fourth, or Nuclear-Renaissance, Objection

But if fission plants such as those in France and in the US have always been risky and uneconomical, someone might ask why there now appears to be a nuclear-construction upswing. Indeed, proponents of atomic energy repeatedly speak of the present as a time of "nuclear renaissance."[68] Is it?

In addition to the 2011 Fukushima Daiichi nuclear catastrophe, outlined earlier, at least 7 reasons show there is no nuclear renaissance. *First*, none of the new nuclear construction is taking place on the market, as chapter 3 showed. Investors such as the World Bank, the European Bank for Reconstruction and Development, the Asian Development Bank, the African Development Bank, the European Investment Bank, and the Inter-American Development Bank all say nuclear power is "uneconomic"; they refuse nuclear loans or investments, as a matter of policy.[69] The World Bank, for instance, reaffirmed its long-standing position of not funding atomic-energy investments because it says nuclear power is "not a least-cost option."[70] That is one reason even the pro-nuclear MIT energy study warned that high construction costs have caused little commercial interest in fission investments.[71] As the CEO of Dominion Energy warned: "We aren't going to build a nuclear plant anytime soon. Standard and Poor's and Moody's [two top debt- and credit-rating agencies] would have a heart attack. And my chief financial officer would too."[72] Given this lack of market interest in fission, as chapter 3 noted, nuclear electricity has been decreasing, as a percentage of global electricity, while the percentage supplied by renewable energy has been increasing. Nuclear plants now supply a much smaller percentage of global energy than they did in the 1990s,[73] as well as a smaller percentage of global electricity.[74] As already mentioned, the nuclear industry itself admits that high costs will rule nuclear "out of consideration" in the future.[75] This is no renaissance. Instead, the few new reactors being built are being promoted and funded by governments, in part by those who want nuclear weapons, as discussed earlier in this chapter. Many poor nations can afford neither to train and equip a large, conventional military force, nor to develop space-based weapons; for them, building nuclear plants and weapons is cheaper and easier than a large conventional-military buildup.[76] Thus, most of the alleged nuclear renaissance is closely linked to having technology to support military programs.[77]

Given government-military, rather than market, interest in atomic energy, a *second* reason (other than a nuclear renaissance) that explains the few new atomic-energy plants is massive taxpayer-government subsidies. Without these subsidies, pro-nuclear economists and nuclear-utility CEOs say there would be no commercial reactors. CEOs from TXU, NRG, Exelon, and elsewhere also say: "to construct a new generation of nuclear reactors will require direct involvement from the federal government."[78] Most economic analyses (including those of the industry itself) likewise admit that "if [future] nuclear plants are to be built, it seems clear that extensive government guarantees and subsidies would be required...for construction cost, operating performance, non-fuel operations and maintenance cost, nuclear fuel cost, decommissioning cost."[79] As already noted in chapter 3, even nuclear proponents admit that global taxpayer nuclear subsidies are already at least $16 billion per year, or nearly 1 cent for every kilowatt-hour of electricity generated.[80] Yet even this figure fails to include one of the most massive health, accident, and financial nuclear subsidies, namely, government-guaranteed liability limits for fission facilities. As already noted in chapter 3, the European Commission recently showed that requiring full nuclear-liability coverage would alone triple costs of nuclear-generated electricity.[81]

Given the nuclear industry's need for massive subsidies—covering 60–90 percent of nuclear-electricity costs, as chapter 1 noted—a nuclear renaissance is especially unlikely in Europe. Why? "European Union law...proscribes (except in specific cases) state aids [or subsidies].....It seems doubtful that such an extensive package of 'state aids' [for commercial reactors] would be acceptable under EU competition law."[82] Yet, as already argued in chapter 3, private investors appear unlikely to do what banks throughout the world refuse to do, and what EU law prevents states from doing: subsidizing or investing in nuclear power. Thus a nuclear renaissance is unlikely.

Besides military agendas and taxpayer subsidies, a *third* reason (other than a nuclear renaissance) that explains the few new nuclear plants—none of which are being built on the market—is industry PR. Chapters 2–3 showed that this PR extends even to using faulty data on reactor emissions, interest rates, plant lifetimes, construction periods, and load-factors. These faulty data make nuclear power erroneously appear carbon free and at least 4 times cheaper than it really is. Thus because fission is neither economical nor carbon free, the nuclear industry—seeking a return on its capital investments—is pushing new reactor construction. It must do so largely with PR rather than with facts. The industry admits that it is now paying PR firms, such as Hill and Knowlton, millions of dollars annually to promote atomic energy and additional government subsidies for the nuclear industry.[83] Yet critics say that if fission power were genuinely desirable, and if there were really a market-based nuclear renaissance, the industry would not have to pay millions of dollars to Hill and Knowlton for a "greenwashing" campaign designed to garner even more taxpayer subsidies.[84]

A *fourth* reason there is no genuine nuclear renaissance is that most of the new plants being built were either begun more than 2 decades ago (and thus are wildly over-budget) or are using outdated, unsafe technology because they are being constructed in the Third World. Of the 22 atomic plants being built around the globe, roughly 80 percent of them (17) are located in Asia, and 16 are being supplied by substandard vendors from India, China, and Russia; none of these substandard vendors has reactors that meet Western safety standards.[85] The Indian units are based on an outdated 1960s Canadian-rector design and, as already noted, may never be completed because India wants the industry to bear liability for reactor accidents. The Chinese units are based on outdated Western designs. None of the Russian units has the safety updates of Western reactors, and they bear the stigma of Chernobyl-design flaws. The safer, latest-design plants, now being built by Western vendors and using up-to-date Western designs, are 4 for China, 1 for Finland, and 1 for Taiwan. Yet 6 reactors is not a nuclear renaissance. Moreover, of the 22 plants now being built, 5 were ordered more than 20 years ago, and 6 were ordered more than 15 years ago.[86] They have enormously high costs, partly because of construction delays. Apart from these 22 plants now being constructed, there are another 14 plants globally on which construction has been stopped.[87] Obviously a nuclear renaissance would not be typified by a 40-percent construction stoppage, an 80 percent use of outdated and substandard technology, and expensive, outdated "hangover" plants whose construction overruns exceed 20 years.

A *fifth* reason there is, and will be, no commercial nuclear renaissance is that, as chapter 3 showed, growth in inexpensive renewable energy has already far outpaced new nuclear plants. If there is a massive energy increase, it is in renewable energy. Wind already generates as much as 15 percent of the electricity in some midwestern US states.[88] Its big advantage is that there will never be a production-decline curve, a fuel that becomes scarce, or one difficult to extract from ore. The Danes already use wind to generate 20 percent of their electricity,[89] and the British say that, by 2020, they can use wind to supply 6 times the planned nuclear increase of 6 plants, and use solar to supply 3 times the planned nuclear increase.[90] As of 2009, nearly 50 percent of Sweden's total energy consumption comes from renewable sources, and the province of Quebec, Canada, satisfies 97 percent of its electricity needs with renewables; Sweden also says that, by 2020, it can replace 100 percent of its nuclear energy, and nearly all of its coal facilities, with renewable sources—partly because Swedish wind power will grow by 2,500 percent.[91] Similarly, solar-panel grid parity is becoming a reality in many countries such as Germany; Germany supplies over half of all global solar energy, in part because it has feed-in electricity tariffs that reduce the external costs of, and provide incentives for, renewable energy; as a result, German and other national markets for solar power are growing as much as 40 percent each year.[92]

As already mentioned in chapter 6, the classic 2004 Princeton University study shows that 6 of only 9 renewable technologies, already long deployed at an industrial scale, could completely solve the climate problem by 2050; the US DOE is even more optimistic, arguing that available renewable technology can provide 99 percent of US electricity by 2020.[93] This is the rough date by which a nuclear plant would be finished if it were begun in 2008. European government studies also have shown that virtually all global energy needs could be supplied through renewables,[94] and the European Renewable Energy Council has shown that renewable energy easily could supply 50 percent of the world's primary energy by 2040.[95] Even Shell Oil has said that one-third to one-half of the world's energy can come from renewables by 2050.[96] Nuclear-renaissance claims also are undercut by the Intergovernmental Panel on Climate Change (IPCC) and the classic Princeton University study. The Princeton authors showed that "a portfolio of technologies now exists to meet the world's energy needs over the next 50 years and limit atmospheric CO_2," and that renewables alone can address climate change.[97] "None of the [renewable-energy] options is a pipe dream or an unproven idea," say the authors, since "today one can buy electricity from a wind turbine, PV array, gas turbine," and "every one of these options is already implemented at an industrial scale and could be scaled up further over 50 years."[98] If only currently-cost-competitive, nonsubsidized renewable energy were used, scientists say they could supply 40 percent of US electricity as soon as 2030.[99]

Two possible drivers for this massive increase in renewable energy—as opposed to an alleged nuclear renaissance—are the facts that many renewables (e.g., wind) are much cheaper than nuclear power, as chapter 3 showed, and that renewables like wind and solar emit fewer greenhouse gases than does the nuclear-fuel cycle, as chapter 2 showed.[100] Besides, as even reports of pro-nuclear governments attest, the current costs of renewables are far more certain than the costs of nuclear plants, given that costs of renewables are decreasing, whereas nuclear costs are increasing because of atomic-energy cost overruns, construction delays, construction- and labor-cost increases, decommissioning, and waste storage.[101] As already mentioned in chapter 3, because nuclear plants are so expensive, even nuclear proponents see reactors as no more than an interim measure (not a source of a nuclear renaissance), until renewables can supply all energy needs.[102] Yet as an interim measure, atomic power makes little sense because even pro-nuclear nations (e.g., the UK Department of Business Enterprise and Regulatory Reform) admit that, even if nuclear-plant construction had begun in 2008, the plant could not be ready to generate electricity until at least 2021.[103] But if new nuclear plants could not be ready for 13 years, at the earliest; if (as chapter 3 noted) wind is already much cheaper than nuclear fission;

and if (as chapter 3 noted) the pro-nuclear US DOE says solar PV will be cost competitive with all existing energy technologies by 2015, there is little reason to use fission power now—even as an interim or transitional technology. Even if atomic energy were cheap and carbon free (and chapters 2–3 showed it is not), it could do little to address climate change, because the plants could not be built quickly enough. Even under the most optimistic nuclear-building scenario of 1,000 new reactors by 2050—a scenario far more optimistic than the industry's own projections—atomic energy could supply no more than 20 percent of global electricity by 2050, roughly the same percentage it supplies now. This is because of increases in global energy demand, because most existing reactors are close to retirement, and because (as already noted earlier in this chapter) the industry says too few new reactors will be built even to replace old ones.[104]

Besides the rapid growth of cheaper, lower-emissions renewable energy, a *sixth* roadblock to any nuclear renaissance is the absence of a permanent waste-disposal facility. Regarding radioactive-waste management, the UK government bluntly says that it is "impossible to guarantee safety and security over such long time periods,"[105] essentially forever. It also says that the waste and proliferation problems are the 2 crucial nuclear issues.[106] Together with high costs and the fact that nuclear subsidies undermine support for renewable energy and efficiency improvements, UK government reports say radioactive waste is a major argument against fission-generated electricity.[107] Even if safely storing radioactive wastes in perpetuity were technically possible, no nation has ever successfully achieved long-term, radioactive-waste management. All US radioactive wastes have leaked within 10 years of their being stored.[108] Yet these wastes began to be created in the 1940s, and ever since then, the government has failed to show they can safety be stored. In 1998, the US government was supposed to begin accepting spent nuclear-fuel waste at the proposed Yucca Mountain (Nevada) repository, but it says that 2017 is the earliest possible date any waste could be accepted; moreover, it is not clear that the proposed Yucca Mountain facility will even win a license,[109] especially since safety problems and cost overruns caused President Obama to withdraw funding for it in 2010.

Blocking any nuclear renaissance, an ongoing problem at Yucca Mountain—and, indeed, at any facility—is that waste sites appear to allow waste migration over the essentially permanent period that the US National Academy of Sciences says that nuclear waste and spent fuel needs to be stored.[110] Similar problems beset all other nuclear-waste-generating nations. The British government claims that it will be at least 2045 before a UK nuclear-waste repository is open,[111] and no nation is able to show it can store the waste safely. The US has long admitted that all permanent nuclear-waste sites will leak and, as a consequence, has repeatedly tried to weaken long-term radiation standards for waste sites, as chapter 5 showed.[112] Besides, given no solution to the radioactive-waste problem, fission is not a sustainable technology. This is one reason that the UK Sustainable Development Commission concluded in 2006 that "there is no justification for a new nuclear power programme at this time....Any such proposal would be incompatible with the government's own sustainable strategy."[113]

A *seventh* obstacle to any nuclear renaissance is concern about safety, poor credit, and lack of liability insurance. After all, the 2011 Fukushima and 1987 Chernobyl accidents are still in many people's minds. As of late 2010, 23 years after Chernobyl and thousands of miles away, sheep and farms in the UK are still under many government health-and-safety restrictions because of continuing radioactive pollution from the faraway Soviet accident.[114] Citizen concerns about safety also are unlikely to allow a nuclear renaissance, given repeated safety violations and government cover-up of serious problems and illegal acts in the US, the UK, Japan, and elsewhere. As this chapter and chapters 4 and 5 showed, fundamental citizen trust regarding government claims about atomic-energy safety probably has been lost. As already mentioned, the UK admitted suppressing the government report that outlined the full extent, harm, and cost of the nuclear accident and fire at Windscale. The facts about the accident were not made public until 30 years later. The official (suppressed) report showed the full extent of the disaster, the many safety and organizational defects that helped cause the disaster, and the many technical shortcomings related to nuclear technology. Scientists now know that the UK Windscale accident generated at least twice as much radioactive material as government originally claimed.[115]

Similarly, after a leaked UK government document showed that about $4 billion could have been saved if the UK had not built the Sizewell B nuclear plant, the House of Commons charged the government with misleading statements about the cost of nuclear energy. Later the UK's Central Electricity Generating Board was forced to admit that the price of nuclear electricity was more than double what it had claimed. The House of Commons said the UK Department of Energy "made no attempt to obtain realistic costings." Likewise the UK Department of Energy admitted in 1990 that, earlier, when it canceled all research into wave power on grounds that it was too expensive, the government actually knew that wave power was much cheaper than nuclear energy.[116] The government had deliberately covered up the economic desirability of wave power by using skewed methods of gross wave-energy data to estimate the productivity of wave farms; these flawed techniques not only were less accurate than those based on exploitable-wave-energy data but also obscured the fact that wave power is more cost-effective than nuclear energy.[117]

Likewise undercutting any notion of a nuclear renaissance, in 1999 Japan ordered an investigation after British Nuclear Fuel (BNF), which is largely owned by the UK government, admitted forging quality-control data for the MOX nuclear fuel that BNF shipped to Japan. In the year 2000, the Japanese refused the flawed, dangerous UK fuel, and the UK government paid Japan about $40 million in compensation. The UK had to send armed boats to Japan, to bring the defective fuel back to the UK. This transport back to the UK cost taxpayers about $225 million.[118] Germany also received the reprocessed, spent uranium fuel from BNF and used it to power its

Unterweser reactor for years; when the falsified records were discovered in 2000, German firms canceled their contracts with BNF—causing $1 billion in losses.[119] Such problems indicate that a nuclear renaissance is unlikely, given citizen safety concerns and serious, continuing nuclear-related cover-ups and illegal acts, even in the most developed nations, like the UK and the US. As noted in chapter 2, the US cover-ups include suppressing the Brookhaven Report (on nuclear risks) for 20 years; putting Navajo uranium miners at great and illegal risk; punishing and even murdering nuclear whistleblowers, like Karen Silkwood; falsifying nuclear-safety data; and weakening radiation standards.[120]

As already argued, any nuclear renaissance also is undercut by the fact that newer generations of reactors are not obviously safer than existing ones. For one thing, most accidents are caused by human error, and there also are no clear ways to correct for human error among reactor operators. Another safety concern is that even pro-nuclear governments note that new reactor "designs incorporate only incremental changes to designs previously built."[121] As a consequence, new-design plants may not be much safer than old ones. Governments admit that, to know that new plants are genuinely safer, one will have to wait many years, until construction is finished and operation has been stabilized. Although several new, generation-III fission plants are planned, they are not evidence of a nuclear renaissance because (as already mentioned) they are government subsidized (like the Areva plant), are unfinished, are already several billions of dollars over cost, and are several years behind schedule. Generation-III plants also have yet to have their bugs worked out; they appear to be more costly than the older plants,[122] and they also could be less safe. Debugging is a crucial safety step and, as chapter 3 showed, all nuclear plants (ever built) have had to operate for years, at far less than their design load, as they debugged their new designs. Besides, as chapter 3 showed, if these new generation-III reactors were really safer, the insurance industry would not have such prohibitively high premiums for market-based, nuclear-reactor-liability coverage, and most governments would not have imposed nuclear-liability limits amounting to only 1–2 percent of worst-case, nuclear-accident costs. All of these problems with nuclear safety, high reactor costs, government cover-up, and lack of nuclear-liability-insurance coverage are likely to prevent any nuclear renaissance.

The Fifth, or Growth-in-Renewable-Energy, Objection

Yet if there is no nuclear renaissance, and if atomic-energy emissions and costs are extraordinarily high, as earlier chapters have argued, some people might pose this question: Why is there not even more renewable energy if it is so inexpensive and desirable, relative to fission? According to the International Energy Agency, as of 2006, renewable energy (including hydropower) supplied 18 percent, and nuclear 16 percent, of global electricity.[123] Since 2006, total electricity generation from renewable sources has been growing by roughly 3 percent each year,[124] while that from fission has been declining. However, why have renewables not grown even faster?

Business publications, such as *Forbes* and the *Economist*, explain why renewable energy has not been adopted more quickly. They claim that campaign donors, lobbyists, and PR firms—funded by the nuclear industry—have skewed reasonable market responses regarding renewable versus atomic energy. They say nuclear fission is not economically defensible, but that special-interest money has skewed US energy subsidies toward atomic energy and away from renewable technologies.[125] As already mentioned, a year-2000 report by MRG Associates showed that, in part at the behest of corporate lobbyists, from 1947 through 1999, the US spent approximately $150 billion of (direct and indirect) energy subsidies for nuclear, wind, and solar power—96.3 percent of which went to nuclear.[126] Yet this funding does not include later subsidies, like the $13 billion dollars in the 2006 Energy Policy Act,[127] or the $85 billion in taxpayer subsidies, promised by President Obama to build new reactors.

Because corporate donations, especially campaign-finance contributions, have skewed US market and energy-subsidy decisions, the US actually has been hurt economically by promoting old, outmoded energy technologies, rather than more lucrative, renewable technologies. As noted earlier, in the early 1980s, the US dominated the wind-energy market, and it also led the world in exploiting wind energy. In 1985, the US had 95 percent of the world's installed wind capacity, with 18 times the total capacity of all of Europe. Yet because of poor US policies of subsidizing nuclear and fossil fuels, by 2003 the US share of installed global wind was only 16 percent. In 2003 alone, the EU added 15 percent more installed wind capacity to its grid than the cumulative amount installed in the US, up to that time.[128]

Such misplaced energy subsidies are a problem not only because they have helped costly and dirty nuclear energy and fossil fuels, while harming cheaper and cleaner renewable technologies, but also because they skew market signals. Markets reflect the true costs and values of goods only when markets operate efficiently and there are no subsidies. Because nuclear power has never operated on the market anywhere, and it always has been heavily subsidized, one cannot expect the market percentages of electricity sources to reflect authentic economics. The preceding chapters, especially 3, revealed that, relative to renewable-energy sources, such as solar and wind, nuclear power appears to have been subsidized (at least by the US) about 25 times more heavily.[129] Thus massive and disproportionate nuclear subsidies explain much of the 16 percent of global electricity supplied by atomic energy, whereas trivial or nonexistent renewable-energy subsidies explain why wind and solar power supply similar amounts of US electricity. Another explanatory factor, already mentioned, is that many nations began nuclear generation of electricity as a covert way to obtain nuclear-weapons capability. Given this motivation and the resulting heavy nuclear subsidies, it is all the more amazing that without comparable subsidies, renewables like wind have grown far more quickly than nuclear fission.

Given enormous nuclear subsidies, it also is amazing that fission power has been decreasing, while renewable energy has been increasing. As already mentioned, for instance, in 1990 the UK generated 30 percent of its electricity from fission, but by 2007, this nuclear share was only 18 percent.[130] As noted in chapter 3, even the International Energy Association says that, as a percentage of global electricity, nuclear will go from its current 16 percent to only 9 percent in 2030, largely because the high capital costs of nuclear plants will "rule them out of consideration"—despite the fact that (as chapter 1 documented) taxpayer subsidies cover 60–90 percent of nuclear-electricity costs.[131] Yet a European Union analysis showed that, from 1995 to 2005, installed wind capacity grew exponentially and increased by a factor of 20–2,000 percent.[132] The excellent economics of renewable energy are one reason that, as the previous chapter showed, renewables and gas-fired cogeneration have been growing far more rapidly than nuclear power. In 2006, solar PV (1.74 GW) brought more capacity online than did atomic energy (1.49 GW), and wind (15 GW) brought 10 times more electricity online than did nuclear. In 2006, distributed renewable energy got $56 billion of private investment, while nuclear got zero.[133] Global net installed wind capacity had grown to 121 GW by 2008, more than doubling wind capacity every year for the last decade; yet nuclear capacity has been stagnating and being phased out, as in Germany and Belgium.[134] As noted in the previous chapter, US wind capacity increased by an astounding 39 percent in 2009, and by nearly the same percentage in 2008, and the nearly the same percentage in 2007. Wind enjoyed $9 billion in private US investments in the year 2007, and even higher investments in 2008 and 2009, while nuclear had no private investments; between now and the year 2015, wind is expected to generate $65 billion in private US investments; in January 2008 alone, in Texas alone, $700 million in new wind farms went into operation.[135] Such figures suggest that nuclear lobbyists may be convincing politicians, to whom they gave campaign donations, but they are not convincing private investors that nuclear fission is a better buy than renewable energy. Such figures also show that, despite nuclear and fossil-fuel subsidies, which harmed renewable-energy growth in the past, the future belongs to renewables.

Rapid growth in renewable energy is also evident from many facts noted in chapter 6, such as that the pro-nuclear International Atomic Energy Agency says global nuclear capacity is shrinking, while renewables like solar PV are massively increasing. As chapters 3 and 6 argued, solar and wind have been greatly surpassing fission growth, largely because they are cheaper. As chapter 3 showed, even when one ignores massive nuclear subsidies and counts only part of the nuclear-fuel cycle, US government data show wind now costs 3.4 cents/kWhr, while nuclear costs about 20 cents/kWhr. Such cost figures explain why Wall Street prefers that taxpayers, through government subsidies, pay for atomic energy. After all, investors know what happened because of Fukushima, because of Three Mile Island, because of the municipal-bond catastrophe surrounding Washington Public Power nuclear construction, because of the bankruptcy of Public Service Company of New Hampshire when it struggled to complete the Seabrook nuclear plant, and because of the shutdown of 7 Japanese nuclear plants due to an earthquake.[136] That is why private investors want 100-percent loan guarantees on all nuclear construction. That is why the US secretary of energy says that without financial incentives and subsidies, atomic power will not be an option.[137] Even with US subsidies—which have effectively paid the entire capital cost of the next 6 US reactors to be ordered—scientists say poor nuclear economics and poor safety have killed fission. They say giving US subsidies to nuclear power is like defibrillating a corpse: It'll jump, but it won't revive."[138]

Also testifying to the strong market support for renewable energy, EU scientists say that between 2005 and 2020, wind will increase up to 1,800 percent, and solar photovoltaic will increase up to 4,200 percent.[139] By 2050, they say renewable energy will supply roughly 70 percent of global electricity, including a 42-percent contribution from wind and solar, with wind being the most important single source of electricity generation.[140] Part of the reason for this remarkable renewable-energy growth is the excellent "rate of learning" curve of wind and solar. As already mentioned, the International Energy Agency shows that solar-photovoltaic costs drop 35 percent for every doubling in installed capacity, while wind costs drop 18 percent for every doubling in installed capacity.[141] Such data suggest that, although the current balance of renewable to nuclear-generated energy reflects past subsidies, the present and the future belong to renewable energy.

The Sixth, or Energy-Intermittency, Objection

Despite these outstanding market reports on renewable energy, some fission proponents say nuclear power is more desirable than renewable energy because the sun does not shine all the time, and the wind does not always blow. They claim renewables can provide only intermittent or "variable" power, while atomic energy can provide continuous or baseload power.[142] Is this claim correct?

In fact, the pro-nuclear, energy-intermittency objection errs on at least 5 points. *First,* proponents of the intermittency objection forget that nuclear energy also has intermittency problems. As chapter 3 noted, and as nuclear advocates admit, in the 1970s and 1980s, fission plants had a severe intermittency problem. Despite more than 30 years of nuclear experience, commercial reactors ran only about half the time.[143] The International Atomic Energy Agency (IAEA) likewise admitted that, after 45 years of experience in generating electricity, in 1990 global commercial reactors had a lifetime-average load factor (percentage of time reactors operated) of only 67 percent.[144] As chapter 3 showed, the lifetime-average load factor of US plants is only about 70 percent. What causes these nuclear intermittencies? As chapter 3 showed, normal maintenance and refueling require at least 10–15 percent reactor downtime, and unforeseen accidents cause additional reactor downtime. For instance, a few years ago, all US reactors of the same type were shut down by government after serious corrosion problems were discovered in Ohio; Japanese and Canadian authorities likewise have ordered fleetwide reactor shutdowns in the face of systemic safety lapses.[145]

A *second* problem with the energy-intermittency objection is that it ignores the fact (outlined in chapter 3) that nuclear intermittencies are about 6 to 18 times more costly, in actual dollars/kWhr, than wind intermittencies. Wind intermittency adds only about $0.00288/kWhr to the cost of wind-generated electricity, if one uses US government empirical data that wind costs are $0.048/kWhr.[146] However, the interest alone on nuclear-construction loans adds about $0.02/kWh to atomic-energy costs.[147] Thus nuclear interest alone adds roughly 10 times more to the cost of electricity than does wind intermittency. Likewise, as already documented in chapter 3, according to the pro-nuclear UK government and other independent scientists, wind intermittency increases the cost of wind-generated electricity only by about 6 percent.[148] Yet because (as chapter 3 showed) nuclear fission costs about 700 percent more than wind energy, wind-intermittency costs are trivial, by comparison. Chapter 3 also explained that in 2008, credit-rating firms said that, after excluding all subsidies, market costs alone of atomic-energy electricity were still greater than $0.15/kWhr.[149] By late 2009, those market nuclear costs had risen to roughly $0.21/kWhr.[150] Yet even nuclear proponents admit that wind now costs only about 4.8 cents/kWhr.[151] This is about one-third the market cost of atomic energy. Thus while there can be a wind or solar intermittency problem—especially if one derives all power from a single windmill or single solar facility, without backup—the relative problem appears far greater for nuclear fission than for wind, the fastest-growing and cheapest current renewable.

A *third* problem with this objection is its ignoring the fact that nuclear intermittencies are far more dangerous, and potentially catastrophic, than are wind or solar intermittencies. The precise nature of fission intermittencies and insecurities (created by high costs, long construction times, low load factors, low credit ratings, risks of accidents, risks of nuclear proliferation, and risks of terrorism) are arguably worse than any energy intermittencies and insecurities created by renewable-energy technologies.[152] This is especially true when one increases the number of terrorist targets by building more reactors, and when one realizes that current atomic plants are not designed to withstand terrorist attacks.[153] This energy and financial insecurity is one reason (already mentioned) that credit-rating companies, such as Standard and Poor's, say they downgrade the credit rating of any utility that has a nuclear plant.[154]

A *fourth* problem with the energy-intermittency objection is that nuclear-fission plants have a difficulty worse than, and the opposite of, the intermittency problem: Reactors cannot be easily turned on or off. Consequently, in order to be more economical, reactors must run even when electricity demand is low.[155] Nuclear plants thus are "inflexible" and cannot increase or decrease their output as quickly as other types of plants. One UK government report notes that although atomic energy has "insufficient flexibility...to match demand effectively,"[156] wind intermittency is "not a major problem for the electricity system" because of the diversity of electricity supply.[157] Thus the British government report concludes that this fission inflexibility is a greater concern than the intermittency that both nuclear plants and renewables share.[158]

A *fifth* problem is that nuclear proponents forget that intermittencies of renewable-energy technologies can be avoided by geographically dispersing them, so that somewhere the sun is always shining, or the wind is always blowing. Solutions include installing many wind turbines offshore, where the wind virtually always blows,[159] as many European nations have done.[160] Properly distributed, offshore wind could easily supply 70 percent of year-2005 US electricity,[161] at costs far below those of new nuclear plants.[162] And as already mentioned, the classic Princeton University study showed that many different technologies can be implemented, immediately, to address climate change and various energy intermittencies.[163] These include utility-scale wind farms, solar power at several different scales, pumped hydropower and natural gas for backup and stabilization, and some types of sustainable biomass.[164] Other technological responses to the intermittency objection were outlined in chapter 6. These include distributing the renewable-energy capacity, using the grid as backup, employing solar PV and wind together, using solar-thermal plants with a few hours of storage to offset early-evening peak demand, and employing electric cars as grid backup. Also, because natural gas produces only 5 percent of the pollution and CC disease, death, and environmental damage of coal, at gas prices in excess of $6.50 per million Btu (roughly current prices), it is economical to use natural gas (idled until needed) as a standby for wind power; soon it also will be economical to use natural-gas backup for solar-photovoltaic; yet solar will drop to 5 to 10 cents/kWh by the year 2015.[165] Even nuclear proponents admit that atomic energy is now more expensive than coal, oil, or natural gas.[166] As a consequence, natural-gas backups are a feasible and economic short-term backup—given intermittencies—until all energy can be supplied by renewables.

For all the preceding reasons, outlined more fully in chapter 6, nuclear-power intermittencies and costs appear far worse than the intermittencies and costs of renewables such as wind and solar-photovoltaic power,[167] mainly because renewable technologies are cheaper than fission and present few intermittency problems, once they are properly implemented. That is one reason the International Energy Agency says that intermittency is not a technical barrier to renewable energy.[168]

The Seventh, or Energy-Mixture, Objection

In response to the preceding analyses, nuclear proponents nevertheless might ask whether an energy mix that includes atomic energy—so that no one technology is forced to produce massive amounts of low-carbon power—might be the surest way to address climate change. Intuitively, such a question makes sense because people diversify their investment portfolios and attempt to avoid heavy reliance on only one solution to a resource problem. Also, because energy use is increasing so rapidly, perhaps quadrupling by 2050,[169] nuclear proponents often claim the world needs a mixture of energy solutions—including nuclear as a "vital component."[170]

The main problems with this energy-mixture argument, however, are (1) that atomic power is not needed at all to address climate change (CC); (2) that building even the maximum number of reactors would reduce only a small portion of CO_2 emissions; (3) that more fission would actually promote CC because it would take funds from cheaper energy options that are more effective at CO_2 abatement; and (4) that new reactors cannot be built as quickly as needed to address CC. Consider each of these 4 problems in order.

Regarding problem (1), that nuclear power is not needed to address CC, both government studies (e.g., from the UK)[171] and university studies (e.g., from Princeton),[172] as already shown, reveal that fission is not needed to address CC. In fact, chapter 6 shows that many nations believe they can become carbon neutral without nuclear energy. They say they can supply most power through renewables by the year 2040. Even the pro-nuclear US DOE argues that renewable energy could easily supply 99 percent of US energy by 2020. Chapter 6 also shows that, even over the near term, wind energy can make the greatest contributions to CC-abatement. The British say that, by the year 2020, they can supply well over 30 GW (the equivalent of more than 30 nuclear plants) using only solar and wind. The Germans and others say much the same thing.

Market investors also do not support an energy mix that includes fission, and their investments confirm the preceding wind facts. As chapter 6 argued, the case of Texas rancher Louis Brooks is fairly typical. He is paid $500 per month to allow 78 wind turbines on his ranch, yet he can use virtually all of the land for grazing and farming.[173] Texan Boone Pickens plans to invest $10 billion and install his own wind farm of 4,000 MW—equivalent to the electricity generated by 4 nuclear plants.[174] His company Mesa Power has already invested $2 billion in building the world's largest wind farm, in Pampa, Texas.[175] While it would cost an estimated $1 trillion to supply 20 percent of US energy using wind, chapter 3 showed that $1 trillion would pay the full cost of only about 7 percent of US energy supplied by nuclear fission. Moreover, each year the US spends more than $700 billion on foreign oil. Because wind installations involve a one-time payment, wind seems a more reasonable way (than fission) to supply electrical energy, especially in an electrical-vehicle-to-grid system, as suggested in chapter 6.[176]

Even McKenzie, a top business-management consulting company that favors new nuclear power plants, admits problems with an energy mix. McKenzie says that, even under the most optimistic nuclear-industry scenario, wind energy will grow at least 55 times faster than fission and be much cheaper; by the year 2030, McKenzie says, global wind capacity will have grown by 700 percent above its 2005 level, while nuclear-energy growth is unlikely and, at best, could increase (with massive government subsidies) by no more than 13 percent above its 2005 level.[177] Although more transmission capacity is needed to deliver wind energy across the nation,[178] as chapter 6 explained, overall US wind potential—in only 1 of 50 US states—exceeds all US nuclear power. Moreover, as already shown in chapters 3 and 6, full costs of nuclear electricity are more than $1.47/kWhr, while US DOE data show that wind costs are 4.8 cents/kWhr, and dropping; DOE affirmed that by 2015, solar will be "cost-competitive with conventional sources of electricity,"[179] so that there could be inexpensive, mass conversion of the entire US to largely solar and wind power. As also mentioned in chapter 6, another reason an energy mix (including fission) is not needed is that three-fourths of all US electricity could be saved through energy efficiency that would cost, on average, about 1 cent/kWh.

Problem (2) with the energy-mix objection is that even the maximum-possible nuclear buildup would help CO_2 abatement only in minor ways. One of the best sources on this point is the classic, pro-nuclear MIT study.[180] It shows that according to even the most optimistic projections for nuclear development, atomic energy could supply only about 20 percent of year-2050 global electricity and could reduce CO_2 emissions only by about one-eighth of what year-2050 emissions otherwise would be.[181] For instance, the UK government says this optimistic nuclear program could reduce only 8 percent of its carbon-equivalent emissions.[182] Yet as previous statistics showed, wind and solar energy both are cheaper than fission, could supply all of US energy needs, and could reduce nearly all carbon-equivalent emissions from electricity generation.

Problem (3) with the energy-mix objection is that building more nuclear plants would actually harm CO_2-abatement efforts. UK government studies show that because reactors are so capital intensive, building new nuclear plants would make addressing CC even harder. New reactors would "reduce support available" for renewable-energy technologies, which are cheaper, promote more economic growth, reduce more greenhouse gases, and could supply more energy than nuclear power; thus any new nuclear plants would likely harm CO_2-abatement efforts.[183] As the UK government repeatedly points out, a major opportunity cost of nuclear subsidies, development, and investment is to "depress the market" for renewable-energy technologies and to divert government subsidies to less effective and more costly strategies for CO_2 abatement.[184] Similarly, as the US assistant secretary for nuclear energy admitted in 2008, because of the high cost of atomic power, "companies cannot underwrite many nuclear plants"; therefore, this high fission cost "underscores the need for more government loan guarantees."[185] But investment, insurance, and loan capital that is spent on atomic energy cannot be spent cost-effectively on cheaper and cleaner technologies, like wind, solar, and natural gas. With less than half the carbon-equivalent emissions of coal, even natural gas is much cheaper, per kilowatt-hour, than nuclear power.[186] Besides, as chapter 6 showed, efficiency, wind, and gas cogeneration actually have negative costs of greenhouse-gas abatement; by using efficiencies, the US could immediately cut carbon emissions to 1990 levels with no net cost to the nation's economy.

Problem (4) with the energy-mixture objection is that nuclear plants cannot be built quickly enough to address CC. Recall the reactor-construction data presented in chapter 3. It showed that average nuclear-construction times ranged from 10–23 years. Yet something needs to be done immediately to abate greenhouse gases. Nuclear proponents admit that, even if fission plants had been started in the year 2011, their high expense and long construction time mean that the very earliest these reactors could begin generating electricity is 2024.[187] As chapter 3 showed, this long nuclear-construction time is a problem because, unless fission can be implemented quickly, it loses virtually all its advantages, given that renewable-energy technologies already are cheaper than atomic energy and are becoming more so.

Thus, although it might appear that using an energy mixture might be "the best of both worlds," in reality this strategy would lead to "the worst of both worlds," as University of London economist David Fleming puts it. Nuclear energy not only would use funds that could be better spent to avert more CC, but also would distract citizens from the real need to address energy efficiency, conservation, and alternative energy. Moreover, an energy mix would not work because a future, efficiency-oriented energy system would have to be flexibly organized, not dependent on nuclear technology that must always operate at full power. For all these reasons, any energy mixture (that includes nuclear fission) is merely clinging to the energy-bankrupt, old-technology past, rather than inventing and building a future that is economical, sustainable, and healthy.

The Eighth, or Uranium-Depletion, Objection

Other objections might challenge the chapter 2 claim that because a severe uranium shortage will occur by 2013, uranium depletion is an obstacle to increased nuclear fission. In response, some might claim, as does James Lovelock, that uranium shortages are not a problem because of the superabundance of low-grade uranium ore in granite, because of plutonium fuel, because of thorium fuel, and because of other uranium sources such as seawater and phosphates.[188] How plausible are these alleged solutions to the problem of uranium depletion? Consider them in order.

Granite appears to provide an abundant supply of uranium. However, the problem is that it contains low-grade (averaging below 0.02 percent) uranium. Chapter 2 showed that, below this level, the amount of energy needed to extract the uranium would be so great that the energy needed to sustain the nuclear-fuel cycle would be greater than the energy produced by it. Moreover, even if one ignores the nuclear-energy bankruptcy caused by trying to use granite as a source of uranium fuel, there are other problems. One year's supply of uranium for only 1 reactor would require 100 million metric tons of granite. Just to supply the 104 US reactors with fuel, for only 1 year, would require (100 × 104) or 10.4 billion metric tons of granite—apart from the difficulty and the energy-intensiveness of the extraction processes. Moreover, the waste-granite tailings for only 1 reactor, for only 1 year, would cover an area 100 meters high, 100 meters wide, and 4 kilometers long. The process to extract uranium from this granite would require 650 petajoules (or 1,000,000 billion joules) of energy, whereas the reactor would supply only 26 petajoules of energy. Thus, because extracting uranium from granite to fuel a reactor for 1 year requires about 25 times more energy than the reactor would produce in 1 year, granite is not a way to address uranium depletion.[189]

Another uranium-shortage proposal is to use plutonium as nuclear fuel, so that breeder reactors not only produce electricity, but also breed more plutonium for the future. In principle, breeder reactors seem plausible. One could bombard uranium-238 with neutrons (from a start-up fuel like uranium-235 or plutonium-239), so that it becomes uranium-239, which decays to neptunium-239, then to plutonium-239, which, in turn, can be used as a start-up fuel to breed more plutonium-239. Nuclear-industry groups say that, if all available ore were used, and if breeder reactors are developed, they could supply 20,000 years' worth of energy.[190]

The problem with breeder reactors, however, is not the preceding principles but the practice. The technology requires breeding, reprocessing, and fuel fabrication— none of which has ever been achieved on a commercial scale. This failure is in part because all 3 processes are so difficult. They all involve highly radioactive materials that either clog and corrode the equipment (breeding, reprocessing) or require operations to be done by remote control (fuel fabrication). Because of these difficulties, there have been only 3 commercial breeder reactors in the world: the Beloyarsk-3 in Russia—which operates but has never done breeding—and the Monju in Japan and the Phenix in France, both of which closed long ago because of safety and technical problems. If these problems could be corrected in 20 or 30 years, and if one could all use existing plutonium supplies (240 metric tons globally), one could fuel up a maximum of 80 breeder reactors by 2035. However, it would still be 2075 before these 80 reactors would have bred enough plutonium to start up 80 more breeder reactors. Yet these 160 breeders by the year 2075 are too trivial a contribution to CC (< 1 percent of global energy needs), given that there are about 3 times as many fission reactors operating, and they now contribute only about 2.1 percent of total global energy, as noted in earlier chapters. This breeder energy would be too little, too late, even assuming that it could work correctly. CC needs to be addressed before 2020, if the worst catastrophes are to be avoided, not by 2075. Breeder technology also is unsafe, given the breeder design. Why? A breeder accident would be so catastrophic that there must be defense-in-depth (DID)—that is, multiple safety systems. This expensive DID and breeder technology requires that reactors be very large, so that they can enjoy economies of scale and be less uneconomical. But this large scale means that no containment dome can withstand a major accident. Without containment, breeders are especially risky. This is why Lawrence Lidsky and Marvin Miller, in a breeder study for Japan, drew a damning conclusion. They said that a successful breeder reactor must have 3 attributes—it must breed, must be economical, and must be safe—and that the laws of physics prevented a breeder from achieving any more than 2 of these 3 requirements.[191]

Another suggested way to address the uranium shortage is to use thorium-232 as a starting point from which to breed nuclear fuel. When plutonium 239 irradiates thorium-232, it becomes thorium-233, which decays to protactinium-233, which decays to uranium-233, which can be used as nuclear fuel. However, the problem with thorium is that its product, uranium-233, can be used for nuclear weapons, which raises proliferation and terrorism concerns, already discussed in chapter 2. Moreover, this thorium-breeding process is even more difficult than plutonium breeding. Consequently, as with plutonium-breeder technology, there is no successful, commercial, reliable, large-scale thorium technology, although several Indian reactors have used small amounts of thorium in their operation. The thorium start-up fuel also is scarce. It could be supplied with uranium-235, but that is the very fuel whose scarcity has necessitated thinking about thorium in the first place. Start-up fuel also could be supplied with plutonium, but there are only about 240 metric tons of plutonium in the world, and it also is scarce. Finally, start-up fuel could be supplied with uranium-233, but that is the final fuel produced by the thorium cycle, and it does not exist until the end of the cycle. Assuming all the preceding technical difficulties could be overcome, experts say that, at best, globally there could be 2 thorium reactors operating by the year 2075—obviously too little (energy), too late to address CC and the uranium-fuel shortage.[192]

Because seawater contains uranium in about 30 parts per billion, some nuclear proponents also have proposed it as a solution to uranium depletion. Would it work? Yes, extracting uranium would work, although it is a massive, 6-stage process that requires significant energy. Thus, as with other nuclear solutions, the problem is not the technology itself, but having a technology that requires more energy than it creates. To operate for 1 year, 1 reactor needs about 200 metric tons of natural uranium—which would require 40,000 cubic kilometers of seawater to be processed. For fuel for 100 reactors, for 1 year, 40,000 cubic kilometers of seawater would need to be processed. Moreover, to supply one reactor with uranium fuel (from seawater), for only 1 year, would require 195–250 terajoules (TJ) or 1,000 billion joules of energy—and yet the reactor would have an electricity yield of only 120 TJ. Thus seawater extraction of uranium faces the problem of energy bankruptcy and hence is no solution to CC and uranium depletion.[193]

Yet another proposal of the nuclear industry is to extract uranium from phosphates, so as to double the global uranium supply.[194] This proposal is problematic, however, both because the extraction process is difficult, and because it requires greenhouse gases—fluorohydrocarbons—whose release during processing would exacerbate CC. Like granite, phosphates also are poor sources of uranium: their average uranium concentration is about 0.01 percent. This means, as chapter 2 already argued, that this low-grade uranium source would cause energy bankruptcy and would yield a negative PREI (practical return on energy investment). In addition, economists say that phosphates are a nearly depleted resource that is facing imminent decline. For all these reasons, uranium from phosphates is not a solution to the uranium shortage. If not, there appear to be no economically effective objections to chapter 2's argument that high-grade uranium depletion threatens any additional reactors.[195]

Conclusion

This chapter answers 8 of the most common and misleading objections of those who want to use nuclear fission to help address climate change. Why did the US even begin using atomic energy, if fission is as expensive and risky as the preceding chapters have argued? Why does France have such an apparently successful atomic-energy program, if fission is as expensive and risky as the preceding chapters have argued? How is it plausible that official government and nuclear-industry-cost estimates could err by 400 or more percent, as previous chapters have argued? Why is there now an apparent renaissance of nuclear-power construction, if this technology is expensive, carbon-intensive, and risky, as this book has argued? Why is renewable energy apparently growing so slowly if it is both cheaper and safer than nuclear fission? How can renewable energy possibly take the place of coal or nuclear power—both of which apparently supply baseload electricity—whereas renewables like wind and solar energy allegedly supply intermittent electricity? Given the severity of CC, why isn't a mixture of various technologies, including nuclear fission (rather than merely conservation, efficiency, and renewable energy alone), a more reliable way to address CC? Why can't other technologies, such as breeder reactors, address the uranium shortage? I call the preceding 8 misleading questions, respectively, (1) the US Objection, (2) the France Objection, (3) the Implausibility Objection, (4) the Nuclear-Renaissance Objection, (5) the Growth-in-Renewables Objection, (6) the Intermittency Objection, (7) the Energy-Mixture Objection, and (8) the Uranium-Depletion Objection. This chapter answers each of these claims.

The market has spoken very clearly about the inadequacies of nuclear fission. Interestingly, the market, citizens' safety concerns, CC, ethical concerns, and common sense all dictate the same course of action: using renewable energy, conservation, and efficiency to address CC. After all, reasonable people know that they must live off their current income, not savings and not borrowed money. People know they should not eat their seed corn. Otherwise, they have no future. The same is true in energy policy. In using nonsustainable fossil and nuclear fuels, society is not living off its current energy supplies, but borrowing against the future, imposing nuclear wastes, risks, costs, and CC on innocent future people.

CHAPTER 8

Conclusions

One of the earliest lessons that children learn is to pick up after themselves. One of the earliest lessons that parents learn is not to reward children who fail to pick up after themselves. Otherwise, children may never learn to do so. As this book has shown, those who have been building nuclear plants have not learned this lesson children are taught, and governments—all of whom massively subsidize those reactors—have not learned this lesson parents come to understand.

As University of London economist David Fleming points out, the nuclear industry has not cleaned up its mess from uranium mining, milling, fuel fabrication, decommissioning closed reactors, and permanently securing the backlog of radio-active waste and spent fuel. Yet utilities are allowed to build new atomic-energy plants—before the half-century-old nuclear mess has been cleaned up. In fact, governments have even rewarded nuclear industries, whose messes have not yet been cleaned up, by giving them taxpayer subsidies for more reactors—subsidies that cover 60–90 percent of nuclear-electricity costs, as chapter 1 showed. This is like loaning more money to someone who has not repaid you, like rewarding a child who ignores repeated requests to clean up his room, like loaning money to someone who has repeatedly filed for bankruptcy. Such behavior appears neither ethically nor economically defensible. The problem is not only that industries and governments should clean up their nuclear messes before making new ones, but also that cleaning up these messes would explicitly reveal that atomic energy is both uneconomical and self-defeating. It requires nearly as much energy, in the various stages of its fuel cycle, including cleanup, as it actually produces. Government fission subsidies, and failure to clean up this cycle, obscure the real energy and economic costs of nuclear power. Yet as chapter 2 revealed, Fleming calculates that roughly one-quarter of reactor-electricity production is required to pay back the front-end, nuclear-energy debts from mining, enrichment, fuel fabrication, and reactor construction; that another one-quarter is required to pay the back-end energy debts of reactor decommissioning, enrichment and other facility clean-up, permanent waste storage, and so on; and that another one-quarter is required to process and store the backlog of existing wastes.[1] This means that three-fourths (75 percent) of current nuclear-energy electricity production is needed for energy payback to the nuclear fuel cycle. Moreover, just because taxpayer subsidies pick up the tab—for much of this enrichment, decommissioning, and waste management—does not mean that the required energy for these nuclear-fuel-cycle processes is free. Rather, it means that people are easily misled about the real energy costs of trying to use nuclear power to help address climate change.

Sixteen Questions

As this book argues, however, people are misled not only about the energy costs of nuclear fission. Rather, they also are misled about fission's climate-emissions costs (chapter 2), its financial costs (chapter 3), its safety costs (chapter 4), its equity and justice costs (chapter 5), and its opportunity costs—because nuclear investments take money away from cleaner, cheaper, safer, more equitable, and more abundant renewable-energy sources (chapter 6).

Chapter 2 argued that those—who claim atomic energy has few greenhouse emissions and is needed to help address climate change—fail to count all the greenhouse-gas (GHG) emissions from the entire, 14-stage, nuclear-fuel cycle. By thus "trimming the data" on nuclear-related GHG emissions, they try to make fission look like a low-carbon technology, when it is not. They also fail to take account of the significantly higher nuclear emissions that arise because of our now using low-grade uranium ore to create reactor fuel. Likewise, they fail to recognize that atomic energy is self-defeating; because it produces only about 25 percent more energy than is required for all the stages of its fuel cycle, it is of little help in averting climate change. Most important, those who claim nuclear fission is needed to help address the potential catastrophe of global warming forget that fission increases the probability of equally serious catastrophes, such as nuclear proliferation and terrorism. Some of the crucial questions that one must ask, after learning in chapter 2 that the full GHG emissions of the nuclear-fuel cycle are roughly equal to those of natural gas, are these.

- Why would nuclear proponents ignore the GHG emissions of the 14-stage nuclear-fuel cycle, count only GHG emissions from reactor operation itself, then claim atomic energy is emissions free, when its full-fuel-cycle GHG emissions are roughly the same as those of natural gas?
- Why would nuclear proponents ignore the energy requirements of the 14-stage nuclear-fuel cycle, then claim atomic energy is needed to address CC, when fission produces only about 25 percent more energy than is required to power all the stages of its fuel cycle?
- Isn't failure to assess life-cycle GHG emissions and life-cycle energy needs as irrational as ignoring the closing costs, down payment, interest rate, insurance, maintenance, mortgage interest, time frame, and yard work, then claiming that home ownership is as inexpensive as renting?

Chapter 3 argued that nearly all nuclear-fission-cost estimates (most of which are produced by the industry) are examples of grossly flawed science, and that this flawed science occurs for 2 main reasons. First, the studies violate standard conflict-of-interest guidelines that are widely accepted in scientific research. Virtually all cost estimates, and all assumptions on which the costs rely, come from the very industries that are trying to sell reactors for a profit and to convince people that they are inexpensive. Second, the industry's nuclear-cost studies are scientifically flawed because they illegitimately "trim the data" on fission costs. They include only several of the 14 stages of the fuel cycle, and they make numerous counterfactual assumptions, such as that reactor lifetimes are double or triple what the actual, empirical data show, or that reactor load factors are 95 percent when, in reality, the lifetime-average for nuclear-load factors is 70 percent. Some of the crucial questions that one must ask, after learning in chapter 3 that the nuclear industry alone estimates all the costs from which it will profit, and that, once one does life-cycle analysis, atomic-energy costs far more than renewables like wind and solar photovoltaic—are these.

- Why should taxpayers (through government subsidies) be forced to invest in nuclear power when free-market bankers and investors absolutely refuse to do so?
- If nuclear energy is as cheap as the industry claims, why won't nuclear vendors provide fixed-price reactor contracts, instead of supplying only cost-plus plants?
- If nuclear energy is as cheap as industry claims, why is the use of atomic-energy plants declining, both nationally and globally, while the use of renewable energy sources, like wind and solar photovoltaic, is increasing as much as 40 percent annually, mainly because of low costs?

Chapter 4 argued that, by using flawed scientific assumptions, flawed models, flawed data, flawed inductive inferences, the nuclear industry and the US government have covered up massive health problems that occurred after the 1979 reactor-core melt and nuclear accident at Three Mile Island, Pennsylvania. Instead, they have blamed the resulting 64-percent cancer increase near Three Mile Island on stress, not radiation from the reactor. Moreover, reliable data from virtually every nuclear nation in the world reveals that even during normal operation, nuclear plants cause statistically significant cancer increases nearby, especially among children, because they are most sensitive to ionizing radiation. Some of the crucial questions that one must ask—after learning in chapter 4 that the nuclear industry has covered up its own massive safety lapses and that it demands (and receives) a government-guaranteed liability limit for nuclear accidents—are these.

- Why should the public believe the industry claims that nuclear fission is safe, when the industry itself demands and receives a government-guaranteed, nuclear-accident liability limit that makes the industry liable for only 1–2 percent of worst-case damages, while the public must pay accident damages even for accidents caused by negligence and violating safety regulations?

- Why should the public believe the industry claims that no one was injured or killed after the Three Mile Island (TMI) accident, when the TMI utility itself spent $80 million, quietly settling TMI victims' damage claims (out of court, and with required gag orders on all plaintiffs), because of resulting cancers, infant retardation, and infant death?
- Why should the public believe industry claims that reactors are safe, when scientists agree that no amount of ionizing radiation is safe, and when normally operating reactors release radiation that, throughout the world, has caused statistically significant increases in cancer, disease, and death?

Chapter 5 argued that the nuclear-fuel cycle and current radiation regulations impose inequitable radiation burdens on poor people, minorities, and children. The chapter shows that most uranium mining is done by poor, indigenous populations who consequently have suffered increased, radiation-induced death and disease, and that, at least in southeastern US, reactors appear to be disproportionately cited in poor communities. Even normal operation of reactors puts children at statistically significant increased risk of cancer, in part because children are up to 40 times more sensitive to ionizing radiation than are adults. Besides their effects on poor people, nuclear-caused environmental injustices are especially burdensome for 3 groups of people: children, radiation workers, and members of future generations. The chapter showed that children are at special risk from the nuclear fuel cycle because the fetus is allowed to receive 5 times more radiation than is an adult, although the fetus is up to 40 times more sensitive to radiation than an adult. Moreover children are roughly 10 times more sensitive than adults to ionizing radiation, and yet radiation standards provide them no extra protection.

The chapter likewise showed that radiation workers are also at special risk because current US regulations allow them to receive an annual dose of radiation that is 50 times greater than that of any member of the public. As a result the chapter showed that classic, International Agency for Research on Cancer (IARC) data show that about 6 additional fatal cancers per year occur for every 500 workers exposed to the maximum-allowable occupational radiation dose of 50 mSv per year. If workers remained in this work for 50 years, and if they received the maximum-allowable radiation dose each year, the chapter showed that their occupational radiation exposure would kill about 1 in every 17 workers from cancer. The chapter also revealed that current radiation standards for permanent nuclear-waste facilities allow members of future generations to be exposed to 4 times the radiation levels that are now allowed from nuclear plants, and that only the average radiation exposure must meet this 4-times-less-protective standard—which means that roughly half the people exposed could receive even higher doses. Some of the crucial questions that one must ask—after learning in chapter 5 that the nuclear-fuel cycle imposes inequitable burdens on poor people, minorities, children, blue-collar workers, and members of future generations—are the following.

- Why are ionizing-radiation protections for children 10 times weaker than those for adults, thus allowing children to be "the canaries in the coal mines" of the nuclear industry?
- Why are low-income, poorly educated US blue-collar workers allowed to receive 50 times more radiation than members of the public, when they probably do not give genuine informed consent to this higher risk and when many European nations protect workers as much as the public?
- Why does this generation have the right to impose some of its heaviest radiation burdens on future generations who have no choice in the matter, and who will not benefit?

Chapter 6 shows that market proponents confirm both that energy efficiency and conservation are the cheapest ways to address climate change and that that wind, solar photovoltaics, and other renewable sources of energy are cheaper than nuclear power. Moreover, it uses the data of market proponents to show that atomic energy will become more expensive in the future, while renewable energy will become even cheaper. The chapter also shows that renewable energy could supply all global-energy needs while nuclear fission could not, that it can be implemented quickly, that it is sustainable, and that it is more militarily secure. Given these strengths of renewable energy, some of the crucial questions that one must ask are the following.

- Why build dirty, risky, expensive nuclear reactors when wind, solar photovoltaic, and other renewable energy sources are cleaner, safer, and cheaper?
- Why build expensive, nonsustainable nuclear reactors that, at best, can supply only about 2 percent of global energy, when wind, solar photovoltaic, and other renewable energy sources are sustainable and can supply virtually all energy needs?
- If market investors—eager to make money on clean, safe, and cheap wind and solar energy—are investing massively in renewable energy, and refusing nuclear investment, how could there be any fundamental objections to using renewable energy instead of atomic energy?

Chapter 7 answered these and other objections to the arguments given in this book. In particular, it showed that the US and most other nations have invested in commercial atomic energy mainly for military reasons, that no reactors anywhere (especially in France) operate on the market and instead are massively subsidized, that there is no nuclear renaissance, that the intermittency of wind and other renewables can be overcome by geographically distributed power sources and a mix of other renewables, and that nuclear investments would actually make investment in renewable energy more difficult because of the massive capital requirements of atomic energy. Given the ability of renewable-energy sources to answer such objections, the crucial questions that one must ask are the following.

- Why has the US allowed other nations—such as China, Denmark, and Germany—to make massive profits from their global leadership in renewable energy, while the US continues to lose this leadership by subsidizing outmoded technologies, like fission and petroleum, that provide no future economic leadership and no sustainable power?
- Why do nuclear proponents say renewable energy won't work—when it now supplies far more energy than does nuclear fission?

Where We Go from Here

One of the interesting things to note about this volume is that much of its emphasis has been on the economics of atomic energy, on the underlying technology of reducing greenhouse gases, and on the quality of the science underlying claims about nuclear safety, as at Three Mile Island and Fukushima, Japan. In other words, the main arguments have attempted to defeat nuclear fission on its own terms— on the basis of claims that it cannot survive on a free market, that it is uneconomical, that epidemiological science reveals its risks, and that its fuel cycle has massive amounts of GHG emissions. In this book, less time has been spent discussing the ethical issues, like environmental injustice associated with atomic energy. Yet those injustices are massive, in part because, as earlier chapters revealed, there is no safe dose of ionizing radiation.

Even if markets, economics, science, technology, and climate change were not aligned against atomic energy, ethics alone would be sufficient to show that it ought not be implemented. As University of London economist David Fleming put it, "Seeding the world with radioactive time-bombs [i.e., reactors and nuclear facilities] which will pollute the oceans and detonate [i.e., allow radiation to escape] at random intervals, for thousands of years into the future, whether there are any human beings around to care about it or not, should be recognized as off any scale calibrated in terms other than dementia."[2] Nuclear proponent Alvin Weinberg had similar worries. Speaking of the problem of radioactive wastes from all 14 stages of the nuclear-fuel cycle, he said that those who use atomic energy are making a "Faustian bargain." In exchange for some fission-generated electricity, nuclear-energy users have sold the soul of the future to the devil, because of the radioactive wastes that will harm our descendants.[3]

The problem with this Faustian bargain is not just that current nuclear users gain some expensive energy, at the cost of the health and safety of future generations but that, if this book is correct, nuclear power not only is not needed to address climate change but also could thwart climate-change efforts because of its high costs. Because atomic energy is not needed, society must tap the most important source of energy to address climate change: the energy of the people. The people—through education, hard work, willingness to conserve, and promoting government policies that are economically and ethically sound—must ensure that society takes immediate action to address climate change.[4]

If the energy of the people is not directed in the right ways, it will be used instead to satisfy unthinking demands for more things that require more energy. If the energy of the people is directed in the right ways, toward sustainable energy and energy efficiencies, it will not only help address climate change, but also help us to be better people.

NOTES

Chapter 1

1. "Doomsday Clock Moves One Minute," *Bulletin of the Atomic Scientists* (Washington, DC: 2010); accessed April 14, 2010, at http://www.thebulletin.org/content/media-center/announcements/2010/01/14/doomsday-clock-moves-one-minute-away-midnight.
2. Viktor Danilov-Danilyan, "Impact of Climate Change Equal to Nuclear War," *Terra Daily* (Moscow: June 29, 2007); accessed April 14, 2010, at http://www.terradaily.com/reports/Impact_Of_Climate_Change_Equal_To_Nuclear_War_999.html.
3. Nyla Sarwar, *Green Movement Acknowledges Nuclear Power as a Feasible Option* (Climatico, 2009); accessed April 14, 2010, at http://www.climaticoanalysis.org/post/nuclear-power-accepted-as-a-feasible-option-by-the-green-movement/.
4. Quoted in Gwyneth Cravens, *Power to Save the World: The Truth about Nuclear Energy* (New York: Knopf, 2008), pp. 259–60; hereafter cited as Cravens, *Power*. Patrick Moore, "Going Nuclear," *Washington Post* (2006): B01; accessed February 5, 2009, at http://www.washingtonpost.com/wp-dyn/content/article/2006/04/14/AR2006041401209.html. Hugh Montefiore, "Why the Planet Needs Nuclear Energy," *The Tablet* (October 23 2004); accessed November 1, 2008, at http://www.thetablet.co.uk/cgi-bin/register.cgi/tablet-00946. Gerald Holton, "Power Surge," *Environmental Health Perspectives* 113, no. 11 (2005): 742–50. Declan Butler, "Energy: Nuclear Power's New Dawn," *Nature* 429, no. 6989 (2004): 238–40. Richard Meserve, "Global Warming and Nuclear Power," *Science* 303, no. 5657 (2004): 433. Steward Brand, "Environmental Heresies," *Technology Review* (May 2005); accessed November 1, 2008, at http://www.technologyreview.com/read_articles.aspx?id=14406&ch=biztech.
5. The 60–90 percent figure is from Travis Madsen, Johanna Neumann, and Emily Rusch, *The High Cost of Nuclear Power* (Baltimore: Maryland Public Interest Research Group, 2009), p. 17; hereafter cited as Madsen et al., *High Cost*. Amory Lovins, *Profitable Solutions for Oil, Climate, and Proliferation* (Snowmass, CO: Rocky Mountain Institute, 2007), p. 3; hereafter cited as Lovins, *Profitable*.
6. Amory Lovins, "Nuclear Is Uneconomic", *Bulletin of the Atomic Scientists* (Roundtable on Nuclear Power and Climate Change, 2007); accessed February 9, 2008, at http://www.thebulletin.org/roundtable/nuclear-power-climate-change/.
7. Lovins, *Profitable*, p. 3.
8. Amory Lovins, *Forget Nuclear* (Snowmass, CO: Rocky Mountain Institute, 2008), pp. 2, 6.
9. Quote is from Nick F. Pidgeon, Irene Lorenzoni, and Wouter Poortinga, "Climate Change or Nuclear Power—No Thanks," *Global Environmental Climate Change* 18 (2008): 69–85. Classic citation for no safe dose of ionizing radiation is National Research Council/National Academy of Sciences (NRC/NAS), *Health Risks from Exposure to Low Levels of Ionizing*

Radiation: BEIR VII, Phase 2 (Washington, DC: National Academy Press, 2006), p. 6; hereafter cited as NRC/NAS, *Health Risks BEIR VII*; see also later notes, esp. in ch. 4.

10. For the $11.92/gallon calculation, see Earth Policy Institute, "The Real Price of Gasoline, 2007 Update," in Lester Brown, *Plan B 4.0: Mobilizing to Save Civilization* (New York: W.W. Norton, 2009); accessed April 5, 2010, at http://www.earthpolicy.org/index.php?/books/pb4/pb4_data. For the $12.75/gallon calculation, see Benjamin Bombard, "Pay at the Pump: Uncovering the True Price of Gasoline," *Catalyst* 29, no. 1 (2010); accessed April 5, 2010, at http://www.catalystmagazine.net/component/content/article/45/1128.

11. German Technical Cooperation, *International Fuel Prices 2009*, 6th ed. (Eschborn, Germany: German Technical Cooperation, December 2009); accessed April 5, 2010, at http://www.gtz.de/de/dokumente/gtz2009-en-ifp-full-version.pdf.

12. Environmental Law Institute, *Estimating U.S. Government Subsidies to Energy Sources: 2002–2008* (Washington, DC: Environmental Law Institute and the Woodrow Wilson International Center for Scholars, September 2009); accessed April 5, 2010, at http://www.elistore.org/Data/products/d19_07.pdf.

13. U.S. Energy Information Administration (EIA), "World Per Capita Total Primary Energy Consumption, 1980–2006," *International Energy Annual 2006* (Washington, DC: US EIA, 2008); accessed February 11, 2010, at http://www.eia.doe.gov/emeu/international/energyconsumption.html.

14. US National Research Council, *Hidden Costs of Energy* (Washington, DC: National Academy Press, 2009); hereafter cited as NAS, Energy, 2009. Nicholas Stern, *The Economics of Climate Change* (Cambridge, UK: Cambridge University Press, 2007); hereafter cited as Stern, *Economics*. Arun Makhijani, *Carbon-Free and Nuclear-Free* (Takoma Park, MD: IEER, 2007), pp. xvi, xx, 1–2; hereafter cited as Makhijani, *Carbon-Free*. Health statistics are from Kristin Shrader-Frechette, *Taking Action, Saving Lives* (New York: Oxford University Press, 2007), ch. 1; hereafter cited as Shrader-Frechette, *Taking Action*. Climate arguments are from Peter Singer, *One World* (New Haven, CT: Yale University Press, 2002), and Stern, *Economics*.

15. Earth Policy Institute, "The Real Price of Gasoline, 2007 Update," in Lester Brown, *Plan B 4.0: Mobilizing to Save Civilization* (New York: W.W. Norton, 2009); accessed April 5, 2010, at http://www.earthpolicy.org/index.php?/books/pb4/pb4_data).

16. Makhijani, *Carbon-Free*, pp. xx, 4–12.

17. NAS, Energy, 2009. Physicians for Social Responsibility, *Coal's Assault on Human Health* (Washington, DC: PSR, 2010). D. Pimentel, S. Cooperstein, H. Randell, D. Filiberto, S. Sorrentino, B. Kaye, C. Nicklin, J. Yagi, J. Brian, J. O'Hern, A. Habas, and C. Weinstein, "Ecology of Increasing Diseases: Population Growth and Environmental Degradation," *Human Ecology* 35, no. 6 (December 2007): 653–68.

18. World Health Organization, *Indoor Air Pollution and Health* (Bonn: WHO, 2005); accessed at http://www.who.int/mediacentre/factsheets/fs292/en/. Commonwealth Scientific and Industrial Research Organization, *Air Pollution* (Aspendale, Australia: CSIRO, 1999); accessed at http://www.csiro.au/index.asp?id=AirPollution&type=mediaRelease.

19. Anna Gosline, "European Deaths from Air Pollution Set to Rise," *New Scientist* 17, no. 51 (2004); accessed July 12, 2005, at http://www.newscientist.com/article.ns?id=dn6364.

20. APHA, "Policy Statements…2000," *American Journal of Public Health* 91, no. 3 (2001): 21.

21. Scientific citations for these claims about air pollution, particularly ozone and particulates, are in Kristin Shrader-Frechette, *Taking Action*, ch. 1.

22. The same study estimated that at least 20,000 Americans die prematurely each year from burning fossil fuels (National Research Council/National Academy of Sciences, *Hidden Costs of Energy: Unpriced Consequences of Energy Production and Use* (Washington, DC: National Academies Press, 2009).

23. Arden Pope, "Cardiovascular Mortality and Long-Term Exposure to Particulate Air Pollution," *Circulation* 109, no. 6 (January 2003): 71–77. C. A. Pope, R. T. Burnett, M. J. Thun, E. E. Calle, D. Krewski, K. Ito, and G. D. Thurston, "Lung Cancer, Cardiopulmonary Mortality, and Long-Term Exposure to Fine Particulate Air Pollution," *Journal of American*

Medical Association 287, no. 9 (2002): 1132–41. ABT Associates, *Particulate-Related Health Benefits of Reducing Power Emissions* (Bethesda, MD: ABT Associates, 2000) is the Bush study. M. L. Bell, D. L. Davis, N. Gouveia, L. Cifuentes, and V. H. Borja-Aburto, "Mortality, Morbidity, and Economic Consequences of Fossil Fuel-Related Air Pollution in Three Latin American Cities," *Epidemiology* 15, no. 4 (July 2004): S44–45. M. L. Bell and D. I. Davis, "Reassessment of the Lethal London Fog of 1952," *Environmental Health Perspectives* 109 (June 2001): 389–94. D. L. Davis, L. Deck, P. Saldiva, and J. Correia, "The Selected Survivor Effect in Developed and Developing Countries Studies of Air Pollution," *Epidemiology* 10, no. 4 (July 1999): S107. L. Cifuentes, V. H. Borja-Aburto, N. Gouveia, G. Thurston, and D. L. Davis, "Assessing the Health Benefits of Urban Air Pollution Reductions Associated with Climate Change Mitigation (2000–2020)," *Environmental Health Perspectives* 109 (June 2001): S419–25. D. L. Davis, T. Kjellstrom, R. Slooff, A. McGartland, D. Atkinson, W. Barbour, W. Hohenstein, P. Nagelhout, T. Woodruff, F. Divita, J. Wilson, and J. Schwartz, "Short-Term Improvements in Public Health from Global-Climate Policies on Fossil-Fuel Combustion," *Lancet* 350, no. 9088 (November 1997). M. L. Bell, D. L. Davis, and G. Sun, "Analysis of the Health Effects of Severe Air Pollution in Developing Countries," *Epidemiology* 13, no. 4 (July 2002): 298. A. D. Kyle, T. J. Woodruff, P. A. Buffler, and D. L. Davis, "Use of an Index to Reflect the Aggregate Burden of Long-Term Exposure to Criteria Air Pollutants in the United States," *Environmental Health Perspectives* 110 (February 2002): S95–102. L. Cifuentes, V. H. Borja-Aburto, N. l. Gouveia, G. Thurson, and D. L. Davis, "Climate Change: Hidden Health Benefits of Greenhouse Gas Mitigation," *Science* 293, no. 5533 (August 2001): 1257–59. See also US Congress, *Implementation of the New Air Quality Standards for Particulate Matter and Ozone*, S. HRG. (Washington, DC: US Government Printing Office, 2004), pp. 108–502. Calculations for Chicago application are in Kristin Shrader-Frechette, *Taking Action, Saving Lives* (New York: Oxford University Press, 2007), ch. 1; hereafter cited as *Taking Action*.

24. European Public Health Alliance, *Air, Water Pollution and Health Effects* (Brussels: EPHA, 2006); accessed at http://www.epha.org/r/54.

25. William Haenzel, David B. Loveland, and Martin G. Sirken, "Lung Cancer Mortality as Related to Residence and Smoking Histories," *Journal of the National Cancer Institute* 28 (1962): 947. Warren Winkelstein, Edward Davis, Charles Maneri, and William Mosher, "The Relationship of Air Pollution and Economic Status to Total Mortality and Selected Respiratory System Morality," *Archives of Environmental Health* 16 (1967): 162.

26. Lester Lave and Eugene O. Seskin, "Air Pollution and Human Health," *Science* 169. no. 3947 (1970): 723–33. Jack Spengler, Richard Wilson, et al., *Health Effects of Fossil Fuel Burning* (Cambridge, MA: Ballinger, 1980). Devra Davis, *When Smoke Ran Like Water* (New York: Basic, 2002), pp. 103, 121; hereafter cited as Davis, *Smoke*. Regarding poor enforcement, see Michael Janofsky, "Study Ranks Bush Plan to Cut Air Pollution as Weakest of 3," *The New York Times* (June 10, 2004); accessed at http://www.nytimes.com/2004/06/10/politics/10air.html?ex=1402200000&en=6d3a4a45d1e13015&ei=5007&partner=USERL AND. Shrader-Frechette, *Taking Action*.

27. D. Pimentel, S. Cooperstein, H. Randell, D. Filiberto, S. Sorrentino, B. Kaye, C. Nicklin, J. Yagi, J. Brian, J. O'Hern, A. Habas, and C. Weinstein, "Ecology of Increasing Diseases: Population Growth and Environmental Degradation," *Human Ecology* 35, no. 6 (December 2007): 653–68.

28. World Health Organization, *WHO Air Quality Guidelines for Particulate Matter, Ozone, Nitrogen Dioxide and Sulfur Dioxide: Global Update 2005* (Geneva, Switzerland: WHO, 2005), p. 5; accessed February 10, 2010, at http://whqlibdoc.who.int/hq/2006/WHO_SDE_PHE_OEH_06.02_eng.pdf.

29. Pieter Tans, *Trends in Atmospheric Carbon Dioxide* (Boulder, CO: National Oceanic and Atmospheric Administration, 2010); accessed February 8, 2010, at http://www.esrl.noaa.gov/gmd/ccgg/trends/.

30. Intergovernmental Panel on Climate Change (IPCC), *Working Group III Contribution to the IPCC: Fourth Assessment Report: Climate Change 2007: Mitigation of Climate Change:*

Summary for Policymakers (Geneva, Switzerland: IPCC Secretariat and UNEP, 2007); accessed October 10, 2007, at http://www.mnp.n./ipcc/doccs/FAR/SPM_%20WGIII_rev5.pdf. Makhijani, *Carbon-Free*, p. xvi.

31. Stern, *Economics*, figure 2. US NAS, Energy, 2009. See next note.
32. *IPCC: Fourth Assessment Report: Climate Change 2007: Mitigation of Climate Change* (Geneva, Switzerland: IPCC Secretariat and UNEP, 2007); hereafter cited as IPCC 2007.
33. IPCC 2007. Makhijani, *Carbon-Free*, pp. xvii, 1–3. United Nations, *Framework Convention on Climate Change* (New York: UN, 1992), pp. 1, 4. See Simon Caney, Stephen Gardiner, Dale Jamieson, and Henry Shue (eds.), *Climate Ethics* (New York: Oxford University Press, 2010); hereafter cited as CE. Stephen Gardiner, *A Perfect Moral Storm* (New York: Oxford University Press, 2010); hereafter cited as PS. E. Crist and H. B. Rinker, *Gaia in Turmoil* (Cambridge, MA: MIT Press, 2009); Paul Harris, *World Ethics and Climate Change* (Edinburgh: Edinburgh University Press, 2009). James Garvey, *The Ethics of Climate Change* (New York: Continuum, 2008); hereafter cited as ECC. Peter Singer, *One World* (New Haven, CT: Yale University Press, 2002); hereafter cited as Singer, *World*. Richard C. J. Somerville, "The Ethics of Climate Change," in *Environment 360*, Roger Cohn (ed.) (New Haven, CT: Yale University School of Forestry and Environmental Studies, 2008); accessed May 12, 2009, at http://e360.yale.edu/contentfeature.msp?id=1365.
34. US Environmental Protection Agency, *Global Greenhouse-Gas Data* (Washington, DC: EPA, 2006); accessed October 19, 2006, at http://www.epa.gov/climatechange/emissions/globalghg.html. Makhijani, *Carbon-Free*, pp. xvi, xx, 1.
35. Intergovernmental Panel on Climate Change (IPCC), *IPCC Assessment Reports*, accessed March 30, 2010, at http://www.ipcc.ch/.
36. Paul Harrison and Fred Pearce, *AAAS Atlas of Population and Environment* (Berkeley: University of California Press, 2000).
37. James J. McCarthy, O. F. Canziani, N. A. Leary, D. J. Dokken, and K. S. White (eds.), *Climate Change 2001, IPCC* (Cambridge, UK: Cambridge University Press, 2001), p. 21; hereafter cited as McCarthy, et al.
38. National Research Council, *Climate Change Science* (Washington, DC: National Academy Press, 2001), pp.1, 3.
39. Intergovernmental Panel on Climate Change (IPCC), *Climate Change 2007: The Physical Science Basis* (Cambridge, UK: Cambridge University Press, 2007); hereafter cited as IPCC 2007 and Fourth Assessment, available at http://www.ipcc.ch/ipccreports/ar4-wg2.htm. IPCC, *Third Assessment Report: Climate Change 2001* (Geneva, Switzerland: IPCC, 2001), p. 152; hereafter cited as IPCC 2001.
40. IPCC 2007, pp. 23, 93–94. Arjun Makhijani, *Carbon Free and Nuclear Free* (Tacoma Park, MD: Institute for Energy and Environmental Research, 2007), pp. xvi–vii, 2–5; hereafter cited as Makhijani 2007.
41. American Meteorological Society, "Climate Change Research," *Bulletin of the American Meteorological Society* 84 (2003); accessed May 1, 2006, at http://www.ametsoc.org/policy/climatechangeresearch_2003.html. See Oreskes 2007.
42. Nicholas Stern, *The Economics of Climate Change* (Cambridge, UK: Cambridge University Press, 2007), pp. i–vff.; available at http://www.hm-treasury.gov.uk/independent_reviews/stern_review_economics_climate_change/sternreview_index.cfm and hereafter cited as Stern 2007.
43. For the 96 percent claim, see Peter Singer, *One World* (New Haven, CT: Yale University Press, 2002), ch. 2, hereafter cited as Singer, OW; Makhijani 2007, pp. 2ff.; previous 10 endnotes, and later citations to Oreskes, Weart, and *The Economist*. For ethicists' responsibility argument, see, for instance, Singer, OW; Caney, et al., CE; Gardiner, PS; and Garvey, ECC.
44. Singer, OW, ch. 2. Makhijani 2007, pp. 2ff. IPCC 2007.
45. Singer, OW, ch. 2. Makhijani 2007, pp. 2ff. IPCC 2007. See previous two notes for ethics arguments.

46. Singer, OW, ch. 2. Makhijani 2007, pp. 2ff. IPCC 2007. See previous three notes for ethics arguments.
47. Singer, OW, ch. 2. Makhijani 2007, pp. 2ff. IPCC 2007. See previous 14 notes for proponents of these initial-allocation rules, such as Jamieson, Singer.
48. IPCC 2007. Makhijani 2007, p. xv, 1.
49. "Americans See a Climate Problem," Time.com, March 26, 2006; accessed May 1, 2006, at http://www.time.com/time/nation/article/0,8599,1176967,00.html. Naomi Oreskes, "The Scientific Consensus on Climate Change," in Joseph F. Dimento and Pamela Doughman (eds.), *Climate Change* (Cambridge, MA: MIT Press, 2007), pp. 65, 94, of 65–99; hereafter cited as Oreskes 2007.
50. Oreskes 2007, pp. 65–66.
51. Spencer R. Weart, *The Discovery of Global Warming* (Cambridge, MA: Harvard University Press, 2003).
52. Oreskes 2007, p. 73. Naomi Oreskes, "Beyond the Ivory Tower: The Scientific Consensus on Climate Change," *Science* 306, no. 5702 (2004): 1686.
53. See David Michaels, *Doubt Is Their Product* (Cambridge, MA: Harvard University Press, 2008); hereafter cited as Michaels, *Doubt*.
54. "The Clouds of Unknowing," *Economist* 394, no. 8674 (March 26, 2010): 84 of pp. 83–86; hereafter cited as *Economist*, "Clouds." Oreskes 2007, p. 92. "Spin, Science, and Climate Change," *Economist* 394, no. 8674 (March 26, 2010): 13; hereafter cited as *Economist*, "Spin."
55. For this argument, see Fred Singer, *The Scientific Case Against the Global Climate Treaty* (Science and Environmental Policy Project, 1997). For a critique of Singer's position, see http://www.exxonsecrets.org/html/personfactsheet.php?id=1, which reveals how ExxonMobil funds Singer's work.
56. Stern 2007. Daniel McDougall, "Stemming the Tide," *Ecologist* 37, no. 10 (December–January 2008): 26–30. *Economist*, "Clouds," p. 84. Arctic Council, *Arctic Climate Impact Assessment* (Oslo, Norway: Arctic Council, 2004); hereafter cited as *Arctic*. Elizabeth Kolbert, *Field Notes from a Catastrophe* (New York: Bloomsbury, 2006). Tim Flannery, *The Weather Makers* (New York: Atlantic Monthly Press, 2006). Oreskes 2007, p. 71.
57. Steven Hayward and Kenneth Green, *Politics Posing as Science* (Washington, DC: American Enterprise Institute, 2007); accessed March 29, 2010, at http://www.aei.org/print?pub=ou tlook&pubId=27185&authors=<a href=scholar/28Steve…and hereafter cited as Hayward and Green, AEI. The American Enterprise Institute is funded, in large part, by the fossil-fuel industry; see later paragraphs in this chapter. See Michaels, *Doubt*, for a critique of this objection.
58. Hayward and Green, AEI.
59. Oreskes 2007, p. 74. *Economist*, "Clouds," pp. 85–86.
60. See, for instance, James Lovelock, *The Revenge of Gaia* (London: Penguin, 2003).
61. J. C. Lashof, et al., Health and Life Sciences Division of the US Office of Technology Assessment, *Assessment of Technologies for Determining Cancer Risks from the Environment* (Washington, DC: Office of Technology Assessment, 1981), pp. 3, 6ff. P. J. Landrigan, "Commentary: Environmental Disease – A Preventable Epidemic," *The American Journal of Public Health* 82, no. 7 (1992): 941–43. See also UNICEF, *State of the World's Children, 2005* (New York: UNICEF, 2005); World Health Organization (WHO), *Effects of Air Pollution on Children's Health* (Bonn: WHO, 2005); and Kristin Shrader-Frechette, *Taking Action*.
62. Hayward and Green, AEI, are two of the many fossil-fuel-industry-funded writers who make these claims.
63. See Janet Raloff, "Climate-Gate," *Science News* (December 12, 2009); accessed March 30, 2010, at http://www.sciencenews.org/view/generic/id/50707/title/Science_%2B_the_ Public__Climate-gate_Beyond_the_embarrassment. For information on this scandal, and how people misuse it to attack climate change, see Union of Concerned Scientists (UCS),

Hacked Emails Are Part of Disinformation Campaign (Washington, DC: UCS, 2009); accessed March 29, 2010 at http://www.ucsusa.org/news/ucs-fact-checker.html.

64. *Economist*, "Spin," p. 13.
65. American Enterprise Institute, *Climate Change* (Washington, DC: AEI, 2008); accessed March 29, 2010, at http://www.aei.org/basicPages/20071211104715244 and hereafter cited as AEI. See also P. Michaels and Robert Balling, Jr., *The Satanic Gases: Clearing the Air about Global Warming* (Washington, DC: Cato Institute, 2000).
66. *Economist*, "Clouds," p. 84.
67. For a CC-denier who makes the cold-winter argument against CC, see Michael Fumento, *Cold, Bitter Winter Is "Proof" of Global Warming* (Washington, DC: Competitive Enterprise Institute, 2010); accessed March 30, 2010, at http://www.globalwarming.org/2010/01/28/cold-bitter-winter-is-%E2%80%9Cproof%E2%80%9D-of-global-warming/
68. See Michaels, *Doubt*. See also Thomas McGarity and Wendy Wagner, *Bending Science* (Cambridge, MA: Harvard University Press, 2008); hereafter cited as McGarity and Wagner.
69. Stephen Schneider, *Global Warming: Are We Entering the Greenhouse Century?* (Washington, DC: Sierra Club Books, 1989). For work on precaution, see Davis, CC; Davis, *Smoke*; Michaels, *Doubt*; McGarity and Wagner; and Kristin Shrader-Frechette, *Risk and Rationality* (Berkeley: University of California Press, 1991), hereafter cited as RR.
70. Michaels, *Doubt*. McGarity and Wagner
71. For a discussion of uncertainty and maximin, see Shrader-Frechette, RR, pp. 100–30. For a discussion of this ethical stance on CC, see also Singer, OW.
72. For instance, this argument is made by AEI; by Hayward and Green, AEI. See also M. Hopkin, "Climate Change 2007: Climate Skeptics Switch Focus to Economics," *Nature* 445: 582–83.
73. Bjorn Lomborg, *Cool It: The Skeptical Environmentalist's Guide to Global Warming* (New York: Knopf, 2007); hereafter cited as Lomborg.
74. Stern 2007.
75. Makhijani 2007, p. 6.
76. F. Valent, D. A. Little, R. Bertollini, L. E. Nemer, G. Barbonc, and G. Tamburlini, "Burden of Disease Attributable to Selected Environmental Factors and Injury among Children and Adolescents in Europe," *Lancet* 363 (2004): 2032–39. Arden Pope, "Cardiovascular Mortality and Long-Term Exposure to Particulate Air Pollution," *Circulation* 109, no. 6 (January 2003): 71–77. See Kristin Shrader-Frechette, *Taking Action*, ch. 1.
77. EPA, *National Water Quality Inventory* (Washington, DC: EPA, 1998), p. ES-3; accessed July 13, 2005, at http://www.epa.gov/305b/98report/. CDC, *Blood Mercury Levels in Young Children and Childbearing-Aged Women* (Washington, DC: CDC, 2004), p. 7; available at http://www.cdc.gov/mmwr/preview/mmwrhtml/mm5343a5.htm. OMB Watch, "One in Five Women Carries Too Much Mercury," *OMB Watch* 7, no. 4 (February 22, 2006); accessed March 10, 2006, at http://www.ombwatch.org/article/articleview/3296/1/429.
78. WHO, *Effects of Air Pollution on Children's Health* (Bonn: WHO, 2005), pp. 20–23. M. Weitzman, et al., "Recent Trends in the Prevalence and Severity of Childhood Asthma," *Journal of the American Medical Association* 268, no. 19 (November 18, 1992): 2673–77. E. Friebele, Weitzman, et al., "The Attack of Asthma," *Environmental. Health Perspectives* 104, no. 1 (January 1996): 22–25. K. Weiss, et al., "An Economic Evaluation of Asthma in the United States," *New England Journal of Medicine* 326, no. 13 (March 26, 1992): 862–66.
79. Shrader-Frechette, *Taking Action*, ch. 1. European Public Health Alliance, *Air, Water Pollution and Health Effects* (Brussels: EPHA, 2006); available at http://www.epha.org/r/54. Centers for Disease Control, "Populations at Risk from Air Pollution," *Morbidity and Mortality Weekly Report* 42, no. 16 (April 30, 1993). D. R. Wennette, and L. A. Nieves, "Breathing Polluted Air," *EPA Journal* (March/April 1992): 16–17.
80. J. T. Houghton, G. J. Jenkins, and J. J. Ephraums (eds.), *Scientific Assessment of Climate Change, IPCC* (Cambridge, UK: Cambridge University Press, 1990). J. P. Bruce, Hoesung Lee, and

E. F. Haites (eds.), *Climate Change 1995* (Cambridge, UK: Cambridge University Press, 1996). R. T. Watson, M. C. Zinyowera, and Richard H. Moss (eds.), *Climate Change 1995, IPCC* (Cambridge, UK: Cambridge University Press, 1996). J.J. MacCarthy, J. T. Houghton, Y. Ding, D. J. Griggs, M. Noguer, P. J. Van der Linden, X. Dai, K. Maskell, and C. A. Johnson (eds.), *Climate Change 2001, IPCC* (Cambridge, UK: Cambridge University Press). Bert Metz, Ogunlade Davidson, Rob Stewart, and Jiahua Pan (eds.), *Climate Change 2001, IPCC* (Cambridge, UK: Cambridge University Press, 2001). Robert T. Watson, *Climate Change 2001, IPCC* (Cambridge, UK: Cambridge University Press, 2001). Spencer R. Weart, *The Discovery of Global Warming* (Cambridge, MA: Harvard University Press, 2003). Oreskes 2007, p. 81.

81. Carl Hempel, *Aspects of Scientific Explanation* (New York: Free Press, 1965). *Arctic*; Oreskes 2007, pp. 83–84; *Economist*, "Clouds," pp. 83–84.

82. D. Stainforth, T. Aina, C. Christensen, M. Collins, N. Faull, D. J. Frame, J. A. Kettleborough, S. Knight, A. Martin, J. M. Murphy, C. Piani, D. Sexton, L. A. Smith, R. A. Spicert, A. J. Thorpe, and M. R. Allen, "Uncertainty in the Predictions of Climate Response to Rising Levels of Greenhouse Gases," *Nature* 433 (2005): 403-406. Oreskes 2007, pp. 86–89.

83. K. R. Briffa and T. J. Osborn, "Blowing Hot and Cold," *Science* 295 (2002):2227–28. E. O. Wilson, *Consilience* (New York: Knopf, 1998). *Economist*, "Clouds," pp. 83–84.

84. Lipton 1991; Oreskes 2007, p. 91.

85. *Economist*, "Spin."

86. *Economist*, "Clouds," p. 83.

87. Leslie Kaufman, "Scientists and Weathercasters at Odds over Climate Change," *The New York Times* CLIX, No. 54,995 (Tuesday, March 30, 2010): A1, A16.

88. Oreskes 2007, pp. 74–75. See Source Watch, *Front Group* (Madison, WI: Center for Media and Democracy, 2009); available at http://www.sourcewatch.org. Sharon Beder, *Global Spin* (Glasgow: Green Books, 2002); hereafter cited as Beder. James Hoggan and Richard Littlemore, *Climate Cover-Up: The Crusade to Deny Global Warming* (Petersburg, VA: Greystone Publishers, 2009); hereafter cited as Hoggan and Littlemore.

89. AEI.

90. Willie Soon, S. Baliunas, S. B. Idso, K. Y. Kondratyev, and E. S. Posmentier, "Modeling Climate Effects of Anthropogenic Carbon Dioxide Emissions," *Climate Research* 22 (2001):187–88 esp. p. 250, Oreskes 2007, pp 75–76. For a discussion of CC misrepresentations, typically by special interests, see Steve Schneider, *Science as a Contact Sport* (Margate, FL: National Geographic Books, 2009).

91. Hoggan and Littlemore. Beder. See next two endnotes.

92. Ross Gelbspan, *The Heat Is On* (Reading, MA: Addison-Wesley, 1997). Ross Gelbspan, *Boiling Point* (New York: Basic Books, 2004).

93. For analysis of the ExxonMobil ad, see Environmental Defense Fund, *Too Slick*, 2005; accessed March 14, 2005, at http://actionnetwork.org/campaign/exxonmobil?source=edac2. Oreskes 2007, p. 78. See Sheldon Krimsky, *Science in the Private Interest* (Savage, MD: Rowman & Littlefield, 2003); hereafter cited as KIrimsky.

94. Tim Dickinson, "The Climate Killers," *Rolling Stone* (January 21, 2010): 35–41; hereafter cited as Dickinson. See Beder, and also the various non-governmental organizations that police corporate-polluter misrepresentations, such as the website of Corporate Accountability International at http://www.stopcorporateabuse.org, the website of Corporate Ethics and Governance Watchdog at http://www.corp-ethics.com/, the website of Corporate Watch at http://www.corpwatch.org/, and the website of Multinational Monitor at http://www.multinationalmonitor.org/. See also Sheldon Rampton and John Stauber, *Trust Us, We're Experts* (New York: Penguin, 2002).

95. Dickinson. See also Shrader-Frechette, *Taking Action*, pp. 39–112, and Krimsky. For groups that check the facts cited by politicians and other groups, see the next note.

96. Dickinson. For sources that enable readers to check the facts of lobbyists who are paid by special interests, see PR Watch, sponsored by the Center for Media and Democracy at the

University of Wisconsin at http://www.prwatch.org, and also the website of Public Citizen at http://www.citizen.org, and the website of the Union of Concerned Scientists at http://www.ucsusa.org/news/ucs-fact-checker.html.

97. Dickinson. See Bill Goodell, "As the World Burns," *Rolling Stone* (January 21, 2010): 31–34, 62; hereafter cited as Goodell. For sources that police media, see the journalistic society Fairness and Accuracy in Reporting (FAIR) and its website at http://www.fair.org/index.php?page=100. To check any media misrepresentation of CC, see also the website of the Intergovernmental Panel on Climate Change (IPCC) at http://www.ipcc.ch/; the website of the Physicians for Social Responsibility at http://www.psr.org/; the website of national academies of science throughout the world, especially their statement on climate change at http://www.nationalacademies.org/onpi/06072005; and the website of the US National Academy of Sciences, esp. its work on climate, at http://dels.nas.edu/climate-change/. The US National Academy has many volumes confirming CC. See, e.g., National Research Council, *Hidden Costs of Energy* (Washington, DC: National Academy Press, 2009).

98. Dickinson. For accurate scientific representations of CC, see the last 5 references in the previous endnote, as well as the website of climate scientist Dr. James Hansen at US NASA at http://pubs.giss.nasa.gov/authors/jhansen.html; the website of climate scientist Dr. Steve Schneider at Stanford University at http://stephenschneider.stanford.edu/; the website of practicing climate scientists (Ph.D.s from NASA, Penn State, NCAR, Norwegian Meteorological Institute, etc.), from around the world; a website for ordinary citizens at http://www.realclimate.org/. For revelations of how scientists (who do not do CC research) are funded by special interests, see Greenpeace, *How Exxon Funds Global Warming Denial* (Washington, DC: Greenpeace Research Unit, 2010); accessed March 30, 2010, at http://www.exxonsecrets.org. For accurate scientific information, see the preceding note, as well as the CC book written by US NASA CC-scientist James Hansen, *Storms of My Grandchildren* (London: Bloomsbury, 2009), and the CC book written by academic CC-scientists Gavin Schmidt and Joshua Wolfe, *Climate Change* (New York: W.W. Norton, 2009).

99. Jonathan Gilligan, *The Age of Fossil Fuels Part I: The Middle Ages through 1973* (Nashville, TN: Vanderbilt University, 2005), pp. 3–4; hereafter cited as Gilligan, *Age*. Barbara Freese, *Coal: A Human History* (Cambridge, MA: Perseus, 2003), pp. 1–2; hereafter cited as Freese, *Coal*. Davis, *Smoke*, p. 34. David Urbinato, *London's Historic 'Pea-Soupers'* (Washington, DC: US Environmental Protection Agency, 1994); accessed January 20, 2010, at http://www.epa.gov/history/topics/perspect/london.htm and hereafter cited as Urbinato, *"Pea-Soupers."*

100. Philip K. Hopke, "Contemporary Threats and Air Pollution," *Atmospheric Environment* 43, no. 1 (January 2009): 87–93. Gilligan, *Age*. Freese, *Coal*.

101. Kimberly K. Smith, *Powering Our Future: An Energy Sourcebook for Sustainable Living* (Lincoln, NE: Alternative Energy Institute, 2005), pp. 68–69; hereafter cited as Smith, *Powering*.

102. Urbinato, *"Pea-Soupers."*

103. Smith, *Powering*.

104. Gilligan, *Age*. Urbinato, *"Pea-Soupers."*

Chapter 2

1. B. Smith, *Insurmountable Risks: The Dangers of Using Nuclear Power to Combat Global Climate Change* (Takoma Park: IEER Press, 2006), p. 23: hereafter cited as Smith, *Insurmountable*; Edward Bryant, *Climate Process and Change* (Cambridge: Cambridge University Press, 1997), p. 194.

2. S. Pacala and R. Socolow, "Stabilization Wedges: Solving the Climate Problem for the Next 50 years with Current Technologies," *Science* 305, no. 5686 (2004): 968–972; hereafter cited as: Pacala and Socolow, "Stabilization." Small parts of this chapter (fewer than 1,000 words) were published as Kristin Shrader-Frechette, "Data Trimming, Nuclear Emissions, and

Climate Change," *Science and Engineering Ethics* 15 (2009): 19–23, and as Kristin Shrader-Frechette, "Greenhouse Emissions and Nuclear Energy," *Modern Energy Review* 1, no. 1 (August 2009): 54–57.

3. Mac-Wan Ho, *The Nuclear Black Hole* (London: Institute for Science and Society, 2008); accessed March 11, 2010, at www.i-sis.org.uk/TheNuclearBlackHole.php, *Nuclear*.

4. R. Shane Johnson (Principal Deputy Assistant Secretary for Nuclear Energy), *Nuclear Energy: Securing Our Energy Future* (Washington, DC: US DOE, 2008); US Department of Energy (DOE), *A Roadmap to Deploy New Nuclear Power Plants in the United States by 2010*, Vol. 1, Summary Report (Washington, DC: US DOE, 2001); N. Deller, A. Makhijani, and J. Burroughs, *Rule of Power or Rule of Law? An Assessment of the US Policies and Actions Regarding Security-Related Treatise* (New York: Apex Press, 2003), pp. 106–110. On the contrary, see Smith, *Insurmountable*; W. S. van Leeuwen, "Secure Energy? Civil Nuclear Power, Security, and Global Warming," in F. Barnaby and J. Kemp (eds.), *CO₂ Emissions from Nuclear Power* (London: Oxford Research Group, 2007), pp. 40–44; here-after cited as: van Leeuwen, "Secure," and Barnaby and Kemp, *Emissions*. Richard Meserve, "Global Warming and Nuclear Power," *Science* 303, no. 5657 (2004): 433; hereafter cited as: Meserve, "Global"; Ansolabehere and John Deutsch, co-Chairs, et al., *The Future of Nuclear Power* (Cambridge: MIT Press, 2003), pp. x, 16; hereafter cited as: Ansolabehere and Deutsch, et al., *Future*; Gwyneth Cravens, *Power to Save the World: The Truth about Nuclear Energy* (New York: Knopf, 2008), p. 368; hereafter cited as: Cravens, *Power*. Bob Percopo, "US Nuclear Power's Time Has Come—Again," *Power* (January 15, 2008); accessed April 6, 2011 at <www.powermag.com/issues/departments/commentary/U-S-nuclear-oiwers-time-as0cine-again_110,html

5. US Department of Energy (DOE), *President Bush Requests $25 Billion for US Department of Energy's FY 2009 Budget* (Washington, DC: US DOE Office of Public Affairs, 2008); Nuclear Energy Institute (NEI), *Nuclear Statistics* (Washington, DC: NEI, 2007); accessed February 15, 2008, at www.nei.org/resourcesandstqats/ nuclear_statistics/costs; P. Bunyard, "Ecologist: Taking the Wind Out of Nuclear Power," *Pacific Ecologist* 11 (Summer 2006): 51–57; hereafter cited as: Bunyard, "Ecologist"; D. Butler, "Energy: Nuclear Power's New Dawn," *Nature* 429, no. 6989 (2004): 238–240.

6. Van Leeuwen, "Secure", p. 41. See F. Barnaby and J. Kemp, "Too Hot to Handle? The Future of Civil Nuclear Power," in F. Barnaby and J. Kemp (eds.), *Emissions*, p. 7 of 7–14; hereafter cited as: Barnaby and Kemp, "Future." Patrick Moore, "Going Nuclear," *Washington Post* (2006): B01; accessed February 5, 2009, at www.washingtonpost.com/wp-dyn/content/article/2006/04/14/AR2006041401209.html; hereafter cited as Moore, "Going." Hugh Montefiore, "Why the Planet Needs Nuclear Energy," *Tablet* (October 23, 2004); accessed November 1, 2008, at www.thetablet.co.uk/cgi-bin/register.cgi/tablet-00946; hereafter cited as: Montefiore, "Planet."

7. Bunyard, "Ecologist," p. 51. Steward Brand, "Environmental Heresies," *Technology Review* (May 2005); accessed November 1, 2008, at www.technologyreview.com/read_articles.aspx?id=14406&ch=biztechl; hereafter cited as: Brand, "Heresies."

8. Matthew L. Wald, "After 35-Year Lull, Nuclear Power May Be in Early Stages of a Revival," *New York Times* (Friday, October 24, 2008): B3–2; hereafter cited as: Wald, "After."

9. F. L. Toth, "Prospects for Nuclear Power in the 21st Century," *International Journal of Global Energy Issues* 30, nos. 1–4 (2008): 4 of 3–27; hereafter cited as: Toth, "Prospects."

10. A. M. Herbst and G. W. Hopley, *Nuclear Energy Now* (Hoboken, NJ: John Wiley, 2007), pp. 93, 443; hereafter cited as: Herbst and Hopley, *Nuclear*; Brice Smith, "The Bulletin Interview," *Bulletin of the Atomic Scientists* 63, no. 6 (November/December 2008): 22–27; Pacala and Socolow, "Stabilization"; Ansolabehere et al., *Future*, p. 3.

11. F. Barnaby and J. Kemp, "Executive Summary," in Barnaby and Kemp (eds.), *Too Hot to Handle? The Future of Civil Nuclear Power* (London: Oxford Research Group, 2007), pp. 7–14.

12. Toth, "Prospects", pp. 6, 24; Cravens, *Power*, p. 58.

13. J. Peter Scoblic, "Nuclear Spring," *New Republic* 238 no. 7 (April 23, 2008): 18–20; Pacala and Socolow, "Stabilization."
14. Jeffrey D. Sachs, "Climate Change after Bali," *Scientific American* 298, no. 3 (2008): 33–34.
15. World Nuclear Association (WNA), *The New Economics of Nuclear Power* (London: WNA, 2005), p. 6.
16. Toth, "Prospects," pp. 20–21, 23–24.
17. Herbst and Hopley, *Nuclear,* p. 58.
18. UK Department of Trade and Industry (UK DTI), "Meeting the Energy Challenge," *CM 7124* (London: UK DTI, 2007), p. 193; accessed January 19, 2009, at commodities-now. com/content/research/includes/assets/UKWPenergy.pdf.
19. See Ansolabehere et al., *Future,* p. 21.
20. Wald, "After," p. B3; Susan Stranahan, "Expensive, Dangerous and Dirty," *Rolling Stone* 1065 (2008): p. 59; see later chapters of this book.
21. Jessica Holzer, "The Joys of Going Nuclear ? ," *Forbes* (2006); accessed February 6, 2009 at <www.forbes.com/2006/05/24/nuclear-power-plants-cx_jh_0525nukes.html>. Steve Thomas, *The Economics of Nuclear Power: Analysis of Recent Studies* (Berlin: Heinrich Böll, 2005), p. 8; hereafter cited as: Thomas, *Economics*; Nuclear Information and Resource Service (NIRS), *Reactor Watchdog Project* (2004); accessed January 26, 2009, at www.nirs. org/reactorwatch/newreactors/profileusreactororder19531978.htm; Ansolabehere et al., *Future,* p. 31.
22. Ansolabehere et al., *Future,* p. 21.
23. Peter Stoett, "Toward Renewed Legitimacy: Nuclear Power, Global Warming and Security," *Global Environmental Politics* 3, no. 1 (2003): 105 of 99–116.
24. International Atomic Energy Agency (IAEA), *Global Public Opinion on Nuclear Issues* (Vienna: IAEA, 2005), pp. 18–20.
25. Shell International, *Shell Energy Scenarios to 2050* (The Hague, Netherlands: Shell International BV, 2008), p. 16; hereafter cited as: Shell International 2008.
26. Shell International 2008; Smith, *Insurmountable,* p. 68; Shell International, "Energy Needs, Choices, Possibilities: Scenarios to 2050," *Global Business Environment* (2001): 9, 38; accessed January 19, 2009, at www.gbn.com/BookClubSelectionDisplayServlet.srv?si=71.
27. Smith, *Insurmountable,* p. 68; UK Department of Trade and Industry (UK DTI), "Energy Whitepaper: Our Energy Future—Creating a Low Carbon Economy," *CM 5761* (London: UK DTI, 2003), p. 12.
28. Thomas, *Economics,* pp. 7, 10.
29. Ibid., p. 10.
30. UK Sustainable Development Commission (UK SDC), *The Role of Nuclear Power in a Low-Carbon Economy: Questions and Answers* (London: UK SDC, 2006).
31. Thomas, *Economics,* p. 11.
32. Ibid., p. 12.
33. Ibid., p. 10.
34. Teresa Weinmeister, *New Plants Update* (Bethesda, MD: AREVA NP Inc., September 2009); accessed March 18, 2010, at www.areva-np.com/common/liblocal/docs/presentation_stat-utEPR/New_Plants_Update_2009.pdf. World Nuclear Association (WNA), *Advanced Nuclear Power Reactors* (2008a); accessed January 21, 2009, at www.world-nuclear.org/info/inf08.html.
35. Note that the military and commercial regulation and promotion of nuclear technology has now been separated. Congressional hearings-reports on the massive nuclear-related safety violations, and so on include US Congress, *Worker Safety at DOE Nuclear Facilities* (Washington, US Government Printing Office, 1999), hereafter cited as: US Congress, *NF*; US Congress, *Worker Safety at DOE Nuclear Sites* (Washington, DC: US Government Printing Office, 1994), hereafter cited as: US Congress, *NS*; US General Accounting Office, *DOE: DOE's Nuclear Safety Program Should Be Strengthened* (Washington, DC: US Government Printing Office, 1999); US Government Accountability Office, *DOE: Clear*

Strategy on Eternal Regulation Needed (Washington, DC: US Government Printing Office, 1998), hereafter cited as: GAO 1998; US Office of Technology Assessment, *Complex Cleanup* (Washington, DC: GPO, 1991), hereafter cited as: OTA 1991. US Government Accountability Office, *Nuclear Safety, GAO-09-61* (Washington, DC: US Government Printing Office, 2008), hereafter cited as GAO, *NS* 2008; US Government Accountability Office, *Nuclear and Worker Safety* (Washington, DC: US Government Printing Office, 2007), p. 5, hereafter cited as: GAO, *NW Safety* 2007; US Government Accountability Office, *NRC's Oversight of … Commercial Nuclear Reactor Units* (Washington, DC: US Government Printing Office, 2008); hereafter cited as: GAO, *Reactor Oversight* 2008; and US Government Accountability Office, *Nuclear Material* (Washington, DC: US Government Printing Office, 2008), pp. 19–23, hereafter cited as: GAO, *Nuclear Material* 2008; US Government Accountability Office, *Nuclear Safety* (Washington, DC: US Government Printing Office, 2007), hereafter cited as: GAO, *Nuclear Safety* 2007. Nuclear-history data are from Kristin Shrader-Frechette, *Burying Uncertainty* (Berkeley: University of California Press, 1993), pp. 17–18; hereafter cited as: Shrader-Frechette, *BU*.

36. Silkwood information is from Jeffrey Stein, "Karen Silkwood: The Deepening Mystery," *Progressive* 45, no. 1 (January 1981): 14–21; Richard Rashke, *The Killing of Karen Silkwood* (Boston: Houghton Mifflin, 1981), p. 5; see also Rashke, *The Killing of Karen Silkwood* (Ithaca, NY: Cornell University Press, 2000). Hans Baer, "Kerr-McGee and the NRC," *Social Science and Medicine* 30, no. 2 (1990): 237–248. Government radiation-experiment information is from US Office of Human Radiation Experiments, *Report of the Advisory Committee on Human Radiation Experiments* (Washington, DC: US Government Printing Office, 1994); accessed June 15, 2005, at http://ris.eh.doe.gov.ohre/roadmap/achre/; hereafter cited as: US Office of Human Radiation Experiments 1994; and US Congress, *American Nuclear Guinea Pigs* (Washington, DC: Government Printing Office, 1986); hereafter cited as: US Congress, *Guinea Pigs*. See also Shrader-Frechette, *BU*, pp. 17–18. For congressional demands for fallout-risk information, see PL 97-144 and National Cancer Institute (NCI). *Estimated Exposures and Thyroid Doses Received by the American People from Iodine-131 in Fallout Following Nevada Atmospheric Nuclear Bomb Tests*, NIH Publication 97-4264 (Washington, DC: National Institutes of Health, 1997), pp. 8.31–8.5. The National Academy of Sciences Study is Institute of Medicine (IOM), *Exposure of the American People to Iodine 131 from Nevada Nuclear Bomb Tests* (Washington, DC: National Academy Press, 1998), esp. p. 42. See D. Rush and J. Geiger, "NCI Study on I-131 Exposure from Nuclear Testing," *Physicians for Social Responsibility* 4, no. 3 (Winter 1997–1998): 1–5. US Congress, *National Cancer Institute's Management of Radiation Studies* (Washington, DC: Government Printing Office, 1998). For fallout cancer estimates, see Steven Simon, Andre Bouville, and Charles Land, "Fallout from Nuclear Weapons Tests and Cancer Risks," *American Scientist* 94, no. 801 (January–February 2005: 48–57. For citizen loss of trust in government handling of fallout exposures, see F. Owen Hoffman, A. Iulian Apostoaei, and Brian Thomas, "A Perspective on Public Concerns about Exposure to Fallout from the Production and Testing and Nuclear Weapons," *Health Physics* 82, no. 5 (2002): 736–748. Warnings about continuing US nuclear risks and experimentation are from two government documents: US Office of Human Radiation Experiments 1994, and US Congress, *Guinea Pigs*.

37. Chernobyl cost and mortality statistics are from Shrader-Frechette, *EJ*, pp. 40, 85–88, 112, 188–191, 201, and from the UN Development Programme and the UN Children Fund, *The Human Consequences of the Chernobyl Nuclear Accident* (New York: UN, January 25, 2002), p. 63; UN General Assembly Report of the Secretary, *Optimizing the International Effort to Study, Mitigate and Minimize the Consequences of the Chernobyl Disaster* (New York: UN, October 8, 2001). Hurricane Katrina costs are from John D. Mckinnon et al., "First Estimates on Katrina Costs for Washington Hit $200 Billion," *Wall Street Journal* 246, no. 47 (September 7, 2005): A1–A4. Hurricane Katrina mortality data are from Genevieve Roberts, "Final Katrina Death Toll Put at 972 as Search Is Called Off," *Independent (London)*,

(October 5, 2005): p. 29. For discussion of nuclear history, the US Atomic Energy Commission, the Brookhaven Report, and the Price-Anderson Act, see Kristin Shrader-Frechette, *Nuclear Power and Public Policy* (Boston: Kluwer, 1983), pp. 1–24, 73–109, hereafter cited as: Shrader-Frechette, *NPPP*. Shrader-Frechette, *Environmental Justice* (New York: Oxford University Press, 2002), pp. 152–162; and Shrader-Frechette, *BU*, 11–12, 17–18. The 1-in-5-lifetime-core-melt probability for 100 US reactors is from US Nuclear Regulatory Commission, *Reactor Safety Study*, WASH 1400 (Washington: NRC,1975), pp. 175 ff. Shrader-Frechette, *NPPP*, pp. 73–109, shows why the American Physical Society criticizes NRC estimates as too low.

38. See earlier notes, next two notes, and Shrader-Frechette, *BU*, pp. 17–18.

39. Four quotations are from, respectively, Frederick Upton, US Rep., Michigan, in US Congress, *NF*, pp. 98–99; Dingell in US Congress, *NS*, p. 159; Dingell in US Congress, *NS*, p. 159. GAO 1998, p. 4, and G. Sawyer, *Report of the State of Nevada Commission on Nuclear Projects* (Carson City: Commission on Nuclear Projects, 1988), pp. 8–9, 13; and James Wells, GAO, in *NS*, pp. 15–22, 25. Some of the many calls for DOE abolition, from 1991 to the present, are repeated in, for instance, GAO, *NS* 2008; GAO 2007, p. 3; GAO, *NW Safety* 2007; John Dingell, "Testimony," in US Congress, *NS*; James Wells, US GAO, in US Congress, *NS*, pp. 3–15; and Tara O'Toole, in US Congress, *NS*, p. 70; OTA 1991, pp. 8, 77, 80, 84, 99–100, 111, 138–143. Claims about poor monitoring and massive nuclear-safety violations are from US Congress, *NF*, and US Congress, *NS*. Claims about Clinton's being forced to provide full coverage are from Gary Jones, GAO, in US Congress, *NF*, pp. 5, 43–49. Claims about current nuclear safety violations are from, respectively, GAO, *NS* 2008; GAO, *Reactor Oversight* 2008, esp. pp. 4–6; GAO, *Nuclear Material* 2008, pp. 19–23; GAO, *Nuclear Safety*, 2007; and GAO, *NW Safety* 2007, pp. 3–4.

40. MIT and EU claims are from "The Nuclear Answer?" *The Economist* (July 7, 2005); accessed July 23, 2005, at www.economist.com/opinion/displayStory.cfm?story_id=4151435; hereafter cited as: "Nuclear Answer." MIT study is E. Moniz and J. Deutsch, *The Future of Nuclear Power* (Cambridge, MA: MIT Laboratory for Energy and the Environment, 2003). For the falsification of 1998–2000 Yucca data, see Naomi Lubick, "Falsification Alleged at Yucca Mountain," *Geotimes* (Alexandria, VA: American Geological Institute, 2005); accessed July 23, 2005, at www.geotimes.org/may05/NN_YuccaFraud.html. National Academy of Sciences quotation is from National Research Council, *Building Consensus through Risk Assessment and Management* (Washington, DC: National Academy Press, 1994). See also R. E. Dunlap, M. E. Kraft, and E. A. Rosa (eds.), *Public Relations to Nuclear Waste* (Durham, NC: Duke University Press, 1993). See prior 6 notes for congressional, GAO, and OTA claims. Inaccurate cost claims are from GAO, *Nuclear Material* 2008, 3–5. 2011 criticisms are From US Office of the Inspector General, *Audit of NRC's Implementation*, OIG-11-A-08 (Washington, DC: US Nuclear Regulatory Commission, 2011).

41. David Fleming, *The Lean Guide to Nuclear Energy* (London: University of London, 2007), pp. 4–7; hereafter cited as: Fleming, *Lean Guide*.

42. B. K. Sovacool, "Valuing the Greenhouse Gas Emissions from Nuclear Power: A Critical Survey," *Energy Policy* 36 (2008): 2940–2953; hereafter cited as: Sovacool, "Valuing."

43. Willem Storm van Leeuwen, *Nuclear Power: The Energy Balance, Energy Insecurity, and Greenhouse Gases* (Chaam, Netherlands: Ceedata Consultancy, 2008); accessed February 8, 2008, at www.stormsmith.nl/ and cited hereafter as Van Leeuwen, *NP*.

44. Van Leeuwen, "Secure."

45. P. Diehl, *Uranium Mining and Milling* (Amsterdam: World Information Service on Energy, 2004); Argonne National Laboratories, *Depleted UF₆ Management Information Network* (Argonne, IL: US Department of Energy, 2007); accessed June 23, 2009, at http://web.ead.anl.gov/uranium.

46. Global Security, *Uranium Feedstock* (Alexandria, VA: Global Security, 2009); accessed March 24, 2009, at www.globalsecurity.org/wmd/intro/u-feedstock.htm.

47. D. Biello, "Finding Fissile Fuel," *Scientific American* (January 26, 2009); accessed March 23, 2009, at www.scientificamerican.com/article.cfm?id=finding-fissile-fuel; hereafter cited as: Biello, "Finding."

48. World Energy Service on Energy (WISE), *Uranium Enrichment Calculator* (Amsterdam: WISE, 2006); accessed March 23, 2009, at www.wise-uranium.org/nfcue.html; Fleming, *Lean Guide*, p. 5.

49. Biello, "Finding."

50. World Energy Service on Energy (WISE), *Uranium Enrichment Calculator* (Amsterdam: WISE, 2006), accessed June 23, 2009, at www.wise-uranium.org/nfcue.html.

51. Energy Information Agency, *Carbon Dioxide Emissions from the Generation of Electric Power in the United States* (Washington, DC: US Department of Energy, 2000).

52. Ho, *Nuclear*.

53. Fleming, *Lean Guide*, pp. 6–7.

54. Biello, "Finding."

55. Mycle Schneider, "2008 World Nuclear Industry Status Report." *The Bulletin of the Atomic Scientists* (16 September 2008); accessed May 20, 2009, at www.thebulletin.org/web-edition/reports/2008-world-nuclear-industry-status-report/.

56. Fleming, *Lean Guide*, esp. pp. 10–19.

57. Ibid., esp. pp. 10–14.

58. Van Leeuwen, *NP*.

59. Uwe Fritsche and Sui-Sam Lim, *Comparison of Greenhouse-Gas Emissions and Abatement Cost of Nuclear and Alternative Energy Options from a Life-Cycle Perspective* (Darmstadt: Oeko Institute, 2006); accessed February 8, 2008, at www.oeko.de/servicegemuis/files/doku/nuclear_c02paper_update2006.pdf; hereafter cited as: Fritsche and Lim, *Comparison*.

60. Central Research Institute of the Electric Power Industry (CRIEPI), *Comparison of CO_2 Emission Factors between Process Analysis and I/O-Analysis* (Tokyo: CRIEPI Working Document, 1995); hereafter cited as: CRIEPI, *Comparison*. International Energy Agency (IEA), *Energy and the Environment, Transport Systems Responses in the OECD—Greenhouse Gas Emissions and Road Transport Technology* (Paris: IEA, 1994); hereafter cited as: IEA, *Energy and the Environment*.

61. Fleming, *Lean Guide*.

62. V. M. Fthenakis and H. C. Kim, "Greenhouse-Gas Emissions from Solar-Electric and Nuclear Power: A Life-Cycle Study," *Energy Policy* 35, no. 4 (2007): 2549–2557; hereafter cited as: Fthenakis and Kim, "Greenhouse"; Barnaby and Kemp, "Future"; Sovacool, "Valuing," pp. 2940–2953.

63. R. E. Hagen, J. R. Moens, and Z. D. Nikodem, *Impact of U.S. Nuclear Generation on Greenhouse Gas Emissions* (Washington, DC: Energy Information Administration of the US Department of Energy, 2001); hereafter cited as: Hagen et al., *Impact*.

64. Fritsche and Lim, *Comparison*; IEA, *Energy and the Environment*; CRIEPI, *Comparison*. See next two notes for discussion of high-grade and low-grade uranium ore.

65. Arun Makhijani, *Carbon-Free and Nuclear-Free* (Takoma Park, MD: IEER, 2007); hereafter cited as: Makhijani, *Carbon-Free*. See later citations to Diesendorf and Christoff and to Fleming.

66. Fleming, *Lean Guide*, pp. 8–9.

67. Mark Diesendorf and Peter Christoff, "CO_2 Emissions from the Nuclear Fuel Cycle," *Energy Science* 2 (2006): 2 of 1–3. Fleming, *Lean Guide*, p. 4.

68. Fleming, *Lean Guide*, pp. 10–12.

69. Ho, *Nuclear*; Bunyard, "Ecologist"; H. W. Ho, P. Bunyard, P. Saunders, E. Bravo, and R. Gala, *Which Energy?* (London: Institute for Science and Society, 2006); hereafter cited as: Ho et al., *Energy*.

70. Fleming, *Lean Guide*, p. 8.

71. W. S. van Leeuwen, *Energy Security and Uranium Reserves* (London: Oxford Research Group, 2006); hereafter cited as: van Leeuwen, *Energy*; see Barnaby and Kemp, "Future," pp. 8–12.

72. Ho, *Nuclear*. See Van Leeuwen, "Secure," p. 40.
73. Ho et al., *Energy*.
74. Van Leeuwen, *Energy*; Barnaby and Kemp, "Future."
75. Cravens, *Power*, p. 368.
76. Meserve, "Global."
77. Bunyard, "Ecologist," p. 51.
78. Brand, "Heresies."
79. Montefiore, "Planet."
80. For example, Hagen et al., *Impact*.
81. K. Barnham, "Secure Energy? Civil Nuclear Power, Security, and Global Warming," in Barnaby and Kemp, *Emissions*, pp. 45–50; hereafter cited as Barnham, "Secure."
82. UK Sustainable Development Commission (UK SDC), *The Role of Nuclear Power in a Low-Carbon Economy: Questions and Answers* (London: UK SDC, 2006), p. 45.
83. Amory Lovins, "Nuclear Is Uneconomic," *Bulletin of the Atomic Scientists*, Roundtable on Nuclear Power and Climate Change (2007); accessed February 9, 2008, at www.the-bulletin.org/roundtable/nuclear-power-climate-change/; hereafter cited as: Lovins, "Nuclear."
84. Smith, *Insurmountable*, p. 62; American Council for an Energy-Efficient Economy, DOE Energy Efficiency R&D and Technology Deployment Programs; accessed June 2, 2006 at www.aceee.org/energy/rdtech.htm.
85. Smith, *Insurmountable*, p. 64; UK Cabinet Office Performance and Innovation Unit (PIU), "The Energy Review" (February 2002): 98.
86. McKinsey and Company, *Reducing US Greenhouse Gas Emissions* (New York: McKinsey and Company, 2007); hereafter cited as: McKinsey, *Reducing*. McKinsey and Company, *How the World Should Invest in Energy Efficiency* (New York: McKinsey and Company, 2008); hereafter cited as: McKinsey, *Efficiency*.
87. World Information Service on Energy (WISE) and Nuclear Information Research Service (NIRS), *Nuclear Power: No Solution to Climate Change* (Tacoma Park, MD: WISE/NIRS, 2005); hereafter cited as WISE/NIRS, *Nuclear*.
88. T. Reichhardt, "No Net Cost in Cutting Carbon Emissions," *Nature* 389, no. 6650 (1997): 429.
89. Pacala and Socolow, "Stabilization."
90. A. Makhijani, "A Reliable Electricity Grid in the United States," *Science for Democratic Action* 15, no. 2 (2008): 9–11; hereafter cited as Makhijani, "Reliable." Iowa Wind Energy Association (IWEA), *Wind Energy Facts* (Estherville, IA: IWEA, 2011).
91. William Sweet, *Kicking the Carbon Habit* (New York: Columbia University Press, 2006), p. 183; hereafter cited as: Sweet, *Kicking*.
92. Van Leeuwen, "Secure," pp. 16–17.
93. Makhijani, *Carbon-Free*, p. 191; Smith, *Insurmountable*.
94. Ansolabehere et al., *Future*.
95. James Kemp, "The Security Background to a Nuclear New Build," in Barnaby and Kemp (eds.), *Emissions*, p. 36 of 36–39; hereafter cited as: Kemp, "Security."
96. Smith, "Bulletin."
97. Barnaby and Kemp, "Future," p. 7.
98. Ibid., pp. 8–12; See Brice Smith, "Insurmountable Risks," *Science for Democratic Action* 36 (August 2006): 2 of 1–2, 5–9; hereafter cited as: Smith, "Risks."
99. Bunyard, "Ecologist."
100. Fthenakis and Kim, "Greenhouse."
101. Smith, *Insurmountable*, pp. 311, 314–16; Matthew Bunn, John P. Holden, Steve Fetter, and Bob Van Der Zwaan, *The Economics of Reprocessing vs. Direct Disposal of Spent Nuclear Fuel: Report for Project on Managing the Atom* (Cambridge: Belfer Center for Science and International Studies, JFK School of Government, 2003), p. 116.
102. See the preceding discussion and chapters 3 and 6.

103. Makhijani, *Carbon-Free*, p. 125; Arun Makhijani and Kevin Gurney, *Mending the Ozone Hole: Science, Technology and Policy* (Cambridge: MIT Press, 1995).
104. E.g., Makhijani, *Carbon-Free*, pp. 145–164.
105. Meserve, "Global."
106. Brand, "Heresies."
107. Moore, "Going."
108. Montefiore, "Planet."
109. Bunyard, "Ecologist."
110. Peter Stoett, "Toward Renewed Legitimacy: Nuclear Power, Global Warming and Security," *Global Environmental Politics* 3, no. 1 (2003): 108 of 99–116.
111. Bunyard, "Ecologist."
112. McKinsey, *Reducing*, p. 27.
113. Smith, *Insurmountable*, p. 50; John Kennedy, Andreas Zsiga, Laurie Conheady, and Paul Lund, "Credit Aspects of North American and European Nuclear Power," *Standard & Poor's* (January 9, 2006).
114. McKinsey, *Reducing*, p. 61.
115. Makhijani, *Carbon-Free*, p. 30; American Wind Energy Association (AWEA), *Congress Extends Wind Energy Production Tax Credit for an Additional Year* (2006); accessed at http://www.awea.org/newsroom/releases/congress_extends_PTC_121106.html.
116. Energy Information Administration, *Annual Energy Review* (EIA AER), Annual Energy Review 2005, Report DOE/EIA-0384(2005) (Washington, DC: DOE, EIA, 2006) pp. 135–136; accessed June 2, 2007 at http://tonto.eia.doe.gov/FTPROOT/multifuel/0338405.pdf; see Makhijani, *Carbon-Free*, p. 15.
117. Ho, *Nuclear*.
118. Smith, *Insurmountable*, p. 200; John Deutch and Ernest J. Moniz, co-chairs, et al., *The Future of Nuclear Power: An Interdisciplinary Study on Nuclear Power* (2003): 71; accessed April 7 2011 at http://web.mit.edu/nuclearpower/pdf/nuclearpowerfull.pdf; hereafter cited as Deutch, *Future*.
119. Smith, *Insurmountable*, p. 302.
120. Ibid., p. 250.
121. Ibid., pp. 71–72; Deutch, *Future*, p. 168.
122. Smith, *Insurmountable*, p. 201; Joanne Omang, "California A-plant Faces License Suspension," *Washington Post* (November 18, 1981).
123. Public Citizen, *Just the Facts: A Look at the Five Fatal Flaws of Nuclear Power* (Washington, DC: Public Citizen, 2006); hereafter cited as: Public Citizen, *Facts*.
124. Smith, *Insurmountable*, p. 321; International Atomic Energy Agency (IAEA), *Model Protocol Additional to the Agreement(s) between State(s) and the International Atomic Energy Agency for the Application of Safeguards* (Vienna: IAEA, 1997), pp. 2–3.
125. Smith, *Insurmountable*, p. 313; International Energy Agency (IEA), *Nuclear Power in the OECD* (Paris: IEA, Organization for Economic Cooperation and Development, 2001), pp. 67–68, 70.
126. Bunyard, "Ecologist."
127. Smith, *Insurmountable*, p. 241.
128. Ibid.
129. Ansolabehere et al., *Future*, pp. 203, 61; Smith, *Insurmountable*, p. 414; Makhijani, *Carbon-Free*, p. 101.
130. Pacala and Socolow, "Stabilization"; the nine renewable options (only six needed to solve climate problems) are efficient vehicles, reduced vehicle use, efficient buildings, wind power for coal power, PV power for coal power, wind for gasoline in fuel-cell car, biomass fuel for fossil fuel, reduced deforestation, and conservation tillage. National Renewable Energy Laboratory (NREL), *Near Term Practical and Ultimate Technical Potential for Renewable Resources* (Golden, CO: US DOE, 2006); hereafter cited as: NREL, *Near*.
131. Barnaby and Kemp, "Future," p. 13.

132. WISE/NIRS, *Nuclear,* p. 14.
133. Pacala and Socolow, "Stabilization," p. 971.
134. Ibid., p. 968.
135. Lovins, "Nuclear."
136. NREL, *Near.*
137. Smith, *Insurmountable,* p. 83; J. Aabakken, *Power Technologies Energy Data Book: Third Edition* (Golden, CO: US DOE, National Renewable Energies Lab, 2005), p. 26.
138. Barnham, "Secure," p. 47.
139. Makhijani, *Carbon-Free,* p. 168.
140. Makhijani, "Reliable", p. 9; Makhijani, *Carbon-Free,* p. 37.
141. US Department of Energy (DOE), *DOE Selects 13 Solar-Energy Projects for Up to $168 Million in Funding: First Funding Awards for Solar America Initiative* (Washington, DC: US DOE Office of Public Affairs, 2007); see Makhijani, *Carbon-Free,* pp. 38–39.
142. Smith, *Insurmountable,* p. 297; Deutch, *Future,* p. 12.
143. Fleming, *Lean Guide,* p. 7.
144. Barnaby and Kemp, "Future," 13.
145. Ibid., 8; see Paul Rogers, "Nuclear Terrorism," in Barnaby and Kemp, *Emissions,* pp. 28–31; hereafter cited as: Rogers, "Nuclear."
146. Barnaby and Kemp, "Future," p. 9; Rogers, "Nuclear," p. 28; Public Citizen, *Facts.*
147. F. Barnaby, "Keeping Nuclear Materials Out of the Wrong Hands," in Barnaby and Kemp, *Emissions,* pp. 22–23; hereafter cited as: Barnaby, "Keeping."
148. Barnaby and Kemp, "Future," p. 9.
149. Rogers, "Nuclear," p. 29.
150. Ibid., pp. 30–31.
151. Smith, *Insurmountable,* p. 321.
152. Bunyard, "Ecologist."
153. Smith, *Insurmountable,* p. 118; Deutch, *Future,* p. 122.
154. Smith, *Insurmountable,* p. 120.
155. Ibid., p. 147.
156. Jurgen Trittin, "Foreword," in Barnaby and Kemp, *Emissions,* pp. 4–5; hereafter cited as: Trittin, "Foreword."
157. WISE/NIRS, *Nuclear,* p. 16.
158. Bunyard, "Ecologist."
159. See F. Barnaby and J. Kemp (eds.), *Secure Energy? Civil Nuclear Power, Security, and Global Warming* (London: Oxford Research Group, 2007).
160. Barnaby and Kemp, "Future," p. 8.
161. Smith, *Insurmountable,* p. 33; Deutch, *Future,* pp. 142, 148.
162. Barnham, "Secure," p. 49.
163. Barnaby and Kemp, "Future," pp. 8–9.
164. Barnaby, "Keeping."
165. Smith, *Insurmountable,* p. 119; Henry Sokolski, "After Iran: Keeping Nuclear Energy Peaceful," *Foreign Policy Agenda* (March 2005): 25.
166. Trittin, "Foreword," p. 4.
167. Arun Makhijani, "Dangerous Discrepancies," *Science for Democratic Action* 36 (2006): 10–15.
168. Makhijani, *Carbon-Free,* p. 170.
169. Smith, *Insurmountable,* p. 143; Office of Technology Assessment (OTA), US Congress, *Nuclear Safeguards and the International Atomic Energy, OTA-ISS-615* (Washington, DC: OTA, June 1995), p. 70.
170. Smith, "Risks," p. 5.
171. See Smith, "Bulletin," pp. 26, 127; Peter Bradford, *Nuclear Is Not an Essential Solution, Bulletin of the Atomic Scientists, Roundtable on Nuclear Power and Climate Change* (2007); accessed

February 9, 2008, at www.thebulletin.org/roundtable/nuclear-power-climate-change/; Public Citizen, *Facts*.

172. Smith, *Insurmountable*, pp. 9, 114; Kenneth Bergeron, *Tritium on Ice: The Dangerous New Alliance of Nuclear Weapons and Nuclear Power* (Cambridge: MIT Press, 2002), pp. 29–30, 32.

173. Barnaby, "Keeping," p. 2 of 22–23; F. Barnaby, "The Risk of Nuclear Terrorism," in Barnaby and Kemp, *Emissions*, pp. 24–27; hereafter cited as Barnaby, *Risk*.

174. F. Barnaby, "From a Civil Nuclear Means to Military Ends", in Barnaby and Kemp, *Emissions*, pp. 32–35; hereafter cited as Barnaby, *Civil*.

175. Smith, *Insurmountable*, pp. 130–138.

176. Barnaby and Kemp, "Future," p. 10.

177. Barnaby, *Civil*, p. 35 of 32–35.

178. Barnaby and Kemp, "Future," p. 12; Kemp, "Security," p. 37.

179. World Nuclear Association (WNA), *The Economics of Nuclear Power* (2008); accessed September 3, 2008, at www.world-nuclear.org/info/inf02.html; International Atomic Energy Agency (IAEA), *International Chernobyl Project: Technical Report* (Vienna: IAEA, 1991).

180. V. K. Savchenko, *The Ecology of the Chernobyl Catastrophe: Scientific Outlines of an International Programme of Collaborative Research* (London/New York: UNESCO and The Parthenon Publishing Group Ltd., 1995), p. xi; hereafter cited as Savchenko, *Ecology*.

181. Ibid., p. 5.

182. Ibid., p. 65.

183. D. L. Henshaw, "Chernobyl 10 Years On," *British Medical Journal* 312, no. 7038 (1996): 1052 of 1052–1053; T. Rytömaa, "Ten Years after Chernobyl," *Annals of Medicine* 28, no. 2 (1996): 83–87.

184. Y. E. Dubrova, O. G. Polshchanskaya, O. S. Kozionova, and A. V. Akieyev, "Minisatellite Germline Mutation Rate in the Techna River Population," *Mutation Research* (2006): xx–yy; Y. E. Dubrova, V. N. Nesterov, N. G. Krouchinsky, V. A. Ostapenko, R. Neumann, D. L. Neil, and A. Jeffreys, "Human Minisatellite Mutation Rate after the Chernobyl Accident," *Nature* 380, no. 6576 (1996): 683–686. See next three endnotes.

185. Dillwyn Williams and Keith Baverstock, "Too Soon for a Final Diagnosis," *Nature* 440 (April 20, 2006): 993–994.

186. T. Hatch, A. A. Derijck, P. D. Black, G. W. Van Der Heiden, P. DeBoer, and Y. E. Dubrova, "Maternal Effects of the Scid Mutation on Radiation-Induced Transgenerational Instability in Mice," *Oncogene* 26 (2007): 4720–4724; R. C. Barber, P. Hickenbotham, T. Hatch, D. Kelly, N. Topchiy, G. Almeida, G. G. Jones, G. E. Johnson, J. M. Parry, K. Tothkamm, and Y. E. Dubrova, "Radiation-Induced Transgenerational Alterations in Genome Stability and DNA Damage," *Oncogene* (2006): 7336–7342.

187. Y. E. Dubrova, P. Hickenbotham, C. D. Glen, K. Monger, H.-P. Wong, and R. C. Barber, "Paternal Exposure to Ethylnitrosourea Results in Transgenerational Genomic Instability in Mice," *EnvironmentalAnd Molecular Mutagenics*. 49 (2008): 308–311; Y. E. Dubrova, "Radiation-Induced Transgenerational Instability," *Oncogene* 22 (2003): 7087–7093.

188. See C. Hohenemser et al., "Agricultural Impact of Chernobyl," *Nature* 321 (1986): 817ff.

189. World Health Organization (WHO), *Health Effects of the Chernobyl Accident: An Overview* (Geneva: WHO, 2006); Elizabeth Cardis, et al., *Reconstruction of Doses for Chernobyl Liquidators* (Atlanta: US Centers for Disease Control; Lyon, France: International Agency for Research on Cancer [IARC], 2003), p. 29.

190. N. A. Beresford, C. I. Barnett, S. M. Wright, and N. M. Crout, "Factors Contributing to Radiocaesium Variability in Upland Sheep Flocks in West Cumbria (United Kingdom)," *Journal of Environmental Radioactivity* 98 (2007): 50–68; N. A. Beresford, C. I. Barnett, S. M. Wright, and N. M. Crout, "Post-Chernobyl Restrictions Still Affecting UK Sheep," *Agra Europe* 2203 (2008): 2; S. Wright, J. Smith, N. Beresford, and W. Scott, "Monte-Carlo

Prediction of Changes in Areas of West Cumbria Requiring Restrictions on Sheep Following the Chernobyl Accident," *Radiation and Environmental Biophysics* 42; (2003): 41–47.

191. International Energy Agency (IEA), *World Energy Outlook* (Paris: IEA, November 2006), p. 25.

192. Nick Middleton, "Environment," *Geographical* 72 (12): 25 of 24–28; P. Kritidis and H. Florou, "Radiological Impact in Greece of the Chernobyl Accident," *Health Physics* 80, no. 5 (2001): 440–446; A. Nisbet and R. Woodman, "Options for the Management of Chernobyl-Restricted Areas in England and Wales," *Journal of Environmental Radioactivity* 51, no. 2 (2000): 239–254. See also L. R. Anspaugh, "Doses to Members of the General Public and Observed Effects on Biota: Chernobyl," *Journal of Environmental Radioactivity* 96 (2007): 13–19.

193. See E. G. Anders Pape Moller and Timothy A. Mousseau, "Reduced Abundance of Insects and Spiders Linked to Radiation at Chernobyl 20 Years after the Accident," *Biology Letters* doi:10.1098/rsbl.2008.0778 (March 18, 2009).

194. John Gofman, "Foreword," in Alla Yaroshinska, *Chernobyl* (Lincoln: University of Nebraska Press, 1995), pp. 1–2; V. M. Zakharov, *Consequences of the Chernobyl Catastrophe* (Detroit: International Scholars, 1988).

195. P. Campbell, "Chernobyl's Legacy to Science," *Nature* 380, no. 5676 (1996): 653.

196. Smith, *Insurmountable*, p. 186; Lynn Anspaugh, Robert Catlin, and Marvin Goldman, "The Global Impact of the Chernobyl Reactor Accident," *Science* 242 (1988): 1513–1519.

197. Makhijani, *Carbon-Free*, p. 170; Raid Qusti, "GCC to Develop Civilian Nuclear Energy," *Arab News* (December 11, 2006); accessed at http://www.saudi-us-relations.org/articles/2006/ioi/061213-gcc-summit.html.

198. Barnaby and Kemp, "Future," p. 11.

199. Makhijani, *Carbon-Free*, p. 170.

200. Ibid., p. 189.

201. Ibid., p. 170.

202. McKinsey, *Reducing*, p. 65.

203. Barnaby, *Risk*, p. 25.

204. Nuclear Regulatory Commission (NRC), *Spent Fuel Pool Accident Risk Report* (Washington, DC: US NRC, October 2000); National Research Council-National Academy of Sciences (NAS-NRC), *Safety and Security of Spent Fuel Storage* (Washington, DC: National Academy Press, 2006); US Government Accountability Office (GAO), *NRC Needs to Do More to Ensure That Nuclear Plants Are Effectively Controlling Spent Nuclear Fuel*, GAO-05-339 (Washington, DC: GAO, 2005); Public Citizen, *Facts*.

205. Barnaby, *Risk*, p. 25.

206. Ibid., p. 26.

207. Ibid.

208. Lovins, "Nuclear."

209. Sweet, *Kicking*, p. 46.

Chapter 3

1. P. A. Rochon, J. H. Gurwitz, R. W. Simms, P. R. Fortin, D. T. Felson, K. L. Minaker, and T. C. Chalmers, "A Study of Manufacturer-Supported Trials of Nonsteroidal Anti-Inflammatory Drugs in the Treatment of Arthritis," *Archives of Internal Medicine* 154, no. 2 (1994): 157–163; E. G. Campbell, K. S. Louis, and M. D. Blumenthal, "Looking a Gift Horse in the Mouth," *Journal of the American Medical Association* 279, no. 13 (1998): 995–999; hereafter cited as Campbell et al., "Looking."

2. For NAS report, see chapter 1. World Coal Institute, *Coal* (Richmond, UK: WCI, 2009), p. 2. Ben Evans, Stephanie Pistello, and Jeff Biggers, "Coal-Free Future Begins in Kentucky," *Louisville Courier-Journal* (February 1, 2010), A7.

3. J. Porritt, Chair of the UK Sustainable Development Commission, quoted in House of Commons Trade and Industry Committee, *New Nuclear? Examining the Issues*, vol. 1 (London: House of Commons, Fourth Report of Session 2005–2006).

4. UK Sustainable Development Commission (UK SDC), *The Role of Nuclear Power in a Low-Carbon Economy* (London: UK SDC, 2006), pp. 1, 4, 17; hereafter cited as UK SDC, *The Role of Nuclear Power*. US Government Accountability Office, *Nuclear Material* (Washington, DC: US Government Printing Office, 2008), p. 3; hereafter cited as US GAO, *Nuclear Material*.

5. S. Thomas, *The Economics of Nuclear Power* (Berlin: Heinrich Böll 2005), pp. 5–6, 8, 19, 20, 26, 30; hereafter cited as Thomas, *Economics*, 2005.

6. European Atomic Forum, *Nuclear Energy* (Brussels: Foratom, 2006); accessed August 10, 2009, at www.foratom.org/index.php?option=com_content&task=view&id=219&Itemid=938.

7. A. M. Herbst and G. W. Hopley, *Nuclear Energy Now* (Hoboken, NJ: John Wiley, 2007), pp. 12, 26; hereafter cited as Herbst and Hopley, *Nuclear*, 2007.

8. Gwyneth Cravens, *Power to Save the World: The Truth about Nuclear Energy* (New York: Knopf, 2008), p. 365; hereafter cited as Cravens, *Power*, 2008.

9. Herbst and Hopley, *Nuclear*, p. 12.

10. Stewart Brand, "Environmental Heresies," *Technology Review* (May 2005); accessed February 18, 2010, at http://www.technologyreview.com/read_articles.aspx?id=14406&ch=biztech.

11. World Nuclear Association (WNA), *The Economics of Nuclear Power* (London: WNA, 2008); accessed September 9, 2009, at www.world-nuclear.org/info/inf02.html; hereafter cited as WNA, *Economics*.

12. McKinsey and Company, *Reducing US Greenhouse Gas Emissions* (New York: McKinsey and Company, 2007), p. 62; hereafter cited as McKinsey, *Reducing*.

13. F. L. Toth, "Prospects for Nuclear Power in the 21st Century," *International Journal of Global Energy Issues* 30, nos. 1–4 (2008): 6; hereafter cited as Toth, "Prospects"; Herbst and Hopley, *Nuclear*, pp. 5, 124; Cravens, *Power*, pp. xiv–v.

14. "Nuclear Dawn," *Economist* 384, no. 8545 (2007): 24–26; hereafter cited as "Nuclear Dawn"; Herbst and Hopley, *Nuclear*, p. 136.

15. Mike Morris, "The Next US Challenge," Address by CEO, American Electric Power, to Detroit Economic Club, June 23, 2008. *Vital Speeches of the Day* 74, no. 9 (2008): 420–422; hereafter cited as Morris, "Next"; see J. Peter Scoblic, "Nuclear Spring," *New Republic* 238, no. 7 (2008): 18; hereafter cited as Scoblic, "Nuclear."

16. Herbst and Hopley, *Nuclear*, pp. 12, 4–7, 36, 43–44, 179, 12.

17. Kristin Shrader-Frechette, "Greenhouse-Gas Emissions and Nuclear Energy," *Modern Energy Reviews* 1, no. 1 (2009): 58–62; Kristin Shrader-Frechette, "Data Trimming, Nuclear Emissions, and Climate Change," *Science and Engineering Ethics* 15, no. 1 (2009): 19–23; hereafter cited as Shrader-Frechette, "Data Trimming"; Benjamin K. Sovacool, "Valuing the Greenhouse Gas Emissions from Nuclear Power: A Critical Survey," *Energy Policy* 36, no. 2940 (2008): 53.

18. Thomas, *Economics*; WNA, *Economics*; World Nuclear Association (WNA), *The New Economics of Nuclear Power* (London: WNA, 2009); accessed October 12, 2009, at www.world-nuclear.org/reference/pdf/economics.pdf; hereafter cited as WNA, *New Economics* 2009; World Nuclear Association (WNA), *The New Economics of Nuclear Power* (London: WNA, 2005), p. 14; hereafter cited as WNA, *New Economics* 2005; Scully Capital Services Inc., *The Business Case for New Nuclear Power Plants: A Report Prepared for the US DOE* (Washington, DC: DOE, 2002); hereafter cited as Scully, *Business Case*; J. Du and J. E. Parsons, *Update on the Cost of Nuclear Power* (Cambridge: MIT Center for Energy and Environmental Policy Research, 2009); hereafter cited as Du and Parsons, *Update*; PB Power, *Powering the Nation* (Newcastle, UK: PB Power, 2006); hereafter cited as PB Power, *Powering*; Royal Academy of Engineering, *The Costs of Generating Electricity* (London: Royal Academy, 2004); hereafter cited as Royal Academy of Engineering, *Costs*;

UK Performance and Innovation Unit (PIU), *The Economics of Nuclear Power* (London: UK Cabinet Office, Performance and Innovation Unit, 2002); accessed January 19, 2009, at www.strategy.gov.uk/downloads/files/Pii.pdf; hereafter cited as UK PIU, *Economics*; Baker Institute for Public Policy, *Japanese Energy Security and Changing Global Energy Markets* (Houston: Rice University, 2000); hereafter cited as Baker Institute, *Japanese Energy*; D. Beutier, *EPR [European Pressurized Water Reactor] Background and Its Role in Continental Europe* (Paris: Areva, 2005); hereafter cited as Beutier, *EPR*; Canadian Energy Research Institute (CERI), *Levelised Unit Electricity Cost Comparison of Alternative Technologies for Baseload Generation in Ontario*, prepared for the Canadian Nuclear Association (Calgary: CERI, 2005); hereafter cited as CERI, *Levelised*; R. Tarjanne and K. Luostarinen, "Economics of Nuclear Power in Finland," in American Nuclear Society (ed.), *International Congress on Advanced Nuclear Power Plants* (Hollywood, FL: American Nuclear Society [ANS], 2002); hereafter cited as Tarjanne and Luostarinen, "Economics"; University of Chicago, *The Economic Future of Nuclear Power* (Chicago: University of Chicago, 2004); hereafter cited as U Chicago, *Economic Future* 2004; International Energy Agency (IAE) / Nuclear Energy Agency (NEA), *Projected Costs of Generating Electricity* (Paris: IEA, 2005); hereafter cited as IAE/NEA, *Projected Costs*; Direction Generale de L'Energie et des Matieres Premieres (DGEMP), *Reference Costs for Power Generation* (Paris: Ministry of the Economy, Finance, and Industry, 2003); hereafter cited as DGEMP, *Reference Costs*; OXERA, *Financing the Nuclear Option* (Oxford, UK: OXERA, 2005); accessed January 16, 2009, at www.oxera.com/cmsDocuments/Agenda_June%2005/ Financing%20the%20nuclear%20option.pdf; hereafter cited as OXERA, *Financing*; UK Department of Trade and Industry, *Nuclear Power Generation Cost-Benefit Analysis* (London: HM Government, 2006); hereafter cited as UK DTI, *Nuclear Power Generation*; S. D. Ansolabehere, J. Deutsch, M. Driscoll, P. E. Gray, J. P. Holdren, P. L. Joskow, R. K. Lester, E. J. Moniz, N. E. Todreas, and E. S. Beckjord, *The Future of Nuclear Power* (Cambridge: MIT Press, 2003); hereafter cited as Ansolabehere et al., *Future*; John Deutsch, Charles W. Forsberg, Andrew C. Kadak, Mujid S. Kazimi, Ernest J. Moniz, and John E. Parsons, *Update of the MIT 2003 Future of Nuclear Power* (Cambridge: MIT Energy Initiative, 2009), pp. 5–6; hereafter cited as Deutsch et al., *Update*; A. B. Lovins, I. Sheikh, and A. Markevich, *Nuclear Power* (Snowmass, CO: Rocky Mountain Institute, 2008); hereafter cited as Lovins, Sheikh, and Markevich, *Nuclear Power*; M. Mariotte, D. D'Arrigo, M. Olson, A. Binette, and D. Keesing, *False Promises* (Takoma Park, MD: Nuclear Information and Research Services, 2008); hereafter cited as Mariotte et al., *False Promises*; Arun Makhijani, *Carbon-Free and Nuclear-Free* (Takoma Park, MD: Institute for Energy and Environmental Research, 2007), pp. 144, 182–184, 188, 190, 192; hereafter cited as Makhijani, *Carbon-Free*; M. Diesendorf and P. Christoff, "*Economics* of Nuclear Power," *Energy Science* (November 2008); accessed October 1, 2009, at http://www.energyscience .org.au; hereafter cited as Diesendorf and Christoff, "Economics"; Brice Smith, *Insurmountable Risks* (Takoma Park: IEER Press, 2006), pp. 44–51, 68, 70, 194, 204, 414; hereafter cited as Smith, *Insurmountable*; Stephen Thomas, Peter Bradford, Antony Frogatt, and David Milborrow, *The Economics of Nuclear Power* (Amsterdam: Greenpeace International, 2007), pp. 6, 31; hereafter cited as Thomas et al., *Economics*; J. W. Van Leeuwen, *Nuclear Power* (The Netherlands: Ceedata Consultancy, 2007); hereafter cited as Van Leeuwen, *Nuclear*; P. Brown, *Voodoo Economics and the Doomed Nuclear Renaissance* (Cambridge: Wolfson College, Cambridge University; London: Friends of the Earth, 2008); hereafter cited as Brown, *Voodoo Economics*; International Atomic Energy Agency (IAEA), *Global Public Opinion on Nuclear Issues* (Vienna: IAEA, 2005); hereafter cited as IAEA, *Global Public Opinion*; University of Sussex and NERA Economic Consulting, *The Economics of Nuclear Power* (London: UK Sustainable Development Commission, 2006); hereafter cited as Sussex-NERA, *Economics*; T. Madsen, J. Neumann, and E. Rusch, *The High Cost of Nuclear Power* (Baltimore: Maryland Public Interest Research Group, 2009); hereafter cited as Madsen et al., *High Cost*.

19. WNA, *New Economics* 2005, p. 14.
20. Royal Academy of Engineering, *Costs*; CERI, Levelised; Tarjanne and Luostarinen, "Economics"; U Chicago, *Economic Future*; IAE/NEA, *Projected Costs*; DGEMP, *Reference Costs*; Ansolabehere et al., *Future*.
21. Scully, *Business Case*; Royal Academy of Engineering, *Costs*; Beutier, *EPR*; Tarjanne and Luostarinen, "Economics"; U Chicago, *Economic Future*; IAE/NEA, *Projected Costs*; OXERA, *Financing*; UK DTI, *Nuclear Power Generation*; Ansolabehere et al., *Future*.
22. Sussex-NERA, *Economics*.
23. Scully, *Business Case*; PB Power, *Powering*; Royal Academy of Engineering, *Costs*; UK PIU, *Economics*; Baker Institute, *Japanese Energy*; CERI 2004; Tarjanne and Luostarinen, "Economics"; U Chicago, *Economic Future*; IAE/NEA, *Projected Costs*; OXERA, *Financing*; UK DTI, *Nuclear Power Generation*; Ansolabehere et al., *Future*.
24. Thomas et al., *Economics*, pp. 6, 31.
25. European Commission (EC), *Solutions for Environment, Economy and Technology* (Brussels: EC, January 2003), p. 132; hereafter cited as EC, *Solutions*; World Nuclear Association (WNA), *Civil Liability for Nuclear Damages* (London: WNA, 2008); accessed May 13, 2009, at www.world-nuclear.org/info/inf67.html; hereafter cited as WNA, *Civil Liability*; A. Heyes, "Determining the Price of Price-Anderson," *Regulation* 25, nos. 4–8 (Winter 2002): 26–30; hereafter cited as Heyes, "Determining."
26. E.g., Scully, *Business Case*; Heyes, "Determining"; D. Spurgeon, "Nuclear Energy: We Must Increase Its Role in Our Future," address by US Assistant Secretary for Nuclear Energy at the Second Annual Global Nuclear-Renaissance Summit (Alexandria, Virginia), *Vital Speeches of the Day* 74, no. 9 (July 23, 2008): 422–425; hereafter cited as Spurgeon, "Nuclear Energy"; T. Slocum, "Nuclear's Power Play: Give Us Subsidies or Give Us Death," *Multinational Monitor* 29, no. 2 (September–October 2008); accessed May 19, 2009, at www.multinationalmonitor.org/mm2008/092008/slocum.html; hereafter cited as Slocum, "Nuclear's Power Play"; American Nuclear Society, *The Price-Anderson Act* (La Grange Park, IL: ANS, November 2005); hereafter cited as ANS, *Price-Anderson*; G. S. Rothwell, *Does the US Subsidize Nuclear Power Insurance?* (Palo Alto: Stanford Institute for Economic Policy Research, January 2002); hereafter cited as Rothwell, *Does the US Subsidize*; Energy Information Administration (EIA), *Federal Financial Interventions and Subsidies in Energy Markets* (Washington, DC: Department of Energy, EIA, 1999); hereafter cited as EIA, *Federal*; B. P. Brownstein, *The Price-Anderson Act*, Cato Policy Analysis No. 36 (Washington, DC: Cato Institute, April 17, 1984), pp. 39–45; hereafter cited as Brownstein, *Price-Anderson*.
27. Makhijani, *Carbon-Free*; Smith, *Insurmountable*; Kristin Shrader-Frechette, *Taking Action, Saving Lives* (New York: Oxford University Press, 2007), pp. 42, 51, 95–97; hereafter cited as Shrader-Frechette, *Taking Action*.
28. Smith, *Insurmountable*, 194; Jim Riccio, *Risky Business* (Washington, DC: Greenpeace, 2001); accessed November 1, 2008, at www.greenpeace.org/raw/content/usa/press/reports/risky-business-the-probability.pdf.
29. E.g., Spurgeon, "Nuclear Energy," p. 423; Slocum, "Nuclear's Power Play"; ANS, *Price-Anderson*; Heyes, "Determining," p. 28; Scully, *Business Case*; Rothwell, *Does the US Subsidize*; EIA, *Federal*; Steve Cohn, *Too Cheap to Meter* (Albany: SUNY Press, 1997), p. 80, hereafter cited as Cohn, *Too Cheap*; Brownstein, *Price-Anderson*.
30. Smith, *Insurmountable*; Shrader-Frechette, *Taking Action*.
31. WNA, *Civil Liability*; J. Schwartz, "International Nuclear-Third-Party Liability Law," in Organization for Economic Cooperation and Development (OECD), Nuclear Energy Agency (NEA), and International Atomic Energy Agency, *International Nuclear Law in the Post-Chernobyl Period* (Paris: NEA, 2006), pp. 37–72.
32. EIA, *Federal*.
33. Deutsch et al., *Update* ; Ansolabehere et al., *Future*.
34. WNA, *Economics*; WNA, *New Economics* 2005.

35. International Energy Agency (IEA), *World Energy Outlook 2005* (Paris: IEA, 2005); hereafter cited as IEA, *World Energy Outlook 2005*.
36. Baker Institute, *Japanese Energy.*
37. Tarjanne and Luostarinen, "Economics."
38. UK PIU, *Economics.*
39. Royal Academy of Engineering, *Costs*; PB Power, *Powering.*
40. Scully, *Business Case.*
41. OXERA, *Financing.*
42. E.g., Cravens, *Power*; Herbst and Hopley, *Nuclear.*
43. E.g., Ronald H. Coase, "Adam Smith's View of Man," *Journal of Law and Economics* 19, no. 529 (1976): 46; Viktor Vanberg, "Spontaneous Market Order and Social Rules," *Economics and Philosophy* 2, no. 75 (1986): 100.
44. Rothwell, *Does the US Subsidize.*
45. ANS, *Price-Anderson*; American Enterprise Institute for Public Policy Research (AEI), *Renewal of the Price-Anderson Act* (Washington, DC: AEI, 1985), pp. 14–15.
46. Andrew Kimbrell, Joseph Mendelson, and M. Briscoe, *The Real Price of Gasoline* (Washington, DC: International Center for Technology Assessment, 1998).
47. See David Pearce, "Environmentally Harmful Subsidies," in Organization for Economic Cooperation and Development (OECD), *Environmentally Harmful Subsidies* (Paris: OECD, 2003), pp. 9–30.
48. See Brownstein, *Price-Anderson.*
49. *US Code of Federal Regulations* (CFR), *Energy*, title 10, part 140 (Washington, DC: US Government Printing Office, 2009).
50. E.g., Spurgeon, "Nuclear Energy," p. 423; Slocum, "Nuclear's Power Play"; ANS, *Price-Anderson*; Heyes, "Determining," p. 28; Rothwell, *Does the US Subsidize*; Scully, *Business Case*; EIA, *Federal*; Cohn, *Too Cheap*, p. 80; Brownstein, *Price-Anderson.* See Kristin Shrader-Frechette, *Nuclear Power and Public Policy* (Boston: Kluwer, 1983), pp. 10–11.
51. E.g., UK Department of Trade and Industry (UK DTI), *Meeting the Energy Challenge* (London: UK DTI, 2007), p. 191; accessed January 19, 2009, at commodities-now.com/content/research/includes/assets/UKWPenergy.pdf; hereafter cited as UK DTI, *Meeting.*
52. Quoted in Heyes, "Determining," p. 28.
53. American Public Health Association (APHA): e.g., APHA, *Reducing Occupational Exposure to Benzene in Workers and Their Offspring*, Policy 2005–6 (Washington, DC: APHA, 2005); APHA, *Preserving Right-to-Know Information and Encouraging Hazard Reduction to Reduce the Risk of Exposure to Toxic Substances*, Policy 2002–5 (Washington, DC: APHA, 2002); APHA, *Trade Agreements and Environmental and Occupational Health Policy*, Policy 9404 (Washington, DC: APHA, 1994); APHA, *Toxic Reduction as a Means of Pollution Prevention*, Policy 9206 (Washington, DC: APHA, 1992); APHA, *Strengthening Worker/ Community Right-to-Know*, Policy 8714 (Washington, DC: APHA, 1987).
54. EC, *Solutions*, p. 132.
55. WNA, *Civil Liability.*
56. Heyes, "Determining," p. 29.
57. Brownstein, *Price-Anderson.*
58. Heyes, "Determining," p. 29.
59. Brownstein, *Price-Anderson.*
60. Makhijani, *Carbon-Free*, p. 192; Smith, *Insurmountable*, p. 230; Matthew Wald, "Interest in Building Reactors, but Industry Is Still Cautious," *New York Times* (April 2, 2005); Nature Editorial, "Nuclear Test: Japan's Response to an Earthquake Highlights Both the Promise and the Pitfalls of Nuclear Power at a Critical Time for Its Future," *Nature* 448, no. 7152 (2007): 387.
61. Heyes, "Determining"; UK DTI, *Meeting.*
62. Brownstein, *Price-Anderson.*
63. Morris, "Next."

64. WNA, *New Economics* 2005, pp. 5, 20; 14, 17–18. Most nuclear economists' failure to include the cost of capital (interest for the reactor-construction loan for a period of 8–30 years), and their instead using a 0 interest rate, or "overnight costs," obviously has the effect of artificially lowering nuclear costs. The need for accurate nuclear-cost information, and for using actual interest rates, should not be confused with arguments about discounting far-distant costs, as related to climate change. In the case of climate-related discounting, the interest rates are largely arbitrary, not real costs, as is the case of those for nuclear construction.

65. Du and Parsons, *Update*, p. 11.

66. Ibid., pp. 5–6.

67. Ibid., esp. pp. 11, 5–6.

68. Morris, "Next"; see Scoblic, "Nuclear," p. 18.

69. "Nuclear Dawn."

70. Thomas, *Economics*, p. 19.

71. International Energy Agency (IEA), *World Energy Outlook* (Paris: IEA, 2006); Antony Froggatt, *Financing Disaster—How the G8 Fund the Global Proliferation of Nuclear Technology* (London: The Royal Institute of International Affairs, June 2001); accessed January 14, 2009, at www.eca-watch.org/problems/fora/documents/G8_eca-nuclear-2001.pdf.

72. Slocum, "Nuclear's Power Play."

73. Makhijani, *Carbon-Free*, pp. 144, 190; see Smith, *Insurmountable*, pp. 51, 97; John Kennedy, Andreas Zsiga, Laurie Conheady, and Paul Lund, "Credit Aspects of North American and European Nuclear Power," *Standard & Poor's* (January 9, 2006), hereafter cited as Kennedy et al., "Credit."

74. Moody's Corporate Finance, *New Nuclear Generating Capacity* (New York: Moody's, 2008); hereafter cited as Moody's, *New Nuclear*.

75. Herbst and Hopley, *Nuclear*, p. 103.

76. Ansolabehere et al., *Future*.

77. Cravens, *Power*, p. 321.

78. Thomas, *Economics*, p. 19.

79. Deutsch et al., *Update* ; Ansolabehere et al., *Future*.

80. U Chicago, *Economic Future*.

81. WNA, *New Economics* 2005, p. 17.

82. Herbst and Hopley, *Nuclear*, pp. 1 7, 36, 179.

83. R. S. Berry, "Tomorrow's Nuclear Power Will Be Different Than Yesterday's Nuclear Power," *Bulletin of the Atomic Scientists*, Roundtable on Nuclear Power and Climate Change (2007); accessed November 9, 2008 at www.thebulletin.org/roundtable/nuclear-power-climate-change/; hereafter cited as Berry, "Tomorrow's Nuclear Power."

84. WNA, *Economics*.

85. Baker Institute, *Japanese Energy*.

86. Scully, *Business Case*.

87. OXERA, *Financing*.

88. Herbst and Hopley, *Nuclear*, p. 46.

89. WNA, *New Economics* 2005, p. 21.

90. WNA, *Economics*.

91. E.g., Herbst and Hopley, *Nuclear*, p. 171; UK SDC, *The Role of Nuclear Power*; Thomas, *Economics*, p. 16.

92. IEA, *World Energy Outlook 2005*; see Thomas et al., *Economics*, p. 35.

93. UK PIU, *Economics*.

94. WNA, *Economics*; Matthew L. Wald, "After 35-Year Lull, Nuclear Power May Be in Early Stages of a Revival," *New York Times* (October 24, 2008), sec. B3.

95. William Sweet, *Kicking the Carbon Habit* (New York: Columbia University Press, 2006), p. 188, hereafter cited as Sweet, *Kicking*; Thomas, *Economics*.

96. Alexandro Clerici and the European Regional Study Group, *The Future Role of Nuclear Energy in Europe* (London: World Energy Council, 2006).

97. Olaf Bayer and C. Grimshaw, *Broken Promises* (Oxford, UK: Corporate Watch, 2007), p. 5.
98. Thomas, *Economics*, p. 8.
99. Scully, *Business Case.*
100. Thomas, *Economics*, p. 26.
101. Slocum, "Nuclear's Power Play."
102. See Smith, *Insurmountable*, p. 414.
103. Thomas, *Economics.*
104. Herbst and Hopley, *Nuclear*, p. 102.
105. Gordon MacKerron, "The Economics of Nuclear Power—Has Government Got It Right?," *Sussex Energy Group Policybriefing* 1, nos. 1–4 (2007): 2; hereafter cited as MacKerron, "Economics"; WNA, *New Economics* 2005, p. 19.
106. WNA, *New Economics* 2005, p. 14.
107. Thomas, *Economics*, p. 30.
108. Herbst and Hopley, *Nuclear*, p. 183.
109. Smith, *Insurmountable*, p. 47.
110. McKinsey, *Reducing*, p. 27.
111. Peter Bunyard, "Ecologist: Taking the Wind out of Nuclear Power," *Pacific Ecologist* 11, no. 51 (2006): 7; hereafter cited as Bunyard, "Ecologist."
112. Peter Bradford, "Follow the Money," *Bulletin of the Atomic Scientists,* Roundtable on Nuclear Power and Climate Change (2007); accessed November 9, 2009, at www.thebulletin.org/roundtable/nuclear-power-climate-change/.
113. Herbst and Hopley, *Nuclear*, pp. 43–44.
114. House of Commons Energy Select Committee, *Fourth Report: The Costs of Nuclear Power* (London: UK House of Commons, 1990).
115. International Atomic Energy Agency (IAEA), *PRIS Database* (Vienna: IAEA, 2007); accessed January 15, 2009, at www.iaea.org/programmes/a2/index.html; hereafter cited as IAEA, *PRIS Database.*
116. Peter Stoett, "Toward Renewed Legitimacy: Nuclear Power, Global Warming and Security," *Global Environmental Politics* 3, no. 1 (2003): 108.
117. International Energy Agency (IEA), *Nuclear Power in the OECD* (Paris: IEA, Organization for Economic Cooperation and Development, 2001).
118. Bunyard, "Ecologist."
119. Makhijani, *Carbon-Free*, p. 30; American Wind Energy Association (AWEA), *Congress Extends Wind Energy Production Tax Credit for an Additional Year* (Washington DC: AWEA, 2006); accessed March 5, 2010, at www.awea.org/newsroom/releases/congress_extends_PTC_121106.html.
120. Smith, *Insurmountable*, p. 50; Kennedy et al., "Credit."
121. Mariotte et al., *False Promises.*
122. WNA, *New Economics* 2005, p. 17.
123. Baker Institute, *Japanese Energy.*
124. Tarjanne and Luostarinen, "Economics."
125. UK PIU, *Economics.*
126. OXERA, *Financing.*
127. Deutsch et al., *Update*; Ansolabehere et al., *Future*; see Herbst and Hopley, *Nuclear*, p. 149; Brice Smith, "Insurmountable Risks," *Science for Democratic Action* 36, nos. 1–2 (2006): 7.
128. Scully, *Business Case.*
129. Royal Academy of Engineering, *Costs*; PB Power, *Powering.*
130. IEA, *World Energy Outlook 2005.*
131. U Chicago, *Economic Future.*
132. Herbst and Hopley, *Nuclear*, p. 149.
133. Cravens, *Power*, p. xiv.
134. E.g., Herbst and Hopley, *Nuclear*, p. 171; UK SDC, *The Role of Nuclear Power*; Thomas, *Economics*, p. 16.

135. Thomas, *Economics*, p. 5.
136. IAEA, *PRIS Database*; Thomas, *Economics*, p. 6.
137. Cravens, *Power*, p. 286.
138. S. Pacala and R. Socolow, "Stabilization Wedges: Solving the Climate Problem for the Next 50 Years with Current Technologies," *Science* 305, no. 5686 (13 August 2004): 968–972; hereafter cited as Pacala and Socolow, "Stabilization Wedges." The 9 renewable options (only 6 needed to solve climate problems) are efficient vehicles, reduced vehicle use, efficient buildings wind power for coal power, PV power for coal power, wind for gasoline in fuel-cell cars, biomass fuel for fossil fuel, reduced deforestation, and conservation tillage. National Renewable Energy Laboratory, *Near Term Practical and Ultimate Technical Potential for Renewable Resources* (Golden, CO: US DOE, 2006); hereafter cited as NREL, *Near Term*.
139. Thomas et al., *Economics*, p. 6.
140. Sweet, *Kicking*, p. 154.
141. Energy Information Administration, *Electric Power Annual* (Washington, DC: Department of Energy, 2009); accessed July 1, 2009, at www.eia.doe.gov/cneaf/electricity/epa/epa_sum.html; hereafter cited as EIA, *Electric Power*.
142. WNA, *New Economics* 2005, pp. 21, 10.
143. Du and Parsons, *Update*, p. 18.
144. Sweet, *Kicking*, p. 182.
145. Mariotte et al., *False Promises*.
146. Herbst and Hopley, *Nuclear*, p. 176.
147. Ibid., p. 174.
148. Christian Parenti, "What Nuclear Renaissance?," *Nation* 286, no. 18 (May 12, 2008): 14; Smith, *Insurmountable*, p. 193; General Accounting Office (GAO), *Nuclear Regulation: NRC Needs to More Aggressively and Comprehensively Resolve Issues Related to the Davis-Besse Nuclear Power Plant's Shutdown* (Washington, DC: GAO, 2004), p. 20.
149. Sweet, *Kicking*, p. 186.
150. Bunyard, "Ecologist"; Herbst and Hopley, *Nuclear*, p. 172.
151. US GAO, *Nuclear and Worker Safety* (Washington, DC: US GPO, 2007), p. 4; hereafter cited as US GAO, *NWS*.
152. V. M. Fthenakis and H. C. Kim, "Greenhouse-Gas Emissions from Solar-Electric and Nuclear Power: A Life-Cycle Study," *Energy Policy* 35, no. 4 (2007): 2549–2557.
153. IAEA, *PRIS Database*.
154. See Thomas et al., *Economics*, p. 31.
155. Thomas, *Economics*.
156. IAEA, *PRIS Database*; see Toth, "Prospects," p. 6; Herbst and Hopley, *Nuclear*, p. 176.
157. IAEA, *PRIS Database*; see Thomas, *Economics*, pp. 5–6.
158. WNA, *New Economics* 2005, p. 17.
159. Westinghouse, *Westinghouse AP1000 Advanced Passive Reactor* (Pittsburgh: Westinghouse, 2003); accessed January 19, 2009, at www.nuclearinfo.net/twiki/pub/Nuclearpower/WebHomeCostOfNuclearPower/AP1000Reactor.pdf.
160. *Nucleonics Week* Editors, "Merrill Lynch Global Power and Gas Leaders Conference," *Nucleonics Week* 47, no. 40 (2006): 4.
161. World Nuclear Association, *Nuclear Power in France* (London: WNA, 2008); accessed January 21, 2009, at www.world-nuclear.org/info/inf40.html; hereafter cited as WNA, *Nuclear Power in France*.
162. Thomas, *Economics*, pp. 8, 20.
163. Tarjanne and Luostarinen, "Economics."
164. OXERA, *Financing*.
165. WNA, *New Economics* 2005, p. 10.
166. Scully, *Business Case*.
167. Royal Academy of Engineering, *Costs*; PB Power, *Powering*.
168. CERI 2004.

169. WNA, *Economics*.
170. UK PIU, *Economics*.
171. Deutsch et al., *Update*; Ansolabehere et al., *Future*.
172. U Chicago, *Economic Future*.
173. IEA, *World Energy Outlook 2005*.
174. UK DTI, *Nuclear Power Generation*.
175. See Mariotte et al., *False Promises*.
176. Deutsch et al., *Update*; Ansolabehere et al., *Future*.
177. Smith, *Insurmountable*, p. 68.
178. Moody's, *New Nuclear*; see Arun Makhijani, "Nuclear Power Costs: High and Higher," *Science for Democratic Action* 15, no. 2 (2008): 2–3; hereafter cited as Makhijani, "Nuclear Power Costs"; Keystone Center, *Nuclear Power Joint Fact-Finding* (Keystone, CO: Keystone Center, 2007); hereafter cited as Keystone, *Nuclear Power*.
179. Cravens, *Power*, p. 253; Smith, *Insurmountable*, p. 70; J. Aabakken, *Power Technologies Energy Data Book* (Golden, CO: US DOE, National Renewable Energies Lab, 2005), pp. 37–39; hereafter cited as Aabakken, *Power Technologies*.
180. Smith, *Insurmountable*.
181. WNA, *New Economics* 2005, p. 7; Herbst and Hopley, *Nuclear*, p. 169.
182. Mycle Schneider, "2008 World Nuclear Industry Status Report," *Bulletin of the Atomic Scientists* (September 16, 2008); accessed May 20, 2009, at www.thebulletin.org/web-edition/reports/2008-world-nuclear-industry-status-report/.
183. Herbst and Hopley, *Nuclear*.
184. WNA, *Economics*, pp. 21, 10.
185. E.g., IAEA, *PRIS Database*.
186. Tarjanne and Luostarinen, "Economics."
187. WNA, *Economics*.
188. Scully, *Business Case*.
189. Royal Academy of Engineering, *Costs*; PB Power, *Powering*.
190. U Chicago, *Economic Future*.
191. IEA, *World Energy Outlook 2005*.
192. OXERA, *Financing*.
193. UK DTI, *Nuclear Power Generation*.
194. Deutsch et al., *Update*; Ansolabehere et al., *Future*.
195. David Fleming, *The Lean Guide to Nuclear Energy* (London: University of London, 2007), p. 7; hereafter cited as Fleming, *Lean Guide*.
196. Deutsch et al., *Update*; Ansolabehere et al., *Future*.
197. Herbst and Hopley, *Nuclear*, pp. 43–44.
198. Moody's, *New Nuclear*.
199. Lovins, Sheikh, and Markevich, *Nuclear Power*.
200. Deutsch et al., *Update*.
201. Daryl Chubin and Edward Hackett, *Peerless Science* (Albany: SUNY Press, 1990), p. 132.
202. E.g., John C. Reinard, *Communication Research Statistics* (London: SAGE, 2006), p. 54; hereafter cited as Reinard, *Communication*.
203. David Sheskin, *Handbook of Parametric and Nonparametric Statistical Procedures* (Boca Raton, FL: CRC Press, 2004), p. 403; hereafter cited as Sheskin, *Handbook*.
204. E.g., M. Wu and Y. Zuo, "Trimmed and Winsorized Means Based on a Scaled Deviation," *Journal of Statistical Planning and Inference* 139, no. 2 (2009): 350–365; M. Wu and Y. Zuo, "Trimmed and Winsorized Standard Deviations Based on a Scaled Deviation," *Journal of Nonparametric Statistics* 20, no. 4 (2008): 319–335; J. A. Cuesta-Albertos, C. Matran, and A. Mayo-Iscar, "Trimming and Likelihood," *Annals of Statistics* 36, no. 5 (2008): 2284–2318; L. A. Garcia-Escudero, A. Gordaliza, A. Mayo-Iscar, and C. Matran, "A General Trimming Approach to Robust Clustering," *Annals of Statistics* 36, no. 3 (2008): 1324–1345;

J. Karvanen, "Estimation of Quantile Mixtures via L-moments and Trimmed L-moments," *Computational Statistics and Data Analysis* 51, no. 2 (2006): 947–959; Z. Leonowicz, J. Karvanen, and S. L. Shiskin, "Trimmed Estimators for Robust Averaging," *Journal of Neuroscience Methods* 142, no. 1 (2005): 17–26.

205. Norman H. Anderson, *Empirical Direction in Design and Analysis* (Mahwah, NJ: Erlbaum, 2001), p. 355; hereafter cited as Anderson, *Empirical*.

206. E.g., Sheskin, *Handbook*, p. 403.

207. Anderson, *Empirical*, pp. 354–356.

208. E.g., Gerald Miller and M. Whicker, *Handbook of Research Methods in Public Administration* (Boca Raton, FL: CRC Press, 1998).

209. E.g., Claes Fornell, Sunil Mithas, and F. Morgeson, "The Statistical Significance of Portfolio Returns," *International Journal of Research in Marketing* 26, no. 2 (2009): 162–163.

210. Sheskin, *Handbook*, p. 403; see R. R. Wilcox, *Applying Contemporary Statistical Techniques* (San Diego: Academic Press, 2003); hereafter cited as Wilcox, *Applying*.

211. Reinard, *Communication*; Sheskin, *Handbook*; S. P. Kothari, Jowell Sabino, and Tzachi Zach, "Implications of Survival and Data-Trimming for Tests of Market Efficiency," *Journal of Accounting and Economics* 39, no. 1 (2004): 129–161; Wilcox, *Applying*; Anderson, *Empirical*, pp. 352–356.

212. Anderson, *Empirical*, p. 356.

213. Ibid., p. 353; Reinard, *Communication*, p. 54.

214. Reinard, *Communication*, p. 54; Anderson, *Empirical*, pp. 353–356; Sheskin, *Handbook*, pp. 403–404.

215. Anderson, *Empirical*, pp. 353–356; Sheskin, *Handbook*, p. 403.

216. Sheskin, *Handbook*, p. 403.

217. Ansolabehere et al., *Future*; Deutsch et al., *Update*.

218. Ansolabehere et al., *Future*, p. 82.

219. IEA, *World Energy Outlook 2005*; UK PIU, *Economics*; see Thomas et al., *Economics*, p. 35.

220. Deutsch et al., *Update*; Ansolabehere et al., *Future*.

221. Deutsch et al., *Update*; Ansolabehere et al., *Future*.

222. Ansolabehere et al., *Future*.

223. E.g., Thomas, *Economics*; Lovins, Sheikh, and Markevich, *Nuclear Power*; Mariotte et al., *False Promises*; Makhijani, *Carbon-Free*; Diesendorf and Christoff, "Economics"; Thomas et al., *Economics*; Van Leeuwen, *Nuclear*; Sussex-NERA, *Economics*.

224. Diesendorf and Christoff, "Economics," p. 2.

225. Ibid.

226. Thomas, *Economics*; Lovins, Sheikh, and Markevich, *Nuclear Power*; Mariotte et al., *False Promises*; Makhijani, *Carbon-Free*; Diesendorf and Christoff, "Economics"; Thomas et al., *Economics*; Van Leeuwen, *Nuclear*; Sussex-NERA, *Economics*.

227. Campbell et al., "Looking"; Diesendorf and Christoff, "Economics."

228. Makhijani, *Carbon-Free*, p. 169. As already noted, most nuclear economists' failure to include the cost of capital (interest for the reactor-construction loan for a period of 8–30 years), and their instead using a 0 interest rate, or "overnight costs," obviously has the effect of artificially lowering nuclear costs. The need for accurate nuclear-cost information, and for using actual interest rates, should not be confused with arguments about discounting far-distant costs, as related to climate change. In the case of climate-related discounting, the interest rates are largely arbitrary, not real costs, as is the case of those for nuclear construction.

229. Van Leeuwen, *Nuclear*, pp. 32, 37, 32, 43, 54.

230. Fleming, *Lean Guide*, pp. 16–19.

231. Morris, "Next," p. 136.

232. MacKerron, "Economics."

233. US Congressional Budget Office (US CBO), *Nuclear Power's Role in Generating Electricity* (Washington, DC: US CBO, 2008), p. 17.

234. Mariotte et al., *False Promises*; Lovins, Sheikh, and Markevich, *Nuclear Power*; Thomas et al., *Economics*; *Nucleonics Week* Editors, "Olkiluoto-3 Costs Weigh on Areva 2008 Profits," *Nucleonics Week* (December 25, 2008): 9.
235. Julio Godoy, *ENERGY: Nuclear Does Not Make Economic Sense Say Studies* (Berlin: International Press Service, February 21, 2010); accessed March 18, 2010, at www.ipsnews. net/news.asp?idnews=50308&utm_source=twitterfeed&utm_medium=twitter).
236. Teresa Weinmeister, *New Plants Update* (Bethesda, MD: AREVA NP Inc., September 2009); accessed March 18, 2010, at www.areva-np.com/common/liblocal/docs/presentation_ statut*EPR*/New_Plants_Update_2009.pdf).
237. Du and Parsons, *Update*, pp. 5–6, 14.
238. E.g., Scully, *Business Case*; U Chicago, *Economic Future*; IAE/NEA, *Projected Costs*.
239. Tarjanne and Luostarinen, "Economics."
240. UK SDC, *The Role of Nuclear Power*, p. 19.
241. UK DTI, *Nuclear Power Generation*.
242. UK SDC, *The Role of Nuclear Power*, pp. 11–12.
243. Diesendorf and Christoff, "Economics," pp. 2–3.
244. UK SDC, *The Role of Nuclear Power*, p. 4.
245. WNA, *New Economics* 2009; WNA, *Civil Liability*; WNA, *New Economics* 2005; Scully, *Business Case*; Du and Parsons, *Update*; PB Power, *Powering*; Royal Academy of Engineering, *Costs*; UK Department for Business Enterprise and Regulatory Reform Meeting the Energy Challenge: A White Paper on Nuclear Power (London: Her Majesty's Stationery Office, 2008; hereafter cited as UK 2008;{ Baker Institute, *Japanese Energy*; Beutier, *EPR*; CERI 2004; Tarjanne and Luostarinen, "Economics"; U Chicago, *Economic Future*; IAE/NEA, *Projected Costs*; DGEMP, *Reference Costs*; UK DTI, *Nuclear Power Generation*; Ansolabehere et al., *Future*; Deutsch et al., *Update*; IAEA, *Global Public Opinion*.
246. WNA, *New Economics* 2009; WNA, *Civil Liability*; WNA, *New Economics* 2005; PB Power, *Powering*; Royal Academy of Engineering, *Costs*; Beutier, *EPR*; CERI 2004; IAE/NEA, *Projected Costs*; IAEA, *Global Public Opinion*.
247. Du and Parsons, *Update*; Baker Institute, *Japanese Energy*; Tarjanne and Luostarinen, "Economics"; Ansolabehere et al., *Future*; Deutsch et al., *Update*.
248. Scully, *Business Case*; UK PIU, *Economics*; U Chicago, *Economic Future*; UK DTI, *Nuclear Power Generation*; Ansolabehere et al., *Future*; Deutsch et al., *Update*.
249. Du and Parsons, *Update*, pp. 5, 10.
250. Ibid., p. 14.
251. E.g., Du and Parsons, *Update*; Tarjanne and Luostarinen, "Economics."
252. Thomas, *Economics*, p. 25.
253. UK PIU, *Economics*.
254. Thomas, *Economics*, p. 26.
255. UK PIU, *Economics*.
256. UK SDC, *The Role of Nuclear Power*, p. 110.
257. Royal Academy of Engineering, *Costs*.
258. PB Power, *Powering*.
259. Thomas, *Economics*, p. 27.
260. Tarjanne and Luostarinen, "Economics."
261. Du and Parsons, *Update*, p. 9.
262. UK SDC, *The Role of Nuclear Power*, pp. 11–12, 19.
263. Tarjanne and Luostarinen, "Economics."
264. Royal Academy of Engineering, *Costs*; PB Power, *Powering*.
265. Bernard Lo, M. J. Field, and the Institute of Medicine, *Conflict of Interest* (Washington, DC: National Academy Press, 2009), p. 6; hereafter cited as Lo et al., *Conflict of Interest*.
266. WNA, *New Economics* 2009; WNA, *Civil Liability*; WNA, *New Economics* 2005; Scully, *Business Case*; Du and Parsons, *Update*; PB Power, *Powering*; Royal Academy of Engineering, *Costs*; UK 2008; Baker Institute, *Japanese Energy*; Beutier, *EPR*; CERI 2004; Tarjanne and

Luostarinen, "Economics"; U Chicago, *Economic Future*; IAE/NEA, *Projected Costs*; DGEMP, *Reference Costs*; UK DTI, *Nuclear Power Generation*; Ansolabehere et al., *Future*; Deutsch et al., *Update*; IAEA, *Global Public Opinion*.

267. WNA, *New Economics* 2009; WNA, *Civil Liability*; WNA, *New Economics* 2005; Scully, *Business Case*; Du and Parsons, *Update*; PB Power, *Powering*; Royal Academy of Engineering, *Costs*; UK 2008; Baker Institute, *Japanese Energy*; Beutier, *EPR*; CERI 2004; Tarjanne and Luostarinen, "Economics"; U Chicago, *Economic Future*; IAE/NEA, *Projected Costs*; DGEMP, *Reference Costs*; UK DTI, *Nuclear Power Generation*; Ansolabehere et al., *Future*; Deutsch et al., *Update*; IAEA, *Global Public Opinion*.

268. OXERA, *Financing*.

269. Lovins, Sheikh, and Markevich, *Nuclear Power*; Mariotte et al., *False Promises*; Makhijani, *Carbon-Free*; Madsen et al., *High Cost*.

270. Thomas, *Economics*; Diesendorf and Christoff, "Economics"; Smith, *Insurmountable*; Thomas et al., *Economics*; Van Leeuwen, *Nuclear*; Brown, *Voodoo Economics*; Sussex-NERA, *Economics*.

271. WNA, *New Economics* 2009; WNA, *Civil Liability*; WNA, *New Economics* 2005; Scully, *Business Case*; Du and Parsons, *Update*; PB Power, *Powering*; Royal Academy of Engineering, *Costs*; UK 2008; Baker Institute, *Japanese Energy*; Beutier, *EPR*; CERI 2004; Tarjanne and Luostarinen, "Economics"; U Chicago, *Economic Future*; IAE/NEA, *Projected Costs*; DGEMP, *Reference Costs*; UK DTI, *Nuclear Power Generation*; Ansolabehere et al., *Future*; Deutsch et al., *Update*; IAEA, *Global Public Opinion*.

272. Scully, *Business Case*; Royal Academy of Engineering, *Costs*; Beutier, *EPR*; Tarjanne and Luostarinen, "Economics"; U Chicago, *Economic Future*; IAE/NEA, *Projected Costs*; OXERA, *Financing*; UK DTI, *Nuclear Power Generation*; Ansolabehere et al., *Future*.

273. UK SDC, *The Role of Nuclear Power*.

274. Royal Academy of Engineering, *Costs*; CERI 2004; Tarjanne and Luostarinen, "Economics"; U Chicago, *Economic Future*; IAE/NEA, *Projected Costs*; DGEMP, *Reference Costs*; Ansolabehere et al., *Future*.

275. Thomas et al., *Economics*.

276. Scully, *Business Case*; PB Power, *Powering*; Royal Academy of Engineering, *Costs*; UK PIU, *Economics*; Baker Institute, *Japanese Energy*; CERI 2004; Tarjanne and Luostarinen, "Economics"; U Chicago, *Economic Future*, IAE/NEA, *Projected Costs*; OXERA, *Financing*; UK DTI, *Nuclear Power Generation*; Ansolabehere et al., *Future*.

277. Du and Parsons, *Update*.

278. Ibid., p. v.

279. Ibid., pp. 11, 10, 14, 15, iii.

280. Ibid., p. 9.

281. Kristin Shrader-Frechette, *Environmental Justice* (New York: Oxford University Press, 2002), p. 131; hereafter cited as Shrader-Frechette, *Environmental Justice*.

282. Du and Parsons, *Update*, p. 21.

283. Shrader-Frechette, *Environmental Justice*.

284. Ibid.; US Congress, *Worker Safety at DOE Nuclear Facilities*, US House of Representatives (Washington, DC: US Government Printing Office, 1999); hereafter cited as US Congress, *Worker Safety*.

285. US National Research Council, *Building an Effective Environmental Management Science Program* (Washington, DC: National Academy Press, 1996).

286. Shrader-Frechette, *Environmental Justice*; US Congress, *Worker Safety*.

287. Du and Parsons, *Update*.

288. Lovins, Sheikh, and Markevich, *Nuclear Power*.

289. Madsen et al., *High Cost*, p. 17.

290. Du and Parsons, *Update*, pp. 4–6, 18, 16, 19, 22.

291. Ibid., p. iii; Mariotte et al., *False Promises*; Moody's, *New Nuclear*.

292. Moody's Corporate Finance, *New Nuclear Generation: Ratings Pressure Increasing*, Report 117883 (New York: Moody's, June 2009).
293. Ansolabehere et al., *Future*.
294. Ibid., p. vii.
295. MIT Laboratory for Energy and the Environment (LEE), *MIT Reports to the President 2001–2002* (Cambridge: MIT LEE, 2003); accessed October 12, 2009, at http://web.mit.edu/annualreports/pres02/03.03.html.
296. Ansolabehere et al., *Future*, pp. 43, 8, 82.
297. OXERA, *Financing*.
298. Ibid., pp. 4, 2, 5.
299. Ibid., p. 3.
300. Ibid.
301. Du and Parsons, *Update*.
302. OXERA, *Financing*, pp. 2–4.
303. Lovins, Sheikh, and Markevich, *Nuclear Power*; Mariotte et al., *False Promises*; Makhijani, *Carbon-Free*; Madsen et al., *High Cost*.
304. Lovins, Sheikh, and Markevich, *Nuclear Power*.
305. Rocky Mountain Institute (RMI), *Helping Businesses/Organizations* (Snowmass, CO: RMI, 2009); accessed October 12, 2009, at www.rmi.org.
306. Mariotte et al., *False Promises*.
307. Nuclear Information and Resource Service (NIRS), *About NIRS* (Takoma Park, MD: NIRS, 2009); accessed October 12, 2009, at www.nirs.orgn/about/nirs.htm.
308. Makhijani, *Carbon-Free*.
309. Institute for Energy and Environmental Research (IEER), *Funders* (Takoma Park, MD: IEER, 2009); accessed October 12, 2009, at www.ieer.org/ieerinfo.html ww.ieer.org/ieerinfo.html.
310. Madsen et al., *High Cost*.
311. Lovins, Sheikh, and Markevich, *Nuclear Power*.
312. Ibid., pp. 1–2.
313. Ibid., pp. 1, 11.
314. Du and Parsons, *Update*; Ansolabehere et al., *Future*, U Chicago, *Economic Future*.
315. Lovins, Sheikh, and Markevich, *Nuclear Power*, p. 10.
316. Ibid., pp. 1–2.
317. Thomas, *Economics*; Diesendorf and Christoff, "Economics"; Smith, *Insurmountable*; Thomas et al., *Economics*; Van Leeuwen, *Nuclear*; Brown, *Voodoo Economics*; Sussex-NERA, *Economics*.
318. Thomas, *Economics*.
319. Brown, *Voodoo Economics*, p. 2.
320. Smith, *Insurmountable*.
321. Ibid., pp. 44–45, 50–51, 97.
322. OXERA, *Financing*, p. 32.
323. Smith, *Insurmountable*, pp. 7, 49.
324. Brown, *Voodoo Economics*, p. 24.
325. Ibid., pp. 24, 31.
326. Ibid., p. 32.
327. Lovins, Sheikh, and Markevich, *Nuclear Power*.
328. Smith, *Insurmountable*, pp. 53, 40–41, 46–47.
329. U Chicago, *Economic Future*.
330. Tarjanne and Luostarinen, "Economics."
331. Du and Parsons, *Update*; Ansolabehere et al., *Future*; Deutsch et al., *Update*.
332. Baker Institute, *Japanese Energy*.
333. S. J. Bird and R. E. Spier, "The Complexity of Competing and Conflicting Interests," *Science and Engineering Ethics* 11, no. 4 (2005): 515–517; J. K. Roberts, F. W. Beard, R. J. Haefeli,

P. E. James, R. W. Jarvis, P. E. Polk, and P. E. Thompson, *National Society of Professional Engineers' Board of Ethical Review Cases* (Denton: Murdough Center for Engineering Professionalism at Texas Tech University, 2001); accessed October 1, 2009, at 88/case85-86.htm; hereafter cited as Roberts et al., *NSPE Board*; S. J. Bird and R. E. Spier, "A Conflict of Interest Disclosure Policy," *Science and Engineering Ethics* 14, no. 149 (2008): 152; hereafter cited as Bird and Spier, "Conflict of Interest."

334. Federal Acquisition Institute (FAI), *Federal Acquisition Regulations, Subpart 9.5—Organizational and Consultant Conflicts of Interest* (Washington, DC: General Services Administration, 2005); hereafter cited as FAI, *Federal Acquisition Regulations*.

335. Lee Stokes, "Key Issues in Conflict of Interest," *Journal of Research Administration* 33, nos. 2–3 (2002): 19–25.

336. Roberts et al., *NSPE Board*.

337. Accreditation Board for Engineering and Technology (ABET), *Standards of Conduct* (Baltimore: ABET, 2009); accessed October 1, 2009, at http://www.abet.org/code.shtml; hereafter cited as ABET, *Standards of Conduct*.

338. FAI, *Federal Acquisition Regulations*.

339. WNA, *New Economics* 2005.

340. Sussex-NERA, *Economics*.

341. Thomas et al., *Economics*.

342. UK SDC, *The Role of Nuclear Power*, p. 13.

343. Bird and Spier, "Conflict of Interest."

344. Ansolabehere et al., *Future*.

345. Lo et al., *Conflict of Interest*, pp. 1–2.

346. Shrader-Frechette, "Data Trimming."

347. ABET, *Standards of Conduct*.

348. National Research Council (NRC), *Sustainable Federal Facilities: A Guide to Integrating Value Engineering, Life-Cycle Costing, and Sustainable Development* (Washington, DC: National Academy Press, 2001), hereafter cited as NRC, *Sustainable Federal Facilities*.

349. Ibid. B. C. Lippiatt, *BEES 4.0: Building for Environmental and Economic Sustainability*, NSTIR 6916 (Washington, DC: National Institute of Standards and Technology (NIST), Office of Applied Economics, 2007); hereafter cited as Lippiatt, *BEES 4.0*.

350. Lippiatt, *BEES 4.0*.

351. NRC, *Sustainable Federal Facilities*, p. 4.

352. Mariotte et al., *False Promises*.

353. E.g., ibid.; Makhijani, *Carbon-Free*.

354. WNA, *New Economics* 2005.

355. Du and Parsons, *Update*.

356. FAI, *Federal Acquisition Regulations*.

357. Ibid.

358. U Chicago, *Economic Future*.

359. Scully, *Business Case*.

360. Shrader-Frechette, *Environmental Justice*; US Congress, *Worker Safety*.

361. Mariotte et al., *False Promises*; Makhijani, *Carbon-Free*; Diesendorf and Christoff, "Economics."

362. UK SDC, *The Role of Nuclear Power*, p. 45.

363. Moody's, *New Nuclear*.

364. Lovins, Sheikh, and Markevich, *Nuclear Power*.

365. Smith, *Insurmountable*; Cravens, *Power*; Aabakken, *Power Technologies*.

366. Lovins, Sheikh, and Markevich, *Nuclear Power*.

367. J. Robert Oppenheimer, "International Control of Atomic Energy," in Morton Grodzins and Eugene Rabinowitch (eds.), *The Atomic Age* (New York: Basic Books, 1963), p. 55.

368. US Department of Energy (DOE), *DOE Selects 13 Solar Energy Projects* (Washington, DC: US DOE, March 8, 2007); accessed June 9, 2009, at www.energy.gov.news.4855.htm.

369. Madsen et al., *High Cost*.
370. Thomas et al., *Economics*.
371. Lovins, Sheikh, and Markevich, *Nuclear Power*.
372. EIA, *Electric Power*.
373. Pacala and Socolow, "Stabilization Wedges"; NREL, *Near Term*.
374. IAEA, *PRIS Database*.
375. Thomas et al., *Economics*.
376. Thomas, *Economics*.
377. Smith, *Insurmountable*; Slocum, "Nuclear's Power Play."
378. WNA, *New Economics* 2005.

Chapter 4

1. Dennis Normile, "Japan's Tsunami Topped 37 Meters," *Science*, April 7, 2011; accessed April 10, 2011, at http://news.sciencemag.org/scienceinsider/japan_quakes.
2. Hiroko Tabuchi and Andrew Pollack, "Strong Aftershock Jolts Japan; Workers at Nuclear Plant Take Cover," *New York Times*, April 8, 2011, p. A14; See Richard A. Kerr, "Fukushima Radiation," *Science*, April 4, 2011; accessed April 10, 2011, at http://news.sciencemag.org/scienceinsider/2011/04/fukushima-radiation-modeling-shows.html.
3. As chapter 4 later reveals, the International Agency for Research on Cancer (IARC) shows that every time 100 workers are exposed to the maximum-allowable annual occupational-radiation dose of 50 mSv, 2.5–5 percent— up to 1 in 20—of their lifetime fatal cancers will be attributable to their workplace-radiation exposures. Thus, given hourly exposures of 500 mSv, half of the fatal cancers of those exposed will be attributable to 1 hour of this Fukushima radiation.
4. Martin Fackler, "Misery and Uncertainty Fill Up Shelters," *New York Times*, March 17, 2011, p. A12; Martin Fackler and Mark McDonald, "Anxiety and Need Overwhelm a Nation," *New York Times*, March 15, 2011, pp. A1, 11; hereafter cited as Fackler and McDonald, "Anxiety and Need." Martin Fackler and Mark McDonald, "Premier Calls Mounting Crisis Worst since World War II," *New York Times*, March 14, 2011, pp. A1, A10; hereafter cited as Fackler and McDonald, "Premier Calls." Tatsujiro Suzuki, "Daily Update from Japan," *Bulletin of the Atomic Scientists*, April 6, 2011; accessed April 10, 2011, at www.thebulletin.org/web-edition/columnists/tatsujiro-suzuki/daily-update-japan; hereafter cited as Suzuki, "Daily Update."
5. Ken Belson, "As Routines Falter, So Does National Confidence," *New York Times*, March 16, 2011, p. A6 of pp. A1, A6; Energy News (2011); accessed May 6, 2011 at http://enenews.com/. See Gretchen Vogel, "Global Reaction to Nuclear Crisis in Japan," *Science*, March 14, 2011; accessed April 10, 2011, at http://news.sciencemag.org/scienceinsider/japan_quakes.
6. See next note. See also Eli Kintisch and Adrian Cho, "The Worst Case: What If the Water Ran Dry in the Japanese Reactors?" *Science*, March 17, 2011; accessed April 10, 2011, at http://news.sciencemag.org/scienceinsider/japan_quakes.
7. William J. Broad and Hiroko Tabuchi, "In Stricken Fuel-Cooling Pools, a Danger for the Longer Term," *New York Times*, March 15, 2011, p. A10; hereafter cited as Broad and Tabuchi, "Stricken." Accident statistics are from US Brookhaven and US Sandia national laboratory reports, as given in Brice Smith, *Insurmountable Risks: The Dangers of Using Nuclear Power to Combat Global Climate Change* (Takoma Park: IEER Press, 2006), p. 194 (hereafter cited as Smith, *Insurmountable*), and in Broad and Tabuchi, "Stricken"; David Jolly, "Japan Weighs Nationalizing a Stricken Utility," *New York Times*, March 30, 2011, p. A8; hereafter cited as Jolly, "Japan Weighs." See Sara Reardon, "Bill Burnett Talks about Radiation in Japan's Seas," *Science*, April 7, 2011; accessed April 10, 2011, at http://news.sciencemag.org/scienceinsider/japan_quakes.

8. Martin Fackler, "Japanese City's Desperate Cry Resonates around the World," *New York Times*, April 7, 2011, p. A1 of pp. A1, 10; h Lauren Schenkman, "What Effect Will the Radiation Have on the Japanese?" *Science*, March 16, 2011; accessed April 10, 2011, at http://news.sciencemag.org/scienceinsider/japan_quakes.

9. Jolly, "Japan Weighs," p. A8. "Come Back in Ten Years' Time," *Economist* 398, no. 8726 (March 26–April 1, 2011): 47–48.

10. David Jolly, "Radioactive Iodine Detected in Ocean," *New York Times*, April 1, 2011, pp. A10–11; hereafter cited as Jolly, "Radioactive Iodine." See Jocelyn Kaiser, "Japan Soil Measurements Surprisingly High," *Science*, March 25, 2011; accessed April 10, 2011, at http://news.sciencemag.org/scienceinsider/japan_quakes.

11. Hiroko Tabuchi and Keith Bradsher, "Fire Adds to Troubles as Japan Seeks Ways to Cool Nuclear Plant," *New York Times*, March 16, 2011, p. A7; hereafter cited as Tabuchi and Bradsher, "Fire."

12. Michael Wines, "Hobbled by Debris and Water, Crews Scour Tsunami Zone for Victims," *New York Times*, March 17, 2011, p. A12; Suzuki, "Daily Update." Jennifer Couzin-Frankel and Eliot Marshall, "Little Protection for Those on the Front Lines," *Science*, March 17, 2011; accessed April 10, 2011, at http://news.sciencemag.org/scienceinsider/japan_quakes.

13. Tabuchi and Bradsher, "Fire," p. A7.

14. Martin Fackler, "As Food Is Rationed, Resolve Is Plentiful," *New York Times*, March 29, 2011, p. A10; hereafter cited as Fackler, "As Food." "Come Back in Ten Years' Time," *Economist* 398, no. 8726 (March 26–April 1, 2011): 47–48.

15. William J. Broad and David Jolly, "UN's Nuclear Chief Says Japan Is 'Far from the End of the Accident,'" *New York Times*, March 27, 2011, p. A10; hereafter cited as Broad and Jolly, "UN's." Nature.com, "Fukushima Disaster: Some Lessons Already Clear," March 22, 2011; accessed April 10, 2011, at http://blogs.nature.com/news/thegreatbeyond/2011/03/fukushima_disaster_some_lesson.html.Michigan and Stanford scientists are Rodney C. Ewing and Jeroen Ritsema, "Underestimating Nuclear Accident Risks," *Bulletin of the Atomic Scientists, May 3, 2011; accessed May 6, 2011 at <www.thebulletin.org/web-edition/roundtables/fukushima-what-dont-we-know>*. Robert Socolow, "Reflections on Fukushima: A Time to Mourn, to Learn, and to Teach," *Bulletin of the Atomic Scientists, March 21, 2011; accessed May 6, 2011 at at <www.thebulletin.org/web-edition/op-eds/reflections-fukushima-time-tomourn-to-learn-to-teach>*

16. Energy News (2011); accessed May 6, 2011 at http://enenews.com/. Nevertheless, the Japanese disaster could have been worse. Only their backup, emergency-diesel cooling stopped additional nuclear-accident threats at Higashidori, at Onagawa, and at Rokkasho Hiroko Tabuchi and Andrew Pollack, "Powerful Aftershock Complicates Japan's Nuclear Efforts," *New York Times*, April 7, 2011, p. A7. At all 4 Fukushima Daini reactors, emergency-core-cooling systems also initially failed, threatening wider catastrophe. Hiroko Tabuchi, Keith Bradsher, and Matthew Wald, "Third Blast Strikes Crippled Nuclear Plant," *New York Times*, March 15, 2011, p. 12 of pp. A1, 12; hereafter cited as Tabuchi, Bradsher, and Wald, "Third Blast." Suzuki, "Daily Update."

17. Shinichi Saoshiro and Jonathan Thatcher, TEPCO Wary of Fukushima Radiaion Leak Exceeding Chernobyl," *Scientific American*, April 11, 2011; accessed May 6, 2011 at <www.scientificamerican.com/article.cfm?id=tepco-wary-of-fukushima-radiation-leak>. *Energy News* (2011); accessed May 6, 2011 at http://enenews.com/. Chernobyl fatalities are from Alexey V. Yablokov, Vassily B. Nesterenko, Alexey V. Nesterenko and Janette D. Sherman-Nevinger, *Chernobyl: Consequences of the Catastrophe for People and the Environment: Annals of the New York Academy of Sciences* (Malden, Massachusetts: John Wiley, 2009).

18. Fackler and McDonald, "Anxiety and Need," p. A11; "Nature Strikes Back," *Economist* 398, no. 8725 (March 19–25, 2011): 29–32.

19. Michael Wines, "Japan's Nuclear Crisis Erodes Farmers' Livelihoods," *New York Times*, March 30, 2011, p. A9.

20. David Jolly and Denise Grady, "Radioactive Iodine Exceeds Levels for Infants," *New York Times*, March 24, 2011, pp. A1, A12; Richard A. Kerr, "How Far Will the Radiation Spread?" *Science*, March 16, 2011; accessed April 10, 2011, at http://news.sciencemag.org/scienceinsider/japan_quakes.

21. Fackler and McDonald, "Premier Calls"; Dennis Normile, "How Is Japan's Energy System Affected?," *Science*, March 22, 2011; accessed April 10, 2011, at http://news.sciencemag.org/scienceinsider/japan_quakes.

22. Mark McDonald, "Worries That Even the Perception of Contamination Could Taint Japanese Brands," *New York Times*, March 20, 2011, p. A11; Elisabeth Rosenthal and William J. Broad, "Marine Life Faces Threat from Runoff," *New York Times*, March 329, 2011, p. A11. See Lauren Schenkman, "Japan Radiation Map Roundup," *Science*, March 24, 2011; accessed April 10, 2011, at http://news.sciencemag.org/scienceinsider/japan_quakes.

23. William Neuman and Florence Fabricant, "Screening the Day's Catch," *New York Times*, April 6, 2011, pp. B1, B4; Hiroko Tabuchi, David Jolly, and Keith Bradsher, "Tainted Water at Two Reactors Increases Alarm," *New York Times*, March 28, 2011, pp. A1–A11. See Ken Belson and Hiroko Tabuchi, "Japan Finds Contaminated Food Up to 90 Miles from Nuclear Sites," *New York Times*, March 20, 2011, p. A8; hereafter cited as Belson and Tabuchi, "Japan Finds." Suzuki, "Daily Update." Jocelyn Kaiser, "What's the Current Radiation Threat to Japan's Food and Water?" *Science*, March 23, 2011; accessed April 10, 2011, at http://news.sciencemag.org/scienceinsider/japan_quakes.

24. Miguel Helft and Nick Bunkley, "Crisis Batters the Supply Chain," *New York Times*, March 15, 2011, pp. B1, 4; Suzuki, "Daily Update." "Come Back in Ten Years' Time," *Economist* 398, no. 8726 (March 26–April 1, 2011): 47–48.

25. Denise Grady, "Precautions Should Limit Health Problems from Nuclear Plant's Radiation," *New York Times*, March 16, 2011, p. A9; Suzuki, "Daily Update."

26. Tabuchi, Bradsher, and Wald, "Third Blast," p. A1.

27. See note 3 for dose-effect calculations.

28. Suzuki, "Daily Update"; see note 3 for dose-effect calculations.

29. Jolly, "Radioactive Iodine," pp. A10–11.

30. Henry Fountain, "Cleanup Questions as Radiation, Spreads," *New York Times*, April 1, 2011, p. A10; Suzuki, "Daily Update." Martin Fackler and Matthew Wald, "Life In Limbo for Japanese Near Damaged Nuclear Plant," *The New York Times,* May 2, 2011, p. A4. Standard radiation-health effects are based on international standards, as described in note 3. Dennis Normile, "Conflicting U.S. and Japan Evacuation Policies Sow Confusion," *Science*, March 23, 2011; accessed April 10, 2011, at http://news.sciencemag.org/scienceinsider/japan_quakes.

31. Ken Belson and Hiroko Tabuchi, "In Setback, Radioactive Water Is Leaking Directly into Sea, Japan Says," *New York Times*, April 3, 2011, p. A11.

32. Andrew Pollack, Ken Belson, and Kevin Drew, "Company Says Radioactive Water Leak at Japan Plant Is Plugged," *New York Times*, April 5, 2011, p. A13; hereafter cited as Pollack, Belson, and Drew, "Company." Belson and Tabuchi, "Japan Finds"; Suzuki, "Daily Update."

33. Martin Fackler, "Prime Minister Defends How Japan Has Handled Nuclear Crisis," *New York Times,* May 1, 2011, pp. A5, A8. Standard methods of calculations of health effects from 20 msv of radiation are in note 3.

34. Helen Caldicott, "Unsafe at Any Dose," *New York Times*, May 1, 2011, p. A10. Regarding mutations and subsequent cancers, see, for instance, R.C. Miller, et al. "The Oncogenic Transforming Potential of the Passage of Single Alpha Particles through Mammalian Cell Nuclei," *Proceedings of National Academy of Sciences USA*, 96 (1999), 19-22; A.M. Stewart, "The Role of Epidemiology in the Detection of Harmful Effects of Radiation" *Environmental Health Perspectives* 108 (2000); 93-96; R.H. Nussbaum and W. Koenlein, "Inconsistencies and Open Questions Regarding Low-Dose Health Effects of Ionizing Radiation," *Environmental Health Perspectives,* 102, no. 8 (1994): 656-667; Y.E. Dubrova et al., "Human Mintitisatellite Mutation Rate after the Chernobyl Accident," *Nature* 380, no. 6576(1996): 683-686; Y.E. Dubrova et al., "Further Evidence for Elevated Human Minisatellite

Mutation Rate in Belarus Eight Years after the Chernobyl Accident," *Mutation Research* 381, no. 2(1997): 267-278; National Research Council, *Health Risks from Exposure to Low Levels of Ionizing Radiation: BEIR VII, Phase 2* (Washington, DC: National Academy Press, 2006).

35. Henry Fountain, "Wind and Rain Steer Radiation's Reach," *New York Times*, March 16, 2011, p. A8; hereafter cited as Fountain, "Wind." Eliot Marshall and Sara Reardon, "How Much Fuel Is at Risk at Fukushima?" *Science*, March 17, 2011; accessed April 10, 2011, at http://news.sciencemag.org/scienceinsider/japan_quakes. Ken Belson, "From Safe Distance, US-Japanese Team Draws Up Plan to Demolish Reactors," *New York Times*, April 8, 2011, p. A14; hereafter cited as Belson, "Safe Distance." "Plutonium and Mickey Mouse," *Economist* 399, no. 8727 (April 2–8, 2011): 33–34.

36. Belson, "Safe Distance," p. A14. See Frank von Hippel, "Containment of a Reactor Meltdown," *Bulletin of the Atomic Scientists*, March 16, 2011; accessed March 22, 2011, at http://thebulletin.org/wcb-edition/features/the-bulletin-archives-containment-of-reactor-meltdown.

37. Broad and Jolly, "UN's," p. A10; Andy Coghlan, "TEPCO under Fire over Handling of Fukushima Crisis," *New Scientist*, April 5, 2011; accessed April 10, 2011, at www.newscientist.com/article/dn20337-tepsi-under-fire-over-handling-of-fukushima-crisis.html.

38. Quoted in James Glanz and William J. Broad, "US Sees New Threats at Japan's Nuclear Plant," *New York Times*, April 6, 2011, pp. A1, A12; hereafter cited as Glanz and Broad, "US."

39. Geoff Brumfiel, "Water Leak Stops at Fukushima, but Big Problems Remain," *The Great Beyond: Nature Brings You Breaking News from the World of Science*, April 6, 2011; accessed April 6, 2011, at http://blogs.nature.com/news/thegreatbeyond/2011/04/water_stops_at-fukushima_but_b.html.

40. Fountain, "Wind," p. A8.

41. Broad and Jolly, "UN's," p. A10.

42. Suzuki, "Daily Update."

43. Belson, "Safe Distance," p. A14. Sara Reardon, "Radioecologists Developing Japan-Response Recommendations," *Science*, March 24, 2011; accessed April 10, 2011, at http://news.sciencemag.org/scienceinsider/japan_quakes.

44. David Bodansky, *Nuclear Industry* (New York: Springer-Verlag, 1996), p. 391; Jeff Sommer, "A Crisis Markets Cannot Grasp," *New York Times*, March 20, 2011, p. A6 of pp. A1, 6; hereafter cited as Sommer, "Crisis."

45. Broad and Jolly, "UN's," p. A10. Hiroko Tabuchi, Ken Belson and Norimitsu Onishi, "In Tokyo, a Dearth of Candor," *New York Times*, March 17, 2011, pp. A1, 11.

46. Hiroko Tabuchi, Norimitsu Onishi, and Ken Belson, "Japan Extended Reactor's Life, Despite Warning," *New York Times*, March 22, 2011, pp. A1, A6; hereafter cited as Tabuchi, Onishi, and Belson, "Japan Extended."

47. Ibid.

48. Ibid., p. A6. " Plutonium and Mickey Mouse," *Economist* 399, no. 8727 (April 2–8, 2011): 33–34.

49. Denise Grady, "Amid Noise on Radiation, Just the Facts," *New York Times*, March 29, 2011, p. D1, D4; hereafter cited as Grady, "Amid Noise." Tom Zeller, "Experts Have Criticized Potential Weakness in Design of Stricken Reactor," *New York Times*, March 16, 2011, p. A8. Frank N. Von Hippel, "It Could Happen Here," *New York Times*, March 24, 2011, p. A29. See Sara Reardon, "Japan Earthquake Holds Lessons, and Warnings, for Pacific Northwest," *Science*, March 11, 2011; accessed April 10, 2011, at http://news.sciencemag.org/scienceinsider/japan_quakes.

50. "Faulty Thinking," *Economist* 398, no. 8725 (March 19–25, 2011): 30; Grady, "Amid Noise," p. D4.

51. Tabuchi, Onishi, and Belson, "Japan Extended," pp. A1, A6; Arjun Makhijani, *Post Tsunami Situation at the Fukushima Daiichi Nuclear Power Plant* (Takoma Park, MD: Institute for Energy and Environmental Research, 2011).

52. John Broder, Matthew Wald, and Tom Zeller, "When All Isn't Enough to Stop a Catastrophe," *New York Times*, March 29, 2011, p. D1 of pp. D1, D4; hereafter cited as Broder, Wald, and Zeller, "When All." Advisory Committee on Reactor Safeguards, Subcommittee on Reliability and Probability Risk Assessment, *Meeting of the Subcommittee*, NRC-744 (Rockville, MD: US NRC, January 24, 2003).

53. US Atomic Energy Commission, *Theoretical Possibilities and Consequences of Major Accidents in Large Nuclear Power Plants*, WASH-740 (Washington, DC: US Government Printing Office, 1957); R. J. Mulvihill et al., *Analysis of US Power Reactor Accident Probability*, PRC R-695 (Los Angeles: Planning Research Corporation, 1965).

54. Norman Rasmussen, *Reactor Safety Study*, WASH-1400, NUREG-75/014 (Washington, DC: US Government Printing Office, 1975).

55. Roger Cooke, "Risk Assessment and Rational Decision Theory," *Dialectica* 36, no. 4 (1982): 334.

56. E.g., Bodansky, p. 391. For arguments to the contrary, see David Lochsbaum, *The NRC and Nuclear Power Plant Safety in 2010* (Cambridge, MA: Union of Concerned Scientists, 2011).

57. See previous 5 notes.

58. See Joshua Pollack, "Guarding against Disaster," *Bulletin of the Atomic Scientists*, March 15, 2011; accessed March 22, 2011, at http://thebulletin.org/web-edition/columnists/joshua-pollack/guarding-against-disaster.

59. S. S. Dosanih, *Melt Progression in Severely Damaged Reactor Cores* (Albuquerque: Sandia, 1987); J. Gonyeau, *Partial Fuel Meltdown Events: The Nuclear Tourist* (Washington, DC: Nuclear Energy Institute, 2005); see www.nei.org and www.nucleartourist.com; Smith, *Insurmountable*, pp. 165–229, esp. 184–196; BBC News, *Timeline: Nuclear Plant Accidents*, July 11, 2006; accessed April 9, 2011, at http://news.bbc.co.uk/2/hi/science/nature/5165736.stm; Jeremy Whitlock, *Safety and Liability, Canadian Nuclear FAQ*; accessed April 9, 2011, at www.nuclearfaq.ca/index.html#top; William Robert Johnston, *Database of Radiological Incidents*, April 1, 2011; accessed April 9, 2011, at www.johnstonsarchive.net/nuclear/revents/net/nuclear/index.html; see also Broder, Wald, and Zeller, "When All," p. D1.

60. "The Risks Exposed," *Economist* 398, no. 8725 (March 19–25, 2011): 34, 36.

61. Heather Timmons and Vikas Bajaj, "India and China Move Ahead While Advanced Nations Back Off," *New York Times*, March 15, 2011, p. B1 of pp. B1, 4.

62. Sommer, "Crisis," p. A6.

63. Rob Stein, "Fear Will Worsen Nuclear Disaster," *Fort Wayne Journal Gazette*; accessed April 10, 2011, at www.journalgazette.net/article/20110316/NEWS04/303169916/-1/NEWS09.

64. World Nuclear Association, Chernobyl Accident; accessed April 10, 2011, at www.world-nuclear.org/info/chernobyl/inf07.html; see, for example, R. ; Giel, "Hoe Erg Was Chernobyl? De Psychosociale Gevolgen van Het Reactorongeluk," *Nederlands Tijdschrift voor Geneeskunde* 135, no. 25 (June 22, 1991): 1137–1141. Vera Rich, "USSR: Chernobyl's Psychological Legacy," *Lancet* 337, no. 8749 (May 4, 1991): 1086–1086.

65. Paul Voosen, "Nuclear Crisis: Psychological Risks Loom in Tokyo Water Warning," *Environment and Energy Daily*; accessed April 9, 2011, at www.eenews.net/public/Greenwire/2011/03242?page_type=print; hereafter cited as Voosen, "Nuclear Crisis"; see Martin Bauer, *Resistance to New Technology* (Cambridge: Cambridge University Press, 1997).

66. General Public Utilities Corporation, *Three Mile Island* (Parsippany, NJ: GPUC. 1980), p. 5. See, for example, L. M. Davidson, R. Fleming, and A. Baum, "Chronic Stress, Catecholamines, and Sleep Disturbance at Three Mile Island," Journal of Human Stress 13, no. 2 (Summer 1987): 75–83. M. A. Dew, E. J. Bromet, H. C. Schulberg, L. O. Dunn, and D. K. Parkinson, "Mental Health Effects of the Three Mile Island Nuclear Reactor Restart," American Journal of Psychiatry 144, no. 8 (August 1987): 1074–1077. M. A. Dew, E. J. Bromet, and H. C. Schulberg, "A Comparative Analysis of Two Community Stressors' Long-Term Mental Health Effects," American Journal of Community Psychology 15, no. 2 (April 1987):

167–184. B. P. Dohrenwend, "Psychological Implications of Nuclear Accidents: The Case of Three Mile Island," Bulletin of the New York Academy of Medicine 59, no. 19 (December 1983): 1060–1076. R. F. Chisholm, S. V. Kasl, B. P. Dohrenwend, B. S. Dohrenwend, G. J. Warheit, R. L. Goldsteen, K. Goldsteen, and J. L. Martin, "Behavioral and Mental Health Effects of the Three Mile Island Accident on Nuclear Workers: A Preliminary Report," Annals of the New York Academy of Sciences 365 (1981): 134–135. R. Goldsteen, J. K. Schorr, and K. S. Goldsteen, "Longitudinal Study of Appraisal at Three Mile Island: Implications for Life Event Research," Social Sciences and Medicine 128, no. 4 (1989): 389–398.

67. Voosen, "Nuclear Crisis"; Fackler and McDonald, "Anxiety and Need." See Robert DuPont, *Nuclear Phobia* (Washington, DC: The Institute, 1980), and see Spencer Weart, *Nuclear Fear* (Cambridge: Harvard University Press, 1989).

68. Tabuchi, Bradsher, and Wald, "Third Blast," p. A12. William J. Broad, "Radiation Over US Is Harmless, Officials Say," *New York Times*, March 22, 2011, p. A6.

69. David Sanger, Mathew Wald, and Hiroko Tabuchi, "US Sees Extremely High Radiation Level at Plant, Focusing on Spent Fuel's Danger," *New York Times*, March 17, 2011, pp. A1, A13.

70. William J. Broad, "Scientists Project Path of Radiation Plume," *New York Times*, March 17, 2011, p. A10.

71. Nuclear Energy Institute, *The Chernobyl Accident* (Washington, DC: NEI, July 2000). The radiation-dose-response curve is discussed in detail later in the chapter.

72. Sheldon Novick, *The Electric War* (San Francisco: Sierra, 1976), pp. 152–153.

73. Andrews Jacob, "Can Hysteria Fell 1,200 Workers? China Says Yes," *New York Times*, July 30, 2009, pp. A1, A12.

74. Vermont Department of Health, *Investigation into Tritium Contamination* (Burlington: Vermont Agency of Human Services, January 21, 2011). Vermont Department of Health, *Vermont Yankee Root Cause Analysis* (Burlington: Vermont Agency of Human Services, June 22, 2010). US Nuclear Regulatory Commission, *Weekly Information Report, SECY-10-0017* (Washington, DC: Office of the Executive Director for Operations, February 5, 2010). See Dave Gram, "Leaks Renew Nuclear Debate," *Louisville Courier-Journal*, February 2, 2010, p. A3. Colin Macilwain, "Tritium Leaks at US Reactor Sparks Crisis for Neutron Source Users," *Nature* 386, no. 6620 (1997): 3–4. Examples of NRC laxness are from Tom Zeller, "Nuclear Agency Criticized for Ties to Industry It Regulates," *New York Times*, May 8, 2011, pp. A1,16-17. For additional discussion of industry capture of regulators, or "regulatory capture," see Kristin Shrader-Frechette, *Taking Action, Saving Lives* (New York: Oxford University Press, 2007), esp. chs. 2–3.

75. J. Kemeny et al., *Report of the President's Commission on the Accident at Three Mile Island* (Washington, DC: Kemeny Commission, 1979), p. 118; hereafter cited as Kemeny et al., *Report*. The industry position is at Nuclear Association (WNA), "Chernobyl Accident," 2008; accessed February 13, 2009, at http://world-clear.org/info/chernobyl/inf07.html; Nuclear Energy Institute (NEI), *Nuclear Statistics* (Washington, DC: NEI, 2007); accessed February 15, 2008, at www.nei.org/resourcesandstats/nuclear_statistics/costs; T. Nakagawa and P. P. Roosen, "Three Mile Island," *American Chronicle*, 2007; accessed February 15, 2009, at www.americanchronicle.com/articles/view/29038; National Heart, Lung, and Blood Institute (NHLBI), *Framingham Heart Study* (Bethesda, MD: NIH, 2009); S. Schorow, "Three Mile Island—Failure of Science or Spin?," MIT Tech Talk, 2009; accessed February 15, 2009, at http://web.mit.edu/newsoffice/2007/threemile.html; P. Moore, "Re-think Nuclear," *IAEA Bulletin* 48, no. 1 (2006): 56–58; Energy Tribune, "Nuclear Schizophrenia," *Energy Tribune*, 2006; accessed February 16, 2009, at www.energytribune.com/articles.cfm?aid=60; Bernard L. Cohen, *Before It's Too Late* (New York: Plenum Press, 1983); Gwyneth Cravens, *Power to Save the World* (New York: Knopf, 2008), p. 188; A. M. Herbst and G. W. Hopley, *Nuclear Energy Now* (Hoboken, NJ: John Wiley, 2007), p. 138.

76. M. Hatch et al., "Cancer Near the Three Mile Island Nuclear Plant," *American Journal of Epidemiology* 132, no. 3 (1990): 397–412; hereafter cited as Hatch et al., "Cancer Near"; E. O. Talbott et al., "Long Term Follow-Up of the Residents of the Three Mile Island Accident

Area: 1979–1998," *Environmental Health Perspectives* 111, no. 3 (2003): 341–348; hereafter cited as Talbott et al., "Long Term."

77. Talbott et al., "Long Term," p. 241; Hatch et al., "Cancer Near"; M. Hatch et al., "Cancer Rates after the Three Mile Island Nuclear Accident," *American Journal of Public Health* 81, no. 6 (1991): 719–724; hereafter cited as Hatch et al., "Cancer Rates."

78. E.g., R. J. Levin, "Incidence of Thyroid Cancer in Residents Surrounding the Three Mile Island Nuclear Facility," *Laryngoscope* 118, no. 4 (2009): 618–628; hereafter cited as Levin, "Incidence"; Hatch et al., "Cancer Near"; Hatch et al., "Cancer Rates"; M. Susser, "Consequences of the 1979 Three Mile Island Accident Continued," *Environmental Health Perspectives* 105, no. 6 (1997): 566–567; hereafter cited as Susser, "Consequences"; S. Walker, *Three Mile Island* (Berkeley: University of California Press, 2004), pp. 37, 78–79, 83, 85–87, 78–112, 116, 122–124, 138, 151, 174, 189, 193–194, 206–207, 219, 229, 231, 233, 235–236; hereafter cited as Walker, *Three.*

79. American Nuclear Society (ANS), *Health Studies* (LaGrange Park, IL: ANS, 2009); accessed March 10, 2009, at www.ans.org/pi/resources/sptopics/tmi/healthstudies.html; hereafter cited as ANS, *Health.*

80. S. Wing et al., "A Re-Evaluation of Cancer Incidence Near the Three Mile Island Nuclear Plant," *Environmental Health Perspectives* 105, no. 1 (1997): 52–57; hereafter cited as Wing et al., "Re-Evaluation"; S. Wing, "Objectivity and Ethics and Environmental Health Science," *Environmental Health Perspectives* 111, no. 14 (2003): 1809–1818; hereafter cited as Wing, "Objectivity."

81. I. Hacking, *The Taming of Chance* (New York: Cambridge University Press, 1990), 214; hereafter cited as Hacking, *Taming.*

82. K. J. Rothman, "Statistics in Non-Randomized Studies," *Epidemiology* 1 (1990): 417–418; hereafter cited as Rothman, "Statistics"; see D. N. McCloskey and Stephen Ziliak, *The Cult of Statistical Significance* (Ann Arbor: University of Michigan Press, 2008); hereafter cited as McCloskey and Ziliak, "Cult."

83. National Research Council/National Academy of Sciences (NRC/NAS), *Health Risks from Exposure to Low Levels of Ionizing Radiation: BEIR VII, Phase 2* (Washington, DC: National Academy Press, 2006); hereafter cited as NRC/NAS, *Health.* The *JAMA*, fallout, EPA, and Nixon claims, respectively, are from official NRC historian Samuel Walker, *Permissible Dose* (Berkeley: University of California Press, 2000), pp. 3–5, 37–38, 89, 51, 71, 75; hereafter cited as Walker, *Dose.*

84. US Environmental Protection Agency (US EPA), *Radiation: Risks and Realities* (2007), p. 2; accessed February 27, 2009, at www.epa.gov/radiation/docs/402-k-07-006.pdf.

85. Nations Scientific Committee on Effects of Atomic Radiation (UNSCEAR), *Sources and Effects of Ionizing Radiation, Report to the General Assembly* (New York: UN, 1994). Note that, for some exposures, absorbed and effective doses are different in their relative biological effectiveness or RBE. For instance, low-energy X-rays (a few tens of KeV) are about twice as damaging as high-energy gamma rays, such as Cs-137, so RBE = 2. Thanks to Dr. Arjun Makhijani for this clarification regarding low-energy X-rays.

86. Walker, *Three*, p. 228. Arnie Gundersen, *Three Myths of the Three Mile Island Accident* (Burlington, VT: Fairewinds Energy Education Corporation, 2009); accessed July 7, 2009, at www.timia.com/march 26; hereafter cited as Gundersen, *Three*; Sue Sturgis, *Investigation: Revelations about the Three Mile Island Disaster Raise Doubts over Nuclear Plant Safety* (Durham, NC: Institute for Southern Studies, 2009); accessed July 7, 2009, at http://southernstudies.org/2009/04/post-4.html; hereafter cited as Sturgis, "Investigation"; Walker, *Three*, 78. Compare to J. May, *The Greenpeace Book of the Nuclear Age* (London: Greenpeace Communications, 1989); hereafter cited as May, *Nuclear Age.,*

87. Walker, *Three*, pp. 87, 122, 124, 151, 189, 219; see May, *Nuclear Age*; M. Lang, *Three Mile Island Unit 2* (Harrisburg, PA: Three Mile Island Alert, 2009); accessed March 9, 2009, at http://www.tmia.com/node/110; hereafter cited as Lang, "Three."

88. Walker, *Three*, p. 233; May, *Nuclear Age.*

89. Walker, *Three*; Wing, "Objectivity."

90. US Nuclear Regulatory Commission (US NRC), *Fact Sheet on the Three Mile Island Accident* (Washington, DC: US NRC, 2008); hereafter cited as US NRC, *Fact*; Walker, *Three*, p. 231.

91. Hatch et al., "Cancer Near," pp. 401–402.

92. Jan Beyea and J. M. DeCicco, *Re-Estimating the Noble Gas Releases from the Three Mile Island Accident* (Philadelphia: Three Mile Island Public Health Fund, 1990), pp. ii, vii, viii, x, ix, 1, 10, 13, 18, 20, 22–29, 43, 70; hereafter cited as Beyea and DeCicco, *Re-Estimating.*

93. Nuclear Information and Resource Service/World Information Service on Energy (NIRS/ WISE), *Radioactive Releases from the Nuclear Power Plants of the Chesapeake Bay Watershed* (Washington, DC: NIRS, 2001). Official NRC readings, Kepford claims, and Carter readings, respectively, are from Walker, *Three*, pp. 130, 207, 182.

94. R. J. Levin, "Incidence of Thyroid Cancer in Residents Surrounding the Three Mile Island Nuclear Facility," *Laryngoscope* 118, no. 4 (2008): 618–628. Helen Caldicott, *Nuclear Power Is Not the Answer* (Melbourne, Australia: Melbourne University Press, 2006), p. 67; hereafter cited as Caldicott, *Nuclear.*

95. Gundersen, *Three*; Sturgis, "Investigation."

96. Walker, *Three*, pp. 79, 85–87, 93, 122–123, 130, 194, 225.

97. The 30,000 rad/hour claim is from the official government report, Walker, *Three*, p. 194, and the Kemeny quotation is from Kemeny et al., *Report*, p. 30.

98. Randall Thompson, Joy Thompson, and David Bear, *TMI Assessment* (Durham, NC: Institute for Southern Studies, 1995); accessed July 7, 2009, at www.southernstudies.org/images/ sitepieces/ThompsonTMIassessment.pdf; hereafter cited as Thompson, Thompson, and Bear, "TMI"; Kemeny et al., *Report.*

99. US NRC, *Fact*; Walker, *Three*, p. 231.

100. Walker, *Three*, pp. 78, 210, 228, notes that the TMI more-than-half core melt was not known by the Kemeny Commission and that it was done under severe time constraints. Beyea and DeCicco, *Re-Estimating*, pp. viii, 20; Wing, "Objectivity," pp. 1809–1810; Hatch et al., "Cancer Near." See later paragraphs for more evidence for each of these points.

101. World Nuclear Association (WNA), *Chernobyl Accident* (London: World Nuclear Association, 2009); accessed March 30, 2010, at www.world-nuclear.org/info/chernobyl/ inf07.html.

102. World Health Organization (WHO), *Fact Sheet* (Geneva: WHO, November 20, 1995).

103. For radiation-induced germ-line mutations as cause of increased rate of Japanese cancers see, for instance, Taisai Nomura, "Transgenerational Carcinogenesis," *Mutation Research/Reviews in Mutation Research* 544, nos. 2–3 (2003): 425–432. For numbers of Japanese radiation fatalities from the two weapons tests, see T. Imanaka, "Casualties and Radiation Dosimetry of the Atomic Bombings," *Radiation Risk Estimates in Normal and Emergency Situations* 9, no. 169690526 (2006): 149–156; Yukiko Shimizu, William Schull, and Hiroo Kato, "Cancer Risk among Atomic Bomb Survivors," *Journal of the American Medical Association* 264, no. 5 (1990): 601–604; William J. Schull, *Effects of Atomic Radiation* (New York: Wiley-Liss, 1995).

104. Other TMI-Hiroshima-Nagasaki caveats are that (3) because the bombs involved a high air burst, bomb radionuclides were mainly blown farther away to other areas than were TMI radionuclides. (4) If the real TMI dose was actually higher than the TMI utility claims, TMI may have released more radiation than Hiroshima and Nagasaki. (5) Admittedly slightly different isotopes, some with different half-lives, were released in the 2 nuclear accidents and the 2 bombings. (6) Admittedly the government/TMI-utility radiation-dose estimates for TMI are much lower than those for Hiroshima and Nagasaki—partly because prompt gamma and neutron radiation from the bomb explosion is of much higher intensity and thus delivered very high doses, especially in the population right below the explosion, which was more concentrated in Japan than at TMI. Thanks to Dr. Arjun Makhijani for helpful discussions (personal communications) on TMI, Hiroshima, and Nagasaki radiation releases. If any errors remain, however, these are the responsibility of the author, not Dr. Makhijani.

105. Imanaka, "Casualties and Radiation Dosimetry," p. 331.
106. H. Wasserman and N. Solomon, *Killing Our Own* (New York: Dell, 1982), ch. 14; hereafter cited as Wasserman and Solomon, *Killing.*
107. M. Rogovin and G. T. Frampton, *Three Mile Island: A Report to the Commissioners and to the Public,* NUREG/CR-1250, vols. 1–2 (Washington, DC: US Nuclear Regulatory Commission, 1980), vol. 2, part 2, p. 728; hereafter cited as Rogovin and Frampton, *Three.* Confirmation that Rogovin and Frampton (see previous note) is the best of the NRC official studies is in Walker, *Three,* p. 217.
108. Opinion of the Court, In Re: *TMI Litigation, 193 F.3d 613 (3rd Cir. 1999),* (Philadelphia: Third Circuit Court of Appeals, 1999), par. 179; Judge S. Rambo, "Three Mile Island: The Judge's Ruling," in *Frontline: Nuclear Reaction Readings* (Alexandria, VA: PBS, 1996); accessed February 24, 2009, at http://www.pbs.org/wgbh/pages/frontline/shows/reaction/ radngs/tmi.html; hereafter cited as: Rambo, "Three"; Lori Dolan et al., In Re: *TMI Litigation,* US Court of Appeals, Third Circuit, 193 F.3d 613 (3rd Cir. 1999), argued June 27, 1997; hereafter cited as: In Re: *TMI Litigation.*
109. Elisabeth Cardis et al., "Risk of Cancer after Low Doses of Ionizing Radiation," *British Medical Journal* 331 (2005): 77–80; hereafter cited as Cardis et al., "Risk"; Elisabeth Cardis et al., "The 15-Country Collaborative Study of Cancer Risk among Radiation Workers in the Nuclear Industry," *Radiation Research* 167 (2007): 396–416. The claims about maximum doses' occurring at least 15 miles from the plant, and thousands of deaths, are in Walker, *Three,* p. 207.
110. Thompson, Thompson, and Bear, "TMI," 9–10; Sturgis, "Investigation." Admittedly, beta doses are less highly penetrating than gamma and X-ray radiation, and admittedly clothing provides some protection from beta doses. Nevertheless, beta radiation is able to cause skin injury and can be harmful if deposited internally through breathing, eating, or drinking. Thus, although beta radiation may be less harmful than other types of radiation, arguably government should always assess it, particularly because TMI victims appear to have displayed skin irritation (see note 112).
111. Walker, *Three,* p. 78; May, *Nuclear Age.*
112. The best official NRC report on TMI is Rogovin and Frampton, *Three,* according to NRC historian Walker, *Three,* p. 217. Laurence Stern, D. J. Balz, M. R. Benjamin, et al., "Crisis at Three Mile Island, (Washington, DC: Washington Post, 1999), ch. 1; accessed July 6, 2009, at www.washingtonpost.com/wp-srv/national/longterm/tmi/stories/ch1.htm; see Rogovin and Frampton, *Three,* pp. 25, 182.
113. Beyea and DeCicco, *Re-Estimating.*
114. E. Epstein, "Science for Sale," *World Information Service on Energy/ Nuclear Information and Research Service Nuclear Monitor* 576 (2002): 9–10; hereafter cited as Epstein, "Science"; May, *Nuclear Age*; Lang, "Three," p. 11.
115. Wing, "Objectivity," pp. 1814–1816; Walker, *Three,* pp. 235–236.
116. Nuclear engineer-physicist Dr. Arjun Makhijani suggested this argument in a personal communication.
117. E.g., Levin, "Incidence."
118. Hatch et al., "Cancer Rates"; Hatch et al., "Cancer Near"; Susser, "Consequences."
119. Wing et al., "Re-Evaluation"; S. Wing, D. Richardson, and D. Armstrong, "A Re-Evaluation of Cancer Incidence near the Three Mile Island Nuclear Plant," *Environmental Health Perspectives* 105 (1997): 266–268; hereafter cited as Wing, Richardson, and Armstrong, "Re-Evaluation"; Wing, "Objectivity."
120. Talbott et al., "Long Term"; E. O. Talbott et al., "Mortality among the Residents of the Three Mile Island Accident Area: 1979–1992," *Environmental Health Perspectives* 108, no. 6 (2000): 545–552; hereafter cited as Talbott et al., "Mortality."
121. Hatch et al., "Cancer Near," pp. 406–407; D. T. Janerich, "Can Stress Cause Cancer?," *American Journal of Public Health* 81, no. 6 (1991): 687–688; J. J. Mangano, "Three Mile Island," *Bulletin of the Atomic Scientists* 60, no. 5 (2004): 30–35; hereafter cited as Mangano, "Three."

122. Hatch et al., "Cancer Near," esp. pp. 398, 401; Hatch et al., "Cancer Rates." Columbia research-ers performed "an investigation of whether or not the pattern of cancer [incidence] occur-rence after the March 28, 1979 [TMI] accident was related to radiation releases from the plant." They performed "an investigation of whether or not the pattern of cancer [incidence] occurrence after the March 28, 1979 [TMI] accident was related to radiation releases from the plant." assigned residents to 69 study tracts whose relative-estimated radiation exposures were grouped into 4 different ordinal levels, lowest to highest exposures. (They gave no car-dinal radiation-exposure estimates.) These 69 study tracts were built from census blocks and shaped like 69 pie pieces, with TMI as the center, and a 10-mile radius.
123. Hatch et al., "Cancer Near."
124. Hatch et al., "Cancer Rates," pp. 397, 719. Strengths of the Columbia studies are that (1) they were commissioned by the industry-funded TMI Public Health Fund and undertaken "as a public charge," as a response to public concern about TMI. (2) The authors also admitted the limits of their non-experimental TMI research. (3) They analyzed the TMI-area population, before and after the accident, instead of comparing the TMI group (which had low cancer rates, typical of a rural area) only to some other state or national group. (4) They studied cancer incidence, not merely cancer mortality, the latter of which has been shown to be a poor indicator of health effects. (5) They excluded chronic lymphocytic leukemia from their cancer-incidence data, as it is thought not to be associated with ionizing radiation.
125. Levin, "Incidence." The NRC maximum-dose claim is in Walker, *Three*, p. 207.
126. Talbott et al., "Long Term," p. 342.
127. Wing "Re-Evaluation," p. 53; S. Wing, *Affidavit in TMI Litigation Cases Consolidated II, Civil Action No 1:CV-88-1452* (Harrisburg: US District Court for the Middle District of Pennsylvania, 1995); hereafter cited as Wing, *Affidavit*. Because the Columbia studies based cancer-incidence rates on residence at diagnosis, they ignored radiation-exposed people who had left the area. (However, all other things being equal, emigrants arguably were more likely to have received higher TMI-radiation doses and injuries than others, in part because they chose to leave the area.) The researchers also counted people as radiation-exposed when they did not live at TMI at the time of the accident, because they assessed merely the TMI-area population, before and after the accident. Similarly, because they failed to consider birth cohorts, over time, increasing numbers of unexposed children were counted as exposed (to TMI radiation) in the study, although the children had not been conceived at the time of the accident. All these problems likely diluted, therefore caused underestimates of, TMI health effects.
128. Levin, "Incidence"; G. MacLeod, "A Role for Public Health in the Nuclear Age," *American Journal of Public Health* 72, no. 3 (1982): 237–238 of 237–239; hereafter cited as MacLeod, "Role"; Wasserman and Solomon, *Killing*, ch. 14; Mangano, "Three"; J. J. Mangano, "Low Level Radiation Harmed Humans near Three Mile Island," *Environmental Health Perspectives* 105 (1997): 786–787; hereafter cited as Mangano, "Low."
129. Wing, "Re-Evaluation"; Wing, *Affidavit*. The Columbia studies had limited statistical power because they considered only rare cancers (which occur in smaller numbers), rather than groups of cancers, such as all respiratory cancers. Were an effect present, these small-sample, low-power studies would have been unlikely to detect it.
130. Wing, "Re-Evaluation"; Wing, *Affidavit*. Because the Columbia studies used national aver-ages for comparison-cancer-incidence data, they failed to correct for geographic variations in cancer. This caused them to underestimate post-TMI effects, given that the rural TMI area has a lower-than-average cancer rate than the rest of the US.
131. Wing, "Objectivity." Although the Columbia studies assessed whether cancer-incidence rates were related to radiation exposure, as already mentioned, the researchers relied on industry and government radiation-exposure estimates. Consequently, they begged the question about the supposed effects of radiation because they were forced to assume that the doses were low. Although this question-begging is partly mitigated by the researchers' using rela-tive, ordinally characterized radiation doses (rather than cardinally characterized doses), as already mentioned, the problem still suggests they may not have had a testable hypothesis

about TMI health effects, given that those effects were required to have come only from assumed low radiation doses.

132. Hatch et al., "Cancer Rates," esp. p. 722.

133. Wing, "Objectivity," p. 1811. The Columbia University TMI studies on accident-related stress share at least 5 weaknesses. These include the facts that (1) as the researchers admit, they had no measure of stress and simply assumed that proximity to the reactor was a surrogate for stress. However, because many epidemiological studies use proximity to the reactor as an indicator of radiation releases and therefore cancer risk (see later remarks), it is difficult for the Columbia scientists to separate stress-related from radiation-related effects. (2) Because the Columbia researchers found that, prior to the accident, proximity to the reactor likewise was related to cancer incidence (odds ratio 1.2)—a result best explained by radiation—it is unclear how much of the post-TMI odds ratio (1.4) is stress-related, not radiation-related. (3) The researchers also failed to consider that a very-high-dose radiation plume, traveling downwind, between the widely spaced later dosimeters, could have caused cancers that, when averaged out, appeared related to reactor proximity, the researchers' proxy for stress. (4) Moreover, contrary to S, although they found an odds ratio for cancer and stress (proximity to the reactor) that was 1.4, the odds ratio for lung cancer and proximity is 1.7. Because most TMI releases were gaseous, radiation (not stress) would have disproportionately caused lung cancers. (5) Also contrary to S, although they found an odds ratio for cancer and stress (proximity to the reactor) that was 1.4, hilltop communities 3–8 miles downwind of TMI had a sevenfold cancer increase within 4 years after the accident. Although the small numbers of cases (2.6 jumping to 19) make definitive medical interpretations problematic, the hilltop communities were more likely to have been affected by a narrow high-dose radiation plume, not by stress.

134. The UNC scientists assessed "associations between [TMI] accident doses [of radiation] and incidence rates" of cancer. Although the Columbia research compared odds ratios for pre- and post-accident cancer-incidence data on the basis of national cancer-incidence data, the UNC scientists (1) corrected for the Columbia scientists' ignoring geographical variation in cancer incidence and for underestimating resulting TMI cancers. They also (2) grouped similar cancers together, e.g., all respiratory cancers, and (3) grouped all leukemias together, thus avoided Columbia's low-power, small-sample studies. The UNC study likewise avoided Columbia's low-power, small-sample studies. They (4) avoided the Columbia inability to detect childhood cancers by considering birth cohorts, and (5) quantified possible radiation-cancer associations by means of a log-linear Poisson regression model, and expressed these associations as the average log percent change in cancer incidence, per unit change in estimated dose. Consequently, the UNC scientists were able to show something the Columbia researchers could not: that "radiation doses are related to increased cancer incidence around TMI" and therefore that R is likely correct. Wing, et al., "Re-Evaluation," esp. p. 52; Wing, *Affidavit*.

135. Mangano, "Three."

136. Other strengths of the UNC researchers are that (1) they discussed the limits of their non-experimental TMI research. (2) They also mitigated the radiation-dose-estimation problem because, although they were investigating the association between cancer-incidence and radiation dose, they interpreted these associations as an indication of the possible coincidence of radiation-plume travel and thus higher cancer incidence. This interpretation allowed the epidemiological analysis both to provide a genuine test of the hypothesis R (whether post-TMI increased cancer rates are related to TMI radiation) and to be interpretable as an indicator of higher possible radiation doses than those estimated by industry and the government. (3) They likewise allowed for the greater sensitivity of cancer incidence to radiation dose because they divided relative radiation-exposure groups into 9 different, ordinally characterized, levels (rather than 4, as Columbia scientists had done). (4) They compared the TMI-area population, before and after the accident, instead of comparing the TMI group only to some state or national group. (5) They studied cancer incidence, not merely cancer mortality, the

latter of which has been shown to be a poor indicator of health effects. Finally, (6) the UNC scientists also excluded chronic lymphocytic leukemia from their cancer-incidence data, as it is thought not to be associated with ionizing radiation. Wing, "Re-Evaluation," pp. 56–57.

137. Following Columbia research, UNC scientists underestimated TMI-induced cancers because they explored TMI effects only within a 10-mile radius, even though airborne radio-nuclides travel hundreds or thousands of miles, and because they oversimplified wind direction, assuming that the north–northwest direction prevailed throughout the accident, although this north–northwest wind direction is atypical, not the prevailing direction, and contrary to where most post-TMI cancers, hypothyroidism, and infant/neonatal mortality arose: e.g., Levin, "Incidence." However, the UNC researchers' consideration of birth cohorts mitigated some of this resulting dilution of TMI health effects, at least in the case of children.

138. Talbott et al., "Long Term," p. 342.

139. Levin, "Incidence"; MacLeod, "Role"; Wasserman and Solomon, *Killing*, ch. 14; Mangano, "Three"; Mangano, "Low."

140. Wing, "Re-Evaluation"; Wing, *Affidavit*.

141. Using relative-risk (RR) regression modeling, they compared post-TMI mortality rates in the 5-mile TMI cohort to mortality rates (standard mortality ratios) in another state population, in order to determine whether TMI radioactivity had any impact on local mortality rates. Unlike the Columbia and UNC researchers, who used ordinal radiation-dose levels (with no cardinal estimates), Pittsburgh scientists divided their 2 exposure groups (estimated maximum gamma exposure and estimated likely gamma exposure) into 4 different estimated-radiation-exposure levels, each of which was characterized by a range of cardinal radiation-exposure estimates. For instance, for the likely gamma exposure, the 4 estimated levels were < 3 rem, 3–7 mrem, 8–15 mrem, > or = 16 mrem. After assessing these data, the researchers concluded that RR was elevated for some cancers. However, because many results failed tests of statistical significance, the researchers rejected R and said "overall cancer mortality in this cohort was similar to [that of] the local population." Talbott et al., "Long Term," esp. pp. 341, 346; Talbott et al., "Mortality."

142. These strengths include the facts that (1) the research was commissioned and funded by the TMI Public Health Fund, as a response to public concern about TMI. (2) Researchers discussed the limits of their non-experimental TMI studies. (3) They used a longer follow-up period, 18 years, than earlier studies. (4) "No other study has followed prospectively a non-occupationally-exposed cohort of this magnitude," roughly 32,000 people. (5) The researchers excluded chronic lymphocytic leukemia and Hodgkin's disease from their results, as both have rarely been linked to radiation. (6) To increase statistical power, the researchers grouped similar cancers together, e.g., total lymphatic-hematopoietic cancers. Talbott et al., "Long Term," esp. pp. 342–348; Talbott et al., "Mortality"; Mangano, "Three."

143. M. Hatch and M. Susser, "Background Gamma Radiation and Childhood Cancers within Ten Miles of a US Nuclear Plant," *International Journal of Epidemiology* 19, no. 3 (1990): 546–552; hereafter cited as Hatch and Susser, "Background."

144. Levin, "Incidence."

145. Ibid.; MacLeod, "Role," pp. 237–238; Wasserman and Solomon, *Killing*, ch. 14; Mangano, "Three"; Mangano, "Low."

146. Arun Makhijani, B. Smith, and M. C. Thorne, *Science for the Vulnerable* (Takoma Park, MD: Institute for Energy and Environmental Research, 2006), pp. 29–31, 37–39, 77; hereafter cited as Makhijani, Smith and Thorne, *Science*.

147. Wing, "Objectivity."

148. Talbott et al., "Long Term," p. 347.

149. US National Cancer Institute (NCI), *National Cancer Institute Brain Tumor Study in Adults* (Washington, DC: National Institutes of Health, 2009); accessed July 22, 2009, at www.cancer.gov/cancertopics/factsheet/risk/brain-tumor-study.

150. Talbott et al., "Long Term," pp. 344–345.

151. Ibid., pp. 341, 346, 347; Hatch et al., "Cancer Rates," pp. 721–722; Hatch et al., "Cancer Near," p. 397.

152. M. San Sebastian et al., "Exposures and Cancer Incidence Near Oil Fields in the Amazon Basin of Ecuador," *Occupational and Environmental Medicine* 58, no. 8 (2001): 517–522; S. M. Llana, "Chevron Fights Massive Lawsuit in Ecuador," *Christian Science Monitor*, May 29, 2009; accessed July 4, 2009, at http://features.csmonitor.com/environment/2009/05/29/chevron-fights-massive-lawsuit-in-ecuador/.

153. Michael Kelsh, Libby Morimoto, and Edmund Lau, "Cancer Mortality and Oil Production in the Amazon Region of Ecuador," *International Archives of Occupational and Environmental Medicine* 82, no. 3 (2008): 381–395.

154. C. Poole and K. J. Rothman, "Our Conscientious Objection to the Epidemiology Wars," *Journal of Epidemiology and Community Health* 52 (1998): 612–618.

155. D. A. Savitz, *Interpreting Epidemiologic Evidence* (New York: Oxford University Press, 2003).

156. S. Greenland, "Randomization, Statistics, and Causal Inference," *Epidemiology* 1, no. 6 (1990): 421–429; hereafter cited as Greenland, "Randomization"; Sander Greenland, "Response and Follow-Up Bias in Cohort Studies," *American Journal of Epidemiology* 106 (1977): 184.

157. Carl Cranor, *Toxic Torts* (New York: Cambridge University Press, 2006), pp. 240–241; hereafter cited as Cranor, *Toxic Torts*.

158. Rothman, "Statistics," p. 417.

159. E.g., Jean Philippe Empana, Pierre Ducimetiere, et al., "Are the Framingham and PROCAM Coronary Heart Disease Risk Functions Applicable to Different European Populations?," *European Heart Journal* 24 (2003): 1903–1911; hereafter cited as Empana et al., "Framingham."

160. R. Curtis Ellison, "AHA Science Advisory on Wine and Health," *Circulation* 104 (2001): e72; hereafter cited as Ellison, "AHA"; R. Curtis Ellison, "Importance of Pattern of Alcohol Consumption," *Circulation* 112 (2005): 3818–3819.

161. International Agency for Research on Cancer (IARC) (2008), *Monograph: Overall Evaluations of Carcinogenicity to Humans*, Supplement 7, 2008; accessed August 27, 2008, at http://monographs.iarc.fr/ ENG/Monographs/suppl7/Suppl7-5.pdf; Kaye M. Fillmore and W. Kerr, "A Bostrom Abstinence from Alcohol and Mortality Risk in Prospective Studies," *Nordic Studies on Alcohol and Drugs* 19, no. 4 (2002): 295–296.

162. Greenland, "Randomization," p. 428; Hacking, *Taming*, p. 206.

163. Garth Anderson, "Genomic Instability in Cancer," *Current Science* 81, no. 5 (2001): 501–507.

164. James Woodward, "Invariance, Explanation, and Understanding," *Metascience* 15 (2006): 56–57 of 53–66.

165. E.g., Empana et al., "Framingham."

166. NRC/NAS, *Health*, pp. 379, 376.

167. Wing, "Objectivity", p. 1815; see McCloskey and Ziliak, "Cult."

168. P. Lipton, *Inference to the Best Explanation* (New York: Routledge, 2004,), pp. 7–20; hereafter cited as Lipton, *Inference*; see C. K. Waters, "Causes That Make a Difference," *Journal of Philosophy* 104, no. 2 (2007): 551–579; hereafter cited as Waters, "Causes."

169. See C. Hempel, *Aspects of Scientific Explanation* (New York: Free Press, 1965), pp. 421–443; B. Van Fraassen, *The Scientific Image* (Oxford: Oxford University Press, 1980); David Lewis, "Causal Explanation," in *Philosophical Papers* (Oxford: Oxford University Press, 1986), vol. 2, pp. 214–240; Lipton, *Inference*; Jonathan Schaffer, "Contrastive Causation," *Philosophical Review* 114, no. 3 (2005): 297–328; Waters, "Causes."

170. J. S. Mill, *A System of Logic*, 8th ed. (London: Longman, Greens, and Company, 1904), III. VII.2; C. Hempel, *The Philosophy of Natural Science* (Englewood Cliffs, NJ: Prentice-Hall, 1966), pp. 3–8, 338; Lipton, *Inference*, pp. 7–90; Waters, "Causes."

171. Hatch et al., "Cancer Rates"; Hatch et al., "Cancer Near," pp. 406–407; Wing, "Re-Evaluation," p. 56.

172. Talbott et al., "Long Term," pp. 343.
173. D.B. Richardson, et al., "Positive Associations between Ionizing Radiation and Lymphoma Mortality among Men," *American Journal of Epidemiology* 169, no. 8(2009): 969-76.
174. MacLeod, "Role," p. 237; Walker, *Three*; World Nuclear Association (WNA), *Three Mile Island: 1979* (London: WNA, 2001); accessed February 24, 2009, at www.world-nuclear.org/info/inf36.html; hereafter cited as WNA, *Three*.
175. Talbott et al., "Long Term," pp. 344-345; Hatch et al., "Cancer Rates."
176. Hatch et al., "Cancer Rates."
177. Ibid.
178. NRC/NAS, *Health*; R. Jones and R. Southwood (eds.), *Radiation and Health* (Chichester: Wiley, 1987).
179. E.g., J. Raingeaud et al., "Pro-Inflammatory Cytokines and Environmental Stress Case p38 Mitogen-Activated Protein Kinase Activation," *Journal of Biochemistry* 270, no. 14 (1995): 7420-7426.
180. E.g., J. MacLeod and G. D. Smith, Re: "Job Stress and Breast Cancer Risk," *American Journal of Epidemiology* 162, no. 11 (2005): 1133-1134; Eva S. Schernhammer, Susan E. Hankinson, Bernard Rosner, Candyce H. Kroenke, Walter C. Willett, Graham A. Colditz, and Ichiro Kawachi, "Job Stress and Breast Cancer Risk," *American Journal of Epidemiology* 160, no. 11 (2004): 1079; D. Prothero et al., "Stressful Life Events and Difficulties and Onset of Breast Cancer," *British Medical Journal* 319 (October 16, 1999): 1027-1030; M. Joffres, D. M. Reed, and A. M. Y. Nomura, "Psychosocial Processes and Cancer Incidence," *American Journal of Epidemiology* 121, no. 4 (1985): 488-500.
181. O. Helgesson, C. Cabrera, L. Lapidus, C. Bengtsson, and L. Lissner, "Self-Reported Stress Levels Predict Subsequent Breast Cancer," *European Journal of Cancer Prevention* 12, no. 5 (2003): 377-381; Hans Schilder, "Stress and Cancer," *British Medical Journal* 319 (October 22, 1999); accessed July 1, 2009, at www.bmj.com/cgi/eletters/319/7216/1015; A. G. Dalgleish, "Stress and Cancer," *British Medical Journal* 319 (October 28, 1999): l; accessed July 1, 2009, at www.bmj.com/cgi/eletters/319/7216/1015.
182. Wing, "Objectivity," p. 1811; Wing, *Affidavit*; Wing et al., "Re-Evaluation."
183. E.g., Levin, "Incidence"; Mangano, "Three."
184. Hatch et al., "Cancer Rates," p. 721.
185. Code of Federal Regulations (CFR), *Protection of Environment, Title 40*, Part 190, *Subsection B 10* (Washington, DC: US Government Printing Office, 2009).
186. Mangano, "Infant," pp. 23-31.
187. E.g., P. Kaatsch et al., "Leukemia in Young Children Living in the Vicinity of German Nuclear Power Plants," *International Journal of Cancer* 1220 (2008): 721-726; hereafter cited as Kaatsch, "Leukemia"; C. Spix, "Do Nuclear Plants Boost Leukemia Risk?," *New Scientist* 2642 (2008): 6; J. J. Mangano, "Excess Infant Mortality after Nuclear Plant Startup in Rural Mississippi," *International Journal of Health Services* 38 (2008): 277-291; J. J. Mangano, "A Short Latency between Radiation Exposure from Nuclear Plants and Cancer in Young Children," *International Journal of Health Services* 36, no. 1 (2006): 113-135; J. J. Mangano, "Infant Death and Childhood Cancer Reductions after Nuclear Plant Closings in the United States," *Archives of Environmental Health* 57 (2002): 23-31; hereafter cited as Mangano, "Infant"; J. J. Mangano, "Improvements in Local Infant Health after Nuclear Power Reactor Closing," *Environmental Epidemiology and Toxicology* 2 (2000): 32-36; J. J. Mangano and J. D. Sherman, "Childhood Leukemia near Nuclear Installations," *European Journal of Cancer Care* 17, no. 4 (2008): 416-418; P. J. Baker and D. G. Hoel, "Meta-analysis of Standardized Incidence and Mortality Rates of Childhood Leukemia in Proximity to Nuclear Facilities," *European Journal of Cancer Care* 16, no. 4 (2007): 355-363; A. V. Guizard et al., "The Incidence of Childhood Leukaemia around the La Hague Nuclear Waste Reprocessing Plant (France): A Survey for the Years 1978-1998," *Journal of Epidemiology and Community Health* 55 (2001): 469-474; C. Busby and M. Scott-Cato, "Death Rates from Leukemia Are Higher Than Expected in Areas around Nuclear Sites in Berkshire and Oxfordshire," *British Medical Journal* 315 (1997): 309; W. Watson and D. Sumner,

"Measurement of Radioactivity in People Living near the Dounreay Nuclear Establishment, Caithness, Scotland," *International Journal of Radiation Biology* 70, no. 2 (1996): 117–130; J. F. Viel and D. Pobel, "Case-Control Study of Leukaemia among Young People near La Hague Nuclear Reprocessing Plant: The Environmental Hypothesis Revisited," *British Medical Journal* 314, no. 7074 (1997): 101–106; J. F. Viel, D. Pobel, and A. Carre, "Incidence of Leukemia in Young People around the La Hague Nuclear Waste Reprocessing Plant," *Statistics in Medicine* 14 (1995): 2459–2472; J. Michaelis et al., "Incidence of Childhood Malignancies in the Vicinity of West German Nuclear Power Plants," *Cancer Causes and Control* 3 (1992): 255–263; Hatch and Susser, "Background"; M. J. Gardner et al., "Results of Case Control Study of Leukemia and Lymphoma among Young People near Sellafield Nuclear Plant in West Cumbria," *British Medical Journal* 300 (1990): 423–434; M. Morris and R. Knorr, *The Southeastern Massachusetts Health Study 1978–1986* (Boston: Massachusetts Department of Public Health, 1994); B. E. Gibson et al., "Leukemia in Young Children in Scotland," *Lancet* 2 (1988): 630; M. A. Heasman et al., "Childhood Leukaemia in Northern Scotland," *Lancet* 1 (1986): 266; Richard W. Clapp et al., "Leukaemia near Massachusetts Nuclear Power Plant," *Lancet* 336 (1987): 1324–1325; D. Forman et al., "Cancer near Nuclear Installations," *Nature* 329 (1987): 499–505.

188. E.g., Hatch et al., "Cancer Rates"; Hatch et al., "Cancer Near," pp. 397–398, 410–411; ANS, *Health*; A. C. Upton, "Health Impact of the Three Mile Island Accident," *Annals of the New York Academy of Sciences* 365, no. 1 (2006): 63–75; Rambo, "Three"; Rogovin and Frampton, *Three*; Kemeny et al., *Report*.

189. Epstein, "Science," pp. 9–10; May, *Nuclear Age*; Lang, "Three," p. 11.

190. Wing, "Objectivity," pp. 1810, 1812; Wing, *Affidavit*; Wing, "Re-Evaluation"; May, *Nuclear Age*; Katagiri Mitsuru and Aileen M. Smith, *Three Mile Island: The People's Testament* (Harrisburg, PA: Three Mile Island Action, 1989), accessed July 7, 2009, at www.tmia.com/mode/118; hereafter cited as Mitsuru and Smith, *Three*; Wasserman and Solomon, *Killing*, ch. 14.

191. Thomas Jefferson National Accelerator Facility, *Radiation Biological Effects* (Newport News, VA: Jefferson Labs, 2004); hereafter cited as TJ, *Radiation*.

192. Ibid.

193. International Commission on Radiological Protection (ICRP), *2005 Recommendations* (Stockholm: ICRP, 2005), 32.

194. H. Yamazaki et al., "Pelvic Irradiation-Induced Eosinophilia Is Correlated to Prognosis," *Radiation Medicine* 23, no. 5 (2005): 317–321; Wing, "Objectivity"; Wing, *Affidavit*; Wing, "Re-Evaluation"; V. A. Shevchenko and G. P. Snigiryova, "Cytogenetic Effects of the Action of Ionizing Radiations on Human Populations," in E. B. Burlakova (ed.), *Consequences of the Chernobyl Catastrophe* (Moscow: Center for Russian Environmental Policy and Scientific Council on Radiobiology, 1996), pp. 23–45; hereafter cited as Shevchenko and Snigiryova, "Cytogenetic"; V. A. Shevchenko, "Assessment of Genetic Risk from Exposure of Human Populations to Radiation," in E. B. Burlakova (ed.), *Consequences of the Chernobyl Catastrophe: Human Health* (Moscow: Center for Russian Environmental Policy and Scientific Council on Radiobiology, 1996), 47–61; hereafter cited as Shevchenko, "Assessment"; Wasserman and Solomon, *Killing*, ch. 14; Robert Del Tredici, *People of Three Mile Island* (San Francisco: Sierra Club, 1980); hereafter cited as Del Tredici, *People*.

195. Pennsylvania Department of Health (PA DOH), *TMI Area Death Rates No Higher Than State Average* (Harrisburg: PA DOH, 1981), Tables 4, 5; Wasserman and Solomon, *Killing*, ch. 14.

196. Talbott et al., "Long Term," pp. 343, 348.

197. Greenland, "Randomization," p. 427.

198. NRC/NAS, *Health*, 6; International Commission on Radiological Protection (ICRP), *1990 Recommendations of the ICRP* (Oxford, England: Pergamon, 1991).

199. Cardis et al., "Risk." Of course, risk numbers from worker studies vary widely, partly because of difficulties with the underlying data from different nations; nevertheless, all the data show the LNT curve.

200. Kaatsch, "Leukemia."
201. E.g., MacLeod, "Role"; Wasserman and Solomon, *Killing*, ch. 14; Mangano, "Three"; Mangano, "Low," pp. 786–787; Levin, "Incidence."
202. Hatch et al., "Cancer Near"; Wing, *Affidavit*; Wing et al., "Re-Evaluation"; Mangano, "Three"; Levin, "Incidence."
203. M. Wahlen, C. O. Kunz, et al., "Radioactive Plume from the Three Mile Island Accident," *Science* 207, no. 4431 (1980): 639–640; hereafter cited as Wahlen, Kunz, et al., "Radioactive"; R. W. Holloway, and C. K. Liu, "Xenon-133 in California, Nevada, and Utah from the Chernobyl Accident," *Environmental Science and Technology* 22, no. 5 (1988): 583–586; hereafter cited as Holloway and Liu, "Xenon"; Mangano, "Three," pp. 32–35.
204. Wahlen, Kunz, et al., "Radioactive"; Holloway and Liu, "Xenon"; Wasserman and Solomon, *Killing*, ch. 14; Mangano, "Three"; Mangano, "Low," pp. 786–787.
205. Wing, "Objectivity"; Wing, *Affidavit*; Wing, Richardson, and Armstrong, "Re-Evaluation"; Wing et al., "Re-Evaluation."
206. Lipton, *Interference*, pp. 119, 139.
207. James E. Gunckel, *Affidavit 9* (Bridgewater, NJ: The Bulletin of the Torrey Botanical Club, 1984); accessed July 7, 2009, at www.southernstudies.org/images/sitepieces/gunckel_affidavit_plants.pdf; Mitsuru and Smith, *Three*; Del Tredici, *People*; May, *Nuclear Age* ; Shevchenko and Snigiryova, "Cytogenetic"; Shevchenko, "Assessment"; Rambo, "Three"; Harvey Wasserman, *People Died at Three Mile Island* (Columbus, Ohio: Free Press, 2009); accessed July 27, 2009, at www.freepress.org/columbus/display/7/2009/1733; hereafter cited as Wasserman, *People*; Wing et al., "Re-Evaluation"; Wing, *Affidavit*.
208. MacLeod, "Role"; Wasserman and Solomon, *Killing*, ch. 14; Mangano, "Three"; Mangano, "Low," pp. 786–787; see Makhijani, Smith, and Thorne, *Science*.
209. Talbott et al., "Long Term"; WNA, *Three*.
210. Greenland, "Randomization," pp. 425–427; C. R. Muirhead, "Invited Commentary: Cancer near Nuclear Installations," *American Journal of Epidemiology* 32, no. 3 (1990): Mangano, "Three."
211. Mangano, "Three," p. 35.
212. E.g., Talbott et al., "Long Term."
213. Makhijani, Smith, and Thorne, *Science*.
214. Mangano, "Three"; Wasserman, *People*; Wing, "Re-Evaluation"; Wing, *Affidavit*.
215. J. L. Bermejo, J. Sundquist, and K. Hemminki, "Risk of Cancer among the Offspring of Women Who Experienced Parental Death during Pregnancy," *Cancer Epidemiology, Biomarkers, and Prevention* 16, no. 10 (2007): 2204–2208.
216. NRC/NAS, *Health*.
217. Ibid.
218. E.g., James Woodward, *Making Things Happen* (Oxford: Oxford University Press, 2003); hereafter cited as Woodward, *Making*; Judea Pearl, *Causality* (Cambridge: Cambridge University Press, 2000); hereafter cited as Pearl, *Causality*.
219. E.g., Peter Machamer, P. L. Darden, and C. Craver, "Thinking about Mechanisms," *Philosophy of Science* 67 (2000): 1–25; hereafter cited as Machamer, Darden, and Craver, "Thinking"; James Bogen, "Analyzing Causality," *International Studies in the Philosophy of Science* 18 (2004): 3–26; hereafter cited as Bogen, "Analyzing"; Stuart Glennan, "Rethinking Mechanical Explanation," *Philosophy of Science* 69 (2002): S342–S353; hereafter cited as Glennan, "Rethinking"; S. Glennan, "Mechanisms and the Nature of Causation," *Erkenntnis* 44 (1996): 47–91; hereafter cited as Glennan, "Mechanisms."
220. Philip Kitcher, "Explanatory Unification and the Causal Structure of the World," in Wesley Salmon and Philip Kitcher (eds.), *Scientific Explanation* (Minneapolis: University of Minnesota Press, 1989), pp. 410–505; hereafter cited as Kitcher, "Explanatory"; see Woodward, *Making*, ch. 8. Of course, no account of causal explanation is wholly compatible with other accounts. Each cannot always take account of different counterexamples and scientific disciplines. Also, various causal accounts are criticized by proponents of other

accounts. Nevertheless, to the degree that different accounts of causal explanation generally agree on particular constraints that should be imposed on causal claims, to that degree are different accounts of causal explanation likely to agree in their assessments of S and R.

221. Woodward explains contrasts such as the difference between the incidence of recovery from a cold among those who take a particular drug (the treatment group), and its incidence among those who do not take the drug (the control group). He says "we should think of this difference between treatment and control in terms of counterfactuals...the difference between what the response (with respect to recovery) would be if a subject...were treated...and how this response compares with what the response would be if the very same...subjects were not treated." In other words, a major motivation for Woodward's counterfactual formulation is that it helps tell scientists what to aim at, in choosing one experimental design or control group rather than another—or in using explicit matching or randomization to choose a control that is relevantly like the treatment group. James Woodward, "Counterfactual and Causal Explanation," *International Studies in the Philosophy of Science* 18, no. 1 (March 2004): 54 of 41–72; hereafter cited as Woodward, "Counterfactual"; Woodward, *Making*, pp. 67–68, 145–146.

222. Woodward, "Counterfactual," p. 66.

223. Woodward avoids two problematic aspects of Lewis's theory, namely, commitment to a strong form of realism about possible worlds other than the actual one, and Lewis's commitment to a view that bears little connection to scientific work. Instead, Woodward characterizes counterfactuals as tied to experiments, as claims "about what would happen if a certain sort of experiment were to be performed." Woodward also avoids Lewis's talk about the similarity among different worlds, and instead uses equations, graphs, and rules to specify what happens under interventions; he uses these interventions to "tell us explicitly just what should be regarded as changed and what should be 'held fixed' when we entertain various counterfactual assumptions." Woodward, "Counterfactual," pp. 42–44; see David Lewis, "Causation," *Journal of Philosophy* 70 (1973): 556–567.

224. At least 5 reasons suggest that the 5 IBE principles (of contrastive explanation, CE) analyze alternative TMI causal hypotheses in ways that are roughly consistent with using Woodward's interventionist-counterfactual scheme.

First, tantamount to experimentation, Woodward would also assess causal relations by manipulating (including counterfactually) putative causes (e.g., radiation, stress) to analyze resulting changes in effects, just as earlier paragraphs varied (or removed) radiation or stress, to examine resulting changes in effects.

Second, consistent with the preceding remarks on the importance of randomization in statistics, Woodward can explain why non-experimental TMI studies—that used classical statistical tests--likely erred. They controlled neither preexisting endogenous causal connections, nor those set exogenously by experimental design. As a result, they were unable to evaluate other potential causes.

Third, Woodward takes CE as mapping onto his interventionist-counterfactual-causal theory, which instantiates Mill's difference principle, as does IBE-CE. As Mill does, IBE-CE principle (2) seeks contrasts supporting one cause over another, while Woodward's account provides a vehicle for finding such contrasts, through counterfactual manipulation.

A *fourth* reason that IBE-CE and Woodward's interventionist-counterfactual accounts might both support R over S is that using IBE-CE principle (3) is similar to Woodward's manipulating putative causes, in order to determine what is invariant and what controls effects. For him, ranges of invariance (e.g., characterizing radiation-dose-response curves) would reveal that R (not S) is a better explainer of TMI harms, just as radiation-dose-response curves would provide principle (3) evidence for R, not S. Woodward's idea is that if one can exploit this (e.g., dose-response) invariance in order to control the effect (e.g., TMI health harms), then there is a causal relationship between some purported cause (e.g., R) and some purported effects (e.g., cancer increases). Woodward emphasizes what would have happened to an effect if the cause had been manipulated differently. Because he does so, the greater the range of invariance of the relationship that supports such counterfactuals, and the greater the range of "What if things had been different?" questions that are successfully answered, therefore the better the explanation.

A *fifth* reason that Woodward's scheme is likely to assess TMI hypotheses S and R in ways that are similar to the IBE-CE assessment is that IBE-CE principle (4) is similar to Woodward's requirement to proceed negatively (to show that counterfactuals can characterize interventions causally). In proceeding negatively, Woodward urges scientists to "formulate conditions that exclude all the other ways" that an intervention that changes an alleged cause might be associated with changes in an alleged effect. Woodward, "Counterfactual," p. 61; Woodward, *Making*, pp. 258–261, 304; see Waters, "Causes"; Pearl, *Causality*; Paul Humphreys, "Invariance, Explanation, and Understanding," *Metascience* 15 (2006): 41 of 39–44; Elliot Sober, "Invariance, Explanation, and Understanding," *Metascience* 15 (2006): 48 of 45–53; hereafter cited as Sober, "Invariance."

225. E.g., Machamer, Darden, and Craver, "Thinking"; Bogen, "Analyzing"; Glennan, "Rethinking"; Glennan, "Mechanisms."

226. This mechanist strategy is similar to part of IBE-CE principle (5), namely, using heterogeneous (e.g., mechanistic) evidence to produce new contrasts to "test" causal hypotheses. Lipton, *Inference*.

227. Because Kitcher's unificationist account requires that better causal explanations unify greater ranges of phenomena with fewer assumptions, inference-patterns, and argument-patterns, it is similar to part of IBE-CE principle (5)—discovering contrasts that unify explanatory schemes. Kitcher argues that the fewer the number of inference patterns used, the more "stringent" they are in imposing constraints on the derivations that instantiate them, and therefore the greater the range of different conclusions derived, the more unified is the explanation. See Kitcher, "Explanatory," and earlier sections of this chapter; see also Woodward, *Making*, ch. 8.

228. Ellison, "AHA."

229. Caldicott, *Nuclear*, p. 67.

230. Wasserman and Solomon, *Killing*, ch. 14; Rosalie Bertell, *Rosalie Bertell on Three Mile Island* (Toronto: International Institute of Concern for Public Health, 1998); accessed March 11, 2009, at www.iicph.org/docs/tmi/htm; Dolan et al., In Re: *TMI Litigation*.

231. Wing, "Objectivity."

232. Cranor, *Toxic Torts*.

233. E.g., Hatch et al., "Cancer Near."

234. K. Shrader-Frechette, *Taking Action, Saving Lives* (New York: Oxford University Press, 2007), p. 187; hereafter cited as Shrader-Frechette, *TASL*.

235. Sharon Beder, *Global Spin* (Glasgow, UK: Green Books, 2002), pp. 134–136, 195–213, 224–225; Sheldon Krimsky, *Science in the Private Interest* (Savage, MD: Rowman and Littlefield, 2003); Kai Koizumi, *R&D Trends and Special Analyses, AAAS Report* (Washington, DC: American Association for the Advancement of Science, 2005–2004); Shrader-Frechette, *TASL*, ch. 3.

236. S. Jablon, Z. Hrubec, and J. D. Boice Jr., "Cancer in Populations Living near Nuclear Facilities," *Journal of the American Medical Association* 265 (1991): 1403–1408. The NCI study admitted it could support no definitive conclusions, yet claimed its evidence showed no higher cancer rates in US counties with nuclear plants.

237. E.g., Hatch and Susser, "Background."

238. Bogen, "Analyzing," for instance, says that because Woodward's deterministic counterfactuals with false antecedents are vacuously true, they are useless for elucidating causal claims. Another objection is that one might illegitimately accept or reject many counterfactual manipulations (removals or varyings) of purported causal factors, when one is attempting to see what hypothesis explains what effects. That is, when one follows IBE-CE principle (3), one might illegitimately accept or reject some manipulations and therefore causal explanations. Obviously, however, if one uses counterfactual manipulation or removal of purported

causes to help elucidate causal claims, one must know how to test them. If so, this objection loses much of its force.

239. Ibid.

240. Woodward, "Counterfactual," pp. 46–47, 63; Woodward, *Making*, pp. 339–342.

241. James Woodward, "Sensitive and Insensitive Causation," *Philosophical Review* 115, no. 1 (2006): 1–50; James Woodward, "Prospects for a Manipulability Account of Causation," in *Logic, Methodology and Philosophy of Science*, ed. P. Hajek, L. Valdes-Villanueva, and D. Westerstahl (London: King's College, 2005), 336 of 333–348; hereafter cited as Woodward, "Prospects"; Sober, "Invariance," p. 48. Against Woodward's account, Sober says he should not claim that causes are necessary to their effects. That is, Woodward claims that the occurrence of c (a cause) is counterfactually dependent on the occurrence of e (an effect) if and only if the following two counterfactuals hold: $O(c) \rightarrow O(e)$ [and] $-O(c) \rightarrow -O(e)$. He thus gives necessary and sufficient conditions for "X causes Y" and says (sufficient condition) that if possible interventions/manipulations "change the value of X such that under such interventions (and no other [intervention]s), X and Y are correlated, then X causes Y." He says (necessary condition) that if X causes Y then "there are possible interventions that change the value of X" such that "under such interventions (and no other interventions), X and Y are correlated." Thus, the objector might say, Woodward appears to believe that if Harry's smoking caused Harry's cancer, this implies that if Harry had not smoked, he would not have gotten cancer. Continuing, the objector might say, because Woodward recognizes that causation can occur in situations that are chancy, he recognizes that token causes are necessary for their effects, but they need not be sufficient. But for the same reason, the objector might say, Woodward should reject the claim that causes are necessary for their effects because "if Harry hadn't smoked, the cancer could still have arisen, by chance."

242. In response to the objection that Woodward should not claim that causes are necessary to their effects, Woodward says he restricts his conditions to a single intervention on X (e.g., smoking) because "without this restriction, correlated interventions on X and Y will produce correlated changes in these variables, even if they are causally unrelated." Moreover, given many different contributing causes, Woodward says that one can employ a combination of different interventions to assess causal relationships. Woodward thus solves the problem of separating multiple possible causes by mentioning the need for multiple interventions to deal with multiple causes and to separate each of them—a multiplicity that goes beyond Lewis's account. To suggest how this might be done, Woodward uses an example from Cartwright. She gives the example of trying to determine the efficacy of a drug, given that the intervention or treatment might be affected by a placebo. She and Woodward both suggest trying to avoid or remove placebo effects by treating everyone overtly the same, whether they receive the drug or a counterfeit of it, or ensuring that everyone has potential placebo effects, while they are being tested for drug efficacy. In other words, Woodward's response is to do multiple interventions for multiple potential causes of some effect—so that one has multiple controls. Woodward, "Prospects," pp. 333–336, 345; Woodward, *Making*, pp. 50–61; Nancy Cartwright, "Modularity: It Can—and Generally Does—Fail," in M. P. Galavotti, P. Suppes, and D. Constantini (eds.), *Stochastic Causality* (Stanford, CA: CSLI Publications, 2001), p. 77.

243. NRC/NAS, *Health*.

Chapter 5

1. Y. E. Dubrova, O. G. Polshchanskaya, O. S. Kozionova, and A. V. Akieyev, "Minisatellite Germline Mutation Rate in the Techa River Population," *Mutation Research* 602, nos. 1–2 (December 1, 2006): 74–82.

2. R. C. Barber, P. Hickenbotham, T. Hatch, D. Kelly, N. Topchiy, G. Almeida, G. G. Jones, G. E. Johnson, J. M. Parry, K. Tothkamm, and Y. E. Dubrova, "Radiation-Induced Transgenerational

Alterations in Genome Stability and DNA Damage," *Oncogene* 25 (2006): 7336–7342. T. Hatch, A. A. Derijck, P. D. Black, G. W. Van Der Heiden, P. DeBoer, and Y. E. Dubrova, "Maternal Effects of the Scid Mutation on Radiation-Induced Transgenerational Instability in Mice," *Oncogene* 26 (2007): 4720–4724.

3. Y. E. Dubrova, P. Hickenbotham, C. D. Glen, K. Monger, H.-P. Wong, and R. C. Barber, "Paternal Exposure to Ethylnitrosourea Results in Transgenerational Genomic Instability in Mice," *Environmental and Molecular Mutagenesis* 49 (2008): 308–311. Y. E. Dubrova, "Radiation-Induced Transgenerational Instability," *Oncogene* 22 (2003): 7087–7093.

4. See Kristin Shrader-Frechette, *Environmental Justice: Creating Equality, Reclaiming Democracy* (New York: Oxford University Press, 2003); hereafter cited as Shrader-Frechette, *EJ.*

5. US Advisory Committee on Human Radiation Experiments, Human Radiation Experiments Associated with the US Department of Energy and Its Predecessors (Washington, DC: US Department of Energy, July 1995); hereafter cited as US Advisory Committee, Human Radiation.

6. Center for World Indigenous Studies, *The Fourth World Documentation Project* (Olympia, WA: CWIS, 1999); World Information Service on Energy, "Uranium Mining and Indigenous People," 2006, accessed June 31, 2008, at http://www.wise-uranium.org/uip.html.

7. Jonathan M. Samet, D. M. Kutvirt, R. J. Waxweiler, and C. R. Key, "Uranium Mining and Lung Cancer in Navajo Men," *New England Journal of Medicine* 310 (June 7, 1984): 1481–1484.

8. US Advisory Committee, *Human Radiation.*

9. Navajo Nation Council, "The Dine Natural Resources Protection Act of 2005," accessed June 31, 2008, at www.sric.org/uranium/DNRPA.pdf.

10. US National Institute for Occupational Safety and Health, *Energy-Related Health Research Program* (Washington, DC: US NIOSH, 2001), accessed October 16, 2005, at http://www.cdc.gov/niosh/2001-133a.html.

11. US Code of Federal Regulations (US CFR), *Standards for Protection against Radiation* (Washington, DC: National Archives and Records Administration, 2005), Title 10, Part 20, sections 1201 and 1301, accessed September 1, 2008, at http://www.access.gpo.gov/nara/cfr/waisidx_00/10cfr20_00.html; hereafter cited as US CFR, *Standards.*

12. National Research Council (NRC), *Biological Effects of Ionizing Radiation VII* (Washington, DC: National Academy Press, 2005), 6; hereafter cited as NRC, *Biological Effects VII.*

13. Shrader-Frechette, *EJ.*

14. Ibid.

15. US Congress, House Committee on Commerce, 106th Cong., 1st sess., 1999, Hearing 106-43, accessed September 1, 2008, at http://frwebgate.access.gpo.gov/cgi-bin/getdoc.cgi?dbname=106_house_hearings&docid=f:58494.pdf; US General Accounting Office, *Report GAO/RCED-98-163: Department of Energy: Clear Strategy on External Regulation Needed for Worker and Nuclear Facility Safety* (Washington, DC: US GAO, May 1998), accessed September 1, 2008, at http://www.gao.gov/archive/ 1998/rc98163.pdf.

16. Kristin Shrader-Frechette, "Trimming Exposure Data, Putting Radiation Workers at Risk: Improving Disclosure and Consent through a National Radiation Dose Registry," *American Journal of Public Health* 97 (August 29, 2007): 1782–1786; hereafter cited as Shrader-Frechette, "Trimming Exposure Data."

17. Shrader-Frechette, "Trimming Exposure Data"; Elisabeth Cardis et al., "Risk of Cancer after Low Doses of Ionising Radiation: Retrospective Cohort Study in 15 Countries," *British Medical Journal* 331 (July 9, 2005): 77–80; hereafter cited as Cardis, "Cohort Study." IARC (Cardis et al.) says 1–2 percent of workers' fatal cancers are attributable to 20 mSv radiation, and thus a 50 mSv dose is responsible for $(2.5 \times 1–2)$ percent, or 2.5–5 percent of cancers.

18. If up to 1 in 20 lifetime fatal cancers of workers (see previous note) are attributable to a 50 mSv radiation dose, and if 1 in 4 people dies of cancer, this 50 mSv dose gives workers a

$(1/20 \times \frac{1}{4})$ or 1 in 80 lifetime chance of fatal cancer. If this maximum dose is received for 40 years, the workers' chance of fatal cancer is $(40 \times 1/80)$ or $\frac{1}{2}$.

19. Kristin Shrader-Frechette, *Burying Uncertainty: Risk and the Case against Geological Disposal of Nuclear Waste* (Berkeley: University of California Press, 1993), 4–6, 69–71, 79–89, 53–57, 161, 169; hereafter cited as Shrader-Frechette, *Burying Uncertainty*; National Research Council (NRC), *Technical Bases for Yucca Mountain Standards* (Washington, DC: National Academy Press, 1994); hereafter cited as NRC, *Yucca Mountain*.

20. Naomi Lubick, "Falsification Alleged at Yucca Mountain," *Geotimes* 50 (May 2005): 10–11; US General Accounting Office, *GAO-02-765T: Nuclear Waste: Uncertainties about the Yucca Mountain Repository Project* (Washington, DC: US GAO, May 2002), accessed September 1, 2008, at http://www.gao.gov/new.items/d02765t.pdf; Shrader-Frechette, *Burying Uncertainty*.

21. Shrader-Frechette, *EJ*; International Atomic Energy Agency and the Organization for Economic Co-Operation and Development, *An International Peer Review of the Yucca Mountain Site Characterization Project* (Paris: Nuclear Energy Agency, 2001).

22. US Environmental Protection Agency (US EPA), *40 CFR Part 197: Public Health and Environmental Radiation Protection Standards for Yucca Mountain, Nevada* (Washington, DC: US Government Printing Office, 2008); hereafter cited as US EPA, *40 CFR Part 197*; Kristin Shrader-Frechette, "Mortgaging the Future: Dumping Ethics with Nuclear Waste," *Science and Engineering Ethics* 11 (December 2005): 518–520.

23. Shrader-Frechette, *EJ*.

24. Kristin Shrader-Frechette and M. Alldred, "Environmental Injustice in Nuclear-Plant Siting," *Environmental Justice* 2, no. 2 (2009): 85–96; hereafter cited as Shrader-Frechette and Alldred, "Environmental Injustice."

25. Kyle Rabin, "Indian Point's Owner Played Role in Attacks on Environmental Justice" (Press Release, Nuclear Information and Resource Service, February 25, 2004); hereafter cited as Rabin, "Indian Point."

26. Southern Nuclear Operating Company (SNOC), "Draft Environmental Impact Statement for an Early Site Permit (ESP) at the Vogtle Electric Generating Plant Site (NUREG-1872)," Southern Nuclear Operating Company, 2009, Draft Report for Comment, ch. 4, p. 59, accessed July 17, 2008, at http://www.nrc.gov/reading-rm/doc-collections/nuregs/staff/sr1872/ index.html; hereafter cited as SNOC, "ESP."

27. US Nuclear Regulatory Commission, "Early Site Permits—Southern Nuclear Operating Company Application for the Vogtle ESP Site," US Nuclear Regulatory Commission, accessed July 17, 2008, at http://www.nrc.gov/reactors/new-licensing/esp/vogtle. html#schedule.

28. US Department of Energy, "Nuclear Plant Deployment Scorecard," US Department of Energy, accessed July 17, 2008, at http://www.ne.doe.gov/np2010/neScorecard/neScorecard_col.html.

29. SNOC, "ESP," ch. 4, p. 59.

30. United States Nuclear Regulatory Commission (US NRC), "SNOC Uses NRC Guidelines Stated in US Nuclear Regulatory Commission," NRR Office Instruction No. LIC-203, Revision 1, Procedural Guidance for Preparing Environmental Assessments and Considering Environmental Issues, May 24, 2004, accessed September 1, 2008, at http://www.nrc.gov/reactors/operating/licensing/renewal/introduction/introduction-files/lic-203rev1.pdf accessed September 1, 2008); hereafter cited as US NRC, "NRC Guidelines"; SNOC, "ESP," ch. 2.5, pp. 26–28.

31. SNOC, "ESP," ch. 2.1, pp. 1.

32. US NRC, "NRC Guidelines."

33. Seymour Jablon, "Cancer in Populations Living near Nuclear Facilities," *Journal of the American Medical Association* 265 (March 1990): 1403.

34. US Census 2000, "Census 2000 Summary Files 1, 3 (SF 1, 3)," 100-Percent Data, Quick Tables, Sample Data, accessed April 20, 2008, at http://factfinder.census.gov/servlet/

QTGeoSearchByListServlet?ds_name=DEC_2000_SF1_U&_lang=en&_
ts=234365620734; US Census 2000, American FactFinder, accessed April 13, 2008, at
http://factfinder.census.gov/home/saff/main.html?_lang=en; hereafter cited as US Census
2000, "Census 2000 Summary."
35. US Census 2000, "Census 2000 Summary."
36. US NRC, "NRC Guidelines."
37. SNOC, "ESP," ch. 4, p. 59.
38. Ibid.
39. US Census 2000, "Augusta City, Georgia," American FactFinder, accessed April 13, 2008, at
http://factfinder.census.gov/servlet/SAFFFacts?_event=&geo_id=16000US1304204&_geo
Context=01000US%7C04000US13%7C16000US1304204&_street=&_county=Augusta&_
cityTown=Augusta&_state=04000US13&_zip=&_lang=en&_sse=on&ActiveGeoDiv=&_
useEV=&pctxt=fph&pgsl=160&_submenuId=factsheet_1&ds_name=ACS_2006_SAFF&_
ci_nbr=null&qr_name=null&reg=&_keyword=&_industry=; SNOC, "ESP," ch. 2, p. 1.
40. SNOC, "ESP," ch. 2, p. 1.
41. US Census 2000, "Waynesboro City, Georgia," American FactFinder, accessed April 13,
2008, at http://factfinder.census.gov/servlet/SAFFFacts?_event=Search&geo_id=&_
geoContext=&_street=&_county=Waynesboro&_cityTown=Waynesboro&_
state=04000US13&_zip=&_lang=en&_sse=on&pctxt=fph&pgsl=010&show_2003_
tab=&redirect=Y.
42. Rabin, "Indian Point"; US NRC, "NRC Guidelines."
43. US Census 2000, American FactFinder, accessed April 13, 2008, at http://factfinder.census.
gov/home/saff/main.html?_lang=en.
44. Shrader-Frechette and Alldred, "Environmental Injustice."
45. Ibid.
46. Richard Morrill, "Geographic Variation in Change in Income Inequality among US States,
1970–1990," *Annals of Regional Science* 34 (March 2000): 109–130.
47. David Fleming, *The Lean Guide to Nuclear Energy* (London: University of London, 2007), 6;
hereafter cited as Fleming, *Lean Guide*. For air- and waterborne radiation releases from normally operating nuclear plants, see the previous chapter, especially references Baker and Hoel,
Busby and Scott-Cato, Clapp et al., Forman et al., Gardner et al. Gibson et al., Guizard et al.,
Kaatsch et al., Mangano, Mangano et al., Spix, Viuel and Pobel, and Watson and Sumner.
48. US Code of Federal Regulations (CFR), *Energy* (Washington, DC: US Government Printing
Office, 2009), title 10, part 140.
49. Joseph J. Mangano, "Excess Infant Mortality after Nuclear Plant Startup in Rural Mississippi,"
International Journal of Health Services 38 (2008): 277–291; hereafter cited as Mangano,
"Excess Infant Mortality"; Joseph J. Mangano, "Improvements in Local Infant Health after
Nuclear Power Reactor Closing," *Environmental Epidemiology and Toxicology* 2 (2000):
32–36; hereafter cited as Mangano, "Improvements"; Joseph J. Mangano, "Infant Death and
Childhood Cancer Reductions after Nuclear Plant Closings in the United States," *Archives of
Environmental Health* 57 (2002): 23–31; hereafter cited as Mangano, "Infant Death."
50. M. Hatch and M. Susser, "Background Gamma Radiation and Childhood Cancers within
Ten Miles of a US Nuclear Plant," *International Journal of Epidemiology* 19, no. 3 (1990):
546–552; hereafter cited as Hatch and Susser, "Background Radiation"; M. Moris and
R. Knorr, *The Southeastern Massachusetts Health Study 1978–1986* (Boston: Massachusetts
Department of Public Health, 1990); R. W. Clapp et al., "Leukaemia near Massachusetts
Nuclear Power Plant," *Lancet* 336 (1987): 1324–1325; Joseph J. Mangano, "A Short Latency
between Radiation Exposure from Nuclear Plants and Cancer in Young Children,"
International Journal of Health Services 36, no. 1 (2006): 113–135; P. J. Baker and D. G. Hoel,
"Meta-analysis of Standardized Incidence and Mortality Rates of Childhood Leukemia in
Proximity to Nuclear Facilities," *European Journal of Cancer Care* 16, no. 4 (2007): 355–363;
Joseph J. Mangano and J. D. Sherman, "Childhood Leukemia near Nuclear Installations,"
European Journal of Cancer Care 17, no. 4 (2008): 416–418.

51. P. Kaatsch et al., "Leukemia in Young Children Living in the Vicinity of German Nuclear Power Plants," *International Journal of Cancer* 1220 (2008): 721–726; hereafter cited as Kaatsch et al., "Leukemia"; C. Spix, "Do Nuclear Plants Boost Leukemia Risk?," *New Scientist* 2642 (2008): 6; J. Michaelis et al., "Incidence of Childhood Malignancies in the Vicinity of West German Nuclear Power Plants," *Cancer Causes and Control* 3 (1992): 255–263.

52. J. F. Viel, D. Pobel, and A. Carre, "Incidence of Leukemia in Young People around the La Hague Nuclear Waste Reprocessing Plant," *Statistics in Medicine* 14 (1995): 2459–2472; A. V. Guizard et al., "The Incidence of Childhood Leukaemia around the La Hague Nuclear Waste Reprocessing Plant (France): A Survey for the Years 1978–1998," *Journal of Epidemiology and Community Health* 55 (2001): 469–474.

53. M. J. Gardner et al., "Results of Case Control Study of Leukemia and Lymphoma among Young People near Sellafield Nuclear Plant in West Cumbria," *British Medical Journal* 300 (1990): 423–434; hereafter cited as Gardner et al., "Sellafield"; D. Forman et al., "Cancer near Nuclear Installations," *Nature* 329 (1987): 499–505; W. Watson and D. Sumner, "Measurement of Radioactivity in People Living near the Dounreay Nuclear Establishment, Caithness, Scotland," *International Journal of Radiation Biology* 70, no. 2 (1996): 117–130; B. E. Gibson et al., "Leukemia in Young Children in Scotland," *Lancet* 2 (1988): 630; M. A. Heasman et al., "Childhood Leukaemia in Northern Scotland," *Lancet* 1 (1986): 266; C. Busby and M. Scott-Cato, "Death Rates from Leukemia Are Higher Than Expected in Areas around Nuclear Sites in Berkshire and Oxfordshire," *British Medical Journal* 315 (1997): 309; Gardner et al., "Sellafield"; Valerie Beral, Eve Roman, and Martin Bobrow, *Childhood Cancer and Nuclear Installations* (London: BMJ, 1993); E. Roman et al., "Cancer in Children of Nuclear Industry Employees: Report on Children Aged under 25 Years from Nuclear Industry Family Study," *British Medical Journal* 318 (1999): 1443–1450; E. Roman et al., "Case-Control Study of Leukaemia and Non-Hodgkin's Lymphoma among Children Aged 0–4 Years Living in West Berkshire and North Hampshire Health Districts," *British Medical Journal* 306, no. 6878 (1993): 615–621; Shrader-Frechette, *EJ,* 158.

54. Mangano, "Infant Death"; Mangano, "Improvements."

55. Kaatsch et al., "Leukemia."

56. D. Laurier et al., "Epidemiological Studies of Leukemia in Children and Young Adults around Nuclear Facilities: A Critical Review," *Radiation Protection Dosimetry* 132, no. 2 (2008): 182–190; hereafter cited as Laurier et al., "Epidemiological Studies."

57. D. Forman et al., "Cancer near Nuclear Installations," *Nature* 329 (1987): 499–505.

58. National Research Council/National Academy of Sciences (NRC/NAS), *Health Risks from Exposure to Low Levels of Ionizing Radiation: BEIR VII, Phase 2* (Washington, DC: National Academy Press, 2006), 6; hereafter cited as NRC/NAS, *Health Risks BEIR VII.*

59. International Commission on Radiological Protection (ICRP), *1990 Recommendations of the ICRP* (Oxford: Pergamon, 1991); hereafter cited as ICRP, *1990 Recommendations.*

60. Cardis et al., "Cohort Study."

61. Shrader-Frechette, "Trimming Exposure Data"; Cardis et al., "Cohort Study." See earlier notes for the calculations.

62. Based on IARC data, this conclusion assumes 25 percent of people die from cancer. See earlier notes for the calculations.

63. Hatch and Susser, "Background Radiation," 549.

64. Arun Makhijani, B. Smith, and M. C. Thorne, *Science for the Vulnerable: Setting Radiation and Multiple Exposure Environmental Health Standards to Protect Those Most at Risk* (Takoma Park, MD: Institute for Energy and Environmental Research, 2006), 29–31, 37–39, 77; hereafter cited as Makhijani et al., *Science for the Vulnerable.*

65. Ibid., 77.

66. Committee on Environmental Health (CEH), "Policy Statement: Ambient Air Pollution: Health Hazards to Children," *Pediatrics* 114, no. 6 (December 2004): 1699–1707; Kristin Shrader-Frechette, *Taking Action, Saving Lives* (New York: Oxford University Press, 2007), pp. 15-29.

67. NRC, *Biological Effects VII*, 6; Mangano, "Excess Infant Mortality"; Mangano, "Infant Death"; Mangano, "Improvements"; United Nations Scientific Committee on Effects of Atomic Radiation, *Sources, Effects, and Risks of Ionizing Radiation* (New York: United Nations, 1994).

68. Makhijani et al., *Science for the Vulnerable*, 39–40.

69. Ibid., 40.

70. Ibid., 36.

71. Ibid., 9.

72. Ibid., 13.

73. NRC/NAS, *Health Risks BEIR VII*, 15; Makhijani et al., *Science for the Vulnerable*, 28.

74. Makhijani et al., *Science for the Vulnerable*, 20–22, 43, 76.

75. National Research Council/National Academy of Sciences (NRC/NAS), *Health Effects of Exposure to Low Levels of Ionizing Radiation: BEIR V* (Washington, DC: National Academy Press, 1990), 358–359; hereafter cited as NRC/NAS, *Health Effects BEIR V*; International Commission on Radiological Protection (ICRP), *2005 Recommendations* (Stockholm: ICRP, 2005), 32; hereafter cited as ICRP, *2005 Recommendations*.

76. Makhijani et al., *Science for the Vulnerable*, 33–34, 44.

77. Ibid., 19–20.

78. Ibid., 33–34, 44.

79. Ibid., 20.

80. Kristin Shrader-Frechette, *Nuclear Power and Public Policy* (Boston: Kluwer, 1983), 29.

81. Code of Federal Regulations (CFR), *Title 40: Protection of Environment* (Washington, DC: e-CFR, April 16, 2007), accessed April 18, 2007, at http://ecfr.gpoaccess.gov/cgi/t/text/text-idx?c=ecfr;rgn=div5;view=text;node=40%3A1.0.1; Environmental Protection Agency (EPA), *Expanded Protections for Subjects in Human Studies Research* (Washington, DC: EPA, 2006),accessed February 6, 2006, at http://www.epa.gov/oppfead1/guidance/human-test.htm; hereafter cited as EPA, *Protections*.

82. CFR, *Title 40: Protection of Environment* 2007; EPA, *Protections*.

83. Kevin Phillips, *Wealth and Democracy* (New York: Broadway Books, 2003); Shrader-Frechette, *Action*, 26–38.

84. NRC/NAS, *Health Effects BEIR V*, 59, 139, 184.

85. Ibid., 65–134.

86. Ibid., 363–364.

87. Ibid., 354–364.

88. CFR, *Standards*, Title 10, Part 20, Sections 1201, 1301.

89. NRC/NAS, *Health Risks BEIR VII*, 6.

90. ICRP, *1990 Recommendations*.

91. Shrader-Frechette, "Trimming Exposure Data"; Cardis, "Cohort Study." See earlier calculations.

92. Based on IARC data, this conclusion assumes 25 percent of people die from cancer. (See earlier calculations in notes 61-62 of health effects)

93. NRC/NAS, *Health Risks BIER VII*, 6. (50 mSv × 40 years) = 2,000 mSv lifetime workplace radiation. Lifetime background radiation for 70 years = (3 mSv × 70) = 210 mSv. Thus lifetime background and workplace radiation = 2,210, whereas for the public, lifetime radiation = 210 mSv. Workers thus could receive lifetime-radiation doses (occupational and background) about 11 times higher than those of the public, given 2,210 ÷ 210.

94. E.g., Health Canada, *What Is the National Dose Registry?* (Ottawa: Health Canada, 2004), http://www.hc-sc.gc.ca/ewh-semt/occup-travail/radiation/regist/what_is-quelle_est_e.html accessed December 15, 2005); hereafter cited as Health Canada, *Registry*; M. Moser, "The National Dose Registry for Radiation Workers in Switzerland," *Health Physics* 69 (1995): 979–986; hereafter cited as Moser, *Registry*; S. Y. Choi et al., "Analysis of Radiation Workers' Dose Records in the Korean National Dose Registry," *Radiation Protection Dosimetry* 95 (2001): 143–148; hereafter cited as Choi et al., "Radiation Workers"; *Energy-Related Health Research Program* (Washington, DC: National Institute for Occupational

Safety and Health, 2001), http://www.cdc.gov/niosh/2001-133a.html accessed October 16, 2005); hereafter cited as *Health Research Program*.

95. Shrader-Frechette, *EJ*, 135–162, argues against the CWD and answers objections of CWD proponents.

96. CFR, *Standards*, Title 10, Part 20, sections 1201 and 130110.

97. I. Linkov and D. Burmistrov, "Reconstruction of Doses from Radionuclide Inhalation for Nuclear-Power-Plant Workers Using Air-Concentration Measurements and Associated Uncertainties," *Health Physics* 81 (2001): 70–75; hereafter cited as Linkov and Burmistrov, "Reconstruction."

98. *Operational Radiation Safety Program* (Bethesda, MD: National Council on Radiation Protection and Measurement, 1998), Report 127.

99. NRC/NAS, *Health Risks BEIR VII*, 6.

100. E. J. Hall, "The Crooked Shall Be Made Straight: Dose-Response Relationships for Carcinogenesis," *International Journal of Radiation Biology* 80 (2004): 327–337.

101. NRC/NAS, *Health Risks BEIR VII*, 6.

102. Ibid., 6.

103. Cardis et al., "Cohort Study."

104. CFR, *Standards*, Title 10, Part 20, sections 1201 and 130110.

105. CFR, *Standards*, Title 10, Part 19.13(b), 835.1. See J. L. Anderson and R. D. Daniels, "Bone Marrow Dose Estimates from Work-Related Medical X-Ray Examinations Given between 1943 and 1966 for Personnel from Five US Nuclear Facilities," *Health Physics* 90 (2006): 544–553; J. Cardelli et al., "Significance of Radiation Exposure from Work-Related Chest X-Rays for Epidemiological Studies of Radiation Workers," *American Journal of Industrial Medicine* 42 (2002): 490–501.

106. Linkov and Burmistrov, "Reconstruction," 70–75; ICRP, *1990 Recommendations*,

107. *Declaration of Helsinki* (Ferney-Voltaire, France: World Medical Organization, 2004).

108. T. L. Beauchamp and J. F. Childress, *Principles of Biomedical Ethics* (New York: Oxford University Press, 1989), especially pages 78ff; R. Faden and T. L. Beauchamp, *A History and Theory of Informed Consent* (New York: Oxford University Press, 1986).

109. NRC/NAS, *Health Risks BEIR VII*, 6.

110. ICRP, *1990 Recommendations*.

111. G. R. Howe et al., "Analysis of the Mortality Experience amongst US Nuclear Power Industry Workers after Chronic Low-Dose Exposure to Ionizing Radiation," *Radiation Research* 162 (2004): 517–526, especially page 518.

112. *Report of the Advisory Committee on Human Radiation Experiments* (Washington, DC: Advisory Committee on Human Radiation Experiments, 1994): ch. 12, sec. 6.

113. *Complex Cleanup* (Washington, DC: US Office of Technology Assessment, 1991), 111, 138–143.

114. *Worker Safety at DOE Nuclear Facilities* (Washington, DC: US Congress, 1999); *Worker Safety at DOE Nuclear Sites* (Washington, DC: US Congress, 1994).

115. *DOE: Clear Strategy on External Regulation Needed for Worker and Nuclear Facility Safety* (Washington, DC: US General Accounting Office, 1998): 4. GAO, *Nuclear Worker and Safety* (Washington, DC: US General Accounting Office, 2007), 3–5.

116. E.g., Health Canada, *Registry*; Moser, "Registry"; Choi et al., "Radiation Workers"; *Health Research Program*.

117. NRC/NAS, *Health Risks BEIR VII*, 6.

118. *I-131 Thyroid Dose/Risk Calculator for NTS Fallout* (Bethesda, MD: National Cancer Institute, 2003), accessed December 1, 2005, at http://ntsi131.nci.nih.gov/accessed.

119. ICRP, *1990 Recommendations*; CFR, "Standards," Title 10, Part 20.

120. Cardis et al., "Cohort Study."

121. L. Krestinina et al., "Protracted Radiation Exposure and Cancer Mortality in the Techa River Cohort," *Radiation Research* 164 (2005): 602–611; hereafter cited as Krestinina et al., "Techa River."

122. Ibid.

123. D. A. Pierce et al., "Studies of the Mortality of Atomic-Bomb Survivors. Report 12, Part 1. Cancer: 1950–1990," *Radiation Research* 146 (1996): 1–27; C. R. Muirhead et al., "Occupational Radiation Exposure and Mortality: Second Analysis of the National Registry for Radiation Workers," *Journal of Radiological Protection* 19 (1999): 3–26.
124. E. S. Gilbert, "Invited Commentary: Studies of Workers Exposed to Low Doses of Radiation," *American Journal of Epidemiology* 153 (2001): 321 of 319–322.
125. A. Smith, *The Wealth of Nations* (New York: Modern Library, 1993).
126. M. Zimmerman, *An Essay on Moral Responsibility* (Totowa, NJ: Rowman and Littlefield, 1988); J. Glover, *Responsibility* (London: Routledge and Kegan Paul, 1970); J. Feinberg, *Doing and Deserving* (Princeton, NJ: Princeton University Press, 1970).
127. CFR, "Standards," Title 10, Part 20, Sections 1208 and 1502; ICRP, *2005 Recommendations*, 45.
128. E. Draper, *Risky Business* (New York: Cambridge University Press; 1991); *Genetic Monitoring and Screening in the Workplace*, OTA-BA-455 (Washington, DC: US Office of Technology Assessment, 1990); R. Jansson et al., *Genetic Testing in the Workplace: Implications for Public Policy* (Seattle: University of Washington, 2000).
129. *National Registry for Radiation Workers* (London: Ministry of Defence, 2005), accessed December 5, 2005, at www.mod.uk/issues/radiation_workers/registry.htm.
130. IARC data (see preceding notes) show a 50 mSv radiation exposure gives people 1 in 80 chance of dying from premature cancer, so that 500 mSv would give a 1 in 8 (or 13 percent) chance of fatal cancer, and a 1 in 4 chance of cancer. For 400 people receiving 500 mSv exposures, IARC data predict (0.13 × 400) = 52 fatal cancers and about 104 cancer incidences. NAS models show roughly 1 in 1,000,000 cancer-incidence risk per 1 mrem exposure, and 500 mSv = 50,000 mrem. Thus 500 mSv causes 50,000 ÷ 1,000,000 risk, or 5 ÷ 100, or a 1 in 20 risk of cancer incidence, according to NAS.
131. Cardis et al., "Cohort Study."
132. Committee on the Medical Aspects of Radiation in the Environment, *The Implications of the New Data* (London: Her Majesty's Stationery Office, 1986).
133. J. Bentham, *An Introduction to the Principles of Morals and Legislation,* ed. J. H. Burns and H. L. A. Hart (London: Athlone, 1970).
134. G. E. Moore, *Principia Ethica* (1903; rpt., Cambridge: Cambridge University Press, 1960).
135. D. B. Berman, *Death on the Job* (London: Monthly Review Press, 1978); K. Viscusi, *Risk by Choice* (Cambridge, MA: Harvard University Press, 1983); Shrader-Frechette, *EJ*, 139–162.
136. W. W. Lowrance, *Of Acceptable Risk* (Los Angeles: William Kaufman, 1976); D. Kahneman and A. Tversky (eds.), *Choices, Values and Frames* (Cambridge: Cambridge University Press, 2000).
137. NRC, *Technical Bases*, 5.
138. US EPA, *40 CFR Part 197,* 52.
139. CFR, "Standards," Title 10, Part 20, sections 1301 and 1402.
140. See above notes showing that for IARC 50 mSv (5 rem), exposures give fatal cancer to 1 in 80 people (or 1.25 percent). But (70 years × 25 mrem) = 1.75 rem and 1.75 ÷ 5 rem = 0.35. Thus (0.35 × 1.25 percent) = 0.44 percent, or about 1 in 250 fatal cancers, or about 1 in 125 cancers.
141. US EPA, *40 CFR Part 197,* 34.
142. See preceding notes. IARC data show each 50 mSv exposure causes 1 in 80 workers to get fatal cancer (1.25-percent chance). This means a waste-repository-lifetime (70 years) dose, each year at the maximum dose of 1 mSv, alone would cause 70 mSv dose—which in turn would cause (70 ÷ 50) × 1.25 or 1.75-percent chance of lifetime fatal cancer in those exposed to maximum annual doses—or roughly a 3.2-percent chance of cancer.
143. Shrader-Frechette, *Burying Uncertainty*, 174–195.
144. Ibid.
145. NRC/NAS, *Health Risks BEIR VII,*15; Makhijani et al., *Science for the Vulnerable*, 28.
146. National Research Council (NRC), *Radiation Dose Reconstruction for Epidemiologic Uses* (Washington, DC: National Academy Press, 1995), 5; hereafter cited as NRC, *Radiation*.

147. See earlier calculations. As already shown, a 50 mSv radiation dose gives a 1 in 80 chance of dying from premature cancer. This means a 1 mSv dose gives a 1 in 4,000 chance of dying from premature cancer.
148. US EPA, *40 CFR Part 197*, sec. III.A.9, 25–26, 64.
149. Ibid., 64, 129.
150. Shrader-Frechette, *Burying Uncertainty*, 42–45.
151. US EPA, *40 CFR Part 197*, 130.
152. NRC, *Radiation*, 161–186.
153. US EPA, *40 CFR Part 197*, 20.
154. Ibid., 129.
155. Ibid., 43, 47–48; see also 39, 58.
156. Ibid., 63, quoting NRC, *Radiation*, 80.
157. US EPA, *40 CFR Part 197*, 66.
158. Ibid., 68.
159. US EPA, *40 CFR Part 197*, 75.
160. Shrader-Frechette, *Burying Uncertainty*, 184ff.
161. US EPA, *40 CFR Part 197*, 74.
162. Shrader-Frechette, *Burying Uncertainty*, 194–195.
163. US EPA, *40 CFR Part 197*, 40.
164. Ibid.
165. Ibid.
166. Ibid., 72.
167. Ibid., 38, 49, 50.
168. Ibid., 52.
169. Ibid., 20.
170. Ibid., 1, 2, 16, 54, 60, 83.

Chapter 6

1. Brice Smith, *Insurmountable Risks: The Dangers of Using Nuclear Power to Combat Global Climate Change* (Takoma Park: IEER Press, 2006), 71–72; hereafter cited as Smith, *Insurmountable*; Stephen Ansolabehere, John Deutch, Michael Driscoll, Paul E. Gray, John P. Holdren, Richard K. Lester, Ernest J. Moniz, and Neil E. Todreas, *The Future of Nuclear Power* (Cambridge, MA: MIT Press, 2003), 168; accessed February 20, 2010, at http://web.mit.edu/nuclearpower/pdf/nuclearpowerfull.pdf; hereafter cited as Ansolabehere et al., *Future*; A. Leiserowitz, E. Maibach, and C. Roser-Renouf, *Climate Change in the American Mind: Americans' Global Warming Beliefs and Attitudes in January 2010* (New Haven, CT: Yale/George Mason University, Yale Project on Climate Change and the George Mason University Center for Climate Change Communication, 2010); accessed February 6, 2010, at http://environment.yale.edu/uploads/AmericansGlobalWarmingBeliefs2010.pdf.
2. Smith, *Insurmountable*, 201; Joanne Omang, "California A-plant Faces License Suspension," *Washington Post*, November 18, 1981.
3. Public Citizen, *Just the Facts: A Look at the Five Fatal Flaws of Nuclear Power* (Washington, DC: Public Citizen, 2006); hereafter cited as Public Citizen, *Just the Facts*.
4. Michael Mariotte, *Safe, Clean Energy Advocates Reject Obama's Call for More Nuclear Power* (Takoma Park, MD: WISE/NIRS, 2010); accessed February 6, 2010, at http://www.nirs.org/press/01-30-2010/2.
5. Smith, *Insurmountable*, 313; International Energy Agency (IEA), *Nuclear Power in the OECD* (Paris: IEA, Organization for Economic Cooperation and Development, 2001), 67–68, 70; hereafter cited as IEA, *Nuclear Power*.
6. See Arun Makhijani, *Carbon-Free and Nuclear-Free* (Takoma Park, MD: IEER, 2007), esp. 125ff; hereafter cited as Makhijani, *Carbon-Free*.

7. See Brice Smith, "The Bulletin Interview," *Bulletin of the Atomic Scientists* 63, no. 6 (November/ December 2007): 24; hereafter cited as Smith, "Bulletin Interview." See chapter 2 for McKinsey study.

8. Makhijani, *Carbon-Free*, 17–21; see S. Pacala and R. Socolow, "Stabilization Wedges: Solving the Climate Problem for the Next 50 Years with Current Technologies," *Science* 305, no. 5686 (13 August 2004): 968–972; hereafter cited as Pacala and Socolow, "Stabilization Wedges."

9. Makhijani, *Carbon-Free*, 141–42; Western Governors' Association (WGA), *Solar Task Force Report* (Denver: WGA, 2006), 40, 44; accessed February 27, 2010, at www.westgov.org/ wga/initiatives/cdeac/Solar-full.pdf

10. Keith Barnham, "If Not Nuclear, Then What?," in Barnaby and Kemp (eds.), *Secure Energy? Civil Nuclear Power, Security, and Global Warming* (London: Oxford Research Group, 2007), 48; hereafter cited as Barnham, "If Not Nuclear."

11. Lester Brown, *Plan B Update 4.0: Mobilizing to Save Civilization* (New York: W. W. Norton, 2009); accessed January 31, 2010, at http://www.earth-policy.org/images/uploads/book_ files/pb4book.pdf.

12. Smith, "Bulletin Interview," 25.

13. See Makhijani, *Carbon-Free*, 40.

14. US Environmental Protection Agency (US EPA), *Clean Energy Strategies for Local Governments: Green Power Procurement* (Washington, DC: US EPA, 2008); accessed January 30, 2010, at http://www.epa.gov/rdee/documents/webcasts/sec7_1_gp_8may.pdf; hereafter cited as US EPA, *Clean Energy*.

15. Tony Reichhardt, "No Net Cost in Cutting Carbon Emissions," *Nature* 389, no. 6650 (1997): 429.

16. Giulio Boccaletti, Markus Loffler, and Jeremy M. Oppenheim, *How Information Technology Can Cut Carbon Emissions* (New York: McKinsey and Company, 2008); accessed February 6, 2010, at http://www.mckinsey.com/clientservice/ccsi/pdf/how_it_can_cut_carbon_mis- sions.pdf.

17. McKinsey and Company, *Reducing US Greenhouse Gas Emissions* (New York: McKinsey and Company, 2007); hereafter cited as McKinsey, *Reducing*.

18. Makhijani, *Carbon-Free*, 196.

19. Dupont Canada, *Corporate Social Responsibility Case Study: Dupont Canada Realizing Sustainable Growth* (Mississauga, Ontario: Dupont Canada, 2010); accessed February 6, 2010, at commdev.org/files/1069_file_dupont_e.pdf.

20. Amory Lovins, "Nuclear Is Uneconomic," *Bulletin of the Atomic Scientists, Roundtable on Nuclear Power and Climate Change* (2007); accessed February 9, 2008, at www.thebulletin. org/roundtable/nuclear-power-climate-change/; hereafter cited as Lovins, "Nuclear Is Uneconomic."

21. US EPA, *Clean Energy*.

22. Xi Lu, Michael McElroy, and Juha Kiviluoma, "Global Potential for Wind-Generated Electricity," *Proceedings of the US National Academy of Sciences* 106, no. 27 (2009): 10933– 10938; hereafter cited as Lu, McElroy, and Kiviluoma, "Global Potential"; Smith, *Insurmountable*, 62; Pacala and Socolow, "Stabilization Wedges"; American Council for an Energy-Efficient Economy (ACEEE), *DOE Energy Efficiency R&D and Technology Deployment Programs: Critically Needed, Sound Investments in the Nation's Energy Future* (Washington, DC: ACEEE, 2001); accessed January 17, 2010, at http://www.aceee.org/ energy/rdtech.htm.

23. US Department of Energy (US DOE), *Obama Administration Launches New Energy Efficiency Efforts* (Washington, DC: US DOE, 2009); accessed February 11, 2010, at http://www. energy.gov/news2009/7550.htm.

24. Smith, *Insurmountable*, 64; UK Cabinet Office Performance and Innovation Unit (PIU), *The Energy Review: A Performance and Innovation Unit Report* (London: UK Cabinet Office, February 2002), 98.

25. Lovins, "Nuclear Is Uneconomic."

26. See Peter Bunyard, "Ecologist: Taking the Wind Out of Nuclear Power," *Pacific Ecologist* 11 (Summer 2006): 51–57; hereafter cited as Bunyard, "Ecologist."

27. World Information Service on Energy (WISE) and Nuclear Information Research Service (NIRS), *Nuclear Power: No Solution to Climate Change* (Tacoma Park, MD: WISE/NIRS, 2005), 9; hereafter cited as WISE/NIRS, *Nuclear Power*.

28. Makhijani, *Carbon-Free*, 5; Energy Information Administration, Annual Energy Review (EIA AER), *Annual Energy Review 2005, Report DOE/EIA-0384(2005)* (Washington, DC: DOE, EIA, 2006); accessed January 7, 2010, at http://tonto.eia.doe.gov/FTPROOT/multi-fuel/0338405.pdf; hereafter cited as EIA AER, *Annual Energy Review 2005*; F. Barnaby and J. Kemp, "Executive Summary," in Barnaby and Kemp (eds.), *Too Hot to Handle? The Future of Civil Nuclear Power* (London: Oxford Research Group, 2007), 7–14; hereafter cited as Barnaby and Kemp, "Executive Summary."

29. Amory Lovins, "Negawatts and Micropower Are Market Winners, While Nuclear Is a Market Loser," *Bulletin of the Atomic Scientists, Roundtable on Nuclear Power and Climate Change* (2007); accessed February 9, 2008, at www.thebulletin.org/roundtable/nuclear-power-climate-change/; hereafter cited as Lovins, "Negawatts."

30. Makhijani, *Carbon-Free*, 171.

31. Ibid., 4, 6; EIA AER, *Annual Energy Review 2005*.

32. Barnham, "If Not Nuclear," 48.

33. Bunyard, "Ecologist."

34. Barnham, "If Not Nuclear," 49.

35. WISE/NIRS, *Nuclear Power*, 13–14; US Environmental Protection Agency (US EPA), *Understanding Cost-Effectiveness of Energy Efficiency Programs: Best Practices, Technical Methods, and Emerging Issues for Policy-Makers* (Washington, DC: US EPA, National Action Plan for Energy Efficiency, Energy and Environmental Economics, Inc., and Regulatory Assistance Project, 2008); accessed February 6, 2010, at www.epa.gov/eeactionplan.

36. V. M. Fthenakis and H. C. Kim, "Greenhouse-Gas Emission from Solar-Electric and Nuclear Power: A Life-Cycle Study," *Energy Policy* 35, no. 4 (2007): 2549–2557; M. W. Ho, P. Bunyard, P. Saunders, E. Bravo, and R. Gala, *Which Energy?* (London: Institute for Science and Society, 2006).

37. WISE/NIRS, *Nuclear Power*, 14.

38. Office of Technology Assessment (OTA), US Congress, *Energy Efficiency in Federal Facilities: OTA-BP-ETI-125* (Washington, DC: OTA, March 1994); Public Citizen, *Renewable Energy* (Washington, DC: Public Citizen, 2006); McKinsey and Company, *Unlocking Energy Efficiency in the U.S. Economy* (New York: McKinsey and Company, 2009); accessed February 6, 2010, at http://www.mckinsey.com/clientservice/electricpowernaturalgas/downloads/US_energy_efficiency_full_report.pdf.

39. Amory Lovins, "Nuclear Remains a Slow, Expensive Option," *Bulletin of the Atomic Scientists, Roundtable on Nuclear Power and Climate Change* (2007); accessed February 9, 2008, at www.thebulletin.org/roundtable/nuclear-power-climate-change/; hereafter cited as Lovins, "Nuclear Remains."

40. A. B. Chang, A. H. Rosenfield, and P. K. McAuliffe, "Energy Efficiency in California and the United States," in Steven Schneider, Armin Rosencranz, and Michael Mastrandrea (eds.), *Climate Change Science and Policy* (Washington, DC: Island, 2007), 13; hereafter cited as Chang, Rosenfield, and McAuliffe, "Energy Efficiency".

41. Lovins, "Nuclear Is Uneconomic."

42. Makhijani, *Carbon-Free*, 9–10; EIA AER, *Annual Energy Review 2005*.

43. Makhijani, *Carbon-Free*, 8; Chang, Rosenfield, and McAuliffe, "Energy Efficiency."

44. Lovins, "Nuclear Is Uneconomic."

45. Lovins, "Nuclear Remains."

46. Renewable Energy Policy Network for the 21st Century (REN21), *Renewables 2011: Global Status Report* (Paris: REN21, 2011); hereafter cited as REN21, *Renewables 2011*.

47. *REN 21, Renewables 2011.* Renewable Energy Policy Network for the 21st Century (REN21), *Renewables Global Status Report: 2009 Update* (Paris: REN21, 2009), 8; hereafter cited as REN21, *Renewables Global Status Report.*

48. Smith, *Insurmountable,* 70; International Energy Agency (IEA), *Renewables for Power Generation: Status and Prospects* (Paris: IEA, 2003), 152, 165; hereafter cited as IEA, *Renewables.*

49. International Energy Agency (IEA), *Technology Roadmap: Wind Energy* (Paris: IEA, 2009); accessed February 5, 2010, at http://www.iea.org/papers/2009/Wind_Roadmap.pdf; Mukund R. Patel, *Wind and Solar Power Systems—Design, Analysis and Operation,* 2nd ed. (Boca Raton, FL: Taylor and Francis Group, 2006), 303.

50. *REN 21, Renewables 2011.* REN21, *Renewables 2007,* 6. US wind-growth figures are from Jad Mouawad, "Wind Power Grows 39 Percent for the Year," *New York Times,* January 26, 2010, B1, B6.

51. Arun Makhijani, "A Reliable Electricity Grid in the United States," *Science for Democratic Action* 15, no. 2 (2008): 10; hereafter cited as Makhijani, "Reliable Electricity"; Makhijani, *Carbon-Free,* 36.

52. Smith, *Insurmountable,* 98.

53. Gwyneth Cravens, *Power to Save the World: The Truth about Nuclear Energy* (New York: Knopf, 2008), 253; hereafter cited as Cravens, *Power.*

54. Bunyard, "Ecologist."

55. US Department of Energy (DOE), primary authors Ryan Wiser and Mark Bolinger, Lawrence Berkeley National Laboratory, *Annual Report on US Wind Power Installation, Cost, and Performance Trends: 2006* (Washington, DC: DOE Energy Efficiency and Renewable Energy, 2007); hereafter cited as DOE, *Annual Report 2006;* see Makhijani, *Carbon-Free,* 36, who places costs between 4 to 6 cents per kWhr; see Smith, *Insurmountable,* 70, who places wind costs between 3 and 7 cents per kWhr.

56. EnerNex Corporation, *Final Report: 2006 Minnesota Wind Integration Study, Vol. 1.* (Knoxville: EneNex, 2006), prepared in connection with the Midwest Independent System Operator and for the Minnesota Legislature and Minnesota Public Utilities Commission; accessed November 14, 2009, at www.puc.state.mn.us/docs/windrpt_vol percent201.pdf; hereafter cited as EnerNex, *Final Report 2006;* Makhijani, *Carbon-Free,* 34; E. A. DeMeo, W. Grant, M. R. Milligan, and M. J. Schuerger, "Wind Plant Integration," *IEEE Power and Energy* 3, no. 6 (2005): 41–42; hereafter cited as DeMeo et al., "Wind Plant".

57. Keystone Center, *Nuclear Power Joint Fact-Finding* (Keystone, CO: Keystone Center, 2007); Lovins, "Negawatts."

58. DeMeo et al., "Wind Plant," 45–46.

59. Smith, *Insurmountable,* 37; Amory Lovins, Imran Sheikh, and Alex Markevich, *Nuclear Power: Climate Fix or Folly?* (Snowmass, CO: Rocky Mountain Institute, 2009); accessed February 6, 2010, at http://www.rmi.org/rmi/Library/E09–01_NuclearPowerClimateFixOrFolly.

60. US Energy Information Administration (EIA), *Electric Power Annual* (Washington, DC: US DOE, 2009).

61. American Wind Energy Association, *U.S. Wind Energy Industry Breaks All Records, Installs Nearly 10,000 MW in 2009* (Washington, DC: American Wind Energy Association, 2010); accessed February 9, 2010, at http://www.awea.org/newsroom/releases/01–26–10_AWEA_Q4_and_Year-End_Report_Release.html.

62. Clifford Krauss, "Move Over, Oil, There's Money in Texas Wind," *New York Times,* February 23, 2008, A1, A13; hereafter cited as Krauss, "Move Over"; American Wind Energy Association, *American Wind Energy Association Annual Wind Industry Report* (Washington, DC: American Wind Energy Association, 2009); accessed February 9, 2010, at http://www.awea.org/publications/reports/AWEA-Annual-Wind-Report-2009.pdf.

63. Krauss, "Move Over," A1; American Wind Energy Association, *Installed U.S. Wind Capacity Surged 45 percent in 2007: American Wind Energy Association Market Report* (Washington, DC: American Wind Energy Association, 2008); accessed February 9, 2010, at http://www.awea.org/newsroom/releases/AWEA_Market_Release_q4_011708.html.

64. Krauss, "Move Over," A13; American Wind Energy Association, *AWEA 2007 Market Report* (Washington, DC: American Wind Energy Association, 2008); accessed February 9, 2010, at http://www.awea.org/projects/pdf/Market_Report_Jan08.pdf.

65. Global Wind Energy Council (GWEC), *Global Wind Power Booms Despite Economic Woes* (Brussels: GWEC, 2010); accessed February 27, 2010, at http://www.gwec.net/index.php?id=30&no_cache=1&tx_ttnews[tt_news]=247&tx_ttnews[backPid]=4&cHash=1196e940a0; hereafter cited as GWEC, *Global Wind Power*.

66. American Wind Energy Association, *AWEA Year End 2007 Market Report* (Washington, DC: American Wind Energy Association, 2008); accessed February 27, 2010, at http://www.awea.org/publications/reports/4Q07.pdf; American Wind Energy Association, *AWEA Annual Wind Industry Report* (Washington, DC: American Wind Energy Association, 2009); accessed February 27, 2010, at http://www.awea.org/publications/reports/AWEA-Annual-Wind-Report-2009.pdf.

67. Teresa Galluzzo and David Osterberg, *A Windfall of Green Energy* (Iowa City: Iowa Policy Project, April 2009); accessed November 14, 2009, at http://www.state.ia.us/government/governor/energy/Renewable_Energy/Docs/090413-windproduction.pdf; hereafter cited as Galluzzo and Osterberg, *Windfall*. See note 90, ch. 2.

68. Makhijani, *Carbon-Free*, 30; American Wind Energy Association (AWEA), *Congress Extends Wind Energy Production Tax Credit for an Additional Year* (Washington, DC: AWEA, 2006); accessed January 26, 2010, at http://www.awea.org/newsroom/releases/congress_extends_PTC_121106.html.

69. Amory Lovins, "Energy Tribune Speaks with Amory Lovins," *Energy Tribune* (November 9, 2007); accessed February 22, 2008, at www.energytribune.com/articles.cfm?aid=672; hereafter cited as Lovins, "Energy Tribune."

70. Krauss, "Move Over," A13.

71. Makhijani, *Carbon-Free*, 34; Global Wind Energy Council (GWEC), *Global Wind Energy Markets Continue to Boom—2006 Another Record Year: Industry Delivered 32 percent of Annual Market Growth Despite Supply Chain Difficulties* (Brussels: GWEC, 2007); hereafter cited as GWEC, *Global Wind Energy Markets*.

72. European Wind Energy Association (EWEA), *Wind in Power 2009 Energy Statistics* (Brussels, Belgium: EWEA, 2010); accessed February 9, 2010, at http://www.ewea.org/fileadmin/ewea_documents/documents/statistics/general_stats_2009.pdf.

73. REN21, *Renewables 2007*, 6.

74. Global Wind Energy Council (GWEC), *More Wind Power Capacity Installed Last Year in the EU Than Any Other Power Technology* (Brussels, Belgium: Global Wind Energy Council, 2010); accessed February 27, 2010, at http://www.gwec.net/index.php?id=30&no_cache=1&tx_ttnews[tt_news]=249&tx_ttnews[backPid]=4&cHash=bda15ad600; Global Wind Energy Council (GWEC), *Global Wind 2008 Report* (Brussels, Belgium: GWEC, 2009); accessed February 27, 2010, at http://www.gwec.net/fileadmin/documents/Global percent20Wind percent202008 percent20Report.pdf; GWEC, *Continuing Boom in Wind Energy—20 GW of New Capacity of 2007* (Brussels, Belgium: GWEC, 2008); accessed February 27, 2010, at http://www.gwec.net/index.php?id=30&no_cache=1&tx_ttnews[tt_news]=121&tx_ttnews[backPid]=4&cHash=f9b4af1cd0.

75. Lovins, "Energy Tribune."

76. Lovins, "Nuclear Remains."

77. William Sweet, *Kicking the Carbon Habit* (New York: Columbia University Press, 2006), 152; hereafter cited as Sweet, *Kicking*.

78. Barnaby and Kemp, "Executive Summary," 14; Barnham, "If Not Nuclear," 45–46.

79. Barnaby and Kemp, "Executive Summary," 13.

80. Smith, *Insurmountable*, 66; Ansolabehere et al., *Future*, 12; Sweet, *Kicking*, 152.

81. REN21, *Renewables 2007*, 7.

82. Makhijani, *Carbon-Free*, 35; DeMeo et al., "Wind Plant," 45.

83. McKinsey, *Reducing*, 19.

84. US Energy Information Administration (EIA), *Annual Energy Outlook 2010 Early Release Overview* (Washington, DC: US Energy Information Administration, 2009); accessed February 9, 2010, at http://www.eia.doe.gov/oiaf/aeo/overview.html.
85. Makhijani, *Carbon-Free*, 32; GWEC, *Global Wind Energy Markets*.
86. Sweet, *Kicking*, 155.
87. Xi Lu, Michael McElroy, and Juha Kiviluoma, "Global Potential for Wind-Generated Electricity," *Proceedings of the US National Academy of Sciences* 106, no. 27 (2009): 10933–10938.
88. Smith, *Insurmountable*, 66.
89. Makhijani, *Carbon-Free*, 31.
90. Makhijani, "Reliable Electricity."
91. Makhijani, *Carbon-Free*, 168; Smith, *Insurmountable*, 66.
92. Walt Musial, *Offshore Wind Energy Potential for the United States* (Golden, CO: National Renewable Energy Laboratory, 2005), slide 10; accessed February 26, 2010, at www.eeere.energy.gov/windandhydro/windpoweringamerica/pdfs/workshops.2005_summit/musial.pdf; Energy Information Administration, Annual Energy Review (EIA AER), *Annual Energy Review 2005, Report DOE/EIA-0384(2005)* (Washington, DC: DOE, EIA, 2006), table 8.2a, full report accessed January 30, 2010, at http://tonto.eia.doe.gov/FTPROOT/multifuel/0338405.pdf; Makhijani, *Carbon-Free*, 36.
93. Makhijani, *Carbon-Free*, 32, 51–52; Smith, *Insurmountable*, 67; Nuclear Regulatory Commission (NRC), *Generic Environmental Impact Statement for License Renewal of Nuclear Plants* (Washington, DC: NRC, 1996), table 8.2; accessed March 5, 2010, at http://www.nrc.gov/reading-rm/doc-collections/nuregs/staff/sr1737/v1.
94. Krauss, "Move Over," A1; Ryan Thomas Trahan, "Social and Regulation Control of Wind Energy—An Empirical Survey of Texas and Kansas," *Texas Journal of Oil, Gas, and Energy Law* 4, no. 1 (2008): 89–110; accessed February 9, 2010, at http://www.tjogel.org/archive/Vol4No1/trahan.pdf.
95. Galluzzo and Osterberg, *Windfall*. See note 90, ch. 2.
96. Krauss, "Move Over," A13; Future Survey, "The Pickens Plan," *Future Survey* 30, no. 11 (2008): 10–11.
97. Brian Parsons, Michael Milligan, J. Charles Smith, Edgar DeMeo, Brett Oakleaf, Kenneth Wolf, Matt Schuerger, Robert Zavadil, Mark Ahlstrom, and Dora Yen Nakafuji, *Grid Impacts of Wind Power Variability* (Reston, VA: Utility Wind Integration Group, 2006), 6; hereafter cited as Parsons et al., *Grid Impacts*; DeMeo et al. "Wind Plant," p. 42.
98. Parsons et al., *Grid Impacts*, 6; DeMeo et al., "Wind Plant," pp. 42, 45–46.
99. EnerNex, *Final Report 2006*, xvii, Table 1; Makhijani, "Reliable Electricity," 9; Makhijani, *Carbon-Free*, 35.
100. Makhijani, "Reliable Electricity," 9; Smith, *Insurmountable*, 80.
101. Smith, *Insurmountable*, 80–82; Paul Denholm, Gerald Kulcinski, and Tracey Holloway, "Emissions and Energy Efficiency Assessment of Baseload Eind Energy Systems," *Environmental Science and Technology* 39 (2005): 1903–1911.
102. Hugh Montefiore, "Why the Planet Needs Nuclear Energy," *Tablet* (October 23, 2004); accessed November 1, 2008, at http://www.thetablet.co.uk/cgi-bin/register.cgi/tablet-00946; hereafter cited as Montefiore, "Why the Planet."
103. The Economist, "The Nuclear Answer?," *Economist* (July 7, 2005); accessed July 23, 2005 at www.economist.com/opinion/displayStory.cfm?story_id-4151435; see Kristin Shrader-Frechette, *Taking Action, Saving Lives* (New York: Oxford University Press, 2007), ch. 2.
104. Marshall Goldberg, *Federal Energy Subsidies* (New York: MRG Associates, 2000).
105. Public Citizen, *Just the Facts.*
106. Smith, *Insurmountable*, 66–67; American Wind Energy Association (AWEA), *Global Wind Energy Market Report* (Washington, DC: AWEA, March 2004), 6; accessed January 18, 2010, at http://www.awea.org/pubs/documents/globalmarket2004.pdf.
107. Sweet, *Kicking*, 193.

108. Makhijani, *Carbon-Free*, 188.
109. Ibid., 182–184; J. Robert Oppenheimer, "International Control of Atomic Energy," in Morton Grodzins and Eugene Rabinowitch (eds.), *The Atomic Age: Scientists in National and World Affairs* (New York: Basic Books, 1963), 55.
110. Smith, *Insurmountable*, 68.
111. Makhijani, "Reliable Electricity," 9.
112. Amory Lovins, Imran Sheikh, and Alex Markevich, "Forget Nuclear," *Solutions* (Spring 2008), appended by the Rocky Mountain Institute April 2008; accessed February 20, 2010, at http://www.rmi.org/sitepages/pid467.php.
113. US Department of Energy (DOE), *President Bush Requests $25 Billion for US Department of Energy's FY 2009 Budget* (Washington, DC: US DOE Office of Public Affairs, 2008); hereafter cited as US DOE, *President Bush*; US Department of Energy (DOE), *DOE Selects 13 Solar-Energy Projects for Up to $168 Million in Funding: First Funding Awards for Solar America Initiative* (Washington, DC: US DOE Office of Public Affairs, 2007); hereafter cited as US DOE, *DOE Selects*; see Makhijani, *Carbon-Free*, 38–39.
114. Makhijani, *Carbon-Free*, 39.
115. S. Kurtz and the National Renewable Energy Laboratory (NREL), *Opportunities and Challenges for Development of a Mature Concentrating Photovoltaic Power Industry*, Technical Report NREL/TP-520–43208 (Golden, CO: NREL of US DOE, 2009), accessed February 14, 2010, at http://www.nrel.gov/docs/fy10osti/43208.pdf; hereafter cited as Kurtz and NREL, *Opportunities*, 2009.
116. REN21, *Renewables 2007*, 6.
117. Makhijani, *Carbon-Free*, 41; PowerLight, *United States Navy Deploys Largest Federal Solar Electric System in the Nation: 750 kW Photovoltaic System Installed at Naval Base Coronado, California* (Berkeley, CA: PowerLight, 2002), accessed November 3, 2009, at http://www.powerlight.com/about/press_2002/11_08_02.html.
118. Kurtz and NREL, *Opportunities*.
119. Jeffrey Sachs, "Climate Change after Bali," *Scientific American* 298, no. 3 (2008): 22; hereafter cited as Sachs, "Climate Change."
120. Mark Cooper, *The Economics of Nuclear Reactors: Renaissance or Relapse?* (South Royalton, VT: Institute for Energy and the Environment, Vermont Law School, June 2009); accessed February 14, 2010, at http://www.vermontlaw.edu/Documents/Cooper percent20Report percent20on percent20Nuclear percent20Economics percent20FINAL percent5B1 percent 5D.pdf.
121. Joseph Romm (Senior Fellow, Center for American Progress Action Fund), "The High Cost of Nuclear Power," *Testimony before the United States Senate Committee on Environment and Public Works and Subcommittee on Clean Air and Nuclear Safety* (July 16, 2008); accessed February 14, 2010, at http://www.americanprogressaction.org/issues/2008/pdf/romm_testimony.pdf.
122. REN21, *Renewables 2007*, 6.
123. Lovins, "Energy Tribune."
124. Barnaby and Kemp, "Executive Summary," 14; Barnham, "If Not Nuclear," 45–46.
125. Erik Kirschbaum, *Germany to Post Record Rise in Solar Capacity* (Berlin: Reuters, November 23, 2009); accessed February 21, 2010, at http://www.reuters.com/article/idUSTRE5AM36E20091123.
126. Dinakar Sethuraman, "Solar Power Generation Capacity May Double in 2010," *Bloomberg* (July 17, 2009); accessed February 21, 2010, at http://www.bloomberg.com/apps/news?p id=20601085&sid=ai3OMQT42TCM.
127. Lovins, "Negawatts."
128. DisplaySearch, *Q3 '09 Quarterly PV Cell Capacity Database and Trends Report* (Austin, TX: DisplaySearch, 2009); accessed February 14, 2010, at http://www.displaysearch.com/cps/rde/xchg/displaysearch/hs.xsl/quarterly_pv_cell_capacity_database_trends_report.asp; Mycle Schneider, "2008 World Nuclear Industry Status Report: Global Nuclear Power,"

Bulletin of the Atomic Scientists (September 16, 2008); accessed February 14, 2010, at http://www.thebulletin.org/web-edition/reports/2008-world-nuclear-industry-status-report/2008-world-nuclear-industry-status-rep.

129. Barnham, "If Not Nuclear," 47.

130. Makhijani, *Carbon-Free*, 168.

131. Ibid., 37; Makhijani, "Reliable Electricity," 9.

132. Makhijani, *Carbon-Free*, 42.

133. Smith, *Insurmountable*, 83; J. Aabakken, *Power Technologies Energy Data Book: Third Edition* (Golden, CO: US DOE, National Renewable Energies Lab, 2005), 26.

134. Vasilis M. Fthenakis, James E. Mason, and Ken Zweibel, "The Technical, Geographical, and Economic Feasibility for Solar Energy to Supply the Energy Needs of the US," *Energy Policy* 37, no. 2 (2009): 387–399; hereafter cited as Fthenakis, Mason, and Zweibel, "Technical."

135. See Makhijani, *Carbon-Free*, esp. 125ff.

136. Bunyard, "Ecologist."

137. US Energy Information Administration (EIA), *International Energy Outlook 2009* (Washington, DC: US EIA, 2009); accessed February 20, 2010, at http://www.eia.doe.gov/oiaf/ieo/highlights.html; hereafter cited as US EIA, *International Energy Outlook 2009*.

138. GWEC, *Global Wind Power*.

139. Mycle Schneider, Steve Thomas, Antony Froggatt, and Doug Koplow, *The World Nuclear Industry Status Report 2009* (Paris: Nuclear Information and Resource Service, August 2009); accessed March 8, 2010, at http://www.nirs.org/neconomics/weltstatusbericht0908.pdf.

140. Lovins, "Negawatts."

141. Lovins, "Nuclear Remains," "Nuclear Is Uneconomic."

142. US EIA, *International Energy Outlook 2009*.

143. Lovins, "Negawatts."

144. Makhijani, *Carbon-Free*, 144, 190; John Kennedy, Andreas Zsiga, Laurie Conheady, and Paul Lund, "Credit Aspects of North American and European Nuclear Power," *Standard & Poor's* (January 9, 2006), hereafter cited as Kennedy et al., "Credit Aspects"; Smith, *Insurmountable*, 44, 51, 97; Charles Komanoff, *Power Plant Cost Escalation: Nuclear and Coal Capital Costs, Regulation, and Economics* (New York: Van Nostrand Reinhold, 1981), 271.

145. REN21, *Renewables 2007*, 18.

146. Smith, *Insurmountable*, 51, 97; Kennedy et al., "Credit Aspects."

147. Scully Capital Services, Inc., *The Business Case for New Nuclear Power Plants: A Report Prepared for the US DOE* (Washington, DC: DOE, 2002); hereafter cited as Scully, *Business Case*.

148. US Department of Energy (DOE), *Moving Forward with Nuclear Power: Final Report of the Secretary of Energy Advisory Board Nuclear Energy Task Force* (Washington, DC: DOE, 2005); R. S. Berry, "Keep All Options on the Table," *Bulletin of the Atomic Scientists, Roundtable on Nuclear Power and Climate Change* (2007); accessed February 9, 2008, at www.thebulletin.org/roundtable/nuclear-power-climate-change/.

149. Dennis Spurgeon, "Nuclear Energy: We Must Increase Its Role in Our Future," Address by US Assistant Secretary for Nuclear Energy at the Second Annual Nuclear Fuel Cycle Monitor Global Nuclear Renaissance Summit, Alexandria, Virginia, *Vital Speeches of the Day* 74, no. 9 (July 23, 2008): 422–425; accessed September 22, 2008, at vsotd.com.

150. A. M. Herbst and G. W. Hopley, *Nuclear Energy Now* (Hoboken, NJ: John Wiley, 2007), 9.

151. Ibid., 6–7.

152. Smith, "Bulletin Interview."

153. Makhijani, *Carbon-Free*, 170.

154. Smith, *Insurmountable*, 230; Matthew Wald, "Interest in Building Reactors, but Industry Is Still Cautious," *New York Times*, April 2, 2005.

155. Makhijani, *Carbon-Free*, 191; Nature Editorial, "Nuclear Test: Japan's Response to an Earthquake Highlights Both the Promise and the Pitfalls of Nuclear Power at a Critical Time for Its Future," *Nature* 448, no. 7152 (2007): 387.

156. Makhijani, *Carbon-Free*, 192.
157. Stan Calvert, Robert Thresher, Susan Hock, Alan Laxson, and Brian Smith, "US Department of Energy Wind Energy Research Program for Low Wind Speed Technology of the Future," *Journal of Solar Energy Engineering: Transactions of the American Society of Mechanical Engineers* 124, no. 4 (November 2002): 456; Declan Butler, "Energy: Nuclear Power's New Dawn," *Nature* 429, no. 6989 (2004): 238–240; Lovins, "Negawatts."
158. Craig A. Severance, *Business Risks and Costs of Nuclear Power* (Washington, DC: Center for American Progress, January 5, 2009); accessed February 26, 2010, at http://climateprogress. org/wp-content/uploads/2009/01/nuclear-costs-2009.pdf; Mukund R. Patel, *Wind and Solar Power Systems—Design, Analysis and Operation*, 2nd ed. (Boca Raton, FL: Taylor and Francis Group, 2006), 303.
159. Scully, *Business Case*; Nuclear Information and Resource Service & World Information Service on Energy (NIRS/WISE), *Nuclear Power: No Solution to Climate Change* (Amsterdam: NIRS/WISE, 2005), 4.
160. Brice Smith, "Insurmountable Risks," *Science for Democratic Action* 36 (August 2006): 7.
161. McKinsey, *Reducing*, 62.
162. John Deutch, Charles W. Forsberg, Andrew C. Kadak, Mujid S. Kazimi, Ernest J. Moniz, and John E. Parsons, *Update of the MIT 2003 Future of Nuclear Power* (Cambridge, MA: MIT Press, 2009); accessed February 21, 2010, at http://web.mit.edu/nuclearpower/pdf/ nuclearpower-update2009.pdf; hereafter cited as Deutch et al., *Update*.
163. The Economist, "Nuclear Dawn," *Economist* 384, no. 8545 (September 6, 2007): 24–26; WISE/NIRS, *Nuclear Power*, 16.
164. S. Pacala and R. Socolow, "Stabilization Wedges: Solving the Climate Problem for the Next 50 Years with Current Technologies," *Science* 305, no. 5686 (August 13, 2004): 968–972; the 9 renewable options (only 6 needed to solve climate problems) are efficient vehicles, reduced vehicle use, efficient buildings wind power for coal power, PV power for coal power, wind for gasoline in fuel-cell cars, biomass fuel for fossil fuel, reduced deforestation, and conservation tillage. National Renewable Energy Laboratory (NREL), *Near Term Practical and Ultimate Technical Potential for Renewable Resources* (Golden, CO: US DOE, 2006); hereafter cited as NREL, *Near Term*.
165. Lu, McElroy, and Kiviluoma, "Global Potential."
166. WISE/NIRS, *Nuclear Power*, 14.
167. Lu, McElroy, and Kiviluoma, "Global Potential."
168. European Council on Renewable Energy (ECRE), *Renewable Energy Scenario, 2040* (Gussing, Austria: ECRE, 2004).
169. Sven Teske, Oliver Schäfer, Arthouros Zervos, Jan Béranek, Stephanie Tunmore, Wolfram Krewitt, Sonja Simon, Thomas Pregger, Stephan Schmid, Wina Graus, and Eliane Blomen, *Energy [R]evolution A Sustainable Global Energy Outlook* (Brussels, Belgium: Greenpeace International and European Renewable Energy Council, 2008), 10, accessed February 27, 2010, at http://www.energyblueprint.info/fileadmin/media/documents/energy_revolu-tion2009.pdf.
170. Shell International, "Energy Needs, Choices, Possibilities: Scenarios to 2050," *Global Business Environment* (2001); accessed March 10, 2010, at http://www.cleanenergystates.org/ CaseStudies/Shell_2050.pdf.
171. Pacala and Socolow, "Stabilization Wedges," 971.
172. Ibid., 968.
173. Vasilis M. Fthenakis, James E. Mason, and Ken Zweibel, "The Technical, Geographical, and Economic Feasibility for Solar Energy to Supply the Energy Needs of the US," *Energy Policy* 37, no. 2 (2009): 387–399; hereafter cited as Fthenakis, Mason, and Zweibel, "Technical."
174. International Energy Agency (IEA), *Technology Roadmap: Wind Energy* (Paris: IEA, 2009); accessed February 5, 2010, at http://www.iea.org/papers/2009/Wind_Roadmap.pdf.
175. Makhijani, "Reliable Electricity," 10.
176. NREL, *Near Term*. See 12 previous notes.

177. Makhijani, *Carbon-Free*, 191; Smith, *Insurmountable*.

178. Sachs, "Climate Change."

179. James Kemp, "The Security Background to a Nuclear New Build," in Barnaby and Kemp (eds.), *Secure Energy? Civil Nuclear Power, Security, and Global Warming* (London: Oxford Research Group, 2007), 36.

180. Smith, "Bulletin Interview," 47.

181. Ansolabehere et al., *Future*.

182. WISE/NIRS, *Nuclear Power*, 9.

183. Smith, *Insurmountable*, 115; Arun Makhijani and Scott Saleska, *The Nuclear Power Deception: US Nuclear Mythology from Electricity "Too Cheap to Meter" to "Inherently Safe" Reactors* (New York: Apex, 1999), 121–122.

184. Makhijani, *Carbon-Free*.

185. Richard Meserve, "Global Warming and Nuclear Power," *Science* 303, no. 5657 (2004): 433.

186. Stewart Brand, "Environmental Heresies," *Technology Review* (May 2005); accessed February 18, 2010, at http://www.technologyreview.com/read_articles.aspx?id=14406&ch=biztech.

187. Bunyard, "Ecologist," 51.

188. Patrick Moore, "Going Nuclear," *Washington Post*, April 16, 2006, p. B01; accessed November 5, 2009, at http://www.washingtonpost.com/wp-dyn/content/article/2006/04/14/AR2006041401209.html.

189. Montefiore, "Why the Planet."

190. Cravens, *Power*, 286.

191. Sweet, *Kicking*, 183.

192. DeMeo et al., "Wind Plant," 40.

193. Barnaby and Kemp, "Executive Summary," 7.

194. Ibid., 8–12; see Smith, *Insurmountable*, 2.

195. Bunyard, "Ecologist."

196. Smith, *Insurmountable*, 191; Federal Aviation Administration (FAA), "Press Release: FAA Restricts All Private Aircraft Flying over Nuclear Facilities," *FAA* (October 30, 2001); accessed March 2, 2010, at http://www.faa.gov/apa/pr/pr.cfm?id=1451.

197. See Bunyard, "Ecologist."

198. Carl Behrens and Mark Holt, *Nuclear Power Plants: Vulnerability to Terrorist Attack. Congressional Research Service Report for Congress, RS21131, February 4* (Washington, DC: Congressional Research Service, 2005).

199. E. S. Lyman, *Chernobyl on the Hudson? The Health and Economic Impacts of at Terrorist Attack at the Indian Point Nuclear Plant* (Washington, DC: Union of Concerned Scientists, 2004).

200. Mark Holt and Anthony Andrews, *Nuclear Power Plant Security and Vulnerabilities* (Washington, DC: Congressional Research Service, 2009); accessed February 27, 2010, at http://fas.org/sgp/crs/homesec/RL34331.pdf; hereafter cited as Holt and Andrews, *Nuclear Power*.

201. Peter Stoett, "Toward Renewed Legitimacy: Nuclear Power, Global Warming and Security," *Global Environmental Politics* 3, no. 1 (2003): 110; Public Citizen, *Just the Facts*.

202. Holt and Andrews, *Nuclear Power*.

203. Public Citizen, *Just the Facts*.

204. Holt and Andrews, *Nuclear Power*.

205. Public Citizen, *Just the Facts*.

206. National Academy of Sciences-National Research Council (NAS-NRC), *Safety and Security of Spent Fuel Storage* (Washington, DC: National Academy Press, 2006); Public Citizen, *Just the Facts*.

207. Holt and Andrews, *Nuclear Power*.

208. Barnaby and Kemp, "Executive Summary," 14.

209. WISE/NIRS, *Nuclear Power*, 16.

210. Smith, *Insurmountable*, 297; Ansolabehere et al., *Future*, 12.

211. Steven E. Miller and Scott D. Sagan, "Alternative Nuclear Futures," *Daedelus* 139, no. 1 (2010): 126–137.

212. Ibid.
213. WISE/NIRS, *Nuclear Power*, 16.
214. Bunyard, "Ecologist."
215. Isaac Wolf, "Recycled Radiation Shows Up at Home," *Journalgazette.net* (June 7, 2009); accessed March 7, 2010, at http://www.journalgazette.net/article/20090607/NEWS03/306079909/1066/NEWS03.
216. Keith Rogers, "Expert Outline Worries of Nuclear Proliferation," *Las Vegas Review Journal* (January 27, 2009); accessed March 1, 2010, at http://www.lvrj.com/news/38442489.html.
217. Matthew Bunn, "Reducing the Greatest Risks of Nuclear Theft and Terrorism," *Daedalus* 138, no. 4 (2009): 112–123.
218. Deutch et al., *Update*.
219. Makhijani, *Carbon-Free*, 170.
220. Matthew Wald, "Getting Power to the People," *Bulletin of the Atomic Scientists* 63, no. 5 (September–October 2007): 26–63.
221. Makhijani, *Carbon-Free*, 19–20; Sweet, *Kicking*.
222. Makhijani, *Carbon-Free*, 165ff.
223. US EPA, *Clean Energy*.
224. Linda M. Kamp, "Socio-technical Analysis of the Introduction of Wind Power in the Netherlands and Denmark," *International Journal of Environmental Technology and Management* 9, nos. 2–3 (2008): 276; Ben Crystall, "Generate a Feed-in Frenzy," *New Scientist* 203, no. 2725 (2009): 39.
225. E.g., Makhijani, Carbon-Free, esp. 165ff.; Smith, *Insurmountable*; International Energy Agency (IEA), *Variability of Wind Power and Other Renewable: Management Options and Strategies* (Paris: IEA, 2005).
226. Sweet, *Kicking*, 188.
227. Makhijani, "Reliable Electricity," 10.
228. Makhijani, *Carbon-Free*, 26.
229. Ibid., 22–23; Makhijani, "Reliable Electricity."
230. Makhijani, *Carbon-Free*, 125; Arjun Makhijani and Kevin Gurney, *Mending the Ozone Hole: Science, Technology and Policy* (Cambridge, MA: MIT Press, 1995).
231. Sweet, *Kicking*, 33.

Chapter 7

1. US Department of Energy (DOE), *President Bush Requests $25 Billion for US Department of Energy's FY 2009 Budget* (Washington, DC: US DOE Office of Public Affairs, 2008), hereafter cited as US DOE, *President Bush*; Nuclear Energy Institute (NEI), *Nuclear Statistics* (Washington, DC: NEI, 2007), accessed February 15, 2008, at www.nei.org/resourcesand-stats/nuclear_statistics/costs.
2. J. M. Deutsch, C. W. Forsberg, A. C. Kadak, M. S. Kazimi, E. J. Moniz, and J. E. Parsons, *Update of the MIT 2003 Future of Nuclear Power* (Cambridge: MIT Energy Initiative, 2009), 19.
3. D. Biello, "Reactivating Nuclear Reactors for the Fight against Climate Change," *Scientific American* (January 27, 2009), accessed May 12, 2009, at www.scientificamerican.com/author.cfm?id=1013&category=&year=2009&month=5&offset=163.
4. Gwyneth Cravens, *Power to Save the World* (New York: Knopf, 2008), 365, hereafter cited as Cravens, *Power*.
5. A. M. Herbst and G. W. Hopley, *Nuclear Energy Now* (Hoboken, NJ: John Wiley, 2007), 12, hereafter cited as Herbst and Hopley, *Nuclear*.
6. World Nuclear Association (WNA), "The Economics of Nuclear Power," World Nuclear Association (2008), accessed September 9, 2008, at www.world-nuclear.org/info/inf02.html, hereafter cited as WNA, "Economics."

7. Arun Makhijani, *Carbon-Free and Nuclear-Free* (Takoma Park, MD: IEER, 2007), 182–183, hereafter cited as Makhijani, *Carbon-Free*; Robert Bacher, "Research and Development of Atomic Energy," *Science* 109, no. 2819 (1949): 2–7.

8. Kristin Shrader-Frechette, *Burying Uncertainty* (Berkeley: University of California Press, 1993), 15–23, hereafter cited as Shrader-Frechette, *Burying*.

9. B. Smith, *Insurmountable Risks* (Takoma Park, MD: IEER, 2006), 10, hereafter cited as Smith, *Insurmountable*; John Ahearne et al., *Nuclear Power* (Washington, DC: National Academy Press, 1992), 31.

10. Smith, *Insurmountable*, 7–8; Arun Makhijani and Scott Saleska, *The Nuclear Power Deception* (New York: Apex Press Saleska, 1999), 87–88.

11. Arun Makhijani, "The Return of the Nuclear Messiahs," *Science for Democratic Action* 36 (2006): 3.

12. William Sweet, *Kicking the Carbon Habit* (New York: Columbia University Press, 2006), 193, hereafter cited as Sweet, *Kicking*.

13. Makhijani, *Carbon-Free*, 188.

14. Ibid., 182–184; J. Robert Oppenheimer, "International Control of Atomic Energy," in Morton Grodzins and Eugene Rabinowitch (eds.), *The Atomic Age* (New York: Basic Books, 1963), 55.

15. Herbst and Hopley, *Nuclear*, 95–96.

16. Bob Percopo, "US Nuclear Power's Time Has Come—Again," *Power* (January 2008): 12.

17. Christian Parenti, "What Nuclear Renaissance?" *Nation* 286, no. 18 (May 12, 2008): 13, hereafter cited as Parenti, "What Nuclear Renaissance?"

18. Herbst and Hopley, *Nuclear*, 102, 110.

19. Olaf Bayer and Chris Grimshaw, *Broken Promises* (Oxford, UK: Corporate Watch, 2007), 19.

20. Herbst and Hopley, *Nuclear*, 110–113.

21. J. H. Crowley and R. S. Kaminski, "What the USA Can Learn from France about Cost Control," *Nuclear Engineering International* 30, no. 371 (1985): 34–36.

22. Modern Power Systems Editors (MPS), "Nuclear Power Progress; Site Work Underway on Finland's 1,600MWe EPR," *Modern Power Systems* (March 15, 2004); Nucleonics Week Editors, "Merrill Lynch Global Power and Gas Leaders Conference," *Nucleonics Week* (October 5, 2006), hereafter cited as Nucleonics, "Merrill Lynch"; Nucleonics Week Editors, "Host of Problems Caused Delays at Olkiluoto-3, Regulators Say," *Nucleonics Week* (July 13, 2006); Nucleonics Week Editors, "Olkiluoto-3 Delays Lower Areva Nuclear Profits by Eur 300 Million," *Nucleonics Week* (October 5, 2006).

23. Makhijani, *Carbon-Free*, 122–123.

24. Herbst and Hopley, *Nuclear*, 102.

25. Makhijani, *Carbon-Free*, 183; Arun Makhijani, *Plutonium End Game* (Takoma Park, MD: Institute for Energy and Environmental Research, 2001).

26. Arun Makhijani, "France's Nuclear Fix?" *Science for Democratic Action* 15, no. 2 (2008): 5; Makhijani, *Carbon-Free*, 186.

27. Ibid., 5.

28. Ibid., 7.

29. Amory Lovins, "Energy Tribune Speaks with Amory Lovins," *Energy Tribune* (November 9, 2007), accessed February 22, 2008, at www.energytribune.com/articles.cfm?aid=672, hereafter cited as Lovins, "Energy Tribune."

30. Makhijani, *Carbon-Free*, 189–190; Smith, *Insurmountable*, 38–42; Energy Information Administration (EIA), *Analysis of Nuclear Power Construction Costs* (Washington, DC: EIA, 1986), xv, xvi, hereafter cited as EIA, *Analysis*.

31. Cravens, *Power*, 211.

32. North Carolina Utilities Commission (NCUC), "In the Matter of: Application for Approval for an Electric Generation Certificate to Construct Two 800 MW State of the Art Coal Units for Cliffside Project in Cleveland," Rutherford Counties, E-7, Sub 790, vol. 6 (January 19, 2007); Makhijani, *Carbon-Free*, 190.

33. Nuclear Energy Institute (NEI), *Nuclear Statistics* (Washington, DC: NEI, 2007), accessed February 15, 2008, at www.nei.org/resourcesandstats/nuclear_statistics/costs.

34. Nuclear Regulatory Commission (NRC), *Standard Review Plant for Decommissioning Cost Estimate for Nuclear Power Reactors NUREG-1713* (Washington, DC: NRC, 2004), accessed February 15, 2004, at www.nrc.gov/reading-rm/-collections/nuregs/staff/sr1713.pdf; Keystone Center, *Nuclear Power Joint Fact-Finding* (Keystone, CO: Keystone Center, 2007), hereafter cited as Keystone, *Nuclear Power*.

35. Arun Makhijani, "Nuclear Power Costs: High and Higher," *Science for Democratic Action* 15, no. 2 (2008): 2–3, hereafter cited as Makhijani, "Nuclear Power Costs."

36. Ibid., 2.

37. Makhijani, *Carbon-Free*, 189–190; Smith, *Insurmountable*, 38–42; EIA, *Analysis*, xv, xvi.

38. Herbst and Hopley, *Nuclear*, 136; Makhijani, "Nuclear Power Costs," 3.

39. E.g., R. S. Berry, "Tomorrow's Nuclear Power Will Be Different Than Yesterday's Nuclear Power," *Bulletin of the Atomic Scientists* (2007), accessed February 9, 2008, at www.thebulletin.org/roundtable/nuclear-power-climate-change/, hereafter cited as Berry, "Tomorrow's Nuclear."

40. Makhijani, *Carbon-Free*, 144, 182–184, 188, 190, 192; Smith, *Insurmountable*, 44–51, 68, 70, 194, 204, 414; Stephen Thomas, Peter Bradford, Antony Froggatt,{ and David Milborrow, *The Economics of Nuclear Power* (Amsterdam: Greenpeace International, 2007), 6, 31; John Kennedy, Andreas Zsiga, Laurie Conheady, and Paul Lund, "Credit Aspects of North American and European Nuclear Power," *Standard & Poor's* (January 9, 2006), hereafter cited as Kennedy et al., "Credit Aspects."

41. Gordon MacKerron, "The Economics of Nuclear Power—Has Government Got It Right?" *Sussex Energy Group Policybriefing*, no. 1 (December 2007): 1–4, hereafter cited as MacKerron, "The Economics."

42. Scully Capital Services, Inc., *The Business Case for New Nuclear Power Plants: A Report Prepared for the US DOE* (Washington, DC: DOE, 2002), hereafter cited as Scully, *Business Case*.

43. Smith, *Insurmountable*, 44–51, 68, 70, 194, 204, 414; T. Slocum, "Nuclear's Power Play: Give Us Subsidies or Give Us Death," *Multinational Monitor* 29, no. 2 (September–October 2008), accessed May 19, 2009, at www.multinationalmonitor.org/mm2008/092008/slocum.html.

44. World Nuclear Association (WNA), *The New Economics of Nuclear Power* (London: WNA, 2005), 14, hereafter cited as WNA, *New Economics*.

45. Peter Bunyard, "Ecologist: Taking the Wind Out of Nuclear Power," *Pacific Ecologist* 11 (Summer 2006): 51–57.

46. Peter Stoett, "Toward Renewed Legitimacy," *Global Environmental Politics* 3, no. 1 (2003): 50–51, 100; see Herbst and Hopley, *Nuclear*, 4–7.

47. Marshall Goldberg, *Federal Energy Subsidies* (New York: MRG Associates, 2000), hereafter cited as Goldberg, *Federal*; Smith, *Insurmountable*, 55, estimates $144 billion in nuclear subsidies.

48. See Smith, *Insurmountable*, 414.

49. Bridgette Blair, "Public Citizen Takes On Big Oil, Battles to Reduce Consumption, Increase Fuel Economy," *Public Citizen News* (January/February 2008): 10; see Smith, *Insurmountable*, 44–51.

50. Shrader-Frechette, *Burying*, 16.

51. Smith, *Insurmountable*, 51, 97; Kennedy et al., "Credit Aspects."

52. Scully, *Business Case*.

53. B. Smith, "Insurmountable Risks," *Science for Democratic Action* 36 (August 2006): 7, hereafter cited as Smith, "Insurmountable Risks."

54. McKinsey and Company, *Reducing US Greenhouse Gas Emissions* (New York: McKinsey and Company, 2007), 62, hereafter cited as McKinsey, *Reducing*.

55. World Nuclear Association (WNA), *The Economics of Nuclear Power* (2008), accessed September 3, 2008, at www.world-nuclear.org/info/inf02.html, hereafter cited as WNA, *Economics*.

56. Ibid.; Matthew L. Wald, "After 35-Year Lull, Nuclear Power May Be in Early Stages of a Revival," *New York Times*, October 24, 2008, p. B3.

57. Alexandro Clerici and the European Regional Study Group, *The Future Role of Nuclear Energy in Europe* (London:World Energy Council, 2006).

58. The Economist, "Nuclear Dawn," *Economist* 384, no. 8545 (September 6, 2007): 24–26; World Information Service on Energy (WISE) and Nuclear Information Research Service (NIRS), *Nuclear Power: No Solution to Climate Change* (Takoma Park, MD: WISE/NIRS, 2005), 16, hereafter cited as WISE/NIRS, *Nuclear Power*.

59. Berry, "Tomorrow's Nuclear."

60. Declan Butler, "Energy: Nuclear Power's New Dawn," *Nature* 429, no. 6989 (2004): 238–240.

61. Sweet, *Kicking*, 188.

62. Makhijani, *Carbon-Free*, 190.

63. Brice Smith, "The Bulletin Interview," *Bulletin of the Atomic Scientists* 63, no. 6 (November/December 2007): 22–27, hereafter cited as Smith, "Bulletin Interview."

64. Scully, *Business Case*.

65. WNA, *Economics*; Smith, *Insurmountable*, 54–59.

66. WNA, *Economics*.

67. Stephen Ansolabehere et al., *The Future of Nuclear Power* (Cambridge: MIT Press, 2003), hereafter cited as Ansolabehere et al., *Future*.

68. E.g., WNA, *New Economics*, 8.

69. European Bank for Reconstruction and Development, *Energy Operations Policy* (July 2006), accessed November 15, 2009, at www.ebrd.com/about/policies/sector/energy.pdf; World Bank, *Environmental Assessment Sourcebook*, vol. 3, Guidelines for Environmental Assessment of Energy and Industry Projects, Technical Report 154 (Washington, DC: World Bank Environmental Department, 1991); Asian Development Bank, *Bank Policy Initiatives for the Energy Sector* (1994, 2000), 10, par. 25, 2000, accessed November 1, 2008, at www.adb.org/work/policies/energy/energy.doc; International Energy Agency (IEA), *World Energy Outlook* (Paris: IEA, November 2006), hereafter cited as IEA, *World Energy Outlook*; Antony Froggatt, *Financing Disaster—How the G8 Fund the Global Proliferation of Nuclear Technology* (London: EU-Enlargement Watch, 2001), accessed January 14, 2009, at www.eca-watch. org/problems/fora/documents/G8_eca-nuclear-2001.pdf.

70. World Bank, "Q and A: Climate Investment Funds," *World Bank* (July 1, 2008), 5, accessed February 8, 2009, at http://siteresources.worldbank.org/INTCC/Resources/Q&A_CIF_July_1_08.pdf.

71. Ansolabehere et al., *Future*.

72. Stephen Thomas, Nuclear Power: Myth and Reality (Washington, DC: Heinrich Boll 2005), 9.

73. F. L. Toth, "Prospects for Nuclear Power in the 21st Century," *International Journal of Global Energy Issues* 30, no. 1–4 (2008): 4, hereafter cited as Toth, "Prospects."

74. Herbst and Hopley, *Nuclear*, 93, 443; Smith, "Bulletin Interview"; S. Pacala and R. Socolow, "Stabilization Wedges: Solving the Climate Problem for the Next 50 Years with Current Technologies," *Science* 305, no. 5686 (August 13, 2004): 968–972, hereafter cited as Pacala and Socolow, "Stabilization Wedges"; Ansolabehere et al., *Future*, 3.

75. WNA, *New Economics*, 14.

76. F. Barnaby and J. Kemp, "Executive Summary," in Barnaby and Kemp (eds.), *Too Hot to Handle? The Future of Civil Nuclear Power* (London: Oxford Research Group, 2007), 12, hereafter cited as Barnaby and Kemp, "Executive Summary," and Barnaby and Kemp, *Too Hot*; James Kemp, "The Security Background to a Nuclear New Build," in Barnaby and Kemp, *Too Hot*, 37.

77. Parenti, "What Nuclear Renaissance?," 13.

78. Herbst and Hopley, *Nuclear*, 9; Nucleonics, "Merrill Lynch."

79. Thomas, Nuclear Power, 32.

80. Cravens, *Power*, 365.

81. European Commission (EC), *Solutions for Environment, Economy and Technology* (Brussels: EC, 2003): 132.
82. Thomas, Nuclear Power, 32.
83. Herbst and Hopley, *Nuclear*, 21.
84. Parenti, "What Nuclear Renaissance?," 13.
85. International Atomic Energy Agency (IAEA), *PRIS Database* (Vienna: IAEA, 2007), accessed January 15, 2009, at www.iaea.org/programmes/a2/index.html, hereafter cited as IAEA, *PRIS Database*; see Jonathan Porritt, chair of the UK Sustainable Development Commission, cited in House of Commons, Trade and Industry Committee, *New Nuclear? Examining the Issue,* Fourth Report of Session 2005–2006, vol. 1 (London: HMPO, 2006), 21–35, hereafter cited as Porritt, *New Nuclear.*
86. Thomas, Nuclear Power, 4.
87. IAEA, *PRIS Database.*
88. Teresa Galluzzo and David Osterberg, "A Windfall of Green Energy: Iowa's Growing Generation of Wind-Powered Electricity," *Iowa Policy Project* (Des Moines: Iowa State Government, April 2009); accessed November 14, 2009, at www.state.ia.us/government/governor/energy/Renewable_Energy/Docs/090413-windproduction.pdf.
89. Arun Makhijani, "A Reliable Electricity Grid in the United States," *Science for Democratic Action* 15, no. 2 (2008): 9, hereafter cited as Makhijani, "Reliable Electricity Grid."
90. Barnaby and Kemp, "Executive Summary," 14; Keith Barnham, "If Not Nuclear, Then What?" in Barnaby and Kemp (eds.), *Secure Energy? Civil Nuclear Power, Security, and Global Warming* (London: Oxford Research Group, 2007), 45–46.
91. "IRENA Calls on Negotiators to Speed Up the Introduction of Renewable Energy in the COP 15 Nations," International Renewable Energy Agency, 2009; accessed November 15, 2009, at www.irena.org/. Swedish data are from the 2005 SSNC report, accessed November 15, 2009 at www.snf.se/pdf.rap-klimat-energipusslet.pdf, and from Eia Lijegren-Palmaer, "Swedish Renewables Can Replace Nuclear by 2020," *Nuclear Monitor* 639 (December 2005): 1–2.
92. Frank N. Laird and Christoph Stefes, "The Diverging Paths of German and United States Policies for Renewable Energy: Sources of Difference," *Energy Policy* 37, no. 7 (2009): 2619–2629.
93. Pacala and Socolow, "Stabilization Wedges." The 9 renewable options (only 6 needed to solve climate problems) are efficient vehicles, reduced vehicle use, efficient buildings, wind power for coal power, PV power for coal power, wind for gasoline in fuel-cell cars, biomass fuel for fossil fuel, reduced deforestation, and conservation tillage. National Renewable Energy Laboratory (NREL), *Near Term Practical and Ultimate Technical Potential for Renewable Resources* (Golden, CO: US DOE, 2006), hereafter cited as NREL, *Near Term.*
94. WISE/NIRS, *Nuclear Power*, 14.
95. European Council on Renewable Energy (ECRE), *Renewable Energy Scenario*, 2040 (Gussing, Austria: ECRE, 2004), hereafter cited as ECRE, *Renewable Energy.*
96. Shell International, "Energy Needs, Choices, Possibilities: Scenarios to 2050," *Global Business Environment* (2001), accessed April 21, 2009, at www.cleanenergystates.org/CaseStudies/Shell_2050.pdf.
97. Pacala and Socolow, "Stabilization Wedges," 971.
98. Ibid., 968.
99. Makhijani, "A Reliable Electricity Grid," 10.
100. See also Kristin Shrader-Frechette, "Data Trimming, Nuclear Emissions, and Climate Change," *Science and Engineering Ethics* 15 (2009): 19–23.
101. Porritt, *New Nuclear*, 9.
102. Cravens, *Power*, 286.
103. P. Brown, *Voodoo Economics and the Doomed Nuclear Renaissance* (Cambridge: Wolfson College, Cambridge University; London: Friends of the Earth, 2008), 25; hereafter cited as Brown, *Voodoo Economics.*

104. Jeffrey D. Sachs, "Climate Change after Bali," *Scientific American* 298, no. 3 (March 2008), accessed April 21, 2009, at www.sciam.com/article.cfm?id=climate-change-after-bali-ext-ver, hereafter cited as Sachs, "Climate Change."

105. UK Sustainable Development Commission (UK SDC), *The Role of Nuclear Power in a Low-Carbon Economy* (London: UK SDC, 2006), 4, hereafter cited as UK SDC, *Role of Nuclear Power.*

106. Ibid., 3.

107. Ibid.; Porritt, *New Nuclear.*

108. Shrader-Frechette, *Burying.*

109. Amanda Leigh Mascarelli, "Funding Cut for US Nuclear Waste Dump," *Nature* 458 (2009): 1086–1087, accessed November 14, 2009, at www.nature.com.proxy.library.nd.edu/news/2009/090429/full/4581086a.html.

110. National Research Council-National Academy of Sciences (NAS-NRC), *Technical Bases for Yucca Mountain Standards* (Washington, DC: National Academy Press, 1995).

111. Brown, *Voodoo Economics.* 23.

112. See also Kristin Shrader-Frechette, "Radiobiology and Gray Science: Flawed New Radiation Protections," *Science and Engineering Ethics* 11, no. 2 (2005): 167–169.

113. Brown, *Voodoo Economics*, 25.

114. Ibid., 10; "Post Chernobyl Monitoring and Controls Survey Report," *Food Standards Agency* (2009), accessed November 14, 2009, at http://www.food.gov.uk/science/surveillance/radiosurv/chernobyl/; Terry Macalister and Helen Carter, "Britain's Farmers Still Restricted by Chernobyl Nuclear Fallout," *Guardian News and Media Limited* (May 12, 2009), accessed December 28, 2009, at www.guardian.co.uk/environment/2009/may/12/farmers-restricted-chernobyl-disaster.

115. J. A. Garland and R. Wakeford, "Atmospheric Emissions from the Windscale Accident of October 1957," *Atmospheric Environment* 41, no. 18 (2007): 3904–3920.

116. Brown, *Voodoo Economics*, 7, 137.

117. M. Folley and T. J. T. Whittaker, "Analysis of the Nearshore Wave Energy Resource," *Renewable Energy* 34, no. 7 (2009): 1709–1715.

118. Brown, *Voodoo Economics*, 7, 19.

119. "BNFL's Faces Contract Loss," *Professional Engineering* 13, no. 6 (2000): 7.

120. Kristin Shrader-Frechette, *Taking Action, Saving Lives* (New York: Oxford University Press, 2007); Kristin Shrader-Frechette, *Environmental Justice* (New York: Oxford University Press, 2002); Shrader-Frechette, *Burying.*

121. Porritt, *New Nuclear*, 2–3.

122. MacKerron, "The Economics," 1.

123. IEA, *World Energy Outlook.*

124. US Energy Information Administration (EIA), *International Energy Outlook 2009*, US Department of Energy (May 27, 2009), accessed December 29, 2009, at www.eia.doe.gov/oiaf/ieo/electricity.html, hereafter cited as US EIA, *International Energy Outlook 2009.*

125. See, for instance, Economist Editors, "The Nuclear Answer?" *Economist*, July 7, 2005, accessed July 23, 2005, at www.economist.com/opinion/displayStory.cfm?story_id=4151435.

126. Goldberg, *Federal.*

127. Public Citizen, *Just the Facts: A Look at the Five Fatal Flaws of Nuclear Power* (Washington, DC: Public Citizen, 2006), hereafter cited as Public Citizen, *Just the Facts.*

128. Smith, *Insurmountable*, 66–67; American Wind Energy Association (AWEA), "Global Wind Energy Market Report," March 2004, accessed November 15, 2009, at www.awea.org/pubs/documents/globalmarket2004.pdf, p. 6.

129. Goldberg, *Federal.*

130. UK Department of Trade and Industry (UK DTI), *Meeting the Energy Challenge*, CM 7124 (London: UK DTI, 2007), 181, accessed January 19, 2009, at commodities-now.com/content/research/includes/assets/ UKWPenergy.pdf, hereafter cited as UK DTI, *Meeting.*

131. WNA, *New Economics*, 14.

132. European Commission (EC) EurObserver, *European Barometer of Renewable Energies, Systemes Solaires* (Paris: EC, 2005); accessed November 15, 2009) at http://ec.europa.eu/energy/res/publicastions/barometers_en.thm.

133. Lovins, "Energy Tribune."

134. US EIA, *International Energy Outlook 2009.*

135. Clifford Krauss, "Move Over, Oil, There's Money in Texas Wind," *New York Times*, February 23, 2008, p. A13, hereafter cited as Krauss, "Move Over."

136. Peter Bradford, "Follow the Money," *Bulletin of the Atomic Scientists* (2007), accessed February 9, 2008, at www.thebulletin.org/roundtable/nuclear-power-climate-change/.

137. US Department of Energy (DOE), *Moving Forward with Nuclear Power* (Washington, DC: DOR, 2005); R. S. Berry, "Keep All Options on the Table," *Bulletin of the Atomic Scientists* (2007), accessed February 9, 2008, at www.thebulletin.org/roundtable/nuclear-power-climate-change/.

138. Amory Lovins, "Nuclear Is Uneconomic," *Bulletin of the Atomic Scientists*, Roundtable on Nuclear Power and Climate Change, 2007; accessed February 9, 2008, at www.thebulletin.org/roundtable/nuclear-power-climate-change/.

139. ECRE, *Renewable Energy.*

140. Ibid.

141. International Energy Agency , *World Energy Outlook* (Paris: IEA,, November 2000), .

142. E.g., UK DTI, *Meeting*, 143; Herbst and Hopley, *Nuclear*, 52–53.

143. Sweet, *Kicking*, 182.

144. Toth, "Prospects," 6.

145. Sweet, *Kicking*, 186.

146. Smith, *Insurmountable*, 70; Jørn Aabakken, *Power Technologies Energy Data Book*, 3rd ed. (Golden, CO: US DOE, National Renewable Energies Lab, 2005), 37, 39.

147. Smith, *Insurmountable*, 47.

148. Ibid., 68; see E. A. DeMeo, W. Grant, M. R. Milligan, and M. J. Schuerger, "Wind Plant Integration," *IEEE Power and Energy* 3, no. 6 (2005): 45, hereafter cited as Demeo et al., "Wind Plant."

149. Moody's Corporate Finance, *New Nuclear Generating Capacity* (New York: Moody's, May 2008).

150. A. B. Lovins, I. Sheikh, and A. Markevich, *Nuclear Power: Climate Fix or Folly?* (Snowmass, CO: Rocky Mountain Institute, 2008).

151. Cravens, *Power*, 253.

152. Makhijani, *Carbon-Free*, 170.

153. UK SDC, *Role of Nuclear Power*, 4.

154. Makhijani, *Carbon-Free*, 144, 190; see Smith, *Insurmountable*, 51, 97; Kennedy et al., "Credit Aspects."

155. UK SDC, *Role of Nuclear Power*, 2; see Brown, *Voodoo Economics.*

156. Porritt, *New Nuclear*, 45.

157. UK SDC, *Role of Nuclear Power*, 2.

158. Ibid., 2.

159. Makhijani, "A Reliable Electricity Grid," 9ff; Makhijani, *Carbon-Free*, 21; Brian Parsons, Michael Milligan, J. Charles Smith, Edgar DeMeo, Brett Oakleaf, Kenneth Wolf, Matt Schuerger, Robert Zavadil, Mark Ahlstrom, and Dora Yen Nakafuji, *Grid Impacts of Wind Power Variability* (Reston, VA: Utility Wind Integration Group, 2006), 10; Demeo et al., "Wind Plant."

160. Makhijani, *Carbon-Free*, 35.

161. Walt Musial, *Offshore Wind Energy Potential for the United States* (Golden, CO: National Renewable Energy Laboratory, 2005), accessed November 23, 2009, at www.eeere.energy.gov/windandhydro/windpoweringamerica/pdfs/workshops.2005_summit/musial.pdf, slide 10; Energy Information Administration, Annual Energy Review (EIA AER), *Annual Energy Review 2005*, Report DOE/EIA-0384(2005) (Washington, DC: DOE, EIA, 2006),

table 8.2a, accessed November 23, 2009. at http://tonto.eia.doe.gov/FTPROOT/multi-fuel/0338405.pdf; Makhijani, *Carbon-Free*, 36.

162. Makhijani, *Carbon-Free*, 36; Arun Makhijani, Lois Chalmers, and Brice Smith, *Uranium Enrichment*, prepared by the Institute for Energy and Environmental Research for the Nuclear Policy Research Institute (Takoma Park, MD: IEER, 2004).

163. Pacala and Socolow, "Stabilization Wedges."

164. Smith, *Insurmountable*; Smith, "Bulletin Interview," 24, 80–82.

165. Makhijani, "A Reliable Electricity Grid," 10; see Makhijani, *Carbon-Free*, 173. Coal-natural gas damage claims are from US National Research Council, *Hidden Costs of Energy* (Washington, DC: National Academy Press, 2009).

166. R. S. Berry, "Nuclear Is More Reliable, Safer Than Before," *Bulletin of the Atomic Scientists* (2007), accessed February 9, 2008, at www.thebulletin.org/roundtable/nuclear-power-climate-change/.

167. Makhijani, *Carbon-Free*, 24.

168. Gul Timur and Till Stenzel, *Variability of Wind Power and Other Renewables* (Paris: International Energy Agency, 2005); Public Citizen, *Just the Facts.*

169. Sachs, "Climate Change."

170. Herbst and Hopley, *Nuclear*, 36, 186; Cravens, *Power*, 16; UK DTI, *Meeting*, 190.

171. UK SDC, *Role of Nuclear Power.*

172. Pacala and Socolow, "Stabilization Wedges."

173. Krauss, "Move Over," A1.

174. Ibid., A13.

175. "Turbine Time," *Economist* 388, no. 8589 (2008): 41–42.

176. "The Pickens Plan," *Future Survey* 30, no. 11 (2008): 10–11.

177. McKinsey, *Reducing*, 19.

178. Makhijani, *Carbon-Free*, 32.

179. US DOE, *President Bush.*

180. Ansolabehere et al., *Future.*

181. Ibid.

182. UK SDC, *Role of Nuclear Power*, 2.

183. Ibid., 1–4.

184. Porritt, *New Nuclear*, 15.

185. Dennis Spurgeon, "Nuclear Energy: We Must Increase Its Role in Our Future," *Vital Speeches* 74, no. 9 (July 23, 2008): 423; accessed September 22, 2008, at www.vsotd.com.

186. Sweet, *Kicking*, 188.

187. UK DTI, *Meeting*, 193.

188. James Lovelock, *The Revenge of Gaia* (London: Penguin, 2003), 106.

189. David Fleming, *The Lean Guide to Nuclear Energy* (London: Economics Department, University of London, 2007), 20–21, hereafter cited as Fleming, *Lean Guide.* Willem Storm Van Leeuwen, *Nuclear Power: The Energy Balance, Energy Insecurity, and Greenhouse Gases* (Chaam, the Netherlands: Ceedata Consultancy, 2008), part D9; cited hereafter as Van Leeuwen, *Nuclear Power.* Willem Storm Van Leeuwen, "Uranium Resources and Nuclear Energy," Appendix E, in *Evidence to the IPCC Working Group III, Fourth Assessment Report Draft for Expert Review* (Chaam, the Netherlands: Ceedata Consultancy, 2006), hereafter cited as *Evidence.*

190. Nuclear Energy Association/International Energy Association (NEA/IAEA), *Uranium 2005* (Paris: OECD, 2006), hereafter cited as NEA/IAEA, *Uranium 2005.*

191. Fleming, *Lean Guide*, 23–24. L. M. Lidsky and M. M. Miller, *Nuclear Power and Energy Security* (Tokyo: Japanese Government, 1998); Willem Storm Van Leeuwen, "Breeders," Appendix C in *Evidence*, hereafter cited as Van Leeuwen, "Breeders." Van Leeuwen, "Reprocessing," Appendix F in *Evidence.*

192. Van Leeuwen, *Nuclear Power.* Fleming, *Lean Guide*, esp. 24–25. Van Leeuwen, "Breeders"; Van Leeuwen, Appendix D, in *Evidence.* World Nuclear Association, *Uranium Production Figures, 1998–2006* (London: WNA, 2007).

193. Fleming, *Lean Guide*, 26–27. Van Leeuwen, *Nuclear Power*, esp. Part D10. Van Leeuwen, "Uranium from Seawater," Appendix E2 in *Evidence*, hereafter cited as Van Leeuwen, "Seawater."

194. NEA/IAEA, *Uranium 2005*.

195. Fleming, *Lean Guide*, 27–28. Van Leeuwen, *Nuclear Power*, esp. Part D10. Van Leeuwen, "Seawater." Van Leeuwen, "Breeders," esp. Part C5.

Chapter 8

1. David Fleming, *The Lean Guide to Nuclear Energy* (London: University of London, 2007), 10–19.

2. Ibid., 36.

3. A. M. Weinberg, "Social Institutions and Nuclear Energy," *Science* 177 (July 7, 1972): 27–34.

4. See Kristin Shrader-Frechette, *Taking Action, Saving Lives* (New York: Oxford University Press, 2007).

INDEX

A
absorbed dose, 129
access to data, 177
accident, 8, 27, 30, 31, 32, 38, 41–43, 64, 65,
72–76, 90, 99, 101, 110–161, 169, 183, 187,
200, 201, 205, 213, 215, 220, 224, 225, 228,
229, 232, 233, 238, 243, 244
accident, Windscale. *see* Windscale accident
accident-liability limit, 72, 73, 161; *see* Price-
Anderson Act
accident-related economic risks, 76
accounting, cost-benefit. *see* cost-benefit accounting
accounting, total-cost. *see* total-cost accounting
Accreditation Board for Engineering and
Technology, 103
accuracy, radiation dose. *see* radiation dose accuracy
Act, Clean Air. *see* Clean Air Act
Act, Clean Water. *see* Clean Water Act
Act, Energy Policy. *see* 2006 Energy Policy Act
Act, Energy Workers' Compensation. *see* Energy
Workers' Compensation Act
Act, Freedom of Information. *see* Freedom of
Information Act
Act, Price-Anderson. *see* Price-Anderson Act
addiction, oil. *see* oil addiction
administration, Bush. *see* Bush administration
Advancement of Science, American Association for.
see American Association for the
Advancement of Science
advantage, competitive. *see* competitive advantage
aerosols, 18, 19
African American, 166
African Development Bank, 77, 223
Agency, Atomic Energy. *see* International Atomic
Energy Agency
Agency, Energy. *see* International Energy Agency
agenda, military. *see* military agenda
agriculture, 11
a-historical ethical principles, 13

aircraft vulnerability, reactor. *see* reactor aircraft
vulnerability
air monitor, general. *see* general air monitor
air pollution, 5, 8, 9, 18, 22, 34
air storage, compressed. *see* compressed-air-storage
Albany, 150
Al Gore, 63
allowances, percentage-depletion. *see*
percentage-depletion allowances
Al Qaeda, 60
Alven, Hannes. *see* Hannes Alven
Alvin Weinberg, 246
Amazon, 10, 141
Amazon Rainforest, 10
American, African. *see* African American
American, Native. *see* Native American
American Association for the Advancement of
Science, 156
American Enterprise Institute, 26
American Medical Association, Journal of. *see*
Journal of the American
Medical Association
American Meteorological Society, 12
American Nuclear Association, 128
American Petroleum, 27
American Public Health Association, 8, 75
amortization formulas, 78
Amory Lovins, xiv, 3, 4
analyses, economic. *see* economic analyses
analysis, cohort. *see* cohort analysis
analysis, epidemiological. *see* epidemiological
analysis
analysis, influence. *see* influence analysis
anecdotal data, 155
aniline, 125
Annals of Internal Medicine, 69
anthropogenic climate change, 16–24, 32
anti-nuclear martyr, 40
Appalachians, 163, 164